ENTRÉE TO JUDAISM

Tina Wasserman

ENTRÉE TO JUDAISM

A Culinary Exploration of the Jewish Diaspora

To Rachel & Wes,
"Eat in Good Health!"
Tina Wasserman

URJ Press
New York, New York

For my husband, Richard
Whose love and encouragement
Make anything possible

Photography by Dave Carlin, Greg Booth and Associates
Food styling by Paige Erin Fletcher and Jane Jarrell
Design by Abbate Design
Cover design by Michael Silber
Composition by Publishing Synthesis, Ltd., New York

Library of Congress Cataloging-in-Publication Data
Wasserman, Tina.
  Entree to Judaism : a culinary exploration of the Jewish diaspora / Tina Wasserman.
     p. cm.
  Includes index.
  ISBN 978-0-8074-1110-0
  1. Jewish cookery. 2. Cookery, International. I. Title.
  TX724.W38 2009
  641.5'676--dc22

                              2009020188

Printed on acid-free paper
Copyright © 2010 by URJ Press
Manufactured in Canada
10 9 8 7 6 5 4 3 2 1

Do not forget the things you saw with your own eyes,
So that they do not fade from your mind as long as you live.
Make them known to your children and your children's children.

DEUTERONOMY 4:9

CONTENTS

LEFT: *Chanukah Chocolate Truffles, pages 190–91* vii

ICONS OF JEWISH COOKING ᖪ 343

FOREWORD

The Talmud (*Nedarim* 50b) records a story about friends sharing recipes. A man makes a financial arrangement to send his servant to study cooking with a friend who was (or had) an accomplished cook. The agreement is that for a fee, the friend is supposed to teach the servant the one thousand ways he knows to

prepare a certain kind of fig. The servant returns having learned eight hundred of the thousand recipes. The man sues his friend and takes him to court. The rabbi presiding over the court sees the episode as an example of epicurean extravagance. He suggests that in more affluent times *maybe* people knew one thousand ways to prepare a single ingredient, but in their world, to know even eight hundred of a thousand recipes is worthy of celebration.

Imagine the kitchen where one would learn to cook a fig a thousand different ways. Smell the vast array of ingredients—fresh, dried, preserved, grown locally, and gathered from around the globe. Watch the techniques expressing an integration of international culture and style with local custom. Listen to the stories that accompany the preparation, words of wisdom that come from experience, small details about origins and adaptation that make a big difference in the final presentation. Taste the richness and history of the Jewish people making their way in the world and around the world in the foods we cook and share. Tina Wasserman is the friend in our generation with one thousand recipes. With this book she invites us to come into her kitchen-

classroom to learn them. Even if we, like the student in the story, are only able to master eight hundred recipes, what a blessing that will be in our lives.

In Tina's recipes each ingredient tells a story. Each recipe expresses an ethical value, explores an historical event, evokes a memory. To study in Tina's kitchen-classroom is to be in a place of challenges and paradoxes, and this book brings that experience to its readers. To cook with Tina, in her kitchen or in our own, is to encounter the place where precision in technique intersects with culinary creativity, intense concentration gives way to laughter, and our personal lives blend with the historic stories of our ancestors.

This book is a little bit like the Talmud, where the story of the one thousand fig recipes originates. It is a compilation of rules and stories, with real life examples and illustrations, a guide not only for preparing certain recipes but for living Jewish life. In this book there are recipes for Jews by birth embracing the history of our people, Jews by choice compiling scrapbooks of memories, interfaith families shaping new shared traditions, college students celebrating Shabbat on their own for the first time, newly married couples hosting holiday celebrations, families balancing work and school and home looking for ways to share a meal. These are recipes that will nourish and nurture not only our bodies but our hearts and minds and souls. Tina Wasserman is an extraordinary chef, teacher, and hostess. *Entrée to Judaism* is our invitation to join her at the kitchen counter and classroom table, and begin the sacred work of learning one thousand recipes for loving and living Jewish life.

Rabbi Debra Robbins
Temple Emanu-El
Dallas, Texas

PREFACE

From the time I was twelve, I knew that I wanted to teach people about food and cooking technique. I loved the creative process and learning about other cultures. I grew up in the 1950s, an era when food was becoming more than sustenance. Our world was expanding. Ethnic foods entered the mainstream as soldiers returning

from two theaters of war brought home new tastes they had acquired overseas. "Hawaiian-style" foods with lots of canned pineapple and Americanized Asian dishes that were deemed authentic because they incorporated soy sauce, and canned bean sprouts found their way onto my kitchen table. My father's specialty of Texas hot wieners with Mexican chili on top was a result of his time spent in the Air Force, and curried chicken over rice was my introduction to Indian cuisine. Although most of my parents' relatives got out before the start of the war, news from Eastern Europe and the popularity of Molly Goldberg on television rekindled the family's interest in traditional Jewish cooking, for food was the connection to the cousins left behind. For all recent immigrants to America, food was the bridge between their cultural observances in their new country and the holiday traditions of their ancestry. They adapted the produce available here to replace the fruits and vegetables of their homelands. If tamarind wasn't readily available, then maybe sour lemons or tomatoes would add the acidity required in a dish.

As ethnic communities were established, entrepreneurs opened food carts and restaurants so people could go out to eat the familiar foods of their former homelands. These foods were familiar to some, intriguing to others. As intrepid food explorers came through the doors of these establishments, they

began to learn about the cultures and enjoy the foods of these exotic lands, and they spread the word. More people came, and more people started to experiment with the new tastes in their own homes. I was a teenager, but I was no different.

Curiosity about food always compelled me to explore. My earliest foray into food experimentation took place when I was three and my mother found me on the kitchen floor with a five-pound bag of flour, one dozen eggs, a rolling pin, and a board . . . I was making a pie! After receiving my master's degree in food and fashion merchandising (I was a junior high school home economics teacher at the time), I traveled with my husband to Europe. We were on a tight budget, as all students were at the time. To save money we ate the prix fixe dinners that were offered at restaurants. Our first stop was Rome, and when my first dinner in Italy included ravioli, I cringed, thinking that I would be eating the Italian equivalent of those little pasta pillows in light red sauce from the can. I had an eye-opening experience when that toothsome piece of pasta filled with flavorful cheese and tinged with green flecks of an herb called basil (yes, young readers, there was a time when all those fresh herbs were not readily available!) entered my mouth. Everything was bursting with flavor, and I wanted to re-create it all when I got home.

After many years of teaching cooking— sometimes Jewish, but always kosher—I experienced an epiphany about my food heritage. I was asked to introduce Claudia Roden at a Jewish book fair in Dallas. Those who knew her work excitedly showed up to hear her speak; many only knew that she had written a new cookbook, *The Book of Jewish Food*. What none of us knew at the time was the world that would be opened to us through the portal of Sephardic cooking. The flavors, the textures, the shapes of those foods were just as much a part of our Jewish lineage to Moses and Abraham as gefilte fish or chopped liver. My time with her taught me to look at each and every recipe as a story of our struggle to survive and thrive. She ignited a passion in me to understand each and every story, and that has brought me to the present.

In 2002 I wrote to Rabbi Eric Yoffie, the president of the Union for Reform Judaism, beseeching him to include articles in *Reform Judaism* magazine about Jewish heritage and continuity through food. The editors of that quarterly publication, Aron Hirt-Manheimer and Joy Weinberg, liked the idea and gave me a chance to write one article. That one published article led to a longtime association with them. They nurtured me and supported my passion to disseminate the folklore and history that surround the culinary tradition of Jews in the Diaspora.

Countless hours have gone into learning about the little links in our cultural chain of fifty-six hundred years. There were times in the quest for the origin of a food, cooking technique, or religious allusion that I would find myself reading deep into the Talmud or the original accounts of first-century Jews by the historian Flavius Josephus. While I may not have shared every detail of these readings in this book, I have tried to connect these historical documents to the recipes I've chosen.

Throughout the history of the Jewish people, the two constants in their lives were the celebration of Shabbat and the commitment to keeping the laws of kashrut. These two observances are the foundation of all Jewish cuisine throughout the world. However, you do not have to be Jewish or keep a kosher kitchen to see or taste the history in this book's recipes. Rather than arranging the recipes by appetizer, main dish, and dessert, I hope that the life experiences and contributions of the Jews who lived in the past can be better understood through the recipes arranged by region or topic. Along the way, I hope you will learn some cooking "tidbits" as well.

It is my sincerest wish that this book will transport you back in time to better understand the culinary roots and heritage of the Jewish people and propel you forward to comprehend the culturally diverse world that we live in today and our children and grandchildren will live in tomorrow.

Eat in good health!

ACKNOWLEDGMENTS

Writing a book is like creating a good recipe; if you don't have the highest quality ingredients the finished product will not be the best. The people who worked with me to complete this book can not be showered with enough accolades, but they must be recognized for all their help and support. It is a pleasure to thank them in these pages.

Rabbi Hara Person championed this book and believed strongly in its concept. When she moved to the CCAR as its publisher and the director of its press, she promised she would find an editor for the URJ Press who would carefully and enthusiastically bring this project to fruition. I could not have asked for a better person to guide me, educate me, and nurture my writing skills than my editor, Michael Goldberg. His calm, straight-forward confidence in his approach to this project continuously made me feel like we were on the right track. He let me keep my voice while orchestrating the content to tell a great story. I am also indebted to Debra Hirsch Corman for her painstaking attention to detail in copyediting that caught the missed word or direction that was crucial to the recipe. Her help was immeasurable. Thanks are also due to Victor Ney, Stephen Becker, Rebecca Rosenfeld, Michael Silber, Jessica Katz, and the rest of the staff of URJ Books and Music. My gratitude also goes to Avvennett Gezahan, who assisted me in collating my research for the book and enjoyed learning about Jewish culture.

My thanks go to Aron Hirt-Manheimer and Joy Weinberg, my editors at *Reform Judaism Magazine*, who encouraged me from the very beginning to deeply explore Torah and Mishnah to better understand the origins and roots of our culinary history; to Rabbi Debra Robbins, my friend, my rabbi, and my mentor, who continued to encourage me to pursue the idea for this book once I had obtained my own voice in the world of Jewish cooking; and to my readers who shared their stories, asked me questions, and encouraged me when I had created recipes that rekindled a fond memory. I thank you all.

Many people spent time telling me their stories about growing up Jewish in the Diaspora. Their personal histories and family recipes educated me far better than any didactic pursuit; their recipes contained the added ingredient, love. Thank you to Rachel Bortnick, Edith Baker, June Penkar, Rita Sasso, Rachel Gomel Israel, Debby Luskey, Libby Zucker, Yvette Feiger, Clemence Barkate, Chantal, Kathy, and Jacques Aferiat, Morton Wechsler, Jacques, Sam, and Albert Capsouto, and J.J. Keki for giving me a better understanding of life as a Jew in the world at large.

A good picture can often say more than words and sometimes it says volumes. Dave Carlin made my food come alive, tell a story, and invite the reader to look closer at the recipe. A joy to work with, he and the staff at Gregg Booth were my cheering squad and good taste testers! Paige Erin Fletcher, a great food stylist, taught me many tricks to make my food look as good as it tastes. She made you want to stick a fork right into the food on the page! One of the greatest joys was having my portrait taken for this book. The photographer made me feel totally comfortable in my kitchen despite the hours of shooting and the lights and reflectors positioned throughout the room. Telling stories and seeing the smile on his face behind the camera made it easy to smile; the photographer was my son Jonathan, and he knew me well. It shows.

A very dear friend believed that "if you saw a turtle on a fence post you knew it took a lot of people to get it there." This book would not have been conceived without the nurturing and support of good friends and wonderful family. My thanks to the "Bridge Buttes" for their love, encouragement, and understanding that my focus couldn't always be on the 5–10 rule; to Liz for sampling food, sometimes as early as 6:45 after walking the dogs, and always

lending an ear and words of advice; to Jerry, Arlene, Jerry, Jan, Joyce, and Tony, who patiently prodded me until I could really understand that I was "supposed to" do what I love to do and could do it with confidence; and to Karel Anne and all my students over the years who reminded me weekly why I love to teach and who were my best recipe testers.

No words of thanks are enough for my family, my best taste testers and guinea pigs. My children, Jonathan and Leslie, lived through lots of "experiments" and knew to eat the "ugly" rugelach. But they also knew that every box of rugelach sent halfway around the world or challah right out of the oven sent overnight to camp had one extra ingredient in the recipe, my love. My husband has the patience of Job. I often neglected his culinary needs while researching this book, and he certainly ate his share of unusual dishes. But his patience and scholarly insight into Judaism helped me focus on the intent of this book, and for that I am ever grateful.

Entrée to Judaism

COOKING IN THE DIASPORA
Adaptation and Reclamation

Jewish communities outside the Land of Israel have existed, and sometimes flourished, since ancient times. Jews settled throughout the Roman Empire, working not only as farmers and artisans but as traders and merchants, connecting with fellow Jews along the Silk Road from Europe to the Middle East and all the way to China. The Middle Ages saw important Jewish communities established in Babylonia, Spain, Germany, and beyond. Jewish history is filled with events that led to mass migrations across oceans and continents. Whether seeking economic freedom, fleeing persecution, or simply searching for a better life, Jewish communities spread to the four corners of the world. Wherever Jews settled, they adapted to the customs, tastes, and ingredients available in their new environment, creating our culinary heritage. This story is still being written as Jewish foods change to meet the times and needs of our communities in kitchens from Texas to Tel Aviv today.

THE LEVANT AND PERSIA

The eastern Mediterranean region that encompasses Iraq, Syria, Lebanon, Jordan, Israel, and parts of Egypt is known as the Levant. This moniker, meaning "to rise," was given in the 1920s by the French to describe the region where the sun comes up. The Levant is the land of biblical lore. With a climate similar to that of southern California, the region produces succulent fruits such as citrus fruits, apricots, figs, grapes, and melons in its temperate areas, as well as dates in the more arid areas. The spice caravans rode through this region, and it is the choice of spices more than anything else that differentiates the cuisine from country to country.

～ SYRIA ～

The first Jew to set foot in this area was Abraham, who was traveling in the Syrian hills on his way to Canaan. Aleppo got its name because Abraham stopped to give some of his goat's milk to the poor of that area, and the Arabic name for the city is Haleb, meaning "he milked." It was the Venetians who adopted the name Aleppo from their transliteration.

Although a Jewish community was said to exist during the time of King David, it was the fall of the First Temple and the Babylonian exile that brought the first major wave of Jewish inhabitants to Aleppo. The trade routes of Byzantium crossed from Asia to the Mediterranean right through the city. Aleppo's Jews didn't benefit from this trade route initially, since the early Christians impeded their financial progress. However, once the Arab

Abbasid dynasty was established, and continuing through the rise of the Ottoman Empire, Aleppo and its Jewish merchants benefitted greatly from all of the culture and commerce centered in its midst. Silks, spices, jewels, and aromatics as well as local wheat, pistachios, almonds, and olive oil were traded to Venice and Livorno and then shipped throughout Europe and the New World.

As the Ottoman Empire began to decline, so did the success and personal freedom of the Jews in Syria. The opening of the Suez Canal in 1869 signaled the end of the trade route through Aleppo, and some Jews left to find work in Cairo and Beirut. The next wave of emigration occurred during World War I, when the Ottoman Empire was looking to conscript Jews to fight for its deteriorating empire.

LEFT: *Chicken Fesenjan with Walnuts and Pomegranate Syrup,* page 10

3

More Jews fled to Europe and the Americas. In 1946, when the French Mandate over the territory ceased, the rise of Arab nationalism and the declaration of 1947 to make Palestine a Jewish state created difficult living conditions for Aleppo Jews. Harsh restrictions and travel bans prevented the Jews from leaving Syria, but in 1992 the ban was lifted and over four thousand Jews living primarily in Aleppo left for the United States and Israel.

Today there are only a handful of Jews left in Syria, but the culinary skills of their women, a prized asset throughout the millennia, live on in Brooklyn and Israel and Europe. Food ingredients from the poorest of poor to the affluent homes of former consuls and merchants have all been incorporated into the cuisine of Aleppo. Whether it is a simple lentil dish or an intricate chickpea dumpling that is encased in a delicately thin bulgur crust, the great reputation of the Jewish cook with Aleppo roots is worldwide.

IRAQ

Iraqi cooking is greatly influenced by its location, agriculture, and prosperity. Turkey to the northwest and Iran to the southeast imparted their culinary proclivities to the Iraqi culinary repertoire. The Turkish love of stuffed vegetables, lamb, rice, and yogurt-based dishes journeyed to Iraq, as did the rice dishes, pickles, and fruit and meat combinations of Persia/Iran.

Hospitality is the hallmark of Iraqi Jews regardless of where they live now. Following the lead of the most famous Iraqi, Abraham, Jews in this region always make more than enough food in case they are visited by unexpected guests.

The Tigris and Euphrates Rivers helped irrigate the surrounding lands and created moist, fertile ground in which to grow an abundance of vegetables. Iraqi dishes containing protein are primarily vegetable-based. Iraq's location on the Persian Gulf put it in direct contact with merchants on the spice trade route. Iraqi cooks use many herbs and spices in their cooking. Thyme, oregano, basil, dill, mint, parsley, and sage are frequently used herbs. Turmeric is used for color, and cardamom, cinnamon, ginger, tamarind concentrate, lemon, and rose water are used as flavoring agents. Even the color of foods plays an active role in menu choices in the Iraqi kitchen, according to Rivka Goldman in her book *Mama Nazima's Jewish-Iraqi Cuisine* (Hippocrene Books, 2006). According to Ms. Goldman, eating yellow vegetables results in laughter and happiness, green fruits or vegetables are considered sources of hope and prosperity, and black vegetables are thought to be unlucky, which is why Iraqis generally peel their eggplants!

ISRAEL

If the foods of the United States are varied because of its vast melting pot of ethnic cuisines, then the food of Israel has multiple personality disorder! Over the last sixty years, Jewish immigrants have come to

Israel from virtually all over the world. They bring with them hopes for the future and cling to culinary traditions from the past. Fusion cuisine takes on new meaning in Israel.

To identify the basis for Israeli cuisine, one need only look in the Bible for the listed seven species. In modern times there is no better example of the use of these wild and domesticated produce than in a meal presented to you by Moshe Basson, the former chef-owner of Eucalyptus Restaurant in Jerusalem. Moshe thrives on the education he gives the patrons of his restaurant every time they sit down to enjoy one of his meals. A history lesson that fills your stomach, mind, and heart all in one forkful is Moshe's best culinary feat. As one of the first participants in the worldwide Slow Food Movement, he strives to initiate people to the wonderful tastes of foods that grow locally in the wild or are cultivated in the region.

The icons of Israeli food in the twenty-first century, falafel, *zatar*, and an abundance of salads,

all highlight foods whose roots literally go back thousands of years. Street vendors and small falafel shops sell the crispy little balls of seasoned chickpea flour rolled up with tahini and stuffed into pita pockets with fresh vegetables and even an occasional French fry!

Large semi-rectangular bagels are sold warm from street carts and served with a small cup filled with *zatar* for dipping. *Zatar* is the spice combination of wild thyme, oregano, sumac, salt, and sesame seeds that is used in conjunction with olive oil as a garnish for bread or for marinating meats.

Sit down at many restaurants in Israel and you will be inundated with the small plates of salads placed before you. Carrot salad with cumin, eggplant roasted and then pureed with spices and tahini, pickled beets—the list goes on and on, and each recipe is better than the next! Are they Greek, Bulgarian, Turkish, Syrian, Persian, Baghdadi? Yes, yes, yes!

ᨓᨘ PERSIA/IRAN ᨓᨘ

*I*f French cuisine was the platform upon which all fusion cuisines were built in the last three hundred years, then Persian cuisine set the bar very high for the ancient world more than twenty-five hundred years ago. Modern-day Iran is the center of the Old Persian Empire and the seat of its culinary heritage.

The origins of this exquisitely flavored, delicate cuisine go back to the time of Cyrus the Great in the sixth century B.CE. Cyrus was the leader of the Pars tribe (Persians) that conquered vast stretches of land from India to Egypt and north to parts of Turkey and Greece. The Silk Road and the spice trade route that passed through Persia were instrumental in introducing new foods and flavorings to the region. It

was through these routes that citrus fruit cultivation, eggplant, and rice were introduced throughout the Middle East.

Persian cuisine is noted for its juxtaposition of sweet and sour tastes in one dish, ground nuts to thicken sauces, and the use of fruits, as well as vegetables, to enhance the flavor of *khoreshes*, stews containing small amounts of lamb or poultry. Marinating and grilling meats as kebabs are also a hallmark of this region. However, Persian cuisine is probably most identified by the many dishes that incorporate rice. Rice is revered whether it is served simply adorned with crisp, golden shreds of fried onion or crowned with prized dried fruits and fragrant almonds. *Chelo*, the crispy base of cooked rice left in the bottom of the pan of properly prepared rice, is a delicacy that is served to special guests or used to garnish the fluffy mound of rice that is presented at table.

The proliferation of fresh herbs in the region coupled with the many spices indigenous to the empire account for the abundance of flavor in Persian cuisine. Basil, chives, dill, parsley, mint, tarragon, and marjoram are some of the many herbs used in Persian cooking to this day. The spice trade route facilitated the inclusion of black pepper, coriander, cardamom, cinnamon, cumin, fenugreek, saffron, sumac, and turmeric into the cuisine as well.

Onions are used in all forms, including scallions and leeks. However, garlic is never used in Persian cooking. That ingredient is left to Persia's surrounding neighbors. Pickles and flatbreads are always served at meals, and meals end with desserts often perfumed with rose water and garnished with bright green pistachio nuts. Diners might find rice offered in this course as well.

Persian Jewish cooks are known for their sumptuous feasts that reflect all of the cooking techniques employed in this region. Because little or no pork is used in Persian cooking and the Persians didn't rely heavily on the use of animal fat in their cooking, the traditions of Persian cuisine are easily adapted to the laws of kashrut.

Millet Pancakes with Fresh Corn

One-third of the world consumes millet as a staple of their diet; in the United States millet is more familiar as birdseed! High in protein, it is often eaten as a cooked porridge. Here it is briefly soaked to retain some of its crunch. Although these pancakes, with their subtle sweetness, are often served for breakfast with honey or syrup, they are equally at home at a cocktail party served warm with caviar and flavored yogurt or sour cream.

½ cup millet seed
1 cup all-purpose flour
½ cup whole-wheat or corn flour
½ teaspoon baking soda
1 teaspoon baking powder
¼ teaspoon salt
2 large eggs
½ cup fresh or frozen corn kernels
2 tablespoons honey
1 teaspoon vanilla

1½ cups milk plus ½ teaspoon lemon juice or vinegar
2 tablespoons unsalted butter for greasing pan
Honey for topping
 or
¼ cup thick Greek yogurt, sour cream, or crème fraiche
¼–½ teaspoon *zatar*
1 teaspoon wildflower honey
Red lumpfish caviar

1. Place millet in a small bowl and cover with hot water. Set aside.

2. Combine the dry ingredients in a medium bowl. Set aside.

3. Beat the eggs in a 1-quart bowl, and add the corn, honey, vanilla, and milk. Set aside.

4. Strain the millet. Place in a 10-inch frying pan over medium heat, and toss until the millet stops steaming and then dries and begins to toast. Rotating the pan gently will allow the millet to toast and "pop" evenly.

5. Add the liquid ingredients to the dry ingredients. Add the toasted millet to the mixture, and stir rapidly but gently until all the ingredients are combined.

6. Heat a nonstick griddle until very hot. Grease with some of the butter and reduce heat to medium. Pour batter into desired size pancakes.

7. When pancakes develop little holes on top, gently flip them over and cook on the other side until golden. Serve with honey or a mixture of the sour cream, *zatar*, and honey topped with a small dollop of red lumpfish caviar.

Yield: 14–20 pancakes, depending on size

TINA'S TIDBITS

- *Corn flour is finely ground cornmeal from the whole kernel of corn (as opposed to cornstarch, which comes only from the endosperm of the kernel).*
- *Adding a little vinegar or lemon juice to milk creates the equivalent of buttermilk.*
- *Use no more than 1 heaping tablespoon of batter if you want to use the pancakes as a base for an hors d'oeuvre.*
- *Zatar is a popular Middle Eastern spice mixture consisting of sesame seeds, sumac berries, thyme, and salt ground together. Often used as a flavoring agent for roasted meats, it is most commonly used in Israel as a seasoning with olive oil to coat the tops of breads.*

GREEN LENTIL AND BULGUR SALAD WITH HAZELNUTS

Bulgur is a culinary staple in the Middle East. Kernels of wheat are steamed, dried, and crushed into coarse, medium, or fine grain. Perhaps the best-known uses of bulgur are in tabbouleh salad and combined with spices and meat for kibbeh. Here the bulgur is paired with small, green French lentils and hazelnuts to create a very elegant and nutritionally balanced dish.

2 large shallots, finely chopped
3 tablespoons tarragon vinegar, divided use
$\frac{1}{2}$ cup green French lentils
Salt and pepper to taste
1 cup medium bulgur
$1\frac{1}{2}$ cups water
1 teaspoon salt

2 stalks of celery cut into $\frac{1}{8}$-inch dice
$\frac{1}{2}$ cup finely shredded carrot (purchased in bags), chopped
2 tablespoons minced fresh tarragon
2 tablespoons hazelnut oil or extra virgin olive oil
$\frac{1}{2}$ cup toasted chopped hazelnuts

1. Combine the shallots and 1 tablespoon of the vinegar in a 1-quart glass bowl. Set aside.

2. Place lentils in a 1-quart saucepan, and cover 2 inches with water. Simmer the lentils for 14–20 minutes or until the lentils are tender but not mushy. Drain well.

3. Add the hot lentils to the shallot mixture, and stir gently to coat the lentils. Season with salt and pepper to taste and set aside to cool.

4. Place the bulgur, water, and salt in a 2-quart saucepan, and simmer covered for 12 minutes or until the water is absorbed. Transfer to a 3-quart serving bowl, and stir to cool (or place **uncovered** in the refrigerator to cool).

5. When the bulgur is cool, add the lentil mixture and the remaining ingredients, and toss to combine. Season with additional salt and pepper if needed.

Yield: About $1\frac{1}{2}$ quarts salad

TINA'S TIDBITS

- *Green lentils are very small, round seeds that are more common in Europe than North America. They are the only lentil sold with their seed coat intact and therefore do not disintegrate during cooking.*
- *To remove the bitter outer skin of the hazelnuts, toast the nuts in a 350°F oven for 7–10 minutes or until they are golden. Immediately encase some of the hot nuts in a terry dish towel and rub firmly. The texture of the towel should remove much of the skin. (I carefully take the towel outside to my herb garden and empty its contents to act as biodegradable mulch!)*

Fattoush Salad

I first tasted this Mediterranean classic at a Lebanese restaurant. Although the main components of the salad are reminiscent of an Israeli salad, the toasted pita chips add a different texture and create a flavorful result. This is a great salad for a Shabbat cold luncheon.

2 large pita breads
1 tablespoon extra virgin olive oil
1 teaspoon *zatar* seasoning (optional)
¼ cup fresh lemon juice
⅓ cup olive oil
Kosher salt
Freshly ground black pepper

½ head romaine lettuce, cut into small pieces
⅔ cup coarsely chopped parsley
5 scallions, thinly sliced into rounds
½ cup coarsely chopped fresh mint
1 cucumber, peeled, seeded, and finely chopped
3 tomatoes, seeded and cut into ¼-inch pieces
½ teaspoon sumac (optional)

1. Brush the tops of the pita bread with the 1 tablespoon olive oil, and sprinkle *zatar* over the tops. Bake at 375°F until golden and crisp. Allow to cool and then break into ½-inch pieces. Set aside.

2. Combine the lemon juice, olive oil, and seasonings in a small, screw-top jar. Adjust seasoning if necessary and set aside.

3. Combine all the vegetables in a serving bowl, and sprinkle with the sumac and pita pieces.

4. Just before serving, toss with the salad dressing.

Yield: 6–8 servings as a side dish

TINA'S TIDBITS

- *Sumac is the small red berry from wild bushes that grow throughout the Levant. Its flavor is suggestive of lemon or a sour candy.*
- *The easiest way to seed a cucumber is to cut it in half lengthwise and run a spoon tip or melon baller down the middle, scraping out the seeds as you go.*
- *To seed a tomato, cut the tomato in half horizontally and gently squeeze each half, cut side down, over the sink. A final shake should release the seeds.*

CHICKEN FESENJAN WITH WALNUTS AND POMEGRANATE SYRUP

This very famous Persian dish is considered a festive dish served for important occasions. Its importance has something to do with the amount of walnuts used to make the rich, flavorful sauce. Although this recipe serves 4-6 people, Persian Jews often served this dish to their extended families, thus requiring significant amounts of walnuts, which were very costly. In the north of Iran the custom is to make this dish with duck or pheasant. Chicken, lamb, and meatballs are also used with this sauce throughout the country.

1 heaping cup of walnut pieces
1 large onion, cut into $\frac{1}{4}$-inch dice (about 2 cups)
3–4 tablespoons extra virgin olive oil
3 tablespoons tomato paste
3 tablespoons pomegranate molasses or syrup
2 tablespoons honey or 3 tablespoons sugar
4 grindings of sea salt or to taste
10 grindings of black pepper

$\frac{3}{4}$ teaspoon cinnamon
1 tablespoon fresh lemon juice
3 tablespoons water
3 chicken breast halves
3 chicken thighs
1 cup of chicken broth or water
2 or more tablespoons lemon juice (as needed)

1. Toast the walnut pieces in a 350°F oven until fragrant (5–6 minutes for large pieces taken from freezer). Remove from oven and cool before finely chopping them in a food processor.

2. Heat a 4-quart Dutch oven for 20 seconds on a cooktop over moderately high heat. Add oil, heat for another 15 seconds, and add diced onion. Sauté for 5–8 minutes or until onions are soft and lightly golden.

3. Add onions to the processor work bowl with the nuts, and pulse the machine on and off for 7 times until a coarse paste is created.

4. In a small glass bowl combine the tomato paste, pomegranate molasses, honey or sugar, spices, and 3 tablespoons of water. Set aside.

5. Remove the skin from the chicken pieces. Rinse and pat dry.

6. Reheat the pan in which you sautéed the onion. If necessary add another tablespoon of oil. Add chicken, meat side down first, and cook for 5 minutes or until slightly browned. Flip meat over and cook for another 5 minutes.

7. Remove chicken from the pan to a platter. Add the onion-walnut mixture to the pot along with the contents from the glass bowl. Add 1 cup water or chicken broth, and stir to combine.

8. Return chicken to the pot, turning pieces so that they are well coated with the walnut mixture. Cover pot and put in 350°F oven for 35–45 minutes or until meat is tender.

9. If necessary, adjust seasonings by adding more sugar or lemon juice to the mixture to get a balanced sweet-and-sour taste. Serve with basmati rice.

Note: This dish tastes even better made 1 day in advance.

Yield: 4–6 servings

TINA'S TIDBITS

- *Because it is hard to skim off fat from this nut-thickened sauce, remove the skin from the poultry before frying to reduce the amount of fat in this already rich dish.*
- *Although tomatoes are not native to the Middle East, many recipes for fesenjan include some tomato paste to slightly thicken the sauce and brighten its color.*

SYRIAN SPICED CHICKEN AND RICE

This is a quicker version of an Iraqi dish that I have created for the busy home cook. You could easily add thin slices of small eggplant, peas, or sautéed cauliflower to the rice mixture before baking for a complete meal.

2 tablespoons extra virgin olive oil
1 medium onion, chopped into ½-inch pieces (about 1½ cups)
1 pound boneless chicken breast or boneless chicken thighs
1 quart chicken stock or two 10.5-ounce cans chicken soup concentrate reconstituted with 2 cans of water

Salt to taste
10 grindings of black pepper or to taste
1 tablespoon extra virgin olive oil
1⅓ cups basmati or jasmine rice
¾ teaspoon ground allspice
½ teaspoon cinnamon
½ teaspoon cardamom
¼ teaspoon turmeric

1. Heat a 3-quart pot over high heat for 20 seconds. Add the 2 tablespoons of olive oil and heat for another 10 seconds until hot but not smoking.

2. Add the chopped onion and sauté over medium-high heat for 8–10 minutes or until the onions are soft and golden brown.

3. Add chicken to the onion mixture in the pot and sauté for 3 minutes or until lightly browned on both sides.

4. Add the chicken stock or diluted chicken soup concentrate to the pot. Add salt if needed and the pepper.

5. Cover pot and bring to a boil. Immediately turn off heat, remove chicken breasts, and cool. If using dark meat, let it remain in hot broth for three minutes.

6. Preheat oven to 325°F.

7. Remove the chicken pieces to a bowl until cool enough to handle.

8. Strain all of the soup, reserving the onions, and measure 3 cups of broth. Reserve the rest for later use.

9. Shred the chicken and return to the bowl. Combine with the onions.

10. Heat a clean 3-quart ovenproof pot or Dutch oven over high heat for 20 seconds. Add the remaining tablespoon of oil and heat for another 10 seconds. Add the rice and stir to coat well. Remove from heat, add the shredded chicken and reserved onions, and stir to combine.

11. Add all of the remaining spices to the 3 cups of broth, and pour this into the chicken and rice.

12. Bring broth to a boil. Cover pot and place in preheated oven for 20–25 minutes or until rice has absorbed all of the liquid.

13. To serve, run a knife along the inside of the pot to separate the rice from the sides. Place a plate over the top and invert so that a smooth cake-like structure comes out. Serve with lemon sauce if desired (see *agristada*, page 86).

Note: If mixture falls apart don't worry; just serve on a platter or in a bowl. It will still taste as good.

Yield: 4–6 servings

TINA'S TIDBITS

- *If you have the time, poach chicken parts, with skin and bone attached, for 40 minutes or until meat is tender. This will yield much more flavorful chicken.*
- *Basmati rice is an ancient, cultivated, long-grain rice originally from the Himalayan mountain region. It gets its nutty, aromatic quality from an aging process that reduces its natural moisture content.*

IRAQI CHICKEN WITH RICE, CHICKPEAS, AND RAISINS

According to Rivka Goldman, the author of Mama Nazima's Jewish-Iraqi Cuisine, *Iraqi cooks typically combine garbanzo beans and raisins with meat or chicken for a sweet-savory flavor component. The following recipe is adapted from one of her family recipes.*

½ teaspoon kosher salt
10 grindings of black pepper
½ teaspoon *pimentón de la Vera* (Spanish smoked paprika) or sweet paprika
½ teaspoon garlic powder
1 teaspoon ground ginger
½ teaspoon ground coriander
½ teaspoon ground cumin
2 chicken breasts
2 chicken thighs

2 chicken legs
1 tablespoon extra virgin olive oil
1 medium onion, chopped (about 1¼ cups)
1 cup basmati rice
One 8-ounce can tomato sauce
1⅓ cups water
2 tablespoons fresh lemon juice
¾ cup dark raisins
One 15-ounce can chick peas, rinsed and drained

1. Combine the first 7 ingredients in a small glass bowl; you should have about 4 teaspoons of mixture.

2. Place 2 teaspoons of the spice mixture in a gallon ziplock plastic bag.

3. Wash the chicken pieces, pull off and discard the skin, and pat dry. Cut chicken breasts and thighs in half horizontally. You may use all breasts or thighs or legs if you wish, but cut large pieces in half.

4. Place chicken pieces in the bag with the spices. Seal bag and shake to coat the chicken. Set aside for at least 30 minutes. If longer, place bag in the refrigerator.

5. Preheat oven to 350°F.

6. Heat a large, ovenproof sauté pan (or decorative casserole that can be used on a cooktop) for 20 seconds. Add the oil and heat for another 15 seconds.

7. Add 4 or 5 pieces of chicken to the hot pan, skin side down, and cook for 4–5 minutes or until lightly gold. Remove cooked chicken to a plate

and repeat with the remaining chicken pieces. Remove from pan and set aside.

8. Add chopped onions to the used sauté pan and fry for 3 minutes or until lightly golden brown.

9. Add the rice and stir to completely coat with oil. Deglaze the pan by adding the tomato sauce, water, and lemon juice and scraping any particles of the chicken from the bottom.

Yield: 4–6 servings

TINA'S TIDBITS

- *In this recipe I use garlic powder instead of fresh garlic. Combining dry powders requires the use of garlic powder for even distribution. Never use garlic salt, since the salt settles to the bottom of the jar, rendering the last few teaspoons very salty with little garlic taste.*
- *Sautéing rice in oil before adding liquid produces rice that is firm and distinct but has more starch to adhere to each other when molded.*

SESAME HALVAH

Halvah or halwa means "sweet" and refers to any firm, sweet confection in the Middle East and India made with nut butter or starchlike rice flour or semolina. In America the most recognized halvah is the one made from sesame seed paste. You could always find the big chunks of halvah at Jewish delis, and a recurrent joke in the 1950s and '60s was that bar mitzvah boys' profiles would be carved out of halvah for their receptions!

2 cups granulated sugar
3/4 cup cold water
1/4 cup egg whites at room temperature (about 2 large egg whites)
1 pound tahini (unflavored sesame paste)

1 teaspoon fresh lemon juice
1 teaspoon vanilla
1/4 teaspoon cinnamon
Pinch of ground cloves (optional)

1. Combine the sugar and water in a 2-quart saucepan. Bring to a boil over medium-high heat, stirring only once or twice until sugar is dissolved. Reduce the heat to medium, and cook for 10–15 minutes or until mixture forms a firm ball when dropped into a small bowl of ice water (approximately 240°F on candy thermometer). Remove from heat when done.

2. Meanwhile, using a handheld mixer, beat the egg whites until firm but no dry peaks form. Set aside.

3. Using the same beaters on the mixer (no need to clean first), combine the sesame paste, lemon juice, vanilla, and cinnamon in a medium bowl.

4. Fold the egg whites into the sesame seed paste until thoroughly combined.

5. Place the bowl on a damp towel. Turn the mixer to medium speed, and slowly pour some of the hot sugar syrup into the sesame mixture, rapidly combining the two. Continue to add the syrup slowly while beating until all the syrup has been used.

6. Pour the mixture into a glass loaf pan or 8-inch square pan, and smooth the top. Cover with plastic wrap, and refrigerate until firm, preferably overnight.

7. To serve, unmold the halvah from the pan and cut into small bars or squares, or just serve with a knife and let guests cut off pieces as they wish.

Yield: 15–20 servings

TINA'S TIDBITS

- *It is important that you always start with fresh, not overly roasted sesame seed paste or the finished halvah will have a burnt or rancid flavor.*
- *Placing a bowl on a damp towel will prevent the bowl from spinning when using a handheld mixer or a whisk. This leaves your other hand free to add ingredients while mixing.*
- *If halvah does not appear firm enough, then freeze or keep refrigerated until ready to serve. It will be easier to slice and pick up.*

SYRIAN APRICOT COMPOTE IN ROSE WATER SYRUP

Apricots originally grew in China thousands of years ago. Today most of our fresh apricots come from California, and the large, prized, dried apricots come from Turkey and Syria. Because apricots bruise easily, their farm to market popularity peaks in June and July. Good-quality dried apricots, however, can be purchased year-round, so I have adapted a classic Middle Eastern recipe to use the dried variety.

6 ounces dried apricots
2 cups water
1 cup sugar

1/2 teaspoon rose water
1/4 cup slivered almonds
1/2 cup pistachios

1. Combine apricots with water in a microwavable bowl. Microwave on high for 2 minutes, and let the apricots sit in the water, covered, for 2 hours or until soft.

2. When apricots are soft, drain them, separate in half (if desired), and reserve the soaking water.

3. Measure ½ cup of soaking water and place in a clean glass bowl. Add the sugar, and microwave on high for 1 minute or until sugar is dissolved. Set aside to cool. Add rose water.

4. Toast slivered almonds in a 325°F oven for 4 minutes or until lightly golden and fragrant.

5. Place the apricots in a serving bowl. Add the pistachios, toasted almonds, and enough rose water syrup to partially cover the bowl. Stir to combine and chill until ready to serve.

Note: This mixture is traditionally eaten alone in shallow dishes but may be served, with additional syrup, over vanilla ice cream, yogurt, or sponge cake for a more Western dessert.

Yield: 4 or more servings

TINA'S TIDBITS

- *Microwaving dried foods submerged in water for 2 or 3 minutes allows them to hydrate significantly faster than letting them soak at room temperature for 5 hours or overnight.*
- *Although the kernel of the apricot pit is used, after roasting, for flavoring sweets and liqueurs, in its raw state the pit is poisonous and should not be used.*

JEWS AND THE ORANGE TRADE

The sweet orange of the twenty-first century has roots that go back thousands of years, and those roots were literally tilled by our Jewish ancestors. The world owes the widespread popularity of this juicy fruit to the farmers and merchants throughout the Mediterranean region; most of these professions were manned by Jews and Arabs.

Oranges trace their roots to the wild variety grown in China and the Cochin region of India and Burma. This orange was very bitter, but it was still popular with the Romans, who were always in search of the new and exotic. They shipped young saplings to the port of Ostia, which was the hub of all Roman commerce. Trees were planted along the Mediterranean coast and on the island of Sicily. Citrus and citron production was very important at the beginning of the first millennium, and because Jews were involved in their cultivation, the citron became the symbol of the Jews on Roman coins, synagogue motifs, and even gravestones. After the fall of the Roman Empire in the fifth century, orange cultivation died out until the Arabs began to conquer the lands throughout the region. Citrus growing began to flourish again in the eighth century due to Arab technology and expertise in irrigation techniques. By the twelfth century Jews were developing groves of citrus fruits in mainland Italy, Sicily, Corfu, southern Spain, and Northern Africa under the Moors' educated eyes.

The Jews were involved in orange agriculture because they had been involved, since ancient times, with the cultivation of another citrus fruit, the *etrog*, or citron. The *etrog* looks like a large (five or more inches), knobby lemon. It is very fragrant but contains little or no juice. It is prized for its fragrance and for its thick rind, which can be candied and is widely popular in baked goods to this day. The Jews cultivated the *etrog* to fulfill the commandment, on Sukkot, in Leviticus 23:40, "On the first day you shall take the product of *hadar* trees, branches of palm trees, boughs of leafy trees, and willows of the brook, and you shall rejoice before the Eternal your God seven days." These are the four species that form the *lulav* and *etrog*.

The *etrog* is not allowed to be used for this ceremony during Sukkot unless it is "perfect." It needs to have a beautiful yellow color, it has to be symmetrical, and most important, it must have a *pitam*, a piece of the stem protruding from the end of the *etrog*. If the *pitam* has fallen off or if the *etrog* has spots or nicks, then the *etrog* is rendered unsuitable for fulfilling the mitzvah of shaking the four species in the sukkah.

Because the *etrog* was so delicate, Jewish merchants needed to personally travel to the lands where they were grown to transport them back to the Jewish community. When they arrived in southern Italy and other coastal Mediterranean regions, they saw the other citrus fruits that the Jews were growing, and they brought some of those new citrus products back to Central, Eastern, and Northern Europe. In fact, Jewish peddlers in London, Amsterdam, and other large cities in Northern Europe continued to sell oranges and other citrus produce from their pushcarts as recently as the late 1900s.

Jewish communities that thrived in mostly Arab lands incorporated oranges into their cooking, and orange blossom water was a common flavoring agent in syrups and sweets.

When I was in Spain, I saw groves of orange trees throughout Cordoba. These trees carried the tart Seville oranges. My guide showed me that you can always distinguish a tart orange from a sweet one because the former has a scalloped leaf that consists of a small leaf near the stem that branches out into a larger leaf. These tart oranges form the basis of the classic English orange marmalade. According to legend, the sweet oranges were later introduced to England by Richard the Lion-Hearted after eating the Jaffa orange during the Crusades in the Holy Land.

Before the cultivation of sweet oranges, Seville varieties were rarely used for cooking. With the addition of sugar, oranges were commonly used in recipes. Perhaps the centuries of involvement with the citrus trade, stemming from a biblical tradition, accounts for the myriad of recipes for orange confections in the cooking of the Jewish Diaspora.

Moroccan Orange and Olive Salad

Jews were the cultivators of the orange groves throughout the Mediterranean region. The Moors brought the bitter oranges (similar in taste to a blood orange) to Córdoba and the south of Spain. From there the taste for oranges migrated south to Morocco.

4–5 large blood or navel oranges
2 tablespoons fresh lemon juice
3 tablespoons walnut oil
2 cloves garlic, finely minced

Salt to taste
1/4 cup Arabian olives (see recipe below)
Chopped fresh mint or paprika for garnish (optional)

1. Slice off the tops and bottoms of the oranges.

2. Using a sharp knife, slice off the peel and the pith from the oranges following the natural curve of the fruit.

3. Cut each orange horizontally into 1/4-inch thick slices. Cut each slice into quarters and place in a bowl.

4. Combine the lemon juice, walnut oil, garlic, and salt in a screw-top jar and shake to combine. Add more lemon juice or salt if needed.

5. Toss some of the vinaigrette with the oranges, and then add the olives and toss.

6. Place salad on a plate, and garnish with some mint or a sprinkling of paprika if desired.

Yield: 4–6 servings

Arabian Olives

I call these olives "Arabian" because the spices represent the Moors' influence on the Spanish palate through the introduction of Middle Eastern spices to Iberian cuisine.

4 ounces pitted green olives, drained
1/4 teaspoon ground cumin
1/4 teaspoon dried oregano
1/4 teaspoon lightly crushed dried rosemary leaves
1/4 teaspoon dried thyme
1 bay leaf
1/4 teaspoon fennel seed
2 cloves garlic, lightly crushed
2 tablespoons sherry vinegar
1 teaspoon grated lemon zest

1. Place the drained olives in a clean glass jar that is just large enough to hold the olives and the remaining ingredients with 1 inch of headroom.

2. Add the remaining ingredients to the jar, and fill the jar with water just to cover all of the olives. Shake well and marinate at room temperature for 2 days.

3. Store indefinitely in refrigerator.

Yield: About 1 cup of olives

TINA'S TIDBITS

- *The best way to tell if a citrus fruit has a good flavor is to scratch the peel with your fingernail. Even if the fruit is tart, the scent should be sweet and full-bodied; a lemon will smell like a lemon lollipop if good.*
- *It is better to add dressing to citrus fruit at the last minute; otherwise the dressing will macerate the fruit or pull the juices out of the fruit.*
- *Use a jar just slightly larger than the one the olives came in so that the olives can be covered with a minimum amount of liquid and lessen the amount of air in the jar.*

Asparagus with Maltaise Sauce

Maltaise always refers to orange, and here you have a hollandaise sauce made with orange juice and zest. For a quick and pareve (nondairy) version, you can whisk orange zest and some juice into a top-grade commercial mayonnaise.

1 pound asparagus
Zest of ½ orange
½ stick unsalted butter
1 large egg yolk

2 teaspoons fresh lemon juice
Pinch of salt
Freshly ground pepper to taste
1 or more teaspoons of orange juice

1. Break the asparagus stalks at the tender point or cut 6 inches in length.

2. Rinse thoroughly and place in a flat baking pan. Cover with plastic wrap and microwave on high for 4 – 4½ minutes or until bright green and crisp tender. Keep warm while making the sauce.

3. Julienne the zest of the orange. Place in a shallow bowl with water to cover, and microwave for 45 seconds. Drain and set aside. Reserve 3 or 4 strands to use as garnish.

4. Melt the butter in a microwavable measuring cup. Set aside.

5. Put the egg yolk, lemon juice, pinch of salt, and pepper to taste in a food processor work bowl, and pulse on and off to combine.

6. With the food processor motor on, add the melted butter in a slow, steady stream. Add the zest and the juice, and process until incorporated.

7. Serve sauce over the warm asparagus, and garnish with the reserved orange zest.

Yield: 6–8 servings

TINA'S TIDBITS

- *If you hold asparagus spears in the middle and at the end and bend them slightly, they will always break where they start to be tender. However, for formal presentation it is better to cut your spears all the same length.*
- *Combine egg yolk and lemon juice at the last minute; otherwise the acidic lemon juice will "cook" the yolk and make it grainy and curdled while waiting to be combined with the other ingredients.*
- *To julienne means to cut into long thin strips. The easiest way to create a julienne of orange zest is with a 5-hole zester. The zest is the colored part of the rind of a citrus fruit with no bitter pith attached.*

SALMON WITH PINK PEPPERCORN CITRUS SAUCE

Lots of ingredients, easy to make, and a perfect example of the positive attributes of citrus fruit! I love serving this sauce with a side of salmon, poached or grilled, as part of my post-Yom Kippur break fast meal. Everything can be made in advance. Just mix the fruits with the sauce at the last minute, and you will wow your guests.

2 teaspoons sherry vinegar
2 teaspoons soy sauce
2 teaspoons pink peppercorns
2 teaspoons finely julienned ginger
$\frac{1}{4}$ teaspoon ground ginger
$\frac{1}{4}$ teaspoon salt
$\frac{1}{8}$ teaspoon celery seed
$\frac{1}{8}$ teaspoon hot red pepper sauce
$\frac{1}{4}$ cup extra virgin olive oil

4 salmon fillets, 5–6 ounces each
Salt and freshly ground black pepper
2 tablespoons chiffonade of cilantro
$\frac{1}{2}$ medium lemon, sectioned and cut into medium dice
$\frac{1}{2}$ medium lime, sectioned and cut into medium dice
1 medium orange, sectioned and cut into medium dice
1 medium Texas ruby red grapefruit, sectioned and cut into medium dice

1. To make the vinaigrette, mix the first 8 ingredients in a glass bowl. Whisk in $\frac{1}{4}$ cup oil in a slow, steady stream. Set aside, reserving 2 tablespoons.

2. Sprinkle the salmon fillets with salt and pepper, and brush with the reserved vinaigrette. Grill over hot coals until done (10 minutes per inch thickness).

3. Stir the remaining 5 ingredients into the vinaigrette, and spoon over each fillet. Serve immediately.

Yield: 4 servings as an entrée, 10 servings as a side dish

TINA'S TIDBITS

- *To chiffonade an herb, lay the leaves on top of each other, roll them up tight like a cigarette, and slice very thin slices through the roll crosswise. The result will be thin wisps of herbs that float through the air like chiffon.*
- *To section a citrus fruit, cut off the top and bottom peel so you can see the fruit inside. Cut one section of the peel completely off from top to bottom. There should be no white pith adhering to the fruit. Using that first cut as a guide, continue to remove the remaining peel in five or six more vertical cuts down the side of the fruit. Next, place your knife parallel to the section membrane and cut to the center. Do the same thing on the other side of that section. It will remove easily. Repeat on the left and right side of each section until all the fruit is removed.*

    This technique works perfectly with all citrus fruit, although it is somewhat easier with oranges and grapefruit because of their larger size.

ORANGE CHICKEN

No orange juice in here, just zest, but since there were Jews in China on and off for over a thousand years, and since this dish is so popular in restaurants, I am including this authentic recipe that just so happens to be kosher!

½ pound chicken, thinly sliced into 1 × 2 × ⅛-inch pieces
1 tablespoon soy sauce
1½ teaspoons cream sherry
1 egg white
Pinch of pepper
1 tablespoon cornstarch
1 teaspoon fresh minced ginger
2 cloves garlic, minced
6 pieces of hot dried red pepper

8 pieces of fresh or dried orange peel (1 × 1 inch)
1 tablespoon cream sherry
1 tablespoon soy sauce
1 teaspoon chili paste (available in Asian food section of store)
2 tablespoons sugar
2 cups oil
1 tablespoon oil
1 teaspoon dark sesame seed oil

1. Marinate the chicken in the first five ingredients. Set aside.

2. Combine the ginger, garlic, dried peppers, and orange peel. Set aside.

3. Combine the remaining sherry, soy sauce, chili paste, and sugar.

4. Heat the 2 cups of oil in a wok until oil begins to shimmer, just before it begins to smoke. Add the chicken in one or two batches, and cook for 2 minutes or until tender. Remove to a platter.

5. Heat a clean wok for 20 seconds, and add 1 tablespoon oil. Swirl the oil about in the pan and heat for 15 seconds. Add the garlic-orange peel mixture and stir-fry for 30 seconds.

6. Return the meat to the wok and then add the sherry-chili paste mixture. Stir-fry until all the moisture is evaporated, and add the sesame seed oil. Serve immediately.

Yield: 2–3 servings or 4–5 servings if part of a full Chinese meal with multiple entrées

---

TINA'S TIDBITS

- *Coating meat with egg white and cornstarch gives the texture of a subtly breaded food without the breading.*
- *I prefer to use cream sherry for cooking because the flavor doesn't dissipate when food is cooked over high heat.*
- *Use an inexpensive steel wok for many types of cooking. It does not require major scouring, and the shape of the wok promotes faster cooking because all sides as well as the bottom are your cooking surface.*
- *Chinese sesame seed oil is not tahini. This is dark clear oil from black sesame seeds.*
- *Almost all authentic Chinese recipes are adaptable to a kosher kitchen because they don't use milk products and rarely use smoked pork. Veal is a perfect substitute for pork, mimicking the color and texture perfectly.*

BAKED APRICOTS IN ORANGE BLOSSOM SYRUP

Orange blossom water is ubiquitous in Jewish cooking from the Levant to the Maghreb.

6–8 ripe apricots
2 tablespoons sugar
2 tablespoons orange juice
2 tablespoons orange liqueur, Grand Marnier, triple sec, or Cointreau
$\frac{1}{4}$–$\frac{1}{2}$ teaspoon orange blossom water

TOPPING:
2 tablespoons sugar
2 tablespoons finely chopped almonds
Fine zest from $\frac{1}{4}$ large orange
1 tablespoon softened butter or pareve margarine

1. Preheat oven to 325°F.

2. Wash the apricots and cut in half along the crease of the fruit. Remove pits. Place apricots cut side up in a buttered dish just large enough to hold the fruit without crowding.

3. Combine the 2 tablespoons of sugar with the orange juice, liqueur, and orange blossom water. Microwave for 20 seconds to partially dissolve the sugar. Pour over the fruit.

4. Combine the topping ingredients with your fingertips, and sprinkle evenly over the center of each fruit half.

5. Bake for 10–15 minutes (depending on the size and ripeness of the fruit).

6. Broil for 3 minutes or until tops are slightly golden.

Yield: 6–8 servings

TINA'S TIDBITS

- *Any stone fruit (fruit with a pit) can be used for this recipe—plums, nectarines, pluots (cross between a plum and an apricot), or cherries.*
- *When a recipe that is baked calls for nuts, the nuts should not be roasted beforehand or they will get overcooked and bitter.*
- *Serve the hot fruit as is or with ice cream or thick yogurt.*

Jaffa Cakes

While researching citrus fruits for this book, I came across the story of McVitie's Jaffa Cakes. In England, cakes and biscuits (cookies) are not taxed, but chocolate-covered biscuits are charged a 15% tax as a luxury item. McVitie's was sued by the government in 1991 because the "cakes" were thought to really be biscuits. McVitie's won its case when it proved that its product became dry and hard when stale, like a cake, unlike a biscuit, which softens when old. The company was able to avoid taxation on its chocolate-covered confection. I was actually more interested in the connection of the name to the port of Jaffa in Israel, known for its orange shipments, so I created this recipe in tribute to the little cookie that isn't a cookie but is!

1 stick unsalted butter
½ cup castor or superfine sugar
1 egg
½ teaspoon vanilla extract
Finely grated zest of ¼ large orange
½ cup flour
¾ cup cake flour
¼ teaspoon salt

½ teaspoon baking soda
¼ cup milk (skim is fine)
1 tablespoon orange juice
6 ounces semisweet or bittersweet chocolate, cut into pieces
1 teaspoon solid shortening (pareve) or oil
6 ounces orange marmalade

1. Preheat oven to 350°F. Line 2 cookie sheets with parchment paper or lightly grease and set aside.

2. Cream the butter and the sugar with an electric mixer on high speed until the 2 ingredients are well combined and light and feathery. Scrape down sides of bowl.

3. Add the egg and beat on medium high until mixture is lemon colored and very creamy. Add the vanilla and orange zest and mix.

4. Combine the flour, cake flour, salt, and baking soda together in a small bowl and set aside.

5. In a small glass measuring cup, measure the milk, and add the orange juice.

6. Add half the milk mixture to the bowl with the butter, sugar, and eggs, and mix on low until mostly combined.

7. Add all of the dry ingredients and the remainder of the milk mixture to the mixing bowl. Mix on low only until ingredients are combined. Do not overmix or finished cookies will be rubbery.

8. Use a 1-ounce ice-cream scoop or a tablespoon to scoop batter onto parchment-lined or greased cookie sheets, leaving 1½ inches between each cookie.

9. Bake for 6–8 minutes or until cookies are lightly golden on the sides and the tops spring back when touched. Remove parchment paper from the hot pans, and let the cookies cool on the paper on the counter or a wire cooling rack until no longer warm.

10. Meanwhile, place the chocolate and shortening in a small saucepan that is placed in a larger saucepan filled with 1 inch of water. Melt chocolate over medium heat. Stir to make sure all chocolate is melted. Remove from heat.

11. To assemble the cookies, spread about $\frac{1}{2}$ teaspoon of orange marmalade on the flat side of each cookie. Let them air-dry for 5 minutes. Spread about 1 heaping teaspoon of the chocolate on top of the marmalade.

12. Let cookies dry at room temperature, or refrigerate until chocolate topping is firm. Cookies may be frozen.

Yield: Approximately 2 dozen cookies

TINA'S TIDBITS

- *Using cake flour will create a finer grain to your baked goods and will lower the gluten in your cookie so it won't be tough and rubbery.*
- *Using solid shortening in the chocolate glaze prevents the chocolate from cracking when cool, and it will remain firm at room temperature, as opposed to using oil.*
- *Avoid using large pieces of rind in the marmalade or your cookie will look bumpy.*

THE MAGHREB AND AFRICA

The Maghreb, which in Arabic means "coming from the land where the sun sets," encompasses three countries that previously had large Jewish populations: Tunisia, Algeria, and Morocco. More than one million Jews lived in this region until the middle of the twentieth century. Today the Jewish population numbers less than two thousand, with most—about fifteen hundred—living in Morocco.

The Jewish presence in North Africa dates back over twenty-five hundred years to the destruction of the First Temple. Folklore tells of fleeing priests who carried one of the Temple doors to the island of Djerba in Tunisia to be used in a synagogue. Hebrews settled in the region with the Phoenicians and lived peacefully alongside the Berbers until the Arab invasion in the seventh century C.E. More Jews settled the region after the Spanish and Portuguese expulsion in the late fifteenth century, and they were joined in the seventeenth century by a number of Italian Jews.

Typical of many of the other countries in this part of the world, after World War II many of the Arab nationalist forces fought for independence, and the countries of the Maghreb were no longer under French control. With the establishment of the State of Israel, these Arab-led countries escalated hostilities toward the Jews. Restrictions were placed on the Jewish inhabitants, and militant factions were allowed to wreak havoc in the Jewish communities. As a result, most Jews left this region for France, North America, South America, and Israel.

ᴄᴀ TUNISIA ᴀᴠ

According to the Web site www.harissa.com, a site devoted to all things Tunisian Jewish, "Tunis Jews have literally adored eating, drinking, and swallowing our culinary patrimony. Very few anorexics in our ranks, but a lot of fat men and women. . . ." A study was conducted at the University of Stockholm where a Jewish Tunis mother was hired to feed all of her ethnic dishes to three gorillas for

three months. After only one week of three meals a day, the gorillas were observed to be attached to the woman, and their demeanor was complacent and relaxed!

These comments give some insight into the wonderfully elaborate and fulfilling food that is part of the culinary heritage of Jews in Tunisia. Tunis Jews make all holidays and life-cycle events into a major celebration centered on copious quantities of many different dishes. Fried foods and other dishes doused with oil are particularly attractive to these Jewish cooks.

Although there have been many attacks on the few remaining Jewish communities, and al-Qaida terrorists ran a bus into the wall of the oldest synagogue in Africa on the Tunisia island of Djerba in 2002, the government has mandated protection for the Jews, and they are granted complete religious freedom.

ALGERIA

Although Algeria is the largest of the three countries in the Maghreb, its Jewish population wasn't as great as that of Morocco. After World War II over one hundred and forty thousand Jews lived in the country. Today fewer than one hundred Jews reside in the cities of Algiers and Oran. Most Algerian Jews immigrated to France in the mid-1960s. Over twenty-five thousand immigrated to Israel.

Algerian Jews historically immersed themselves in the culture of the peoples who governed them while maintaining their own religious identity and customs. When the Arabs governed, Algerian Jews learned their grammar, read their literature, studied their science, and spoke Judeo-Arabic, but they never forsook their religious traditions. They were welcoming to European Jews coming to settle there and their community became one of the most sophisticated and Westernized Jewish communities in North Africa. After the immigration of Italians to Tunisia in the seventeenth and eighteenth centuries, the Jews added Italian to their language repertoire, along with Berber, Arabic, Spanish, Ladino, and Hebrew. In the early 1800s, Algerians were given French citizenship, and French schools were established throughout the country. This foundation made it much easier to immigrate to France and assimilate into the French culture when most Algerian Jews left in the two decades after World War II.

MOROCCO

The history of Moroccan Jews is not dissimilar to that of their brethren elsewhere in the Maghreb. Inhabitants of the land since ancient times, the rise and fall of the Jewish population followed the ebb and flow of living conditions at home and abroad. During World War II the Jews were subjected to the harassment of the Vichy government of France, which controlled Morocco.

Shortly after the establishment of the State of Israel, there were riots in Oujda and Djerada in which forty-four Jews were killed, and an official economic boycott was prompted against Moroccan Jews.

When Morocco gained its independence in 1956, Jewish immigration to Israel was suspended. In 1963 the immigration prohibition was lifted. Though the undertones of anti-Semitism are still present, Morocco has one of the most tolerant environments for Jews in the Arab world today.

Although the Jewish population is aging and many young Moroccan Jews don't return after studying abroad, the Moroccan community has established a ritual of making pilgrimage to some of the tombs of ancient sages. This brings back the Moroccan Jewish émigré to the land and helps keep the community's roots alive while the newer generations are growing up in relatively peaceful surroundings.

THE FOOD OF THE MAGHREB

Although you will find couscous in all three countries of the Maghreb, the flavors and ingredients used in each cuisine are not the same. According to Simone Gozlan, a French émigré from Morocco, the food of her youth is not the same as that of her husband, who grew up in Tunisia. Moroccans use a lot of dried fruits in their cooking, and their couscous contains chickpeas as well as raisins. Prunes stuffed with almonds and other fruits are often cooked with meats for a rich and complex flavor, and cumin and cinnamon are often the spices of choice in these preparations. Olives and preserved lemons are used in many recipes for a tart flavor addition. The famous dish *bestilla*, made with chicken in a flaky crust or phyllo dough, is flavored with sugar, cinnamon, and almonds as well as cilantro, onions, and parsley.

Tunisians do not use sugar at all in their cooking; coriander seed and caraway seed are more common, and chickpeas are never used. Other spices used to enhance the flavor of their dishes are aniseed, cumin, saffron, cinnamon, and harissa, a fiery mixture of spices made into a paste with olive oil. Olive oil is used for frying *briks*, a Tunisian specialty of deep-fried, flaky dough filled with meats or vegetables.

Algerian cooking bears some resemblance to Moroccan cooking, but the French influence is more readily seen in many of its dishes. Ginger, cumin, cinnamon, and pepper reflect the influence of the spice trade on this region. Olives are incorporated into many of its dishes. Salads are dressed with olive oil, although mayonnaise is used in some dishes, showing the French influence. Almonds are prevalent, and one of the best-known desserts in Algeria is the gazelle's horn, the crescent-shaped almond paste cookie found in most bakeries throughout the world today.

ETHIOPIA

The Beta Israel of Ethiopia trace their ancestry back thousands of years. Theories abound as to their origins, including that they are the lost tribe of Dan, descendants of Jews who fled Israel for Egypt after the destruction of the First Temple in 586 B.C.E., or descendants of King Solomon and the Queen of Sheba.

The Beta Israel Jews lived peacefully in the hills of Ethiopia until 1973, when regime changes in Ethiopia, the Yom Kippur War, and a threat of an Arab oil embargo if relations were maintained with Israel caused great hardships for this segregated group of Jews. Thousands of Betas were killed or injured during riots, and many fled to squalid refugee camps in the Sudan. Beginning in 1984 with Operation Moses and in 1991 with Operation Solomon, over twenty-five thousand Jews (nearly 85 percent of the Ethiopian Jewish community) were successfully, albeit clandestinely, airlifted out of Ethiopia via Sudan to Israel. In the years since, Ethiopians have slowly integrated into fully industrialized Israel from their rural, tribal existence. With over 60 percent of the Ethiopian Jewish population under the age of eighteen, educating the next generation is their hope for successful assimilation.

ᥡ UGANDA, GHANA, AND ZIMBABWE ᥡ

In the 1880s, British missionaries converted the powerful Bagandan warrior Semei Kakungulu to Christianity. By the turn of the century, his Old Testament Bible reading had drawn him to Judaism. By 1919 he had converted himself, his family, and his community to Judaism. Difficult times befell the "People of Judah" during the reign of Idi Amin, but over five hundred members of the community kept their faith and continue to reach out to the world to let them know they exist. The Abayudaya community originally relied solely on subsistence farming of mangoes, cassava, pineapples, and bananas. They are now developing coffee cooperatives to bring in additional revenue to modernize their community.

In Western Ghana, the Jewish community is called "the House of Israel." They believe they are descendants of Jews who migrated south through the Ivory Coast. This community was founded in the latter part of the twentieth century.

The Lemba are a group of a few thousand black Jews in the region of Zimbabwe whose genetics link them to the *kohanim* (priests) of Palestine. Although their religious practices date back millennia, they have only been actively practicing their belief in one God since the early 1900s.

The white South African Jewish community is the most Westernized group in all of Africa. The history of this community follows similar migratory patterns of Europeans to the New World. Beginning with the pogroms in the 1800s all the way to World War II, the Jews who immigrated to Cape Town and Johannesburg did so to escape religious persecution and to make a new life for themselves. Ashkenazi Jews make up the overwhelming majority of the Jewish community. Food traditions follow Eastern European culinary tastes with the addition of local produce and meats.

EAST AFRICAN GROUNDNUT (PEANUT) SOUP

The peanut was originally cultivated in South America. When Columbus came over, he was introduced to the peanut and brought it back to Spain. The trade routes set up throughout the Near and Far East, with the help of many Jewish traders, spread the use of the peanut, and the African slaves brought peanuts back to the New World and particularly the southern states of the U.S. Considered to be the food of the poor, the peanut was not widely consumed in this country until the Civil War and was not in full production as a major industry until the beginning of the twentieth century when new methods of cultivation and production were introduced in the South, the area with the most former African citizens, the original importers.

2 chicken breasts, preferably boneless and skinless
One 10.5-ounce can chicken broth concentrate
2 chicken broth cans of water
1 onion, peeled and cut into eighths
1 large leek
2 carrots, peeled and coarsely chopped

$\frac{1}{4}$ cup long-grain rice
1 small dried hot red chili pepper
$\frac{1}{2}$ teaspoon salt
$\frac{1}{2}$ cup peanut butter, preferably smooth (although chunky is okay)
3 tablespoons chopped roasted peanuts

1. Rinse the chicken breasts in cold water. Place them in a 3-quart saucepan with the chicken stock concentrate and the 2 cans of water.

2. Trim off all but 2 inches of the green part of the leek. Slit the leek in half lengthwise and rinse thoroughly under cold running water. Coarsely chop the leek and add to the chicken in the pot.

3. Add chopped onion and carrots to the other ingredients in the pot. Bring to a boil, simmer, covered, over moderately low heat for 20–25 minutes or until chicken meat is cooked.

4. Remove the chicken from the soup. Shred the meat and set aside.

5. Place the soup and the vegetables in a blender, and blend until very smooth. Return the soup to the saucepan, and bring to a boil.

6. Add the rice, chili pepper, and salt. Cover and reduce the heat to low. Cook for 20 minutes until rice is cooked through.

7. Slowly pour $\frac{1}{2}$ cup of the soup into the peanut butter and whisk to make a smooth mixture.

8. Add the peanut butter mixture to the soup, cover, and simmer for 5 minutes.

9. Top each bowl of soup with some shredded chicken meat and a sprinkling of chopped peanuts.

Yield: 4 servings

TINA'S TIDBITS

- *In order to hasten the production of the soup, boneless chicken breasts are used. However, real canned chicken broth must be used to compensate for the lack of extra flavor from whole pieces of chicken with skin and bones.*
- *The green parts of leeks are never used in cooking other than to wrap around edible foods. They are too tough to eat. Always cut the leek at the point where the green starts to show and discard the green parts.*
- *Leeks grow in very sandy soil, so slit the leek down the middle and open out the leaves as if you were shuffling a deck of cards in order to let rinsing water remove any sand trapped on the inside.*
- *Always add liquid slowly to peanut butter so that it will be free of lumps and not look curdled in your soup.*

ARTICHAUD AU CITRON
(ARTICHOKES WITH LIME)

Rachel Gomel Israel's family escaped the Spanish Inquisition and made their home in Egypt. In 1956 Rachel's father, who manufactured Nasser's uniforms, was abducted with other prominent members of the Jewish community. After two months of incarceration, he was released, and in 1958 the family was forced to leave Egypt and moved to Brazil. Her family founded the Sao Paolo synagogue, Major Haim, named after the last great rabbi of Egypt, Haim Nahum, who was a family member. Rachel and her husband moved to the United States in the 1970s. She is a vibrant, intelligent woman whose culinary skills equal her love of life. Here is a recipe that has been in her family for decades. The French name is due to the French influence on cooking and language in Egypt when she was growing up.

2 packages of frozen artichoke hearts (preferably Egyptian or French)
1–2 tablespoons extra virgin olive oil
4 large cloves of garlic, finely minced

Juice of 3 limes
½–¾ cup chicken broth (or water with 2 teaspoons chicken bouillon)

1. Defrost artichoke hearts and pat dry. Set aside.

2. Heat a large (10- to 12-inch) frying pan over high heat for 15 seconds. Add enough olive oil to lightly coat the entire bottom of the pan. Heat oil for another 10 seconds. Reduce the heat to medium, and add the garlic. Sauté garlic until oil is fragrant and just beginning to turn lightly golden.

3. Halve the limes horizontally, and remove the juice using a reamer or a fork to press out the liquid while squeezing the halves. Add the juice to the frying pan along with the broth or water and bouillon. There should be about ¼ inch of liquid in the bottom of the pan.

4. Carefully place each artichoke heart into the frying pan, making sure that they are placed in one layer.

5. Simmer the artichoke hearts for 10 minutes, basting occasionally with the liquid. If liquid runs low, add additional broth or seasoned water. If after 10 minutes there is an abundance of liquid, remove the artichokes to a serving dish and boil the liquid down until syrupy before pouring over artichokes. Check to see if salt is needed (most bouillon and canned broth provide enough).

6. Serve immediately as a side dish with rice and an entrée.

Yield: 4–6 servings

TINA'S TIDBITS

- *Frozen artichokes are flash frozen and taste most like fresh without all of the extra work. Canned are soft and preserved with citric acid, which alters the flavor of this dish immensely.*
- *The acid in this dish preserves the color of the artichokes as well as giving the dish a wonderful flavor.*
- *Do not waste the zest of the limes because they are not used in the recipe; instead, use a zester to remove thin strips of zest from the limes before you cut them in half. The zest may then be frozen in plastic wrap for future use.*
- *If you scratch a lime with your fingernail, the scent will tell you how sweet and full-flavored the lime juice will taste. The sweeter the smell, the sweeter the taste.*

TUNISIAN SPICED CARROTS

Harissa is to Tunisia what ketchup is to America, the traditional accompaniment to many foods. Harissa can be very hot, as it is a spicy mixture of chilies, garlic, cumin, coriander, caraway seeds, and olive oil. Different foods absorb this condiment differently, so always adjust to your own preference.

1 pound carrots, thinly sliced
1 teaspoon whole caraway seeds
½ tablespoon of harissa, or to taste
2 large cloves of garlic, minced
2 tablespoons extra virgin olive oil

1 or more teaspoons red wine vinegar
Kosher salt to taste
Freshly ground black pepper to taste
Fresh mint, finely chopped for garnish (optional)

1. Add ½ inch of water to a 3-quart saucepan. Lightly salt the water.

2. Add carrots and cook over moderate heat until tender when pierced with a fork (10–15 minutes).

3. Drain the carrots and place in a serving bowl.

4. Add the caraway seeds and harissa to the carrots, and gently stir with a rubber spatula or wooden spoon. Set aside or refrigerate for later use.

5. Place the remaining ingredients in a small screw-top jar, and shake to thoroughly combine. Let the dressing rest for 30 minutes, if possible, to allow the garlic to infuse the oil.

6. Pour dressing over carrots and toss well. Sprinkle with mint, if using, and serve.

Yield: 4–6 servings

TINA'S TIDBITS

- *Never use large amounts of water when cooking vegetables or you will lose some of the nutrients if the vitamins are soluble in water. Vitamin A, found in carrots, is actually fat soluble, but the color of the cooked carrot will be diminished if cooked in too much water.*
- *If you do not like biting into bits of raw garlic, just crack the garlic open with the side of a broad knife and add it to the olive oil mixture. After half an hour or so, the flavor will be imparted to the oil, and you can discard the whole garlic.*

BESTILLA
(MOROCCAN PIGEON PIE)

This classic Moroccan dish is often served on Shabbat by the Jews of the region, but this could also be the wow dish you prepare for company, as we do in our house at my husband's request (this recipe is one of his absolute favorites). The chicken mixture may be frozen after step 2. When ready to complete the bestilla, reheat the chicken and onion mixture in the microwave to facilitate removing the skin. Proceed with step 3 to continue to complete the dish.

1 pound onions, grated
$3/4$ cup minced parsley
5 tablespoons sugar
2 tablespoons snipped coriander
1 cinnamon stick
1 teaspoon ground cinnamon
1 teaspoon freshly ground black pepper
$1/2$ teaspoon salt
$1/2$ teaspoon saffron threads
3 pounds chicken pieces

2 tablespoons margarine
7–12 eggs well beaten
Vegetable oil
1 cup slivered almonds
$1/4$ cup granulated sugar
$1^1/2$ teaspoons cinnamon
1 cup melted pareve margarine
1 pound phyllo dough
Confectioners' sugar & cinnamon (for garnish)

1. Combine the first 9 ingredients in a large Dutch oven.

2. Add the chicken pieces and coat with the onion mixture. Add the 2 tablespoons of margarine, and heat the mixture to boiling. Reduce the heat and simmer for 1 hour, turning meat frequently.

3. Remove the chicken, and save all of the onion mixture. Scrape off as much of the onion mixture from the chicken as possible. Skin and bone the chicken and tear meat into shreds. Set aside.

4. Stirring often, cook the onion mixture over medium-high heat until mixture is quite thick, about 20 minutes. Discard the cinnamon stick.

5. Beat 7 eggs in a bowl. Add to the onion mixture and stir as you would when making scrambled eggs. Add more eggs, if necessary, to get a firm egg mixture. Set aside.

6. Heat $1/2$ inch oil in a small frying pan, and cook the almonds for 1 minute or until golden. Drain and coarsely chop. Combine the almonds with the sugar and cinnamon and set aside.

7. Brush some melted margarine on a 12- to 14-inch pizza pan, and place a sheet of phyllo dough with the edge of the dough at 12 o'clock and the extra hanging off the pan at 6 o'clock. Add 7 more layers, making sure that you brush each layer thoroughly with the margarine and that the overhang of the dough looks like a pinwheel. *Note*: I place the dough hanging off the pan like the hands of a clock: 6, 9, 12, and 3; then 7, 10, 1, and 4 o'clock.

8. Spread the egg mixture evenly over the dough but not up the rim of the pan. Spread the chicken mixture over this. Sprinkle with the almond mixture. Gently fold each layer of dough over the filling, brushing with additional margarine if layers become dry.

9. Layer 4 sheets of dough (12, 3, 6, and 9 o'clock), with margarine brushed in between, over the enclosed filling. Fold all of these layers under, using the sides of your pinkies to tuck the dough under so you don't tear it.

10. Flip the pie onto another greased pizza tin, and brush all loose leaves of dough with margarine. Repeat the procedure in step 9 to this side of the pie. Tuck the ends under. Invert the pie back into the original pan, and cover with the last 2 phyllo leaves, which have been brushed with melted margarine and placed centered and at right angles to each other.

11. Place in a **cold** oven and set the temperature at 350°F. Bake until top is golden. Carefully invert the pie into the second pizza pan, and bake for 20 more minutes.

12. Sprinkle with confectioners' sugar and cinnamon to make a nice design, and serve immediately.

Yield: 1 12-inch pie, 8–12 servings

TINA'S TIDBITS

- *Never have a moist towel come in direct contact with phyllo dough or it will get soft and stuck together irreparably.*
- *When filling phyllo pastries, the drier the ingredients the more likely your dough will crisp evenly.*
- *The chicken can be cooked in advance and frozen with all of its onion mixture. When ready to assemble, defrost the chicken and reheat so that the onions and sauce can be easily scraped off the meat and the skin can be easily removed.*
- *Shaped bestilla can be prepared and kept tightly covered for 2-4 hours before baking. If it is very cold from the refrigerator, then bring to room temperature before placing in cold oven.*

Sanbat Wat
(Ethiopian Shabbat Stew)

Often declared the national dish of Ethiopia, a wat *is a stew, and* doro wat *is a spicy chicken stew eaten with one's fingers using injera bread to scoop up the morsels of food and gravy and to temper the heat of the seasonings. Sanbat means "Sabbath," and Ethiopian Jews, no matter how poor, would find a way to add a little bit of chicken to their daily stew to elevate their food for their Sabbath table.*

Although my assistant, Avvennett, is from Ethiopian lineage, I took my direction from Joan Nathan and adapted her recipe from The Foods of Israel Today *to create this wonderful dish. More pepper flakes, hot harissa, or Berber seasoning may be added to spice this dish to your palate.*

3 large onions, finely chopped
Salt and freshly ground black pepper
3 tablespoons corn or peanut oil
4 large cloves of garlic, finely minced
2 teaspoons freshly grated peeled ginger
1 tablespoon cumin
1 tablespoon nutmeg
1 tablespoon ground coriander

½ teaspoon red pepper flakes
¾ cup water
1 teaspoon cinnamon
1 teaspoon turmeric
One 8-ounce can of tomato sauce
1 chicken, cut into 8–12 pieces (if large, cut thighs and breasts in half)

1. Heat a large skillet or casserole for 20 seconds over medium-high heat. Add the onions, sprinkle with salt and pepper, and sauté in the dry pan for 2 minutes.

2. Add the 3 tablespoons of oil and stir to evenly coat the onions. Add the garlic and ginger and continue to sauté until the onions are soft. Do not let the garlic brown or it will become bitter.

3. Add the cumin, nutmeg, coriander, pepper flakes, and ½ cup of the water. Combine well and simmer for 4 minutes.

4. Add the remaining spices, the remaining ¼ cup water, and the tomato sauce, and cook at a boil for 5 minutes.

5. Add the chicken pieces, turning to coat thoroughly with the sauce. Cover. Reduce temperature to medium or a gentle simmer, and cook for 30–40 minutes until the chicken is tender. Serve with rice and injera (Ethiopian flatbread).

Yield: 4–6 servings

TINA'S TIDBITS

- *Part of the Ethiopian cooking technique for* wat *is to sauté the onion in a dry pan first. This helps break down the onion so that it will thicken the sauce.*
- *Spices, especially brown ones, should be stored in the freezer to retain their flavor.*
- *Fresh ginger is easily peeled using the edge of an ordinary spoon*

Moroccan Chicken Kebabs

Whether served as part of an assortment of mezes, or small plates, or laid on a bed of couscous as part of a Moroccan meal, kebabs can be found throughout the Middle East and North Africa. This method of cooking and the use of spice demonstrate the recipe's migration westward with the Moors.

½ medium onion, diced
2 tablespoons lightly packed chopped fresh mint
⅓ cup extra virgin olive oil
¼ teaspoon crushed red pepper
1 large clove garlic, minced

1 teaspoon ground coriander
½ teaspoon ground cumin
1 tablespoon lemon juice
1 pound boneless chicken breasts

1. Combine the first 8 ingredients in a 1-quart nonreactive bowl.

2. Remove the fillet from the chicken breasts, and cut all parts of the chicken into ½-inch cubes.

3. Combine the chicken with the marinade in the bowl and allow it to sit for at least ½ hour, but longer is better.

4. Skewer the chicken on metal skewers or on bamboo sticks, and grill for about 6 minutes, basting occasionally with the remaining marinade. Serve as a first course to a Moroccan meal.

Yield: 6–8 servings

> ## TINA'S TIDBITS
>
> - *To identify the fillet of the breast for removal, look for the pearlized white membrane running lengthwise through the triangular piece of meat. Pull gently on that piece and it will slide out of its thin membrane pocket. If you don't see the membrane, it might have already been removed before sale.*
> - *Although the membrane can be eaten, it is best to remove it before grilling so that the meat won't curl up when the membrane becomes tight and pulls on the delicate chicken breast.*

Moroccan Lamb Tagine with Prunes

The following recipe is very easy to make and is incredibly delicious. Make this recipe a day or two in advance to let the flavors meld, or you can make it far in advance and freeze it. Don't add the nuts until just before serving.

¼ cup extra virgin olive oil
1 large or 2 medium onions, grated
3 cloves of garlic, minced
2 pounds boneless lamb shoulder or 4 lamb shanks
¼ teaspoon saffron threads
½ teaspoon ground ginger
½ teaspoon coriander

2 teaspoons cinnamon
2 cups pitted prunes
3 cups water
½ cup almond slivers
1 teaspoon sesame seeds
1 tablespoon honey
1 or more teaspoons lemon juice or to taste

1. Heat the oil in a large Dutch oven or tagine, and sauté the onion and garlic for a minute until soft. Add the lamb and cook for 2 more minutes until the meat and bones (if meat isn't boneless) begin to lightly brown.

2. Add the spices, prunes, and water to the meat and onion mixture, and simmer covered for 1 hour.

3. While the meat is cooking, lightly toast the almonds in a 350°F oven for 5 minutes and the sesame seeds on a different baking pan for 2 minutes. Do not let them burn! Set aside until needed.

4. After the hour, if the meat is tender, add the honey and adjust the tagine's sweetness with the lemon juice. Sprinkle the top of the tagine with the almonds and sesame seeds just before serving.

Yield: 6–8 servings

TINA'S TIDBITS

- *Lamb shoulder is often not one solid piece of meat. Be sure to remove obvious chunks of fat and gristle before using.*
- *Smaller pieces of meat allow the flavors of the sauce to permeate better. Don't cut the meat smaller than 1-inch cubes, however, as they might disintegrate upon cooking and won't be visually appealing.*
- *Foods cooked with fruit and/or spices actually benefit from sitting a day or so before serving.*
- *If you are feeding only one or two people, you can freeze smaller portions in 1-quart freezer bags that lie flat and require little freezer space.*

Moroccan Meatball Tagine with Couscous

This dish is terrific for company in the sukkah. Incorporating the fall vegetables, pumpkin or butternut squash, with the sweetness of the raisins and prunes makes this a delicious addition to your holiday meal. In addition, the tagine tastes even better the next day and is easily portable outside to the sukkah in its casserole dish.

1½ pounds ground beef
½ medium onion, grated
2 tablespoons finely chopped parsley
1 egg
½ cup unseasoned bread crumbs
½ cup tomato sauce
Salt and freshly ground black pepper to taste
3 tablespoons extra virgin olive oil, divided use
5 medium onions, thinly sliced

1 quart water
½ cup dark raisins
8–12 soft pitted prunes
½ cup slivered almonds, lightly toasted
2 pounds pumpkin or butternut squash, peeled and cut into 1-inch chunks (about 4 cups)
½ cup brown sugar
1 teaspoon cinnamon

1. Place the meat in a 2-quart mixing bowl and add the grated onion, parsley, egg, bread crumbs, tomato sauce, salt, pepper, and 1 tablespoon of the olive oil. Mix the mixture well and set aside until ready to make the meatballs.

2. Heat a large Dutch oven and add the remaining 2 tablespoons of olive oil. Sauté the sliced onions in the oil until golden brown.

3. Add the water to the onions and bring to a boil.

4. Shape the meat into walnut-sized balls, and drop into the simmering liquid. Cook the balls until firm, about 10–15 minutes.

5. Combine the raisins and the prunes in a small glass dish and cover with water. Microwave on high for 3 minutes, and let sit while the meatballs cook.

6. When the meat is firm, transfer the meat, onions, and all liquid to a 13 × 9-inch casserole.

7. Drain the fruits and add them to the casserole along with the almonds and pumpkin.

8. Sprinkle the brown sugar and cinnamon over the food, and bake in a preheated 350°F oven until the squash is tender and almost all of the liquid has been absorbed. Serve with couscous.

Yield: 6–8 servings

Couscous

1½ cups water or chicken broth
1 tablespoon butter or margarine
1 cup couscous

1. Bring liquid and margarine to a boil in a 1-quart saucepan.

2. Add the couscous and stir to combine. Immediately cover and turn off the heat.

3. Allow the couscous to sit for 5 minutes. Fluff with a fork. Place in the middle of a large serving platter with the meat and vegetables around it, or serve separately from a bowl.

Yield: 6–8 servings

TINA'S TIDBITS

- *Caramelizing the onions means cooking the onions until the natural sugars in the onions start to turn brown. In this recipe, if the onions aren't a distinctive brown, the gravy will not be well balanced in flavor and will have little color. The onions will not caramelize if cooked with water or another vegetable high in water content.*
- *When making meatballs, do not squeeze the meat together heavily or the meatballs will be very tough.*
- *Microwaving dried fruit or beans in water for 3 minutes is the equivalent of soaking for 1 hour in warm water.*

TABIKHA
(ALGERIAN FESTIVE STEW)

This tabikha is an Algerian Jewish beef stew. Its name comes from the Arabic, meaning "a cooked dish." The implication is that it was slow cooked in an ovenlike setting. Although one might associate the cooking time with a Shabbat meal cooked overnight, Clifford Wright, the food historian, says that this dish was more often served to brides following their wedding eve bath and for bar mitzvah celebrations, thus giving it a prestigious stature.

4 tablespoons extra virgin olive oil, divided use
2–2½ pounds beef stew meat, cut into 1-inch chunks
2 medium onions, finely chopped (about 2 cups)
2 tablespoons finely minced garlic (about 4 large cloves)

2 tablespoons prepared harissa, or to taste
1 14.5-ounce can diced tomatoes with their liquid
1 8-ounce can tomato sauce
1 cup water
Cilantro or mint leaves for garnish (optional)

1. Heat a 3- or 4-quart saucepan for 15 seconds over high heat. Add 2 tablespoons of the olive oil to the pan and heat for another 10 seconds. Reduce heat to medium high and add half of the meat. Brown on all sides, and remove to a bowl. Add the rest of the meat to the pan and cook until brown. Remove to the bowl with the meat and set aside.

2. Return the pan to the stove and heat on high for 5 seconds. Add the remaining 2 tablespoons of olive oil to the pan, and add the finely chopped onions. Sauté onions over medium-high heat until lightly caramelized and golden brown.

3. Add the garlic and the harissa to the onions, and stir over low heat for 2 minutes to thoroughly combine the ingredients.

4. Return the meat to the pan and stir to coat well. Add the diced tomatoes, tomato sauce, and water, and bring to a boil.

5. Reduce the heat, cover, and cook until the meat is tender (1–3 hours, depending on how tough and lean the meat is).

6. Serve with couscous or rice garnished with the optional chopped cilantro or mint.

Yield: 6–8 servings

TINA'S TIDBITS

- *Cooking oil should never be added to a cold pan because it will adhere to the pan and cause the food to stick more readily. Always heat the pan first for 15-20 seconds; then add the oil and heat for 10 seconds before adding any food. Cooking and cleaning the pan will be much easier using this technique.*
- *Browning meat first, rather than just combining all of the ingredients, will add significant flavor to this dish. It will also add a rich color to the finished stew.*
- *Always pat your meat dry first or it will not brown.*

Ugandan Fall Harvest Fruit Salad

I created this recipe for Reform Judaism *magazine to honor the Abayudaya Jews and their leader J. J. Keki, whom I met when he came to Dallas for a fundraiser. This salad contains the three most eaten fruits in Uganda: bananas, mango, and jackfruit. Bananas are actually a staple of the Ugandan's diet. Per capita consumption is 500 pounds a year! Many of the spices in this recipe are now grown in Uganda, a legacy of the spice trade route through Africa centuries ago.*

3 ripe mangoes, peeled and cubed, divided use
1 20-ounce can of jackfruit in syrup
1 cup coarsely chopped mixed dried fruits (apples, peaches, pears, apricots)
2 bananas, peeled and sliced into ½-inch slices
1 small can mandarin oranges, drained

Pinch of kosher salt
1 cup sweetened shredded coconut
1 teaspoon prepared garam masala or to taste
1 teaspoon tamarind liquid concentrate or lemon juice
Honey (optional)

1. Use a mango cutter to remove the fruit from the pit, or slice from the stem to the bottom of the mango, running your knife along the edge of the pit on both sides. Cut the flesh away from the skin of the mango, and cut into ½-inch dice.

2. Puree about ⅓ to ½ of the mango cubes to make 1 cup of mango puree. Place puree in a serving bowl with the remaining cubed mango.

3. Remove and drain the jackfruit, and cut the translucent white ovals into strips lengthwise. Add to mango mixture.

4. Add the dried chopped fruits, sliced bananas, mandarin oranges, and salt to the bowl, and gently stir with a rubber spatula. Set aside.

5. In a small processor work bowl, combine the coconut, garam masala, and tamarind concentrate (or lemon juice). Turn the machine on, and pulse the mixture until it forms a paste.

6. Stir the spice paste into the mixed fruit carefully, using a rubber spatula. Taste to see if any honey is needed.

7. Refrigerate until ready to serve. May be served for dessert or as an accompaniment to grilled meats.

8. Just before serving, you can sprinkle a little extra coconut on top as a garnish.

Yield: 8–10 servings

TINA'S TIDBITS

- *To ripen mangoes, place them in a brown paper bag. Adding a banana to the bag will hasten the process.*
- *To dice a mango easily, cut it in half along the seed and remove the seed. Score the meat just to the skin by slicing lengthwise and then crosswise about 1/2-inch apart. Bend the skin back and the meat stands up like a porcupine's back. Run a knife along the skin to dislodge the fruit and you will have a perfect 1/2-inch dice!*

TUNISIAN GUIZADA

The shipping port of Livorno in Italy did much trading with Tunisia in the sixteenth century. As a result, many Livornese Jews settled in Tunisia and brought their culinary customs with them. Here the almond paste cookies of Italy are transformed with the local ingredients of North Africa with its Arab ingredients, pistachio nuts, and orange blossom water.

1¼ cups shelled pistachio nuts
½ cup extra fine or bar sugar
1 tablespoon imported orange blossom water

1 large egg
1 large egg yolk
⅛ teaspoon almond extract

1. To chop the nuts, use a large French chef's knife and rock it back and forth over the pistachios until very small pieces are formed. If you have a processor, place pistachios in the processor's work bowl and pulse the machine on and off 50 times to chop the nuts into small pieces but not so finely chopped that they look like meal.

2. Preheat the oven to 350°F.

3. Add the remaining ingredients to the nuts, and stir well to thoroughly combine.

4. Line mini muffin pans with paper liners, and drop 1 tablespoon of nut mixture into each cup (about 18–20 cups).

5. Bake for 14–18 minutes (depending on whether you have a standard or convection oven), until tops are slightly golden and a toothpick inserted into the center of a *guizada* comes out clean but moist. You don't want them to be too hard when cool.

6. Remove from oven and immediately turn the filled papers on their side. When cool, store in an airtight container or heavy plastic storage bag.

Yield: 2 dozen pastries

TINA'S TIDBITS

- *Imported orange blossom water is more concentrated and therefore doesn't burn out during baking and adds a better flavor to the finished product. I use a brand from Lebanon or other parts of the Middle East.*
- *When using a processor to chop nuts, it is very important to pulse the machine rather than just turning it on. Pulsing throws the nuts up and chops them evenly rather than having them circulate on the bottom of the bowl, creating nut butter.*
- *Always turn your muffins on their sides immediately after baking to avoid the bottoms "sweating" from the steam. This prevents gummy bottoms.*
- *When mixtures contain fruit or strong flavoring, their flavors will be enhanced if they are made a day in advance of eating.*

Moroccan Mint Tea

This recipe is simple to make and a refreshing, authentic addition to your Moroccan meal, whether served hot or cold. Moroccans like their tea sweet, so add sugar to your taste.

1 tablespoon green tea
1/3 cup packed fresh mint leaves
1/4 cup sugar or more to taste

2 drops orange blossom water
1 quart boiling water

1. Pour some additional boiling water into the teapot you will be using, and swirl it about to warm the pot. Discard the water.

2. Add all of the ingredients to the prepared teapot and stir. Let steep for 6 minutes, and strain into decorative glasses or tea cups.

Yield: 1 quart mint tea

TINA'S TIDBIT

- *Dried mint should never be used to make mint tea. Always use fresh mint to avoid a musty, bitter taste.*

SPAIN

After the destruction of the First Temple in 586 B.C.E., when all Jews were expelled from Judea, and before the Arab conquest of Spain in 711 C.E., Jews dispersed along the coastline of the Mediterranean in North Africa and southern Spain. For more than a thousand years they lived in communities where they were

sometimes treated very well and sometimes persecuted, but they thrived. They were established traders, craftsmen, and agrarians who added to the economic growth of the communities where they lived. Nowhere was this success more evidenced than in Spain.

For three hundred years after the Arab conquest of Spain in 711 C.E., the Jews lived successful, influential, and peaceful lives under Muslim rule. Toledo, Granada, and Córdoba were centers of Jewish learning and commerce. However, following the capture of Córdoba in 1148 by the Almohads, who imposed Islam on Christians and Jews alike, life became very difficult, and many Jews immigrated to Egypt and the Middle East. Probably the most famous émigré from Spain was Moses Maimonides, who left Córdoba and settled in Egypt.

In 1492, the seven-hundred-year Arab reign in Spain came to an end simultaneously with the termination of two thousand years of rich Jewish history in that country. However, because of the Jewish expulsion, 1492 also marked the beginning of the spread of a distinct culinary heritage throughout the entire Mediterranean that affected all the cuisines from Italy to Turkey to Greece and the Balkans. The established Arab trade routes had introduced spices, melons, oranges, eggplant, olives, wheat, grapes, and rice into Spanish kitchens.

The culinary practices using these ingredients were subsequently dispersed throughout the world to wherever the Spanish Jews emigrated.

The laws of kashrut required Jews to cook differently than their Christian counterparts in Spain. Jews fried foods in olive oil rather than lard, since pork products were forbidden. They grew their own grapes and became vintners to ensure the wine would be kosher. They raised their own cattle to provide the milk and the properly slaughtered meat for their diets.

The prohibition of cooking on Shabbat inspired the creation of many dishes that could either be made in advance and preserved with vinegar or slow cooked from Friday until the dish could be eaten on Saturday afternoon. These culinary practices helped the "secret Jews" (crypto-Jews) who remained in Spain adapt in a world where many had converted to Christianity to escape the Inquisition. The Conversos, or Marrano Jews (the word *marrano* is likely derived from the Spanish word for "pig"), went to church and outwardly lived the lives of Christians. However, it was the basic precepts of kashrut observance that were used during the Inquisition to convict the crypto-Jews. Maids and neighbors turned in people who they saw setting the table in a decorative way on Friday nights or whose chimneys were smokeless because they ate only cold foods on Saturdays. Eating flat "crackers" in the spring or not eating at all for twenty-four hours in the early fall was associated with Passover or Yom Kippur and rendered an indictment against the crypto-Jews.

Many holidays fell into oblivion in this world of the Converso, but Passover, the High Holy Days, and Shabbat were observed as best as the secretive Jew could follow.

In 1492 over two hundred thousand Jews were expelled from Spain. Today, only fifteen thousand Jews live in that country, most of whom arrived in the twentieth century and have no connection to the once-great community of the Golden Age of Spain.

MARINATED OLIVES

Olives and oranges are often combined in foods of the Mediterranean. Here the ingredients almost call out their location as foods of Morocco and Spain are joined to create a great nibble at cocktail parties, as a part of a meze or tapas assortment.

8 ounces garlic-stuffed green olives, drained
1 medium orange
1 teaspoon dried pepper flakes
1 tablespoon finely snipped cilantro leaves
½ teaspoon kosher salt

1 teaspoon Spanish smoked paprika (*pimentón de la Vera*) or sweet paprika
1–2 tablespoons extra virgin olive oil, preferably Spanish or Italian
1 tablespoon fresh orange juice (optional)

1. Place drained olives in a 1-quart glass bowl.

2. Remove the zest, or peel, from the oranges with a zester, creating long thin strands. Add to the olives.

3. Add the remaining ingredients and stir to coat olives well. If olives appear too dry, add 1 tablespoon of fresh orange juice to the mixture.

4. Return olives to their original container and chill, preferably overnight.

5. Serve as part of a mixed platter of mezes with wine and cheese.

Yield: 2 cups olives

TINA'S TIDBITS

- *In general, I prefer the fine, featherlight shards of orange peel (or zest) that you get from using a rasplike grater. However, in this recipe the zest is used for color and variety of shape in addition to being a flavor enhancement.*
- *A zester is a 5-inch tool with a slightly curved metal head that has five or six holes at the top that create strands of citrus peel when scraped along the fruit.*
- *If garlic-stuffed olives are not available, pitted olives may be substituted, with 2 large, finely diced cloves of garlic added to the mix.*

TORTILLA ESPAÑOLA (SPANISH TORTILLA)

In Spain this dish is called tortilla de patata; *in the rest of the world it is called Spanish tortilla. It resembles a potato frittata with egg binding the ingredients together, but this is potatoes with a little egg rather than the other way around. This is a wonderful tapas to serve because it can be cut into wedges or little squares for individual bite-sized portions. It can be served at room temperature and so can be made in advance. The fact that it is always made with olive oil instead of lard raises the question of whether or not it was originally a Jewish dish.*

3–4 large white baking potatoes, peeled
1 large onion
1 cup olive oil

Coarse salt
4 large eggs

1. Thinly slice the potatoes by hand or with the 3-mm cutting blade on your processor.

2. Thinly slice the onion.

3. Heat the oil in a 10-inch frying pan.

4. Layer the potatoes and the onion in the hot oil, alternating potatoes and then onions, and sprinkling each layer with a little coarse salt.

5. Every few minutes turn the mixture over in the pan to cook the potatoes and onions lightly. The mixture should not brown, and care should be taken not to break up the slices of potato.

6. When the potatoes are tender, drain the mixture in a colander, reserving 3 tablespoons of oil.

7. Beat the eggs in a large bowl, and add the potato mixture. Gently press down on the mixture to allow the eggs to cover. Let sit for 15 minutes.

8. Heat 2 tablespoons of the reserved olive oil in a large skillet until very hot. Quickly add the potato mixture and spread it out evenly. Reduce heat to medium.

9. When the mixture begins to brown on the bottom, invert a large round plate over the pan, and flip the pancake over onto the plate.

10. Slide the pancake from the plate into the frying pan, raw side down, and cook until light brown on the bottom. Repeat the process 2 more times so that each side has been cooked twice. If the mixture sticks the first 2 times, don't worry, just patch it up. The egg mixture will hold it together.

12. Serve the tortilla at room temperature, cutting it either into wedges or into bite-sized squares for appetizers.

Yield: 8–10 servings

TINA'S TIDBITS

- *Use a rubber spatula or turner when turning the potatoes and onions so that you can maintain some of the layering. A metal turner will cut into the potato and create too many little pieces.*
- *Always use a plate that is larger than your frying pan when flipping your tortilla over, and wear a protective mitt on the hand holding the plate over the pan.*
- *For larger parties I cut the circle into 1-inch squares and put a toothpick in each so guests can help themselves. They then become* banderillas, *or skewered pieces of meat or food. The name comes from the barbed dart used in bullfighting.*

CROSTINI WITH TAPENADE

Tapenade is the quintessential Mediterranean spread. Create your own unique version with the addition of garlic in the mix, or more sun-dried tomatoes and less roasted peppers. Freshly roasted peppers are always the best to use, but I have never had a complaint when I used the jarred peppers instead.

12 or more thin slices of French bread
1 large clove of garlic, cut in half
¼ cup extra virgin olive oil
20 large Calamata or other cured olives

One-half 7-ounce jar roasted peppers or 1½ freshly roasted red bell peppers
2 pieces of sun-dried tomatoes (about 1 tablespoon)

1. Preheat the oven to 400°F.

2. Rub one side of each slice of bread with the cut sides of the garlic.

3. Brush the olive oil over the garlic-seasoned sides.

4. Place the bread on a cookie sheet and bake for 5 minutes or until golden.

5. Meanwhile, make the tapenade. With the flat side of a heavy knife, crack the olives and remove the pits.

6. Place the olives in a processor work bowl and process until fairly smooth. Scrape down the sides of the work bowl.

7. Drain the roasted peppers and pat dry. Add the peppers and the sun-dried tomatoes to the olive mixture and process until smooth.

8. To serve, spread tapenade over the bread crostini, and serve at room temperature.

Note: The tapenade mixture can be stuffed into mushrooms, covered with a little mozzarella, and baked until the mushrooms are hot and the cheese has melted.

Yield: ¾ cup

TINA'S TIDBITS

- *If garlic starts to get dry, either cut a sliver off the edge to expose a new layer or make hatch marks on the cut side to release its juices.*
- *The best way to remove the smell of garlic from your hands is to rub them on a stainless steel sink or a pot in your kitchen. The metal neutralizes the smell.*
- *Most supermarkets are happy to take your baguette or ficelle (thin baguette) and put it through the bread-slicing machine. This will save you time and from having to clean up all the crumbs from slicing the bread.*

MANCHEGO CHEESE WITH QUINCE PRESERVES

The nuttiness of the manchego *coupled with the sweet-tart taste of the* membrillo *is a great combination. Jews were instrumental in growing quince and were cheese makers five hundred years ago.*

Two ¼-pound wedges well-cured *manchego* cheese

½ pound quince paste (*membrillo*) or quince marmalade

1. Trim the rind from each cheese wedge. Place the wedge on its side, and slice into ¼-inch-thick triangles.

2. Slice the *membrillo* paste into the same size triangles as the cheese, and place a slice of the *membrillo* on top of a slice of the cheese. If you are using the marmalade, gently spread some of the marmalade on top of each cheese slice.

3. Serve at room temperature.

Yield: 2 dozen or more portions

TINA'S TIDBIT

- *I like to cut little flowers out of a strip of* membrillo *and put that on top of the cheese for a more decorative presentation.*

Tostada con Salsa Tomaquet
(Catalan Bread with Tomato Spread)

A standard offering at a tapas bar, this is perfect peasant food to make when tomato season is at its height. This recipe is probably the forerunner of crostini with tapenade.

1 loaf dense country bread or 2-inch wide country baguette
1 large clove garlic, cut in half lengthwise
3 medium red tomatoes (about 1 pound)
Coarse salt and freshly ground black pepper

$\frac{1}{4}$ teaspoon sugar
$\frac{1}{2}$ teaspoon red wine or sherry vinegar
$\frac{1}{4}$ cup extra virgin olive oil
$\frac{1}{4}$ cup lightly packed whole basil leaves

1. Preheat the oven to 400°F.

2. Slice the bread or baguette into $\frac{1}{2}$-inch slices. Rub the cut side of the garlic over the bread slices, and place them on a large cookie sheet. Bake the bread slices until golden and crisp (6–7 minutes). Remove from the oven and set aside.

3. Cut tomatoes in half crosswise. Remove the seeds by slightly squeezing the tomato, cut side down, over a sink.

4. Using a coarse hand grater, grate the tomatoes over a 1-quart bowl. Discard the skins.

5. Add the salt and pepper, sugar, and vinegar to the tomato pulp. Stir in the olive oil.

6. Stack the basil leaves, and roll them into a tight cigar. Finely slice the roll crosswise. Add the basil strips to the tomato mixture and stir well to combine. Refrigerate until ready to use.

7. When ready to serve, spread some of the tomato mixture over the bread slices and serve sprinkled with a little coarse sea salt on top.

Note: A small piece of cheese can be placed on top, or drizzle a little bit of oil on top of the mixture before sprinkling with salt.

Yield: 8–10 servings

TINA'S TIDBITS

- *Similar to a bruschetta, another way Spaniards make this tapas is to literally rub the cut side of the tomato on the hard crisp baguette slices and let the bread do the grating!*
- *Although this mixture can be made in advance, it is generally not a good idea to mix sugar and vinegar with a fruit for a long time, as it will pull moisture out of the food.*

PECHUGA DE POLLO CON PORTO
(BONELESS CHICKEN BREAST WITH PORT)

So much has been said about the expulsion of Jews from Spain that one must also remember that a short seven years later they were expelled from Portugal, and the Inquisition followed the Jews all the way to Brazil! This dish is a modern creation, using two ingredients that best typify their countries of origin: port wine from Oporto, Portugal, and orange juice from Valencia, Spain.

6–8 boneless, skinless chicken breasts
1/2 cup flour
Salt, freshly ground black pepper, and pinch of allspice
3 tablespoons olive oil
1 cup port wine (preferably Tawny Port), divided use
3/4 cup fresh orange juice, divided use

2 teaspoons lemon juice
1 tablespoon brandy
1 teaspoon Kitchen Bouquet
2 teaspoons cornstarch
1/2 teaspoon salt
Freshly ground black pepper to taste
4 drops Tabasco sauce

1. To prepare the chicken breast for this recipe, first remove the fillet. The fillet is the separate, tender piece of chicken breast that is located in a clear membrane sack on the underside of each breast half. The chicken fillet or "tender" can be recognized by a thin, white pearlized tendon that runs through it.

2. Once the fillet is located, gently pull it away from the chicken breast and out of its sack. Note that the sack may have been cut when filleting the breast, so do not worry if it is not visible on inspection.

3. To remove the tendon from the fillet, hold onto the thick end of the white tendon and gently scrape a knife blade along it to slightly separate it from the fillet meat. Hold the meat back with the knife while the blade rests against the tendon. Slowly jiggle the tendon as you pull it away from the knife. The blade will scrape the meat away from the tendon as it is pulled out of the fillet.

4. Place the breast meat on a cutting board with the smooth side down. Cover with a plastic storage bag and gently pound with the heel of your hand or a smooth mallet until the chicken is 1/2 inch thick. If pieces are very large, they may be cut in half crosswise.

TINA'S TIDBITS

- *Chicken doesn't need to be pounded for tenderizing, just for uniformity of thickness.*
- *It is better to pound meat under a plastic bag instead of waxed paper, because shards of wax can get embedded in the meat.*
- *Port is a sweet fortified wine that is named after the city Oporto, from where it is shipped. A very acceptable flavored port from New York State can be purchased for under $10 a bottle and used for cooking. Because it is fortified, port does not need to be refrigerated after opening.*
- *Kitchen Bouquet is a vegetable-based brown-colored sauce used solely to darken a sauce and make it look richer. It can be eliminated in most cases if needed.*

5. Lightly dust the chicken in flour that has been seasoned with salt, pepper, and a pinch of allspice.

6. Heat a large frying pan for 20 seconds. Add the oil and heat for an additional 15 seconds. Sauté the chicken breasts 1 minute on each side, until lightly browned. Add half the port and $\frac{1}{4}$ cup orange juice, and simmer over low heat for 5–7 minutes or until the chicken is tender. Transfer the chicken to a warm platter and keep hot.

7. Blend the remaining ingredients. Add to the frying pan and cook until the sauce thickens. Return the chicken to the pan and turn the meat in the sauce until all pieces are coated and reheated. Serve.

Note: May be made in advance and frozen or refrigerated until ready to reheat.

Yield: 6–8 Servings

FLAN

Flan can be thick and heavy or thin and light. But a good flan should be smooth as silk and firm, but not hard, with a golden caramel that has a strong flavor but is not burnt tasting. Here is my all-time favorite. For a taste from the Maghreb, use orange blossom water, as my friends at Café Marrakesh in Dallas taught me, in place of all or some of the vanilla for a wonderfully subtle floral essence.

1 cup sugar
½ cup water
3 cups milk, preferably whole or 2%
¾ cup sugar

4 large eggs
2 egg yolks
2 teaspoons vanilla or orange blossom water

1. Preheat the oven to 350°F.

2. To make the caramel, place the sugar and water in a 1½-quart saucepan, and cook over moderate heat for 10 minutes or until the sugar becomes an amber color.

3. Using 6–8 individual ramekins, pour the caramel immediately into the cups, turning the cups around to coat the bottom and sides thoroughly. Set aside while you make the custard.

4. Heat the milk and sugar in a 2-quart saucepan.

5. In a mixing bowl, whisk the eggs and the yolks until smooth.

6. Pour about ¼ cup of the hot milk **slowly** into the eggs, stirring constantly. Add the remainder of the milk into the eggs, and whisk to thoroughly combine. Flavor with the vanilla, and strain the mixture through a sieve into a large liquid measuring cup or pitcher.

7. Pour the mixture into the caramel-coated molds.

8. Line a 13 × 9-inch baking dish with paper towel. Place the ramekins in the pan, and pour hot water around them halfway up the sides of the mold. Bake for 25–30 minutes until the custard is firm (but still jiggles a little) and has shrunk slightly away from the sides.

9. Remove from the water bath, cool to room temperature, and then refrigerate.

10. To unmold, slightly turn the mold to see if the flan is loose. If necessary, run a small, sharp knife around the inside edge of the cup. Place a plate over the ramekin and invert rapidly. Let the caramel pour out onto the flan and serve.

Yield: 8 servings

TINA'S TIDBITS

- *Egg whites are responsible for the firm edge to a flan; yolks give the flan its richness and weight.*
- *Never stir a sugar mixture after it has dissolved, or you will set up a crystalline structure in the sugar that might yield a pot of sugary sand.*
- *As water evaporates from a sugar solution, the bubbles get bigger and slower. This is a clue that the mixture will soon begin to caramelize.*
- *To see if the custard is done, slightly poke a small, sharp knife into the center of the dish. If the knife comes out clear, then the custard is done. The flan will firm up when it is cold.*
- *Cooked flans can be refrigerated for a day or two and then unmolded just before serving. Make sure the dishes are tightly covered with plastic wrap to prevent drying.*
- *Sugar syrup is **very** hot. Always use a pot holder or glove on the hand that will be holding the ramekin when you add the syrup.*

ITALY

*I*taly is home to the oldest, continuously inhabited Jewish community in Europe. The first Jews arrived in southern Italy and Rome after the destruction of the First Temple. By the time of the destruction of the Second Temple, Jews made up almost 9 percent of the Roman Empire's population. Their living conditions were

tolerable until the beginning of the fourth century when Constantine I established Christianity as the official religion of the Roman Empire. After this decree, the Jews were consistently subjected to higher taxes, exclusion from owning property, and exclusion from most professions.

Life became even worse in the twelfth century when Pope Innocent III ordered every Jew to be singled out in the community by wearing an identifying badge proclaiming his religion. In the thirteenth century Pope Gregory IX promoted the process of the Inquisition in Central and Western Europe and began to focus on the Jewish community as well as Christian heretics. The only places where Jews were not greatly harassed were in major commercial centers like Venice, Florence, Genoa, and Pisa as well as southern French cities like Avignon, Marseilles, and Arles, where the important contribution of Jews to the financial success of the papacy afforded some limited protection.

The first Jewish ghetto was established on an island in Venice in 1516. The island was referred to as the ghetto because of the foundry (*geto* in Italian) on the island. Subsequent ghettos were set up in other major cities, especially after the southern Italian Jews were expelled and crowded the northern cities. Immigrants from the Spanish expulsion in 1492 moved to the north of Italy—almost forty

thousand Jews lived on the islands of Sicily and Sardinia, then Spanish territories, and they were expelled as well.

As with all Jewish cuisine in the Diaspora, the movement of the Jews meant the migration of their regional dishes. Sicilian and Spanish cooking highlighted the seven hundred years of Arab influence. When the Jews moved east and north, they brought with them the custom of using oil instead of pork fat for frying. Eggplant, artichokes, spinach (often with raisins), and rice were the cornerstones of Italian Jewish cuisine.

Holidays influenced the foods prepared. According to Claudia Roden, using saffron to color rice or adding spinach and raisins was a way to elevate simple foods for the celebration of Shabbat. Risotto alla Milanese and other risotto dishes incorporating vegetables were the creations of observant Jews. The prohibition of cooking on the Sabbath created dishes that either slow cooked overnight or were served cold. Again, according to Roden, only the Jews ate cold pasta and rice dishes, and foods preserved with vinegar and sugar like caponata were served on Shabbat because they could be prepared in advance.

Relatives, dispersed throughout the world by the Inquisition, exchanged new foods with each other. Because of their connections in the New World and because Jews were traders, tomatoes, pumpkins, corn, and green beans were associated with the Jews in Italy. The Spanish brought these foods to Italy, but the Jews distributed their use throughout the north.

When the names of dishes include adjectives like *alla giudia*, *all' ebraica*, and *alla mosaica* (such as *carciofi alla guidia*, "artichokes Jewish style") or the names of cities that had large Jewish populations like Ancona, Livorno, Ferrara, and Venice, they quietly announce their Jewish roots.

SALMONE AFFUMICATO CON MELONE (SMOKED SALMON WITH MELON)

Here I have taken a little license and "tweaked" an icon of Italian cuisine to conform to our dietary laws. Prosciutto e melone *is traditionally made in Italy by rolling a slice of the Parma ham around a wedge of rock melon. In this recipe, cubes of juicy, sweet honeydew or cantaloupe melon are wrapped with glistening, pink strands of smoked salmon to re-create the salty-sweet taste contrast of the original.*

½ small, ripe honeydew or cantaloupe
4 ounces of thinly sliced smoked salmon (lox)

1 lemon
Italian flat leaf parsley for garnish (optional)

1. Cut the melon in half. Remove the seeds, and cut the flesh into 1-inch cubes.

2. Cut each slice of smoked salmon lengthwise into ½-inch strips.

3. Wrap one strip of salmon around a cube of melon, and secure it with a toothpick. Repeat with remaining ingredients.

4. If using, finely mince some Italian parsley and set aside, covered with plastic wrap.

5. Just before serving, squeeze a little lemon juice over each cube and sprinkle with a little parsley.

Yield: Approximately 3 dozen pieces, or 9–12 servings

TINA'S TIDBITS

- *Melon can be cut into 1 1/2-inch wedges and the salmon wrapped around crosswise for individual appetizer portions.*
- *Finely grated lemon zest sprinkled on the top also makes a delicious garnish.*
- *Do not expose fish to acidic liquids for long periods of time or they will "cook" the fish that comes in contact with the juice and toughen the delicate meat.*

Fiori de Zucca Ripieni
(Stuffed Zucchini Blossoms)

Zucchini blossoms are found in frittatas, in salads, or stuffed and/or fried throughout Rome in summer and early fall. Although one can find recipes calling for all types of cheese or even rice fillings, the combination of mozzarella and anchovy is most strongly associated with the cooking of the Roman Jewish ghetto.

One summer I grew zucchini plants not for the vegetable but just for the blossom! It is now easier to find blossoms in high-end supermarkets in late summer. Thin slices of zucchini or eggplant can be used as a delicious but somewhat messier alternative.

12 zucchini blossoms, with stems preferably
6 ounces soft, fresh mozzarella
½ tablespoon anchovy paste or 6 canned anchovy fillets
¾ cup all-purpose flour
¾ cup water or club soda

¼ teaspoon salt
Additional flour for dredging
Olive oil for frying
Marinara sauce, store-bought or freshly made (optional)

1. Remove stamen from inside of the flower. Rinse flower thoroughly in case any insect pollinator is present. Shake off excess water. Set aside.

2. Combine mozzarella with anchovy paste or fillets in a small processor work bowl, and using the metal blade, pulse the machine on and off until the cheese and anchovies are coarsely combined. Place mixture in a 1-quart plastic bag.

3. Place ¾ cup flour in a 1-quart bowl. Gradually add water or club soda to the flour, whisking constantly until a thick, creamy consistency is achieved. Add the salt and mix well. Set aside.

4. Place about ½ cup flour in a shallow soup bowl.

5. Cut a ¼-inch hole in the corner of the bag and squeeze gently at the top of the bag until the cheese mixture starts to extrude from the hole.

6. Hold the tip of the bag just inside the blossom, and squeeze about 1 tablespoon of cheese mixture inside the blossom. Gently twist the open end of the blossom to keep it closed. Set aside and proceed with the remaining blossoms.

7. Heat about 1 inch of olive oil in a 2-quart saucepan or 10-inch frying pan.

8. Lightly coat each blossom with the flour in the shallow soup bowl, and then dip into the flour-water batter to completely cover.

9. Fry the blossoms in 3 or 4 small batches until golden brown and crisp (about 3 minutes).

10. Drain on paper towel and serve as is or with warm marinara sauce.

Yield: 6–12 servings

TINA'S TIDBITS

- *Long-stemmed flowers that do not have baby zucchinis attached to them are male and need to have the interior stamen removed before stuffing.*
- *To make the coating adhere better to food, always dip the moist food in flour before coating with batter. The flour adheres to the food and the batter adheres to the flour so it doesn't slide off when put into the hot oil.*
- *Two canned anchovy fillets equal 1/2 teaspoon anchovy paste.*

Pumpkin Ravioli from Mantua

During the Renaissance the Jews lived very well in Mantua under the Gonzaga duchy. They were very familiar with pumpkin because of New World exploration and the Portuguese and Converso connections throughout the world. Although this dish is very popular in restaurants throughout the world right now, the recipe is five hundred years old. This recipe was adapted from Joyce Goldstein's cookbook, Cucina Ebraica.

2 pounds fresh pie pumpkin or butternut squash, or
  1 pound canned pumpkin puree
$\frac{1}{4}$ cup freshly grated Parmesan cheese
1 cup Italian amaretti cookies (about 2 ounces)
$\frac{1}{4}$ teaspoon nutmeg
$\frac{1}{2}$ cup finely chopped raisins (soaked in hot water
  for 15 minutes if too dry and hard)

Sugar to taste
1 egg
2 tablespoons dried plain bread crumbs
1 egg yolk mixed with 2 tablespoons water for sealing
  dough
1 stick butter melted, until light brown
$\frac{1}{4}$ cup chiffonade of fresh mint

1. To prepare the pumpkin or squash, roast in a 400°F oven for 50 minutes or until soft. Cool, cut in half, and remove all seeds and stringy fibers. Scoop the meat of the squash into a bowl and mash with a fork until smooth.

2. If puree is watery, spread the puree on a rimmed baking sheet, and bake at 300°F for 10 minutes or until it appears dry. Let cool before using, or use 1 pound of canned pumpkin.

3. In a large bowl, combine the pumpkin with the next 7 ingredients and set aside while you make the dough.

Dough

2 large eggs
1 tablespoon extra virgin olive oil
2 tablespoons ice water
2 cups bread flour

1. Place the eggs, oil, and water in the food processor work bowl, and mix by turning the processor on and off twice.

2. Add 1 cup of the bread flour, and turn the processor on for 5 seconds. Scrape the sides of the bowl. Add the other cup of flour and process for 10 seconds longer. The dough will be crumbly. Pinch a little bit of dough; if it holds together, it is ready to be rolled.

3. Remove the dough and divide in half. Place on a lightly floured surface, cover, and allow to rest for 10 minutes or longer if you are rolling the dough by hand.

4. Make pasta according to machine directions. If rolling pasta by hand, divide dough into fourths and then roll out each portion as thin as possible. Cut dough into 3-inch rounds, or use a ravioli form.

5. Place 1 tablespoon of filling in the center of each circle or each template on the ravioli form. Brush a little of the egg yolk mixture on the edges of the dough, and cover with another circle of dough (or sheet if using the ravioli plate). Press dough firmly from the filling outward to remove any air trapped in the middle and seal the dough.

6. Bring a large pot of salted water to a boil and add 1 tablespoon of oil. Cook pasta until al dente. Drain and place in a large serving bowl.

7. Drizzle brown butter on top of ravioli, and sprinkle with the fresh mint chiffonade.

Yield: 4 servings

TINA'S TIDBITS

- *Although fresh pie pumpkin has a more distinct flavor, canned pumpkin will work if you are short on time.*
- *Never use salt in the pasta dough. It will make the dough tough and hard to roll.*

Winter Squash Gnocchi with Wilted Spinach and Pine Nuts

I don't remember the first time I made this wonderful version of gnocchi, but I do remember mispronouncing the name in the little South Jersey Italian restaurant thirty-five years ago. I pronounced the dish "gunochee," but its proper pronunciation is "nyoki." However you say it, these firm but not hard cylinders of cooked pasta are absolutely wonderful, especially when made with the pumpkin or butternut squash.

1½ pounds butternut squash or pie pumpkin
¾ pound russet or Yukon Gold potatoes
1 large egg, lightly beaten
½ cup grated Romano cheese
½ teaspoon minced fresh thyme or 1 pinch dried thyme
½ teaspoon finely chopped pineapple sage or pinch of dried sage
salt and freshly ground white pepper to taste

Good-sized pinch of nutmeg
¾ cup flour
6 tablespoons unsalted butter
0.5 ounce dried porcini mushrooms
¼ cup pine nuts
9 ounces fresh baby spinach leaves
½ teaspoon kosher salt
Additional Romano cheese for garnish
Freshly ground black pepper, as needed

1. Preheat the oven to 425°F. Place the butternut squash or pumpkin and the potato on the middle rack of the oven, and roast the vegetables until soft, about 40 minutes. Remove from oven and cool until easy to handle.

2. Cut the squash or pumpkin in half lengthwise and remove seeds. Scoop out the flesh, and place in a medium bowl. Mash until smooth, and measure ¾ cup of the puree. Reserve the remainder for another use.

3. Place the squash or pumpkin puree on a jellyroll pan.

4. Cut the potato in half, and scoop out the flesh into a small bowl. Mash with a fork or potato masher until smooth, and add to the pan with the squash or pumpkin puree. Place in the freezer to cool completely, but do not freeze.

5. Return the cooled puree mixture to a medium bowl, and stir in the egg, cheese, thyme, sage, salt, pepper, and nutmeg.

6. Add the flour, and stir to combine. Knead the dough on a lightly floured board for about a minute until dough holds together and is soft and still slightly moist.

7. Divide dough into thirds. Shape each portion into a rope that is about ½-inch thick. Cut rope into ½-inch pieces. If knife gets sticky, dust it with some extra flour.

8. Lightly flour a kitchen towel, a dinner-size fork, and your thumb. Holding the front of the fork facing you, pushing with your thumb, roll a piece of dough from the bottom of the fork tines, against the curve, up to the tip of the fork and then flick the dough off the fork onto the prepared towel. Repeat with the remaining dough.

9. Melt 3 tablespoons of unsalted butter in a 10-inch skillet. Keep warm while you make the gnocchi.

10. Bring a large pot of salted water to a boil, and cook ⅓ of the gnocchi for about 3 minutes or

until the centers are no longer raw. Stir once after the gnocchi rise to the top of the pot. When the gnocchi are done, remove with a slotted spoon to the heated butter in the frying pan. Lightly toss to coat with the butter. Repeat with the remaining gnocchi until all are warmed in the butter. Keep warm while you prepare the spinach and mushrooms.

11. Cover the dried mushrooms with water, and microwave on high for 3 minutes. Allow to sit for 10 minutes or until soft.

12. Carefully remove the mushrooms from the liquid, and cut into julienne strips. Melt 1 tablespoon of butter in a small frying pan, and sauté the mushrooms until they have given up their juices. Sprinkle with a little kosher salt and set aside.

13. Melt the remaining butter in a large nonstick frying pan, and add the pine nuts. Toss the nuts over medium heat until lightly golden. Immediately add all of the spinach and the salt, and toss lightly. Reduce the heat, cover, and wilt the spinach for 2 minutes.

14. To serve, divide the spinach among 6–8 plates. Place gnocchi equally on top of spinach on each plate, and spoon some of the mushrooms over all. Top with some additional grated Romano cheese and a few grindings of pepper. Serve as a first course.

Yield: 6–8 servings

TINA'S TIDBITS

- *Butternut squash is easy to find in most supermarkets. However, in early fall look for small, round, sweet, firm-fleshed pie pumpkins to enhance the flavor of the dish.*
- *When a recipe requires cooked squash, it is much easier to bake the vegetable whole and then scoop out its flesh than to try to peel the hard, slippery rind off before boiling.*
- *Do not overhandle the dough or you will activate the gluten in the flour, and the gnocchi will be dense and heavy instead of light.*

PASTA WITH SALSA CRUDA

This pasta dish is a variation of the famous insalata Caprese *made up of the season's freshest tomatoes and basil and fresh mozzarella found on the island of Capri in the very fertile region of the Campania surrounding Naples. The essence of summer, this dish must be made with the freshest and sweetest produce and soft mozzarella. The original Caprese salad is a staple at every Roman Jewish restaurant I visited. The addition of pasta makes a hearty main dish or side for fish.*

3/4 pound (2–3 large) tomatoes
1/2 pound, fresh soft mozzarella
1/2 cup lightly packed basil leaves
2 cloves garlic, finely minced
1/2 cup extra virgin olive oil

1/4 teaspoon kosher salt
Freshly ground black pepper to taste
8 ounces dried rotelle (spirals) or penne rigati
Freshly grated Parmesan cheese

1. Cut the tomatoes into 1/2-inch cubes, and place them in a 3-quart glass or ceramic serving bowl.

2. Cut the mozzarella into 1/2-inch cubes, and add to the tomatoes.

3. Layer the basil leaves, and roll them up lengthwise like a cigarette. Slice thinly crosswise through the roll to make a chiffonade—thin strands of basil that "float" like chiffon—and add to the tomato mixture.

4. Add the garlic, olive oil, salt, and pepper to the bowl, and stir to combine. Cover the bowl, and set aside at room temperature for at least 1 hour.

5. When ready to serve, cook the pasta in boiling salted water until al dente. Drain and immediately toss with the raw tomato mixture.

6. Serve at once with freshly grated Parmesan cheese and more black pepper if desired.

Yield: 6–8 servings

TINA'S TIDBITS

- *Pasta in shapes like macaroni, shells, or twists will hold onto small particles of food in chunky sauces better than long, smooth pasta.*
- *The heat of the drained pasta will wilt the basil and slightly soften the cheese to bring out their full flavor. Therefore, do not rinse pasta, as it will cool it.*
- *Eliminate the cheese for a meat meal or if you need to make the dish in advance, since the melted cheese will clump when cold.*

Pasta Riminata

This is an incredible dish, with a creamy sauce made with pine nuts and raisins and no cream. This recipe can be prepared in advance and is so delicious. Don't tell anyone that the base of the sauce is cauliflower. Leave out the Parmesan and you have a wonderful side dish for a meat meal. The pine nuts and raisins imply the Spanish origins, and the olive oil the Jewish connection.

1 head cauliflower, cut into florets, or one 1-pound
   bag frozen cauliflower
1½ cups water
½ teaspoon salt, divided use
4 tablespoons extra virgin olive oil
1 large onion, cut into ½-inch dice

2 tablespoons pine nuts
2 tablespoons dark raisins
Freshly ground black pepper to taste
1 pound rigatoni
½ cup freshly grated Parmesan cheese or to taste

1. Combine the cauliflower, water, and ¼ teaspoon salt in a 3-quart saucepan, and bring to a boil. Cover, reduce heat, and simmer until very tender, about 10 minutes.

2. Drain the cauliflower, and reserve the cooking liquid. Mash the cauliflower with a fork until relatively smooth and set aside.

3. Heat a large frying pan for 20 seconds, add 3 tablespoons of olive oil, and heat another 10 seconds. Sauté the onion in the olive oil for 5 minutes or until soft and very slightly golden.

4. Add the pine nuts, raisins, remaining salt, and pepper to taste to the onion mixture, and stir for 2 minutes or until nuts begin to turn golden.

5. Add the mashed cauliflower and ¼ cup of the reserved cooking liquid to the onion mixture, and simmer for 15 minutes or until thick, stirring often. If the mixture is getting too dry, add more of the reserved liquid to prevent sticking. When mixture is done, set aside until ready to serve.

6. Cook the pasta in boiling salted water and add 1 tablespoon of olive oil. Cook until pasta is al dente. Drain and place in a large serving bowl.

7. Pour ⅓ of the sauce over the pasta and toss. Place remaining sauce over the pasta, garnish with the Parmesan cheese, and serve.

Yield: 6 servings

TINA'S TIDBITS

- *The amount of time it takes to cook cauliflower varies. Therefore, cook the vegetable until it is really very tender. Your finished sauce will be much smoother and creamier.*
- *Add some chopped anchovies or brined olives instead of cheese to create a pareve (nondairy) dish, another inventive way to utilize the foods and flavors of a country without compromising the Jewish dietary laws.*

Spinaci con Pinoli e Passerini (Spinach with Pine Nuts and Raisins)

At Walter's Ristorante d'Italia in Providence, Rhode Island, you can experience the two-thousand-year-old cuisine of Italian Jews. I had the good fortune to eat an authentic historically accurate Jewish meal when I was there, and Walter put this dish on my radar screen. It seems that whenever you see pine nuts and raisins together and especially with spinach, the dish is screaming that it has Jewish roots from the Moorish influence in Spain. This dish is made easier by using tender baby spinach leaves. No sand, no removal of stem, and no chopping!

4 cups baby spinach (about $\frac{1}{3}$ pound)
2 tablespoons extra virgin olive oil
$\frac{1}{2}$ medium onion, finely chopped

3 tablespoons pine nuts
3 tablespoons dark raisins, soaked in water if hard
Kosher salt and freshly ground pepper to taste

1. Rinse the spinach in water if gritty and drain well. Set aside.

2. Heat the olive oil in a large nonstick frying pan for 20 seconds. Add the onion and sauté for 5 minutes or until onions are lightly golden and soft.

3. Add the pine nuts and sauté until the nuts are light golden in color.

4. If the raisins have been soaking, drain. Add the raisins to the pine nuts and onions, and stir to combine.

5. Add all of the drained spinach and lightly stir the mixture just a little. Place a lid on the pan and cook over low heat for 2 minutes or until the leaves are wilted.

6. Sprinkle mixture with salt and pepper, and stir until all of the spinach is soft but still a bright green. Serve hot or at room temperature.

Yield: 4–6 servings

TINA'S TIDBITS

- *One easy way to wash spinach is placing all the leaves in a large bowl of water. The leaves will float, and the gritty sand will sink.*
- *Always dry spinach leaves well so that they don't soak up the water when cooking.*
- *If you must use frozen spinach, make sure the spinach is thoroughly defrosted and squeezed dry before sautéing with the onions. The dish will be acceptable but will not have the bright color or taste of the fresh.*
- *Use baby spinach and you will never have to devein or cut up a leaf again. In addition to its ease in use, there is no waste in volume with the small, tender leaves.*

PESCE EN SAOR
(FISH IN SWEET AND SOUR SAUCE)

This recipe was originally prepared for sailors at sea because the sauce preserved the fish over long journeys. However, the presence of pine nuts and raisins signals the Moorish influence and draws a distinct link between the Spanish Jewish émigrés and their culinary traditions. Frying foods, specifically in oil, and then preserving them in a vinegar sauce originated on the Iberian peninsula by Jews and was a necessity to fulfill the laws of Shabbat, since the food could be prepared in advance, eliminating the need to work on the day of rest. This dish is traditionally made with sardines (sarde en saor), but small, firm fillets of fish may be used as well.

2 pounds whole sardines or red mullets, or 1 pound sole fillets
Salt and freshly ground black pepper to taste
1/2 cup flour
1/4 cup extra virgin olive oil

MARINADE:
2 tablespoons extra virgin olive oil
1 pound yellow onions, cut in half and thinly sliced
1 1/4 cups balsamic vinegar
1 tablespoon honey
Pinch of saffron (optional)
1/2 cup raisins
1/4 cup pine nuts

1. If using whole fish, make sure that the fish is thoroughly gutted and scaled. The head of larger fish may be removed; sardines may be left whole.

2. Rinse fish or fish fillets and pat dry. Season lightly with salt and pepper.

3. Place the flour in a gallon plastic bag and season with a small amount of salt and pepper. Add a few pieces of fish to the bag and toss until completely coated. Remove fish from the bag and repeat with the remaining fish.

4. Heat a 10-inch skillet over high heat for 20 seconds. Add the olive oil and heat for 10 seconds more. Add the fish to the hot oil and fry until lightly golden brown on both sides. This should take no more than a total of 3 minutes per fillet or sardines and no more than a total of 4–5 minutes if using other small, whole fish. Drain on paper towel. Place in a nonreactive glass or porcelain casserole that just fits the fish; fish may overlap slightly. Set aside to cool completely.

5. Meanwhile, heat a clean sauté pan over high heat for 20 seconds. Add the 2 tablespoons of olive oil to the pan, and heat for an additional 10 seconds. Reduce heat slightly if oil begins to smoke.

6. Add the thinly sliced onions to the pan and sauté until the onions are soft and lightly golden. Add the vinegar, honey, saffron (if using), and raisins to the pan, and cook over moderate heat for 5 minutes or until mixture has reduced slightly.

7. Lightly roast the pine nuts in a 350°F oven for 4 minutes. Add the pine nuts to the onion mixture and remove from the heat. Adjust amount of vinegar or honey if needed.

8. When the onion mixture is warm to the touch of your finger, spoon the mixture over the fish.

9. Although the fish may be served immediately, historically the fish is allowed to marinate in the refrigerator for 1–2 days to absorb all the flavors.

10. Serve at room temperature.

Yield: 4–6 servings as an appetizer, 3–4 as a main dish

TINA'S TIDBITS

- *Traditionally, vinegar, wine, and a wine concentrate are used in this dish. However, balsamic vinegar has a richer and thicker consistency and is a perfect substitute for the concentrated wine-vinegar mixture.*
- *If the raisins are particularly sweet, honey is not needed.*
- *Another word for this type of preparation—frying and then marinating in a vinegar sauce—is escabeche.*

Zucca Gialla in Agrodolce
(Squash in Sweet and Sour Sauce)

I first saw this dish in Joyce Goldstein's Cucina Ebraica. *I was intrigued by the flavor combinations. The sweet-and-sour flavoring is so much a part of the Jewish culinary culture, and the use of vinegar implies that this dish was made in advance for the Sabbath day meal. The following is an adaptation of Joyce's recipe.*

2 pounds butternut squash
2–3 tablespoons olive oil, or as needed
Kosher salt as needed
½ cup chiffonade of fresh mint
2 large cloves of garlic, sliced lengthwise into thin
    slivers

½ cup balsamic vinegar or red wine vinegar
½ cup sugar (less if using balsamic vinegar)
⅛ teaspoon cinnamon
Kosher salt and freshly ground black pepper to taste

1. Cut the squash in half lengthwise, peel it, and remove all seeds and fibers from the inside. Cut each half lengthwise again and slice crosswise into ¼-inch slices.

2. Toss the squash slices with 2 tablespoons of olive oil to coat, and place the squash slices on a nonstick cookie sheet or roasting pan. Sprinkle very lightly with some kosher salt.

3. Bake for 15 to 20 minutes at 400° F or until squash is tender but firm—if the tip of a sharp knife is easily inserted and removed from the squash, it is done.

4. Layer the cooked squash with the mint and garlic slivers in a serving dish.

5. Pour any pan drippings from the squash into an 8-inch nonstick sauté pan. If there is very little oil, add 1 tablespoon of olive oil to the pan. Heat on medium for 10 seconds.

6. Add the balsamic vinegar and sugar first to dissolve, and then add the cinnamon to the pan. Cook, stirring constantly, until the mixture bubbles and thickens slightly, about 4 minutes.

7. Pour the hot syrup over the squash, and gently move and lift the squash with a rubber spatula or large plastic serving spoon (these utensils won't cut into the pieces of squash) to distribute the sauce evenly.

8. Serve at once or at room temperature, which is perfect for a buffet.

Yield: 6–8 servings

TINA'S TIDBITS

- *To chiffonade a leafy herb, layer 5–10 leaves on top of each other, and roll the leaves tightly together into a long log like a cigarette. Cutting across the log, make thin slices. When you are done, there will be thin strands of herb that almost float when you toss them in the air—hence the reference to chiffon!*
- *Balsamic vinegar is made from white trebbiano grapes. The juice is allowed to age in different types and sizes of wood barrels that impart the special sweet-tart flavor to the vinegar.*

ZABAGLIONE

This light custard is a perfect way to end a meat meal. The egg yolks are flavored and cooked gently over simmering water to allow the yolks to expand and thicken. If the egg yolk gets too hot, it will cook and you will have very delicious scrambled eggs! The classic version of this sauce is made with Marsala wine. The French use champagne and call it sabayon. Either way, this is delicious over fruit and/or a simple pound cake.

4 egg yolks
¼ cup sugar
3 tablespoons Marsala wine

1 tablespoon water
1 tablespoon apricot brandy
2 pints fresh berries or fruit

1. Place the egg yolks and the sugar in the top of a double boiler or in a 1-quart saucepan, and whisk together until a thick ribbon of mixture pours off the whisk.

2. Place the pan with the sugar-egg mixture over another pan containing hot, but not boiling water. The mixture shouldn't be so hot that it will cook the eggs.

3. Add the Marsala, water, and brandy to the sugar-egg mixture. Whisk constantly over the warm water for 4 minutes until a nice thick custard is formed.

4. When the custard has thickened, **immediately** remove from the heat or you will have fancy scrambled eggs!

5. Have your fresh berries divided into 5 or 6 serving dishes or glasses. Pour the zabaglione over the fruit and serve.

Yield: 6 servings

TINA'S TIDBITS

- *Egg yolks are used for flavor and as a coloring and thickening agent in sauces and baked goods.*
- *Using a whisk while the sauce is cooking incorporates air into the yolks, and the yolks cook in their volumized state, creating the light, airy consistency.*

TURKEY AND THE OTTOMAN EMPIRE

For almost three thousand years there has been a Jewish presence in the region of the world now associated with Turkey. At one time the Ottoman Empire encompassed lands from the Persian Gulf in the east to Hungary, Bulgaria, and Greece in the northwest, and from Egypt and Palestine in the south to the Caucasus mountains in the north, with Istanbul designated its capital. According to the famous Jewish historian Josephus, the great Greek philosopher Aristotle met with Jews on a trip throughout western Asia.

During the Byzantine period Jews experienced great persecution in a heightened Christian environment. In 1453, however, the Ottomans conquered the region and bestowed many privileges on the Jews. Life was so good that a letter was sent from Rabbi Yitzchak Sarfati to Jewish communities in Europe encouraging them to leave the persecutions they were experiencing in Christian Europe and come to Turkey (Anatolia, as it was called then). The Jews were encouraged to live in Constantinople and set up their own governing communities.

When the Jews were expelled in 1492 from Spain, Sultan Bayazid II actively encouraged the immigration of the Spanish refugees to his shores. He is quoted as commenting that Ferdinand was not very wise, since he stripped Spain of all its assets when he expelled the Jews. Turkey prospered, and so did the people in the Jewish communities of Constantinople, Izmir, Safed, and Salonika. In 1856 the Ottoman Empire established equality for all citizens of its country. This meant that the Jews no longer governed themselves but were part of the greater civic community.

The twentieth century brought some difficult times to this region. The Ottoman Empire declined after siding with the Germans during World War I, and the rise of anti-Semitic activities led many Jews to move to Western Europe, the Americas, and Palestine, which became a British mandate after World War I. However, those Jews left behind during World War II were protected due to Turkey's hard-won neutrality. Although Turkey's diplomats fought to save their Jewish citizens from camp deportation while they were in Nazi-occupied territories, a shipload of Romanian Jewish émigrés on their way to Palestine were denied asylum when their ship broke down, and the ship sank into the Black Sea, killing all but one of the 769 passengers.

Today the rich heritage of the Sephardic Jews is still felt in Turkey, though only twenty-six thousand remain to carry on their rich, ancient traditions.

Rachel Amado Bortnick, a Sephardic historian, Ladino instructor, and the founder of the online group Ladinokomunita (a virtual community made up of over nine hundred Ladino-speaking members worldwide, found at www.sephardicstudies.org/komunita), sat with me in her kitchen and related stories from her childhood in Izmir, Turkey. A descendant of Spanish Jews on both sides of her family, her history mirrored countless textbooks on post-expulsion migration. The Amado family migrated from Spain, probably to Portugal and then to Bayonne, where they lived for at least two centuries before moving to Izmir in the eighteenth century. Her mother's side of the family was named Algranti, which means "from Granada."

Growing up in Izmir meant picking a young, green almond fruit off the tree in the yard, sprinkling it with a little salt and biting into its slightly tart fruit. In the center was a viscous sweet gel where the almond nut had not yet begun to form. Figs were so large that they were peeled to reveal their purple fruit. Izmir apricots tasted like no other in the world, and that's why most of the large dried apricots produced in Turkey come from there. All varieties of melons abounded and were there for the choosing. Is it any wonder that the only definition of dessert on an Izmir table was fruit?

The meal consisted of three courses, with a variety of small vegetables or salads always served on the side. This is very typical of this region of the world. Shabbat meals always started with fish in lemon sauce.

The first course would be the vegetable course, which was the vehicle for any protein on the menu. *Irviya kon gayina*, for example, is peas with chicken. The chicken is listed second, implying that you will find small pieces of chicken supplementing the peas and other vegetables rather than the other way around. Chicken was rarely served except on Shabbat and special occasions. Lamb was the more common meat used in the mostly vegetarian community.

The second course consisted of a rice or noodle dish. Sometimes a little of the first course was added to the rice, but generally this was eaten unadulterated with the salads on the side.

The third course was always fruit. Apples were served peeled, as were oranges and tangerines. Rachel demonstrated how to present an orange. The finished product looked like an orange on a decorative stand. See instructions on page 95. Fruits were always served without sauce.

Sweets, many of which Turkey is famous for, are never served at meals. They are for entertaining and snacking.

Liptauer Cheese

Liptauer cheese is actually a sheep's milk cheese from the Liptauer province in Hungary. However, in most German-speaking regions of Europe, Liptauer refers to a cheese highly flavored with herbs and seasoned and colored with the indigenous sweet paprika that Hungary is known for producing.

¼ pound cottage cheese
4 ounces cream cheese
½ stick unsalted butter
1 tablespoon gin
1 teaspoon anchovy paste
½ teaspoon dry mustard

1 tablespoon caraway seeds
1 tablespoon *fresh* Hungarian sweet paprika
Salt and pepper to taste
1 tablespoon capers
2 tablespoons chopped chives

1. Place the cottage cheese in a processor work bowl, and pulse on and off until relatively smooth.

2. Add the cream cheese and butter to the work bowl, and process until the butter-cheese mixture is thoroughly combined. You might need to stop and scrape down the sides of the bowl a few times until the mixture is smooth.

3. Add the gin, anchovy paste, dry mustard, caraway seeds, paprika, and salt and pepper, and process until well combined.

4. Add the capers and pulse on and off 10 times to distribute them evenly.

5. Spoon into a serving bowl and refrigerate for at least a few days to "ripen."

6. Just before serving, fold in the chopped chives and mound on a plate or shape into a ball. Chill until firm.

Yield: 1 cheese ball, 8–10 servings

TINA'S TIDBITS

- *The major flavor component in gin is juniper berries.*
- *One teaspoon of anchovy paste is equal to 4 canned anchovies.*
- *Unless you can buy paprika in very small quantities, it is best to store your paprika in the freezer to retain its flavor and color.*

OTTOMAN WATERMELON AND OLIVE SALAD

I first tasted this wonderful combination of flavors on the island of Santorini in the Adriatic Sea. As bright as the iconic sun-drenched, white stucco walls and blue domed rooftops are on this island, this dish is vibrant with color and flavor to match its surroundings. Enjoy this dish any time of year but especially when watermelon is at its sweetest!

3 cups watermelon, cut into ½-inch cubes
1 very small red onion, cut into thin rings (or ½-cup sliced half rings)
½ cup pitted Calamata olives
½ cup crumbled feta cheese
¼ cup extra virgin olive oil

2 tablespoons lemon juice
Salt and freshly ground pepper to taste
Pinch of sugar
2 tablespoons chiffonade of fresh mint
1 teaspoon sumac (optional)

1. Arrange the watermelon, onion rings, and olives on a platter. Sprinkle with the crumbled feta cheese.

2. Combine the olive oil, lemon juice, salt, pepper, and sugar together in a small, screw-top jar.

3. Sprinkle the mint over the platter, and drizzle the vinaigrette over the salad.

4. Dust the salad with the sumac and serve.

Yield: 4–6 servings

TINA'S TIDBITS

- *If preparing the salad in advance, keep ingredients in separate bowls so that the flavor of the onions doesn't overpower the other ingredients.*
- *It is important to dress the salad (pour dressing on it) at the last minute so that the watermelon won't absorb the liquid and become mushy.*
- *Sumac is a red berry grown on bushes throughout the Middle East whose flavor is tart like a lemon. Paprika may be substituted for color, but the flavor will be different.*

ORZO WITH DRIED CHERRIES

Orzo is more closely associated with Greece and the Ottoman Empire, but it is actually a form of pasta that in Italian means "barley," because of its shape. All the flavorful ingredients in this recipe belie the delicate taste of the finished product.

1 cup orzo
¼ teaspoon crumbled saffron threads
4 teaspoons grated orange zest
4 tablespoons orange juice
Salt to taste

1 tablespoon hazelnut oil
¼ cup dried cherries or raisins
2 tablespoons lightly toasted, coarsely chopped
   hazelnuts or slivered almonds
1 scallion, thinly sliced

1. Bring 2 quarts salted water to a boil. Add the saffron and the orzo, and cook for 7–10 minutes or until orzo is al dente. Drain, rinse under cold water, and drain well. Place orzo in a serving bowl.

2. In a small bowl, combine the orange zest, juice, and salt to taste. Whisk the hazelnut oil into the juice mixture until it is incorporated.

3. Toss the dressing with the orzo, and add the cherries, almonds, and scallion. Serve at room temperature.

Yield: 6 servings

TINA'S TIDBITS

- *Dijon mustard (1/4 teaspoon) can be added to the zest and juice before the oil is added. The mustard will help bind the oil to the juice, creating an emulsion. This will make a more uniform sauce for the orzo.*
- *Pasta will break down and become mushy if mixed with a high-acid food for a prolonged period of time, so don't make this dish more than a few hours in advance of serving.*

Ottoman Tsatsiki
(Cucumber Yogurt Dip)

All tsatsikis are not created equal. Eaten as a side salad on a tray of mezes or as a dip with pita chips, this authentic recipe bears no resemblance to the packaged variety in the supermarket.

1 large cucumber
1 cup Greek yogurt or ½ cup unflavored yogurt and
  ½ cup sour cream
2 cloves garlic, coarsely chopped
1 tablespoon olive oil

Lemon juice to taste (2–3 teaspoons)
Salt (very little) and freshly ground black pepper to
  taste
2 tablespoons chopped fresh dill or mint

1. Peel the cucumber and cut it in half lengthwise. Remove the seeds from both halves.

2. Coarsely cut half of the cucumber and place in a processor work bowl. Cut the other half into ¼-inch dice. Set aside.

3. Add the yogurt and the garlic to the work bowl with the cucumber, and pulse on and off until the mixture is coarsely smooth and there are no large pieces of garlic floating around.

4. Pour the mixture into a bowl and add the olive oil, lemon juice, salt, pepper, and dill or mint.

5. Add the diced cucumber, reserving 1 tablespoon for garnish. Stir to combine well. Pour into a serving bowl. Garnish with the remaining diced cucumber and possibly a sprig of dill. Serve with lavash crackers or toasted pita.

Yield: 4 or more servings

TINA'S TIDBITS

- *In most recipes using cucumber, the seeds should always be removed to prevent a very watery finished product.*
- *The easiest way to remove cucumber seeds is to cut the cucumber in half lengthwise and run the tip of a spoon down the middle, scraping the seeds away.*
- *Commercially prepared American yogurt does not have the same consistency as Greek or Middle Eastern yogurt. Greek yogurt must be used so that the final mixture won't be thin and watery. If necessary, sour cream may be substituted as per recipe.*

Mamaliga
(Romanian Polenta)

When corn was introduced to Europe after the discovery of the New World, it was widely received. However, growing conditions were not favorable in many regions, and colloquial biases to certain grains such as oats or rye diminished interest in corn. The Romanians loved the corn and the porridge made from its grain, mamaliga. *The Jewish community subsisted on the cornmeal porridge morning, noon, and night, adding slightly different ingredients to each meal to vary the taste. The love for* mamaliga *was so great that Romanian Jews were referred to as "Mamaligas" long after they crossed the Atlantic.*

2 cups milk, preferably whole or 2%
2 cups water, divided use
1 cup polenta or coarse corn meal
$\frac{1}{2}$ teaspoon salt, or to taste (depends on saltiness of feta)
10 grindings of fresh white pepper

2 tablespoons butter (salted butter is okay if desired)
2 ounces feta cheese, drained and crumbled
$\frac{1}{2}$ cup small-curd 4% fat cottage cheese
2 tablespoons finely grated Parmesan cheese
Sour cream (optional)

1. Heat 2 cups of milk and 1 cup of water in a microwave oven for $1\frac{1}{2}$ minutes. Set aside.

2. Combine 1 cup polenta with 1 cup of water, salt, and pepper in a 2-quart saucepan.

3. Add the hot liquid to the polenta mixture and place over medium heat, stirring constantly with a whisk for about 7 minutes, until the milk has been absorbed by the meal. The mixture will feel thick but still runny. Remove from the heat.

TINA'S TIDBITS

Variations on this recipe include:
- *Use all water and pareve margarine and serve with stews or pot roast.*
- *Add cream cheese instead of feta and 2 tablespoons of sugar and even add some raisins for a sweet, but not traditional, alternative.*
- *At Walter Potenza's restaurant I first tried the following polenta fritters stuffed with anchovy paste. Joyce Goldstein, in her book* Cucina Ebraica, *calls them* Rebecchine de Gerusalemme. *Using this recipe for* mamaliga, *the fritters are even more rich and delicious.*
  1. *Place one tin of anchovy fillets with the oil in the can in a small frying pan, and cook over low heat, mashing the anchovies into a paste.*
  2. *Cut slices from the* mamaliga *that are 1/2-inch thick and as wide as they are tall.*
  3. *Carefully slice each square in half so that each side is 1/4-inch thick.*
  4. *Spread a little anchovy paste over one half, and sandwich both sides together.*
  5. *Beat 1 egg with 1 teaspoon of water in a shallow bowl, and cover a plate with 1/2 cup of flour.*
  6. *Heat a frying pan for 20 seconds. Add 1/4 inch of oil in the pan, and heat for another 10 seconds.*
  7. *Dip the polenta squares in the egg to moisten, and coat thoroughly with the flour.*
  8. *Add coated squares to the frying pan 3 or 4 at a time, and fry over moderately high heat until the squares are crisp and lightly golden. Remove from oil, drain on paper towel, and serve immediately or when still warm.*
  9. *Serves 4–6 if you don't use all of the* mamaliga *and don't double the anchovies.*

4. Stir in the butter, crumbled feta, and cottage cheese. Mix until butter has melted and cheeses are evenly distributed throughout the mixture.

5. Preheat an oven to 350°F.

6. Grease an 8-inch square baking dish. Stir the cornmeal to break up any lumps, and pour mixture into pan. Smooth top and sprinkle with the Parmesan cheese.

7. Bake for 30 minutes or until top is golden brown. Serve immediately or at room temperature, or chill and cut into slices and brown in butter in a frying pan. Serve as is or topped with a little sour cream.

Yield: 16 2-inch × 2-inch pieces

TURKISH STUFFED GRAPE LEAVES

At the end of the grape harvest, the leaves are washed and brined to preserve them for later use. Ottoman and Middle Eastern Jewish cooks made use of everything that was available to feed their families regardless of their wealth. Since most meals consisted of little meat and copious amounts of vegetables and fruit along with starch, stuffed grape leaves were an important addition to any meal or party. This recipe is vegetarian, and the addition of the cinnamon and allspice along with the raisins and pine nuts hints strongly of its Sephardic roots in Spain, with its Moorish influence.

2 tablespoons olive oil
2 medium onions, chopped
1 clove garlic, minced
One 8-ounce jar grape leaves in brine
1 cup uncooked long grain rice plus 2 cups water
3 tablespoons toasted pignoli nuts (pine nuts)
4 scallions, finely chopped
2 tablespoons minced fresh dill
2 tablespoons finely chopped Italian parsley
2 tablespoons minced fresh mint
½ teaspoon cinnamon
½ teaspoon allspice
3 tablespoons raisins
1 teaspoon kosher salt
¼ teaspoon freshly ground pepper or to taste
⅔ cup olive oil
cup lemon juice
⅔ cup water, plus additional as needed during cooking
1 teaspoon sugar
Broken grape leaves or lettuce leaves for the bottom of the pot

1. Heat 2 tablespoons olive oil in a large skillet, and sauté the onion for 5 minutes. Add the garlic and sauté until onions are lightly golden. Place mixture in a 2-quart mixing bowl.

2. Soak the separated grape leaves in a bowl of warm water for 5 minutes while you make the filling.

3. Combine the rice with the 2 cups water, and microwave on high for 5 minutes. Drain.

4. Toast pine nuts in a 350°F oven for 3–4 minutes until lightly golden.

5. Add the rice, scallions, dill, parsley, mint, cinnamon, allspice, pine nuts, and raisins to the onion mixture. Season with the salt and pepper.

6. Remove the leaves from the bowl of water and rinse under cold running water. Separate the leaves and place shiny side down on a board. If the leaves are small, place two together.

7. Remove any stems from the leaves.

8. Place 2 teaspoons of the rice mixture near the stem end of the leaves. Fold leaf over filling once. Fold in sides and then proceed to tightly roll up leaf until the end to make a neat roll.

9. Place some broken vine leaves or lettuce leaves in the bottom of a 4-quart Dutch oven so the rolls won't stick to the bottom of the pot. Arrange the rolls in the pot seam side down.

10. Combine the remaining ⅔ cup oil, lemon juice, ⅔ cup of the water, and sugar, and pour over the rolls in the Dutch oven.

11. Place a heavy plate or a plate and some weights on top of the rolls, and simmer 40 minutes.

12. Add the remaining water as needed, and cook for a total of 50 minutes or until the rice is tender.

13. Cool and serve at room temperature. May be refrigerated until later use, but bring to room temperature before serving, as olive oil will solidify in the refrigerator and the rolls will be hard to separate.

Yield: 3–4 dozen rolls

TINA'S TIDBITS

- *I find it helpful to partially cook the rice beforehand, thus preventing the possibility of crunchy, undercooked rice in the finished product.*
- *Toasting the pine nuts before adding to the filling significantly enhances the flavor of the filling.*
- *Do not substitute another nut for the pine nuts. Most nuts will be too hard and destroy the mouth feel of the finished product.*

Tomat Reynado
(Turkish Stuffed Tomatoes)

When meat was expensive and difficult to come by, stuffing vegetables was a perfect way to extend the small amount of protein in a meal. Vegetables were plentiful and perfect vehicles for the meat. Here is a recipe that Rachel Bortnick described to me in her home; it was a family favorite.

1 pound ground beef
1 medium onion, grated
2 tablespoons fine semolina (quick cream of wheat is okay)
2 eggs, divided use
2 tablespoons chopped parsley
1 tablespoon finely chopped fresh basil (optional)

½ teaspoon salt
½ cup flour
Salt and freshly ground black pepper to taste
10 medium tomatoes
Pinch of salt and sugar
Extra virgin olive oil, as needed

1. Combine beef, onion, semolina, 1 slightly beaten egg, parsley, and basil in a 2-quart bowl. Mix first with a fork and then with your hands, but do not overhandle the mixture. Set aside.

2. Cut tomatoes in half. Remove and discard seeds. Hollow out tomato halves and reserve pulp. Salt interiors, turn upside down on paper towels, and pat dry.

3. Fill tomato halves with meat mixture.

4. Season flour with salt and pepper, and place in a small, shallow bowl.

5. Beat the remaining egg in another small, shallow bowl.

6. Heat a 10-inch frying pan over high heat for 15 seconds. Add enough oil to cover the bottom of the pan to a depth of ¼ inch. Reduce heat to medium high.

7. Dip the tops of the meat-filled tomato into the flour and then into the beaten egg.

8. Place the stuffed tomatoes floured side down into the hot oil, and fry for 1 minute until tops are golden brown.

9. Turn over tomatoes and arrange tomatoes with browned filling side up in an ovenproof dish.

10. Finely chop reserved tomato pulp Add pinch of salt and sugar to taste. Place some tomato mixture on top of each tomato.

11. Bake stuffed tomatoes in a 350° F oven for 10–15 minutes or until meat is firm and tomatoes still hold their shape.

Yield: 8–10 servings

TINA'S TIDBITS

- *Semolina is coarse grains of wheat. If there are no sources of finely ground grain in your area, use the quick, but not instant variety of cream of wheat cereal.*
- *Handle ground meat lightly to prevent the mixture from getting too dense.*
- *Use a less lean form of ground meat for this recipe so that the semolina can absorb the juices and swell, creating a moist, light filling.*

Bulgarian Baked Chicken with Barley

Delicious, comforting, and very easy to make, this is a classic Shabbat dish in Bulgaria and is transformed into a festive dish when served with agristada *(see page 86).*

1 chicken cut into eighths or 4 large breasts or
thighs with skin and bone
1 onion, peeled but left whole
2 tablespoons extra virgin olive oil

1 cup pearled barley
Salt and pepper to taste
Lemon slices for garnish (optional)
Chopped parsley (optional)

1. Rinse chicken pieces under cold running water and place in a 4-quart saucepan.

2. Pierce the onion 6 times with the point of a sharp knife, and add it to the chicken. Cover ingredients with water, and add the oil.

3. Bring the chicken to a boil, and then partially cover and reduce heat so that the water just simmers. Cook until the chicken is tender, about 30–45 minutes.

4. Remove the chicken from the liquid, and keep warm and covered while you make the barley.

5. Pour the broth from the saucepan into a measuring cup and measure out $3\frac{1}{2}$ cups. If necessary, add some water. Place in a 2-quart saucepan.

6. Add the barley and cook, partially covered, over low heat for 25 minutes or until barley starts to swell but is still tough.

7. Lightly oil a baking dish large enough to hold the chicken in one layer but not larger than you need or the barley will dry out too much.

8. Place the barley and remaining cooking liquid in the baking dish, and top with the chicken, skin side up. Sprinkle chicken with salt and pepper, and bake in a preheated 350°F oven for 20 minutes or until the liquid has been absorbed and chicken skin has browned.

9. Garnish with the lemon slices or chopped parsley and serve.

Note: Delicious eaten as is, or serve with *agristada* (see page 86).

Yield: 4 servings

TINA'S TIDBITS

- *Chicken skin should not be removed before stewing, as it imparts a rich flavor to the broth. The fat can always be removed after chilling the broth, and the skin can later be removed from the meat.*
- *Pearled barley has had the bran removed and is steamed and polished.*

AGRISTADA
(EGG LEMON SAUCE)

Agristada is definitely an offshoot of the well-known avgolemeno *sauce from Greece, to the south of Bulgaria. In this recipe whole eggs are used to lighten the intensity of the egg yolk flavor. I prefer this delicate flavor to the more metallic taste that can result when using solely egg yolks.*

2 eggs
2 tablespoons extra virgin olive oil
2 tablespoons all-purpose flour
2 cups chicken broth (may be made from bouillon cube or canned)

2 tablespoons fresh lemon juice
Kosher salt and freshly ground pepper to taste
Zest of 1 lemon in long strips
1 tablespoon minced fresh parsley

1. Beat the eggs in a 1-quart bowl with the oil until combined.

2. In a small dish, combine the flour with enough chicken broth (about 3 tablespoons) to make a smooth paste, and slowly add to the eggs as you whisk the mixture.

3. Gradually add the remaining chicken broth and lemon juice, stirring constantly to combine.

4. Pour mixture into a 2-quart saucepan and stir constantly over medium heat until mixture thickens and coats the back of a spoon. Season to taste with salt and pepper.

5. Strain the mixture directly into a serving dish and serve warm, not hot, garnished with the lemon zest and parsley.

6. Serve over chicken or vegetables.

Yield: Approximately 2¼ cups, enough to sauce two cooked chickens.

TINA'S TIDBITS

- *There is no substitute for fresh lemon juice, so throw away the green bottle!*
- *Lemons should be stored at room temperature to yield the most juice. If refrigerated, microwave lemons for 25 seconds before juicing.*
- *Strain any type of custard mixture before pouring into serving containers or baking to remove thick egg-white strands that might have formed when adding liquid.*
- *To serve this sauce over fish, substitute fish or vegetable broth for the chicken broth.*
- *To produce a lighter, more ethereal sauce, separate the eggs and then whip the whites to a soft peak before folding them into the sauce.*

GREEK LAMB STEW

This is a dish representative of all the culinary influences of the region—spices from the Middle East, olives and oranges from the Mediterranean, and lamb from the hills. The only ingredient that makes this recipe more contemporary and less Jewish is the wine. In ancient times Jews didn't cook with wine.

½ cup golden raisins
½ cup plus 3 tablespoons cream sherry
2 pounds boneless lamb, cut in 1-inch cubes
1 cup fresh orange juice
4 cloves minced garlic
2–4 tablespoons extra virgin olive oil, as needed
1½ cups frozen pearl onions, defrosted
1 teaspoon saffron threads or ⅛ teaspoon powdered saffron
2 teaspoons ground coriander

2 teaspoons dried thyme
1½ teaspoons ground cumin
½ cup slivered almonds
1 tablespoon flour
½ cup dry red wine
Salt and freshly ground pepper to taste
3 medium tomatoes, seeded and cubed
½ cup halved, pitted Calamata olives
2 tablespoons fresh lemon juice

1. Soak the raisins in the ½ cup cream sherry for 1 hour or longer.

2. Marinate the lamb in the orange juice and garlic at least 2 hours at room temperature. Drain and reserve the marinade.

3. Heat 2 tablespoons of the olive oil in a Dutch oven and brown the lamb. Do not crowd the meat. Brown in two batches if necessary. Remove the lamb to a bowl with a slotted spoon.

4. Add the remaining 2 tablespoons of oil to the pan if pan is dry. Heat for 10 seconds. Add onions and sauté until a light golden brown. Add the spices and the almonds, and sauté for another 5 minutes.

5. Stir in the flour with a whisk and cook for 1 minute. Add the raisins with the sherry, the reserved marinade, and the red wine. Stir to mix, and season to taste with the salt and pepper.

6. Return the lamb to the pot, add the tomatoes and the olives, and cook until the meat is tender, about

1½ hours. If the sauce is too watery, remove meat from pot, boil sauce until preferred thickness, and then return meat to sauce.

7. Add the 3 remaining tablespoons of cream sherry and the lemon juice. Reheat all of the ingredients and serve.

Note: The stew can be made with dark chicken thigh meat instead of lamb.

Yield: 6–8 servings

TINA'S TIDBITS

- *I use cream sherry in recipes because the fortified liquor does not lose its flavor during cooking and it adds a richer flavor to the dish than does dry sherry.*
- *An acid food must always be present in a marinade, because it is the agent that tenderizes the meat.*
- *Be aware of the form of your saffron. If you are using the powdered form, 1/16 teaspoon is equivalent to a pinch of saffron strands!*

GREEK PSARI SAGANAKI

In Greece this dish is most often made with shrimp. To conform to the Jewish dietary laws that prohibit eating shellfish, I took the bright colors and flavors of this dish and incorporated fish indigenous to the waters around Greece in order to be able to serve it in my own home. Basically, that is how Jewish cooks throughout time have adapted local recipes for their kosher kitchens.

1 pound branzino fillets (about 2 fish) or tuna steaks
Juice of ½ lemon
4 tablespoons extra virgin Greek olive oil, divided use
1 medium onion, diced
2 large cloves garlic, peeled and cut in half
One 28-ounce can crushed tomatoes
½ teaspoon sugar

1 tablespoon fresh oregano, chopped
Salt and pepper to taste
1–2 tablespoons ouzo or other licorice liqueur (amount depends on your taste)
2 tablespoons Metaxa or other brandy
1 cup feta cheese, cubed

1. Place the fish fillets in a 7 × 11-inch glass dish. Add the lemon juice and coat the fish well. Set aside.

2. Heat 2 tablespoons of the olive oil in a 3-quart saucepan. Add the onion and halved garlic, and cook until lightly golden.

3. Add the crushed tomatoes, sugar, oregano, and salt and pepper to taste, and cook uncovered over moderate heat for 20 minutes or until thickened. Remove the pieces of garlic.

4. Heat a cast-iron skillet or heavy, uncoated sauté pan for 15 seconds. Add the remaining 2 tablespoons of olive oil and heat for another 15 seconds. Drain the fish. Season lightly with salt and pepper, and place in the hot skillet. Cook over moderately high heat for 2 minutes or until the fish is lightly golden on one side.

5. Turn the fish over, and add the ouzo and the brandy to the frying pan. Heat for 10 seconds and then ignite the liquids. When the flames die out, place the fish in a 2-quart ovenproof serving dish.

6. Cover the fish with the warm tomato sauce, and top with the cheese.

7. Place the dish in a preheated 400°F oven and bake until the cheese is melted but not browned. Serve with pasta or rice as desired.

Yield: 4 servings

TINA'S TIDBITS

- *Soaking fish in lemon juice imparts a subtle flavor to the meat, which will remain even after baking with a strongly flavored sauce. However, do not let the fish sit in the juice more than 15-30 minutes or the acid will start to "cook" the fish and make it tough.*
- *Brandy and liqueurs must be warm in order for them to ignite. However, if the liquid is heated too long, the alcohol content will burn off and no flame will be produced.*
- *If finishing a sautéed fish dish in the oven, make sure the initial cooking of the fish isn't too long or your completed dish will be tough and dry.*

KATAIFI WITH CREAM FILLING (KONOFA)

This is a multinational dish; kataifi dough is associated with Greece, while the dish is a popular dessert for special occasions in Egypt and Syria, according to the food historian and writer Claudia Roden. A few years ago I made this for a large Rosh Hashanah gathering at my home, and it has been one of the most requested desserts ever since. The Muslim community prefers to use a mild white cheese in the filling, but Jewish cooks prefer the rice flour-milk filling.

SYRUP:
2½ cups granulated sugar
1¼ cups water
Juice of ½ small lemon
2 tablespoons orange blossom water

FILLING:
¾ cup rice flour
5 cups milk
½ cup sugar
1 teaspoon vanilla extract
½ cup heavy cream

DOUGH:
1 pound *kataifi* dough, defrosted
½ pound unsalted butter, melted
½ cup chopped pistachios or walnuts for garnish (optional)

1. To make the syrup, boil the first 3 ingredients for 10 minutes. Add orange blossom water and cool completely in a shallow bowl in the refrigerator or freezer if you are in a hurry. Syrup **must** be cold but not frozen.

2. Mix the rice flour with enough milk to make a thin paste. Heat milk in a 2-quart saucepan until boiling. Add rice flour paste and mix with a whisk until smooth. Simmer over low heat for 15 minutes. Stir constantly at first, using a rubber spatula, until mixture thickens. Be careful not to let it burn on the bottom. Stir in sugar and vanilla when it is thick.

3. Place mixture in a bowl and cool for ½ hour. Add heavy cream when cool.

4. Place *kataifi* dough in a 4-quart bowl and carefully pull the strands apart. Pour the melted butter over the dough and lightly toss with fingers until all the strands are coated.

TINA'S TIDBITS

- *Do not attempt to substitute another starch for the rice flour. The flour not only thickens the mixture, but it imparts a taste reminiscent of rice pudding.*
- *In place of the orange blossom water, 1 1/2 teaspoons vanilla may be used to flavor the syrup. However, nothing compares in flavor to the orange blossom water, and a bottle will last for a very long time on your pantry shelf. Treat yourself—this ingredient is worth seeking out in the stores.*
- *Kataifi looks like shredded wheat and is actually phyllo dough that has been extruded into thin threads.*
- *If you can't find kataifi, use phyllo dough and assemble the mixture using layers of phyllo brushed with butter as for baklava (see pages 92-93).*

5. Spread half the dough in the bottom of a 13 × 9-inch baking dish. Spread the filling over the dough, and spread the remaining dough over the filling. Press down lightly with your palms.

6. Preheat oven to 350°F. Bake pastry for 1 hour. With pastry still in the oven, raise the temperature to 425°F and continue baking for 15 minutes or until lightly golden.

7. Remove from oven and immediately pour syrup over pastry. Run a knife along the sides of the pan to allow syrup to seep to the bottom.

8. Cut into squares, and serve warm or at room temperature.

Yield: 20–25 servings

Baklava

Baklava can be traced back to Assyria in the eighth century B.C.E., when it was originally made with a bread dough layered with some nuts and honey. Although it became popular throughout the Ottoman Empire and Syria, it is most associated with Greece. This may be because the Greeks invented phyllo dough, the dough used for construction of the baklava layers. Phyllo actually means "leaf," and the dough is, in fact, as thin as a leaf.

4 cups walnut pieces, almonds, pistachios, or a
  mix—depending on country of origin
1 cup sugar
$3/4$ teaspoon ground cinnamon
$1/8$ teaspoon ground cloves
1 pound phyllo dough
2–3 sticks melted unsalted butter

SYRUP:
1 cup water
$1\frac{1}{2}$ cups sugar
$1/2$ cup honey
1 cinnamon stick
2 strips of lemon zest, $1/2$ inch wide and length of
  lemon
1 tablespoon lemon juice

1. Place half of the nuts in a processor work bowl and pulse on and off until a fine texture. Place them in a medium bowl. Add the remaining nuts to the work bowl and repeat the procedure. Add the sugar, cinnamon, and cloves to the nuts. Mix well and set aside.

2. Butter a 13 × 9-inch baking pan.

3. The phyllo dough is folded in the box lengthwise before it is rolled. Unroll the dough. Take one of the sheets of dough and place it folded in the pan so that it fits perfectly. Open up the fold of the sheet of dough and brush the inside with butter. Refold the other half over the dough. You have just created two layers of dough. Brush the top of the dough with the melted butter, and place another sheet of folded dough on top. Open dough, brush with butter, and then close the "page." Do this 4 more times with 4 more full sheets of dough so that you have used a total of 6 sheets of dough.

4. Spread $1/3$ of the nut mixture on top. Layer 6 more folded sheets of dough using the previous method. Spread with $1/2$ of the remaining nut mixture.

5. Spread 6 more folded sheets of dough on top of this, making sure to brush the butter in between each layer. Top with the remaining nut mixture, and layer the remaining dough on the top. Brush the top with melted butter.

6. Score the top of dough with a sharp knife, making parallel lines $1\frac{1}{2}$ inches apart. Score on a diagonal again $1\frac{1}{2}$ inches apart. Make the cuts about $1/4$ inch deep.

7. Bake in a 325°F oven for 45–50 minutes or until golden. Meanwhile, make the syrup while the baklava is baking.

8. Combine all of the ingredients for the syrup in a saucepan, and heat for 30 minutes over a low heat to barely simmer. Remove from the heat and discard the cinnamon stick and lemon peel.

9. Allow the baklava to cool for 10 minutes, and then evenly pour the syrup over all of the pastry. Wait at least 30 minutes or until thoroughly cool, and cut completely through the dough to make the individual pieces. Place pieces on cupcake papers and serve.

Yield: 4–5 dozen pieces

TINA'S TIDBITS

- *Baklava is actually easy to make; just make sure you keep unused sheets of phyllo covered with plastic wrap and then with a damp towel. Don't let the damp towel come in contact with the dough, or it will get soggy and stick together.*
- *Most packages of phyllo have sheets that are about 13 inches wide and 18 inches long. If you place the edge of the short end of dough inside up against the long end of the pan, you can brush butter on that half sheet and then fold the rest of the phyllo over it to fit into the pan perfectly. This creates even layers of dough without having to fold the excess dough under and creating thick edges.*

SERVING FRESH ORANGES IN THE TURKISH STYLE

According to Rachel Bortnick, fresh fruit was the dessert of choice in Turkish homes. Sweets were relegated to snacks and entertaining. The following instructions for cutting and presenting an orange at a meal are from her hometown of Izmir.

1. Cut a small slice of rind off the bottom of the orange so that the orange will sit flat on a plate. Do not cut so deeply as to cut into the fruit.

2. Make 6–8 cuts from the top of the orange, through the peel to within ½ inch of the bottom of the orange.

3. Carefully separate each section of the peel away from the fruit. Do not remove it from the fruit or break the rind.

4. Gently roll each section of peel inwards toward the fruit to create a tight roll of peel at the base.

5. Repeat this technique with the remaining sections of peel. The finished product will look like the orange is nestled in a decorative base.

6. For added flair, gently separate each section so the orange looks like it is in bloom.

Yield: 1 serving

Borekitas kon Kalavasa (Bulgarian Squash-Filled Cookies)

The migration of the Sephardi culture is reflected in this recipe. Since the Moors brought squash from the Middle East, and Columbus introduced pumpkin from the New World, one can find squash recipes (mostly used in sweetened fillings for ravioli, borekas, and pastries) in communities that were established following the same routes that the Jews traveled when escaping the Inquisition.

Typical of most European pastries, these little filled cookies are not very sweet. They could be sprinkled with sugar before baking, but that is not the traditional method of preparation.

$1\frac{3}{4}$ cups all-purpose flour
2 tablespoons granulated sugar
$\frac{1}{4}$ teaspoon salt
1 stick unsalted butter
$\frac{1}{2}$ cup water
10 ounces frozen cubed butternut squash or 1 cup canned pumpkin

$\frac{1}{3}$ cup granulated sugar
$\frac{1}{2}$ cup finely ground ($\frac{1}{16}$-inch pieces) walnuts
$\frac{1}{2}$ teaspoon ground cinnamon
2 tablespoons unflavored dry bread crumbs
1 egg mixed with 1 tablespoon water
Sugar for topping (optional)

1. To prepare the dough, place flour, sugar, and salt in a 2-quart bowl and stir to combine.

2. Place the stick of butter in a 1-cup glass measuring cup and microwave on high for 45 seconds or until butter is melted. Add the water to the cup until the foam line comes to the 1-cup line.

3. Stir the butter-water mixture as you pour it into the bowl of flour.

4. Using a wooden spoon or spatula, quickly combine the flour-butter mixture until a smooth, slippery soft dough is formed.

5. Refrigerate dough for 15 minutes or longer while you prepare the filling.

6. Cook squash in the microwave for 4 minutes with no additional water.

7. Blot the squash dry with a towel, and mash with a fork until no lumps remain. You should have 1 cup cooked squash.

8. Combine the squash with the sugar, walnuts, cinnamon, and bread crumbs.

9. Remove dough from the refrigerator and roll out on a floured surface to about $\frac{1}{8}$ inch thick. Cut 2- to 3-inch circles from the dough.

10. Place 1 teaspoon of filling in the center of each circle and fold dough over filling, matching edges and pressing down to seal with the side of your pinkie. Place on a parchment-lined cookie sheet.

11. Using the tines of a fork, crimp the pinched edges together to seal and make a decorative design. Bend the cookie slightly to form crescents.

12. Brush the tops of the cookies with the egg-water mixture, and if desired (but not traditional), sprinkle some additional sugar on top.

13. Bake in a preheated 375°F oven for 18–20 minutes or until golden. Makes about 2 dozen cookies.

Note: There will be some filling left over, which can be frozen for future use or used to stuff ravioli.

Yield: 2–3 dozen pastries

TINA'S TIDBITS

- *Squash can be very watery, so use only butternut squash or pie pumpkin to make this filling.*
- *Bread crumbs are often used in European baking to absorb excess liquid, whether it is in a filling or in between phyllo layers in a strudel.*
- *This dough is like the classic* pâte à choux, *or cream puff dough, except there are no eggs in this batter.*
- *Pressing edges of pastry with the tines of a fork is effective in creating a seal so the filling will not ooze out during baking.*

INDIA

India's Jews come from four distinct groups: the Bene Israel, the Cochin Jews, the Sephardic Jews from Europe, and the "Baghdadis" from Iraq. The Bene Israel and the Cochin Jews claim to be the longest Jewish inhabitants of India.

The "black" Cochin Jews (Cochin is a city in southwest India) are dark-skinned Jews who trace their ancestry to the lost ten tribes who came with King Solomon in search of spices. The "white" Cochin Jews were in India as early as the thirteenth century, coming from Spain and later from Portugal and Holland in search of spices and, judging from the time frame, probably to establish themselves far from the Inquisition. However, this group of Jews had to move from their original home in Cranganore to Cochin in the late fifteenth century to escape the wrath of Portuguese invaders. The maharajah welcomed the Jews to Cochin, and they settled in an area of the city that was called Jew Town. The name of the city remains the same to this day. The Cochin Jews were always involved in the spice trade. The Malabar Coast was certainly known for its pepper, but cinnamon, ginger, cloves, nutmeg, cardamom, and other spices also grew in the region. The division of labor saw the white Cochins directly involved with the trading of the spices and the black Cochin Jews more involved with the handling, curing, and manufacturing of the ground spice. Under the Dutch in the seventeenth and eighteenth centuries, the Cochin community flourished. When trade in the region of Cochin declined, its importance and its Jewish population diminished. Some Jews migrated north, but mostly they left for Israel.

The Bene Israel also claim that they are descendants of the ten tribes of Israel. Their ancestors were shipwrecked off the west coast of India on the Konkan Coast in the second century B.C.E. after escaping persecution in the Galilee region. According to legend, only seven couples survived, and their offspring were cut off from other Jewish communities until they were discovered in the eighteenth century by traders from Baghdad. Although they had assimilated into local communities, they maintained the practices of Jewish dietary laws, circumcision, and observance of Shabbat as a day of rest. In the early 1990s, Tudor Parfitt, a Jewish studies professor at London's School of Oriental and African Studies, initiated a research study examining the DNA of four thousand Bene Israel to see if information could corroborate the link to the ancient tribes of Israel. The study indicates they are probable descendants of Israelite *kohanim*.

The last group of Jews to arrive in India are the Baghdadi Jews. They established a trading network stretching from Syria and Baghdad to Bombay and Calcutta, all the way to Hong Kong and Japan. By the late eighteenth century, Bombay was home to the largest Jewish community in India, which included Bene Israel Jews as well as Iraqi and Persian Jews.

Although this is the last of the three major sects of Jews in India, the last migration to this country took place during and after World War II, with the

Eastern European Jews escaping the Holocaust. By the end of the 1940s, the Jewish population in India numbered some twenty-six thousand. After the war, the rise of Indian nationalism made it uncomfortable for the Jewish communities, which were closely associated with the British. Almost all Jews migrated to Israel, England, or the United States, leaving a handful of elderly Jews behind.

As in all Jewish communities around the world, Indian Jews translated their culinary tastes and the laws of kashrut to embrace the foods of the region. Living along the spice route meant that pepper, cinnamon, allspice, nutmeg, and cloves were readily used in their dishes. Hot peppers, especially green ones, figured prominently in Indian cuisine, as did coconut milk. The latter was utilized often in the Indian kosher kitchen, since there was no dairy in the coconut liquid and it could be used to enhance many meat dishes.

Mango Salad Dressing

Indians are very fond of mangoes, which are in season only from March to May. They are so beloved that they preserve many of their mangoes in chutneys and pickles to enjoy long after the season is over. Here is a delicious dressing to use over any salad.

½ cup finely chopped mangoes
¼ cup rice wine vinegar
3 tablespoons oil

2 tablespoons honey
1 teaspoon chopped mint
1 teaspoon chives

1. Combine all ingredients in a screw-top jar and shake until combined.

2. Serve with mixed greens tossed with some nuts or dried fruit bits, like cherries or cranberries.

Yield: 1 cup dressing

TINA'S TIDBITS

- *Rice wine vinegar is not as tangy as other vinegars and makes a perfect base for a fruit-flavored dressing*
- *If you would like a smooth, slightly thick dressing, place the mangoes, vinegar, and honey in a food processor work bowl and pulse on and off 5 times or until the fruit is pureed. Slowly pour in the oil while the machine is running until an emulsion is formed. Add the mint and chives and pulse on and off 8 times, just until the herbs are chopped but not pureed.*

BENE ISRAEL SHABBAT CHICKEN CURRY

June Penkar lives in Dallas and was my personal guide to the cooking of the Bene Israel Jews from the west coast of India. Her great-grandfather was a justice in the maharajah's court, and her grandfather went to school with the princes. The Jews were never discriminated against and were allowed to prosper in India.

The different regions where her grandparents grew up influenced her culinary style; different regions emphasize different flavors and ingredients. The hallmark of Bene Israel cooking is the use of coconut milk, which is pareve, to thicken sauces and a good amount of garlic, ginger, onions, and tomatoes. Although garam masala is used throughout India, its use in Indian Jewish cooking is prominent. Chicken was the most common dish for Shabbat. The following recipes are all from my friend June, a wonderful woman, Hadassah president, and fantastic cook!

3 jalapeño peppers
2-inch piece of fresh ginger, peeled and cut into 6 pieces
5 large cloves of fresh garlic
1 bunch cilantro leaves and top stems
2 tablespoons oil
3 whole cardamom pods
3 whole cloves
2-inch stick of cinnamon, broken into two pieces
2 large onions, finely chopped (about 4 cups)
4 Roma tomatoes, seeded and chopped
2 tablespoons ground coriander

½ teaspoon turmeric
1 teaspoon ground cumin
3 pounds assorted chicken pieces, no wings
1 russet potato, peeled and cut into 12 chunks
Salt and freshly ground black pepper to taste
½ cup water or chicken bouillon
One 5.5-ounce can of coconut milk (about ½–¾ cup)
1–2 teaspoons prepared garam masala (Caution: All garam masala are not created equal. Some are so hot that ½ teaspoon is more than enough. Taste a little first to decide what amount to use.)

1. Place the peppers, ginger, and garlic in a processor work bowl and pulse on and off until the contents are coarsely chopped. Add the cilantro and pulse on and off to create a coarse paste. Set aside.

2. Heat a large, deep frying pan for 20 seconds over high heat. Add the oil and heat for 15 more seconds. Do not allow the oil to smoke. Reduce the heat to medium high and add the whole cardamom, cloves, and cinnamon. Sauté for 1 minute or until the spices become fragrant.

3. Add the onion to the pan and sauté until golden brown.

4. Add ¼ cup (or more depending on how hot you like your curry) of the fresh jalapeño-cilantro paste to the pan and sauté for another 2 minutes.

5. Add the chopped tomatoes and the dried spices to the mixture and cook until the mixture looks fairly dry.

6. Remove all of the skin from the chicken parts, and add the chicken to the frying pan, making sure that you turn the chicken pieces around to coat with the onion-spice mixture. Add the potato pieces and do likewise.

7. Add salt and pepper to taste and ½ cup water or bouillon, and stir gently to combine.

8. Cover the pan and cook over low heat for 30–45 minutes or until the chicken pieces are tender.

9. Remove chicken pieces to a platter. Add the coconut milk and garam masala to the pan and stir to thoroughly combine.

10. Return the chicken to the pan and cook for another 5–10 minutes to combine flavors.

11. Place chicken on a serving platter, pour sauce over, and serve with rice—preferably fragrant basmati rice.

Yield: 4–5 servings

- *When processing a mixture that contains a large quantity of green herbs, always process the herbs last. Overchopping in the processor brings out the chlorophyll taste in the herbs and makes your mixture taste "grassy."*
- *Always sauté your onions alone before adding other vegetables. The golden brown is the natural caramelizing of the sugars in the onion, which gives the onion its sweet taste. Sautéing with other vegetables initially will stew the onions and not bring out the sweetness.*
- *Nowadays chicken has more fat under the skin; therefore it is advisable to remove the skin before cooking.*
- *To seed a tomato, cut it open horizontally, hold it over the sink cut side down, and give a squeeze and a shake and it's seeded!*
- *The easiest way to cook rice: Combine water, salt (if using), and rice in covered glass casserole. Microwave on high for 5 minutes, on medium for 15 minutes, and then let sit for 5 minutes. That's it!*

NIRVANA CHICKEN WINGS

I call these wings "nirvana" because they could transport you to paradise. They are easy to make, messy to eat, and loads of fun—a modern interpretation of Indian cuisine that's far from "Shabbat chicken."

4 tablespoons pareve margarine
2 tablespoons curry powder
¼ cup dry white wine
2–3 pounds chicken drummettes

1 cup mango chutney
¼ cup shredded coconut
1 tablespoon finely chopped scallion
2 tablespoons finely chopped peanuts

1. Melt the margarine in a saucepan, and stir in the curry powder. Cook for 2–3 minutes, and add the wine. Remove from heat.

2. Remove any excess fat from the chicken parts. Wash and pat dry. If using whole wings, discard the tip and cut the two-bone section and drummette apart.

3. Place the chicken parts in a roasting pan, and baste with the curry sauce. Bake for 20 minutes in a 350°F oven.

4. Chop up any large pieces of mango in the chutney, and spread the chutney over the chicken parts. Bake for 30 minutes or until chicken is tender.

5. Place the chicken on a serving platter, and pour sauce into a 1-quart saucepan. Reduce the sauce by one-third over moderate heat.

6. Pour the sauce over the chicken, and sprinkle with the coconut, scallions, and peanuts. Serve.

Note: May be made in advance and reheated in the microwave or oven. Garnish with the coconut, scallion, and peanuts only after reheating and before serving.

Yield: 8–10 servings as an appetizer

TINA'S TIDBITS

- *Classic Indian cooking technique calls for cooking the spice for a brief period to bring out the flavor. However, when working with powder, be very careful not to brown the spices or they will taste bitter.*
- *It is not necessary to remove the tip or third portion of the chicken wing if you are serving the wings in a casual setting with lots of napkins. Cut them into drummettes and wing sections for a more formal cocktail party as instructed above.*

CURRIED TURKEY AND RICE (WITH VEGETARIAN OPTION)

This recipe incorporates all the components of an Indian curry dish, including the accompaniments. However, this is a creation from my own kitchen at a time when I had leftover turkey and all cookbooks called for milk or cream as the base of the sauce. As our ancestors did, I tweaked an established recipe to conform to the dictates of kashrut, and a new recipe was born.

4 tablespoons pareve margarine (or butter if vegetarian)
1 onion, diced
⅓ cup flour
1 tablespoon curry powder or to taste
¾ teaspoon salt
2 cups chicken broth or vegetable substitute
2 cups diced cooked turkey or assorted cooked vegetables

1 cup frozen peas, defrosted (optional)
Raisins
Peanuts
Coconut
Chutney
1 cup basmati, jasmine, or long-grain rice
2 cups water
1 teaspoon salt

1. Melt the margarine or butter in a 2-quart saucepan.

2. Add the diced onion and sauté until the onion is golden.

3. Whisk in the flour, curry powder, and salt until well combined (about 20 seconds).

4. Add the broth slowly but steadily while you whisk the mixture. Keep whisking until the mixture begins to bubble and thickens. Add the turkey or vegetables.

5. Reduce the heat and add the peas, if using.

6. Serve the mixture with rice (see recipes below), and top with the other ingredients if desired.

Yield: 4 servings

BASIC METHOD FOR COOKING RICE

1. Combine 1 cup rice with 2 cups water and 1 teaspoon salt in a 3-quart saucepan.

2. Bring the rice mixture to a boil. Cover the pot, reduce the heat to low, and cook for 20 minutes or until all the water has been absorbed. Serve.

MICROWAVE METHOD FOR COOKING RICE

1. Combine 1 cup of rice with 2 cups of water and 1 teaspoon of salt in a 2-quart covered glass casserole. Place in microwave oven and heat for 5 minutes on high.

2. Gently swirl mixture in casserole, return to microwave, and cook on medium power for 15 minutes. Let casserole sit for 5 minutes before removing cover and tossing rice with a fork to fluff. Serve.

TINA'S TIDBITS

- *Curry is actually a combination of many spices. Use a good-quality curry powder from a reputable source if you are not going to make your own mixture.*
- *A velouté sauce is a white sauce that uses chicken, beef, or vegetable stock in place of milk or cream.*
- *Unflavored liquid soy creamer may also be used as a milk substitute for a pareve sauce.*

CURRIED LENTILS AND VEGETABLES

The British, Dutch, and Portuguese traders sailed the spice trade route starting in the South China Sea, with major stops in the Moluccas (Spice Islands) for nutmeg, mace, and cloves, to Sri Lanka and the Malabar Coast on the southwestern tip of India, where cinnamon and black pepper were exclusively grown. These spices plus the chilies and cardamom from inland routes were the basis of many curry spice blends of the region.

1 cup red lentils
2 tablespoons olive oil
2 medium onions, chopped
1 tablespoon minced garlic
1 teaspoon ground coriander
1 teaspoon ground cumin
1 teaspoon turmeric
1/2 teaspoon chili powder
1/4 teaspoon ground cardamom
2 good pinches of ground cloves
1/4 teaspoon cinnamon
4 ounces sliced mushrooms

3 yellow crookneck squash, sliced
2 carrots sliced
1 cup vegetable broth
One-half 6-ounce can tomato paste
Salt and freshly ground black pepper to taste
One 8-ounce can chickpeas, drained
1/2 cup roasted peanuts (optional)
3 cups cooked basmati or jasmine rice (1 cup raw rice + 2 cups water)
1/2 cup unflavored yogurt (thick Greek yogurt is best) (optional)

1. Boil lentils in enough water to cover for 15 minutes or until they are soft but not mushy. Set aside.

2. Heat the oil in a 3-quart saucepan and sauté the onion and garlic over medium heat until the onions are soft but the garlic does **not** brown.

3. Add the spices and the vegetables and sauté for 3 minutes.

4. Add the broth, tomato paste, and salt and pepper to taste. Add the chickpeas. Cover and simmer for 8 minutes or until vegetables are tender.

5. Drain the lentils and add to the vegetables. Add the nuts and serve over the rice with the yogurt if desired.

Yield: 4–6 servings

TINA'S TIDBITS

- *Different varieties of lentils vary little in flavor, but the color choice enhances this recipe.*
- *Curry is not a single spice but a mixture of many. This recipe includes the individual spices and creates a wonderful flavor not equaled by store-bought mixtures. In an emergency, 1 1/2 to 2 tablespoons of Madras curry powder may be substituted.*
- *Basmati and jasmine rice add a subtle nutty flavor to your dish. White or brown rice may be substituted, but "converted" or polished rice should never be used as it will not absorb the flavors appropriately.*

Indian Coconut Rice Pudding

Here's another recipe I adapted from June Penkar. This is a perfect dessert for a meat meal or for anyone who is lactose intolerant. There is no butter or milk in this recipe, but this dish is still creamy and delicious, especially if you like a subtle hint of coconut flavor.

½ cup basmati rice
½ cup water
One 13.5-ounce can coconut milk
2 cans of water
¾–1 cup sugar

Large pinch of kosher salt
½ cup raisins, optional
Powdered cardamom
Toasted sliced almonds for garnish (optional)

1. Combine the rice and ½ cup water in a small glass bowl, and microwave on high for 2 minutes.

2. Pulse the partially swelled rice and any remaining water in a processor 10 times until grainy.

3. Place the rice in a 3-quart saucepan, add the coconut milk, and stir. Fill the empty can twice with water and add it to the rice.

4. Cook over medium-high heat until mixture begins to boil. Add the sugar, salt, and raisins to the pot, and reduce heat to a simmer. Stir every 5 minutes to prevent scorching the rice. Cook the mixture for 30–40 minutes or until the liquid is reduced enough to see the grains of rice on the surface of the pudding.

5. Transfer pudding to a serving casserole or individual dishes. Sprinkle surface of the rice pudding with cardamom, and add the toasted sliced almonds if using. Serve warm or at room temperature.

Yield: 6–8 servings

TINA'S TIDBITS

- *For a more American version, add 1 teaspoon vanilla extract to the finished pudding and sprinkle cinnamon on top.*
- *Brown basmati rice may be used for this recipe. Cover rice with 1 cup of water before microwaving on high for 5 minutes, and then proceed with the remaining directions.*
- *According to June, this pudding gets more liquid if refrigerated and does best if allowed to remain at room temperature. I suggest that you refrigerate after a day.*
- *Rice pudding will always appear more liquid when hot, so don't overcook unless you want to re-create your grandmother's version that gets cut with a knife into squares!*

JEWISH TRADERS ON THE SPICE ROUTE

"Worth your weight in gold" might be a compliment today, but in ancient times "worth your weight in salt" would mean a financial windfall for the recipient. Spices of all sorts were in such demand that they were often used as currency. The word "salary" derives from the salt payment that was given to Roman soldiers, and

the Visigoths demanded three thousand pounds of pepper as partial payment for sparing Rome in the fifth century. Salt was the only method of food preservation in ancient times. Spices such as pepper, cinnamon, and cloves were necessary to make the food palatable and counteract the saltiness.

Jews played a significant role in the spice trade as early as biblical times (tenth century B.C.E.). Chapters 5 and 10 of I Kings recount Solomon's inheritance from King David of vast lands that gave him control of the major trade routes between Egypt, Mesopotamia, and Anatolia (often referred to as the Kings Highway) and routes to the southern Arabian peninsula, where the vast majority of spices were traded. His three-year trade expedition with Hiram, as told in I Kings, referred to a long sea voyage from Ezion-Geber (near Eilat) to the island of Chryse, somewhere in the Indian Ocean east of the Ganges River, to seek out spices. The hardships and dangers encountered on long expeditions over sea and land made the transport very costly and the price of spices very expensive, but it only fueled the desire for the exotics more. This desire ushered in the age of exploration. Christopher Columbus—often thought to be a Converso—set sail on the last days of the Jewish expulsion from Spain in 1492.

The Portuguese explorer Vasco da Gama sailed east for a quick route to the Spice Islands in 1497, and Magellan sailed across the Pacific for similar reasons in 1521. During the fourteenth and fifteenth centuries, Jews were restricted from oversees trade. However, the Italians soon replaced Christian intermediary traders with Jews, which moved the Jewish traders back into the spice trade with the Orient.

The Inquisition sent many Jews and "New Christians" to Amsterdam, South America, and the West Indies. From the mid-sixteenth century to the late eighteenth century, Jews who settled in Amsterdam built a trading empire on a scale that was unimaginable in the past. Their business acumen made a significant contribution to the colonial expansion of the Dutch Empire in the seventeenth century. In the mid-1600s the Jewish Mendes family (former Conversos from Spain and Portugal) built a commercial fortune controlling the major portion of the pepper and spice trade in Northern Europe. During this period Jews were actively trading in spices from Yemen, India, and the Dutch East Indies to Europe and the New World. The Mendes family was one of the first Sephardic families to grow and prosper in New

York, Philadelphia, and Newport, based on its trading skills with Jews in Holland.

The flavors of cinnamon, cloves, pepper, and ginger can be found in many recipes prepared in Jewish homes throughout the Diaspora and especially in major trading centers such as Aleppo in Syria, Cochin in India, the Moluccas Islands in Dutch East India (Indonesia), Cape Town in South Africa, and Amsterdam.

SPICE ROUTE NASI GORENG

The first time I ate nasi goreng *(Indonesian fried rice) was at the Bali Restaurant in Amsterdam, and it was one of many dishes on a* rijsttafel *or "rice table." The Dutch adopted the style of offering many dishes on a table that resembled a Ferris wheel during their occupation of Indonesia at the height of their involvement in the spice trade from the late seventeenth century.*

I have combined the basic concept of nasi goreng *with the spices from Indonesia and the west coast of Africa near Elmina, the major Dutch trading port in west Africa that sent spices, gold, palm oil, and timber to Europe and the New World.*

2 cups basmati or medium-grain rice
3½ cups chicken broth
¼ cup oil
2 medium onions, cut into ½-inch dice
3 cloves garlic, minced

2 cups cooked chicken or leftover turkey, julienned
2 tablespoons *tsire* (see recipe below)
4 tablespoons peanut butter, chunky or smooth
¼ pound *merguez* (lamb sausage), Italian sausage, or smoked turkey, cubed

1. Combine the rice and the broth in a large saucepan and bring to a boil. Reduce the heat, cover, and simmer for 20 minutes.

2. Spread the cooked rice on a rimmed cookie sheet to cool and dry for 1 hour. May be placed, uncovered, in the refrigerator to cool faster.

3. Make the *tsire* peanut and spice mix (see recipe below). Set aside.

4. Heat a wok or 4-quart pot over medium-high heat for 20 seconds. Add the oil and heat for another 15 seconds. Sauté the onion over medium heat for 5 minutes, and add the garlic and sauté 5 minutes more or until the onions are lightly golden. Do not burn the garlic.

5. Add the rice, and stirring constantly, cook the rice for 5 minutes or until it is lightly browned.

6. Add the prepared *tsire,* peanut butter, and meats to the pot, and cook over low heat for 10 minutes or until heated through. Stir occasionally.

TSIRE PEANUT AND SPICE MIX

10 cloves
½ teaspoon whole allspice (about 30)
2-inch piece of cinnamon stick
½ teaspoon red chili flakes
½ teaspoon ginger
½ teaspoon ground nutmeg
½ teaspoon salt
½ cup dry roasted or cocktail peanuts

1. Heat a small frying pan or saucepan for 15 seconds. Add the cloves, allspice, and cinnamon and stir until the spices become fragrant. Remove from heat, cool, and grind the spices to a powder in a spice grinder or mortar and pestle. Place in a small processor work bowl.

2. Add the remaining spices and the peanuts to the work bowl and process until finely chopped.

Yield: 6–8 servings

TINA'S TIDBITS

- *Fully cooked deli chicken or turkey can be sliced 1/2-inch thick at the market counter, and then you can easily cut it into 1/2-inch cubes at home.*
- *Six cups of leftover rice (save the containers of Chinese takeout rice!) can be substituted, but you will not have the added flavor of the chicken broth.*
- *Store dark spices in your freezer to preserve their flavor, especially if you don't use certain varieties very often.*

Syrian Spiced Meat with Eggplant and Prunes

The English traders would sail the spices across the Arabian Sea up the Gulf of Suez to the Mediterranean to Syria and Turkey. The major center of trade connecting the spice trade route of the sea with the Silk Road over land was in Syria and Turkey. Aleppo, in northern Syria, had a large Jewish population involved with trade, and the Jewish women of that city were renowned for their culinary abilities.

2 pounds ground chuck meat
2 teaspoons ground allspice
2 teaspoons ground cinnamon
1 teaspoon kosher salt
Pepper to taste
3 tablespoons corn or canola oil
6 medium onions, halved lengthwise and cut into fourths crosswise
4 large red potatoes, halved lengthwise and cut into 1-inch slices
12 ounces pitted prunes

1 large eggplant, quartered lengthwise and cut into 1-inch slices
Two 6-ounce cans of regular tomato paste (not flavored)
¼ cup light brown sugar
¾ cup fresh lemon juice
1 tablespoon Worcestershire sauce
½ tablespoon tamarind concentrate (optional), available in Asian markets
Salt and pepper to taste

1. In a 2-quart bowl, combine the ground meat with the allspice, cinnamon, salt, and pepper. Distribute the spices evenly by first mixing with a fork and then with your hands.

2. Place the oil in the bottom of a 6-quart Dutch oven or metal casserole.

3. Place half of the onion slices in the bottom of the pot, and cover with half of the meat, making sure that you press the meat evenly and firmly into the onions.

4. Scatter half of the potatoes, prunes, and eggplant over the meat.

5. Repeat with the remaining onions, seasoned meat, potatoes, prunes, and eggplant.

6. In a 3-quart bowl, combine the tomato paste with the remaining ingredients along with salt and pepper to taste into a smooth sauce. Pour the sauce evenly over the meat and vegetables and gently swirl the pan to allow the sauce to evenly permeate the dish. I sometimes poke holes in the mixture to allow the sauce to initially penetrate the interior.

7. Cover the pot and bring to a boil over medium-high heat. Keeping the liquid at a medium simmer, cook the mixture for 2 hours or until the potatoes are tender and the sauce is thickened. If you prefer, the mixture can be cooked in a preheated oven at 300–350°F for about the same amount of time. Just make sure that the sauce is simmering so that it will thicken properly in a reasonable amount of time.

8. Serve with rice flavored with some pine nuts and sautéed onions if you like.

Yield: 10–12 servings

TINA'S TIDBITS

- *Ground meat used in a casserole should not be too lean or it will become very hard after prolonged cooking. Eighty to ninety percent lean is acceptable for these purposes.*
- *Ground meat will become tough and rubbery if it is squeezed tightly when combined with other ingredients. Using a fork or your fingertips is a better technique for mixing.*
- *Like all stews that contain many ingredients, this recipe tastes even better the next day.*

GRILLED FISH WITH SPICE RUB

This simple recipe for fish duplicates the itinerary of a ship sailing the spice route! The honey, lemon juice, and olive oil bring it right to the port in Alexandria or Istanbul. Any firm fish can be used as long as it holds together when grilling.

1 tablespoon cumin seed
1 tablespoon coriander seed
1 tablespoon whole black peppercorns
$\frac{1}{3}$ cup salted pistachio nuts
3 large cloves of garlic, finely chopped
1 tablespoon finely chopped candied ginger
1 tablespoon sweet paprika
$1\frac{1}{2}$ teaspoons ground cinnamon

$\frac{1}{2}$ teaspoon salt
1 teaspoon wildflower honey
3 tablespoons extra virgin olive oil
1 tablespoon fresh lemon juice
2 tablespoons chopped fresh parsley
$1\frac{1}{2}$ pounds fillet of fish such as halibut, tuna, or salmon, $\frac{3}{4}$ inch thick

1. Combine all of the ingredients for the rub in a small processor work bowl. Process until a coarse paste is formed. Set aside. Alternatively, place the first 5 ingredients in a bowl or plastic bag and press with the back of a spoon or rolling pin until coarsely crushed. Add remaining ingredients to the bowl and set aside.

2. Rinse the fish and pat dry.

3. Rub the fish with some of the spice rub to coat well. Allow to sit for 20 minutes at room temperature. If marinating for several hours, keep food in the refrigerator but bring to room temperature before grilling.

4. Grill the fish for 3 minutes per side or until firm but springy to the touch.

Yield: 3–4 servings

TINA'S TIDBITS

- *Always choose a firm fish for grilling so it won't fall apart.*
- *Never place your brush or hand into the bowl of spice rub, then onto the meat, and back to the marinade. You will contaminate the mixture, and any leftovers could be dangerous to your future health.*
- *Never let fish sit in a marinade or rub containing a lot of acid for longer than 30 minutes; otherwise the acid in the mixture will "cook" the fish, and grilling will cook the same fish twice, making it tough.*
- *To avoid the smell of fish in your kitchen, remove the paper wrapped around the fish and discard immediately. Most of the time it's the paper that's the culprit in causing bad odors.*

Grilled Chicken with Spice Rub

Here is a similar recipe (for chicken instead of fish) but one could say the ship went north, since all sweetness is eliminated in this recipe and there are more garlic and herbs.

1 tablespoon cumin powder
1 tablespoon curry powder
1 tablespoon paprika
1 tablespoon coriander seed, crushed
1 tablespoon black peppercorn, crushed
1½ teaspoons cinnamon

½ teaspoon salt
3 tablespoons extra virgin olive oil
1 large clove of garlic, chopped
1 tablespoon minced fresh oregano
2 tablespoons minced fresh cilantro
2 pounds boneless, skinless chicken breasts

1. Combine all of the ingredients for the rub in a small bowl. Mix well and set aside.

2. Separate the fillet from the chicken breast, and remove the pearlized white tendon from the fillet (for detailed instructions see page 52). Cut the chicken pieces in half crosswise. Rinse and pat dry.

3. Rub the chicken with some of the spice rub to coat well. Allow to sit for 20 minutes at room temperature. If marinating for several hours, keep food in the refrigerator but bring to room temperature before grilling.

4. Grill the chicken for 3 minutes per side or until firm but springy to the touch.

Yield: 6–8 servings

> ### TINA'S TIDBITS
>
> - *Using crushed seeds not only gives the chicken texture, but it absorbs and retains the oil on the surface better.*
> - *If your grilled chicken has ever come out raw on the inside, the only explanation is that you didn't remove the fillet or "tender" from the breast and heat couldn't penetrate to the interior. Look for a white, pearlized string running through the meat and pull the piece of meat containing it away from the breast.*

SPICED ANGEL PECANS

I call these angel pecans because they truly are heavenly! A perfect treat to make in the fall when pecans are freshly harvested, you can serve them to guests in your sukkah.

1 egg white
1 tablespoon unsalted butter, melted
1 teaspoon vanilla
1 pound pecan halves
$\frac{1}{2}$ cup sugar

$1\frac{1}{2}$ teaspoons cinnamon
$\frac{1}{4}$ teaspoon ground allspice
$\frac{1}{2}$ teaspoon nutmeg
$\frac{1}{2}$ teaspoon salt

1. Preheat oven to 250°F.

2. Place egg white in a 2-quart bowl and beat with a whisk until light and foamy.

3. Fold melted butter and vanilla into the whites. Add the nuts and gently stir to coat all the nuts with the egg white mixture.

4. In a small bowl, combine the sugar, cinnamon, allspice, and salt, and gently fold into the nuts to coat evenly.

5. Spread the nuts onto a jelly roll pan lined with parchment paper, and bake for 45 minutes, stirring the nuts after the first 25 minutes. Nuts should be very crisp and dry.

6. When completely cool, store in an airtight container or freeze in ziplock freezer bags until ready to use.

Yield: 4 cups

VARIATIONS

For Savory Nuts: Substitute 1 teaspoon Worcestershire sauce for vanilla, and use $1\frac{1}{2}$ teaspoons Lawry's seasoned salt, $\frac{1}{4}$–$\frac{1}{2}$ teaspoon garlic powder, and $\frac{1}{4}$ teaspoon curry powder instead of the spices. Prepare as directed above.

For Orange-Spice Nuts: Substitute 1 teaspoon orange extract for the vanilla, and use $\frac{1}{2}$ teaspoon cardamom instead of the nutmeg. Prepare as directed above.

TINA'S TIDBITS

- *Beating the egg white for coating provides more surface area for the sugar to adhere to and makes the pecans more crunchy and "heavenly"!*
- *Pareve margarine or oil may be substituted for butter to make it suitable to serve at meat meals.*

EAST AND SOUTHEAST ASIA

*T*here have always been two major factors in the spread of the Jewish Diaspora: commerce and persecution. The arrival of Jewish émigrés in East Asia and their subsequent egress from that region were no exception.

One hundred years ago a letter was found in Western China that was written by a sheep merchant in 718 petitioning for the right to sell his animals. It was written in Persian-Hebrew. Evidence of traders coming from the Near East—Persia, Mesopotamia—has been found all along the Silk Road. Around the year 960, a group of Persian Jews arrived in the city of Kaifeng, which at that time was the capital of the Sung Dynasty and the center of trade on the Silk Road. The Kaifeng museum has a stone tablet dated in 1489 that commemorates an old synagogue that the Jews were given permission to build at the time of the first millennium. There is also a street in the old Jewish quarter whose name is "The Lane of the Sect That Teaches the Scriptures."

There is no documentation of the survival of Jewish practices in that region until the new waves of Jewish immigrants started to arrive in the mid-nineteenth century. The first groups to arrive in Shanghai were Sephardic Jews from Iraq and Bombay. Two families, the Sassoons and Hardoons, were instrumental in establishing very successful Jewish business and religious communities in that city.

Thousands of Russian Jews came to China in the early twentieth century to escape pogroms. They migrated to northern China through Siberia and remained in that part of the country until 1931, when the Japanese invaded Manchuria. Many

Russian Jews then moved to Shanghai, where they joined the already thriving Ashkenazi and Baghdadi communities. In 1937 mainland China was invaded by the Japanese, who later occupied the Shanghai region. From December 1941 to 1945 the Japanese created a ghetto in Hong Kou where they interned those Shanghai Jews who were associated with Allied countries and the "stateless" Jewish refugees who had escaped from Germany, Austria, and Poland—over twenty-one thousand Jews. Deemed from neutral countries, Shanghai's Iraqi and Russian Jews were left alone. At the end of the war, many Jews were found living in all areas of the Far East after having escaped from Nazi tyranny. There were estimates of over twenty-four thousand Jews in Shanghai alone. With the rise of Communism, most of the community migrated to the United States, Australia, Israel, and Hong Kong. At one point there were seven synagogues in Shanghai. Today, there are two, and the seven-hundred-seat Ohel Rachel Synagogue, the first built in that city, has only been allowed to be open since 1999, one day at a time, for Rosh HaShanah, Chanukah, and Passover.

With commerce opening up between China and the rest of the world, the Jewish community in the city of Shanghai now numbers a few hundred. They hold services and even have a kosher restaurant. This restaurant reflects the food heritage of the Chinese Jewish community. Like many other

Jewish communities in the Diaspora, the common denominator for food preparations is to have the local cuisine conform to the laws of kashrut; no pork or shellfish is consumed, and food is not prepared with any milk products. The Jews of old Kaifeng were actually referred to as the "people who removed the sinew," a tradition whose origins stem from Jacob wrestling with the angel in Genesis 32.

Asian cuisine is probably the easiest to adapt to a kosher kitchen. The substitution of veal (not chicken) for pork renders a dish identical in taste and texture to a recipe that calls for pork. The sauces are almost always vegetable-based. Oyster sauce is not allowed, but thick "dark soy" can be substituted without a problem. Thai fish sauce is usually made with anchovies, and although traditional red curry paste is made with 5 percent dried shrimp paste, there are many high-quality brands available in North America that are vegetarian, do not contain anything *t'reif* (nonkosher), and have excellent flavor. If ingredients are added in the proper order, a homemade Chinese dish will taste just as good, if not better, than one served in any restaurant you can imagine.

ASIAN SPINACH SALAD WITH CANDIED WALNUTS AND FRIED TOFU CROUTONS

This is not an ancient recipe, but it is a good example of how observant Jews in far-reaching areas of the world used the ingredients readily available to build upon the foundation of Jewish dietary laws.

⅓ cup corn oil
2 tablespoons dark sesame seed oil
3 tablespoons rice wine vinegar
1 tablespoon cream sherry
2 × ½-inch strip of lemon zest
1 teaspoon soy sauce
1 scallion, white part and 2 inches of green, sliced ½ inch thick
1 teaspoon minced ginger
1 clove garlic, minced
Pinch of crushed red pepper
Salt and freshly ground pepper to taste
1 teaspoon brown sugar
1 tablespoon minced fresh basil
10 ounces fresh baby spinach or spinach-mesclun mix

1 cup fresh bean sprouts
⅓ cup julienne-sliced bamboo shoots
½ cup blanched snow peas, finely sliced lengthwise
3 ounces extra firm tofu, cut into ½-inch cubes (about 25 cubes)
1 tablespoon honey
1 teaspoon soy sauce
Oil for deep-frying
1 egg white (about 3 tablespoons)
½ cup dried panko bread crumbs
¼ cup water
¼ cup sugar
2 teaspoons five-spice powder
1 teaspoon salt
1½ cups walnut pieces

1. Combine the first thirteen ingredients in a blender and blend until relatively smooth. Set aside in a screw-top jar until ready to use.

2. Rinse and dry the spinach and bean sprouts. Place in a large salad bowl with bamboo shoots and snow peas.

3. Marinate the tofu squares in honey and soy sauce for 10 minutes. Heat oil in a 1-quart saucepan to a depth of 1 inch. Roll the tofu in the egg white, and coat thoroughly with the bread crumbs. Fry the tofu until golden, and drain on paper towel.

4. Preheat the oven to 375°F. Bring the water, sugar, five-spice powder, and salt to a boil in a 1-quart saucepan.

5. Add the walnuts and stir for 1 minute. Spread the nuts onto a nonstick jellyroll pan or a pan lined with parchment paper. Bake walnuts for 7 minutes or until they are dark golden and most of the liquid has evaporated.

6. Remove the nuts from the baking pan and cool on an oiled counter or cookie sheet. When cool, break the pieces up and store in freezer until ready to use.

7. To assemble the salad, toss the greens with some of the vinaigrette until lightly moistened. Top salad with some of the walnuts and the tofu croutons and serve with remaining vinaigrette on the side.

Yield: 4–6 servings

TINA'S TIDBITS

- *"Blanching" literally means "to whiten," but with reference to vegetables it means cooking in boiling salted water for 30 seconds to 1 minute and then plunging the vegetables into ice water to stop the cooking process. This is done to set the bright color and heighten the flavor of the food by bringing out the natural sugars in the food. This technique should always be used on green vegetables that are to be served cold in a salad or as crudités with dip.*
- *Panko is a type of bread crumb from Japan that is large and irregular in shape and gives food an excellent crunchy coating.*

SZECHUAN COLD SPICY NOODLES

This is the real McCoy—an original that I have been making for over thirty years before bottled dressings were the norm. Made with jarred sesame paste (not tahini!), it has a wonderful musty flavor. However, peanut butter is a great substitute. Thinking like a Jew in ancient China, I would prepare this cold dish in advance and serve it for Shabbat lunch. Remember, it was the Chinese who gave the world noodles!

1 chicken breast, cooked, boned, and shredded
1 pound fresh or frozen Chinese egg noodles (lo mein) or ½ pound dried
2 tablespoons corn, canola, or peanut oil
1 tablespoon sesame oil

SAUCE:
3 tablespoons Chinese sesame seed paste or peanut butter
6 tablespoons soy sauce
1 tablespoon red wine vinegar
1 tablespoon chili pepper oil
1 teaspoon sugar
2 tablespoons chopped scallion
½ tablespoon chopped ginger
½ tablespoon chopped garlic
½ teaspoon ground pepper
1 tablespoon Chinese black sesame seed oil
1 tablespoon chopped roasted peanuts
1 tablespoon chopped fresh scallions

1. Put the noodles into boiling water and cook until water returns to a boil. Immediately add ½ cup **cold** water to the pot and return to a boil. Noodles should be tender shortly after the water has come to the boil for the second time. Drain the noodles, but **do not rinse.**

2. Place 2 tablespoons vegetable oil on a large rimmed platter. Add noodles and top with the 1 tablespoon sesame oil. Toss the noodles until well coated with the oils.

TINA'S TIDBITS

- *The Chinese method for cooking noodles is easy and always produces a product that is not too soft. Stopping the cooking action by adding the cold water is the secret to perfect noodles.*
- *When buying jarred Asian sesame seed paste, make sure the paste isn't too dark, which could be a sign of over-roasting and bitterness.*
- *Chili pepper oil is clear and bright orange. Any liquid hot sauce can be substituted, but add a little more vegetable oil to the sauce to keep the proper consistency.*
- *Coating the noodles with the two oils first is imperative so that they don't stick together and to prevent the noodles from absorbing all the sauce and clumping.*
- *To prepare in advance, toss the noodles with the oils and shred the chicken on top. Store the sauce and chopped vegetables separately, and combine everything just before serving.*
- *I like to serve this in a shallow rimmed platter so I can present it and then toss at the table without the noodles falling out of the serving dish.*

3. Shred the chicken by hand or with a coarse grater directly onto the center of the noodles. Cover with plastic wrap and refrigerate until ready to serve.

4. Combine the sesame seed paste (or peanut butter) and the soy sauce in a processor work bowl. Process until mixture is smooth. Add the remaining sauce ingredients and pulse on and off until combined. If too thick, add a little more oil, water, or soy sauce to get the desired consistency and flavor you want.

5. When ready to serve, pour the sauce over the chicken and noodles, and sprinkle the chopped peanuts and scallions on top. Toss to combine and serve. For a pretty presentation, toss the noodles at the table just before serving.

Note: Half a cucumber, finely shredded, may be added to this dish along with the chicken or instead of the chicken for a vegetarian variety.

Yield: 6–8 servings if part of a Chinese meal with several courses

SOBA NOODLES WITH SHITAKE MUSHROOMS AND TOFU

Here's another noodle dish, but this one is Japanese. The meaty mushrooms and the tofu provide a substantial meat alternative for a vegetarian dish. These noodles are made from the same grain as kasha, which is really not a grain but a seed, so one could argue that these noodles (if 100% buckwheat flour) are kosher for Passover. Check the package to make sure wheat flour wasn't used as well.

8 large dried shitake mushrooms
$\frac{1}{4}$ cup cream sherry
$\frac{1}{4}$ cup soy sauce
$1\frac{1}{2} \times \frac{1}{4}$-inch piece of fresh ginger, peeled
2 teaspoons brown sugar or honey
8 ounces dried soba (buckwheat) noodles

1 tablespoon peanut oil
6 ounces firm tofu, cut into $\frac{1}{2}$-inch cubes
2 scallions, finely cut in $\frac{1}{8}$-inch rounds
$\frac{1}{4}$ cup carrot strips made with a zester or very finely julienned
Wasabi for extra flavoring (optional)

1. Place the mushrooms in a 1-quart bowl and cover with at least 1 cup of water. Microwave uncovered for $3\frac{1}{2}$ minutes, and soak for 15 minutes or until very soft.

2. Squeeze the mushrooms over the bowl (reserving the liquid), and slice the mushrooms into $\frac{1}{8}$-inch strips, discarding the stems. Set aside.

3. Strain the mushroom liquid into a measuring cup using a paper coffee filter or double mesh strainer, or very carefully pour out the liquid so the sandy sediment stays in the bowl. You need to have $\frac{3}{4}$–1 cup mushroom liquid. Set aside.

4. In a 1-quart saucepan, bring the sherry to a boil and ignite with a flame. Swirl the pan until the flame disappears. Add the soy sauce, mushroom liquid, fresh ginger, and brown sugar, and boil over medium heat for 10–15 minutes or until liquid is reduced to $\frac{3}{4}$ cup (about half).

5. Meanwhile bring 2 quarts of water to a boil in a 4-quart pot. Add the soba noodles, and when the water returns to a full boil, pour $\frac{1}{2}$ cup of cold water into the pot. Bring to a boil again and cook for 5 minutes more or until the noodles are cooked but still al dente. Drain. Rinse noodles with cold water and place in a serving bowl.

6. Heat 1 tablespoon of peanut oil in a nonstick pan,. Lightly sauté the tofu for 2 minutes. Add the shitake mushroom slices and sauté until heated.

7. Remove the ginger slice from the hot sauce, and pour half of the sauce into the mushroom-tofu mixture. Heat this mixture, stirring, until tofu and mushrooms are coated with the sauce. Add the remaining sauce to the soba noodles and toss well. Pour the mushroom mixture over the soba, and garnish with the sliced scallion and carrot slivers. Serve warm or at room temperature, with wasabi on the side.

Yield: 4 servings

TINA'S TIDBITS

- *I am probably the only cooking instructor who would recommend using cream sherry in Asian cooking. However, most recipes call for a small amount of sugar, and using this sherry, which is sweeter, eliminates the necessity for added sweetner. Cream sherry retains its flavor when exposed to high heat, so it is a very good choice for hot stir-frying.*
- ***Never*** *buy cooking sherry! By law it has a certain percentage of salt added to it. This goes back to Victorian times, when the cook couldn't be monitored in the downstairs kitchen! Buy a decent bottle of domestic cream sherry for about $7 that is palatable and useful for many purposes.*

Tamarind Marinated Grilled Salmon with Thai Curry Sauce on Rice Flake Noodles

With or without the noodles, this dish is terrific. My only regret is that I can't just eat the sauce with a spoon! Actually, this sauce could be thinned down to be a soup with pieces of chicken and canned straw mushrooms as a garnish.

2 large cloves garlic, finely minced
2 tablespoons tamarind or Thai fruit concentrate
1/3 cup water
1/2 teaspoon salt
2 teaspoons ground coriander

1 1/2 teaspoons brown sugar
1/4 teaspoon freshly ground black pepper
1 tablespoon vegetable oil
1 1/2 pounds skinless salmon fillet, cut crosswise into 1 1/2-inch strips

1. Combine all of the ingredients except the salmon in an 11 × 7-inch rectangular dish. Add the salmon to the marinade and coat well. Let the mixture marinate for at least 15 minutes but no more than 1/2 hour.

2. When ready to grill, heat a grill on high and cook the salmon for 3 minutes per side or until the fish is firm but still springy to the touch. Estimate 10 minutes per inch of thickness for the cooking time of the salmon.

3. Serve as is or with the following Thai curry sauce over wide rice flake noodles.

Thai Curry Sauce

One or two 5-ounce bags rice flake or *Chantaboon* noodles
2 tablespoons vegetable oil
2 large cloves of garlic
1 1/2 tablespoons finely minced fresh peeled ginger
3/4 teaspoon ground coriander
1/2 tablespoon curry powder

2 teaspoons Thai red curry paste
1/2 tablespoon sweet paprika
3/4 teaspoon ground cumin
1 1/4 cups unsweetened coconut milk
1 tablespoon tomato paste
1 tablespoon soy sauce
1 1/2 tablespoons light brown sugar

1. Bring a 3-quart pot of water to a boil, and just before making the following sauce, cook the noodles. Drop noodles into the boiling water and add a cup of cold water to the pot. Bring the water to a boil again, and check noodles after 2 minutes to see how soft they are. Meanwhile, make the curry sauce.

2. Heat a 1-quart saucepan for 20 seconds. Add the oil and heat for 15 seconds. Add the garlic and ginger and sauté for 20 seconds over moderately high heat but **do not burn** the garlic.

3. Combine the coriander, curry powder, curry paste, paprika, and cumin. Whisk the spices into

the garlic mixture and stir over low heat for 20 seconds. Whisking constantly, add the remaining ingredients and heat thoroughly. Do not boil.

4. When the noodles are done, drain them, place on a platter, and toss with some of the sauce. Top with the grilled salmon fillets and enough remaining sauce to coat well. Reserve any remaining sauce to pass. Serve.

Yield: Serves 4–6 people

TINA'S TIDBITS

- *Premeasured ingredients can be combined in a small bowl if they are to be added to the recipe at the same time and if they are either all dry or all liquid. Mixing the two in advance can often result in loss of flavor or texture.*
- *Coconut milk is not made from milk. It is the pulverized meat of the coconut and water, and the Jews of India and Thailand utilized its pareve properties to the fullest.*

Steak with Cellophane Noodles

The technique and the ingredients in this recipe are the cornerstone for all beef and lamb stir-fry dishes; lamb with scallions, beef with bok choy or snow peas, and so on all use the same marinade and technique. This recipe, with the substitution of green bell peppers instead of the broccoli, is the iconic dish known as pepper steak that was found in all Cantonese restaurants in the 1950s. The cellophane noodles are the fried "Styrofoam" noodles that are used for a garnish. They are fun and wow your guests but are not necessary for the success of this dish.

1 ounce cellophane noodles (optional)
$\frac{1}{2}$ pound steak, preferably partially frozen
3 tablespoons soy sauce
$1\frac{1}{2}$ tablespoons cream sherry
$1\frac{1}{2}$ teaspoons cornstarch
1 teaspoon sugar

1 small bunch broccoli, stems sliced and florettes, separated
2 teaspoons finely chopped ginger root
$\frac{1}{8}$ teaspoon cayenne pepper or to taste (optional)
2 cups corn or peanut oil (if making noodles)
3 tablespoons corn or peanut oil

1. Over a deep bowl, use a pair of sharp scissors to cut the cellophane noodles into 4-inch lengths. Separate the noodles. Set aside.

2. Using a sharp chef's knife or cleaver, trim off and discard any fat on the meat, and thinly slice the meat on a diagonal against the grain. This can be done more easily if the meat is almost frozen. Sliced meat should be about 2 inches long and $\frac{1}{2}$ inch wide and as thin as can be.

3. In a small bowl, combine the soy sauce, cornstarch, sugar, and sherry. Add the sliced meat and toss it until it is well coated. Set aside.

4. Have the noodles, steak, broccoli, ginger, cayenne, and oil ready and within easy reach. If not making noodles, proceed to step 6.

5. Heat the 2 cups oil in a deep pot or wok until it is almost smoking. A noodle dropped into oil will cook in **1 second**. If oil is ready, drop in a handful of noodles at a time. Cook for 3 seconds and immediately remove to paper towels. Fry the remainder in the same way.

6. Heat a wok for 30 seconds. Add 1 tablespoon oil and heat for 30 seconds. Turn the heat down if the oil begins to smoke. Add the broccoli stems and stir-fry for 1 minute. Add the florets and cook until a bright emerald green. Remove both to a bowl.

7. Add another 2 tablespoons of oil to the wok and heat. Add ginger root and stir-fry for 5 seconds. Add the meat and cayenne and stir-fry for 1 or 2 minutes.

8. Add the broccoli to the pan and stir-fry to combine thoroughly and reheat.

9. Serve immediately by placing the meat mixture in the center of a large heated platter. Arrange the noodles around the perimeter.

Note: As a main course this will serve 4. This recipe can be doubled, but never use more than 1 pound of meat in a stir-fry dish or the flavor of the dish will change unfavorably.

Yield: 4–6 servings

TINA'S TIDBITS

- *Remember, if you are not making the cellophane noodles, then this recipe needs only 3 tablespoons oil!*
- *The entire area of a wok is your cooking surface so it is imperative to keep the food moving in order to cook it in 2–3 minutes.*
- *Because stir-frying is very fast, all of your ingredients must be premeasured and ready to go. However, premeasuring small quantities of oil in a little bowl will result in inaccurate quantities, since much of the oil will adhere to the bowl.*

PUMPKIN WITH SPICED COCONUT CUSTARD

Although this recipe is Thai in origin, it mimics the preparation that the Puritan settlers first used when introduced to this native plant. A rabbi at the Chabad house in Bangkok told me that pumpkin, which is readily available in Thailand, is often used for Jewish holidays in the Sephardi manner to represent all-encompassing prosperity.

One 4- to 5-pound pie pumpkin
3 eggs
½ cup dark brown sugar
Pinch of salt

1 teaspoon cornstarch (optional)
⅛ teaspoon cinnamon
⅛ teaspoon ground cloves
One 14-ounce can coconut milk

1. With your knife angled 45 degrees toward the center, cut a large hole in the top of the pumpkin.

2. Remove and discard all of the stringy fiber from the interior of the pumpkin (discard seeeds if you don't want them for roasting), but save the lid.

3. Lightly scrape the inside of the pumpkin with the tines of a fork. Set aside.

4. Preheat the oven to 350°F. Line a low-sided jelly roll pan with foil.

5. Whisk the eggs until well beaten, and add the remaining ingredients. Whisk until well combined.

6. Pour the mixture into the prepared pumpkin, and replace the top of the pumpkin.

7. Bake for 1½–2 hours until pumpkin is soft and custard is set. Serve hot or warm, scooping out some of the cooked pumpkin with the custard.

Yield: Serves 4–6

TINA'S TIDBITS

- *Use a round pie pumpkin (stores will state this), not a jack-o-lantern variety, for this dish. Kabocha or white pumpkin can be used as well.*
- *The acidity of the pumpkin will determine if custard looks curdled. It isn't really curdled and will taste just as good, without having to use starch to bind the custard together and change the custard's texture.*

RUSSIA AND CENTRAL AND EASTERN EUROPE

*T*he Jews of this continuously altered political region are the Jews with whom most North American Jews are most familiar. In the thirteenth and fourteenth centuries, the Polish monarchs encouraged Jews to come to Poland to help develop the trade and market economy of the region. At this time Jews were being persecuted

throughout Europe. If they weren't responsible for the death of Christ, they were responsible for the plague. If they were not beaten or executed, they were required to live in dark, overcrowded ghettos or small villages where they could barely survive. Of course, another way to deal with the Jewish scourge was to expel them altogether.

Poland looked good in those days, so thousands of Jews from the beginning of the Crusades to the end of the fifteenth century resettled from Germany, Austria, Hungary, and Lithuania into the land then known as Poland. The French and Northern Italian Jewish immigrants who immigrated to Germany in the tenth century created a language within their newly assimilated Jewish communities that combined elements of their Laaz (Jewish/French dialect), medieval German, biblical and mishnaic Hebrew, and Aramaic. This came to be the primary language of Western European Jews. When these Jews migrated to Poland, they introduced this language to the Polish Jewish community. Using Hebrew as the common denominator and introducing the Slavic language into the mix, Yiddish as we know it today was born. This language helped to define a community and protect them, because non-Jews didn't understand this language. On the other hand,

Yiddish defined who was a Jew to the outside world and made them targets for persecution.

In the middle of the seventeenth century, there was a Cossack revolt, and the Polish army was overthrown. The Cossacks, under the leadership of Bogdan Chmielnicki, joined with the Polish peasants in attacking the Jews. The Chmielnicki massacres, as they were called, were carried out over a period of eight years. One hundred thousand Jews were killed, tortured, or poorly treated. As a result, many Jews fled back to Germany, Holland, Central Europe, and the Balkans. The Yiddish language went with them as well.

Beginning in 1790, and into the early twentieth century, Western European Jews were slowly emancipated and allowed to interact with all members of the community, secure jobs in these communities, and pursue their own religious beliefs without restrictions. Eastern European Jews were also thriving, although their community was still insular, with little contact with the outside world. At this same time Russia was expanding her borders westward, and more than 1.2 million Jews in Poland and Lithuania came under her rule. By 1835 the Pale of Settlement, stretching from the Baltic Sea to the Black, was established. Jews were forced to leave their homes east and west of this territory and were evacuated from their homes in the big cities of this region to move into shtetls, or little villages, throughout this area.

As a result of the success of the Jews within the non-Jewish communities of Germany and parts of Eastern Europe and the need for a scapegoat for Russian economic and political decline, Jews became targets of fear and jealousy, and by the 1880s anti-Semitism was on the rise. Pogroms (Russian for "violent mass attacks") began in 1871 in Odessa and continued for the next thirty-five years. In Romania, the government's support of anti-Semitism in the late 1800s was responsible for the migration of over seventy thousand Jews to the United States.

Russia tried to diminish its Jewish population by conscription into the army. Boys were taken away at twelve, before bar mitzvah, forced to eat pork, and required to serve for twenty-five years. The government hoped that after this long time the soldiers would forget that they were ever Jewish. This was the major impetus for the migration, often illegally, to the United States, Palestine, and South Africa. By 1900 New York City had the largest Jewish population of any city in the world. By 1904 over sixty-four thousand Jewish families lived in six thousand tenements on the Lower East Side.

Many recipes you expect to find in this section are dispersed throughout the book and most likely in the Icons section—and with good reason. Because of the mass migration of over two million Jews from Eastern Europe, the Pale of Russia, and Romania at the end of the nineteenth century and the beginning of the twentieth, generations of Jews in America viewed only the foods coming out of this area as Jewish. The recipes have been tweaked to adapt to foods readily available—people in the South use red snapper in their gefilte fish because it is plentiful in the Gulf—but the roots are still in the Ashkenazic kitchen of the past. Most Americans don't know that bagels are a peasant snack from the shtetls in the Pale, but all know they are found throughout America and well loved.

Although we no longer subsist on herring, black bread, and an onion as our midday meal, we can see the connection in foods that were "dressed up" for Shabbat or holidays in the poverty-stricken homes of this region.

"Homemade" Pickled Herring in Cream Sauce

Today most of the traditional Ashkenazic dishes are available already prepared in delis and supermarkets. We no longer brine our own fish to preserve it. However, we can add fresh ingredients to the prepared product to elevate the taste and heighten the memory. This recipe is one such example. Auntie Yetta taught it to me when I was in my teens, and I have made her recipe every year since.

2-pound jar of pickled herring snack bits (no sour cream sauce)

1 medium Bermuda or Spanish onion
1–2 cups heavy sour cream

1. Drain herring and jarred onions, reserving the liquid. Place herring pieces and pickled onions in a medium mixing bowl.

2. Thinly slice the onion into rings and add to the herring, along with enough sour cream to be thick but still slightly runny. Refrigerate for a day or longer, and add additional sour cream or reserved juice if needed.

3. Store and serve in a glass bowl.

Yield: 2 quarts

> ## TINA'S TIDBITS
>
> - *Although I have given you the traditional preparation above, I generally cut the onion in half to create half moons. This prevents a ring from hanging by the spoon's handle and dripping sour cream all over your tablecloth or rug!*
> - *Always keep herring in a glass container; plastic will absorb the odor, and metal will change the flavor or color of this highly acidic preparation.*

RUSSIAN CABBAGE BORSCHT

My mother was a first-generation American. She learned to speak Yiddish when her cousins escaped Poland in the early 1930s to come and live near her. She was poor growing up, and her cooking as an adult reflected the reverence she had for the simplest of ingredients. I still feel guilty when I throw a salad together for dinner. When I was growing up, we started dinner every evening with our own individual salad bowls garnished with four tomato wedges, a green pepper ring, and a radish rose centered on top. She didn't make elaborate or ethnic foods, but her sound, basic Ashkenazic cooking was always perfectly cooked and presented.

This soup is a perfect representation of less is more and the love affair the Eastern European cooks had with all things sweet and sour. The original recipe was shown to me with a shiterein (a handful or a pinch—a nondescript amount of ingredient—of this and that). Here is my recipe for another generation.

3 strips of flanken meat (short ribs), about 1½ pounds
2½ quarts water
1 large onion
One 15.5-ounce can peeled tomatoes in liquid
One 8-ounce can tomato sauce

1 medium or ½ large head of cabbage, finely sliced into shreds
Salt and freshly ground pepper to taste
1 cup dark raisins
¼ cup dark brown sugar or to taste
Lemon juice (optional)

1. Rinse off meat and place in a 4-quart pot. Add the water, bring to a boil, and simmer for 30 minutes, skimming the top of the soup occasionally to remove the brown foam.

2. Add the onion, after piercing it 4 or 5 times with a sharp knife. This technique allows the flavor of the onion to permeate the soup without the onion disintegrating.

3. Squeeze the canned tomatoes through your fingers so that you get uneven strings of crushed tomato. Add this and any liquid from the can to the pot. Add the tomato sauce.

4. Add the shredded cabbage, salt and pepper to taste, and the raisins to the soup pot, and cook for 1½ hours partially covered.

5. After 1½ hours, add the brown sugar and adjust the seasonings to your taste, using some lemon juice, if needed, to balance the sweet-and-sour taste.

6. Cook for ½ hour more. Remove the onion, break up the meat into pieces, remove the bones, and serve.

Yield: 6–8 servings

TINA'S TIDBITS

- *This soup, like most soups, tastes even better the second day and freezes very well.*
- *If the soup is too thin for you, either add additional tomato sauce or thicken with an einbrenne, which is a mixture of equal parts pareve margarine and flour that is added in small amounts to the hot soup to create the desired thickness.*
- *Flour can never be added directly to a hot liquid without creating little floating lumps. Mixing it into a fat first will allow the flour to dissolve slowly and evenly.*
- *When preparing soup, it is always a good idea to cook meat alone in water for the first 30 minutes. The coagulated blood and any other impurities from the bone rise to the surface as a foam that is easily removed, which helps clarify the soup.*

LENTIL SOUP

Although lentils are more often associated with India and the Near East, Jewish traders helped bring these staples of Middle Eastern regions to Eastern Europe. Easy and delicious—all you need is some hot bread and maybe a salad, and that's dinner.

2 cups lentils
1½ pounds flanken or short ribs
2 quarts water
2 tablespoons oil
1 large onion, diced

3 carrots, diced
2 stalks celery diced
Salt and pepper to taste
2–3 Polish sausages or frankfurters

1. Place lentils in a glass bowl and cover with 2 inches of water. Microwave for 3 minutes and then set aside for 1 hour or until slightly softened. Drain and set aside.

2. In a 3-quart pot, bring the 2 quarts of water to a boil with the meat. Simmer for 30 minutes, skimming off the foam that rises.

3. Heat an 8-inch frying pan for 15 seconds. Add the oil and heat for another 15 seconds. Add the diced onion and sauté in the oil until it is golden. Add to the pot with the meat.

4. Add the lentils and the remaining ingredients, except the sausage, to the pot, and simmer for 1 hour or until the meat and lentils are tender.

5. Remove the flanken to a plate. Remove bones and cartilage, and cut the meat into small pieces if not eating the meat separate from the soup.

6. Place the soup in a food mill or blender and process until smooth.

7. Return the soup to a clean pot, and add the sliced Polish sausage and cubed meat, if desired. Simmer for another 10 minutes or until the sausage has imparted its flavor to the soup and is completely heated through. Serve.

Yield: 4–6 servings

TINA'S TIDBITS

- *This soup is pureed; however, if you want to leave the soup chunky, take extra care to cut your vegetables in uniform shape.*
- *A blender does a much better job of pureeing soups than a processor because all the ingredients are pulled down to the blade by the whirlpool effect. If you are using a processor, you must add only the solids to the work bowl first or the soup will have a coarse texture.*
- *An alternative method of serving this recipe is to keep the flanken whole after the soup is cooked. Serve the soup first and the meat as an entrée accompanied by a starch and a vegetable.*

PRUNE TZIMMES

Tzimmes has its origin in medieval Germany, where it was the custom to have meat stews that contained fruit and vegetables. Perhaps the Persian and western Asian culinary habit of using fruits with meat made it up the Rhine. The sugar-beet-growing region of southwestern Poland surely influenced the addition of sugar to the recipe, and the use of sweet potatoes is only a few centuries old, since the sweet potato wasn't introduced to Eastern Europe from America until the sixteenth century.

1 pound pitted prunes
1 tablespoon peanut oil
1 small onion (about 3 inches in diameter), finely diced
1 large clove garlic, minced
4–5 pounds brisket or boneless chuck roast

Salt and freshly ground black pepper to taste
4 carrots, pared and sliced into 1½-inch chunks
2 sweet potatoes, pared and cut into eighths
¼ cup sugar
1 tablespoon lemon juice (or to taste)

1. Cover prunes with cold water. Microwave on high for 3 minutes, and let soak for 30 minutes or longer, until soft.

2. Heat a large Dutch oven for 20 seconds. Add the oil and heat for another 10 seconds. Add the onion and garlic and sauté for a few minutes until the onion is golden. Do not let the garlic brown or it will become bitter. Add the meat and sear on all sides. The meat probably won't lie flat; don't worry, just sear all sides.

3. Transfer the meat to a large roasting pan, preferably one with a lid (if not, use heavy-duty foil to cover). Add prunes and soaking water to the meat and bring to a boil on your cooktop. Add salt and pepper.

4. Cover roasting pan tightly and transfer to a preheated 300°F oven. Cook the meat for 3–4 hours, depending on the size and thickness of your brisket.

5. Remove the meat and prunes from the pan. Put the potato and carrot chunks in the bottom of the pan, and place meat and prunes on top.

6. Sprinkle sugar and lemon juice into the gravy. Stir to combine, and cover tightly with lid or heavy-duty foil.

7. Place the roasting pan in a 350°F oven for 45–60 minutes or until the meat and potatoes are tender. Adjust the seasonings if necessary.

8. Remove the meat and cool, preferably overnight in the refrigerator.

9. Slice the meat when it is firm, and return to the vegetables and gravy to reheat.

Note: If your meat is small enough to fit into a large Dutch oven or pot, you may cook it on the top of the stove for 2 hours and then proceed to step 5.

Yield: 8–10 servings

TINA'S TIDBITS

- *A Dutch oven is a large, squat, 4- to 6-quart pot with two small handles.*
- *The dull side of the foil should always be facing up when roasting in the oven because the dull side absorbs the heat and helps the roasting process. However, **never** use the dull side up on a turkey, because it will dry out the white meat—use shiny side up for that.*
- *To freeze the vegetables and fruits, remove from the gravy, cool completely and then place in a freezer bag, place a straw in the bag, and close the bag up to the straw. Suck out all the air in the bag and then seal. This will prevent ice crystals in the air from piercing the vegetables and making them soggy. Freeze the gravy in a jar or bag in the same way*

KASHA VARNISHKAS

Kasha is probably the grain most identified with Eastern European Jews, but the grain (actually a seed) least eaten by contemporary American Jews. This earthy, chewy grain could easily replace rice or potatoes on the modern Jewish table, but it doesn't. What a pity! There is nothing like pot roast gravy on a pile of little brown granules mixed with golden fried onions and mushrooms to transport one back to the "good ol' days" that weren't so good but are long, long gone.

"Try it, you'll like it"... and it's good for you too!

1 cup kasha
1 egg, slightly beaten
¼ cup oil
1 medium onion, finely diced
4 ounces sliced mushrooms

2 cups boiling water
2 beef or vegetable bouillon cubes
½ teaspoon salt
Freshly ground black pepper to taste
8 ounces pasta bow ties

1. Heat a 2-quart saucepan over medium-high heat and add the kasha. Pour the beaten egg over all of the kasha and stir constantly until egg evenly coats the grains and each grain separates from the rest of the kasha. This should be done over a medium heat so that the egg does not cook before it coats the kasha grains. Put kasha in a bowl.

2. Reheat pan for 10 seconds then place the oil in the used pan and sauté the onions for 3 minutes. Add the sliced mushrooms and sauté another 3–5 minutes or until the mixture is golden.

3. Return the kasha to the pan with the onions and mushrooms. Add the boiling water, bouillon cubes, salt, and pepper, and stir to dissolve the bouillon. Cover and cook over a low flame for 15 minutes or until the kasha is tender.

4. Meanwhile cook the pasta bow ties according to package directions.

5. Combine the kasha and bowties and serve as is or with some gravy from your meat entrée on top.

Yield: 4–6 servings

TINA'S TIDBITS

- *Coating the uncooked granules with the raw egg prevents the kasha from swelling up. If you eliminate this step, you will feel like you are eating a bowl of Wheatena.*
- *Always sauté onions alone initially before adding other vegetables with a high water content. This allows the sugars in the onion to caramelize and makes the onion sweeter.*
- *Although any pasta shape can be used, bow tie pasta is to kasha what grape jelly is to peanut butter!*

POTATO KUGEL

There's a famous Yiddish song that says, "Monday a potato, Tuesday a potato . . . and for Shabbat a potato kugel!" Whole books with variations have been written about kugel as well—as they should, since a kugel, or pudding, was an inexpensive way to bulk up an ingredient like potatoes or carrots to fill up a family. If your grandmother fried her onions first, do so. If mushrooms and carrots were added in your family's kugel, go ahead. This is a delicious, proportionately correct potato kugel for you to enhance to your liking and memory.

6–8 large white or Yukon Gold potatoes, raw
1 medium onion
3 eggs, beaten well
1 tablespoon salt
½ teaspoon freshly ground pepper

½ cup matzah or cracker meal
¼ cup oil or rendered chicken fat
Additional oil or chicken fat for greasing pan and
   coating top of kugel

1. Wash and grate the raw potatoes by hand or in a processor fitted with the grating disc; there is no need to peel potatoes. Put grated potatoes in a colander, rinse with cold water, and drain well. Place in a large bowl.

2. Grate the onion as you did the potatoes. If you are using a processor, change to the cutting blade, and add ¼ of the grated potatoes to the grated onion and pulse on and off to make a coarse paste. Add this mixture to the grated raw potatoes in the bowl.

3. Add the eggs and the remaining ingredients, including the ¼ cup oil or chicken fat and mix well. (Use your hands if you need to.)

4. Oil a 2-quart casserole or 13 x 9 pan, and pour potato mixture into the prepared pan. Drizzle an additional tablespoon of oil or room temperature chicken fat over the top of the mixture, and lightly spread with your hand to coat evenly.

5. Bake in a preheated 350°F oven for 45 minutes or until top is crisp and golden. If need be, kugel may be placed under broiler for 3 minutes or until top is golden.

Yield: 12–15 servings

TINA'S TIDBITS

- *Potatoes absorb a great deal of salt, so more salt than you would normally need must be added to make your kugel taste right.*
- *The reason potatoes discolor is the oxidation of the potato starch in the tuber. If the potato is rinsed well and drained, your kugel will not be gray on the inside.*
- *Never grate the onion with the potato, because when you drain the mixture, a great deal of the onion flavor will be lost.*

COULIBIAC

Not everyone in Russia was poor. Some advisors to the czar, or "court Jews," lived well, if only for a short time.

This recipe is long, but not difficult. It can be prepared in advance and even frozen, since the salmon has already been poached (you can buy it that way if you like). Each step can be made separately and then put together when you want.

1 recipe for rice-cheese filling (see page 138)
1 recipe for mushroom duxelles (see page 138)
1 recipe for herbed crepe (see page 139)
½ pound salmon, cut into 1½-inch strips
1 cup water

½ cup dry white wine
1 package frozen puff pastry
1 egg white combined with ½ tablespoon water for egg wash
Port wine cream sauce (optional; see page 139)

1. Prepare recipes for mushroom duxelles, rice and cheese filling, and herbed crepe. Set aside until you are ready to prepare salmon and assemble coulibiac.

2. Combine water and wine in a 10-inch sauté pan with lid. Bring to a simmer and add the salmon. Lower heat, cover, and cook for 4 minutes or until salmon is springy to the touch and just cooked through. Immediately remove from liquid and place on a cloth towel to drain.

3. Roll one sheet of the puff pastry into an 18 × 16-inch rectangle. Place the herbed crepe centered over the dough.

4. Spread half the rice and cheese filling down the middle third of the crepe.

5. Spread half the mushroom duxelles over the rice, and lay the poached salmon strips down the center.

6. Cover the salmon strips with the remaining duxelles, and cover with the remaining rice and cheese filling.

7. Draw the long edges of the dough together over the filling, and pinch to seal. Draw up the sides, cutting off any excess dough, and pinch decoratively to seal. Place the rolled dough seam side down on a parchment-lined cookie sheet that has low sides.

8. Brush the coulibiac with egg white wash, and cut 2 ¼-inch steam holes on top. Decorate the top with any rolled dough scraps, and brush decorations with the egg wash as well. Refrigerate for at least 30 minutes.

9. When ready to bake, remove coulibiac from the refrigerator, and preheat the oven to 425°F.

10. Bake the coulibiac for 10 minutes at 425°F, then reduce the oven to 350°F, and continue to bake for 10–15 minutes longer or until golden. Insert a metal tester in the center of the roll to make sure the interior is hot. Cover with foil (shiny side facing up) if the dough is golden and the mixture needs more time to heat through.

11. Serve sliced with port wine cream sauce if desired (see page 139).

Yield: 8–12 servings

Mushroom Duxelles

½ ounce dried porcini mushrooms
¼ cup cream sherry
1½ pounds fresh mushrooms
½ stick unsalted butter
1 shallot, finely chopped

½ cup finely chopped onion
½ teaspoon thyme
½–¾ teaspoon salt
Nutmeg to taste (should be subtle)
Pepper to taste

1. Rinse the dried porcini mushrooms with cold water and drain well. Place in a glass bowl and add the sherry. Microwave for 20 seconds and allow the mushrooms to soften in the liquid while you prepare the rest of the ingredients for the duxelles.

2. Wash and drain the fresh mushrooms, and mince in a processor until finely chopped.

3. Melt the butter in a 2-quart saucepan. Add the shallot and onion, and sauté for 5 minutes or until golden.

4. Add the minced mushrooms and the seasonings, and stir to combine.

5. Place the soaked mushrooms (reserve the liquid) in a processor work bowl (be careful not to get any sand from the liquid in the work bowl). Pulse the machine on and off until a fine paste is formed. Add the soaking liquid and process to puree. Add this mixture to the saucepan.

6. Sauté over low to medium heat until the duxelles is reduced and thickened. Be careful that the mixture doesn't stick. Adjust seasonings. Set aside until ready to use. May be refrigerated for a day or two or frozen for later use.

Rice and Cheese Filling

2 tablespoons butter
¼ cup finely minced scallions
2 tablespoons flour
1 cup milk

2¼ cups leftover cooked rice (or ¾ cup raw rice cooked in 2¼ cups water for 20 minutes)
2 tablespoons minced dill
¼ cup parmesan cheese
Nutmeg to taste
Salt and pepper to taste

1. Melt the butter in a saucepan and sauté the scallions until wilted. Whisk in the flour and cook for 1 minute over low heat.

2. Add the milk all at once and rapidly mix the sauce until thickened.

3. Add the remaining ingredients and adjust seasonings if necessary. Set aside until ready to assemble coulibiac.

Herbed Crepe

2 teaspoons vegetable oil
2 eggs
½ cup flour
1 cup milk (preferably 2% or whole)

Pinch of salt
1 tablespoon chopped fresh chives
1 tablespoon chopped fresh parsley
1 tablespoon chopped fresh dill

1. Brush a nonstick jelly roll pan with the oil. Set aside.

2. Beat eggs with a handheld electric mixer for 30 seconds or until pale yellow.

3. With mixer on medium, add the milk in a steady stream, and then add the flour until a smooth batter is formed.

4. Add the remaining ingredients and mix just to combine. Let mixture rest at room temperature for 20–30 minutes.

5. Preheat oven to 425°F.

6. Spread the mixture in the prepared jelly roll pan and bake for 12 minutes. Let cool in pan until ready to assemble.

Note: This mixture will get a little rubbery if made far in advance of assembly.

> ### TINA'S TIDBITS
>
> - *Although the puff pastry readily available in your supermarket freezer is quite good, it is pareve. It would be worth a little time to find butter-based puff pastry for this dish. It is superb.*
> - *Nutmeg should always be added to recipes containing cheese or mushrooms. The flavor enhances the natural taste of those ingredients. Make sure, however, that your cheese sauce doesn't smell like egg nog!*
> - *The base of the sauce for the rice and cheese filling is a classic medium white sauce that is also the base for a macaroni and cheese sauce: 2 tablespoons of butter to 2 tablespoons of flour, with 1 cup of milk. Substitute margarine and chicken broth to that proportion and you have a velouté sauce, which is often used to create a non-dairy sauce for a meat dish that will conform to the laws of kashrut.*

Port Wine Cream Sauce

5 tablespoons unsalted butter, divided use
¼ cup minced shallots
½ cup port wine

½ cup heavy cream
½ teaspoon fresh lime juice
Salt and pepper to taste

1. Melt 2 tablespoons butter in a heavy saucepan and add the shallots. Sauté for 3 minutes or until soft.

2. Add the port wine, and over high heat, reduce the liquid by half.

3. Add the lime juice and cream. Heat just to the boiling point and then reduce to a low simmer.

4. Whisk in the remaining butter 1 tablespoon at a time. Remove from the heat. Adjust seasonings, and serve with coulibiac.

RUGELACH

Thirty-five years ago I sat in Mrs. Goodman's kitchen and she gave me this recipe. It was the first time I had ever made them and they were great. Over the years I realized that although everyone seems to have the same recipe with the same proportions, mine always came out lighter and flakier. I pass on my three "secrets" to you in my Tidbits. At one time I used to make a thousand of these at a time for the largest kosher caterer in Philadelphia. Nowadays, I am content to make a double batch of 150 for my friends and family.

8 ounces cream cheese
8 ounces salted butter
2 cups all purpose flour
1½ cups sugar

2–3 teaspoons ground cinnamon
1 cup raisins
¾ cup chopped walnuts
Confectioners' sugar

1. Cream the cheese and butter together on high speed with an electric mixer until well combined and light and fluffy (the mixture should feather out from the edge of the bowl). Scrape down the sides of the bowl. Add flour and turn your mixer on and off **only** until dough looks like the flour has been incorporated. Remove the dough from the bowl and lightly drop it on a smooth surface a few times until it forms a compact mass. (Pressing with your hands could soften the butter and change the consistency of your finished product.)

2. Divide mixture into 8 cylinders, and refrigerate 1 hour or until dough is firm.

3. Roll each portion of dough onto a board that is heavily "floured" with confectioners' sugar. Roll out into a 6 × 9-inch rectangle.

4. Combine the sugar, cinnamon, raisins, and walnuts in a bowl.

5. After the dough is rolled out, sprinkle with some of the sugar-nut mixture. Roll dough into a log from the long side. Pinch the seam together on the bottom and the ends slightly under.

6. Cut filled logs into 8 or 9 pieces, and place on an ungreased or parchment-lined cookie sheet. Repeat with remaining dough logs.

7. Bake in a 350°F oven for 12–15 minutes or until golden. Cool completely before freezing.

Yield: 5–6 dozen cookies

TINA'S TIDBITS

- *Using salted butter in a pastry is the exception. Here it is necessary to evenly distribute salt in non-liquid dough.*
- *Handling this dough as little as possible keeps the fat content from dissolving into the flour, with the result more like puff pastry instead of cookie dough.*
- *Always roll this dough on a board covered with confectioners' sugar. This sugar helps balance the richness of the dough with the sweet filling.*
- *Confectioners' sugar contains 2–3 percent cornstarch, which helps absorb moisture and prevent the dough from sticking to the counter or rolling pin.*
- *The raw dough or the baked rugelach can be frozen for later use.*

WESTERN EUROPE

᪥ GERMANY ᪥

Jews first traversed the Alps to the land of modern-day Germany and eastern France during the Roman period. They settled by rivers because they were primarily traders. The Radenites (from Persian for "knowing the way") were Jewish traders in the ninth century who journeyed between China and the Frankish kingdoms, bringing furs, beaver pelts, swords, slaves, and eunuchs to China and bringing spices, silks, and metal to Arabia, Persia, North Africa, Germany, and France. Jews were primarily involved in this profession because of the basic distrust between Muslims and Christians. They also were fluent in many languages so they acted as interpreters during transactions.

The Jews were never accepted by the Christian communities, nor were they allowed to live near them or associate with them. They lived in fenced-off villages. However, for a time they were tolerated and were permitted to enter into business transactions with the Christians. The Crusades ended this era. Although the Crusades officially began in 1096, a crazed Monk named Peter started his own drive to the Holy Land a year earlier. On his way he pillaged and massacred any "enemy of God" on his path. The church didn't condone this but was unable to prevent the mass slaughter of Jews in Worms.

In medieval times, Jews who traveled could not reliably expect a kosher meal in the villages where they traded. They were known for taking large loaves of bread on their journeys and subsisting on preserved fish and vegetables. Some inns on their trade routes kept a pan aside that was retained solely for kosher sauces, but this practice was not common.

At home, each village had a kosher communal oven and even a few cauldrons set aside for large festivities like weddings. These ovens were used to bake challah and slow-cooked stews for Shabbat and matzah for Pesach. German Jews preferred to eat goose and duck over chicken, liked sweet-and-sour flavors in foods from meat to cabbage to fish, and baked goods encasing cheese or fruit or both, such as *fludens* or *chremslach*, and sweet crackers were their desserts of choice.

The great German migration to America peaked in the mid- to late 1800s. German Jewish merchants, financiers, and manufacturers quickly rose to prominence in the economic landscape, and German Jews were the major force behind the growth of Reform Judaism in America. The next major wave of German-Jewish immigration was in the early 1930s as Hitler was coming to power. In 1933 there were almost 600,000 Jews living in Germany; 240,000 German Jews managed to escape to the United States, and another 130,000 made it to South America.

Jews have lived in France since the Roman period. Initially they were scattered and isolated from their coreligionists. However, after the Roman conquest of Jerusalem in 70 C.E., many Jews sought asylum in Bordeaux, Arles, and Lyon in southern France. By the ninth century, good-sized Jewish communities with communal ovens, *mikvaot*, and venues for religious practice (if not actual synagogues) existed in Paris, Rouen, Alsace-Lorraine, Blois, and Lyon in addition to the already established region in Provence. Jews were active in medicine and commerce. They were so successful that they were accredited vendors to the royal court. They were also significant in the viniculture community, supplying not only the kosher wines needed by the Jews but also wines for general consumption and for church mass. In the tenth century, one of the most famous commentators of the Talmud, Rashi, established his school in Troyes, southeast of Paris, while he tended his extensive vineyard.

The First Crusade had no impact on the Jewish communities in France; however, by the Second Crusade in the mid-twelfth century, the long reign of persecution, ascribed attire, looting, taxation, and mass murders had begun. In 1240 whole communities of Jews were expelled from France. The kingdom confiscated all personal goods and property. Two years later the Talmud was put on trial and burned.

In the middle of the fourteenth century, the plague struck, and Jews were blamed for it, because they seemed to have escaped most of its effect—most likely because the Jews were not allowed to associate with the Christian community and had higher standards of personal hygiene. Nevertheless, retaliatory massacres of Jewish communities in the east and southeast of France occurred. The Jews in the south were protected from most persecution because the papal seat had moved to Avignon and the pope needed the business acumen and trade contacts of the Jews to finance the Roman Catholic Church. Jews in this region lived well in comparison to their brethren in other regions.

In the next two centuries, Marrano Jews escaped from Portugal and settled in the area of Bayonne just over the Pyrenees. Jews escaping the Chmielnicki massacres in the Ukraine and Poland came to Alsace and Lorraine.

The French Revolution granted full citizenship to its Jewish inhabitants, but that didn't stop the establishment of anti-Jewish measures to restrict where Jews could live and how they could assimilate into French society. Despite some restrictions, Jews became prominent in many social circles. The Rothschild and Pereire families were prominent financiers. Baron Edmond de Rothschild helped establish what was to become Israel's thriving wine industry by setting up vineyards in Rishon LeZion with cuttings from his own famous vineyards. The renowned novelist Emile Zola used his writing skills to protest the mishandling of the Dreyfus case, which prompted Theodor Herzl to write his treatise on the establishment of a Jewish state.

The pogroms in Eastern Europe and North Africa increased Jewish immigration to France, but World War II and the establishment of the Vichy government depleted over 25 percent of the three hundred thousand French Jewish population. In February 1941 there were forty thousand Jews interned in southern French camps. By April 1942 only eleven thousand Jews remained. It is not known whether or not the Jews were released or deported.

After the establishment of the State of Israel, anti-Semitism rose in the Middle East. Algeria and Morocco were agitating for their own independence from France (which they won in 1962 and 1956, respectively). The Jews identified with the French influence in that region, which angered the Arab inhabitants even more, leading many of the region's Jews to move to France. The Jewish community in France has thrived since the latter half of the twentieth century, though increasing anti-Semitism in recent years has led many French Jews to immigrate to Israel and North America. Still, France has the largest Jewish population in Europe and the largest Jewish population outside Israel and the United States.

ENGLAND

The first Jews came to England from Rouen, France, in 1066 with William the Conqueror. They were mostly moneylenders, dealing with the barons and advancing money to the Crown to support the monarchy. Jews were allowed this occupation because it was not a lucrative business for Christians, who were not permitted to charge interest to their fellow parishioners. Because they were an asset to the Treasury, the Jews were afforded protection by the Crown.

When the Crusades began, being Jewish in England was a major liability. Many Crusaders felt they needn't wait to get to Jerusalem to fight the "infidel" when so many Jews were in their midst at home. The Jews were forced to wear identifying large swatches of cloth on their clothes representing a Torah or Jewish star, their property was taken away, loans to Christians were declared null and void, and in the worst cases, Jews were tortured or killed after being accused of the infamous blood libel.

On July 18, 1290, all the Jews in England were expelled. This date coincided with Tishah B'Av, the day on the Jewish calendar marking the day the First and Second Temples in Jerusalem were destroyed. Estimates of the number of people expelled varies between five thousand and sixteen thousand, but all those who survived crossing the English Channel settled in France.

Jews did not receive permission to resettle in England for over 350 years. The level of anti-Semitism in England was so great that two of her most famous playwrights, Marlowe and Shakespeare, used stereotypic Jewish protagonists in their plays of 1589 and 1597. The irony is that no one in England had ever seen a Jew in 300 years!

In 1655 Oliver Cromwell was petitioned to authorize the return of Jews to England. No official authorization was granted, but the first synagogue was erected in 1657 by Sephardic Jews from Holland. The next immigrants were German Jews, beginning in 1690. In 1698 a decree legalized practicing Judaism in England.

Bevis Mark, a Sephardic synagogue still functioning today, was founded in 1701. By 1734 six thousand Sephardic and Ashkenazic Jews lived in England. Jews were knighted and held public office, and in 1858 the Christian oath of Parliament was changed to allow Jews to take their oath on the Hebrew Bible. Since that time there has never been an English Parliament without Jewish members.

Today almost two-thirds of England's Jewish population reside in London, the neighborhoods of Golders Green and Edgmere being the biggest Jewish hubs. Both sections of London house a branch of Bloom's Deli. Often referred to as London's Second Avenue Deli, this establishment was founded in 1920 in the heart of Jewish London by a Lithuanian immigrant, Morris Bloom. But Morris wasn't the only famous Jewish culinary impresario in England.

Back in the sixteenth century when Portuguese Jews came to England as crypto-Jews fleeing the Inquisition, they introduced their special style of fish preparation to the country. Batter-dipped, deep-fried fish fillets served cold became popular. Even Lady Judith Montefiore in her 1846 cookbook, *The Jewish Manual: Practical Information in Jewish and Modern Cookery with a Collection of Valuable Recipes and Hints Relating to the Toilette*, offered a recipe for "Fried Fish in the Jewish Style." In 1860 Joseph Malin, a Jewish immigrant from Eastern Europe, left his fish shop, Malin's of Bow in the East End, to go to an Irish potato shop.

There he took some of their fried potatoes, added them to some of his fried fish, wrapped it up in newspaper, and sold it. His new combination was a great hit, and he is credited with being the first in England to sell fish and chips. Here was a true amalgam of cultures: Ashkenazic, Sephardic, and Irish immigrants all lent their culinary heritage to create a new dish for their new homeland.

DILL PUFFS WITH CAVIAR

I created this recipe by combining the flavors of dill, smoked salmon (lox), and cream cheese in a vehicle that was more appropriate for entertaining than bagels, lox, and cream cheese. Here again is the classic technique for making pâte à choux, *but dill and nutmeg are added to complement the filling's flavor.*

1 cup water
1/2 teaspoon salt
Pinch of nutmeg
Pinch of pepper

3/4 stick unsalted butter
1 tablespoon minced fresh dill
1 cup flour
4 eggs

1. In a medium saucepan, combine the first six ingredients and bring just to a boil.

2. **Immediately** remove the pan from the heat and add the flour all at once. Stir rapidly with a firm wooden spoon or spatula until a ball is formed.

3. Return the pan to the stove. Over medium heat, beat the flour ball for a minute or two, until a film forms on the pan. Remove the pan from the heat and cool for a minute.

4. Beat in 1 egg at a time, making sure that the previous egg has been totally incorporated before you add the next egg. Beat vigorously!

5. Bake for 20 minutes at 425°F. Remove and turn off the oven. Cut a little slit in the sides of the puffs to let out the steam, and return to the turned-off oven for another 5–10 minutes. Let cool completely and then fill with caviar filling (see recipe on the following page). The puffs may be frozen **unfilled** for later use.

TINA'S TIDBITS

- *I strongly advise using fresh dill in the puffs rather than dried dill weed, which can be bitter.*
- *It is important that the puffs have a dry interior so that they will hold their shape and not get too soft when filled.*
- *To successfully freeze puff shells that won't be used on the day they were made, make sure puffs are completely cooled, place on a cookie sheet in the freezer until frozen, and then remove from the sheet and place in a plastic freezer storage bag. Using a common straw, suck all the air out of the freezer bag to prevent ice crystals from forming.*
- *If you don't have fresh chives for the filling, you can always substitute the green section of scallions for an equivalent volume.*
- *If you are making the filling a day in advance, don't add the caviar to the cream cheese until the filling is at room temperature. This prevents the eggs from breaking open when mixed into the cream cheese.*

Caviar Filling

8 ounces cream cheese
¼ cup heavy cream
6 chives, about 8 inches long, ripped into 1-inch pieces
1 teaspoon fresh lemon juice

Finely grated zest from ½ medium lemon
4 ounces smoked salmon, cut into 1-inch pieces
2 tablespoons red lumpfish caviar

1. Cut the cream cheese into 8 pieces and place in a processor work bowl. Pulse the processor on and off to make the cream cheese smooth. Scrape down the sides of the bowl.

2. Add the cream and pulse on and off until combined. Add the chives, lemon juice, and zest and process for 5 seconds.

3. Add the smoked salmon pieces and pulse until the fish is small and distributed evenly. Pour the cheese mixture into a bowl, and fold in the caviar. Chill until ready to fill the puffs.

Yield: 2–3 dozen

GOUGERE

Take the classic French recipe for pâte à choux *(cream puff paste), add cheese and herbs to the mixture, and bake long enough to have the outside crisp and the inside creamy and you have a perfect appetizer for entertaining.*

1 cup water
3/4 teaspoon salt
Pinch of freshly ground pepper
1/2 teaspoon dried marjoram or thyme
Pinch of nutmeg
3/4 stick unsalted butter

1 cup flour
4 eggs
1 cup grated Swiss or Parmesan cheese
1 teaspoon dry mustard
Pinch of cayenne pepper

1. In a medium saucepan, bring the water, salt, pepper, marjoram, nutmeg, and butter just to a boil. Immediately remove from the heat and **rapidly** add the flour all at once. Beat the flour mixture until a ball is formed.

2. Return the pan to medium heat, and over medium heat beat the flour ball for another minute or two, until a film forms on the pan.

3. Remove the pan from the heat and cool for 1 minute. Using a wooden spoon or handheld electric mixer beat in 1 egg at a time, making sure that the previous egg has been totally incorporated into the dough before you add the next egg. Beat vigorously!

4. After the dough is made, beat the cheese, dry mustard, and cayenne into the dough.

5. Drop dough by tablespoon, or pipe a 1-inch circle using a pastry bag and #6 tip, onto a greased or parchment-lined cookie sheet.

6. Bake at 375°F for 25–30 minutes or until puff is golden and easily removed from the paper. Puffs will have a moist, cheese-filled center.

Yield: 3–4 dozen

TINA'S TIDBITS

- *Have all of your ingredients measured out so that the water won't boil for long and lose some of its volume.*
- *Always remove the dough from the heat before you add the eggs or you will get a thick sauce rather than a dough that will puff up in the oven.*
- *If piping your dough onto the cookie sheet, press the little points of dough down with a fingertip moistened with water. This will prevent the top of the dough from burning.*

THREE-POTATO CHEESE GRATIN

An elegant variation of potatoes dauphinois, this gratin is colorful and rich with the addition of the Montrachet goat cheese. Serve with grilled fish and a salad and you have an impressive but easy meal.

2 tablespoons unsalted butter
2 leeks, white part only, thinly sliced
8 purple potatoes, thinly sliced
8 small Yukon Gold or fingerling potatoes, thinly
    sliced
1 long large yam, peeled and thinly sliced
6 tablespoons all-purpose flour

1½ teaspoons salt
Freshly ground black pepper
1½ cups whole milk
½ cup heavy cream
10 ounces herbed Montrachet goat cheese
8 chives, thinly sliced
½ cup freshly grated Parmesan cheese

1. Preheat the oven to 350°F.

2. Melt the butter in a large skillet over high heat until it starts to brown. Reduce the heat to medium. Add the sliced leeks and sauté until tender.

3. Toss the potatoes in a bowl with the flour, salt, and pepper. Add to the leek mixture. Stir gently with a rubber spatula to combine.

4. Combine the milk, heavy cream, goat cheese, and chives, and add to the pan. Cook until cheese is melted and the mixture is bubbly.

5. Butter a 2-quart gratin pan or casserole. Pour the potato-cheese mixture into the prepared pan and sprinkle with the Parmesan cheese.

6. Bake for 35 minutes or until top is golden and potatoes are tender when pierced with the tip of a knife.

Yield: 6–8 servings

TINA'S TIDBITS

- *Leeks grow in very sandy soil. To remove the sand, cut off the white portion of the leek and then cut in half lengthwise up to, but not including, the root. Under running water, fan the leaves of the leek as you would shuffle a deck of cards so that the water can rinse away the sand.*
- *Eight ounces of cream cheese may be substituted for the goat cheese.*
- *A gratin may be made in advance and reheated in a microwave until hot, about 2-3 minutes depending on the depth of the mixture.*
- *When reheating in a microwave, it is most desirable to bring the gratin to room temperature first so that reheating takes the minimal amount of time and preserves the dish's proper consistency.*

CHEESE FONDUE

The word fondue *is derived from the French word for* melt. *This recipe, however, is from Switzerland. Jews have been documented as living in Switzerland since the thirteenth century. The first immigrants were from the southeast region of France, thus influencing the culinary heritage of the Swiss inhabitants and possibly the creation of this dish.*

1 clove garlic
1¼ cups dry white wine
1 pound aged Gruyère or Emmenthaler cheese, grated

1½ tablespoons cornstarch
3 tablespoons Kirschwasser
Pinch of nutmeg and pepper

1. Cut the clove of garlic in half, and rub the inside of the fondue pot with garlic. Discard the garlic clove.

2. Heat the white wine in the fondue pot on the stove until the wine is just simmering.

3. Add the cheese by thirds and stir constantly with a wooden spoon until melted and barely simmering.

4. Combine the cornstarch with the Kirschwasser and add to the cheese mixture. Stir until bubbly and add the seasonings.

5. Transfer the fondue pot to a Sterno or candle warmer. Keep warm but do not allow to boil.

6. Serve with wedges of French bread or pieces of apple if you like.

Note: If mixture gets too thick, add a little extra wine or water. If mixture starts to separate, combine 1 teaspoon cornstarch with 1 tablespoon wine and add to cheese mixture.

Yield: 6 servings

TINA'S TIDBITS

- *Alcohol will burn off somewhat during cooking, but this mixture is still strong. Substitute unsweetened grape or apple juice for all or part of the wine if you prefer.*
- *Cornstarch is used in this mixture to bind the cheese and wine together without imparting a flavor. Cornstarch thickens clear and shiny, as opposed to flour, which makes a mixture opaque.*
- *Kirschwasser is a German clear cherry brandy that enhances the flavor of the cheese. It is distilled from cherries and cherry pits.*
- *Nutmeg should always be used subtly in cheese mixtures, as it complements the flavor of the cheese beautifully.*

FIVE-ONION FRENCH ONION SOUP

The biggest problem with creating classic French onion soup in a traditional Jewish home is that the base for the soup is beef and the appeal of the soup is the copious amounts of melted cheese on the top. My sister, Sherry, came up with this delicious broth for the base, and a trip to Crested Butte, Colorado, gave me the idea of using many different textures and colors of onion in the soup. Jewish culinary ingenuity at work again!

BROTH

5 quarts water
1/3 cup pareve beef-flavored bouillon
2 packets or cubes vegetarian or mushroom bouillon
   (for color as well as flavor)
1 large onion, coarsely chopped
1 1/2 cups coarsely chopped celery, leaves and tops
   included

1 1/2 cups carrots, cut into 2-inch lengths
1 cup turnips, cut into 1-inch cubes
12 peppercorns
2 sprigs parsley
1 bay leaf
1 teaspoon dried thyme
2 cloves garlic, coarsely chopped

1. Place all of the ingredients into a large Dutch oven. Bring to a boil and simmer for 3 hours.

2. Strain the stock through a fine sieve or cheesecloth, and refrigerate until needed.

ONION SOUP

3 tablespoons unsalted butter
1 leek, white part only, sliced lengthwise in half and
   into 1/4-inch crosswise strips
1 large red onion, thinly sliced
1 large Bermuda onion, thinly sliced
10 ounces pearl onions, peeled but kept whole
5 scallions, white part only, thinly sliced
Salt to taste

Freshly ground black pepper to taste
4 tablespoons flour
2 cups dry white wine
2 or more cups of prepared broth (see recipe above)
8 slices French bread
1 clove garlic, split in half
8 ounces Gruyère cheese, grated

1. To make the soup, melt the butter in a 3-quart saucepan, add the onions and salt and pepper to taste, and slowly sauté the onions until they are very soft and lightly golden. Scrape the pot well to incorporate any of the brown residue.

2. Sprinkle the onions with the flour and stir for 2 minutes.

3. Add the wine and stir frequently until mixture comes to a boil. Add 2 cups of reserved broth and heat for 15 minutes. Add more broth if you want a different consistency. There is no right or wrong amount.

4. Meanwhile, rub both sides of the slices of bread with the cut edge of the garlic, and toast the bread on a cookie sheet in a 475°F oven until golden.

5. Pour the hot soup into a large tureen or 8 individual ramekins, making sure that you evenly distribute the onions.

6. Cover each serving with a piece of toast and sprinkle generously with the cheese.

7. Place in the hot oven for 20 minutes or until the soup is hot and the cheese is melted, or heat the soup in a microwave before placing in ramekins and topping with bread and cheese. This will prevent the bread from getting tough in the microwave.

Note: The ramekins may be placed under the broiler for a minute or two if you like the cheese browned more.

Yield: 8 servings

TINA'S TIDBITS

- *A Dutch oven is a 4- or 6-quart lidded pot with two short handles that can be used on the top of the stove, instead of the oven, to make "pot" roast and thus conserve a great deal of energy. It can also be used in the oven when you don't want direct heat cooking your food.*
- *Adding flour to the onions is a way of creating a roux for thickening the soup without the chance of burning the flour before the vegetables are cooked.*
- *Rubbing garlic on the bread before toasting imparts a distinct but mild flavor of garlic to the bread without the need for oil to carry the garlic flavor.*

CLASSIC POT ROAST

Although pot roast is classic to American Jewish kitchens, none of our ancestors, regardless of location, used this quantity of meat in one recipe. Most meat dishes around the world were vegetables enhanced with bits of meat. The affluence of the modern Jewish community was more often displayed on the dining room table than on material possessions.

2 large onions
1/4 cup vegetable oil
One 3- to 4-pound piece of brisket or chuck roast
1 teaspoon of salt or to taste

Freshly ground black pepper to taste (about 1/4–1/2 teaspoon)
1 teaspoon or more garlic powder (or 2 teaspoons finally chopped fresh garlic)
4 or more cups water (to almost cover meat)

1. Slice the onions in half lengthwise, and slice each half into thin strips.

2. Heat a large pot or Dutch oven for 20 seconds, add oil, and heat for another 10 seconds. Add the sliced onion and sauté over moderately hot heat until the onions are very dark but not yet burnt.

3. Wash off the meat and pat dry. Add to the large pot and sear on all sides. (Searing adds flavor to the gravy and helps prevent the meat from drying out.)

4. Sprinkle the meat with the salt, pepper, and garlic powder, and add enough water to almost cover the meat.

5. Cover the pot and bring the liquid to a simmer. Reduce the heat to low and cook the meat until the gravy has reduced to make thin but strong gravy and the meat is tender, about 2 hours. Check for seasonings. Remove the meat and cool the meat and the gravy separately.

6. If you desire thicker gravy, prepare an *einbrenne* by melting 2 tablespoons of margarine and adding 2 tablespoons of flour to it, stirring until mixture is brown. Add this to the gravy and heat until gravy is desired thickness. Adjust seasonings if necessary.

7. Slice the meat when it is cool. If there is time, refrigerate meat until firm, then slice. (Refrigerated meat is even easier to cut). Return the meat slices to the gravy. Reheat in the microwave and serve.

Yield: 6–8 servings

TINA'S TIDBITS

- *The rich color and taste of the gravy are directly proportional to the length of time the onions are cooked. If you make a pot roast and you deem it "tasteless," there's a good chance that you were in a rush that day and didn't take the time to brown the onions sufficiently and the final product was bland.*
- *This dish, like most meat dishes, tastes much better the next day. In addition, the meat is much easier to slice cold.*
- *Potatoes and carrots could be added to the meat during the last hour of cooking if desired.*

SOUPE DE POISSONS (BOUILLABAISSE)

There has been a strong Jewish presence in southern France since the fall of the Second Temple, when Jewish captives were brought by Roman legions to that region. In the fifteenth and sixteenth centuries, many Jews arrived in Provence from Spain and Portugal to escape the Inquisition. The following recipe illustrates the culinary influence of these Jews, with the inclusion of fennel, orange, and saffron from the Iberian Peninsula.

⅓ cup extra virgin olive oil
1 onion, thinly sliced
1 leek, white part only, thinly sliced
One 8-ounce package of prepared fish stock
 concentrate or 1 pound fish head and bones plus 1
 cup of water
2½ cups water
1 cup dry white wine
1½ pounds ripe Roma tomatoes, cut into eighths
¼ teaspoon fennel seeds, lightly crushed
1 clove garlic, chopped
One 1 × 3-inch strip of orange zest

1 sprig of parsley
1 bay leaf
1 pinch of saffron threads or one tiny pinch of saffron
 powder
Salt and freshly ground pepper to taste
1 clove garlic, sliced in half lengthwise
4 large, thick slices of country French bread
1 pound sea bass or halibut
1 pound snapper or sole
Rouille (optional; see recipe on the following page)
Freshly grated Parmesan cheese (optional)

1. Heat a 4-quart Dutch oven over high for 20 seconds. Add the olive oil and heat for 10 seconds. Add the sliced onion and the sliced leeks, and sauté over medium heat for about 5 minutes until the onion is soft but not turning brown.

2. Add all of the ingredients through the salt and pepper to the Dutch oven, cover, reduce the heat to low, and simmer for 45 minutes.

3. When the soup is done, strain the mixture through a fine strainer into a clean 3-quart saucepan. Press down gently on the vegetables to extract their juices. Discard the vegetables and bones (if using).

4. Adjust the salt and pepper to taste.

5. Rub the cut edge of the garlic over the surfaces of the bread slices.

6. Toast the bread in a preheated 350°F oven for 5 minutes or until firm and lightly golden.

7. Bring the soup to a simmer and add 2-inch pieces of two or more varieties of fish. If one fish is thicker than the other, add the thicker fish to the stock first and cook for 3 minutes before adding the remaining fish. Cook the fish for a total of no more than 5 minutes. Fish will continue to cook in the hot broth even after removing from heat.

8. To serve, ladle some soup in a soup bowl and place a slice of bread on top. Spoon some rouille on top of the bread and sprinkle with freshly grated Parmesan cheese if you like.

Easy Rouille

2 large cloves of garlic
6 fresh basil leaves
2 ounces drained, roasted red bell peppers
¼ cup fresh bread crumbs

1–2 tablespoons hot soup
1 cup good-quality mayonnaise
Cayenne, salt, and freshly ground black pepper to taste

1. Combine the garlic, basil, and roasted red peppers in a processor work bowl and process until pureed.

2. Add the remaining ingredients and process until smooth. Refrigerate until ready to use.

Yield: 6 or more servings

TINA'S TIDBITS

- *If you are only using one or two very mild fish, then you could add some of the rouille to the soup (by first adding some soup to the rouille in a small glass bowl until a smooth paste is formed and then adding to the soup). This would give you a slightly thicker and more flavorful soup.*
- *There are three ways to remove zest, depending on the final result desired:*
  1. *Use a vegetable peeler to get one long strip of zest for flavoring.*
  2. *Use a zester to get thin strands for flavoring and garnish.*
  3. *Use a rasp grater to get fine shreds for flavoring that will blend into food.*

Easy Sauerbraten (German Brisket)

Sauerbraten normally takes time to make, since the meat has to marinate in the vinegar mixture for days. Here is a faster version that comes close to its German roots.

2 tablespoons extra virgin olive oil
1 large onion, chopped into ½-inch dice (about 2 cups)
2- to 3-pound cut of brisket or other cut suitable for slow cooking
1 large clove of garlic, minced
1 tablespoon flour
5 grindings of black pepper

⅓ cup apple cider vinegar
1½ cups water
4 teaspoons pickling spice
1 inch piece fresh ginger, peeled
2 or more tablespoons light brown sugar to taste
1 pound baby carrots
6–8 ginger snap cookies

1. Heat a 4-quart Dutch oven over high heat for 20 seconds. Add oil and heat for another 10 seconds. Reduce the heat to medium high.

2. Add the chopped onion to the pan and sauté for 3 minutes or until lightly golden.

3. Rinse the meat and pat dry with a paper towel. Add meat to the onion and brown on both sides—about 3 minutes per side.

4. Add the garlic, flour, and pepper and stir to combine with the onions and meat.

5. Combine the vinegar, water, pickling spice, fresh ginger, and 2 tablespoons brown sugar in a liquid measuring cup. Pour over the meat and stir to deglaze the pan.

6. Preheat the oven to 300°F while you bring the liquid to a boil.

7. Cover the meat with a lid and place the pot in the preheated oven. Bake for 2 hours and then add the baby carrots. Return the meat to the oven and bake for another hour or until the meat is fork tender.

8. Remove the meat from the liquid.

9. Add 6–8 ginger snaps to the pan and stir until they are completely dissolved and the mixture has thickened. Boil for a few more minutes if the gravy is too thin. Adjust seasonings if necessary. Skim off excess fat from the gravy, or refrigerate and remove the fat from the gravy when the mixture is cold.

10. Chill the meat before slicing. Place sliced meat in a casserole dish and add the gravy to the meat. Reheat in a low oven or microwave. Serve with potato pancakes or noodles.

Yield: 6 servings

TINA'S TIDBITS

- *The German origins of this are evident by the use of ginger (in the pickling spice) and ginger snaps to create the piquant, spicy flavor.*
- *For this recipe, it is important to use a cut of meat marbled with some fat to keep the meat from drying out during cooking.*
- *If you do not have pickling spice, use 1 bay leaf, 1 cinnamon stick, 1 teaspoon coriander seeds, 1 teaspoon allspice, and 1 teaspoon mustard seeds to approximate some of the flavors in the commercially prepared mixture.*
- *Using 1/4 cup rice wine vinegar and 1/4 cup apple juice for the apple cider vinegar will cut some of the "bite" in the sauerbraten sauce, especially if your ginger snaps have a real peppery taste.*

Sweet and Sour Red Cabbage with Apples

Although the last two ingredients in this recipe indicate their modern influence, this was a typical recipe among Jewish peasants throughout Eastern Europe. Everyday cabbage and onions were slightly elevated by the precious apple, and the vinegar helped preserve it for Shabbat or later use.

1 small red cabbage (about 1½ pounds)
¾ cup red wine vinegar
¼ cup sugar
½ tablespoon salt
2 Braeburn or Gala apples
2 tablespoons cooking oil

1 small onion, cut in half lengthwise and thinly sliced
1 whole onion, peeled and pierced with 6 whole cloves
4 cups boiling water
¼ cup dry red wine
3 tablespoons red currant jelly or raspberry jam

1. Wash and core the cabbage, and cut into quarters lengthwise. Cut each quarter crosswise into ¼-inch strips. Place in a large bowl with the vinegar, sugar, and salt.

2. Peel, core, and thinly slice the apples.

3. In a 5-quart Dutch oven, heat the oil and sauté the sliced onion for 4 minutes until it is lightly golden. Add the apple and sauté for 5 minutes longer.

4. Put the cabbage and the whole onion in the Dutch oven with the apples.

5. Pour the boiling water over all the cabbage and bring to a boil.

6. Reduce the heat to moderate and cook for 1 hour, stirring occasionally to prevent sticking.

7. When cabbage is ready, remove from heat, stir in the wine and jelly, and season to taste with salt, pepper, and more sugar if necessary.

Yield: 4–6 servings

TINA'S TIDBITS

- *Although this dish can be served freshly made, it tastes better refrigerated overnight and then served warm.*
- *The secret to preserving the beautiful purple color in cooked red cabbage is to cook it with apples and/or vinegar.*

SUMMER FRUIT SOUP

There are no cherries in here to epitomize a Hungarian fruit soup, but the fresh flavors of summer are represented deliciously. Jewish homes rarely served sweets for dessert. Meals often ended with fresh fruit or fruit compotes. Here is a wonderful way to bridge the divide between European custom and American palates.

2 pounds of frozen peaches or 2 ½ pounds of fresh peaches
1 cup orange juice
1 cup water
½ teaspoon cinnamon

⅔ cup honey
Juice of ½ lemon
1 large (3–4 pounds) cantaloupe
¼ cup apricot brandy
Blueberries (for garnish)

1. If using fresh peaches, peel and pit the fruit. Cut the peaches into chunks and place in a 2-quart saucepan with the orange juice, water, cinnamon, honey, and lemon juice. Simmer for 15 minutes or until peaches are tender.

2. Using a slotted spoon, transfer the peach chunks to a processor work bowl and puree. Pour into a large bowl and add the liquid from the saucepan.

3. Peel, cut into chunks, and puree the cantaloupe. Combine with the peach mixture and the apricot brandy, and chill.

4. Serve garnished with blueberries in individual bowls.

Yield: 8–10 servings

TINA'S TIDBITS

- *If fresh fruit is not available or at its flavor peak, substituting frozen fruit is an excellent alternative. Growers often process their fruit on location, and the blanching process locks in the color and sweetness of the produce.*
- *For a delicious alternative, try freezing this mixture according to ice-cream maker directions. Make sure the puree is cold before adding to the machine.*
- *The apricot brandy not only adds flavor to the soup, but it will prevent the mixture from freezing rock hard, so it will make a perfect sorbet.*

CHOCOLATE CHIP MERINGUES

The first documented example of meringue was in an English cookbook written by Lady Elynor Fettiplace in the early 1600s for her family. She called them "white biskit bread." Since the first sugar refinery in England wasn't established until the 1540s this commodity wasn't readily available to home cooks and might have only been used in the royal houses of Europe at that time. However, in 1692 Francois Massialot published a cookbook with the recipe for meringues and since then these light-as-air confections have been considered French in origin. This treat is very popular at Passover because no flour or matzah meal needs to be used.

½ cup egg whites (about 4–5 large egg whites), at room temperature
Scant ¼ teaspoon salt
¼ teaspoon cream of tartar (optional for Passover)

1 cup sugar
1 teaspoon vanilla extract
8 ounces semisweet chocolate chips or chopped chocolate pieces

1. Preheat the oven to 275°F. Cover 2 cookie sheets with parchment paper or aluminum foil. Set aside.

2. In a medium, clean, grease-free bowl, with an electric mixer on high speed, whip egg whites until foamy.

3. Add the salt and cream of tartar, and whip until soft peaks form.

4. Add half the sugar gradually, whipping until stiff but not dry peaks form.

5. Add the vanilla and continue to beat in the remaining sugar until the mixture no longer feels gritty when rubbed between two fingers.

6. Fold in the chocolate chips.

7. Drop by rounded teaspoon 2 inches apart on covered cookie sheets.

8. Bake until completely firm and dry, but still white, about 25 minutes; you should be able to lift cookies easily from the paper or foil.

9. Remove paper or foil from the cookie sheet with the meringues still attached to cool cookies completely. Store in an airtight container when thoroughly cooled.

Yield: 3–4 dozen

TINA'S TIDBITS

- *Never grease a cookie sheet to be used for baking meringues; they need to anchor to their base in order to puff up properly.*
- *When covering a cookie sheet with foil, **always** put the foil on dull side up. The dull side absorbs the heat and helps brown the underside of the baked product.*
- *Although cream of tartar acts as a leavening and stabilizing agent in meringues, these pastries can be made without it and would be suitable for Passover. Just make sure that you add the sugar slowly and beat the whites until formed into stiff but shiny peaks.*
- *Stiff peaks are defined by how firmly the egg white mixture stands up on its own when the beaters are pulled up out of the mixing bowl.*

TAHITIAN CROISSANT BREAD PUDDING

Many Portuguese Jews escaping the Inquisition settled in Bayonne, France, and earned a reputation as excellent bakers and chocolatiers. The following are some classic recipes with a little modern help in honor of those creative Jews who put French pastry on the map.

8–10 croissants, about 27 ounces
12 ounces bittersweet, semisweet, or milk chocolate, cut into ½-inch chunks (Lindt or Dove bars are very good)
1 cup heavy cream

1 Tahitian vanilla bean or 2 teaspoons vanilla extract
1 cup sugar
3 large eggs
3 egg yolks
3 cups milk

1. Butter a 13 × 9-inch glass baking dish. Preheat the oven to 350°F.

2. Break or slice the croissants into 1-inch pieces, and place half in the prepared pan. Evenly distribute the chocolate chunks over the bread, and cover the chocolate with the remaining croissant pieces.

3. If using a vanilla bean, heat the cream in a measuring cup in the microwave for 2 minutes. Cut the vanilla bean in half lengthwise, and place it in the cup, completely covered by the cream. Allow the bean to steep for at least 5 minutes or longer if the bean is fairly dry. When the bean is softer, scrape out all of the vanilla seeds from the inside of the bean into the warm cream. Discard the hull of the bean. If using vanilla extract there is no need to heat the cream. Just add extract to cream and then proceed to step 4.

4. In a medium bowl, combine the sugar with the eggs and egg yolks, whisking well. Add the milk and the flavored cream, and stir to incorporate thoroughly.

5. Pour the egg mixture through a sieve directly over the croissants. Lightly press down on the bread to make sure it is covered with the custard.

6. Place the pan in a larger pan, and pour hot water in the larger pan to a depth of 1 inch.

7. Bake in the preheated oven for 45 minutes or until a sharp, thin knife inserted into the center of the pudding comes out wet but clear. Serve warm, with rum sauce if desired (see recipe on the following page).

TINA'S TIDBITS

- *It is not necessary to heat the cream if you are using vanilla extract. Heating the extract will cause some of the flavor to dissipate with the heat.*
- *I recommend that you **always** strain a custard mixture before you bake it. Straining removes any bit of invisible solid egg white or partially cooked yolk that would make the finished custard lumpy.*
- *Placing a custard-based mixture in a pan over a pan of water is referred to as using a bain-marie or "Mary's bath." This is the equivalent of a double boiler in the oven and protects the custard from getting tough and rubbery.*

Rum Sauce

1 stick unsalted butter
1 cup sugar

1 egg
⅓ cup rum

1. Melt the butter in the top of a double boiler over simmering water.

2. Whisk the sugar and the egg together in a small bowl and add to the butter. Stir until the sugar is dissolved and the egg is cooked. The sauce will appear thick.

3. Allow the sauce to cool for 10 minutes. Stir in the rum and serve alongside the bread pudding.

Note: This sauce can be refrigerated until later use and warmed slightly in the microwave or over simmering water.

Yield: 10–12 servings

CROQUEMBUCHE

This confection was invented by the famous French pastry chef Antoine Careme in the late 1700s. The cake is served at festive occasions and weddings. Although Careme lived in Paris, the creative center for French patissiere was actually in Bayonne, just over the Pyrenees from Portugal. The pastry industry was heavily influenced by the Converso confectioners who came from Portugal after the Inquisition and established themselves in this region. Their access to the finest ingredients was due in large part to their relatives' involvement in the trade industry throughout the world.

2 containers of frozen miniature cream puffs (about 60 total)
1 cup sugar

⅓ cup water
3 tablespoons white corn syrup

1. Defrost cream puffs in their container in the refrigerator or use frozen.

2. To make the caramel, combine the remaining ingredients in a heavy 2-quart saucepan and bring to a boil over medium-high heat.

3. When the sugar is dissolved (mixture will be clear), cover saucepan and allow syrup to boil until bubbles thicken, about 5 minutes (this allows the steam to wash the sides of the pan, dissolving all of the sugar crystals).

4. Remove the lid and boil the mixture until it begins to caramelize (mixture will boil slower and the bubbles will get bigger before the color turns from beige to amber). The mixture will continue to get dark after heat is turned off, so do not let it get too dark or it will taste burnt. Remove from heat.

5. Place a round of 10 cream puffs on your serving plate.

6. Dip the remaining cream puffs lightly in the syrup to coat the bottom, and immediately stack the puffs to form a pyramid or "tree."

7. Take a fork and dip it into the sugar mixture. Pour this mixture off the fork, holding the fork high above the cream puffs so that the sugar forms strands. Moving the fork through the air, drape the "tree" with sugar "tinsel."

8. To serve, use forks or spoons to pull some of the puffs off the mound and place on plates, or pull off with your fingers and pop in your mouth!

Yield: One tower, 20 servings

TINA'S TIDBITS

- Croquembouche *means to "crack in your mouth."*
- *Originally shaped like a fez hat (with a flat top) it is now often served in a conical shape.*
- *For a more decorative presentation, candied fruit or nuts can be attached to the cream puffs after stacking but before coating with the spun sugar.*
- *This preparation is similar in concept to teiglach and would make an interesting addition to a Rosh HaShanah lunch.*

DACQUOISE

Do not panic! Dacquoise can be made in little mounds and served as cookies with or without the chocolate ganache in the middle. However, if you really want to wow your guests and live up to culinary heritage, this cake is worth making.

4 ounces toasted whole almonds
4 ounces toasted hazelnuts
1½ tablespoons cornstarch
1¼ cups sugar, divided use
6 large egg whites
½ teaspoon cream of tartar
¼ teaspoon salt
½ teaspoon almond extract
1½ teaspoons vanilla extract

¾ cup half-and-half cream
6 egg yolks
1 cup sugar
2 squares unsweetened chocolate
1 pound unsalted butter, softened at room temperature
3 tablespoons Kirschwasser, clear framboise, Grand Marnier, or rum
1 teaspoon vanilla extract
1 cup toasted sliced almonds

1. Make an outline of a 9-inch heart, 8-inch round, or 16 × 5-inch rectangle pan, 3 times on 2 sheets of parchment paper to fit 2 cookie sheets. Set aside.

2. Preheat the oven to 400°F.

3. Place the toasted nuts in a processor work bowl, and pulse until the nuts are fairly fine. Add the cornstarch and **1 cup** of the sugar, and pulse to combine into a fine mixture. Set aside.

4. Beat the egg whites with an electric mixer until foamy. Add the cream of tartar and the salt, and begin to beat at high speed, adding 2 tablespoons of the remaining sugar. Add the almond and vanilla extracts and the remaining sugar, and continue beating until stiff but not dry peaks are formed.

5. Sprinkle the nut-sugar mixture over the egg whites, and gently but rapidly fold it in until the mixture is evenly distributed but still very light.

6. Fill a 14-inch pastry bag fitted with a #6 plain tip with some of the meringue, and pipe along the edges and in the center of the shapes. Refill bag as needed to make three heart, round, or rectangular shapes. Gently smooth over the meringue with a small spatula and place in the oven. **Immediately** reduce oven to 275°F and bake for 1½ hours or until dry.

7. Cool on pans for 15 minutes and then carefully peel the paper away.

8. To prepare the butter cream, scald the half-and-half in a 2-quart saucepan. While the cream is heating, whisk the egg yolks and the sugar in a small bowl. Add the scalded cream to the egg mixture, whisking constantly until combined. Return the cream-egg mixture back to the saucepan and stir constantly as you heat the mixture over medium-low heat until it thickens. **Don't boil the mixture.**

9. Pour the custard into the bowl of an electric mixer and place the bowl either in the refrigerator

or over another bowl of ice to bring the mixture to near room temperature. Meanwhile, melt the chocolate in a dish over hot water. Set aside.

10. When the mixture has cooled down, return the bowl to the mixer, and beat the butter into the custard piece by piece until all of the butter has been incorporated. If the mixture curdles, return it to the saucepan and whisk rapidly over low heat until the mixture smoothes out.

11. Add the liqueur and the vanilla to the mixture, and divide the mixture $2/3$ and $1/3$ into clean bowls. Add the chocolate to the $1/3$ mixture and stir well to combine. Chill the buttercreams for a little while if they are too soft. Do not let them harden.

12. To assemble the cake, place one of the meringues on a plate. Spread $1/3$ of the natural buttercream over the meringue. Cover with another meringue, and spread half of the remaining natural buttercream over that. Top with the last meringue. Spread the top of the cake with the chocolate buttercream, reserving some of the frosting to pipe rosettes or designs on top of the cake when it is completed.

13. To finish the cake, spread the remaining natural buttercream around the sides of the cake, and using your hand, gently press the toasted sliced almonds into the buttercream. Using a medium star tip, pipe the remaining chocolate buttercream along the top edge in whatever design you want. Refrigerate until ready to serve.

Yield: One cake, 16 servings

TINA'S TIDBITS

- *Before grinding roasted hazelnuts, remove their skins by covering the hot nuts in a dish towel for 5 minutes. Rub the nuts in the towel to loosen most of the skins and then proceed with the recipe.*
- *Separate the yolk from the white over a small bowl in case the yolk breaks. The yolk is high in fat and any presence of fat in egg white will prevent the white from expanding.*
- *Egg whites that are at room temperature will yield a larger volume when whipped than cold egg whites.*
- *Meringues may be sealed airtight and frozen until ready to assemble the cake.*

THE NEW WORLD
AND LATIN AMERICA

A few years ago, before Castro became ill, I had the opportunity to visit Cuba as part of a Jewish humanitarian medical mission. I was very anxious to meet with the remaining Cuban Jews and learn about their surviving culinary traditions on an island that had been sequestered from the Western world and Jewish practice for almost fifty years.

Today's Cuban Jewish food bears little resemblance to the flavorful recipes of prerevolutionary kitchens. Traditionally, the tastes of Spain, Africa, and the Caribbean were blended with exotic spices brought from the Middle East and China. Cookbooks by expatriate chefs show, for example, that the ubiquitous sofrito (a combination of onion, green pepper, and tomatoes with other optional ingredients) added color and flavor to many entrées and side dishes. Today, those ingredients are luxuries that seldom enhance the food of the average Cuban meal.

South American cuisine has always represented an amalgam of regional foods and spices coupled with the food habits of the Spanish, Portuguese, French, and Dutch settlers who arrived in that region over the last five hundred years. Although the first Jew to set foot on Latin American soil was Christopher Columbus's translator, Luis de Torres (although he was converted to Christianity just before he got on the ship!), the real history of the Jews in Latin America can be traced to the first Jews who came to Recife, Brazil, in 1500 from Portugal to escape the Inquisition. When the Inquisition was officially enforced for Portugal by the pope in 1531, the lives of Jews or Conversos in Portuguese Brazil were made difficult. As Jews were persecuted and their lands confiscated, they moved to other parts of South America and the Caribbean, wherever the Inquisition couldn't hurt them.

After World War II, there was also a substantial influx of Eastern European Jews to Argentina, Columbia, Venezuela, and Brazil. Today, Argentina has the largest population of Jews in Latin America.

The following recipes represent both the old and new cooking in Latin America.

Sopa de Elote
(Mexican Corn Soup)

When I was Chef Field at Marshall Field in Dallas, I ran a weekly program with guest chefs from local restaurants. This recipe is one I have taught in my classes based on a recipe given to me by a private chef in one of our local Mexican restaurants. This soup is a perfect beginning to an otherwise light dairy meal and is representative of the Mexican palate.

6 cups milk
⅔ cup masa harina
1 pound frozen kernels of corn
2 tablespoons cornstarch dissolved in ¼ cup milk
4 tablespoons unsalted butter
½ medium onion, diced

1 teaspoon chili powder
1 teaspoon cumin powder
1 teaspoon garlic powder
1 teaspoon freshly ground black pepper
1 teaspoon salt
1 ounce canned diced green chilies (optional)

1. Combine the first 4 ingredients in a large bowl and set aside while you sauté the onion.

2. Heat a 4-quart pot for 20 seconds. Add butter and sauté the onion in the butter until lightly golden. Add the spices and seasonings, and cook over low heat for 3 minutes.

3. Combine all of the ingredients and puree in a blender.

4. Place pureed mixture in a clean 4-quart pan and heat over low heat, stirring often until mixture is very hot and thick. If necessary, add more milk to get the desired consistency.

5. Stir in chilies, if using, just before serving.

Yield: 8–10 servings

TINA'S TIDBITS

- Masa harina *means "dough flour," and it is actually made from the lime-treated corn that is made into masa for tortillas. It is a variety of fine corn flour.*
- *This soup will freeze well and can be reheated, but it will probably need to be thinned out with additional milk or water.*
- *Because the soup is so thick, garlic powder is better than fresh garlic for uniform flavoring.*

CHILEAN PASTEL DE CHOCLO

A very popular casserole all over South America, this particular recipe is a favorite in Chile. The spices, olives, corn, and hard-boiled eggs show the Iberian influence in this dish.

1 pound boneless chicken breast
1 carrot, peeled and cut into 8 pieces
½ onion, peeled and cut in half
1 small stalk of celery, cut in half
Salt and pepper to taste
3 cups water
¼ cup raisins
½ cup water
2 tablespoons extra virgin olive oil
2 pounds ground beef
4 medium onions, coarsely chopped
1 clove garlic, minced
¼–½ teaspoon red chili flakes

2 teaspoons ground cumin
1 teaspoon sweet paprika
Salt and freshly ground black pepper to taste
4 hard-boiled eggs, cut into quarters lengthwise (optional)
½ cup pitted black olives
2 cups frozen corn kernels, thoroughly defrosted and drained
2 tablespoons soy creamer
6 large leaves of basil, finely minced
1 tablespoon extra virgin olive oil
1–2 tablespoons sugar

1. Place the chicken breasts, carrot, onion, celery, and a little salt and pepper to taste in a 3-quart saucepan with the water. Bring to a boil and reduce the heat to a low simmer. Cover the pan and cook for 10 minutes or until the chicken is tender and just cooked through. Discard the vegetables; reserve the stock, if desired, for another use; and when cool enough to handle, shred the chicken. Set aside, covered, until ready to use.

2. Microwave the raisins and a ½ cup water for 3 minutes on high. Set aside until needed.

3. Heat a large frying pan for 20 seconds. Add the 2 tablespoons of olive oil and heat for another 10 seconds. Add the ground beef and stir well, breaking up any clumps of meat that form.

4. Reduce the heat to low-moderate, and add the onions, garlic, drained raisins, red chili flakes, cumin, paprika, salt, and pepper. Cook uncovered for 15 minutes, and transfer the meat mixture to a deep 3- to 4-quart casserole. Lay the quartered eggs over the meat, if using. Sprinkle the olives evenly over the eggs.

5. Arrange the shredded chicken evenly over the olives.

6. Preheat the oven to 350°F.

7. Place the defrosted and drained corn kernels and the soy creamer in a blender container. Cover and blend on high for 30 seconds or until puree is relatively smooth. Add basil and blend for 10 seconds to disperse the chopped herb.

8. Heat the 1 tablespoon of olive oil in a medium nonstick skillet and cook the corn mixture for approximately 5 minutes over moderate heat until the mixture looks like thick cream of wheat cereal. Stir occasionally to prevent clumping.

9. Pour the corn mixture over the chicken and smooth out the surface of the puree. Sprinkle with the sugar and bake for 20 minutes.

10. Raise the oven heat to 450°F but do not remove the casserole from the oven. Bake for an additional 5–10 minutes or until the corn puree is golden brown. Serve.

Yield: 6–8 servings

TINA'S TIDBITS

- *To save time, leftover roasted chicken, skinned and boned, may be used instead of the cooked chicken breasts.*
- *If you put the beef and chicken in a 13 × 9-inch casserole, you might need to make a double recipe of the corn topping to adequately cover the casserole. Cook for the same amount of time as above.*
- *Since corn is processed right after it is picked, frozen corn is sweeter than fresh corn sold in the supermarket a week after it was pickd.*

GRILLED CHICKEN BREASTS WITH SOFRITO

About fifteen years ago, the Jewish community in Cuba petitioned Castro to provide them with chicken for Shabbat in order to fulfill their religious obligation! The government conceded to provide chicken for communal dinners, and every Friday night the Jews of Havana congregate at the Patronato for dinner and services. Smaller gatherings occur in a few smaller Jewish communities in Cuba as well.

The cooks told me that they either bake chicken with a simple marinade or make chicken fricassee with a basic sofrito. I have adapted the marinade to use with boneless chicken breasts, which are then grilled or sautéed. The sauce can be spooned on top of the grilled breasts or added to the frying pan after the chicken is cooked.

1–1½ pounds boneless chicken breast
¼ cup lime juice
2 tablespoons extra virgin olive oil

1½ teaspoons ground cumin
1 tablespoon soy sauce

1. Separate the fillet from the underside of the chicken breasts.

2. Combine all of the remaining ingredients in a glass bowl or casserole.

3. Add the chicken breasts and fillets and marinate for 2 or more hours in the refrigerator.

4. Grill on both sides until chicken is done but still moist and tender, about 7 minutes total; **or** heat 1 tablespoon of oil in a frying pan and sauté the chicken until golden on both sides and done in the center, about 7–8 minutes. Reserve the marinade. Set chicken aside and keep warm until ready to serve with the sofrito sauce (see recipe below).

SOFRITO

3 tablespoons olive oil
1 large onion, cut into ½-inch dice
1 green pepper, cut into ½-inch dice
3 Roma tomatoes, seeded and chopped
4 large cloves of garlic, minced
1 bay leaf
¼ teaspoon ground cumin

¼ teaspoon crushed dried oregano
⅓ cup cream sherry
3.5 ounces pimento-stuffed green olives, coarsely sliced
½ cup dark raisins
Salt to taste

1. Heat a 10-inch frying pan over high heat for 20 seconds. Add the olive oil and heat for another 10 seconds. Add the onion and sauté for 4 minutes or until lightly golden.

2. Add the diced green pepper and the chopped tomatoes to the pan and continue to cook for another 4–5 minutes, until the vegetables are soft.

3. Add the remaining ingredients, except the olives and raisins, and let it cook over low heat for 3 more minutes. Set aside. May be made in advance and refrigerated until needed.

4. After chicken is cooked, reheat the sofrito and add the marinade.

5. Bring sofrito and marinade to a boil over medium heat, and add the olives and raisins. Simmer for 3 minutes.

6. Return sautéed chicken to the pan with the sauce to warm and serve. Alternatively, serve grilled chicken on a platter topped with sauce. This dish is traditionally served with rice.

Yield: 4–6 servings

TINA'S TIDBITS

- *The fillet of the chicken breast has a white pearlized tendon running through it. The fillet needs to be removed to ensure even cooking of the breast.*
- *To seed a tomato, cut the tomato in half crosswise and hold the tomato over the sink, cut side down. Gently squeeze and shake once, and all the seeds should fall out.*
- *The sofrito may be used with other meats and fish, with or without the olives, raisins, and marinade. It is also a great filling for empanadas (Cuban knishes!).*
- *Leftover chicken can be diced and added to the sofrito for a great meal alternative.*

Fao de Queijo
(Brazilian Cheese Puffs)

A São Paulo restaurant chain opened its first restaurant in the United States in Dallas, of all places. On each table was a basket filled with these puffs. One of my dear friends, Debby Luskey, is a phenomenal cook who happens to be from Brazil, and she gave me the following recipe for the Brazilian equivalent of miniature Yorkshire puddings.

½ cup milk
½ cup vegetable oil or melted butter
2 eggs
1½ cups *polvilho doce* (yucca flour)—found in
    Hispanic markets

½ teaspoon salt
½ cup Parmesan cheese
½ teaspoon garlic powder
⅛–¼ teaspoon cayenne pepper
Butter or nonstick spray for the pans

1. Preheat oven to 350°F.

2. Combine the milk, oil or butter, and eggs in a blender container and blend.

3. Add the *polvilho doce*, salt, cheese, and spices, and blend thoroughly.

4. Spray or grease 24 mini muffin pans.

5. Fill the muffin cups ¾ full. Bake for 12–15 minutes or until large golden puffs are formed.

6. Serve immediately, although they are still good at room temperature.

Yield: 2 dozen puffs

TINA'S TIDBITS

- *Unused batter may be stored, covered, in the refrigerator for days and then poured into prepared pans and baked.*
- *Unused batter does not need to be reblended if it was made with oil. Just stir and use the batter.*
- *Refrigerated batter that contains butter needs to be brought to room temperature to avoid uneven distribution of fat in the finished product.*

GRILLED STEAK WITH CHIMICHURRI SAUCE AND ORANGE SLICES

The use of sherry vinegar, cumin, and oranges speaks volumes about the Iberian influence on the cooking of South America.

½ cup tightly packed parsley
¼ cup chopped onion
4 cloves of garlic, chopped
1 teaspoon ground cumin
¼ teaspoon dried oregano
¼ teaspoon cayenne pepper
½ teaspoon coarse salt

1 teaspoon black peppercorns
2½ tablespoons sherry vinegar
⅓ cup extra virgin olive oil
1½ pounds steak (rib eye, skirt, or club)
4 navel or Valencia oranges
Flour tortillas (optional)

1. Combine the first 8 ingredients in a processor work bowl. Pulse on and off until the garlic and parsley appear to be minced and make a coarse paste.

2. Add the vinegar and olive oil, and pulse until well blended. Let the mixture sit for a few hours to allow the flavors to meld.

3. Brush steaks with 2 tablespoons of the sauce and let sit for ½ hour. Marinate skirt steak in half of the sauce for 3–4 hours to tenderize.

4. Cut the tops and bottoms off the oranges and cut away all of the rind, leaving a ball of orange. Slice the oranges horizontally into ¼-inch slices. Set aside.

5. Grill the steak over medium-hot coals until medium rare (about 10 minutes per inch of meat.)

6. Slice the steak across the grain and place on the center of a platter. Place the orange slices around the meat and drizzle with some of the remaining chimichurri sauce.

Note: If you like, you may place some of the meat, sauce, and oranges in a tortilla and wrap it up, like eating fajitas. This is not traditional but fun!

Yield: 4 servings

TINA'S TIDBITS

- *The acid in a marinade will help tenderize tougher cuts of meat. Tender cuts use the marinade for its flavor alone.*
- *Regardless of the tenderness of your meat, always slice meat on a diagonal to avoid cutting directly on the grain of the muscle, which would create long strings of chewy meat. This is most true with beef.*

Huachinango Veracruz (Veracruz-Style Snapper)

Fresh ingredients, bright sunny colors, and tender juicy fish—this is a classic recipe equally at home on the Costa del Sol of Spain or the Gulf Coast of Mexico.

1½ pounds fish fillets (preferably snapper, redfish, or trout)
1 large or 2 medium limes
3 tablespoons olive oil
1 large onion, sliced thin
2 medium green peppers, sliced in strips
2 cloves garlic, finely minced

2 medium tomatoes, seeded and diced
One 6-ounce can tomato juice
2 jalapeño peppers, sliced, or 2 teaspoons jarred peppers
¼ cup sliced pimento-stuffed green olives
1 bay leaf
¼ cup dry vermouth

1. Preheat oven to 350°F.

2. Place the fish in a 13 × 9-inch glass baking dish, and squeeze the lime juice over the fish. Shake the dish to make sure that all of the juice comes in contact with the fish. Set aside.

3. In a large sauté pan, heat the olive oil and sauté the onions for 5 minutes or until golden.

4. Add the green pepper and sauté for 3 more minutes.

5. Add the garlic and tomatoes and sauté until the tomatoes start to give up their juices.

6. Add the tomato juice, jalapeño peppers, olives, and bay leaf, and bring to a boil.

7. Remove from the heat and add the vermouth.

8. Drain the fish, spoon tomato-pepper mixture on top.

9. Bake for 18–22 minutes or until fish is firm but springy. Serve.

Yield: 4–6 servings

TINA'S TIDBITS

- *Fish should not be exposed to highy acidic foods for more than 1/2 hour or the fish will begin to "cook." Exposure to citrus-juice marinades for a few hours can make the fish very tough when it is ultimately cooked over heat.*
- Huachinango *means "snapper" in Spanish.*

PECAN-CRUSTED FISH TACOS WITH PINEAPPLE SALSA

Here is a perfect example of the migration of Jewish cooking. I created this taco to incorporate all the flavors of the Southwest United States while adhering to the tenets of kashrut.

1 pound fish fillets, skin removed (salmon, sea bass, halibut, or black cod), cut into 1-inch strips
¼ cup soy sauce
1 tablespoon light brown sugar
6 ounces regular (not lite) beer
2 large cloves garlic, finely minced
1 cup pecans, coarsely chopped

2 tablespoons flour
¼ teaspoon salt
Freshly ground black pepper to taste
2 tablespoons extra virgin olive oil
1 tablespoon unsalted butter
4–6 flour tortillas

1. Combine the soy sauce, brown sugar, beer, and minced garlic in a glass loaf pan or small casserole. Add the fish and marinate for no more than 1 hour.

2. Combine the chopped pecans, flour, salt, and pepper on a plate. Firmly press all sides of the fish into the pecan mixture to coat well.

3. Preheat the oven to 400°F.

4. Heat a cast-iron skillet over high heat for 20 seconds. Add the olive oil and butter and heat until the butter is melted and bubbling.

5. Reduce the heat to medium high, and add the fish fillets to the pan. Cook on one side for 1–2 minutes until the nuts are golden brown.

6. Flip fish over, place the entire frying pan in the oven, and bake for 3–4 minutes more or until the fish is firm but still springy.

7. Serve on a flour tortilla with the following accompaniments.

Yield: 4 servings

PINEAPPLE-MINT SALSA

½ ripe pineapple, peeled, cored, and finely diced
½ jalapeño pepper, seeds and inner ribs removed, finely diced
⅓ cup finely diced red onion
1 tablespoon finely minced fresh Mexican mint marigold (or tarragon)
1 tablespoon finely minced fresh mint
Juice of half a lime
Pinch of sugar (optional, if pineapple isn't sweet)

Combine all of the ingredients and refrigerate.

ANCHO CHILI–MARGARITA MAYONNAISE

¼ cup mayonnaise
1 teaspoon Tequila
½ teaspoon Grand Marnier or triple sec
Fresh lime juice to taste
⅛–¼ teaspoon ancho chili powder

1. Whisk the mayonnaise in a small bowl until smooth.

2. Add the remaining ingredients and stir to combine.

TINA'S TIDBITS

- *Never fry in just butter, because it has a tendency to burn. Use half the amount of butter called for in a recipe, and substitute olive oil for the difference. This will give your food a higher smoking point so it won't burn and you will still have the flavor of butter.*
- *Never use salted butter for frying under any circumstance, as it will burn even faster and the salt will pull moisture out of the environment and cause more splattering.*
- *Mexican mint marigold grows in warmer climates but tastes very similar to tarragon, for an easy substitution. Basil could be used as well.*

MERMELADA DE GUAYABA
(GUAVA MARMALADE)

Throughout Cuba, ice cream made from evaporated or sweetened condensed milk was served for dessert. However, the communities of Santa Clara and Sancti Spiritus served us guayaba (guava) marmalade on little plates. It is very easy to make and incredibly intense in flavor, unadulterated by any added ingredients other than fruit and sugar.

Here is my version of the marmalade, which I serve over pound cake or banana ice cream. It is also great as a dip for strawberries or other fruits.

1 pound fresh or 1-pound bag frozen guavas (look for it in Hispanic markets)

$3\frac{1}{2}$ cups sugar
$\frac{1}{4}$ cup water

1. Cut the fruit in half crosswise, scoop out all the insides including the seeds, and place in a 2-quart heavy saucepan.

2. Add the sugar and water, and stir until the sugar is moist. Heat pan on medium high.

3. Stir **only** until sugar is dissolved, and then simmer about 10 minutes or until a teaspoon of the mixture, dropped into a dish of ice cubes and water, comes out thick and syrupy.

4. Put sauce through a food mill or fine strainer to remove all of the seeds, and place the sauce in screw-top jars. Store in the refrigerator. (If mixture is too thin, you can return the sauce to a clean pan and cook it down until it is the right consistency.)

5. Serve as a sauce over ice cream or as a dip for fresh fruit. If your final mixture is very thick, serve as a spread on bread or with crackers and cheese.

Yield: 1 pint sauce

TINA'S TIDBITS

- *Putting ice cubes in the water prevents the water temperature from rising and gives you a better idea of the consistency of the syrup at room temperature.*
- *Overstirring a mixture high in sugar can cause the sugar to crystallize and make your mixture very gritty when it is cooled.*

Cuban Rugelach—"Guavalach"

Combine a love of cooking with all things Jewish, add one Jewish Cuban expat, and you have a recipe for "guavalach," courtesy of Libby Zucker, which I have adapted for the modern kitchen. This is how Jewish recipes are born!

In Cuba, guava paste is eaten with cream cheese. In Hispanic bakeries one can find guava pies often having a layer of cheese. It is one of those perfect food combinations transformed into an Ashkenazic classic pastry beloved by all.

1 cup all-purpose flour
Pinch of salt
4 ounces of cream cheese
1 stick unsalted butter
11 vanilla wafers

⅔ cup finely chopped walnuts
4 tablespoons of brown sugar
Guava paste—found in the Hispanic food aisle in a round metal tin, round plastic tin, or long box
Confectioners' sugar for rolling out dough

1. Place flour and salt in a processor work bowl. Pulse on and off 3 times to combine.

2. Cut cream cheese and butter in small chunks, and sprinkle as evenly as possible over the flour in the food processor. Pulse the processor on and off until all the ingredients come together and almost form a ball.

3. Divide dough in half and shape into 2 logs. Cover dough with plastic wrap and refrigerate for 1 hour or overnight.

4. Preheat the oven to 350°F degrees.

5. Put vanilla wafers into the food processor and process into crumbs. Combine with the chopped walnuts and set aside until needed.

6. Remove the dough balls from the refrigerator. Sprinkle confectioners' sugar over your rolling board and pin. Roll out one log of dough into a 6 × 12-inch rectangle. Sprinkle half of the wafer mixture over the dough, and sprinkle 2 tablespoons of the brown sugar over that.

7. Cut strips of guava paste into ¼-inch-wide lengths. The length of the strip will vary depending on the package of the guava paste. Place a line of guava paste 1 inch from the long side of the bottom of the dough. Place another line of guava paste 1 inch from the long side of the top of the rectangle of dough. Place a third line in the middle of the dough equidistant from the other strips. Sprinkle half (⅓ cup) of the vanilla wafer/chopped walnut mixture evenly over the dough.

8. Tightly roll up the dough from the bottom over the filling, and pinch the edges together to seal. Turn the sides under, and place seam side down, pressing the roll together to make it compact and slightly longer.

9. Cut the log into 1½-inch pieces and place on a parchment-lined cookie sheet.

10. Repeat with the other log of dough, and bake for 15–20 minutes or until the cookies are light brown.

Yield: 6–8 servings

TINA'S TIDBITS

- *Vanilla wafers are an inexpensive alternative to walnuts to create a crunch in the center of the cookies.*
- *Because the guava paste is not spreadable, the spacing of the lines of the guava will help distribute the fruit paste evenly throughout the pastry.*
- *Rolling dough on a board "floured" with confectioners' sugar not only prevents the dough from sticking, but also creates a light sugar glaze on the surface of the pastry.*

JEWS AND THE VANILLA AND CACAO TRADE

*V*anilla is a baking staple in everyone's kitchen. Attempt to make a chocolate chip cookie without it and your taste buds will immediately notice its absence. Usually, the only topic of discussion concerning vanilla is whether to use vanilla bean, vanilla extract, or vanillin in your recipe.

A much more interesting topic centered on this member of the orchid family would be how we are indebted to seventeenth-century Jewish settlers in South America for its popularity.

The first Jews to settle in South America were predominantly Portuguese. The native Indians liked these new, gentle immigrants and trusted them more than the French or Spanish conquistadores, who came to the New World to plunder their peaceful villages and take over their lands.

In 1660 a grant was given to David Nassy to create a settlement in Cayenne (an island city now part of French Guyana) for a group of Jewish colonists from Brazil and Amsterdam. However the Dutch governor, Jan Classen Lagedijk, did not want the Jews in his territory. It was the local Indians who convinced the governor to let the Jews stay, and they settled in Remire, establishing a close bond with the native Arawaks. This bond would prove to be very important to the Jews.

Jewish inhabitants of Guyana and the Caribbean mainly concentrated on sugar production. However, as they became successful, local colonists became resentful and implored the governing countries to put restrictions on the Jews so they wouldn't monopolize the sugar industry. The English tried to inhibit the Jewish involvement in this industry by establishing very restrictive laws. Jews were not allowed to hire Christians (most of the slaves or indentured servants were converted to Christianity when they arrived in the New World). They were also restricted to owning only one or two slaves (depending on the island). They had to look for other agricultural industry that was less labor intensive.

Because the Indians trusted the Jews more than any other people in the region, they taught them the secrets of vanilla cultivation and the process of extracting the flavor from the bean without it spoiling. No one else was entrusted with this secret. This is documented in a letter sent to the Dutch West India Company in 1684 from the Dutch commander of Pomeroon, lamenting the death of Salomon de la Roche, who took the secret of vanilla extract production to his grave and depleted the regional vanilla supply as a result.

At this time, cacao was being exported to Amsterdam and promoted only as a medicinal preparation. The introduction of sugar and then vanilla from South America and the Caribbean elevated the interest in cacao significantly. No longer were cacao beans used only as a medicinal elixir.

Benjamin d'Acosta de Andrade, a Portuguese Converso, is credited with establishing, in the mid-1600s, the first cacao processing plant in French territory on the island of Martinique. As Jews became more successful in this endeavor and powerful in the shipping community, they were perceived as threats to society. In 1685 the "Black Code" stipulated that all commerce had to be transferred to French hands and all Jews were to be expelled from the islands of Martinique and Guadeloupe. Many Jewish families relocated to the island of Curaçao. Curaçao, situated off the coast of Venezuela, is a great source for cacao beans. The Jews began to process cacao for export and ship it to the thriving Dutch merchants in Holland. This trade depended on the network of Jewish traders in Amsterdam. Because Jews are not allowed to charge interest to each other (Exodus 22:24), it was easier for trading to exist among Jews on "futures" of cacao for the necessities that were needed to reestablish their businesses on Curaçao.

Jewish growers of sugar and vanilla sent their products, along with the cocoa they were processing and refining, to their Portuguese relatives in Amsterdam and Bayonne, France. (Bayonne is considered the birthplace of French pastry because the Portuguese Jewish bakers used these ingredients in their dessert creations.) From there, chocolate as we know it spread through the Jewish network of traders throughout Europe.

Budino Cioccolato (Italian Chocolate Pudding)

This Italian recipe shows the strong influence of its Spanish/South American roots. Essentially a chocolate flan, the subtle cinnamon flavor is reminiscent of Mexican chocolate.

1 cup sugar
½ cup water
1½ cups milk
3-inch piece of stick cinnamon
3 ounces dark sweet chocolate

3 large eggs
3 egg yolks
⅓ cup sugar
1 teaspoon vanilla

1. Preheat the oven to 350°F.

2. To make the caramel, place the sugar and the water in a saucepan and cook over moderate heat until the sugar dissolves and caramelizes to a light golden brown.

3. Using 6–8 individual ramekins, pour the caramel immediately into the cups, and turn the cups around to coat the bottom and sides. It is much easier to do this if you work with one cup at a time and keep the pan of sugar over a very low flame so it won't harden before you get all of the cups coated.

4. Heat the milk, cinnamon stick, and chocolate in a small saucepan until the chocolate dissolves. Do not let the milk boil. Keep warm over a low flame.

5. Beat the eggs, egg yolks, sugar, and vanilla in a 2-quart bowl until thickened, about 3 minutes.

6. Discard the cinnamon stick, and add the milk mixture to the egg mixture, beating constantly until thoroughly combined.

7. Strain the mixture into a large pitcher, and carefully pour the custard into the prepared ramekins.

8. Arrange the ramekins in a 13 × 9-inch pan lined with a paper towel, and pour boiling water in the pan so that the water comes halfway up the sides of the ramekins.

9. Bake for 25–30 minutes or until the custard is firm and pulls slightly away from the sides (or a thin, sharp knife inserted partially in the center of the custard comes out clean).

10. Remove from the water bath and cool. Before serving, invert each ramekin on a plate and allow the caramel sauce to coat the custard and plate. Serve.

Yield: 6–8 servings

TINA'S TIDBITS

- *When caramelizing sugar, never stir the sugar mixture once the sugar is dissolved. Stirring can cause the thickened syrup to crystallize and result in a gritty mass.*
- *Using a cinnamon stick steeped in liquid imparts the flavor of the spice without the grittiness of the powder.*
- *Straining a custard mixture before pouring into molds helps remove any particle of egg white that might have solidified when mixed with a hot liquid.*

ROULAGE LEONTINE

Dionne Lucas was on television long before Julia and Emeril, and she introduced the American cook to this classic French recipe. It is actually quite easy to make. (I baked my first roulage when I was ten!)

5 large eggs, separated
3/4 cup sugar
6 ounces dark, sweet chocolate
3 tablespoons coffee or 3 tablespoons water with 1
   teaspoon instant espresso

Pinch of salt
1 teaspoon vanilla
1 cup heavy cream
1 tablespoon confectioners' sugar
1 teaspoon vanilla

1. Lightly oil a 15 × 10-inch jelly roll pan. Insert a piece of waxed paper or parchment paper cut exactly to fit on the bottom of the pan. Lightly oil the top of the paper. Set aside.

2. In a medium bowl, beat the sugar into the egg yolks until it is a light, creamy consistency and pale yellow in color.

3. Break the chocolate into pieces and combine it with the 3 tablespoons of liquid in a small saucepan. Place this pan into another larger pan filled with 1 inch of water. Cook over a medium flame and stir until the chocolate melts. Set aside to cool slightly.

4. Add chocolate, salt, and vanilla to the egg yolk mixture, and stir well.

5. With clean beaters, beat the egg whites until stiff. **Gently** fold the egg whites into the chocolate mixture until well combined.

6. Gently spread the mixture over the prepared pan to prevent the loss of air in the batter.

7. Bake at 400°F for 5 minutes. Reduce the temperature to 350°F and bake for an additional 15 minutes.

8. Remove from the oven, and cover the cake with a damp cloth or paper towel and allow to cool for 10 minutes.

9. Remove the cloth carefully, and loosen the roll from the sides of the pan. Cover the pan with clean waxed or parchment paper, and invert the cake. Gently peel off oiled paper and discard.

10. Place the bowl you will be using for whipping the cream in the freezer for 15 minutes.

11. Beat the cream until slightly thickened. Add the sugar and vanilla, and continue beating until the cream is stiffly beaten and spreadable.

12. Spread the roll with whipped cream. With the help of the paper on the bottom, roll the cake up from the narrow side. Sift with confectioner's sugar just before serving. This cake freezes well. Just defrost in the refrigerator 1 hour before cutting. Dust with confectioners' sugar before serving.

Yield: One cake, 10–12 servings

TINA'S TIDBITS

- *Egg whites that are at room temperature will yield a larger volume when whipped than cold egg whites.*
- *Whipping heavy cream over a bowl of ice will prevent it from turning yellow when it sits.*
- *Because a double boiler has an indented rim on the top it is not a good idea to use it when melting a small quantity of food. I prefer a one-quart saucepan over a two-quart saucepan or over an 8-inch frying pan to create the double boiler effect.*

MUSTACCHIONI

I adapted this recipe from Claudia Roden's Book of Jewish Food. *The recipe is from Trieste, which was a major port of call in northeastern Italy, once a part of the Austrian Empire. The ships from Livorno would stop there before or after embarking on trade routes throughout the Mediterranean. The prevalence of the almonds and the chocolate speaks to its Converso roots.*

7 ounces dark bittersweet chocolate
1 cup lightly roasted slivered almonds
3 eggs

½ cup sugar
2 tablespoons orange liqueur (such as Hallelujah from Israel or Grand Marnier)

1. Preheat oven to 350°F, Place paper cups in mini muffin pans. Set aside.

2. Break the chocolate into relatively small pieces and place in a processor work bowl along with the remaining ingredients.

3. Pulse the processor on and off until the mixture forms a relatively smooth paste (it will still be a little coarse).

4. Fill mini muffin papers ⅔ full, and bake for 10–12 minutes or until tops are crisp but insides are still soft. Allow muffins to cool, and store in an airtight container.

5. Alternatively, you can use cooking spray on the mini muffin pans or an 8-inch round cake pan. If using the cake pan, bake for 20–25 minutes until set.

Yield: 18 miniatures or one 8-inch cake

TINA'S TIDBITS

- *Always pulse your processor when you have nuts or chocolate in the work bowl. This will throw the food up as it is cut rather than risking some portion of the food turning into a paste while the rest is not broken down properly.*
- *When a recipe calls for eggs, always use large eggs. Large eggs are 24 ounces per dozen. If you use jumbo eggs (which are 30 ounces per dozen), you would effectively add the equivalent of an extra egg to this recipe and change the consistency of the finished product.*
- *Cacao comes from trees that have to be grown within 20 degrees of the equator.*

Mexican Dark Chocolate Bark

Thinking about Montezuma's love of chocolate and the ingredients the Aztecs used with their cacao beans to make his favorite elixir, I created the following modern incarnation of the beverage in candy form.

12 ounces semisweet Callebaut or Scharffenberger chocolate or chocolate chips
1/4 teaspoon chipotle chili powder

3/4 teaspoon cinnamon
2 tablespoons coarsely ground coffee

1. Break the chocolate into pieces if not using chips. Place dark chocolate in a glass bowl and microwave for 45 seconds on medium high (level 8). Stir the chocolate gently with a rubber spatula.

2. Return the bowl to the microwave for another 30 seconds on medium high (level 8). Remove the bowl from the microwave and stir chocolate gently until all pieces are melted. This time should be enough even for thick chocolate chunks.

3. Combine the remaining ingredients with the chocolate and spread on a piece of parchment paper or waxed paper. Do not make the chocolate too thin or the bark will melt too easily when handled.

4. Chill the bark at room temperature and cut or break into pieces.

Note: Raisins or nuts may be added as well or used to replace the coffee grounds if desired.

Yield: about 2 cups or 1 pound of chocolate bark

TINA'S TIDBITS

- *Chipotle chilies are jalapeños that have been dried and smoked. You can also use ancho chili powder, but it is fruitier and not so spicy. Ancho chilies are dried poblano peppers.*
- *Because you are not carefully tempering the chocolate (melting and cooling the chocolate to specific temperatures, which creates a chocolate that is more malleable and shiny), the finished chocolate will have a matte finish.*
- *An extra sprinkling of cinnamon or coffee grounds on top will adhere to the bark if sprinkled on before the chocolate hardens.*
- *Another alternative is to use Thai curry powder and coconut in place of the chilies and ground coffee.*

CHANUKAH CHOCOLATE TRUFFLES

Although the connection of coins to Chanukah celebrations is traced back to the Hasmoneans' minting their own state coin after their victory, giving children money and then subsequently chocolate coins is a decidedly European tradition whose origins are probably in the late eighteenth century and the early nineteenth. Jews figured prominently in chocolate manufacturing in Europe at that time, and creating coins of chocolate would allow even poor children to participate in the growing tradition of giving gelt to children at Chanukah. These chocolate morsels are as rich as any to be found in Europe then or now. Wrapped in malleable gold foil or aluminum foil, they can be flattened to look like a coin or just covered in foil in the shape of a ball.

6 ounces chocolate, dark, milk, or white
¼ cup sweet unsalted butter
2 egg yolks
1 tablespoon coffee liqueur, cognac, or Grand
  Marnier

Dried sweetened cherries, cranberries, or raisins
Cocoa
Gold foil paper or aluminum foil

1. Place the chocolate in a 1-quart bowl. Place the bowl in a 1-quart saucepan filled with hot but not boiling water. (A small double boiler may be used if you prefer, but scrape all the chocolate out of the ridge of the pan.) Over low heat, melt the chocolate and stir to remove any lumps.

2. Remove the bowl of chocolate from the hot water bath.

3. Cut the butter into 4 pieces and gradually whisk in the butter one piece at a time until all the butter is incorporated.

4. Whisk in the yolks until thoroughly combined. The mixture may look grainy and separated, but don't worry.

5. Whisk in the cognac or other flavoring. This should smooth out the mixture.

TINA'S TIDBITS

- *Truffles get their name from the hard-to-find, irregularly shaped, wrinkled fungus that grows 3 to 12 inches below ground. After being sniffed out by pigs or dogs, the truffle is carefully dug up, with much dirt clinging to its crevices. These luxurious fungi are mimicked in equally rich chocolate morsels that are traditionally coated in unsweetened cocoa to resemble the dirt of the vegetation of the same name.*
- *White chocolate is not really chocolate at all, since it is made with only cocoa butter and not any of the chocolate solids. As a result, working with white "chocolate" is more difficult, and you will often find the finished product grainier. Since we are adding even more fat to this confection with the butter and yolks, the mixture will separate when mixing. However, the alcohol will bind the mixture together in the final mixing. These truffles must be kept cold at all times, as they melt more easily than the dark or milk truffles.*
- *The yolks in this recipe are essentially cooked by the alcohol in the liqueur, so there is no need to worry about the raw yolks.*
- *Coffee enhances the flavor of chocolate markedly, which is why Kahlua or other coffee liqueur is my first recommendation. The French often use champagne, but that is too subtle for my personal taste.*

6. Cover and refrigerate for an hour or until the mixture is firm but not rock hard.

7. Working quickly, so that your hands do not melt the truffles, place a heaping teaspoon of chocolate in your hand. Press a dried cherry (or other fruit) into the center of the chocolate and shape into a rough ball about ¾ inch in diameter, completely encasing the fruit. Handle the chocolate as little as possible to prevent melting.

8. Roll the truffle in cocoa, using only your fingertips. Place on a plate lined with plastic wrap and refrigerate until firm.

9. Wrap the truffles in gold foil or aluminum foil to resemble coins or place in little paper petit four cups and refrigerate covered until ready to serve.

Note: If truffles are stored in paper cups they might need to be redusted with cocoa before serving.

Yield: 2–3 dozen truffles

CHOCOLATE CHIP CAPPUCCINO BROWNIES

The expulsion from Spain and Portugal at the end of the fifteenth century sent many Jews fleeing to Holland, Brazil, and the Far East. Trade routes were set up from the Caribbean and the Far East to Holland, and Jewish immigrants were directly responsible for the brisk trade in cocoa and coffee from their newfound countries to their relatives trading on the Dutch market. Combined with the spice trade, these brownies are emblematic of all the routes!

Two college students in Seattle were waxing ecstatic about a brownie they had gotten from a friend, one at home in Texas and one at camp in California. After fifteen minutes of discussion, they realized that they were both talking about the same girl and the same brownie! Here's my daughter's favorite care package from home.

1½ sticks unsalted butter
1 pound light brown sugar
1–1½ teaspoons instant espresso powder
1 tablespoon water
¾ teaspoon cinnamon
2 eggs

2 tablespoons vanilla extract
2 cups all-purpose flour
2 teaspoons baking powder
½ teaspoon salt
6 ounces chocolate chips or white chocolate chips

1. Place the butter in a 3-quart saucepan and add the brown sugar. Stir over medium heat until the butter melts and the sugar dissolves. Remove from heat and add the espresso powder, water, and cinnamon, and stir to combine. Set aside to cool while you measure the other ingredients.

2. Preheat the oven to 350°F. Line the bottom of a 9 × 9-inch pan with parchment paper, and butter or spray the sides of the pan to prevent sticking.

3. Meanwhile, using a handheld mixer, beat the eggs and the vanilla into the butter mixture (still in the saucepan). Add the flour, baking powder, and salt, and mix to combine. Using a rubber spatula, add the chocolate chips and stir by hand to thoroughly incorporate without melting the chips.

4. Spread the mixture in the prepared pan and bake for 20–25 minutes or until a toothpick comes out clean when inserted in the center of the pan. The mixture should be very moist, but not liquid.

5. Cool and cut into 1½-inch squares.

Note: This recipe may be doubled and baked in a 16 × 11 × 1-inch pan for 30 minutes.

Yield: 3–4 dozen small bars

TINA'S TIDBITS

- *Do not overbake these brownies! When they're done, a toothpick inserted into the center of the pan will come out clean.*
- *Never cut brownies while they are hot or the sides will mash down.*
- *I keep a jar of instant espresso in the freezer to use whenever a recipe calls for some coffee flavoring.*

Vanilla Custard Ice Cream

Ice cream made from a custard base will be smoother and creamier than one made from an uncooked base. Here the little specks of vanilla bean add color and texture to a wonderful frozen dessert.

2 cups whole milk
⅔ cup sugar
2 teaspoons vanilla extract or 1 vanilla bean, cut open lengthwise

6 egg yolks
Pinch of salt
1 cup heavy cream

1. Combine the milk and the sugar in a 1-quart saucepan. If using the vanilla bean, add it now. Stir constantly over medium heat until the milk begins to scald and the sugar is dissolved. Scrape the inside of the vanilla bean into the milk mixture and discard the outer bean. If using vanilla extract, add it now and stir to combine.

2. In a small bowl, whisk the egg yolks with the salt until a light lemony color.

3. Whisking rapidly, slowly add some of the hot milk to the egg yolks until combined and the egg yolks are warmed. Return the milk and egg mixture to the saucepan with the rest of the milk mixture.

4. Cook over low heat, stirring constantly until the mixture forms a thick custard and coats the back of a spoon. This will take 5–7 minutes.

5. Strain the mixture through a sieve into a clean bowl, and place the bowl in a larger one filled with ice.

6. Stir in the heavy cream and allow to cool completely.

7. Place in an ice-cream maker and follow the manufacturer's instructions.

Yield: About 1 quart

TINA'S TIDBITS

- *Because the whole milk is cooked with the yolks first, the finished ice cream will not be grainy with ice crystals.*
- *Vanilla bean can be reused. Rinse it off, pat it dry, and bury it in a pint of sugar. After a week the sugar will be subtly vanilla scented.*
- *Straining a liquid containing cooked egg ensures a smooth finished product.*

CRÈME BRÛLÉE

The translation of this dish is "burnt cream." The correct method for making this vanilla-scented custard is listed below. Many restaurants now pour a custard over fruit and then glaze it with sugar melted to the hard crack stage and call it by the same name . . . it's not the same.

2½ cups heavy cream
¼ cup sugar
4 egg yolks
1 teaspoon vanilla extract

1 tablespoon Kirschwasser or cognac liqueur, or ½ tablespoon orange blossom water
½ cup sugar

1. Preheat the oven to 300°F.

2. Scald the cream in a heavy saucepan. Stir in the ¼ cup sugar to dissolve and set aside.

3. Beat the yolks until smooth. Slowly add a few drops of cream to the mixture while you stir rapidly with a spatula or whisk. **Do not** whisk so rapidly that you cause the mixture to foam. Add the remainder of the cream in a slow and steady stream as you constantly stir to prevent the egg from "cooking." Add the vanilla and your choice of liqueur or orange blossom water. Stir to combine.

4. Strain the mixture into a large measuring cup and then pour into individual brûlée ramekin cups.

5. Place cups in a paper-towel-lined pan to prevent sliding, and add hot water to come halfway up the sides of the ramekins.

6. Place in the oven and bake for 25 minutes or longer (depending on size of the pan) until set and a small, sharp knife inserted in the center of the dish comes out clean. Remove the dishes from the water and refrigerate.

TINA'S TIDBITS

- *To scald means to bring the milk to just below boiling point. Little bubbles will appear around the edge of the liquid.*
- *A piece of paper towel in the bottom of the pan prevents the ramekins from sliding in the boiling water and burning you when removing them from the oven.*
- *Always add a few drops of hot liquid to eggs before adding the eggs to the bulk of the mixture. This prevents the egg from cooking and creating lumps.*
- *Kirschwasser is a very delicate, clear cherry liqueur that is often mistaken for vanilla; cognac adds a subtle flavor; and orange blossom water transforms this custard into an exotic, nonauthentic but delicious North African–French dessert.*
- *It is very important that the layer of sugar is not too thick or it will be gritty under the crisp, glazed topping.*

7. Place the chilled ramekins in a larger pan filled with ice cubes.

8. Sift the ½ cup sugar lightly over the crème no thicker than 1/16 inch. Lightly pack the sugar down.

9. Place dishes 8 inches from the broiler and broil for 2–3 minutes or until the sugar is caramelized, or evenly pass a blowtorch flame over the sugar to caramelize. Remove from the ice-cube pan and serve or refrigerate from 1–8 hours before serving. Refrigeration longer than 8 hours could result in the caramel getting soft.

Yield: 7–8 servings

ARUGULA SALAD WITH DATES AND CHÈVRE

Vanilla is generally associated with desserts, not salads. However, the subtle sweetness this extract brings to the dressing really complements the salad ingredients.

Sephardic Jews often serve pomegranates for the New Year because they are a new fruit of the season and common myth says they contain 613 seeds, which correspond with the 613 mitzvot, or commandments, in the Torah.

4 ounces arugula, about 4 cups
8 large, pitted, soft Medjool dates
¼ cup diced red onion
4 ounces crumbled goat cheese (see note)

¼ cup dry-roasted, shelled sunflower seeds
Freshly ground black pepper
¼ cup pomegranate vanilla vinaigrette (see recipe below)

1. Rinse the arugula and pat dry with paper towels. Place in a salad bowl.

2. Lightly oil a cutting knife and cut the dates in half lengthwise. Cut each half crosswise about 2 or 3 times. Set aside.

3. Toss the arugula with ¼ cup of the dressing. Place on 4 or 5 individual plates. (Alternatively, see step 6.)

4. Evenly distribute the dates, onion, crumbled goat cheese, and sunflower seeds on each plate.

5. Grind a little black pepper on top, and drizzle with the remaining dressing.

6. You can also toss everything together in one large bowl and serve.

Note: ¼-inch-thick rounds of goat cheese whose edges are rolled in cracked pepper may be added to individual salads as an alternative to the crumbled goat cheese.

Yield: 4 servings

POMEGRANATE VANILLA VINAIGRETTE

½ cup extra virgin olive oil
¼ cup unseasoned rice wine vinegar
¼ cup pomegranate molasses (available in Middle Eastern markets)
2 teaspoons sugar or 1 teaspoon honey
1 teaspoon Adams Best vanilla or any rich vanilla extract
Salt and freshly ground pepper to taste

Combine all of the ingredients in a screw-top jar. Shake until well blended.

TINA'S TIDBITS

- *If you are presetting your salad plate on the dinner table for a party, reserve the chopped onion in a dish in the refrigerator, and sprinkle on at the last minute to avoid having the room filled with the scent of onions.*
- *Medjool dates are the large, soft date variety that are easily cut or mashed into a paste if needed. Try to avoid a package of chopped dates, as they are heavily coated with sugar to prevent sticking.*
- *Adams Best vanilla is only available in the Southwest or online. It is a blend of vanilla and vanillin and tastes somewhat like Mexican vanilla without the bad chemicals. I like it because the flavor doesn't dissipate when exposed to high heat. A good-quality vanilla extract will certainly do.*

CELEBRATION OF THE JEWISH HOLIDAYS THROUGHOUT THE WORLD

LEFT: *Kneidlach (Matzah Balls), page 219*

SHABBAT

Rabbi Abraham Joshua Heschel taught that God could have made a mountain or a spring that he created holy, but he didn't, he made time holy: "The Sabbaths are our great cathedrals; and our Holy of Holies is a shrine that neither the Romans nor the Germans were able to burn."*

For most of us today, our spirituality is enhanced by the concrete activities of observance in our lives. On Shabbat, the only holy day mentioned in the Ten Commandments, we are commanded to rest—an activity that was never afforded to our ancestors in Egypt—and, like God, reflect on all that we have created during the week. How we celebrate Shabbat gives us a spiritual connection to God, and how we look upon and assess our activities of the previous week gives us the opportunity to right the wrongs we have committed and devote our time toward spiritual learning and enlightenment. For many of our ancestors, Shabbat was a chance to emotionally escape from the world of harsh abuse and persecution. For us today, Shabbat can be the much-needed respite from material pursuit and inner pressures and a chance to find inner peace and spiritual renewal.

How does the Torah instruct us to "keep the Sabbath" with regard to food? And how have the interpretations of the laws in the Talmud affected our culinary traditions? We are instructed to eat three distinct meals on Shabbat. Since Shabbat is often referred to as "the Queen," all food prepared for Shabbat should be befitting of a queen. Even

the poorest of households would elevate their daily provisions. For members of Bene Israel living on the western coast of India, fish was plentiful, but on Shabbat they would prepare chicken, which was not readily available, to honor the Sabbath. Ethiopian Jews would serve the famous chicken stew *doro wat* for the same reason.

Poor Eastern European Jews living in shtetls in the Pale would elevate the foods of their daily diet for Shabbat. The salted herring, black bread, and onion of daily sustenance were combined with a sweet apple, a biblical fruit, to create chopped herring. This dish is still served at Shabbat *Kiddush* and festive occasions. Whole-grained dark breads were replaced with finely milled white flour, as prescribed in Leviticus 24:5, "You shall take choice flour and bake of it twelve loaves." The braided white challah is the most recognizable icon of Shabbat.

The many prohibitions related to eating and working on Shabbat created some of the most well-known foods associated with Jewish cuisine. The cholent and tzimmes of the Ashkenazic world, the Sephardic *hamins* in the Middle East, and the tagine in the Maghreb (North Africa) all derive their roots from Sabbath cuisine.

---

* Abraham Joshua Heschel, *The Sabbath* (New York: Farrar, Straus and Giroux, 1951), p. 8.

There is a midrash that says that God told Israel that if they accepted the Torah and followed it, they would have a share in the world-to-come—not heaven, but the messianic age. When Israel asked what that would be like, God said to them, "Shabbat will give you a taste of what it will be like."

SCHMALTZ (RENDERED CHICKEN FAT)

This recipe should probably be listed under icons, but since our ancestors found every possible use for the Sabbath chicken, I thought it would be appropriate to include it here. You can find rendered chicken fat in the kosher frozen foods section of many supermarkets, but if you make your own, it will taste ten times better.

8 ounces chicken fat
1 medium onion, cut into $\frac{1}{2}$-inch dice

1. Cut the raw chicken fat into $\frac{1}{2}$-inch chunks.

2. Heat a 10-inch skillet over medium heat and add the chicken fat.

3. After about $\frac{1}{4}$ inch of liquid fat forms, add the diced onion and cook over medium heat until the onion is a dark golden brown and the fat is completely melted. The once invisible membrane on the fat will now be crisp and mixed in with the fried onion.

4. Remove all solids from the rendered fat and save for a later use. Pour the liquid fat into a clean jar and refrigerate for months for later use.

Yield: Approximately $\frac{3}{4}$ cup

TINA'S TIDBITS

- *Every time you cook a chicken and remove some of the raw fat, freeze the fat in a freezer bag until you have enough to render some fat.*
- *Rendered chicken fat will freeze very well and you can scoop out whatever amount you need when you need it.*
- *Chicken fat has the least amount of cholesterol of any animal fat, including butter.*
- *Rendered chicken fat will be liquid at room temperature. For over thirty years Sammy's Roumanian, on the Lower East Side of New York, has served liquefied schmaltz in IHOP-type syrup bottles on their tables so that you could pour it on your potatoes.*
- *Don't throw the onion mixture away! The* griben, gribbenes, greebeners *(in Texas), as it's called in Yiddish, is incredible mixed into mashed potatoes or just spread on matzah if you like.*

CHOPPED LIVER

Another by-product of the Shabbat chicken—thank goodness those Eastern European Jews didn't waste anything! Copious amounts of golden onions are added to softly cooked chicken livers and chopped to the degree of smooth that your grandma made.

Is it any wonder that the foie gras industry was run by Jews? They knew their chopped liver!

3 medium onions, finely diced
3 tablespoons chicken fat or oil
8 ounces chicken livers

3 hard-boiled eggs (see recipe below)
Salt and pepper to taste
More oil or mayonnaise (optional)

1. Sauté the onions in the fat until a dark golden brown.

2. Remove any green membrane from the livers. Broil the livers just until lightly seared. Add the livers to the onions and sauté just until the livers lose their pink, raw color.

3. Put the liver, onions, and hard-boiled eggs through a meat grinder or combine in a food processor until a desired texture is achieved. Season with salt and pepper and add more oil or mayonnaise if the mixture is too dry. Serve with crackers or on a bed of lettuce as a first course.

Yield: 1½–2 cups

HOW TO HARD-BOIL AN EGG

1. Place eggs in a non-aluminum pot with cold water to cover and a little salt. Bring to a boil.

2. When water boils, cover the pot, turn off the heat, and allow eggs to sit for 15 minutes. Peel under cold running water, and you will have perfect hard-boiled eggs.

TINA'S TIDBITS

- *Green on the liver does not mean that the liver is spoiled. It is just some of the bile that would make the chopped liver taste bitter, which is why it should be removed.*
- *Do not overcook your eggs or they will not blend well with the liver when chopped.*
- *Modern cooks often use mayonnaise to moisten the liver mixture. I prefer oil or rendered chicken fat, and then I season the mixture with salt and pepper to taste.*

VEGETARIAN CHOPPED LIVER

I was a child when Uncle Barney had his eightieth birthday party in a Jewish vegetarian restaurant. I still remember the mound of "chopped liver" on a bed of lettuce with some tomato slices. Over the years I compared recipes for vegetarian chopped liver, and I will say that my students like the taste of this mock chopped liver even more than the real thing. I know the ingredients sound bizarre in this day and age of fresh or high-quality frozen vegetables, but try it, you will be surprised how much you like it.

3 large onions, sliced
2 tablespoons oil
1-pound can cut green beans, drained
1-pound can green peas, drained
16 Ritz crackers

6 hard-boiled eggs
½ cup chopped walnuts
Salt and pepper to taste
2 tablespoons mayonnaise

1. Sauté the onions in the oil until a dark golden brown.

2. In a food processor, combine the green beans, peas, onions, crackers, eggs, and walnuts using a pulsing action to chop the mixture fairly fine.

3. Season with salt and pepper, and moisten with a little mayonnaise if needed to have it resemble real chopped chicken livers. Serve with bread or crackers.

Yield: 6–8 servings

TINA'S TIDBITS

- *Because you cannot use chicken fat here, I would recommend the use of mayonnaise to season and bind the mixture together rather than oil.*
- *Whipped salad dressings are never a substitute for high-quality mayonnaise.*
- *Never use fat-free or low-fat mayonnaise in this mixture unless you are planning to serve it right away. The cellulose used to thicken the mayonnaise to make it appear like the original variety will absorb moisture from the vegetables and make the mixture thick and gummy.*

Bukharan Shabbat Chicken Palov

Cultures might remain the same, but in this day and age countries often change borders and names. Bukhara is now Uzbekistan and Tajikistan, but its culinary heritage can best be defined as an amalgam of Turkish and Iranian food traditions. Here is a recipe for a Shabbat chicken dish from this region that I adapted for the cook who has no time to wait for chicken to boil and then be deboned!

1½ pounds boneless chicken breasts
Salt and freshly ground pepper to taste
2 tablespoons corn or peanut oil, divided use
1 medium onion, chopped into ½-inch dice
2 cups coarsely shredded carrots (about 2)
2 apples such as Jonagold or Gala (if available,
    substitute quince for 1 apple)

½ cup raisins
1 teaspoon ground cumin
½ teaspoon cinnamon
2 cups canned chicken broth
1 cup basmati rice

1. Slice the boneless chicken breasts into ¼-inch slices. Sprinkle with salt and pepper.

2. Heat a 3-quart saucepan over high heat for 20 seconds. Add 1 tablespoon of the oil and heat for 10 seconds. Reduce heat to medium high if oil begins to smoke. Add the chicken pieces and sauté for 2 minutes until lightly golden. Remove to a plate and set aside.

3. Add the remaining tablespoon of oil and heat for 10 seconds. Add the onions and sauté until lightly golden.

4. Add the carrots and apples or apples and quince and sauté an additional 5 minutes until soft.

5. Return the chicken to the pot and stir to recombine.

6. Add the raisins and all of the seasonings to the chicken-fruit mixture.

7. Microwave the broth and the rice, covered, for 5 minutes on high.

8. Add the rice and broth to the pot with all the ingredients. Stir gently to combine.

9. Reduce the heat to medium. Cover the pot and simmer the mixture for 15 minutes or until the rice is tender.

Yield: 6 servings

TINA'S TIDBITS

- *Although sautéing boneless chicken breasts is quicker than poaching whole chicken pieces in water, you need to be very careful not to overcook the boneless white meat for fear of it drying out. If available, try boneless chicken thighs for a more foolproof alternative.*
- *Do not add salt to rice cooked in prepared chicken broth, as the broth contains enough salt.*
- *Thin julienne of carrots is available in small bags at many markets. These may be substituted for the 2 coarsely shredded carrots.*

YEMENITE FRUIT AND NUT STUFFED ROASTED CHICKEN

The following recipe utilizes the many fruits and nuts indigenous to Yemen. I combined these ingredients with the classic Yemenite hot condiment zhoug, *which adds a kick to the chicken. Not your usual Shabbat chicken dinner!*

1 tablespoon olive oil
½ cup uncooked rice
1 cup boiling water
6 moist dried figs, diced
½ cup walnut pieces
½ cup slivered almonds

½ cup raisins
2 teaspoons sumac
1 teaspoon kosher salt
1 roasting chicken
2 cups orange juice
2 teaspoons red *zhoug* or *shatta*

1. Heat the oil in a 1-quart saucepan over medium heat. Add the rice and sauté until rice is lightly golden.

2. Add the boiling water to the rice, cover, and simmer over low heat until all of the water is absorbed, about 10–15 minutes.

3. Add the figs, walnuts, almonds, raisins, sumac, and salt to the rice. Combine well.

4. Stuff the chicken with the rice mixture and place in a roasting pan. Combine the orange juice and *zhoug* or *shatta* and pour over the chicken.

5. Bake in a 350°F oven for 1½ hours. Baste often with the juices while baking. Serve.

Yield: 4 servings

TINA'S TIDBITS

- Shatta *is a condiment that is often sold as "red"* zhoug. *The use of red chilies instead of green makes it more mild, but don't be fooled; it's still quite hot and a perfect complement to the slightly sweet orange juice.*
- *If available, 1 1/2 cups of leftover cooked rice may be substituted for the 1/2 cup of raw rice and 1 cup of water in the recipe. Omit step 2 and proceed with the remainder of the recipe.*

SHABBAT ROASTED TURKEY WITH VEGETABLES

Cooking the turkey over a bed a vegetables keeps the meat very moist and gives you a fantastic side vegetable and clear gravy. Once you give up the notion of thick, opaque turkey gravy, you will fall in love with this flavorful version. My grandfather had a deli during the Depression, and this is my mother's version of her father's recipe, so I am a little biased!

1 turkey, 10–18 pounds
5 carrots, peeled and coarsely chopped
3–4 large onions, diced
3 stalks of celery, coarsely chopped
½ pound mushrooms, sliced

½ pound chicken livers, chopped (see note under Tina's Tidbits)
One 28-ounce can crushed peeled tomatoes
2–3 cloves garlic, finely chopped
Salt, pepper, paprika, and garlic powder, to taste
1 tablespoon chicken fat or margarine

1. Salt the cavity of the turkey and rinse. Set aside.

2. Place the carrots, onions, celery, mushrooms, chicken livers, and tomatoes in the bottom of a large roasting pan. Season to taste with the seasonings and the fresh garlic, being light-handed with the salt if using a kosher turkey.

3. Place the turkey on top of the vegetables, breast side up. Season the turkey all over with the salt, pepper, paprika, and garlic powder.

4. Rub the tablespoon of fat all over the turkey skin with your hand. Use a little more fat if necessary to cover the wings and legs well. Cover with a tent of aluminum foil, being sure that the **shiny side** is facing out.

5. Roast the turkey at 325°F for 15–18 minutes per pound or until the internal temperature of the breast meat is about 170°F and thigh meat 180°F. Baste often with the juices in the pan. If necessary, you can add 1 cup of boiling water to the bottom of the pan.

6. Allow turkey to rest outside of oven for 15 minutes before carving.

7. Remove vegetables with a slotted spoon and place in a serving dish. Pour remaining liquid into a gravy boat. Skim the excess fat off the top of the gravy either with a spoon or by laying paper towels gently on the surface to absorb the fat. Serve.

Yield: 8 or more servings

TINA'S TIDBITS

- *If you keep kosher, first broil the chicken livers until almost done (which removes all of the blood) before dicing and adding to the vegetable mixture.*
- *Turkey cooked this way can be made the day before. Just slice the meat and place it in a large baking dish. Store the gravy and vegetables separately in the refrigerator. When ready to serve, pour some of the clear gravy over the sliced meat and reheat in the microwave. Reheat the vegetables and remaining gravy in the same way and serve. Your turkey will be moist and flavorful, and you won't have any last-minute mess in your kitchen!*
- *Foil only protects the breast meat from drying out if the shiny side is facing out, because that side reflects the heat away from the bird. If the dull side was placed facing out, it would absorb the heat and overcook the meat, making it dry.*

BREAD STUFFING

If you think culinary migration only existed in the "Old Country" centuries ago, think again. My classic, non-bacon bread "stuffing" was met with curiosity by my Texas students, whose "dressing" always used cornbread as the base. Eighteen hundred miles and many colloquial traditions apart—not much different than our ancestors' culinary traditions between Spain and Turkey.

3 tablespoons extra virgin olive oil, plus additional for greasing the pan
1 onion, diced
2 ribs celery, chopped
2 cups chopped mushrooms
7 cups white bread cubes with crusts (approximately 1-pound loaf)
1 teaspoon dried thyme
½ teaspoon crushed rosemary
½ teaspoon sage
¼ teaspoon marjoram
¼ teaspoon nutmeg
Salt and pepper to taste
2½ cups chicken broth or vegetable broth
1 egg

1. Sauté the onion in the olive oil until lightly golden. Add the celery and mushrooms and sauté until the vegetables are soft and have given up their juices. This will take an additional 10 minutes.

2. Place bread cubes in a large bowl.

3. Combine the seasonings with the chicken broth and egg. Mix well.

4. Grease a 2-quart casserole with some additional olive oil. Set aside.

5. Add the onion mixture to the bowl with the bread cubes and toss.

6. Add the broth and egg mixture, and stir until the mixture is **very moist** and almost runny. If necessary, add a little more broth.

7. Pour mixture into the prepared casserole and bake at 350°F for 30–40 minutes.

Yield: 8 servings

TINA'S TIDBITS

- *For a very soft stuffing, bake for the first 25 minutes covered with foil, and then remove foil for the remainder of cooking time.*
- *Any bread can be used, but remember that different breads absorb different amounts of liquid. If in doubt, let stuffing rest for 15 minutes before placing in the oven to bake. If the mixture looks too solid, add some more broth, **not** another egg.*
- *Baking stuffing separately means no waste left in the bird and less chance of bacteria growing in the stuffed cavity.*

Not So Basic Chicken Salad

There is absolutely nothing better for chicken salad than cooked soup chicken. It is soft, flavorful, and just the right consistency. Make this salad on Friday and your Saturday lunch is taken care of in advance. This is a technique I learned from my mother-in-law, Gladys Wasserman.

3 cups shredded cooked chicken (from soup chicken; see page 347, *Basic Chicken Soup*)
1¼ cups finely diced celery
3 or more carrots

1 tablespoon grated onion or to taste
Salt and pepper to taste
1 cup mayonnaise
1 can jellied cranberry sauce (optional)

1. Place the shredded chicken into a large bowl.

2. Dice the celery and add it to the chicken.

3. Clean the carrots, trim both ends, and grate them into the bowl with the chicken and the celery.

4. Add the onion, seasonings, and mayonnaise and mix until well blended and moistened. If necessary, add more mayonnaise.

5. Line a bowl with plastic wrap and spoon the chicken mixture into it. Press down firmly on the chicken so that it will mold. Refrigerate until ready to serve.

6. Slice the cranberry sauce into ½-inch slices. Using a decorative cutter or sharp knife, cut out designs in the sauce.

7. To serve, turn the bowl with the chicken salad upside down on a serving plate. Remove the bowl and plastic wrap, and coat the chicken salad with a thin layer of mayonnaise. Garnish with the cranberry sauce cutouts, and serve with crackers or rolls.

Yield: 6–8 servings

TINA'S TIDBITS

- *It is much easier to remove the chicken meat from the skin and bone when it is warm. If chicken soup was made in advance, reheat the meat in the microwave for 1 1/2 minutes or until the skin easily slides off the bone.*
- *Shredded chicken is easier to mold than cubed chicken. The added advantage is that as you shred the meat with your fingers, you can catch that stray piece of wishbone or cartilage.*
- *Grated carrot will add moisture to the chicken salad, but it will not be runny because the meat is in shreds and absorbs some of the good juices.*

GRILLED CHICKEN WITH BASIL-GARLIC TOMATO SAUCE

Shabbat chicken doesn't have to mean soup chicken or whole roasted chicken. It is better not to stress over the meal and enjoy Shabbat than to prepare an elaborate meal and not enjoy the shared experience with loved ones and friends. Here is an easy, delicious dish that can be made in the dead of winter because it does not rely on fresh tomatoes, and chicken can always be grilled outside as long as the grill is not covered in 6 feet of snowdrifts!

1–1½ pounds boneless chicken breast
2 tablespoon extra virgin olive oil
2½ tablespoons balsamic vinegar
2 cloves garlic, finely minced
One 1-pound can imported peeled plum tomatoes

1 teaspoon olive oil
1 large clove garlic, minced
1 tablespoon minced shallot
1 tablespoon chiffonade of fresh basil

1. To prepare the chicken breast for this recipe, first remove the fillet. The fillet is the separate, tender piece of chicken breast that is located in a clear membrane sack on the underside of each breast half. The chicken fillet or "tender" can be recognized by a thin, white pearlized tendon that runs through it.

2. Once the fillet is located, gently pull it away from the chicken breast and out of its sack. Note that the sack may have been cut when filleting the breast, so do not worry if it is not visible on inspection.

3. To remove the tendon from the fillet, hold onto the thick end of the white tendon and gently scrape a knife blade along it to slightly separate it from the fillet meat. Hold the meat back with the knife while the blade rests against the tendon. Slowly jiggle the tendon as you pull it away from the knife. The blade will scrape the meat away from the tendon as it is pulled out of the fillet.

4. Cover the breast meat with a plastic bag, and lightly pound the meat to a uniform thickness. Cut the breasts into 4-ounce pieces if they are unusually large.

5. Combine the olive oil, vinegar, and garlic in a nonreactive bowl and add the chicken pieces. Turn to coat well and marinate for at least ½ hour.

6. When ready to cook, start the grill and begin to make the sauce.

7. Remove the tomatoes from the can and coarsely chop them into approximately ¼-inch pieces. Place in a measuring cup. If necessary, add some of the liquid from the can to make 1 cup of tomatoes.

8. Heat the olive oil in a medium sauté pan, and add the garlic and shallots. Reduce the heat to low and sauté for 2 minutes.

9. Add the tomatoes and simmer for 5 minutes or until sauce is reduced slightly. Season with salt, if necessary, and a little pepper. Keep warm until chicken is done.

10. Meanwhile, grill the chicken over hot coals for 2–3 minutes per side, until the chicken is done but still very moist.

11. Add the chiffonade of basil to the sauce, spoon the sauce over the chicken, and serve.

Yield: 4–6 servings

TINA'S TIDBITS

- *Do not overcook grilled chicken! The rule is to estimate cooking time based on the thickness of the meat. Plan on 10 minutes per inch. Chicken breasts usually cook in 5 minutes.*
- *The easiest way to peel garlic is to lay a large knife on its side over the clove of garlic and smack it lightly to crack the garlic. This will dislodge the paper-like skin on the garlic clove and make it very easy to remove. It is also much easier to mince fresh garlic once it has been smacked flat.*
- *To chiffonade basil, layer the basil leaves and roll them up like a cigarette. Slice thin slices through all thicknesses. This will give you thin, delicate strips of the herb.*
- *Because canned tomatoes often contain seeds, and seeds can make a tomato-based sauce bitter, an old Italian cooking trick is to add a little bit of sugar to the sauce.*

MANDELBRODT

This is a classic recipe for mandelbrodt. *They are very satisfying dunked in a "glass" of hot tea. This Eastern Europe tradition was popular way before biscotti came into vogue in the twentieth century.*

2³/₄ cups flour
2 teaspoons baking powder
¹/₄ teaspoon salt
1 cup sugar
6 tablespoons oil
Juice of ¹/₂ orange

3 eggs
1 tablespoon grated zest of orange
1 teaspoon vanilla
¹/₂ cup slivered almonds
Cinnamon and sugar mixture for topping

1. Combine the flour, baking powder, and salt in a small bowl and set aside.

2. Cream sugar and oil until light and well combined. Add juice, eggs, zest, and vanilla and beat well.

3. Stir in the flour mixture and almonds and mix well.

4. On a greased cookie sheet, form 2 loaves of dough about 4 inches wide and 10 inches long. Sprinkle the tops with cinnamon and sugar, and bake for 45 minutes at 350°F.

5. Remove the loaves from the oven. Cut the loaves on a diagonal into ¹/₂-inch slices. Place each slice cut side down on the cookie sheet and return to the oven for 5–7 minutes or until lightly golden. Turn each slice over and return to the oven for an additional 5 minutes. Cool and serve.

Yield: 4 dozen

TINA'S TIDBITS

- Mandelbrodt *literally means "almond bread" in Yiddish.*
- *In Hungary and some other Eastern European countries, this cookie is called* kamishbread.
- *The use of oil points directly to Jewish origins, because baking throughout Europe and the Iberian Peninsula before the twentieth century utilized either butter or lard.*

ZIMSTERNE COOKIES

Zimsterne cookies are traditionally served after the Havdalah service. Shaped like stars to represent the three stars that signify the end of Shabbat, the cookies are made with honey and spice so that some of the sweetness of Shabbat can be taken into the new week. The spices mimic those found in the b'samim box used during Havdalah.

1 stick unsalted butter
8 tablespoons (½ cup) solid white shortening
1½ cups sugar
1 egg
2 tablespoons honey
½ teaspoon vanilla
2½ cups all-purpose flour
½ cup cake flour
¼ teaspoon salt
1 teaspoon baking soda

2 teaspoons cinnamon
2 teaspoons ginger
2 teaspoons cloves
Confectioners' sugar for rolling dough

DECORATIVE ICING:
1 cup confectioners' sugar
¼ teaspoon vanilla
1–2 tablespoons milk

1. Using an electric mixer, cream the butter, shortening, and sugar together until light and fluffy. Add egg, honey, and vanilla and beat well, scraping down the sides of the bowl if necessary.

2. Add the dry ingredients and mix well. Form the dough into a ball, flatten it slightly, place it in a plastic bag, and refrigerate for 1 hour or longer.

3. Roll the dough out ⅛-inch thick on a surface that is lightly coated with confectioners' sugar (instead of flour). Cut the dough with a 2-inch star cookie cutter.

4. Bake on a parchment-lined cookie sheet at 375°F for 6–8 minutes or until cookies are lightly golden. Remove from the oven.

5. Allow cookies to cool for 5–10 minutes while you make the icing.

6. To make the icing: Place the cup of confectioners' sugar in a small bowl. Whisk in the vanilla and 1 tablespoon of the milk until smooth. If the mixture is too thick, whisk in some more milk until the mixture resembles mayonnaise in consistency.

7. Brush the icing over the tops of the warm cookies and allow them to sit at room temperature until the cookies are cool and the icing is dry and no longer sticky. Store in an airtight container at room temperature, or freeze until later use.

Yield: 5 dozen

TINA'S TIDBITS

- *Hydrogenated fat, such as solid white shortening, will make the cookie harder or crisper. Margarine may be substituted, but it will change the "spread" of the cookie.*
- *The high concentration of sugar in this recipe will make the cookie firm but also chewy. Using all honey would make it even chewier, so a combination of the two is recommended.*
- *Dark spices, such as cinnamon and cloves, should always be stored in the freezer to protect their flavor, especially if you do not use them often.*

ROSH HASHANAH
AND YOM KIPPUR

We incorporate certain foods into our celebration of the High Holy Days because of custom, not biblical dictate. The only prescription in the Talmud for this celebration is for *hidur mitzvah*, taking the extra time to exalt God by making our holiday table and ourselves more beautiful by using our best china and silver or getting our hair cut and wearing new clothes for the holiday. Through these actions, we enhance the meaning of the High Holy Days.

The choices of food to represent the holiday have depended on the region, societal customs, and socioeconomic standing of the Jews. Ashkenazic Jews express their wish for a sweet and fruitful year by dipping apples and challah in honey. Kreplach, toothsome pockets of meat-filled dough served in chicken soup, is a modern interpretation of a medieval German custom of placing a wish for the New Year into a piece of dough and then wearing it as an amulet around the neck. Sephardim conduct seders serving seven foods and reciting seven blessings. They also serve fruit in covered baskets so no one knows what's inside, just as no one knows what the New Year will bring.

Normally, two loaves of elongated challah are served for Shabbat, but for the High Holy Days a round challah, sometimes containing raisins, is customary. The round challah is fraught with meaning. It is symbolic of the crown of God, our Sovereign; it represents a year filled with never-ending good. A ladder of dough placed on top represents the question of who will ascend or descend in health or wealth in the coming year. A lesser-known custom is to bake the challah in the shape of a bird, based on Isaiah 31:5, "As hovering birds, so will the Eternal protect Jerusalem."

It is customary to eat foods that symbolize sweetness, abundance, and fertility. Sight association and sound/word plays on names of foods lend themselves to using these foods symbolically as positive reflection for the coming year.

The following are some of the foods that Jews worldwide serve for the New Year:

- **Carrots:** *Meren*, Yiddish for "carrots," also means "more." In addition, sliced carrots look like gold coins.

- **Pomegranates** are supposed to contain as many seeds as the 613 mitzvot, and they represent a new fruit of the season.

- **Apples:** The *g'matria* (number association) of *tapuach* (Hebrew for "apple") is equal to that of *seh Akeidah*, "lamb of the binding," referring to the story of Abraham and Isaac. Apples also represent fertility and the story of Sarah and Isaac.

LEFT: *Round Challah, page 219*   217

- **Fish**: The whole fish or head is served. This represents a wish for a year placing you at the "head" of life. Another interpretation is that a fish never closes its eyes and, like God, is ever watchful over us.

- **Beets**: In Hebrew the word relates to "removal," as removal of our sins and our enemies.

- **Leeks**: In Hebrew the word sounds like "to cut"—may our spiritual enemies be cut down.

- **Pumpkin** represents the hope that as a thick covering protects the vegetable, God will protect us.

Cooking for Yom Kippur is an oxymoron. Or is it? How does one write about food for a holiday when you aren't supposed to ingest anything for twenty-five hours?

Actually food is prominent in the traditions of Yom Kippur, starting with the *s'udah hamafseket*, the meal preceding Yom Kippur. This meal is obviously important because we need to build up reserves of energy and water to make it through the fast. Although this is pragmatic, the Talmud states that "just as it is a mitzvah to fast on the tenth of Tishrei, it is a mitzvah to eat on the ninth" (*Yoma* 81b). Much joy and preparation therefore go into the Erev Yom Kippur meal before the *Kol Nidrei* service ushers in the Day of Atonement.

Chicken is often the entrée of choice for Jewish holiday meals. However, there is also an old ritual associated with Yom Kippur called *kaparot*, which is a ceremony using a chicken as a scapegoat for one's sins. A chicken is waved around one's head while the person recites a prayer requesting that the chicken be sacrificed instead of the waver. The bird is then slaughtered and given to the poor or its value donated to charity. Because of its magical underpinnings, this ceremony hasn't survived in this format. Today, if this ritual is performed, coins are substituted for the chicken. They are placed in a handkerchief, waved over one's head, and then donated as *tzedakah* for the poor.

There are no prescribed foods for the meal preceding or following the fast of Yom Kippur; however, there are many customs based on common sense. According to Dr. Elliot Berry, a clinical nutritionist at Hebrew University Hadassah Medical School, you should drink water frequently throughout the day prior to fasting and avoid salty or highly sweetened foods that will make you thirsty. Cutting down on caffeine intake the week before Yom Kippur will help avoid withdrawal headaches while fasting. This is common sense, but did you know that you should include foods like pasta, sweet potatoes, or whole-grain breads in your *s'udah hamafseket* because stored complex carbohydrates in the liver help you retain water? So that's why I have no ankles after Pesach!

Common sense and custom prevail as well for breaking the fast. If you break the fast with a noncarbonated drink and a piece of bread or dry cake, your blood sugar won't spike, and afterwards you will be able to enjoy a full meal. This is probably why synagogues offer these items directly after the close of the *N'ilah* service before people go home.

Most customs throughout the Diaspora prescribe breaking the fast with wine or tea and a simple bread or cookie. Once these are ingested, a light meal follows, usually consisting of dairy foods and salted fish. One advantage to this type of meal is that you can prepare almost everything in advance—a necessity if you are going to spend your time in synagogue praying for forgiveness and redemption, rather than thinking about cooking times and slicing techniques!

ROUND CHALLAH

Moist, cake-like challah is a big hit at my Rosh HaShanah open house. Divide the dough into two-thirds and one-third to make two loaves, but never use all the dough to make one giant crown or the center will surely be raw after the normal baking time is reached.

7–8 cups bread flour, divided use
2 packages rapid rise yeast
1½ cups water
2 sticks pareve margarine, butter, or ½ cup oil and 1 stick margarine
¼ teaspoon yellow food coloring

¾ cup sugar
2 tablespoons poppy seeds (optional)
1 tablespoon salt
4 large eggs
1 cup raisins (optional)
Egg wash: 1 egg mixed with 1 tablespoon water

1. In a large mixer bowl combine **6 cups** of the flour and the yeast. Stir to combine.

2. Heat the water, margarine, food coloring, sugar, poppy seeds, and salt in a saucepan until very warm (140°F). Water should be uncomfortably hot to your finger but not hot enough to burn you. (It will feel like hot tap water.)

3. Add the warm liquid mixture to the flour while the mixer is on low. As the liquid is being incorporated, add the eggs. Mix thoroughly.

4. Gradually add the remaining flour **only** until a fairly firm dough is formed. This process should take about 7 minutes whether you are using the dough hook on your mixer or are kneading it by hand. The mixture will be satiny smooth.

5. Preheat your oven to 400°F for 1 **minute**. Lightly grease a bowl with some oil, and turn the dough in the bowl to oil all sides. Cover with plastic wrap and place in the **turned off** oven until doubled in size, about 30–45 minutes.

6. Punch down the dough and divide in half or in thirds. Roll each piece into a rope about 15 inches long. Hold one end 2 inches above the work surface and wrap the rest of the dough around it to make a large coil. Pinch the ends together to prevent unraveling while baking. Place the formed breads on parchment-lined or greased cookie

sheets, and let rise in the previously warmed oven until light and doubled, about 25 minutes.

7. Remove loaves from oven and reduce to 375°F. Brush the tops of the loaves with the egg wash and bake for 25–35 minutes, depending on the size of the loaves. When the bread is done, it will be golden brown and have a hollow sound when tapped.

Yield: 2–3 loaves

TINA'S TIDBITS

- *As no amount of eggs will make the challah look golden, coloring is added. You can substitute 1/8 teaspoon saffron or turmeric for color.*
- *The amount of flour you use will be directly related to the weather; on dry, wintry days you will need less flour than on a rainy spring day, because the cold dry air will make the dough drier and the moist air in spring will require more flour to absorb the extra moisture. The amount of flour is dictated by the feel of the dough.*
- *To let the dough rise overnight, spoon 1 tablespoon of oil inside a 2-gallon ziplock bag and rub to distribute. Place the dough in the bag, squeeze out any excess air, seal, and place in the refrigerator overnight. In the morning, remove the bag from the refrigerator and let it sit at room temperature for 30 minutes before proceeding with step 6.*
- *Never cut bread hot from the oven. The steam will cause the knife to drag through the loaf and mat the dough together.*

Dulce de Manzana (Apple Preserves)

Turkish Sephardic Jews serve this sweet apple preserve as they wish their family and friends a sweet New Year.

3 cups granulated sugar
1½ cups water
2 pounds apples, Jonagold, Gala, or Delicious

Juice of ½ lemon
1 tablespoon rose water or 1 teaspoon vanilla
¼ cup slivered almonds

1. Place the sugar and water in a 3-quart saucepan and bring to a boil over medium-high heat.

2. While the mixture is heating, peel the apples and grate them by hand with a coarse grater or use a coarse grating disk on your processor. Immediately add the apples to the hot sugar syrup.

3. Reduce the temperature to medium and cook for 30–45 minutes or until most of the liquid has evaporated and the mixture is quite thick. (Note: The amount of time depends on the variety of apple and its juice content.) Stir the mixture occasionally to prevent sticking.

4. While the mixture is cooking, toast the almonds in a 350°F oven for 4 minutes or until lightly golden. Set aside.

5. When the mixture is thickened (it will get thicker when it cools), add the rose water or vanilla and place in an open container until cool. The toasted almonds may be added to the mixture at this time or sprinkled on top as a garnish just before serving. Refrigerate until serving.

Yield: 3–4 cups

TINA'S TIDBITS

- *Do not use a soft apple like McIntosh for this recipe. Jonagold are my first choice for flavor and consistency, but any firm apple will do.*
- *When grating the apples by hand, use long strokes so that the apple shreds remain intact when cooked in the sugar syrup.*
- *Fruit mixtures become well balanced and mellow when allowed to sit for 24 hours.*
- *A teaspoon of hot apple mixture dropped into a bowl of ice and water will give a good indication of what the mixture will be like when chilled.*

LUBIYA
(SEPHARDIC BLACK-EYED PEAS)

I have a theory about this dish. For over two thousand years, Ethiopian Jews have celebrated the New Year by eating these peas. I think it is possible that the culinary custom spread to West Africa over the spice trading route and that slaves learned this recipe and brought it, and the tradition of eating them at the beginning of the New Year, with them to the southern United States.

3 tablespoons extra virgin olive oil
1 medium onion, diced into ¼-inch pieces
2 large cloves of garlic, minced
1½ cups water

3 tablespoons tomato paste
1 pound fresh or frozen black-eyed peas
½ teaspoon cumin
Salt and freshly ground black pepper to taste

1. Heat a 3-quart pot over high heat for 20 seconds. Add the olive oil and heat for another 10 seconds. Add the onion and garlic and sauté over medium heat until the onions are lightly golden.

2. Add the water and tomato paste, and bring to a boil. Reduce the heat to low. Add the peas and cumin, and cook covered for 1–2 hours or until the peas are tender. It might be necessary to add a small amount of additional water to the pot if the mixture looks too dry. Conversely, if the mixture is too soupy, continue to cook uncovered until some of the liquid has evaporated.

3. Remove from the heat, and add salt and freshly ground black pepper to taste. Serve hot or at room temperature. Serve alone or over rice.

Yield: 8 servings

TINA'S TIDBITS

- *Peas need time to absorb water and expand. Either soak the peas for a few hours before cooking, or cook them for a long time until they reach the desired consistency.*
- *Never put salt in the water prior to cooking beans, as it will harden the beans and prevent them from absorbing the water and becoming soft.*
- *Save leftover tomato paste by scooping out tablespoons of the paste onto a sheet of plastic wrap. Place them in the freezer, and when frozen, peel off the plastic and store in a freezer ziplock bag until needed.*

MAPLE-GLAZED CARROTS

Carrots symbolize prosperity for the New Year, and sliced they look like gold coins. The maple syrup adds the sweetness for a sweet year ahead.

5 pounds carrots, peeled and sliced ¼ inch thick on the diagonal
1 stick sweet, unsalted pareve margarine
8 scallions, white part only, thinly sliced

Finely grated zest from 1 large lime
¾–1 cup pure grade A medium amber maple syrup
Juice of 1 lime
Kosher salt and pepper to taste

1. Place 1 inch of water that has been lightly salted in a 3-quart pot. Add the carrots, cover, and cook over moderate heat until they are tender but not soft, about 15 minutes. Drain.

2. Heat a large frying pan (big enough to hold all the carrots) for 20 seconds. Add the margarine and melt completely.

3. Add the sliced whites of the scallions and the lime zest, and sauté until the scallions are soft and just beginning to turn golden. Do not burn or the flavor will be bitter.

4. Add the maple syrup and lime juice and bring to a boil. Boil the mixture for 5 minutes or until it is reduced by half.

5. Add the carrots and gently stir with a rubber spatula to coat thoroughly. Add salt and pepper to taste and serve.

Yield: 20 servings or more if part of a buffet

TINA'S TIDBITS

- *Cooking vegetables in a small amount of water prevents the water-soluble vitamins in the food from leaching out.*
- *When stirring tender vegetables, it is better to use a rubber spatula so you won't bruise the edges of the food.*

SALMON EN PAPILLOTE

Here is my foolproof answer to entertaining large groups of people. The fish will last for days in the refrigerator, although I prefer to make it the morning of an event or the day before if it is for a Yom Kippur break fast.

1 tablespoon unsalted butter
2- to 4-pound side of salmon fillet, skin removed
1–2 limes

Cayenne pepper
Fresh ginger, peeled

1. Tear off a piece of heavy-duty foil that is 4 inches longer than the side of salmon.

2. Rub the butter all over the shiny side of the foil. Place the fish on the foil with what would have been skin side down. Set aside.

3. Remove the zest from the limes in long strips with a zester and place the strips in a small glass dish. Cover with water and microwave for 45 seconds to soften. Set aside.

4. Cut away all of the white pith from the limes, and cut out each section of the limes. Set aside.

5. Season the fish lightly with cayenne. Grate some fresh ginger directly over the fish, using about 1 inch of ginger. Decorate the top of the fish with the lime sections and julienned zest.

6. Bring the long edges of the foil together. Fold over the foil lengthwise 2 times to seal tightly but leave a little room for steam over the fish. Fold up the sides as you would a present, on a diagonal from each side and then over twice to seal the edges.

7. Place the foil packet on a rimmed cookie sheet and bake at 450°F for 16–17 minutes. Immediately open the foil or the fish will continue to cook. Place on a platter and serve immediately or at room temperature.

8. If making in advance, refrigerate the cooked fish out of the foil and covered tightly with plastic wrap. Bring to room temperature before you serve.

SAUCE

1/2 cup mayonnaise
1 teaspoon Dijon mustard
1 tablespoon dry white wine
1 tablespoon finely minced fresh dill, basil, tarragon, or lemon thyme or 1 teaspoon dried herbs

1. Place the mayonnaise in a small bowl and stir to a smooth consistency.

2. Add the remaining ingredients, using more wine if the mixture appears too thick.

3. May be served immediately, although the flavors meld when made in advance.

Yield: 10–15 servings

TINA'S TIDBITS

- *Scrape the outside of the lime with your nail to ascertain the flavor of the fruit before buying (a sweet fruit will have a sweet smell). In this recipe the natural oils and flavor of the zest are important.*
- *The dull side of the foil will absorb heat faster, and the shiny side is less reactive to acid, so it is important to place the fish on the shiny side of the foil with the dull side facing out.*
- *It is imperative that the foil is sealed tightly so that the fish steams. That said, it is important to bake it on a rimmed cookie sheet so any juices that might escape don't wind up on the oven floor!*
- *When making a mayonnaise-based sauce, you must stir up the mayonnaise before you add any other ingredients or the sauce will appear lumpy.*

Sogliola con Pinoli e Passerine
(Sole with Pine Nuts and Raisins)

The Sephardic community often serves sweet-and-sour fish for breaking the fast. This flavor, as well as the pickling liquid used by Eastern European Jews, helps replenish some of the salt lost during fasting. The following Italian recipe illustrates the Spanish influence on Mediterranean cuisine. The use of raisins and pine nuts is a giveaway that this recipe probably was introduced into Italy by the Jews fleeing the Inquisition.

¼ cup olive oil
2 tablespoons red wine or balsamic vinegar
2 teaspoons honey
¼ cup dark raisins
3 tablespoons lightly toasted pine nuts
2 tablespoons chopped fresh parsley

½ cup dry bread crumbs or matzah meal
Salt and freshly ground black pepper to taste
1½ pounds fillet of sole or other thin fish (about 5–6 fillets)
1 cup dry white wine
2 tablespoons unsalted butter

1. Lightly oil a 2-quart casserole that will be able to accommodate all of the fish rolls. Set aside.

2. Combine the first 8 ingredients in a 1-quart bowl.

3. On a flat surface, place the fish rough side up. Spread about 1–2 tablespoons of the raisin-nut mixture over the fish and roll the fish, starting from the wider end of the fillet.

4. Place the rolled fillets in the prepared casserole, seam side down.

5. Gently pour the white wine around the fillets and sprinkle any remaining filling bread crumbs over the top of the fish. Dot each fish fillet roll with some butter.

6. Bake in a 400°F oven covered with greased foil for 10 minutes. Uncover and bake for 5–10 more minutes or until fish appears firm and crumb topping is golden.

Yield: 4–6 servings

TINA'S TIDBITS

- *Thicker pieces of fish can be used; however, do not try to roll thick fillets. They look unsightly and the filling will fall out. Instead, place the filling on top of each thicker fillet and proceed with the recipe.*
- *Toast the nuts at 325°F until lightly golden, about 3 minutes.* **Remember:** *Nuts roast in their own oils, so even though you remove the nuts from the oven—the source of heat—you are not removing them from the roasting source and they will continue to brown outside of the oven.*
- *Grease the foil on the shiny side. The dull side will face outward and will absorb the heat better and prepare the fish perfectly.*

SAUTÉED "FISH" WITH PECAN BUTTER

Since fish is symbolic of the eyes of God watching over us for the New Year, I created this fish with "scales" to represent the fish of folklore. It's a little time-consuming cutting out the "scales," but the finished dish is delicious and fun to see.

1–1½ pounds bass, snapper, or sea trout fillets, cut into 4 pieces
Salt and freshly ground pepper
Flour
1 egg lightly beaten
2–3 russet potatoes
6 tablespoons butter

⅔ cup pecans, chopped into ¼-inch pieces
Pinch of black pepper
Pinch of cayenne
4 tablespoons butter
1 tablespoon lemon juice
2 tablespoons minced parsley

1. Season the fish with salt and pepper and lightly coat with flour.

2. Peel the potatoes, and then using the peeler, slice thin slices of potato. Place the potato slices in a bowl of salted water.

3. Brush the tops of the pieces of fish with the beaten egg. Using a 1-inch round cutter, cut circles from the potato slices and overlap the circles on the egg side of the fish to make lines that look like scales.

4. Clarify the butter by melting the 6 tablespoons of butter very slowly in a small saucepan over low heat. Skim the foam off the top and discard. Carefully remove yellow clarified butter with a spoon or gently pour butter into a clean dish. Discard any water from the bottom of the pan. This should yield about 4 tablespoons of clarified butter.

5. Brush the potato "scales" with clarified butter, and refrigerate for at least ½ hour.

6. When ready to cook, heat the remaining clarified butter in a large sauté pan. Place the fish, potato side down, in the pan and cook for 4 minutes or until golden. Carefully turn the fish over and cook until done. Remove to a warm plate. Drain the pan.

7. To make the pecan butter, sprinkle the pecans with the two peppers, and heat the butter in the sauté pan used for cooking the fish.

8. Sauté the pecans for 3 minutes or until lightly golden. Turn off the heat and add the lemon juice and parsley.

9. To serve, place 1 fillet on each plate and top with some pecan butter.

Yield: 4 servings

TINA'S TIDBITS

- To keep a coating adhering to your food when frying, always coat the food with flour first, then egg, and then the starch (breading or potato). Flour sticks to the moist fish, egg adheres to the flour, and the starch adheres to the egg. Refrigerating the fish for 30 minutes cements the layers together.
- Clarified butter is clear butter minus any milk solids in the melted butter. Removal of milk solids allows the fish to be fried at a higher temperature without the butter burning.
- If you have time, clarify butter and then place the entire pan in the refrigerator. Butter will solidify and solids and water can be easily discarded.

Keftes de Prasa Con Carne
(Turkish Leek and Meat Patties)

Adapted from a recipe by Rachel Bortnick, this is a favorite Sephardic recipe served as part of the Rosh HaShanah seder. Leeks are an important symbolic ingredient for the New Year, especially in Turkey.

6 medium leeks, white and light green part only
   (about 4 pounds before trimming)
2 medium russet potatoes (1½ pounds)
¾ pound lean ground beef
1 egg
1 teaspoon salt or to taste
Freshly ground black pepper to taste

¼ cup very lightly packed parsley (no big stems)
1 medium tomato, seeded and cut into eighths
1 cup flour
2 eggs, lightly beaten in a shallow bowl
Oil for frying
Prepared mild tomato or marinara sauce or lemon
   wedges

1. Cut off all the dark green leaves of the leeks and discard. Cut the white part lengthwise to the root and rinse thoroughly under running cold water. Cut the leeks crosswise into ¼-inch semicircles and place in a 2-quart saucepan with lightly salted water. Simmer 15 minutes and drain in a colander.

2. Meanwhile, peel the potatoes and cut into eighths. Place in a 1-quart saucepan with salted water and cook until tender, about 15 minutes. Drain and let sit in the pot to cool and dry off. Do not rinse the potatoes.

3. Press the leeks in batches in your hands to squeeze out excess liquid and then pat some more in a paper towel (this is **very** important to allow the *keftes* to hold together). Place the leeks in the work bowl of a processor fitted with the metal blade.

4. Add the meat and then the potatoes, and pulse the processor on and off until the mixture starts to combine. You might need to stop the processor a few times to scrape down the sides of the bowl.

5. Add the 1 egg, seasonings, parsley, and the tomato sections, and pulse until the mixture is well combined and a thick, slightly sticky mass is formed.

6. Have the flour ready on a flat plate, the remaining 2 eggs beaten with a fork in a shallow bowl, and about ¼ inch of oil in a large frying pan heating on medium high.

7. Take a rounded soup spoon of the mixture and drop it onto the flour. With floured fingers, lightly toss the meat mixture to coat well on both sides, and form into round patties about ½ inch thick.

8. Carefully coat both sides of the patty with the egg, and gently place it in the hot oil. Repeat with the remaining patties, and fry until golden brown on both sides.

9. Drain on paper towel and serve hot or at room temperature, with tomato sauce or freshly squeezed lemon juice. Makes about 3 dozen.

Yield: 6–8 servings

TINA'S TIDBITS

- *This mixture barely holds together, which is why you lightly toss it in the flour with your fingertips. Handling the mixture roughly will create heavy, pasty spheres instead of light meat pancakes.*
- *Turkish cooking often involves dipping the food in egg last to give the dish a finished "cap."*

MAPLE-GLAZED CHICKEN BREASTS WITH APPLES

Quick, sweet, savory, contains apples—what more could you want from a New Year dish?

1½ pounds boneless chicken breasts
⅓ cup Dijon mustard
7 tablespoons good-quality maple syrup, divided use
1½ tablespoons chopped fresh rosemary
1 tablespoon cooking oil

¾ teaspoon salt
Freshly ground black pepper to taste (about ¼ teaspoon)
4 Southern Rose, Winesap, or Granny Smith apples

1. Remove the fillet from each of the chicken breasts. Remove the white membrane from each of the fillets.

2. Combine the Dijon mustard with 3 tablespoons of the maple syrup, the rosemary, oil, salt, and pepper in a bowl.

3. Place the chicken in the bowl and turn to coat all pieces well. Allow chicken to marinate for at least 30 minutes.

4. When ready to cook, heat a grill on high and, when hot, place the chicken smooth side down. Grill for 4 minutes. Turn the meat over and cook until the chicken is firm but has some "give," about 2–3 more minutes. Remove from heat and keep warm until the apples are ready.

5. Peel the apples and cut into 16 wedges each.

6. Pour 1 tablespoon of cooking oil into a hot frying pan. Sauté the apples until they are a light, golden brown.

7. Reduce the heat to low and add the remaining 4 tablespoons of the maple syrup. Sauté the apples until they are tender. (The sautéed apples may be made in advance and then briefly reheated before serving.)

8. To serve, place the grilled chicken on a serving platter, and spoon the apples and sauce over the chicken.

Yield: 4–6 servings

TINA'S TIDBITS

- *The tender or fillet of the chicken breast can often make the breast look thick and plumped up. If it is not removed, the breast will not cook evenly and the center will be raw. Look for the white, pearlized membrane to determine if the fillet is still intact.*
- *It is better to reheat food in the microwave than to warm it in an oven. Microwaves will agitate the water molecules in food to make them hot, but even a low oven can still dry out the food.*

Rosh HaShanah Noodle Kugel

Here's a delicious noodle kugel that incorporates all the symbols for a sweet and fruitful New Year. The kugel is moist, not too sweet, and contains no dairy products, so it can be served with a meat meal or for dessert.

12 ounces extra-wide dried egg noodles
$\frac{1}{3}$ cup vegetable oil (corn or canola)
4 large eggs
Two 3.9-ounce (snack size) containers or 1 cup unsweetened applesauce
$\frac{1}{3}$ cup wildflower or clover honey
$\frac{1}{4}$ cup frozen apple juice concentrate
1 teaspoon cinnamon
$\frac{1}{4}$ teaspoon ground ginger

$\frac{1}{4}$ teaspoon nutmeg
3 Jonagold or Gala apples, pared, cored, and sliced into thin semicircles (reserve 8 slices for garnish on top of kugel)
$\frac{1}{2}$ cup golden raisins (optional)
$\frac{1}{4}$ cup sugar mixed with $\frac{1}{2}$ teaspoon cinnamon (for topping)
Nonstick cooking spray or pareve margarine

1. Preheat oven to 350°F. Grease a 13 × 9-inch baking dish with nonstick spray.

2. Cook noodles according to package directions. Drain but do not rinse. Place in a large mixing bowl. Add the oil and stir gently with a rubber spatula to coat and separate all the noodles.

3. In a 2-quart mixing bowl, lightly beat the eggs with a fork. Add the applesauce, honey, apple juice concentrate, cinnamon, ginger, and nutmeg and combine.

4. Using a spatula, add the apple semicircles and raisins (if using) to the egg mixture.

5. Pour the apple mixture into the noodles. Mix gently, but thoroughly, and pour into the prepared pan. Place reserved apple slices down the center of the casserole.

6. Lightly grease the shiny side of a sheet of foil with nonstick spray and cover the casserole, greased side down.

7. Bake for 45 minutes and remove from the oven. Uncover, sprinkle with the cinnamon and sugar mixture, and lightly spray with cooking spray or dot with margarine. Return the uncovered casserole to the oven for an additional 15 minutes or until lightly golden.

Yield: 12–15 servings

TINA'S TIDBITS

- *Because honey is 1–1 1/2 times sweeter than sugar, less is needed to sweeten most recipes.*
- *Covering a casserole with foil, dull side out, will help the food absorb heat from the oven without drying out.*
- *Always bake a noodle kugel immediately after adding the egg mixture or the mixture will settle and create a rubbery layer on the bottom and the noodles will be dry on top.*

Koliva
(Sweetened Wheat Berry Pudding)

This Greek pudding is called by many names in the Middle East. Sephardim serve this for Rosh HaShanah and Tu BiSh'vat. The addition of pomegranate seeds and dates makes it appropriate for the New Year.

1 cup whole soft spring wheat berries
4 cups water
½ cup sugar
¼ cup wildflower honey
Pinch of salt
1 teaspoon cinnamon

1 cup almonds, walnuts, pistachio nuts, or a mixture
1 cup raisins or mixed dried fruit bits
4 Medjool dates, cut in half lengthwise and pitted (for garnish)
Pomegranate seeds for garnish

1. Place wheat berries in a glass bowl and cover with boiling water. Soak the berries for 2 hours or until they are slightly softened. Drain the water. Place in a 3-quart saucepan.

2. Add the 4 cups of water to the pan and bring the water to a boil. Simmer for 45–60 minutes, or until the wheat berries are tender but firm. Drain.

3. Add the sugar, honey, salt, and cinnamon to the pot and cook over moderate heat until the honey and sugar are completely melted and thoroughly coating the wheat berries.

4. Toast the nuts in a 350°F oven for 5 minutes. Set aside.

5. Add the nuts and the dried fruit to the mixture, and spoon into a serving bowl.

6. Garnish with the sliced dates and pomegranate seeds if desired. Serve at room temperature or cold.

Yield: 8–10 servings

TINA'S TIDBITS

- *Never cook beans or grains with salt, as the salt will toughen the food and require a lengthy cooking time. Add salt afterwards if necessary.*
- *Nuts should always be stored in the freezer to keep them from becoming rancid.*

TEIGLACH

Three weeks prior to Rosh HaShanah, all the New York Jewish bakeries put up signs urging customers to place their teiglach orders. Most Texans, as well as many other American Jews outside of New York, are not familiar with this great dessert. I have fond memories of sitting around the table discussing politics and picking on this dessert, trying to dislodge a sweet morsel. This recipe is much easier than the original technique of cooking the dough in the honey syrup, and the results are perfect every time!

3 eggs
3 tablespoons oil
2 tablespoons water
$\frac{1}{2}$ teaspoon vanilla
$2\frac{1}{2}$ cups flour
$\frac{1}{4}$ teaspoon salt
$\frac{1}{4}$ teaspoon ginger
1 teaspoon baking powder

1 pound wildflower honey (any honey is OK, but
   wildflower is the best)
$\frac{1}{2}$ cup sugar
$\frac{1}{2}$ teaspoon ginger
One 2-inch piece of orange zest, $\frac{1}{2}$ inch wide
1 cup toasted hazelnuts, peeled
$\frac{1}{2}$ cup candied cherries or raisins

1. Preheat the oven to 375°F.

2. Combine the eggs, oil, water, and vanilla, and beat with a fork or whisk until light and combined.

3. In a medium bowl, combine the flour, salt, ginger, and baking powder.

4. Add the liquid ingredients to the bowl with the dry ingredients and stir with a fork until well combined. Knead with your hands for a few minutes until the dough is smooth and shiny. Cover with plastic wrap and let rest for 10 minutes.

5. Roll out small chunks of dough into long $\frac{1}{2}$-inch-wide snakes and cut into $\frac{1}{3}$-inch pieces. Roll the dough pieces briefly in your hands to make balls, and place them on ungreased cookie sheets. Bake for 20–22 minutes or until golden brown.

6. Meanwhile, combine the honey, sugar, ginger, and orange zest in a heavy 3-quart saucepan and bring slowly to a boil. Simmer for exactly 10 minutes.

7. Add the *teiglach* balls, the nuts, and the raisins or cherries to the honey mixture and stir with a wooden spoon to coat well. Place in a pie plate or individual tart tins mounded to form a pyramid.

Yield: 12 servings

TINA'S TIDBITS

- *The balls of dough can be made and frozen until you are ready to assemble the* teiglach.
- *Always freeze baked goods after they are thoroughly cooled. Place in a freezer bag and close almost all the way. Insert a straw and suck out all of the air and then seal. Defrost before using.*
- *Always stir a hot sugar syrup with a wooden spoon. Metal will conduct the heat and get too hot and plastic will melt.*

Hadgi Badah
(Almond Macaroons)

The following recipe is a variation of the ubiquitous Sephardic almond macaroon. This recipe is undeniably Iraqi, because of the inclusion of the cardamom, and it is traditionally served following the conclusion of the N'ilah service at the end of Yom Kippur. The cookies are very easy to make, especially if you use the food processor to combine all of the ingredients. Longer baking will make them hard but more golden.

8 ounces almond slivers
⅔ cup sugar
1 egg

2 teaspoons rose water
¼ teaspoon ground cardamom

1. Preheat the oven to 350°F, and cover 2 cookie sheets with parchment paper. Set aside.

2. Place almonds in a food processor work bowl and pulse the machine on and off to grind the nuts until they are fairly fine.

3. Add the sugar and pulse on and off 10 times to combine well and grind until very fine.

4. Add the remaining ingredients and pulse on and off until the mixture is well combined and a thick batter is formed.

5. Lightly shape into balls or drop by teaspoon onto the prepared cookie sheets. A sliver of almond is sometimes pressed into the top of the cookie before baking.

6. Bake for 14 minutes or until lightly golden. The longer you bake this cookie, the harder it becomes. This is a matter of personal taste and strong teeth!

7. Store in a plastic bag when cool. Keeps for a week or more.

Yield: 2–3 dozen

TINA'S TIDBITS

- *When buying nuts by weight, the rule is to double the weight of the nuts and convert that amount to cups to determine the volume. For example, 8 ounces of nuts will yield approximately 2 cups of nuts.*
- *When grinding nuts in a processor, always pulse the machine on and off to finely grind. Pulsing throws the nuts up and allows them to fall to get chopped, preventing a paste or "butter" from forming on the floor of the work bowl.*
- *Never seal food in a plastic bag while still warm. The steam given off by the warm baked good will make your product soggy and hastens the formation of mold in the bag.*

Fresh Apple Cake

Grated apples make this cake moist and delicious. It is a simple dessert when served dusted with confectioners' sugar, but the original West Texas version calls for a coconut-pecan topping as rich as the region's oil wells.

2 cups flour
1 teaspoon baking soda
½ teaspoon salt
1 teaspoon cinnamon
1¼ cups oil
2 cups sugar
3 eggs

2 teaspoons vanilla
3 cups grated apple (peel does not need to be removed if finely grated)
1¼ cups coarsely chopped pecans
Confectioners' sugar for dusting top (if not making the topping below)

1. Combine the flour, soda, salt, and cinnamon in a small bowl and set aside.

2. In a large mixing bowl, beat the oil and sugar together until well blended. Add the eggs and beat until the eggs are totally incorporated and the mixture is a light lemon color.

3. Mix in the vanilla and then add the flour mixture, the grated apple, and the pecans and mix well.

4. Pour into a 10-inch springform tube pan or a Bundt pan that has been sprayed with nonstick cooking spray. Bake at 350°F for 50–55 minutes or until a toothpick inserted in the center of the cake comes out clean. Remove from the oven and cool. When cool, remove from the pan and place on a serving tray. Dust with some confectioners' sugar **or** top with the following topping if desired.

Topping

6 tablespoons unsalted butter
2 tablespoons milk
¾ cup brown sugar

½ cup shredded coconut
½ cup chopped pecans

1. Combine all ingredients in a medium saucepan. Bring to a boil and boil for 1 minute.

2. Pour over top of cake and cool before serving.

Yield: 12 servings

TINA'S TIDBITS

- *It is very important to thoroughly combine the eggs, sugar, and oil in a cake batter before adding other ingredients. If the oil is not completely incorporated into the eggs, the finished product will be very greasy and heavy instead of light and moist.*
- *When a recipe calls for oil, it refers to vegetable oil like corn, canola, or soybean oil. Never use olive or peanut oil unless specified, because they have distinctive flavors.*
- *Once a sugar mixture comes to a boil, it should not be stirred. Stirring will create a grainy, coarse texture instead of a smooth mixture.*

SUKKOT

Many historians believe the Pilgrims' first celebration of giving thanks was patterned after the Jewish festival of Sukkot. Jews made pilgrimage to Jerusalem after the fall harvest to give thanks not only for the bounty of the earth they had just gathered but also for God's deliverance to the Promised Land. Likewise, the Pilgrims lived in temporary huts and gave thanks to God for their deliverance to the New World and the first harvest that would sustain them through the winter.

The Torah refers to Sukkot as *HaChag*, "The Festival." The symbols of this festival are the sukkah, the three-sided hut with its profusion of fall fruits and vegetables hanging from the open, star-illuminated roof; the *lulav*, with its palm, myrtle, and willow branches; and the *etrog*, or citron, a citrus fruit that looks like a huge bumpy lemon.

The Talmud (*Beitzah* 30b) recommends using nuts, almonds, peaches, grape branches, and jugs of freshly pressed olive oil to decorate the sukkah but does not suggest what to eat. One of the mitzvot of the holiday is to actually eat meals in the sukkah and invite guests to partake of the meals with you. The great kabbalist, Rabbi Isaac Luria, offered an invitation to the *ushpizin*—symbolic guests Abraham, Isaac, Jacob, Joseph, Moses, Aaron, and David—who were all great wanderers of our heritage who lived in huts.

The Torah does not dictate what should be eaten in the sukkah. Fruits, vegetables, and grains figure prominently in the harvest foods of Sukkot, as they did in the Mediterranean diet. Wheat, barley, and lentils were cultivated. Grapes, figs, and dates are cited often in the Bible. In Leviticus 20:24, "a land flowing with milk and honey" refers to the honey-sweet dates from the date palm tree whose fronds are the "backbone" of the *lulav*.

For Sukkot, Jewish cooks throughout the Diaspora have traditionally made foods that are rolled or stuffed, symbolic of the abundance of the holiday harvest. Rice and couscous dishes made with seasonal fruits and vegetables and cooked fruit compotes are prominent on menus for Sukkot as well. Most dishes are prepared as casseroles because they are easily transported from the kitchen to the sukkah.

The sukkah represents the transient nature of our material wealth. What our homes contain is temporary; what our hearts contain can lead to caring for others and *tikkun olam* (repair of the world).

LEFT: *Sweet Potato-Pumpkin Cazuela, page 248*

BUTTERNUT-APPLE SOUP

Butternut squash was cultivated millennia before Columbus discovered it. The smooth texture of the squash lends itself to creating a thick, creamy soup without all the cream. Perfect for a dairy luncheon, this soup can easily be made pareve by using soy creamer and margarine in place of the cream and butter. Fall pie pumpkin may be substituted. Great for a sukkah meal.

One 2-pound butternut squash
2 McIntosh or Gala apples, peeled, cored, and cut up,
   or 1 cup unsweetened applesauce
2 tablespoons butter
1 cup apple cooking liquid or vegetable stock
$\frac{1}{2}$ cup half-and-half

$\frac{1}{2}$ tablespoon loosely packed Mexican mint marigold
   or tarragon
$\frac{1}{2}$ teaspoon nutmeg
Salt and freshly ground black pepper to taste
$\frac{1}{3}$ cup toasted pine nuts

1. Pierce the squash with a fork in 2 places and bake in a 350°F oven for 40 minutes or until a knife easily cuts into the flesh.

2. Place the cut apple pieces in a small saucepan and add water to a depth of $\frac{1}{4}$ inch. Cook covered for 8 minutes or until the apples are very soft.

3. Cut the squash in half lengthwise, remove the seeds, and scoop out the flesh. Remove apples from cooking liquid and reserve liquid. Place the squash flesh and the apples in a food processor work bowl and process until smooth.

4. Add the remaining ingredients **except** the pine nuts and process until well blended. Add additional cooking liquid if the soup is too thick.

5. Place the mixture in a clean saucepan and heat thoroughly over moderate heat for about 6 minutes.

6. Serve in individual soup bowls or little pumpkins, sprinkled with some toasted pine nuts.

Yield: 4–6 servings

TINA'S TIDBITS

- *It is much easier to bake a whole butternut squash than to try to peel it and cut it into cubes. However, if roasting a pierced squash, always do so on a low-rimmed cookie sheet to prevent any juices from spilling over and burning on the oven floor.*
- *Toast the pine nuts for 3–4 minutes or until lightly golden and fragrant. Do not let them get too dark or they will continue to fry in their own oils outside of the roasting oven and will burn.*
- *Nuts are not roasted in the oven; they fry in their own oils that are heated by the oven. As a result, removing nuts from the oven only removes them from the heat source, not from the frying source.*

Autumn Pâté

French Jews were often associated with the foie gras industry. Fattening the geese so that their livers were exceedingly large and riddled with fat in order to produce the best pâté is considered by many contemporary Jews to be inhumane and anathema to the Jewish dietary laws. Luckily, this pâté is made with chicken livers and the bird wasn't force-fed. This pâté is not smooth, but rather more like a country pâté, because of the fruits and sautéed onions included with the chicken livers.

2 stalks of celery, preferably with some leaves attached
6 black peppercorns
1 bay leaf
1/2 teaspoon finely ground sea salt
2 quarts water
1/4 cup sweetened dried cranberries
1/4 cup water
8 tablespoons (1 stick) pareve margarine
4 tablespoons rendered chicken fat
1/2 cup chopped onion

1 clove garlic
1 pound chicken livers
2 teaspoons dry mustard
1/4 teaspoon ground nutmeg
1/8 teaspoon ground allspice
4 tablespoons of apple brandy
Salt and freshly ground pepper
1/4 cup finely diced unsweetened canned apples or cooked fresh apple
1 teaspoon sugar

1. Combine the first 5 ingredients in a 3-quart saucepan and bring to a boil. Simmer for 10 minutes.

2. Meanwhile, combine the dried cranberries with the 1/4 cup water and microwave for 1 1/2 minutes. Set aside until ready to use.

3. Heat an 8- to 10-inch frying pan for 20 seconds. Add the margarine and chicken fat and melt. Fry the onion over medium heat until the onion is soft. Add the garlic and continue to sauté until the mixture is very lightly golden. Do not allow the garlic to burn. Set aside while you cook the livers.

4. Pick over the chicken livers to remove any yellow membrane. Check for and remove any green spots (this would be from the bile and would make the livers bitter). Broil the livers 1 minute on each side until lightly browned. (This is to prepare them according to the laws of kashrut.)

5. Place the livers in the simmering water mixture and reduce the heat to low. Cover and cook for 10 minutes. Turn off the heat and let rest for 2 minutes. The livers will be very tender and barely pink inside.

6. Drain the livers and discard the celery, peppercorns, and bay leaf. Place the livers in the container of a food processor.

7. Add the sautéed onion-garlic mixture with all the fat from the pan and all the spices to the livers and process until fairly smooth. Scrape down the sides of the work bowl and add the apple brandy. Process until the mixture is very smooth. Add salt and pepper to taste.

8. Place the liver mixture in a 2-quart bowl. Set aside.

9. Drain the soaking dried cranberries and combine with the diced apples and sugar.

10. Fold the cranberry-apple mixture into the liver mixture, and pour into a 1-quart bowl or mold that is lined with plastic wrap. Tap the mold on the counter 1 or 2 times to settle the mixture. Cover well and refrigerate until firm and ready to serve.

11. To serve, unmold the pâté onto a plate and serve with toasted pita or French bread.

Note: Orange liqueur and other dried fruits can be substituted, or try adding 1 heaping tablespoon drained green peppercorns to the mixture instead of the fruits.

Yield: 12 servings

TINA'S TIDBITS

- *Although pâté can be made with any liver (chicken, beef, or calf), chicken liver is the smoothest and mildest-tasting liver of the three to use.*
- *Golden raisins and pear can be substituted for the dried cranberries and apple. Poire William, a pear liqueur, can be used as well with this combination.*

MIXED-FRUIT CRANBERRY RELISH

Every fall I am approached after Thanksgiving and told stories about proud hostesses whose guests waxed ecstatic about the cranberry relish they were served. Here is a recipe that is easy to make, tastes delicious, and, because of the high sugar content and alcohol, lasts for a month or more in the refrigerator. Your Sukkot fruit relish becomes your Thanksgiving accompaniment. Enjoy the rave reviews!

12 ounces fresh cranberries
2 apples, pared, cored, and cut into chunks
2 pears, pared, cored and cut into chunks
1 cup dark raisins
1 cup sugar

$\frac{1}{2}$ cup fresh orange juice
1 tablespoon grated orange zest
$1\frac{1}{4}$ teaspoons cinnamon
$\frac{1}{3}$ cup orange liqueur

1. Put all of the ingredients **except** the liqueur into a heavy saucepan. Bring to a boil and then reduce the heat to a slow simmer.

2. Cook uncovered for 25–40 minutes or until the mixture thickens slightly. Stir occasionally to prevent sticking. Remove from the heat.

3. Add the liqueur and stir until thoroughly blended.

4. Refrigerate for at least three hours. This mixture lasts for months in the refrigerator and freezes well.

5. Serve chilled as an accompaniment to a poultry dinner or on a sandwich.

Yield: 1$\frac{1}{2}$ quarts

> ### TINA'S TIDBITS
>
> - *The alcohol and sugar in this recipe act like preservatives and allow the sauce to last for months in the refrigerator.*
> - *Make a double batch so the leftovers from Sukkot can be eaten for Thanksgiving or even Chanukah!*

DOLMAS
(TURKISH STUFFED GRAPE LEAVES)

Stuffed grape leaves and cabbage are ubiquitous in the cuisines of the Jews. At Sukkot, every Jewish community has its specialty. The use of the sweet spices along with the pine nuts and raisins shows the strong Arab influence in this dish.

2 tablespoons olive oil
2 medium onions, chopped
1 clove garlic, minced
One 8-ounce jar grape leaves in brine (2 if leaves are small)
1 cup uncooked long-grain rice
4 scallions, finely chopped
2 tablespoons minced fresh dill
2 tablespoons finely chopped Italian parsley
2 tablespoons minced fresh mint
$\frac{1}{2}$ teaspoon cinnamon
$\frac{1}{2}$ teaspoon allspice

3 tablespoons toasted pine nuts
3 tablespoons raisins
1 teaspoon salt
$\frac{1}{4}$ teaspoon freshly ground pepper or to taste
$\frac{2}{3}$ cup olive oil
$\frac{1}{3}$ cup freshly squeezed lemon juice
$\frac{2}{3}$ cup water, plus additional as needed during cooking
1 teaspoon sugar
Broken grape leaves or lettuce leaves for the bottom of the pot

1. Heat 2 tablespoons of olive oil in a large skillet and sauté the onion for 5 minutes. Add the garlic and sauté until the onions are lightly golden. Place this mixture in a 2-quart mixing bowl.

2. Soak the separated grape leaves in a bowl of warm water for 5 minutes while you make the filling.

3. Place the rice in a 1-quart glass bowl, cover with water, and microwave on high for 5 minutes. Drain.

4. Add the rice, scallions, dill, parsley, mint, cinnamon, allspice, pine nuts, and raisins to the onion mixture. Season the mixture with the salt and pepper.

5. Remove the leaves from the bowl of water and rinse under cold running water. Separate the leaves and place shiny side down on a board. If the leaves are small, place two together, overlapping at the stem end.

6. Place 2 teaspoons of the rice mixture near the stem end of each leaf, and roll up the leaf once to cover filling. Fold in both sides of the leaf to cover the filling, and proceed to tightly roll the leaf up toward the tip to make a neat roll.

TINA'S TIDBITS

- *Dolmas can be made in advance and stored in the refrigerator. Serve cool or at room temperature.*
- *Never use "real" lemon juice from a bottle! It bears no resemblance to the real thing. Two to three lemons will yield 1/3 cup juice.*
- *When buying lemons, scrape the outside with your fingernail and sniff. The fragrance will indicate the flavor of the lemon juice.*
- *Any remaining filling may be frozen in an airtight container for later use.*

7. Place some broken vine leaves or lettuce leaves in the bottom of a 4-quart pot or Dutch oven, so the rolls won't stick to the bottom of the pan. Arrange the rolls in the pot, seam side down, piling the rolls on top of each other as much as necessary.

8. Combine the remaining ⅔ cup oil, lemon juice, ⅔ cup water, and sugar and pour over the rolls in the Dutch oven.

9. Place a heavy plate or a plate with a weight (a heavy glass will do), on top of the rolls to prevent unraveling while cooking, and cover the pot. Simmer 40 minutes.

10. Add more water as needed to maintain about ½ inch of liquid on the bottom of the pot and cook for a total of 50 minutes or until the rice mixture in the rolls is tender.

11. Cool and serve at room temperature.

Yield: 3–4 dozen

STUFFED CABBAGE

Whether they were called holipkes, golishkes, goluptzi, *or* prakkes, *everyone who was summoned to dinner knew they were having stuffed cabbage. Let the Jews to the south stuff their meat and rice into teeny, tiny packets of grape leaves; the peasants in Poland and Russia were using big cabbage leaves to disguise the fact that there wasn't too much meat inside the tasty rolls. These rolls were traditionally served at Sukkot, probably because they were using the produce of the region and because it was transportable to the sukkah. No need to wait for any holiday to enjoy these.*

$\frac{1}{3}$ cup uncooked rice
2 cups boiling water
1 large onion
1–1$\frac{1}{2}$ pounds ground beef
1 tablespoon salt
$\frac{1}{2}$ cup water

1 large or 2 small heads of cabbage
Two 8-ounce cans of unflavored tomato sauce
2 cups water
3 tablespoons brown sugar or to taste
$\frac{1}{2}$ cup raisins
Fresh lemon juice, to taste

1. Cook the rice in 2 cups boiling water for 10 minutes. Drain.

2. Cut onion into $\frac{1}{2}$-inch dice. Combine with the meat, drained rice, salt, and $\frac{1}{2}$ cup water in a bowl and mix well. Set aside while you prepare the cabbage for stuffing.

3. Cut the core out of the cabbage and place the cabbage, core side down, in a 4-quart pot, covering $\frac{2}{3}$ of the cabbage with water. Cover the pot, bring the water to a boil, and cook the cabbage for as long as it takes to make the cabbage tender enough to remove some of the leaves, about 15 minutes. If some of the cabbage is still hard, return it to the water and cook while you start to stuff the soft leaves.

4. To fill the cabbage leaves, first cut a small inverted V out of the thick stem end of the cabbage leaf and discard. On a flat surface, place the leaf with the stem end toward you.

5. Place 2–3 tablespoons of the meat mixture at the stem end of the leaf and fold over once. Fold in both sides of the leaf, and continue rolling up the remaining cabbage to the end of the leaf. Fill the remaining leaves in the same way.

TINA'S TIDBITS

- *Rather than buy one very big cabbage, consider buying two smaller ones. The rolls will be a little bit smaller, but it will be easier to get the leaves soft.*
- *A modern trick to this old technique is to microwave the cabbage until its leaves are soft enough to roll. The advantage to this trick is that it will also cook the cabbage from the inside out.*
- *Placing some leftover or broken leaves on the bottom of the pan prevents any of the rolls from sticking and possibly scorching.*
- *Check the pot every once in a while to make sure that most of the rolls are covered with sauce.*
- *Traditionally the rice is added raw to the meat. However, partially cooking it results in rice that will ultimately blend in more with the other filling ingredients, and the filling won't fall apart when the cabbage roll is cut.*

6. Place any broken or small leaves in the bottom of a 4-quart Dutch oven. Layer the cabbage rolls over the small leaves, placing them seam side down so that they won't unravel when cooking.

7. Combine the tomato sauce, 2 cups of water, brown sugar, and raisins and pour over the cabbage rolls. Simmer for 2 hours, until the cabbage rolls are very tender.

8. Taste the sauce and add a tablespoon or more of lemon juice and more brown sugar, if needed, to properly adjust the sweet-and-sour taste. Cook for another 20 minutes.

9. Although stuffed cabbage can be served immediately, it will taste even better the next day or later.

Yield: 8–10 servings

Pear Salad with Jicama and Snow Peas

I originally taught this recipe as part of my spa cuisine class because it is very low in fat and high in fiber and flavor. I am including it here because it is the perfect salad to serve your ushpizin *in the sukkah.*

3 tablespoons pine nuts or pecans	1 teaspoon Dijon mustard
2 cups snow peas	1 clove garlic
2 ripe pears	2 tablespoons corn oil
1/2 tablespoon lemon juice	2 tablespoons olive oil
3 cups fresh baby spinach	1 scallion, thinly sliced crosswise
1 cup jicama	Freshly ground black pepper to taste
2 tablespoons balsamic vinegar	1 tablespoon chopped basil

1. Toast the nuts in a 350°F oven for 5 minutes or until lightly golden. Set aside.

2. String the snow peas. Blanch them in boiling salted water for 30 seconds and then plunge them into ice water. Cut them lengthwise into 1/4-inch strips.

3. Peel and core the pears, cut them into 1/4-inch strips lengthwise, and toss with the lemon juice.

4. Rinse the spinach well and remove any large stems. Pat dry and place in a serving bowl.

5. Peel the jicama and cut into 2-inch lengths, 1/4 inch wide.

6. In a small bowl, whisk the vinegar, mustard, and garlic together. Slowly add the oils while you whisk rapidly to form an emulsion. Lightly whisk in the scallion, pepper, and basil. Allow to set for 15 minutes.

7. To arrange the salad, add the snow peas, pears, and jicama to the spinach and toss with the dressing. Spoon onto individual plates and sprinkle with the toasted nuts. Serve immediately.

Yield: 6–8 servings

TINA'S TIDBITS

- *To string snow peas, hold one pod by the top stem in your right hand and then place your thumb into the pod on top in the middle and pull the stem down. If pods are stringy, both stringy sides will peel away.*
- *The little bit of mustard in the vinaigrette will help the oil bind to the vinegar and create a creamy dressing rather than a clear liquid that will separate.*

Vegetarian Couscous

This Moroccan-inspired dish, adapted from The Gourmet Jewish Cook *by the cookbook author and cooking teacher Judy Zeidler, is a perfect way to exploit the wonderful vegetables available during Sukkot. It makes a beautiful edible centerpiece for your dinner table in the sukkah. Served hot or at room temperature, it is equally enjoyable.*

2 tablespoons olive oil
2 large cloves garlic, finely chopped
1 medium onion, cut into ½-inch dice
2 carrots, sliced into ¼-inch rounds
One 8-ounce can tomato sauce
¾ cup dark raisins
½ teaspoon salt or to taste
1 teaspoon ground cumin
2½ cups vegetable stock, divided use

2 small zucchini, sliced into ¼-inch rounds
1 small (1 pound) eggplant, cut into 1-inch dice
2 yellow crookneck squash, sliced into ¼-inch rounds
4 ounces mushrooms caps (any type—see Tidbit below), cut into quarters
One 15-ounce can chickpeas, rinsed and drained
4 tablespoons butter or margarine
1 cup couscous
1–2 tablespoons finely minced parsley for garnish (optional)

1. Heat a large frying pan for 30 seconds and add the oil. Heat the oil for 15 seconds and sauté the garlic and onion until lightly golden. Do not burn the garlic.

2. Add the carrots, tomato sauce, raisins, salt, cumin, and 1 cup of stock to the pan. Cover and simmer the mixture for 10 minutes or until the carrots are tender.

3. Add the zucchini and the eggplant and cook for 10 minutes. Add the crookneck squash, mushrooms, and chickpeas. Cook until all of the vegetables are tender.

4. In a large saucepan, heat the remaining 1½ cups stock and butter or margarine. Add the couscous. Cover, remove from the heat, and allow the pan to sit for 5 minutes.

5. To serve, spoon the couscous in the center of a large rimmed dish, and surround with the cooked vegetables. Pour the sauce evenly over all. Sprinkle with a little parsley for garnish if you like.

Yield: 4 servings as a main course or 8 as a side dish

TINA'S TIDBITS

- *Always heat the pan first before adding the oil. This prevents the oil from adhering to the pan and the food from sticking to the oil.*
- *You may vary the vegetables in the recipe, but always add first the vegetables that need more cooking time.*
- *Like all stews, this dish tastes even better the next day. Make the couscous right before serving, and reheat the vegetables in the microwave for 4 minutes or until hot.*
- *The fins of a portabella mushroom will blacken foods. Scrape the fins off with a spoon and discard them before using a portabella mushroom in this or any recipe.*

Sweet Potato–Pumpkin Cazuela (Casserole)

Here's a dish that is perfect for Sukkot and very easy—especially if you use the canned potatoes and pumpkins. Pumpkins are believed to have originated in North America between 7000 and 5500 B.C.E. Although prevalent in the Far East, pumpkins gained popularity in Europe beginning in the sixteenth century after their discovery in the New World. This recipe would be perfect for Thanksgiving as well as Sukkot. Substitute pareve margarine for the butter for a dairy-free dish. Don't be afraid of the coconut milk. It is very subtle and rounds out the flavors.

2 tablespoons unsalted butter or pareve margarine
$\frac{2}{3}$ cup granulated sugar
$\frac{1}{3}$ cup dark brown sugar
2 tablespoons all-purpose flour
$\frac{1}{2}$ teaspoon salt
$\frac{2}{3}$ cup unsweetened canned coconut milk
2 eggs
One 15-ounce can unflavored pumpkin puree or 1 small pie pumpkin (see instructions for cooking in Tina's Tidbits)

One 29-ounce can of yams in light syrup, drained and mashed, or 3 large yams
$\frac{1}{4}$ cup water
$\frac{1}{8}$ teaspoon ground ginger
2-inch piece of stick cinnamon, broken into pieces
$\frac{1}{4}$ teaspoon fennel seeds
3 whole cloves

1. Place the butter or margarine in a 2-quart glass bowl and microwave for 45 seconds.

2. Whisk the sugars, flour, and salt into the butter to combine.

3. Whisk the coconut milk into the mixture until thoroughly blended. Add the eggs and combine.

4. Add the pumpkin puree and the mashed yams and whisk until a smooth batter is formed.

5. Combine the water with the spices in a small glass cup and microwave on high for $1\frac{1}{2}$ minutes. Let the mixture steep for 5 minutes. Strain the spiced water through a fine-mesh strainer into the pumpkin-potato mixture and stir to incorporate.

6. Butter a 2-quart casserole and pour the mixture into the prepared dish.

7. Bake covered in a preheated 350°F oven for 1 hour. Serve.

Yield: 8–10 servings

TINA'S TIDBITS

- *Always use a small sugar pie pumpkin when cooked pumpkin is called for. Larger pumpkins are more watery and more like acorn squash.*
- *To cook a pumpkin, cut into large chunks, peel, and cook in boiling salted water until tender— about 20 minutes. Drain and mash.*
- *Coconut milk is not milk or dairy. It is the liquid formed from ground, fresh, hydrated coconut.*
- *This dish freezes beautifully! Just cool completely before freezing so no ice crystals form. Defrost and reheat in the microwave.*

PUMPKIN MOUSSE

All the good taste of pumpkin pie without the crust. It can be made with nondairy creamer for a pareve dessert that can easily be transported outside to the sukkah.

2 teaspoons unflavored kosher gelatin
2 tablespoons dark rum
1 cup canned unsweetened pumpkin
$\frac{1}{2}$ cup sugar
1 egg yolk
$\frac{1}{8}$ teaspoon nutmeg

Pinch of allspice
$\frac{1}{2}$ teaspoon cinnamon
$\frac{1}{4}$ teaspoon ginger
1 teaspoon vanilla
$\frac{1}{4}$ teaspoon salt
1 cup heavy cream or nondairy whipped topping mix

1. Sprinkle the gelatin over the rum in a small glass custard cup and let it soften for a few minutes.

2. Combine the remaining ingredients **except** the heavy cream in a medium bowl.

3. Place the custard cup with the rum and gelatin in a frying pan that contains $\frac{1}{2}$ inch of simmering water. Stir the rum mixture until the gelatin is dissolved.

4. Whisk the hot gelatin mixture into the pumpkin mixture until thoroughly combined.

5. Whip the cream in a small bowl until it forms soft peaks and fold it carefully into the pumpkin mixture.

6. Spoon into six 4-ounce ramekins and refrigerate until set, about 3–4 hours.

Yield: 6 servings

TINA'S TIDBITS

- *Soaking the gelatin in the rum helps it swell so that when it is warm it will melt and be evenly distributed in the mousse.*
- *If a frozen, pre-whipped dairy or pareve topping is available, you may substitute 2 cups of that already whipped product for the 1 cup of whipping cream, however, the taste will be slightly different.*

CHANUKAH

*T*heme parties aren't new. One year I created a birthday cake for my son that covered an entire table with cupcakes, licorice, and cookies, transforming the table's surface into a giant Pac Man grid. I used modern media to enhance my creativity. Jewish cooks eight hundred years ago found their creative stimulus in themes from

the Bible, regional folklore, and daily life. The Chanukah story of the rededication of the Temple and the single vial of oil that lasted eight days instead of one prompted the use of large amounts of oil or rendered goose fat to make specialty dishes for Chanukah celebrations.

The original Chanukah culinary expression often served in Jewish homes over one thousand years ago was a cheese pancake commemorating Judith's heroic efforts on the part of her brethren. Dairy products were readily available in the warmer climates of the Diaspora. The Jews in Eastern Europe did not have easy access to dairy products, and Chanukah was celebrated sometime in December, when the weather was very cold. Historically, raising geese was a Jewish occupation, and in December the fattened geese were ready to provide the meat, fat, and down that would be needed during the cold months. Potatoes were cheap and readily available, so the Jews in the cold north reinterpreted the latke into a crisp, golden potato galette.

Symbolism is incorporated into culinary custom; foods that are regionally available dictate the expression of that symbolism. If you mix some goose or chicken fat with a plentiful supply of

radishes in the shtetl, you create a salad that was, according to folklore, one of the Maccabees' favorite foods. (Perhaps this story comes from the fact that the Roman word for *radish* means "root" and hiding in the mountains required the Maccabees to survive eating mostly root foods.)

Middle Eastern dishes made with bulgur always graced the Chanukah table, especially if delicate, but crisp, fried kibbeh was served too. North African Jewish communities relied on couscous to create a festive table, and the Dutch saw a parallel to the Hasmoneans' struggle in the siege of Leyden in 1574. At that time the Dutch organized a surprise attack on the invading Spanish camps at dinnertime, and the Spanish soldiers were forced to flee, leaving their simmering pots of stewed vegetables with meat behind. Many Dutch Jews serve a mashed stew of vegetables with garlic sausage called *hutspot* on Chanukah to commemorate this battle.

An entire chapter could be devoted to the myriad variations of fried doughnuts served around the world to commemorate this holiday, and latkes take on an entirely different meaning in Italy when made with arborio rice, raisins, and pine nuts. The common denominator of all these choices is the story of Chanukah and the survival of the Jewish way of life.

Chanukah Radish Salad Canapés

The Torah states that radishes were one of the mainstays of the Jewish slave's diet in Egypt. Both the Jerusalem and Babylonian Talmud refer to eating radishes. The red radish first became widely available in the sixteenth century, and a poor peasant's meal in Eastern Europe and Russia often consisted of black bread and radish. The addition of a little goose fat to this combo often elevated this simple food to a holiday treat. Geese were fattened in the fall and killed in the winter to save their fat for future use. A goose was often served for Chanukah, and its rendered fat was used in holiday preparations such as this.

1 pound large fresh red radishes (about 2 dozen)
2 large scallions
2 tablespoons rendered chicken fat
1½ tablespoons apple cider vinegar
½ teaspoon kosher salt or sea salt
½ teaspoon freshly ground black pepper (about 10 grinds)

1 teaspoon sugar or honey
Westphalian pumpernickel bread or whole-wheat pita
Extra chicken fat for spreading on bread (optional)
Coarse sea salt for garnish (optional)

1. Thinly slice the radishes crosswise by hand or using a thin slicing blade on a food processor.

2. Trim off the very ends of the scallions. Slice the scallions lengthwise in half through the white part. Cut the scallions crosswise into thin slices, using all of the green part as well. You should have about ⅔ cup.

3. Combine the radishes, scallions, chicken fat, vinegar, salt, pepper, and sugar or honey in a medium bowl and toss gently. Refrigerate for ½ hour to meld flavors.

4. Meanwhile cut thin pumpernickel slices in half on the diagonal or cut wedges from the pitas. Lightly toast the breads so that they are slightly crisp.

5. When ready to serve, spread a little bit of additional chicken fat on the tops of the bread triangles, and place a small mound of radish salad on the tops of the toasts. Sprinkle the tops of each radish mound with a pinch of coarse sea salt, if desired.

   Alternatively, place a few lettuce leaves on a salad plate, and mound some of the radish salad on the lettuce. Place a few triangles of bread on the side and serve.

Note: If you prefer, fragrant extra virgin olive oil may be substituted for the chicken fat.

Yield: 24 canapés or 6–8 servings

TINA'S TIDBITS

- *Red radishes tend to bleed their color when exposed to acidic foods for long periods of time. Either add vinegar an hour before serving or serve the same day as preparation.*
- *Spreading a thin layer of oil or fat on a bread base prevents the bread from getting soggy, especially when covered with a moist filling.*

Frituras de Malanga (Taro Root Fritters)

A few years ago I went on a humanitarian medical mission to Cuba. We made a trip to the central synagogue of Havana, the Patronato, where I met some of the staff. It was here and on our mission to other cities where the small Jewish populations live that I learned some of their simple ways of cooking for Shabbat and some of the holidays.

Malanga, or taro root, has very little flavor and is very light and crisp when fried. This is how Tanya at the Patronato taught me to make them.

2 medium malanga, about 1 pound
1 small onion
1 teaspoon white or apple cider vinegar
1½ teaspoons salt
1 egg

1 tablespoon finely chopped parsley (optional in Cuba, but a nice addition)
Freshly ground black pepper (optional in Cuba, but a nice addition)
Vegetable oil for frying

1. Peel the malanga. Grate the malanga using the finest grating disk on your processor. Grate the onion in the same way. Replace the grating disk with the steel blade and pulse on and off about 20 times, until the pieces of food are quite small but not a mush. Transfer to a bowl. **Alternatively**, grate the malanga and onion on the fine side of a grater and place in a bowl.

2. Add the remaining ingredients **except** the oil and mix well.

3. Heat about 1 inch of oil in a frying pan or deep fryer until very hot, about 375°F.

4. Drop the mixture by teaspoon into the hot oil. Fry until golden on each side.

5. Drain on paper towel.

6. Serve immediately with *mojo* sauce (see recipe on the following page), sour cream, and applesauce, or purchased salsa.

Yield: 6–8 servings

TINA'S TIDBITS

- *The addition of a small amount of vinegar prevents the fried food from absorbing excess oil.*
- *For a crispy coating, use this malanga mixture on floured fish before frying.*
- *Garlic should never be allowed to brown, as it becomes very bitter.*
- *Crumble paper towels to have more surface area to absorb oil from fried foods.*

Mojo Sauce

Sour orange juice is a common ingredient in Cuba, confirming its roots in Spanish and possibly Jewish cooking. The ubiquitous orange trees in Andalusia are not the sweet variety that we associate with Valencia, and these oranges must have been brought to this region with the Spanish conquistadores.

¼ cup olive oil
6 large cloves garlic, finely minced
½ cup sour orange juice or ¼ cup orange juice and
   ¼ cup lime juice

½ teaspoon ground cumin
Salt and freshly ground black pepper to taste

1. Heat a 1-quart saucepan for 20 seconds. Add the olive oil and heat for 10 seconds over medium heat.

2. Add the garlic and cook for 20 seconds or until it just starts to get lightly golden. Do **not** let the garlic brown or the sauce will be bitter.

3. Add the remaining ingredients; be careful, as the sauce may steam. Bring to a rolling boil and cook for 3 minutes. Remove from heat, adjust the seasonings if necessary, and chill until ready to serve with the fritters or on top of vegetables, meats, or fish.

Yield: 6 servings

LATKES
(POTATO PANCAKES)

Latkes are traditionally served for Chanukah because they are cooked in oil (to commemorate the vial of oil lasting for 8 days). However, since they are pareve when served without sour cream, they are also a perfect accompaniment to a beef or chicken entrée. For an elegant appetizer, prepare as small rounds and top with sour cream and caviar.

6–8 large thin-skinned potatoes, California long whites or Yukon Gold
3 eggs, beaten well
1 tablespoon salt
½ teaspoon freshly ground pepper

½ cup matzah meal or cracker meal
1 large onion, cut into 8 pieces
Oil for frying
Applesauce (optional)
Sour cream (optional)

1. Grate the raw potatoes using the large grating disk on a processor or the largest holes on a grater if doing it by hand. Place the grated potato in a colander, rinse with cold water. Set aside to drain.

2. Combine eggs, salt, pepper, and matzah meal or cracker meal in a 3-quart bowl. Mix thoroughly.

3. Change to the cutting blade on your processor. Add the onions to the work bowl. Pulse on and off 5 times. Add ¼ of the grated potatoes to the onion and pulse on and off to make a coarse paste. Add to the egg mixture and stir to combine.

4. Add the drained potatoes to the bowl and mix thoroughly, using a large spoon or your hands.

5. Heat a large frying pan or large skillet for 20 seconds. Add enough oil to cover the pan to a depth of ¼ inch and heat for an additional 10 seconds. Drop mounds of potato mixture into the pan. Fry on both sides until golden. Drain the fried latkes on a platter covered with crumpled paper towels. Serve with applesauce and sour cream.

Yield: 2–4 dozen depending on size

TINA'S TIDBITS:

- *Grated potatoes turn black when exposed to air. Rinsing the potatoes under running water washes away excess starch, the discoloring culprit.*
- *Always grate the potatoes separately from the onions so that you don't lose any of the flavorful onion juice when you drain the potatoes.*
- *The best way to drain fried foods is on a plate covered with crumpled paper towels. Crumpling them yields more surface area for absorption.*

LEMON RICOTTA PANCAKES

In deference to the heroine Judith, who saved the Jews from annihilation by feeding salty cheese and wine to General Holofernes, getting him drunk enough so she could behead him and scare off his troops, I have created this updated version of classic kaese latkes. *A delicious treat all year long, not just for Chanukah.*

1 tablespoon unsalted butter
1 cup whole milk ricotta
2 eggs
2 tablespoons light brown sugar
Zest of $\frac{1}{2}$ medium lemon, finely minced
$\frac{1}{2}$ teaspoon vanilla extract

$\frac{1}{8}$ teaspoon ground nutmeg
$\frac{1}{4}$ teaspoon salt
2 tablespoons whole-wheat flour
2 tablespoons all-purpose flour
Unsalted butter for frying

1. Place the 1 tablespoon of butter in a 1$\frac{1}{2}$-quart glass bowl and microwave on high for 40 seconds or until the butter is melted.

2. Add the ricotta and eggs and mix well with a whisk to thoroughly combine.

3. Add the brown sugar, lemon zest, vanilla, nutmeg, salt, and the two flours and stir well.

4. Heat a griddle over medium-high heat and rub the end of a stick of butter all over the surface of the pan to coat it well.

5. Drop heaping tablespoons of batter onto the griddle and cook for 3 minutes or until the underside of the pancake is golden brown and the top is slightly dry.

6. Gently flip the pancakes over (it might be easier to use 2 small spatulas to do this), and cook for another 2 minutes until the edges are barely crisp and both sides are golden brown.

7. Serve drizzled with additional melted butter, honey, or a dollop of sour cream, if desired.

Note: Recipe may be doubled if desired.

Yield: About 20 silver-dollar-sized pancakes, 4–6 servings

TINA'S TIDBITS

- *These pancakes are as light as air and delicate, so turning is best achieved using two spatulas, one in each hand, to evenly brown both sides.*
- *Whole-wheat flour contains more gluten than white flour, so less is needed in delicate foods to bind ingredients together.*
- *A rasp-type grater is perfect for creating fine shards of lemon zest that will flavor the batter evenly without any bitter white pith from the inner peel.*

STUFFED KIBBEH

Kibbeh is a popular national dish of Syria, Lebanon, Jordan, and Iraq. Kurdish Jews call this dish kubba, *and in Egypt it is called* kobeba. *A woman was judged on her prowess in forming the kibbeh into long, torpedo-shaped, shelled dumplings. If a baby girl was born with a long finger, she was considered blessed. Making the crust is much easier now that a food processor can be used to make the paste. However, all the hard work of pounding the bulgur with the meat and shaping the crust into a thin shell to be stuffed has been alleviated by the more modern technique of layering the cooked filling in between the crust layers and baking the entire kibbeh instead of frying individual pieces. As a result, this dish can be made by hand without the use of electrical equipment.*

In the Middle East, dishes made with bulgur always graced the Chanukah table.

CRUST:
1¼ cups bulgur
2 cups water
1 cup coarsely chopped onion (about one 3-inch onion)
1 pound ground beef or lamb
½ teaspoon salt
10 grindings of black pepper
1 teaspoon cinnamon

FILLING:
2 tablespoons extra virgin olive oil
2 cups finely chopped onion (about ½ of large sweet onion)
¼ cup pine nuts
½ pound ground beef or lamb
½ teaspoon salt or to taste
12 grindings of black pepper
¼ teaspoon allspice
½ teaspoon cinnamon
1–2 tablespoons extra virgin olive oil for coating

1. To make the crust, combine bulgur and water in a 1-quart glass bowl and microwave on high for 2 minutes. Let the bulgur soak for 10–15 minutes. Drain in a mesh sieve, pressing out most of the liquid. Set aside.

2. Place the 1 cup of onion in a processor work bowl with the metal blade and pulse the machine to chop the onion fine.

3. Add the rest of the crust ingredients (meat, salt, pepper, and cinnamon) and turn the machine on for 10 seconds to form a paste. Add the drained bulgur and process until a smooth paste is formed.

4. Spread half of this meat mixture ½ inch thick over the bottom and up the sides of a 10-inch glass pie plate. Set aside while you make the filling.

5. Heat a 10-inch sauté pan on high for 20 seconds. Add the olive oil and heat for another 10 seconds. Reduce the heat to medium high and add the finely chopped onions. Sauté the onions until they are soft and lightly golden.

6. Add the pine nuts and sauté until they are lightly golden.

7. Add the meat to the pan along with the remaining filling ingredients. Break the meat up with a fork or the back of a large spoon. Cook the meat until it loses its pink color, but do not overcook or the meat will be tough and rubbery.

8. When the mixture is cooked, pour into the center of the meat shell.

9. Wet your hands with cold water and gently spread the remainder of the crust meat mixture smoothly over the top, covering the filling completely.

10. Spread 1–2 tablespoons of olive oil over the top of the kibbeh. With the tip of a sharp knife, lightly score the meat on the diagonal every $1\frac{1}{2}$ inches to create a diamond pattern.

11. Place in a 400°F oven and bake for 30–35 minutes, until the top is golden brown and slightly crisp.

12. Cut the kibbeh in wedges and serve as a main course, or cut along the scored lines and serve little diamonds as an appetizer.

Yield: 4–6 servings

TINA'S TIDBITS

- *A food processor is not necessary to make this recipe if fine bulgur is used and you chop the onion very small.*
- *Bulgur is wheat that has been steamed, dried, and crushed. It comes in coarse, medium, and fine grain. If you are not using a processor, make sure you use medium- or fine-grain bulgur.*
- *Bulgur (or bulghur) should not be confused with cracked wheat, which has not been previously treated.*

Moroccan Sweet Couscous with Mixed Dried Fruits

This dish is now a staple on my buffet table for all fall Jewish holidays, since I like to incorporate a new fruit (pomegranate) or fall fruits (raisins, apples, pears in their dried form) for Rosh HaShanah and Sukkot. In reality, this traditional Moroccan dish is served for Chanukah, but I can't relegate it to just that one holiday. I have streamlined the preparation time by using dried fruit that is already chopped, and you can use any combination of dried fruit that you want. This is a very kid-friendly recipe and a great way to get those iron-packed fruits into their diet.

1 cup Israeli couscous
2 tablespoons unsalted butter or pareve margarine
¼ cup sugar
½ teaspoon cinnamon
One 7-ounce package of chopped mixed dried fruit
or 1½ cups assorted dried fruits

⅓ cup whole almonds, roasted and coarsely chopped
2 tablespoons pine nuts, lightly roasted
⅓ cup milk with 3 drops of almond extract added
Cinnamon, pitted Medjool dates, pomegranate seeds, and/or apricot slivers for garnish

1. Cook couscous in a large pot of boiling salted water for 7 to 10 minutes or until tender but still firm. Drain, but do not rinse, and place in a large mixing bowl.

2. Melt the butter or margarine in a 1-cup bowl in the microwave for 35 seconds. Add the sugar and cinnamon and stir to combine. Pour the mixture over the couscous to coat thoroughly.

3. Add the dried fruit and roasted nuts.

4. Mix the 3 drops of almond extract into the milk. Add just enough of the milk to the couscous to moisten it. Do not add too much or the mixture will be runny. Reserve excess milk in case the couscous is dry. Remoisten before you garnish.

5. Pile the couscous into a mound or pyramid shape on a serving platter. Sprinkle with additional cinnamon and garnish with Medjool date halves, pomegranate seeds, and/or apricot slivers.

Yield: 10 or more servings as part of a holiday buffet

TINA'S TIDBITS

- *Israeli couscous is a large, milled ball of pasta approximately 1/8 inch in diameter.*
- *Coating couscous with butter or margarine prevents the mixture from clumping. However, it still holds together beautifully when mounded.*
- *Made with wheat berries, this dish is Greek koliva, and Sephardim serve this tooth-resembling grain to celebrate a baby's first tooth.*

DUTCH HUTSPOT

History often gets transformed into a culinary creation and people often use a recipe to symbolize a part of that historical event. Although all countries have a favorite fried recipe for Chanukah, Dutch Jews also serve this rich mixture of vegetables at Chanukah to recount a Dutch tale. During the Spanish siege of Leyden in 1574, the Dutch made a surprise attack on the Spanish camps at dinnertime, and the soldiers were forced to flee, leaving their simmering pots of stewed vegetables and meat behind. This stew is symbolic of that siege and its parallel to the Maccabean fight.

1 tablespoon rendered chicken fat or vegetable oil
2 medium-large onions, diced
3 large Yukon Gold or California white potatoes, peeled and cut into eighths
2 large carrots, peeled and cut into eighths
2 cups water or chicken broth

Salt and freshly ground black pepper to taste
Additional tablespoon chicken fat (optional)
Cayenne pepper (optional)
1 garlic-flavored Polish sausage or knockwurst, finely diced (optional)

1. Heat a 3-quart saucepan over high heat for 20 seconds. Add the chicken fat or oil and heat for 10 seconds. Add the onions and sauté for 5 minutes or until golden brown but not dark.

2. Add the potato chunks and carrots to the saucepan. Add the water or broth, which should not cover the vegetables more than halfway.

3. Bring the vegetable mixture to a boil, and then cover and reduce the heat to a simmer. Cook the vegetables until they are very tender.

4. Remove the pan from the heat and carefully drain the liquid from the pot. Reserve the liquid for another use, if desired.

5. Mash the drained vegetables until they form a fairly smooth mass. (Carrots and onions may be pureed in a processor, but mash the potatoes by hand—do **not** use a processor for the potatoes.) If the mixture appears too watery, return it to the stove and cook over moderate heat until the excess moisture evaporates. Stir occasionally to prevent scorching.

6. Add seasonings and an additional tablespoon of chicken fat if desired. Stir to combine. Add the diced sausage, if using. Reheat just before serving.

Yield: 1½ quarts or 8 or more servings

TINA'S TIDBITS

- *Never use a processor to mash white potatoes. You will always get a consistency akin to wallpaper paste if you do!*
- *Yukon Gold and California whites are more dense varieties of potato that create a creamier consistency and less water in the finished mash. They are also thin-skinned and do not require peeling unless specifically called for in a recipe.*
- *Browning onions caramelizes the natural sugars in the onion and brings out the sweetness that enhances most dishes.*

Frittelle di Riso (Italian Rice Pancakes)

According to the Italian Jewish culinary authority Edda Servi Machlin, these rice pancakes are traditionally served for Chanukah. I have adapted her recipe so that the pancakes are not saturated in oil and the use of eggs is decreased. I have also roasted the nuts first to enhance their flavor and crispness.

Served with cinnamon and sugar or honey, these frittelle *make a very acceptable dessert or breakfast. However, because they are pareve, they would make a welcome side dish to any main course. Recipes that call for raisins and pine nuts in Italian cuisine strongly suggest the influence of the Jewish émigrés from Spain in the fifteenth century.*

1 cup arborio rice
2¼ cups water
1 teaspoon salt
½ cup slivered almonds or pine nuts
1 cup dark raisins

Finely grated zest of 1 lemon
4 large eggs or 2 whole eggs and 3 egg whites
3–5 tablespoons extra virgin olive oil
¼ cup sugar mixed with 1 teaspoon cinnamon or honey (optional)

1. Place the rice, water, and salt in a 2-quart saucepan and bring to a boil. Cover the pan and lower the heat. Simmer for 20–25 minutes, until the water is absorbed.

2. Roast the nuts on a cookie sheet in a 350°F oven for 5 minutes or until lightly golden.

3. Add the nuts, raisins, and lemon zest to the rice and stir well to combine. Let the mixture sit for 20 minutes to cool.

4. Lightly beat the eggs in a bowl and add them to the rice mixture.

5. Heat a large, nonstick frying pan over high heat for 20 seconds. Add 3 tablespoons of olive oil and heat for 15 seconds. Reduce the heat if the oil begins to smoke.

6. Drop about 2 tablespoons of the mixture into the hot pan. Repeat with more rice mixture until the pan is full but not crowded.

7. Cook the pancakes on one side for 3 minutes or until golden. Flip them over and cook for another 2 minutes or until crisp and golden. Transfer the pancakes to a pan lined with paper towels.

8. Add additional tablespoons of oil to the pan as needed, and make the remaining pancakes.

9. Serve the pancakes immediately with the optional cinnamon and sugar or honey.

Yield: 24 pancakes

TINA'S TIDBITS

- *Converted rice or "minute" rice cannot be used in recipes that require the mixture to bind together, because they do not contain enough starch.*
- *Arborio rice is a short-grain, highly starchy rice. When not available, any short- or medium-grain rice that has not been polished will suffice as a good substitute.*

Halvah de Semola
(Sephardi Semolina Pudding)

Halvah refers to any Middle Eastern or Asian sweet that is made with sweetened cooked grain. Originally a staple of the Sephardic repertoire, halvah gained popularity in this country in the Ashkenazic community as a confection made from ground sesame seeds and sugar. Even the comprehensive Food Lover's Companion *dictionary defines halvah as a sesame seed treat. This recipe is actually much easier to make and is probably the ultimate Sephardic comfort food. This recipe is served for Chanukah by Bulgarian Jews and is a nice alternative to fried pastries.*

1 stick unsalted butter
1½ cups semolina (or cream of wheat cereal), *not* semolina flour
3 cups water
1 cup granulated sugar (honey may be substituted, although not traditional)

1 teaspoon vanilla extract
½ cup finely chopped walnuts (chopped finely, but *not* a paste)
Cinnamon for sprinkling on top (optional)

1. Melt the butter in a 2-quart saucepan over moderate heat.

2. Add the semolina and stir to completely coat the grains of wheat with the butter.

3. Continue to cook and stir the semolina until the mixture is light brown, about 10 minutes.

4. Meanwhile, combine the water and sugar in a small saucepan and bring to a boil. Boil for 3 minutes.

5. Stir the semolina mixture constantly while you carefully pour the boiling syrup into the pot. Avoid burning yourself with the spattering liquid.

6. Remove the pan from the stove and continue to stir for about 4 minutes until the mixture becomes thick.

7. Gently stir in the vanilla and the finely chopped walnuts until well combined.

TINA'S TIDBITS

- *Cream of wheat is a good substitute for semolina but will not create as fine a grain as semolina.*
- *For a more Middle Eastern flavor, substitute 1 1/2 teaspoons rose water for the vanilla, and add 1/2 teaspoon ground cardamom. Finely ground pistachios may be added to the mixture instead of the walnuts.*
- *For a more Indian influence, add the zest of 1/2 orange to the hot sugar syrup, and substitute 1/4 cup raisins and 1/4 cup grated coconut for the walnuts.*

8. Cover the pot with a double layer of dishtowel and let the mixture set for about 30 minutes or until thick and all the moisture has been absorbed.

9. Lightly butter an 11 × 7-inch glass casserole or six to eight 4-ounce ramekins. Stir the mixture one more time and spread the semolina mixture evenly in the chosen container, smoothing out the top.

Sprinkle with cinnamon. Let mixture set for $\frac{1}{2}$ hour or chill. Cut into diamond shapes and serve warm or at room temperature.

Note: If using ramekins, chill and then unmold before you sprinkle with some cinnamon.

Yield: 2–3 dozen pieces

TU BISH'VAT

For the Eternal your God is bringing you into a good land,
a land with streams and springs and fountains issuing from plain and hill;
a land of wheat and barley, of vines, figs, and pomegranates,
a land of olive trees and honey.

DEUTERONOMY 8:7–8

*T*u BiSh'vat, the fifteenth of Sh'vat, is the celebration of the Jewish new year for trees. The holiday occurs in late January or early February, four months after the holiday of Sukkot. Sukkot marks the beginning of the rainy season in the Land of Israel, and after four months, the rain-soaked ground is ready to support the young roots of trees to help them flourish in the parched Israeli desert.

Originally a celebration coinciding with the tithing of agricultural products, in Talmudic times Tu BiSh'vat became a minor holiday celebrating God's blessings on the community and its fields. A quick look at the Jewish calendar and you can see that major holidays center around the agricultural harvests. Pesach coincided with the barley harvest, wheat and the first fruits and vegetables were harvested at the time of Shavuot, and on Sukkot we celebrate the final wheat, grape, and vegetable harvests of the year.

Sixteenth-century kabbalists instituted the custom of having a Tu BiSh'vat seder, similar to a Passover seder. This seder had no specific order but included the blessing and enjoyment of at least the seven species of agricultural products listed in the Bible. In modern times, with Jews dispersed throughout the world, it is a celebration of our connection to the actual Land of Israel; congregations encourage families to plant trees in Israel through the Jewish National Fund, and many fruits and grains indigenous to the region are eaten as part of the celebration. As a child, I remember being given a piece of *bokser*, or carob, to chew on. In this country, we mainly consider carob a healthy substitute for chocolate. However, in ancient times, exiles of the region would take carob with them because it was one of the few agricultural products from Israel that could survive the long voyage to a foreign land.

On Tu BiSh'vat it is customary to eat foods containing the seven species and to bless them. These are wheat, barley, grapes, figs, pomegranates, dates, and olives. Although not mentioned in Deuteronomy, almonds also figure prominently in this celebration, as they are the first tree to flower in Israel at that time of year.

✎ ALMONDS ✎

Their father Israel said to them,
". . . Take from among the land's choice products in your bags,
and bring the man [Joseph] an offering—
a bit of balm, a bit of honey, some laudanum,
mastic, pistachios, and almonds."

GENESIS 43:11

Almonds are seeds of the fruit *Prunus dulcis*, which is an inedible fruit closely related to peaches and plums. Almond trees resemble peach trees, but their fruit cracks open, revealing the seed (or nut) when it is ripe.

There are two kinds of almonds—sweet, the almond we commonly eat, and bitter. The bitter almond contains poisonous prussic acid and must be roasted to be consumed as a nut. In small amounts this bitter almond was used for medicinal purposes and as a flavoring agent. Our modern almond extract is a mixture of bitter almond oil, water, and alcohol.

Almonds are considered to be the oldest cultivated nut, dating back ten thousand years. Some feel that the first documentation of almond cultivation was in the Torah, Numbers 17:23: "There the staff of Aaron of the house of Levi had sprouted: it had brought forth sprouts, produced blossoms, and borne almonds." Almonds and pistachios are the only nuts cited in the entire Torah.

The almond originated in the mountains of western China and was brought along the Silk Road to be cultivated in western Asia, Greece, Turkey, and ancient Persia. Its popularity extended to Rome, where it was often served sugar-coated at festivities. These sugared nuts were considered to be one of the first sweetmeats, or desserts, in history. Almonds were seen as a sign of fertility, probably because they were the first tree in the Mediterranean region to flower each spring. Roman and then European tradition included serving almonds to wedding guests and/or throwing almonds at newlyweds to wish them fecundity.

The route of the almond mirrored, in many ways, the route of the olive and grape. From the Middle East, almond production eventually centered in Italy and Spain. Conquistadors from Spain brought the trees to the New World, and Franciscan monks planted almond trees around their missions up the Pacific coast of California. Today, California is the only state in the union to produce almonds on a commercial scale.

Spanish Jews first introduced the use of almond meal, or finely ground almonds in cakes such as *pan d'Espanya*, a technique used especially at Passover. In Toledo, where there was a large Jewish population, it was the Jewish confectioners who perfected the art of making marzipan, a mixture of almond paste and sugar, bitter almond, and sometimes egg white.

ᦄ FIGS ᦄ

Then the eyes of both of them were opened,
and, realizing that they were naked,
they sewed fig leaves together
and made themselves skirts.

GENESIS 3:7

Figs were one of the first fruits to be cultivated over five thousand years ago. Grown predominantly in the Arabian Peninsula and the Mediterranean, they were brought to Northern Europe in the early sixteenth century and to Mexico by Cortez at approximately the same time. Franciscan monks introduced the fig throughout the California missions, and that variety of fig came to be known as the mission fig.

Figs are mentioned in Genesis 3:7, as the first addition to Adam and Eve's wardrobe. The fig appears often in the Bible and was revered by many cultures and religions. The founders of Rome, Romulus and Remus, were said to be nurtured by the she-wolf under a fig tree, which was later declared a sacred tree. Arabs regarded figs as their most esteemed fruit. Athenians, who were enamored of figs, were dubbed sycophants (*syke* means "fig eaters"). This word took on a new meaning after some Athenians informed

authorities about illegal fig exportation in order to gain favor with the leaders of the community. Next to wine and olive oil, figs were the most important crop of Greece.

Figs were primarily eaten when they were succulent and fresh. However, the best-quality figs were also dried individually or strung on thread. Lesser-quality figs were also mashed into cakes, which became invaluable during long winters or long sieges. Remnants of first-century fig cake were found in the storehouses on top of Masada, the last remaining Jewish stronghold against the Roman invasion in 73 C.E.

Aside from their nutritive value and wonderful flavor, figs were purported to have medicinal powers as well. In II Kings 20:7, the prophet Isaiah healed Hezekiah by telling his aides, "'Get a cake of figs.' And they got one, and they applied it to the rash, and he recovered." Evidently, there is historical evidence that using fig paste as a poultice was an ancient

Assyrian practice. Pliny of Rome, in the first century C.E., thought that figs were restorative and suggested that people who were suffering from long illness would recover if they ate figs. He also said that figs would "preserve the elderly in better health and make them look younger with fewer wrinkles." Does that mean they should eat them or put cakes on their faces, like Hezekiah?

Although figs were popular with the Greeks and Romans, it was the Arabs' cultivation of the trees and irrigation skills that produced superior figs in the lands they inhabited.

Figs ripen between July and September. They should be purchased when firm but have some give to them when pressed. Varieties of figs can range in color from green to brown to mottled purple. If a fig is hard and green, it is immature, regardless of the variety. Figs can be eaten raw (skin and all), poached, stewed, dried, pureed, used for jam, or made into a strong beerlike drink.

ᐱᐁ GRAPES AND WINE ᐁᐱ

The fig tree has put forth its green figs,
and the vines with their tiny grapes have given forth their fragrance;
arise, my beloved, my fair one, and come away.

SONG OF SONGS 2:13

Grapes are mentioned throughout the Torah as one of the symbols, along with olives and figs, of the fertility of God's Promised Land to the Israelites. The first mention of grapes, and their by-product, wine, takes place in Genesis 9:20–21, which records Noah's planting of the first vineyard and his subsequent drunken state. The more beautiful references to grapes, however, appear in Solomon's moving verses in Song of Songs.

Wine was used as a drink offering in the Temple, and in Exodus 29:40–41 specifics are given for the quantity and frequency of its use during the consecration of Aaron and the priests.

In order for a wine to be considered kosher, only Jewish hands could be involved in the planting, cultivating, and pressing of the grapes for the purpose of producing wines. These laws stem from the reality that in ancient biblical times wine was used in many pagan rituals and was a product of idolatry. The only way to guarantee that the wine hadn't been prepared for less honorable use than as a drink offering in the Temple was to have every aspect of its production supervised by a rabbi and Sabbath-observant Jewish workers.

There are two types of kosher wine, non-*mevushal*, which is the wine described above, and *mevushal*, which are kosher wines that go through an extra process of flash pasteurization. This process subjects the wine to very high heat for a few seconds—it is not boiled, as often thought—and renders the wine unfit for idolatrous worship. Today this technique allows the wine to be certified kosher even when served at a banquet by non-Jewish servers, which conforms to the needs of the Orthodox community.

Because Jews were generally not allowed to own their own land and were often uprooted from their homes with little notice, wine production has taken on different definitions in different parts of the world. Raisins and other fruits and vegetation helped create many ceremonial kosher wines. Necessity was the mother of invention.

Many people think that kosher wine is synonymous with the very sweet Concord grape wine produced in upstate New York. Of course, nowadays this isn't the only source of kosher wine, and many grape varietals are used to produce excellent drinking wines. However, when Jewish émigrés came to this country in the mid-1800s, they needed to make ritual wine, and the only grapes available were the big, plump grapes growing near Concord, Massachusetts. When the grapes produced extremely bitter wine, our resourceful ancestors added sugar to the liquid and a new Passover icon was born!

Jewish tradition and custom mandate the ceremonial and medicinal drinking of wine, and on Purim we are commanded to imbibe enough wine so that we get confused between the names of Haman and Mordecai. What you will not find amid Jewish customs is traditional Jewish food preparation containing wine (other than *charoset*). This practice is not prohibited, it just wasn't done. Until now . . .

⁓ POMEGRANATES ⁓

On the hem of the robe they made pomegranates
of blue, purple, and crimson yarns, twisted.
They also made bells of pure gold,
and attached the bells between the pomegranates,
all around the hem of the robe, between the pomegranates.

EXODUS 39:24–25

Pomegranates have been around the Middle East and the Mediterranean region for thousands of years. King Solomon cultivated large groves of pomegranates and likened the beauty of his love to the fruit in his sensual Song of Songs.

The beauty of the fruit inspired the use of its design in the High Priests' robes as well as the columns in the holy Temple. Muslims called it the "fruit of paradise" in the Koran. The Moors were so enamored of the fruit that they renamed their fortress city in Andalusia Granada (Spanish for "pomegranate"). The Spanish missionaries brought pomegranates as well as figs and almonds to the missions of California and its central valley.

The pomegranate is traditionally eaten on the second night of Rosh HaShanah as a symbol of the new fruit of the season. Sephardim connect the supposed 613 seeds that are found in a pomegranate to the 613 mitzvot we are to fulfill every day.

When buying a pomegranate, look for a bright red or pink fruit with firm shiny skin that feels dense for its size.

Although Cleopatra was purported to use the juice of the pomegranate as "lipstick," the fruit's ability to stain often becomes a culinary liability. Separating the seeds from the inedible white pith in a bowl, under water, is the best way to seed a pomegranate without turning your fingers red. The seeds sink to the bottom of the bowl, and any loose pith floats to the surface, making it very easy to remove. Pomegranate seeds are used to garnish dishes, the juice is used in sauces, and a concentrate of the juice, often referred to as pomegranate molasses, is used in marinades and sauces that require a tart-sweet component.

∽ DATES ∾

The date palm is thought to have originally grown in the Persian Gulf region, and in biblical times it was growing densely in the areas around the Nile River in Egypt and the Euphrates River in Mesopotamia. The earliest records of its presence in the Land of Israel were found near the site of Jericho.

The migration of the date plant can be traced to the nomads who planted saplings whenever they came to an oasis. The Moors brought the date palm to Spain when they came from North Africa in the eighth century.

The date got its name from the Greek *daktulos*, "fingers," because the growth of dates on the tree resembles a cluster of fingers.

The date palm is important to Jewish tradition as well as to everyday life in the countries where it is grown. The fronds of the tree are used as part of the *lulav* during Sukkot, and syrup made from crushed and boiled dates is considered the "honey" referred to in Leviticus 20:24, "a land flowing with milk and honey." The fronds were also used for thatching, and the bark was used for its fibers to make ropes and baskets. Pakistani syrup made from ripe dates is used to make a viscous coating for pipes to prevent leaks. This is not to be confused with delicious *halek* or *hullake*, date syrup made in India or the Middle East, which is used as a sweetener or as a base for *charoset* during Passover.

Prior to the 1991 war, Iraq was the number one producer of dates in the world, growing over twenty-two million date palms and exporting over six hundred thousand tons of dates annually. Dates also come from other countries in the Middle East and are grown very successfully in the Central Valley of California.

Rarely can you buy a fresh date in North America. The first time I ate a fresh date was in Israel. Its consistency was reminiscent of a ripe plum, and it was not as sweet as the dried, but plump Medjool date I was used to in the United States. When buying dried dates, look for dates that are slightly wrinkled but not hard. The drier the date, the sweeter it will be because of the concentration of sugar. I prefer to buy pitted whole dates and chop them myself to avoid the excessive sugar that commercially chopped dates contain.

WHEAT AND BARLEY

Wheat and barley have been growing in the Land of Israel for thousands of years. Barley is indigenous to this region. The original wild strains of wheat were very hard and difficult to grind. The grains were consumed at every meal but rarely in the form of bread; the production of flour, being very laborious, required hours of pounding, grinding, and sifting. Any bread made from this grain was dense and dark, and all were produced without using yeast. The bread of display brought to the Temple was more like pita bread than like our modern-day challah. Lighter loaves were produced when more tender strains of wheat, higher in gluten and easier to mill, were cultivated, and yeast—developed by the Egyptians—was incorporated into the dough.

In biblical times, most grains were heartily consumed in the form of porridges, pilafs, soups, salads, and even beverages. Today whole barley is regaining its popularity on the dinner table, but the major portion of the modern barley crop is used for making beer.

Stir-Fried Chicken in Hoisin Sauce

Not what you might expect in this book except that Jews have had a presence in China and Asia for over one thousand years. Although not exactly a traditional Jewish food, this dish can be an unexpected way to bring almonds to your Tu BiSh'vat table.

1 pound boneless chicken breast
1 tablespoon cornstarch
1 tablespoon cream sherry
1 tablespoon soy sauce
4 tablespoons oil, divided use
1 medium green pepper, cut into $\frac{1}{2}$-inch cubes

8 water chestnuts, cut into quarters
$\frac{1}{4}$ pound fresh mushrooms, cut into $\frac{1}{2}$-inch cubes
Salt to taste
3 tablespoons hoisin sauce
$\frac{1}{4}$ cup whole almonds, roasted

1. Cut chicken into $\frac{1}{2}$-inch cubes.

2. Place chicken in a large bowl and sprinkle with cornstarch. Toss lightly to coat evenly. Pour in the sherry and soy sauce, and toss again to coat well.

3. Place all of the ingredients within easy reach.

4. Set a 12-inch wok or 10-inch skillet over high heat for 20 seconds. Pour 1 tablespoon of the oil, swirl it about in the pan, and heat for another 10 seconds, turning the heat down to moderate if the oil begins to smoke.

5. Immediately add the green peppers, water chestnuts, mushrooms, and salt, and stir-fry briskly for 2–3 minutes.

6. Scoop out the vegetables with a slotted spoon and set them on a plate.

7. Pour the remaining 3 tablespoons of oil into the pan, heat almost to the smoking point, and drop in the marinated chicken. Stir-fry over high heat for 2–3 minutes until the chicken turns white and firm.

8. Add the hoisin sauce, stir well with the chicken, and add the reserved vegetables. Cook for 1 minute.

9. Add the almonds. Stir to heat them through, transfer the contents of the wok to a heated platter, and serve at once.

Yield: 4 servings

TINA'S TIDBITS

- *When stir-frying in a wok, cut all the foods in similar shapes and sizes to facilitate the cooking process.*
- *Vegetables are often cooked separately from meat in stir-frying, because they require a different amount of time to cook. The separation of foods also ensures that the flavor of the vegetables will be distinct from the flavor of the meat, imparting layers of flavors to the dish.*
- *Because every soy sauce has its own level of saltiness, use caution when adding salt to this dish.*

MINIATURE CHOCOLATE ALMOND TORTES

I first saw this recipe in Claudia Roden's The Book of Jewish Food. *I realized that it could be made for Passover, and garnishing it with a ganache rose would make it extra special for Tu BiSh'vat or any festive occasion.*

1 cup slivered almonds
7 ounces high-quality bittersweet chocolate
3 eggs

½ cup sugar
2 tablespoons brandy, rum, or Jack Daniels (optional)
1 recipe chocolate ganache (see the following page)

1. Roast the almonds in a 350°F oven until lightly golden. Do not burn. Let cool.

2. Break the chocolate into little squares and place in a processor work bowl fitted with the metal blade. Pulse on and off until the chocolate is in small pieces.

3. Add the roasted almonds and pulse on and off to grind the almonds and soften the chocolate. Add the remaining ingredients to the processor and process until the mixture becomes a slightly coarse but thick and creamy paste. You might need to stop the machine periodically and scrape the sides of the bowl.

4. Place a heaping tablespoon of batter into mini muffin paper cups and bake in a 350°F oven for 8–10 minutes or until firm but still very moist.

5. Remove from mini muffin pans or turn them on their sides until cool. These tortes store very well in an airtight container for 4–6 days.

Note: Mixture may be poured into a greased 8-inch springform pan and baked for 18 minutes or until a toothpick comes out clean when poked into the center of the cake.
Yield: 18–24 pieces

TINA'S TIDBITS

- *Slivered almonds are the little sticks of blanched (all white, no skin) almonds.*
- *Sliced almonds are flat slices of almond with brown skin attached around the edges.*
- *Scalding means the milk product begins to bubble around the edges and/or a thin skin forms on the top of the simmering liquid, which can easily be removed if needed.*

Quick Chocolate Ganache for Frosting or Rosettes

Two 3-ounce bars of high-quality bittersweet chocolate (or 5 ounces semisweet chocolate chips and 1 ounce unsweetened baking chocolate)

¾ cup heavy cream or soy creamer
1 tablespoon brandy or flavored liquor

1. Break the bars of chocolate into small squares and place in a processor work bowl. Process until the chocolate is fairly fine.

2. Heat the cream in a microwave oven until it is scalded. Add it to the running processor until all of the chocolate is melted and a smooth paste is formed.

3. Transfer the ganache to a bowl, and when cool, add the liquor. Chill until the consistency is firm but spreadable.

4. Using a pastry bag and star tip, pipe a rosette of ganache on top of each cake or spoon some of the ganache on top. Chill until ready to serve.

TUSCAN BISCOTTI

If this recipe looks similar to mandelbrodt, *it could be the coincidence that Jews were sea traders, and sea traders took these hard, dry biscuits on board their ships for long voyages, knowing they would remain edible for months.*

$3\frac{1}{2}$ **cups flour**
3 tablespoons cornstarch
1 teaspoon baking powder
$\frac{1}{4}$ **teaspoon baking soda**
$\frac{1}{2}$ **teaspoon salt**
$\frac{1}{3}$ **cup finely ground almonds**
1 cup sugar
1 cup vegetable oil, preferably corn oil

3 eggs
Zest of 1 lemon, grated
$\frac{1}{2}$ **tablespoon vanilla extract**
$\frac{1}{2}$ **teaspoon almond extract**
$\frac{1}{2}$ **cup toasted almonds, chopped into large pieces**
1 tablespoon sugar
$\frac{1}{2}$ **teaspoon cinnamon**

1. Combine the flour, cornstarch, baking powder, baking soda, salt, and ground almonds in a 1-quart bowl and set aside.

2. Cream 1 cup sugar and the oil in a 2-quart bowl on high speed until light and fluffy. Add the eggs, zest, vanilla, and almond extract and mix until thoroughly combined.

3. Stir in the flour mixture and mix well. Add the toasted chopped almonds and combine.

4. Line 2 cookie sheets with parchment paper. Divide the dough into 4 portions. Lightly oil your hands and gently form each portion into a log 10 inches long and 2 inches wide. Place 2 logs on each prepared sheet. Gently shape the soft dough into a uniform log that is now probably 12 inches long.

5. Sprinkle the tops of the loaves with the cinnamon and sugar mixture. Bake at 350°F for 20 minutes or until the edges are golden brown.

6. Remove the loaves from the oven. Let cool for 5 minutes. Slice each loaf crosswise into $\frac{1}{2}$-inch cookies. Place cookies cut side up and bake for another 5 minutes. Turn slices over and bake for another 5 minutes. Cool and store in an airtight container for 2 weeks or freeze.

Yield: 3–4 dozen

TINA'S TIDBITS

- *Sixteenth-century Italian sailors would bring these twice-baked cookies on long sea voyages because their dry consistency prevented the cookies from getting soft or moldy.*
- *The addition of cornstarch gives the cookie a dense, but smoother consistency.*
- *Ground almonds and oil make this cookie very hard, which is perfect for dipping into hot coffee or tea.*

ALMOND HONEY STICKS

Nut confections "glued" together with honey are prevalent in most cultures. One of the most common candies for Passover is individually wrapped sesame bars from the Middle East. Almond candies are also prevalent in that region so I created this recipe as a special treat all year round. Any shape can be created as the mixture is malleable until it hardens. One end of each bar could be dipped in chocolate for a truly decadent treat.

15 ounces slivered almonds
½ cup honey

1. Toast the almonds in a 325°F oven until golden, about 5–9 minutes. **Do not burn!**

2. In a large skillet, bring the honey to a boil. Add the almonds. Stir the almonds for 2 minutes until they start to stick together. **Note:** If you don't cook the honey long enough, the mixture won't hold together when cool.

3. Lightly oil a board, your hands, and a metal spoon, and then chill your hands by grabbing a bag of frozen vegetables in your freezer.

4. Pour 1 tablespoon of the mixture out onto the board in a small mound. Repeat with 4 or 5 more mounds at a time. Working quickly, shape the mounds into compact 2-inch sticks. Repeat with the remaining honeyed almonds until all sticks are formed.

5. Cool completely before storing in airtight containers.

Yield: 2–3 dozen pieces

TINA'S TIDBITS

- *Boiling the honey reduces its moisture content so that when it cools it will be hard and bind the almonds together.*
- *Hot honey and sugar mixtures both reach a very high temperature (over 350°F) so caution must be taken when making these candies, especially if working with children.*
- *If the mixture gets too hard before you get a chance to shape the sticks, place the cookie sheet in a 300°F oven for a minute or so until the mixture is more pliable. If you are too late then you just serve little mounds. They are still delicious and better tasting than burnt honey.*

FRESH FIGS WITH GOAT CHEESE AND HONEY

Upscale restaurants and caterers are serving this combination of fruit and cheese that Middle Easterners enjoyed thousands of years ago. Although this is a simple preparation, the quality of each component must be very high for it to taste fantastic. It is best when figs are at the height of ripeness.

12 ripe Mission or Brown Turkey figs, cut in half
4 ounces good-quality chèvre goat cheese

3–4 tablespoons wildflower or berry honey
French bread or crackers (optional)

1. Place figs on a plate cut side up.

2. Spread some of the goat cheese on each fig.

3. Drizzle with some honey and serve with bread or crackers.

Yield: 6 or more servings

TINA'S TIDBITS

- *Alternatively, serve a plate with all of the ingredients and allow your guests to prepare their own. You can also serve them on a bed of lettuce as a first course.*
- *Mission figs are named for the California Franciscan missions where they have been cultivated since 1770.*

MOSHE'S STUFFED FIGS

I ate at Moshe Basson's Jerusalem restaurant Eucalyptus while attending an HUC-JIR board meeting a number of years ago. I had heard about his knowledge of biblical foods but was not prepared for the breadth and depth of his information. He was personable, relaxed (hard to believe for a man who had evaded an intifada against him), a great cook, and an incredible teacher. Ten of us sat around a large round table while Moshe brought dish after dish to our table and explained about this vegetable and that herb. We were all so thrilled to have had the opportunity to experience Moshe's expertise. After the meal, however, one fellow diner said that he couldn't decide which he enjoyed more, the food on the table or the rapturous look on my face! The following is an adaptation of Moshe's creative genius for the home cook.

One 8- or 9-ounce package dried calimyrna figs
   (about 24 figs)
2 cups water
2 tablespoons extra virgin olive oil
2 small onions (about 6 ounces), finely diced
8 ounces boneless chicken breast, finely diced
$\frac{1}{8}$ teaspoon ground cardamom
$\frac{1}{4}$ teaspoon ground allspice
$\frac{1}{4}$ teaspoon ground cinnamon
Kosher salt and freshly ground pepper to taste

SAUCE:
3 tablespoons tamarind paste
Additional water as needed
3 tablespoons brown sugar
$\frac{1}{8}$ teaspoon ground cardamom
$\frac{1}{4}$ teaspoon ground allspice
$\frac{1}{4}$ teaspoon ground cinnamon
Kosher salt and freshly ground pepper to taste

1. Place dried figs in a glass bowl and cover with 2 cups water. Microwave on high for 3 minutes, and set aside while you make the filling.

2. Heat a 10-inch sauté pan over high heat for 20 seconds. Add the oil and heat it for another 10 seconds. Reduce the heat if the oil is beginning to smoke.

3. Add the diced onions to the pan and sauté until golden brown.

4. Add the finely diced chicken breast, the spices, and the salt and pepper to the onions. Sauté the chicken over medium-high heat until the chicken has lost its color and the spices are evenly distributed. Remove the contents to a small mixing bowl to cool while you prepare the sauce.

TINA'S TIDBITS

- *If using fresh figs, cut the upper half of the figs in half and scoop out most of the seeded flesh. (Reserve the flesh to make jam if you like.) Proceed with stuffing the figs, and cook for 10 minutes or until the figs are soft but not overcooked.*
- *Some adaptations of this recipe use onions and eggplant along with the figs for stuffing. If you find yourself with excess stuffing, then consider adding other vegetables to the pot.*
- *Although a food processor can be utilized to finely chop the chicken, I find it pulverizes it into a mass that is hard to separate when cooked. Using ground turkey or veal instead of chicken, with the onions and spices used for the filling, would work well.*
- *Using the soaking liquid from the figs helps impart the fig essence to the sauce without overcooking the figs and yields the same result.*

5. Drain the figs, reserving the soaking water. Measure the liquid and add enough water to make a total of 2 cups.

6. Add the tamarind paste, water, and sugar to the used, unrinsed frying pan. Add the spices and the salt and pepper to the sauce, and bring the mixture to a boil. Stir to dissolve the tamarind concentrate, and cook until the mixture is smooth and slightly thickened. Set aside while you stuff the figs.

7. Insert your forefinger into the opening at the top of the fig to enlarge the opening for stuffing.

8. Using your fingers, stuff the figs with the chicken mixture, and place the figs in the pan with the sauce.

9. When all the stuffed figs are placed in the pan, turn the heat on and bring the sauce to a boil. Cover the pan, reduce the heat, and simmer for 15 minutes.

Note: Moshe suggests serving with rice or couscous.

Yield: 4–6 servings as an entrée

HERBAL GRAPE SORBET

Anya Von Bremzen is an expert on Spanish culture and cuisine. I was intrigued by a recipe in her book, The New Spanish Table, *for a grape granita. Since Mexican mint marigolds were thriving in my garden, I thought I would play around with this food concept. Here is my adaptation.*

1 pound seedless green or red grapes
5 small leaves of Mexican mint marigold, tarragon, or basil
4 ounces sweet dessert wine—Riesling, Moscato d'Asti, or Gewürztraminer

Juice of ½ medium lemon
2 or more tablespoons of simple syrup (see recipe below)

1. Cut the grapes in half and place them in a processor work bowl. Pulse the machine on and off until most of the grapes are pulverized.

2. Add the herbs and process the mixture until it is fairly smooth. Let the mixture sit and the flavors steep for 15 minutes.

3. Place the grape-herb mixture in a fine-mesh strainer over a 2-quart mixing bowl. Press on the grape pulp to extract as much juice as possible.

4. Add the wine and lemon juice and 2 tablespoons of simple syrup to the grape liquid. Taste to see if more syrup is needed (this will depend on the sweetness of the grape). Chill.

5. Place in the container of an ice-cream maker, and follow the manufacturer's directions to make the sorbet. The sorbet may be served immediately or stored in an airtight container in the freezer until ready to serve.

Yield: 1½ pints

SIMPLE SYRUP

1 cup granulated sugar
1 cup water

2 teaspoons orange blossom water (optional—but terrific!)

1. Combine the sugar and water in a 1-quart saucepan. Bring the mixture to a boil, stirring until the mixture begins to clear.

2. When the mixture is clear and all the sugar is dissolved, remove from heat, add the orange blossom water, and pour into a jar. Store in the refrigerator indefinitely. Use in sorbets or drinks, or pour some over fresh berries just before serving.

TINA'S TIDBITS

- *Using a simple syrup ensures that your sorbet won't be grainy and gives a little more body to the frozen product than using undissolved granulated sugar.*
- *Orange blossom water hints of the Moors' influence in Andalusia, the region that had a very large Jewish population before the expulsion.*
- *Simple syrup must be very cold or sorbet won't freeze in an ice-cream maker.*

Sopi di Bina
(Curaçao Wine Soup)

The Jewish community of Curaçao was established over 350 ago years and its Mikvé Israel-Emanuel is the oldest continuously operating synagogue in the Western Hemisphere. As in all Jewish communities in the Diaspora, cooking traditions from countries of origin mingled with the foods readily available to create new preparations that conformed to the Jewish dietary laws. The following is adapted from their community cookbook, Recipes from the Jewish Kitchens of Curaçao.

3 cups water
6 ounces pitted prunes (about 20)
1 cinnamon stick
4 tablespoons cornstarch

$\frac{1}{2}$ cup water
One 750 ml bottle of Zinfandel or Shiraz wine
$\frac{1}{3}$–$\frac{1}{2}$ cup sugar, depending on sweetness of prunes

1. In a 3-quart saucepan, bring the 3 cups water to a boil and add the prunes and cinnamon stick. Reduce the heat and simmer until the prunes are soft.

2. Using a slotted spoon, remove the prunes from the pot and reserve them in a bowl. Discard the cinnamon stick, and return the saucepan with the liquid to the stove.

3. In a small dish, combine the cornstarch with the $\frac{1}{2}$ cup water to make a smooth paste. Slowly add the cornstarch to the prune liquid, stirring constantly to combine.

4. Reheat the liquid over moderate heat. Stir constantly until the liquid thickens.

5. Increase the heat to bring the liquid to a boil, and add the wine and the sugar. Stir constantly until the sugar is dissolved. Add a little more water if the soup is too thick. Return the prunes to the soup. Serve warm or refrigerate until ready to serve cold.

Yield: 6–8 servings

TINA'S TIDBITS

- *Cinnamon stick adds flavor to liquid without adding the grittiness that results from using the powdered version.*
- *Cornstarch requires the mixture to come to a boil in order for it to thicken properly. Its use makes the mixture thicken clear, compared to flour, which thickens a mixture opaque.*
- *Add 2 or more tablespoons of curaçao liqueur to the soup after it is cooled to add a touch of orange, and the signature liqueur of the island, to your soup.*

Sangria de Curaçao

This recipe is unique for sangria since it has a minimal amount of fruit juice added to the wine. However, the cinnamon-scented syrup, plus the limes and nutmeg, highlight the versatility of wine and the resulting beverage is very refreshing.

1 cup water
¾ cup sugar
2 cinnamon sticks
One 750-ml bottle red wine (Shiraz, Zinfandel, or Burgundy)

2–3 limes
¼ teaspoon nutmeg

1. Combine the water, sugar, and cinnamon sticks in a 1-quart saucepan. Bring to a boil and cook over moderately high heat for 5 minutes or until the bubbles get larger and slower. Remove from the heat and cool until room temperature.

2. Remove the zest from two of the limes in long thin strips. Cut away all of the white pith and peel, and discard.

3. In a large pitcher, combine the sugar mixture, wine, two peeled whole limes, zest, and nutmeg. Let it steep, covered, for a number of hours or overnight.

4. To serve, remove the limes, and add 1 cup hot water and the juice from one of the limes. Taste and add more lime juice if necessary (this will depend on the fruitiness of the wine you use).

5. Serve in 4- to 6-ounce glasses.

Yield: 8–10 servings

TINA'S TIDBITS

- *If you prefer a more Spanish variation, oranges may be used instead of the limes.*
- *Boiling sugar and water puts the sugar into solution, and it will stay that way, refrigerated, for months. This is called a simple syrup.*
- *Simple syrups are used in liquid recipes because they distribute throughout the beverage and do not make the drink grainy.*

WINE JELLY

I first learned about wine jelly when I was in graduate school at NYU. Exploring foods from around the world, Mr. Tarantino exposed us to new preparations (at least new for the early 1970s!). Serve this as an addition to a cheese platter or with a scoop of the pear-wine sorbet from the poached pear recipe that follows.

2 cups red wine (I prefer Shiraz or Zinfandel)
4 whole allspice berries
One 3-inch stick of cinnamon

3 cups of sugar
One 3-ounce pouch of liquid fruit pectin

1. Combine the wine with the spices in a 2-quart saucepan. Heat the wine until it is warm. Turn off the heat and allow the wine and spices to steep for 30 minutes.

2. Add the sugar to the spiced wine and heat to a rolling boil. Stir constantly for 1 minute or until the sugar is totally dissolved.

3. Add the pectin and return the mixture to a rolling boil. Stir for 1 minute and pour into clean glass jars or a decorative mold.

4. Allow the jelly to cool at room temperature before covering and refrigerating. Unmold before serving.

5. If desired, decorate with frosted grapes (see recipe below).

Yield: 1 two-cup mold or 16 small servings

FROSTED GRAPES

1. To frost the grapes, either rinse them under water or toss them in slightly beaten egg whites.

2. Place a few tablespoons of sugar in a small dish, and roll the moist grapes in the sugar.

3. Place the sugared grapes on a plate or rack, and allow the sugar to dry completely before using as an edible decoration.

TINA'S TIDBITS

- *If you plan to serve the jelly with cheese and crackers, pour it into a mold or a shallow container that will easily release the jelly.*
- *Using liquid pectin prevents any chance of lumps from forming or having to heat the wine too long while waiting for a powder to dissolve.*
- *Frosting grapes with egg white helps the sugar adhere better and longer. However, if you are uncomfortable with using raw eggs, water will do the trick.*

POACHED PEARS IN RED WINE

It was hard to decide in which section of the book this recipe should appear, but it was easy to decide to include it. This is a perfect use for sweet pears, and here I have taken the flavorful cooking syrup, redolent with spice and pear essence, and turned it into a delicious sorbet to serve with the pears and/or wine jelly.

1½ cups water
Juice and zest of ½ lemon
1 cup red wine, preferably Zinfandel or Shiraz
1 cup sugar

½ teaspoon vanilla
3 medium Anjou pears or 4 small Seckel pears, peeled and halved if large

1. Place the water, lemon juice, lemon zest, wine, sugar, and vanilla in a 2-quart saucepan. Bring to a boil for 5 minutes.

2. If the pears are small and you are keeping them whole, use a long corer to remove the seeds and core from the bottom of the pear upward. Keep the stem intact on top. If you are using larger pears, cut the pears in half lengthwiseand remove the core with the seeds using a melon baller to scoop out the center of the core. As you finish preparing each pear, put it into the pan with the wine mixture.

3. Bring the pears and the liquid to a boil. Reduce the heat, cover, and simmer for 10 minutes or until a knife easily pierces the fruit. Turn off the heat and allow the pears to soak in the poaching liquid until ready to eat. Mixture may be refrigerated for up to a week. Once the poaching liquid is cold you may proceed to make the following sorbet, if desired.

Yield: 6 servings

SPICED PEAR INFUSED WINE SORBET

2–3 cups poaching liquid from Poached Pears recipe (see above)
1 ice-cream maker, preferably 1- to 2-quart size

1. Chill the poached pears in the wine poaching liquid for 2 or more hours or until the liquid is quite cold.

2. Remove the pears from the liquid and set aside in a glass or plastic bowl.

3. Pour the liquid into the frozen container of a small ice-cream maker and follow the manufacturer's directions until a soft, but thoroughly frozen mixture is formed. Store the sorbet in a sealed plastic container and serve when ready to use.

TINA'S TIDBITS

- *Alcohol will lower the freezing point of the sorbet so that the mixture will never get rock hard.*
- *If you don't have an ice-cream maker, freeze the liquid in a tray and use a fork to shave off portions. This is called a granita and is just as delicious.*

Mushroom Barley Soup

One of the best Jewish delis and caterers on Long Island was Andel's in Roslyn, New York. Estelle Areman, the owner, was a fantastic cook and a good friend of my family. Knowing that I was pursuing a career in foods and education, she always took the time to teach me some new culinary tricks and some great recipes. I think that this is one of the all-time best soups that I have ever tasted. The secret to the thickness of this soup is the lima beans. They are peeled and therefore disintegrate into the stock when fully cooked. Do not panic—they peel very easily if soaked long enough and you use large beans.

1 cup dried large lima beans
0.5 ounces dried imported mushrooms, preferably porcini
2 slices of flanken (short ribs cut into long thin slices)
2 quarts water
2 tablespoons oil

1 onion, finely diced
1 stalk celery, finely diced
8 ounces fresh mushrooms, diced
Salt and pepper to taste
1 carrot, diced
¼ cup medium pearl barley

1. Cover the lima beans with 1 inch of water. Microwave on high for 3 minutes, and let them soak for 1 or more hours or until the skins easily slide off.

2. Cover the dried mushrooms with water. Microwave for 2 minutes, and let them sit for ½ hour.

3. Place flanken in a soup pot and cover with the 2 quarts water. Bring to a boil and cook for ½ hour, skimming off the foam periodically.

4. Meanwhile, remove the skins from the lima beans by gently squeezing on one end; the bean will just slide out.

5. Carefully lift the dried mushrooms out of the water, and gently squeeze them over the bowl to save the juices. Dice the soaked, dried mushrooms and set aside.

6. Add the beans and the diced, dried mushrooms to the soup pot. Strain the mushroom liquid into the pot as well.

7. Heat a 10-inch skillet for 20 seconds, add oil, and heat for another 10 seconds. Sauté the onion in the oil for 2 minutes. Add the celery and fresh mushrooms, and cook until wilted and translucent. Add to the soup pot.

8. Add the diced carrot and salt and pepper to taste. Cook for 1 hour, stirring occasionally so that the mixture does not stick.

9. Add the barley and cook for ½–1 hour longer or until the meat is tender, the lima beans disintegrate, and the soup is thick. Check the seasoning.

Yield: 10–12 servings

TINA'S TIDBITS

- *Because the lima beans and barley make this soup thick, additional water might be necessary to give the soup the proper consistency.*
- *Do not make the mistake of buying small lima beans. It will take you forever to peel them!*
- *Always initially cook your meat in the water alone so that you can remove any coagulated impurities (foam) from the water first, before it adheres to any of the solid foods added to the broth later. This is true for chicken soup as well.*
- *Sautéing your vegetables in oil caramelizes the natural sugars in the vegetables and produces a far superior soup.*

1654 Barley Salad

I created this salad for Reform Judaism *magazine in celebration of the 350th anniversary of Jews in America. The method of gardening in Plymouth, Massachusetts, inspired this salad. Small squares of land were cultivated next to the house to provide food for the family. The Native Americans taught the pilgrims how to commingle different crops in one square bed to enhance the growth of all. A fish head was buried in the center of a three-foot square. Corn was planted directly on top to absorb the nitrogen from the decomposing head. Pole beans were planted around the corn to protect and fertilize the corn as well. Cucumbers or squash were planted around the perimeter because their rough leaves kept animals and playful children away from the vegetation. Tomatoes were native to the Americas but not necessarily used in salads until much later, but I have included them for the modern palate.*

4 large cloves of garlic, finely minced
1/4 cup finely chopped parsley
24 red grape tomatoes, cut in half horizontally
1 teaspoon minced fresh rosemary or 1/4 teaspoon dried rosemary
1/2 teaspoon cinnamon
Pinch of cloves
1 jalapeño pepper, seeded and finely diced
1/4 cup extra virgin olive oil
1/2 teaspoon coarse kosher salt

Freshly ground black pepper to taste
2 cups frozen yellow corn, defrosted
1 cup frozen cut green beans, defrosted
4 cups water
3/4 cup barley
3 scallions, finely sliced
1/4 cup roasted red pepper, jarred or fresh, diced
One 15-ounce can black beans, drained and rinsed
Additional salt and freshly ground pepper to taste

1. Combine the first 10 ingredients in a large, glass serving bowl. Let marinate for at least 1/2 hour at room temperature.

2. Defrost the corn and green beans. Discard any accumulated liquid.

3. Bring the 4 cups water to a rolling boil. Add a pinch of salt and the barley. Stir to combine, cover, and reduce the heat to low. Cook the barley for 40 minutes or until tender but not mushy.

4. Prepare the remaining ingredients while the barley cooks.

5. When the barley is done, quickly drain it and pour it over the tomato mixture. Toss with the remaining ingredients. Add more salt and pepper if needed.

Yield: 10–12 servings

TINA'S TIDBITS

- *The easiest way to peel a clove of garlic is to lightly smash it under the flat side of a knife. The peel then easily pulls away.*
- *Small grape and cherry tomatoes do not need to be seeded; large ones do because the seeds are slightly bitter.*
- *When working with hot peppers, place your hand in a plastic bag before holding the pepper to slice.*
- *For a great additional flavor to salads, roast cobs of corn over a fire, and cut the kernels off the cob using a large knife.*

PURIM

Sweet foods, filled foods, and an abundance of alcohol are prescribed for the joyous celebration of Purim. All are rich in symbolism. Filled foods are served because they represent the secrets and intrigue of Esther and Mordecai as they uncovered Haman's wicked plot to destroy the Persian Jews. It has also become

the custom to consume sweet foods, much like on Rosh HaShanah, to convey the wish for a sweet future. One theory suggests that making all the sweets to give as gifts, *shalach manot*, was a great way to rid the home of flour before Passover. Finally, while it is true that Jewish tradition says one should drink enough on Purim so as to be unable to distinguish between Haman and Mordecai, it is also true that giving charity to the poor is a mitzvah associated with the holiday.

Sephardic Jews tend to eat cookies that are fried or baked in the shape of Haman's ear. Ashkenazic Jews eat cookies that are filled with fruit or nut filling and shaped in triangles. This shape has been referred to as Haman's hat or pocket or even as representing the three Patriarchs, Abraham, Isaac, and Jacob.

Poppy seeds are often used in Purim confections. Aside from their widespread popularity in Eastern Europe and the Middle East, they are symbolic of the many lots cast by Haman and the promise God made to Abraham to spread his seed throughout the world, the very antithesis of the annihilation Haman planned. If you've ever dropped a spoonful of poppy seeds, then you know how quickly they disperse! In Israel, many Purim foods are prepared with poppy seeds in keeping with this promise.

Poppy seed filling is called *mohn* in Yiddish. *Mohn*-filled triangle cookies were very popular in medieval Central Europe. These confections were called *mohntaschen*, "poppy seed pockets." *Mohntaschen* sounded enough like *hamantaschen*, "Haman's pockets," that these cookies were adopted as the first unofficial Purim treat in the eleventh century.

Prune filling, the other widely popular filling for these triangular cookies, became traditional in 1731. David Brandeis, a plum preserve merchant, was acquitted after being charged with poisoning some plum preserves. He was released from prison just before Purim. In order to celebrate his freedom, the townspeople of Jungbunzlau in northeastern Bohemia (now part of the Czech Republic) filled the hamantaschen with *povidl*, plum preserves, and referred to the holiday as Povidl Purim.

When Rhineland Jews moved east to Poland, Russia, and Hungary, they brought the hamantaschen tradition with them. The Jews remaining in Western Europe, however, made gingerbread men to represent Haman and enjoyed gobbling off his head!

Today you can buy prepared poppy seed (*mohn*) filling as well as prune (lekvar) and other fruit fillings for hamantaschen. Hamantaschen cookies can often be found in bakeries throughout the United States all year round, another example of a traditional Jewish food going mainstream in America.

HAMAN'S EARS

This recipe is a variation of fried Italian dough, which was commonly prepared in Italian kitchens but had no association with Purim. It is a perfect example of one ethnic holiday custom infiltrating general society. The Italian flavoring of choice was anisette for some of the brandy in this recipe. The addition of finely grated lemon zest is a more "Jewish" variation. In European countries, pastries were often shaped like parts of Haman's body so that people could "eat him into oblivion."

2 cups all-purpose flour plus additional for rolling
2 tablespoons sugar
$\frac{1}{4}$ teaspoon salt
$\frac{1}{2}$ teaspoon baking powder
Finely grated zest of $\frac{1}{2}$ small lemon
$\frac{1}{3}$ cup milk
1 egg

1 egg yolk
2 tablespoons olive oil
2 tablespoons brandy
$1\frac{1}{2}$ teaspoons vanilla
Vegetable oil for frying
Confectioners' sugar

1. Combine the first 5 ingredients in a mixing bowl. Set aside.

2. Combine the remaining liquid ingredients for the dough in a small bowl and whisk together until well combined. Proceed immediately to add this mixture to the flour, and stir by hand or machine until a soft, slightly sticky dough is formed.

3. Turn out the dough onto a generously floured board and gently knead for 15 strokes to form a soft ball of dough. Cover with the inverted used mixing bowl and let the dough rest for $\frac{1}{2}$ hour.

4. Divide the dough in half and roll one half on a moderately floured board until it is very thin (1/16 inch) and almost transparent.

5. Pour 3 inches of oil into a deep pot or fryer and heat to 375°F.

6. Cut strips of dough that are about 4 inches in length by 1 inch. As you lift up each strip, the dough will stretch a little, which is OK. Bring the two ends of the dough together and lightly press them to form a sagging O.

7. Fry the dough 3 or 4 pieces at a time until golden. Drain on crumpled paper towels.

8. When all the dough is fried, place on a serving tray and sprinkle liberally with confectioners' sugar while still warm. Serve.

Yield: 3–4 dozen pieces

TINA'S TIDBITS

- *Dough made with oil will always appear to be sticky, even when its consistency is correct. Use a little more flour than usual on your board when rolling out the dough to prevent it from sticking.*
- *It is important to keep the temperature of the frying oil consistent so that the dough does not get soggy. Never add too much food to the oil at once or the temperature will drop and change the quality of your finished product.*
- *Whenever a recipe calls for draining food on paper towels, always crumple the paper into loose balls first before putting them on a tray. The crumpling creates more surface area for the excess oil to be absorbed, resulting in less greasy foods and fewer used towels.*
- *Confectioners' sugar will adhere much better when it is sprinkled on food that is warm rather than cool.*

MOHNBRODT

As early as the Middle Ages, cookies for Purim were made in stick shapes to denote the finger of accusation pointed at the Jews by Haman. Children would use the cookie to represent a character in the M'gillah and act out the story with their pastry. The addition of the poppy seeds, or mohn, *to this sweet is very common in Israel, as are other dishes using this seed. The seeds represent God's promise that the seed of Israel would spread throughout the world, rather than Haman's wish to obliterate the Jews.*

3³/₄ cups flour
2 tablespoons cornstarch
1 teaspoon baking powder
¹/₄ teaspoon baking soda
1 teaspoon salt
2 tablespoons poppy seeds
1 cup sugar

1 cup peanut oil
3 eggs
Zest of 1 lemon, grated
2 teaspoons lemon juice
1¹/₂ teaspoons vanilla
1 tablespoon sugar
¹/₂ teaspoon cinnamon

1. Preheat oven to 350°F.

2. Combine the flour, cornstarch, baking powder, soda, salt, and poppy seeds in a bowl and set aside.

3. Cream the sugar and oil on high speed until light and fluffy. Add the eggs, zest, juice, and vanilla and mix until thoroughly combined.

4. Stir in the flour mixture and mix well.

5. Line 2 cookie sheets with parchment paper. Lightly oil your hands, and divide the dough into 4 portions. Lightly handle each portion as you form a loose log that is about 10 inches long and 2 inches wide. Place 2 logs on each cookie sheet. Gently shape the soft dough into a uniform log that is now probably 12 inches long.

6. Sprinkle the tops of the loaves with the cinnamon and sugar mixture.

7. Bake for 20 minutes, or until the edges are golden brown.

8. Remove the loaves from the oven. Let cool for 5 minutes. Slice horizontally into ¹/₂-inch cookies. Place cut side up and bake for another 5 minutes. Turn the cookies over and bake for another 5 minutes. Cool and store in an airtight container for 2 weeks or freeze.

TINA'S TIDBITS

- *The use of cornstarch in this recipe creates a dough that is more compact and smooth. This type of dough is much easier to cut into uniform cookies after it is partially baked.*
- *Whenever a recipe for a baked good calls for a large amount of oil, it is imperative that the oil, eggs, and sugar be beaten together well to form an emulsion. If this step is followed properly, you will never have a greasy cake or cookie. Your finished product will be light and airy instead of dense and greasy.*
- *This type of "bread," or biscotto, was invented in Italy, probably by Jewish seamen. The double baking process rendered the finished pastry very dry, so it could withstand the humidity of the ocean air for long periods of time without becoming rancid.*

Yield: 3–4 dozen cookies

Hamantaschen Dough (Dairy)

Here's another dough that is firm but lighter, because of the baking powder.

1 stick unsalted butter
$\frac{1}{2}$ cup sugar
2 large eggs
$\frac{1}{2}$ teaspoon vanilla extract
$\frac{1}{2}$ teaspoon pure almond extract

2 cups all-purpose flour
1 teaspoon baking powder
$\frac{1}{4}$ teaspoon salt
Confectioners' sugar (optional)
Filling of your choice, canned or homemade

1. Preheat oven to 350°F. Line cookie sheets with parchment paper.

2. Using an electric mixer, cream the butter and sugar together until thoroughly combined.

3. Add the eggs, vanilla, and almond extract, and beat until lighter in color and fluffy.

4. Add the flour, baking powder, and salt, and mix just until the mixture starts to hold together.

5. Very gently knead the dough on a lightly floured surface about 10 strokes or until the dough is smooth and holds together. Cover with plastic wrap and refrigerate for at least 15 minutes.

6. Roll the dough out on a board that is lightly covered with flour or confectioners' sugar. **Note:** The sugar will slightly glaze the baked cookie and make it a little sweeter.

7. Cut the dough into $2\frac{1}{2}$-inch circles, and place 1 scant teaspoon of filling in the center of each circle.

8. Shape into triangles by using your thumbs to push up from the bottom of the circle and your forefingers to pull down from the top sides. Pinch the top seams of the dough well to securely enclose almost all of the filling. A little should peek through the top of the opening. See diagram on page 336.

9. Pinch the dough together so that the filling is exposed only at the top of the cookie.

10. Bake the hamantaschen in the preheated oven for 10 minutes or until golden. Store in a plastic bag or container when cool, or freeze for later use.

Yield: $1\frac{1}{2}$–2 dozen hamantaschen

TINA'S TIDBIT

• *Do not overwork the dough when kneading it or you will toughen it and the hamantaschen will be heavy.*

Hamantaschen Dough (Pareve)

Another version of dough when you want your pastry to be dairy-free.

2 sticks unsalted pareve margarine
1½ cups sugar
2 large eggs
1½ teaspoons vanilla extract
Zest of ¼ of a large orange
5½ cups all-purpose flour

1¼ teaspoons baking powder
¼ teaspoon salt
½ cup orange juice
Filling of your choice, canned or homemade (see
    recipes on the following page)
1 egg plus 1 tablespoon water for glaze

1. Cream the margarine and sugar until well combined. Add the eggs, vanilla, and orange zest, and mix until light and fluffy.

2. Combine the flour, baking powder, and salt in a 1-quart bowl. Add half the flour mixture to the mixing bowl, and stir until almost incorporated. Add half the orange juice and combine.

3. Repeat with the remaining flour mixture and the remaining orange juice until a soft, smooth dough is formed. Refrigerate the dough for 15 minutes or longer before rolling out.

4. Roll out the dough to ¼-inch thickness on a lightly floured board, and cut into 2½-inch circles.

5. Place 1 scant teaspoon of filling in the center of each circle. Shape into triangles by using your thumbs to push up from the bottom of the circle and your forefingers to pull down from the top sides. Pinch the top seams of the dough well to securely enclose almost all of the filling. A little should peek through the top of the opening. See diagram on page 336.

6. Combine the remaining egg with the 1 tablespoon of water, and brush the egg wash on the tops of the hamantaschen.

7. Bake at 350°F on parchment-lined cookie sheets for 12 minutes or until lightly golden.

Yield: 3–4 dozen hamantaschen

TINA'S TIDBITS

- *The addition of orange juice not only adds flavor, but the acid breaks down some of the gluten in the flour. This will make your cookie tender.*
- *Never use whipped or diet margarine. You will add too much air and water to the dough and change its consistency, making it harder to roll out and shape.*

Hamantaschen Fillings

Although there are many good canned fillings on the market, it is good to know how to make the fillings from scatch.

Prune Filling (Lekvar)

1 pound soft pitted prunes
$\frac{1}{4}$ cup sugar
1 teaspoon lemon juice
Grated zest of $\frac{1}{2}$ lemon

$\frac{1}{4}$ teaspoon cinnamon
$\frac{1}{2}$ teaspoon vanilla
$\frac{1}{3}$ cup finely chopped walnuts

1. Combine the prunes, sugar, lemon juice, lemon zest, cinnamon, and vanilla in a processor work bowl. Process the mixture until smooth.

2. Transfer the mixture to a bowl and fold in the finely chopped walnuts. Cover and refrigerate until ready to use.

Mohn Filling

1 cup poppy seeds (about 4 ounces)
$\frac{1}{4}$ cup sugar
$\frac{1}{3}$ cup honey
Grated zest of $\frac{1}{2}$ lemon

$\frac{2}{3}$ cup raisins
1 teaspoon vanilla
$\frac{1}{2}$ cup finely chopped walnuts

1. Place the poppy seeds in a 1-quart bowl, and pour boiling water over to 1 inch above the seeds. Set aside for 15 minutes and drain thoroughly.

2. Place the poppy seeds, sugar, honey, lemon zest, raisins, and vanilla in a processor work bowl. Process until well ground.

3. Transfer the mixture to a bowl and fold in the finely chopped walnuts. Cover and refrigerate until ready to use.

Yield: About 2 cups each

How to Shape Hamantaschen

1. Roll the dough out to $\frac{1}{8}$-inch thickness, and cut into 3-inch circles.

2. Place a teaspoon of filling in the center of each circle. Regular fruit preserves with lots of fruit pieces can be used, but **don't** use jelly, as it will melt and dissipate, leaving you with an empty cookie.

3. Hold your hands so that the tips of your thumbs touch and your forefingers are straight up in the air, so that the left hand makes an L and the right hand makes a J. Place your thumbs at the bottom of the circle (B) and slightly lift up the dough. Bring your forefingers down at an angle (between A and C and between A and D) and gently push up the dough from all sides until the dough forms an equilateral triangle. Gently pinch the top edges together and you will have a perfect, professional-looking hamantaschen.

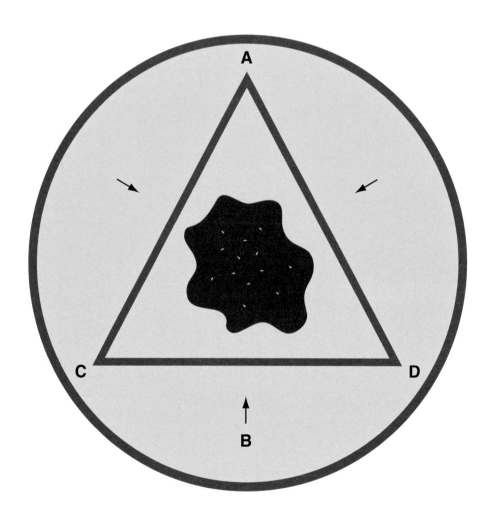

Hamentaschen de Panama

The following recipe epitomizes the transformation of a Jewish recipe due to immigration. I received the cookbook of the Panama chapter of the Women's International Zionist Orgranization from a friend of mine in Mexico City. The recipes were all in Spanish, but my high school teacher would have been proud! I came across a recipe titled Orejas de Haman para Purim *(Haman's Ears for Purim). But instead of a recipe for fried dough, the ingredients and diagram were for hamantaschen. To blur the lines of transition even further, many of the ingredients (including the brandy) were more typical of Middle Eastern fried dough than the Eastern European pastry* murbeteig *or* pâte sucrée. *There is a large Sephardic population from Syria and Lebanon in Latin America, and of course there is a substantial Ashkenazic community as well. Their traditions were commingled probably through shared celebrations to produce the following dessert.*

Enjoy this dish, adapted from a recipe by Rita Sasso, for its taste as well as for its history.

3¼ cups flour
½ cup sugar
½ teaspoon salt
Zest of 1 small lemon
1 stick margarine, cut into eighths
1 stick unsalted butter, cut into eighths
1 egg yolk

1½ teaspoons vanilla
2 or more tablespoons of brandy or rum
Milk (optional)
Confectioners' sugar
Commercially prepared poppy seed, prune, or apricot filling

1. Place the flour, sugar, salt, and lemon zest in the work bowl of a food processor fitted with the metal blade. Pulse the machine on and off to combine the ingredients.

2. Add the margarine and butter, and pulse on and off about 20 times or until the dough resembles a coarse meal.

3. Quickly combine the egg yolk, vanilla, and brandy or rum in a small bowl.

4. Immediately add the liquid mixture to the processor while it is running, and mix only until a ball of dough starts to begin to form. Do not overmix. If the dough looks very dry, you may add another tablespoon of brandy or some milk. The dough should not be too moist or the cookie will be heavy.

5. Turn the dough out on a lightly floured board and lightly knead into a ball. Divide the dough into 2 or 3 portions and refrigerate, covered, for 20 minutes.

6. Remove the dough and roll out to ⅛-inch thickness on a surface that has been liberally coated with confectioners' sugar.

7. Cut the dough into 3-inch circles, and place a small amount of prepared filling in the center of each circle. Shape the dough into triangles, pinching the edges together.

8. Place the cookies on parchment-lined cookie sheets, and bake for 12–15 minutes in a preheated 350°F oven until golden brown.

Yield: 3 dozen or more, depending on size

TINA'S TIDBITS

- *Pastry that contains alcohol or fruit juice will taste even better the next day, as the flavors need time to mellow.*
- *Liquid is necessary, even in small amounts, to bind the flour and fat in pastry together. A processor is so efficient that dough could be formed without it, but it will fall apart when rolled or baked.*
- *Always roll sweet pastry in confectioners' sugar instead of flour. The cornstarch in the sugar prevents sticking, and the sugar creates a light, glistening glaze over the finished product..*

Yolanda's Mother's Best Cookies

When Yolanda first gave me this recipe it was all in pounds and ounces. That is tricky when you are weighing flour, so I made the recipe user-friendly. This makes a great hamantaschen dough as well as a rolled-out cookie dough or even a log, coated in sugar and then cut into slices. All-purpose!

1 pound unsalted butter
½ pound minus 1 tablespoon confectioners' sugar
1 tablespoon corn syrup
2 teaspoons vanilla

½ teaspoon salt
4½ cups all-purpose flour
Confectioners' sugar if rolling cutout cookies

1. Cream the butter, sugar, and corn syrup together on high speed until light and fluffy.

2. Add the vanilla and salt, and mix until incorporated.

3. Add the flour and mix only until the dough starts to come together.

4. Remove the dough from the bowl and lightly knead the dough into a ball.

5. Divide the dough in half and either flatten it into disks (for rolling out) or shape it into two logs (for slice and bake). Cover with plastic wrap and refrigerate until ready to use, at least 1 hour.

6. Preheat the oven to 300°F.

7. Roll the dough out in confectioners' sugar, and cut into desired shapes. For hamentashen, cut dough into 2–3 inch circles. Place a teaspoon of prepared filling in the center of the circle. Shape into triangles by using your thumbs to push up from the bottom of the circle and your forefingers to pull down from the top sides. Pinch the top seams of the dough well to securely enclose almost all of the filling. A little should peek through the top of the opening. See diagram on page 302.

8. For slice and bake, roll the logs in colored sugar, and slice into ⅛-inch slices. Place flat on parchment-lined cookie sheets.

9. Bake the cookies for 15–20 minutes, until light golden brown.

Yield: 4–5 dozen cookies

TINA'S TIDBITS

- *Confectioners' sugar makes the dough very firm and smooth, ideal for shaping cookies.*
- *The addition of corn syrup enhances the golden color of normally pale cookies.*
- *Never mix scraps of dough (second-generation dough from cutouts) with dough that has not been rolled (first-generation dough). The cookie won't lie as flat and might brown unevenly.*

EASY PALMIERS

This light, crunchy pastry is often referred to as "pig's ears" in America. However, the French Jews serve these "ears" at Purim, attributing their shape to Haman's misshapen ones. Ears are often associated with the villain Haman because medieval Europe had a ritual of cutting off a villain's ear prior to execution.

This is a very easy recipe, especially because you don't have to make the dough from scratch. I have given you detailed steps, but the cookies can be prepared in very little time.

Purchased puff pastry sheets are pareve, so this can be served with tea after a meat meal.

One 17.3-ounce box of puff pastry sheets
Granulated sugar

1. Remove the two frozen sheets of dough from the box and defrost at room temperature for 20–30 minutes.

2. Spread about ¾ cup of sugar over a pastry board or countertop, and press the sugar into both sides of one sheet of dough.

3. Roll the sheet lengthwise on the sugar surface until the dough is slightly thinner and about 16 inches long. Do not change the width of the sheet.

4. Find the center of the dough on the long side and make a little mark with a knife.

5. Starting from each short end, tightly roll up the dough so that each side meets in the middle. Wrap with plastic wrap and freeze for 30 minutes. Repeat the procedure with the other sheet of dough.

6. When ready to bake, line a cookie sheet with parchment paper or use foil, dull side up, which you have lightly sprayed with cooking oil.

7. Slice the dough into ½-inch slices.

> **TINA'S TIDBITS**
>
> - *Because the pastry consists of many fine layers of dough, it is important when working with any leftover pieces that the scraps be layered and not just bunched into a ball.*
> - *This recipe often calls for confectioners' sugar instead of granulated. I prefer the extra crunch one gets from the granulated.*
> - *Another alternative is to cut the dough into circles, cut the circles in half, and pinch the dough in the middle of the straight edge to resemble an ear.*
> - *When cutting shapes from puff pastry, never twist the cookie cutter. This motion will stretch the dough out of alignment, and the pastry will bake slanted.*

8. Sprinkle additional sugar on your board or counter. Using a rolling pin, gently roll each slice, cut side down, in the sugar until the dough is about ⅛ inch thick. Turn the dough over, and coat the other cut side with sugar. Place it on the cookie sheet, with about 1½ inches between pastries.

9. Place in a preheated 400°F oven and bake for 12–15 minutes, until the bottom and sides of the cookies are caramelized.

10. Remove the cookie sheets from the oven, and gently turn the cookies over, using two spatulas.

11. Return them to the oven and bake for another 3–5 minutes, until the bottoms are golden.

12. When thoroughly cool, remove the cookies from the sheets. Store in an airtight container for a week or freeze until needed.

Yield: 3–4 dozen

PASSOVER

I renovated part of my house for Passover. Really! I tore down the archway between the living and dining rooms to create a large, open space. Each year I remove all the furniture from the living area, put up five long folding tables, and transform the space so the seder can be shared with forty people. You see, my family knows that I take to heart the command in the Haggadah, "Let all who are hungry come and eat." Aside from my husband and children, none of the forty are relatives, but they are all family.

Passover is a time when I feel steeped in my heritage and have fond memories of my mother's kitchen. I still take out the wooden bowl and hand chopper that I used as a child to make the *charoset*. With the acquisition of a food processor, these utensils are obsolete; I no longer need to chop by hand, but my daughter prefers it. She also prefers— no, I take that back—she demands that we must **always** be home for Passover so that we can have at least one seder at our house. She loves the way her father conducts the seder, the way each person has a sound to make while singing *"Chad Gadya,"* and the constancy of familiar faces. She is not alone in her feelings. Passover is celebrated by over 77 percent of Jewish households in America, making it the most

observed Jewish holiday, according to the most recent National Jewish Population Study.

Julius Lester, in the CCAR Haggadah *The Open Door,** describing his preparation for Passover, says, "Passover is a blending of history and religion, of celebration and commemoration, a drama of remembering, of transforming history into personal memory so that it is I who am emerging from bondage in Egypt." Our memories connect us to our past, and the seder opens our hearts and minds to our people's suffering and triumph over persecution. The possibility of creating memories for our children and grandchildren is very enticing. Maybe this is the true explanation for Passover's popularity.

---

* Sue Levi Elwell, ed. (New York: Central Conference of American Rabbis, 2002), p. 6.

Kneidlach (Matzah Balls)

This recipe is so old (from my mother) that I can't bring myself to change the first line that calls for a rotary beater—the kind you crank with your hand while the beaters go around. I did, however, adjust the seasonings a little, because most people are used to the boxed mix. These are lighter than air and might not form a perfectly shaped ball, but that is OK. Just read the tidbits for an education in Matzah Ball 101.

4 eggs separated
½ cup cold water
¼ cup chicken fat or peanut oil
1 teaspoon salt
Freshly ground black pepper to taste

¼ teaspoon garlic powder
1 tablespoon finely minced parsley
Large pinch of ginger
1¼ cup matzah meal
2 quarts water with 1 chicken bouillon cube added

1. Beat egg whites with a rotary beater (or a whisk) until slightly fluffy. Beat or mix egg yolks with the water until foamy. Combine egg whites and yolk mixture, and beat with the rotary mixer until combined and foamy.

2. Add fat or oil, salt, pepper, garlic powder, parsley, and ginger to the egg mixture and beat well to form an emulsion.

3. Add the matzah meal and stir with a fork until thoroughly combined. Cover the bowl with plastic wrap and refrigerate overnight or at least 2 hours before making the balls.

4. When ready to cook matzah balls, bring water and bouillon to a boil in a 3-quart pot. Make sure the bouillon cube is dissolved. Reduce the temperature so water is at a low simmer.

5. Lightly grease your hands with a little oil and form balls. Drop them into the simmering seasoned water. If the water is boiling too rapidly, the matzah balls will fall apart.

6. Cover the pot and cook for 20 minutes over moderate heat. **Do not lift the top off the pot before the time is up.**

Yield: 12–15 matzah balls

TINA'S TIDBITS

- *Commercial mixes all have a leavening agent in them. This recipe doesn't and only uses the air beaten into the egg whites to make the* kneidlach *light.*
- *Using garlic powder lets the seasoning evenly distribute throughout the mixture. The result is better than using freshly minced garlic, although I prefer using fresh garlic in food preparation.*
- *If you prefer heavier matzah balls, add some more matzah meal to the recipe. Make sure the lid of the pot isn't raised while the matzah balls are cooking. This way you'll avoid matzah balls that shrink, become dense, and have a raw, translucent center.*

PASSOVER BAGELS

A practical dilemma during Passover is taking one's lunch to work or school without finding a brown bag filled with egg salad adhering to shards of matzah pieces in the bottom. Here's my answer—bagels! Made like the classic pâte à choux *dough for cream puffs, these rolls turn out crisp on the outside and soft on the inside.*

2 cups matzah meal
1 teaspoon salt
1 tablespoon sugar

1 cup water
½ cup peanut or vegetable oil
4 eggs

1. Combine the matzah meal, salt, and sugar in a medium bowl. Bring the oil and water to a boil and add to the matzah meal mixture all at once. Stir well to combine.

2. Using a wooden spoon or stiff spatula, beat in eggs thoroughly one at a time until each is incorporated into the dough. Let stand covered for 15 minutes.

3. With oiled hands, scoop up about 2 heaping tablespoons of dough and shape into rolls. Place on a greased or parchment-lined cookie sheet.

4. Grease your forefinger. Insert your finger into the middle of the roll and twirl your finger around until a hole is formed in the center.

5. Bake at 375°F for 40–50 minutes.

Yield: 12 bagels

TINA'S TIDBITS

- *Have all of the ingredients premeasured in the bowl and saucepan. If the water mixture boils too long, the proportion of matzah meal to water will be off and will result in dense bagels.*
- *Oiling your hands serves two purposes: the dough won't stick when you're shaping it and making the hole in the center, and it helps to lightly "fry" the top to give the bagel a crisp crust.*
- *The **most important** rule for working with matzah meal is **always** allowing the mixture to sit covered for at least 15 minutes. Matzah meal needs time to hydrate (absorb the water). Many people make the mistake of adding more meal when the mixture looks too thin. Their finished product is always too heavy and dry.*

MATZAH BRIE

Any way you look at it, matzah brie is French toast. But I refuse to tell you that this is the right way to make it. Family traditions should not be trampled! The 1930 edition of Tempting Kosher Dishes, *by the B. Manischewitz Co., suggests making this dish either as a single slice or frittata style, like the following recipe, because Manischewitz doesn't want to decide for you either! It is your choice, but the technique is the same for all. Enjoy!*

3–4 egg or plain matzot
2 eggs
¹⁄₂ cup milk
1 teaspoon salt

¹⁄₂ teaspoon vanilla extract
¹⁄₄ teaspoon cinnamon (optional)
1 tablespoon unsalted butter

1. Break each matzah into 5 or 6 large pieces.

2. Place the matzot in a bowl containing enough warm tap water to cover all the pieces. Soak until soft.

3. Combine the eggs, milk, and the seasonings in a medium bowl.

4. Drain the matzot very well, lightly pressing on the matzot to remove a lot of the water. Don't crush.

5. Add the matzot to the egg mixture and coat well.

6. Heat the butter in a 10-inch frying pan (preferably nonstick).

7. Add the matzah mixture and fry on both sides until brown on the outside and firm but not dry on the inside.

8. Serve with maple syrup or cinnamon and sugar.

Yield: 2–4 servings

TINA'S TIDBITS

- *In order to make matzah pliable, it must be soaked. Warm water is more effective for this than cold.*
- *Using slightly more milk will make the mixture more layered and less solid.*
- *For a savory matzah brie, add sautéed mushrooms and peppers to the milk mixture, and serve with a tomato salsa. Omit the vanilla and cinnamon for this version.*

Mr. Wechsler's Memory Matzah Muffins

Some years ago, Mr. Wechsler wrote and asked me to help him re-create his aunt's matzah muffin recipe. He gave me the ingredients and I tried my best. These were good, he said, but didn't match his memory. I think that this recipe combined with the following one might fit the bill for him. This is probably the best part of my job as a columnist for Reform Judaism *magazine—I get to try to make people happy by connecting them with their fond food memories. It doesn't get better than that!*

½ cup unseasoned, leftover mashed potatoes
2 eggs, lightly beaten with a fork
Pepper to taste
½ teaspoon salt (omit if potatoes were seasoned)

2–3 tablespoons chicken stock or water
½ cup matzah meal
Cooking spray or oil for muffin tin

1. Preheat oven to 325°F.

2. Oil or spray 12 muffin cups. Set aside.

3. Combine the potatoes with the remaining ingredients until the mixture is smooth. Add additional stock if necessary to make a mixture that is thick but still pourable.

4. Spoon 2 heaping tablespoons of mixture into each cup, and bake for 20 minutes or until puffy and lightly browned on top.

Yield: 12 servings

TINA'S TIDBITS

- *If muffins are slightly underbaked, they will sink but still be soft. If you bake them too long, they might be too hard and dry.*
- *As an alternative, try adding 1/2 cup finely chopped sautéed mushrooms to the mixture with a pinch of nutmeg and/or thyme.*

Burmolikos
(Bulgarian Matzah Puffs)

When I visited with Edith Baker in her art-filled home, the retired artist, art dealer, and Bulgarian Holocaust survivor waxed ecstatic about the little matzah puffs that were eaten for Passover and year-round in her home. After experimenting with the recipes she gave me, I understood her ecstasy. These are light, soft puffs that bear no resemblance to heavy matzah fritters. They will transform your Passover breakfast.

2 sheets plain matzah
2 eggs
1 egg yolk
1/8 teaspoon salt

Canola or cottonseed oil
1/2 cup sugar mixed with 1/2 teaspoon cinnamon
(optional)

1. Break the matzot into large pieces and soak in a bowl of warm water until soft, about 15 minutes.

2. Drain the matzot and squeeze handfuls until almost all of the water is removed. Place in a 1-quart bowl.

3. Add the eggs, egg yolk, and salt to the clumps of matzot and combine well with a fork.

4. Heat the oil in a small saucepan or deep fryer to a depth of 2 inches. If you use a 1-quart saucepan you will use only about 1 cup of oil but will only be able to make 2 puffs at a time; however, they cook fast, so it is up to you.

5. When the oil is hot, drop the mixture by oval soup spoon into the fat and fry on one side until golden, about 1 minute. Turn the puff over and fry on the other side until golden—another minute. Drain on paper towels. Drizzle with honey or coat with granulated sugar or sugar that has been mixed with cinnamon, and serve.

6. *Burmolikos* can also be served with jam or honey.

Yield: 10–12 puffs

TINA'S TIDBITS

- *If you choose not to deep-fry the* burmolikos, *make sure you splash some of the oil in the pan over the batter when it first goes in the oil to achieve a more rounded look in the finished product.*
- *One of the reasons the mixture puffs is that the water in the soaked matzot is turned to steam by the hot oil.*
- *Never crowd food in hot oil. First, there won't be enough room for expansion of the cooked product; and second, the temperature of the oil will decrease and cause the food to absorb more oil and be greasy.*

Mina de Maza

Although it is common to see recipes for matzah lasagna or pies in cookbooks, it is not an invention of the American Jewish kitchen. Throughout the Mediterranean, Turkish minas, *Italian* scacchi, *and Greek pitas have been prepared for at least a thousand years with matzah used for dough during Passover. The following is a variation of the classic Turkish* mina *and a meatless* scacchi.

2 tablespoons pine nuts
2 tablespoons butter
1 medium onion, finely diced
One 10-ounce package frozen chopped spinach, defrosted
½ pound feta cheese, crumbled
7.5 ounces dry curd farmer cheese (pot cheese)
2 eggs, lightly beaten
Salt and freshly ground pepper to taste
¼–½ teaspoon nutmeg, to taste
1 tablespoon minced fresh dill

2 tablespoons unsalted butter
1 large clove garlic, finely minced
8 ounces sliced mushrooms
8 ounces defrosted artichoke hearts
Salt and freshly ground black pepper to taste
2 cups warm mushroom or vegetable broth
6 plain matzah squares
1 egg
¼ cup grated Parmesan cheese
Additional butter for greasing pan

1. Preheat oven to 350°F.

2. Lightly grease a 13 × 9-inch pan with some additional butter. Set aside.

3. Toast pine nuts in a 350°F oven for 4–6 minutes until lightly golden brown.

4. Melt 2 tablespoons of butter in a 2-quart pan. Sauté the onion until golden.

5. Squeeze out all of the excess moisture from the spinach. Add the spinach to the onions and cook over low heat until most of the moisture has evaporated. Stir occasionally. Add the feta, farmer cheese, eggs, seasonings, and dill and combine. Set aside.

6. Melt the remaining 2 tablespoons of butter in a small sauté pan. Add the garlic and cook for 20 seconds over medium-high heat. Add the mushrooms and sauté until they have given up most of their moisture.

7. If the artichoke pieces are large, cut them in half. Add to the mushroom mixture and stir to heat through. Add the toasted pine nuts and season with salt and pepper. Set aside.

8. Heat the 2 cups of broth in the microwave for 1½ minutes. Pour into an 8-inch square casserole or a deep dish that will hold the liquid, and soak 2 sheets of matzah until soft and pliable. As they become soft, fit them into the bottom and sides of the 13 × 9-inch buttered dish. Repeat with 2 more sheets so that the entire bottom and some of the sides of the pan are covered with matzah.

9. Spread the spinach mixture over the matzot, and top with the mushroom mixture.

10. Soak the remaining 2 sheets of matzah in the broth and cover the filling. Trim or tuck the sides in to make it look neat.

11. Add the remaining egg to the remaining broth in the dish. (Note: If no broth is left, combine ½ cup of additional broth with the egg.) Pour it evenly over the entire casserole.

12. Sprinkle the Parmesan cheese over the top and bake for 30–35 minutes until golden brown and bubbling. Serve hot or at room temperature.

Yield: 10–12 servings

TINA'S TIDBITS

- *Nuts will continue to roast even after removing them from the heat of the oven. They fry in their own oils so do not let them get too brown in the oven.*
- *Onions must always be sautéed alone for part of their cooking time to caramelize the natural sugars that make fried onions sweet.*
- *One 10-ounce package of frozen chopped spinach is equal to 1 pound of fresh spinach (minus all the large stems), and you don't have to wash, de-stem, or chop the frozen variety.*

CAPSOUTO FRÈRES POTATO MINA

When the Capsouto brothers make this recipe in their New York City restaurant, Capsouto Frères, for their annual charitable community seder, they usually start out with more than forty pounds of potatoes and ninety eggs. I have adapted the recipe to make a deep 13 × 9-inch casserole that will be sure to please many hearty eaters. The flavor is delicate, more southern France than eastern Poland.

4 pounds russet potatoes (4 large)
1 tablespoon kosher salt for cooking potatoes
8 large eggs
1 cup finely grated Parmesan cheese
1 tablespoon kosher salt or to taste
15 grindings (or ½ teaspoon) black pepper

7 boards of matzah
2 eggs
½ cup milk
3 tablespoons extra virgin olive oil, divided use
½ cup grated Parmesan cheese for topping

1. Wash and cut potatoes into eighths, and place in a large pot. Cover with water, add about 1 tablespoon of salt, and bring to a boil. Cook for 20 minutes or until a knife inserted into the potatoes comes out easily.

2. Drain potatoes, peel when cool, and mash in a 4-quart bowl.

3. Add the eggs and stir with a flat whisk or fork until thoroughly combined. Add the 1 cup Parmesan cheese, salt to taste, and the pepper, and mix well. Set aside.

4. Preheat oven to 350°F.

5. Place 3 inches of water in a glass dish wide enough to hold a board of matzah. Microwave the water for 3 minutes or until very warm.

6. In another bowl or dish large enough to hold a board of matzah, combine the remaining 2 eggs, milk, and 2 tablespoons of oil with a pinch of salt.

7. To assemble the *mina*, grease a 13 × 9-inch glass dish with 1 tablespoon of olive oil. Place in the oven for 2 minutes.

8. Meanwhile soak 2 boards of matzah in the warm water until slightly soft. Lift from the water and dip each board in the egg-milk mixture. Remove the baking dish from the oven, and lay the 2 boards of matzah in the bottom of the dish. They will lie flat and be slightly narrower than the pan. That's OK.

TINA'S TIDBITS

- *Because potatoes absorb a great deal of salt, it is necessary to add more salt to this dish than you normally would.*
- *If you are salt restricted, add a seasoning from one of the variations to enhance the flavor.*
- *Because this dish already contains a milk product, you may choose to enrich the dish by using butter.*
- *When cooking with butter, **always** use unsalted butter.*

9. Place half of the potato mixture over the matzot and spread evenly. Repeat step 8 and then cover with the remaining potatoes.

10. Repeat step 8 again with the last three boards of matzah, using the third matzah to fill in on the sides if necessary. Pour the remaining egg mixture, if any, over the matzot, and sprinkle with the remaining ½ cup Parmesan cheese.

11. Bake for 35–40 minutes until the top is golden and a knife inserted into the center comes out hot.

12. Serve hot or at room temperature.

Note: This tastes even better reheated the next day!

Yield: 12–15 servings

VARIATIONS

Here are three variations on this recipe:

Add 1 small grated onion to the potato mixture.

Add 2 tablespoons finely chopped basil.

Sauté 1 cup chopped onion until lightly golden. Add 8 ounces chopped mushrooms and cook until the mushrooms are done. Layer half of this mixture over each potato layer. Follow the remaining instructions.

CARROT TZIMMES WITH DUMPLINGS

When I was young, I loved Mrs. Adler's jarred carrot tzimmes. I created this recipe in Texas when it was no longer available. It's great for Passover too!

1 pound carrots, steamed and sliced, or 1 pound cooked frozen carrots
$\frac{1}{3}$ cup chicken stock (or pareve bouillon)
$\frac{1}{3}$ cup orange juice
$\frac{1}{4}$ teaspoon ginger
$\frac{1}{3}$ cup honey

1 tablespoon pareve margarine
$1\frac{1}{2}$ teaspoons potato starch dissolved in 3 tablespoons water
Leftover matzah balls, quartered, or 12 miniature matzoh balls prepared according to instructions in step 1.

1. Make matzah ball mixture according to your favorite recipe. Use part of the mixture to make miniature balls by shaping $\frac{1}{2}$ teaspoon of dough into a ball in your oiled hands and adding it to the boiling water. Cook and reserve matzah balls for later.

2. Place sliced cooked carrots, stock, orange juice, ginger, and honey in a saucepan and heat to boiling.

3. Reduce heat and add margarine.

4. Give potato starch mixture a stir to recombine and add to the carrots. Stir constantly until mixture thickens.

5. When mixture has thickened, add the reserved matzah balls and gently combine until the dumplings are coated and heated through.

Yield: 8–10 servings

TINA'S TIDBITS

- *If you want to make a portion of carrots look larger, slice them on the diagonal.*
- *Always stir a hot mixture as you add a potato starch-water mixture to it. Potato starch will congeal instantly if not stirred rapidly.*
- *An easy way to make little matzah balls is to put the mixture in a pastry bag fitted with a number 6 tip. Squeeze out 1/2 inch of dough and cut it off with a knife over the pot of boiling water.*

DELUXE MATZAH KUGEL

This kugel is moist and flavorful and can be adapted to any assortment of vegetables or fruit to re-create your bubbe's (unless hers was rock hard and dry—then you'd better write to me!). It can be made in advance and briefly warmed in the microwave, but do not reheat it for a long time in the oven.

3/4 cup plus 1 tablespoon oil or chicken fat
1 cup diced onion
1 cup diced celery
1 cup diced fresh mushrooms, crimini or portabella preferred
1 box matzah farfel
1 1/4 teaspoons salt or to taste

1/2 teaspoon freshly ground black pepper
1/2 teaspoon garlic powder
3 garlic cloves, finely minced
1 tablespoon paprika
2 eggs, well beaten
3 cups canned chicken broth or more if needed

1. Sauté the onion in a 4-quart saucepan using 3/4 cup of the oil or chicken fat until golden brown. Add the celery and mushrooms and sauté some more, until the celery is translucent. Add a little more oil if the vegetables appear to be sticking to the pan.

2. Add the farfel and toss thoroughly so that all the farfel is coated with the vegetables and fat and lightly toasted. Place mixture in a large bowl.

3. Combine the seasonings, eggs, and broth and pour over the farfel mixture. The mixture should be loose. If needed, add more broth.

4. Grease a 9 × 13-inch roasting pan with 1 tablespoon of shortening (preferably chicken fat). Pour in farfel mixture and bake at 350°F for 45 minutes or until golden brown.

Yield: 12–15 servings

TINA'S TIDBITS

- *Scrape the fins away from the underside of a portabella mushroom with a teaspoon before using. This will prevent the mushrooms from turning the mixture inky black when they are sautéed.*
- *A box of matzah can replace a box of farfel. Place broken sheets of matzah in a plastic bag and use a glass or rolling pin to break them into smaller pieces.*
- *Always sauté onions alone until lightly golden before adding other vegetables. The moisture in the other vegetables will stew the onion if you add them all at once and will change the flavor of the mixture markedly.*
- *For a sweeter kugel, use 3/4 cup onion, 1 1/2 cups apple chunks, and orange juice for all or part of the broth.*

After-the-Seder Frittata

While I was researching for this book, it became clear that our forebears utilized every bit of food that was available to them to create nutritious, satisfying meals. Frittata-style pancakes were common in Iraq and Persia as well as in southern France and Italy. I must have inherited this cooking philosophy, because one year I took a look at all of the leftover ingredients in my refrigerator that were a result of overzealous Passover shopping and created this recipe.

1/4 cup extra virgin olive oil
1 medium onion, cut in half lengthwise and sliced
   very thin
10 baby redskin new potatoes, unpeeled, thinly sliced
5 large eggs
1 tablespoon finely minced parsley

1 teaspoon (or more) prepared horseradish in the jar
Salt and freshly ground pepper to taste
10 cooked asparagus, cut into 1-inch lengths
1/4 cup Passover mayonnaise
1 tablespoon Passover ketchup
1 teaspoon Concord grape wine, or to taste

1. Heat an 8- to 10-inch nonstick pan over high heat for 20 seconds. Add the oil and heat for another 10 seconds.

2. Add the onions to the pan and cook for 2 minutes. Add the sliced potatoes to the pan, reduce the heat to medium, and cook until potatoes and onions are golden. Remove from the heat.

3. Whisk the eggs, parsley, horseradish, salt, and pepper in a 2-quart bowl until well combined. Add the asparagus and all of the contents of the frying pan. Gently mix together so that the egg is evenly distributed.

4. Place the empty frying pan back on the burner over medium-high heat. Pour the egg mixture into the pan and flatten slightly.

5. Cover the frying pan and cook the egg-potato mixture over medium heat for 6–7 minutes until the sides are golden and most of the center is cooked.

6. Remove the frying pan from the heat. Cover the pan with a large plate and flip the pan over so that the frittata goes onto the plate.

7. Return the pan to the heat and gently slide the frittata back into the pan, cooked side up.

8. Cook the frittata for an additional 3–4 minutes until the bottom is golden and the frittata is cooked through.

9. Meanwhile, combine the last three ingredients to make a sauce. Serve with the frittata.

Yield: 4–6 servings

TINA'S TIDBITS

- *Adding salt to eggs serves two purposes: in addition to flavoring the eggs, the salt breaks down the egg white so it will uniformly blend with the other ingredients, eliminating those tough white strands throughout your frittata.*
- *Obviously any leftover vegetable such as broccoli, spinach, cauliflower, or sautéed mushrooms may be used in this recipe. Just make sure that the size of your vegetable is no larger than 3/4 inch thick so that it will be properly encased by the egg.*

Braised Lamb Shanks in Merlot

Since leg of lamb is technically not kosher (because the sciatic nerve runs through it), lamb shanks are the meat of choice when you want a flavorful lamb dish on your seder table. Slowly braising the shanks in an aromatic liquid flavored with kosher wine yields a moist, tender, fall-off-the-bone delicacy.

2–4 lamb shanks
2 tablespoons mixed fresh herbs (basil, rosemary, oregano, or mint), finely minced
1 cup of orange juice or the juice of 2 oranges
Grated zest of 1 orange

2½ cups full-bodied Merlot
4 large or 6 medium cloves of garlic, minced
Salt and freshly ground black pepper
2 tablespoons of extra virgin olive oil
1 cup low-salt chicken stock or water

1. Rinse the lamb shanks and place them in one layer in a wide glass dish.

2. Combine the mixed herbs, orange juice, orange zest, Merlot, and garlic and add to the shanks. Turn the shanks over so they are coated with the marinade.

3. Cover with plastic wrap and let the shanks marinate at room temperature for 2 hours or overnight in the refrigerator. Every half hour, turn the shanks to coat well.

4. Remove the shanks from the marinade, and pat them dry with a paper towel. Reserve the marinade.

5. Preheat the oven to 450°F.

6. Lightly season the shanks with freshly ground black pepper and a pinch of salt. Heat a large skillet over high heat for 20 seconds. Add 2 tablespoons of olive oil and heat for 10 seconds. Reduce the heat to medium-high and add the lamb shanks.

7. Cook each side for approximately 2 minutes, until the shanks are brown on all sides.

8. Place the shanks in a single layer in an ovenproof casserole. Pour the chicken stock into the hot pan. Scrape up any meat particles, add them to the reserved marinade, and pour over the shanks in the casserole. Cover with a lid.

9. Put the casserole in the preheated oven, and immediately reduce the temperature to 350°F. (The hot oven will sear the meat initially, but the

---

TINA'S TIDBITS

- *Because the shanks are cooked for a long time, it is important to use a wine whose flavor won't be lost after prolonged heating. Full-bodied reds like Cabernet Sauvignon, Merlot, and Syrah/Shiraz fit the bill and balance the strong flavor of lamb.*
- *In general, avoid using white wines in dishes with acidic ingredients such as orange juice. Wine flavors tend to grow stronger during cooking, and white wines tend to reduce to a more acidic finish, which may throw your more acidic recipe off balance.*

mixture needs to cook at a lower temperature or the meat will toughen.)

10. Roast the shanks for 45 minutes. Remove from the oven and baste with the sauce. Return the casserole to the oven and roast for an additional 1–1½ hours, or until the meat is very tender and easily pulls away from the bone. If the liquid has reduced greatly, add ½ cup of water to the pan.

11. Remove the meat from the pot and put on a serving platter and keep warm. If the gravy is too watery, boil the liquid down for about 5–10 minutes or until it has thickened to the consistency of tomato sauce. Drizzle some of the sauce on each shank and serve.

Yield: 4 servings

PASSOVER GRANOLA

This recipe will make your Passover week! It is delicious with milk for breakfast, and a healthy snack for school or work. If you must satisfy your sweet tooth further, make the chocolate candies at the end of this recipe.

3 cups matzah farfel
$2/3$ cup slivered almonds
$1/2$ cup sweetened or unsweetened coconut
$2/3$ cup pecans, broken into large pieces
$1/4$ teaspoon salt
$1^1/2$ teaspoons cinnamon

$1/4$ teaspoon nutmeg
6 tablespoons unsalted butter or pareve kosher for Passover margarine
$1/3$ cup wildflower or clover honey
$1^1/2$ cups chopped dried mixed fruit of your choice including raisins or 7-ounce bag of dried fruit pieces

1. Preheat oven to 325°F.

2. Combine the farfel, almonds, coconut, pecans, salt, cinnamon, and nutmeg in a 3-quart mixing bowl.

3. Melt the butter and honey in a small glass bowl in a microwave for 1 minute until butter is melted and honey is more fluid.

4. Stir the butter mixture into the farfel mixture until all farfel is lightly coated with the butter.

5. Spread the mixture over a large jelly roll pan with 1-inch sides and bake for 15 minutes until deep golden brown. Halfway through baking, stir to brown evenly.

6. Remove from oven. Cool completely and toss with the dried fruit.

7. When totally cooled, store in a ziplock bag or airtight storage container for all eight days of Passover—if it lasts that long!

Yield: 1–1$1/2$ quarts

VARIATION: CHOCOLATE GRANOLA TREATS

1. Melt 8 ounces of Passover chocolate chips and mix them with 1$1/2$ or 2 cups of the prepared granola. Stir to coat well.

2. Drop by teaspoonful onto parchment paper, and allow the mounds to firm up before you devour them!

3. These can be stored in a sealed container at room temperature or frozen. Chocolate might appear chalky after freezing, but this does not alter the taste.

Yield: 2–3 dozen pieces

TINA'S TIDBITS

- *To prevent burning, never pre-roast nuts if they will be baked in the oven.*
- *This recipe can be made with old-fashioned oatmeal when Passover ends.*
- *Salt should always be added in a small quantity to a sweet mixture to bring out the flavors of the individual foods but not lend a salty taste to the dish.*
- *If making ahead, leave out fruit until the day you want to use it so farfel doesn't get soggy.*

PASSOVER LINZER TORTE

This is my signature Passover dessert. Debby Stahl's German mother-in-law gave the two of us this recipe over thirty years ago. Many students have told me that their families love this so much they make it year-round.

Spanish Jews were the first to use ground nuts in place of some or all of the flour to make their tortes, especially for Passover, when flour was prohibited.

½ cup cake meal
½ cup potato starch
1 cup unsalted pareve kosher for Passover margarine
½ cup sugar
1 cup unpeeled, finely ground hazelnuts, almonds, or a combination

½ teaspoon cinnamon
2 large eggs, separated
½ cup kosher for Passover raspberry jam, preferably seedless

1. Combine the cake meal and the potato starch in a processor work bowl.

2. Using the cutting blade, add the margarine and pulse on and off until the mixture is well combined.

3. Add the sugar, hazelnuts or nut mixture, cinnamon, and egg yolks, and mix until smooth and well blended.

4. Take ⅔ of the dough and press it over the bottom and 1 inch up the sides of an ungreased 9-inch springform pan. Leave a 1-inch-wide rim of dough around the top.

5. Spread with ½ cup or more of raspberry jam.

6. Gently squeeze egg-sized balls of remaining dough between your fingertips over the top of the jam to simulate weaving ropes for the lattice top.

TINA'S TIDBITS

- *Springform pans often leak butter during baking, so always place the filled pan on a rimmed cookie sheet to avoid burnt oil spills on the bottom of your oven.*
- *When grinding nuts in a food processor, always pulse the mixture on and off rather than just turning the machine on. This will prevent nut butter from forming on the bottom of the bowl and your nuts will be more uniform in size.*
- *This recipe should be made with preserves or jams, not jelly, so that its volume will remain intact after baking.*
- *Nuts do not have to be pre-roasted if they are contained in pastry that is baked for over 40 minutes.*
- *The recipe can be increased 1 1/2 times to cover a 13 × 9-inch pan, which can be cut into 2-inch squares.*
- *If you are planning to make more than one torte and/or want to freeze it after baking, tightly line the base of the springform pan with aluminum foil. Freeze the torte in the pan, remove the cake with the foil attached, and put it back in the freezer in a freezer bag. You must place the frozen cake back on the springform base or directly on the serving plate **while still frozen**. This cake is delicate.*

This dough cannot easily be handled, but don't worry because the ropes don't have to be perfect, as they become smooth during baking.

7. Fasten the dough rope to the rim of dough, and smooth it out with your fingertip, pressing lightly.

8. Beat the egg whites slightly and brush over the top of the lattice. As you brush, the ropes will get smoother and more uniform.

9. Place the springform pan on a cookie sheet that has very low sides and bake at 325°F for 1 hour and 15 minutes.

10. Partly cool before removing the rim of the pan. Do not attempt to remove the base of the pan. Serve the cake from the base.

Yield: 12 or more servings

SABAYON FOR PASSOVER

Earlier in this book there is a recipe for zabaglione. It is very similar to this one. However, geographic region and Jewish culinary custom dictate how a dish is prepared. This recipe is a perfect example. Sabayon is the French name for the Italian egg custard sauce that is served with fruit or cake. The French chefs use the local sparkling white wine from the Champagne region of France to flavor their custard instead of the Italian fortified Marsala wine. Passover dictates what liqueur can be used, so a different combination of flavors might result in a variation. This is ultimately how Jewish food developed throughout the Diaspora, keeping tradition and using the foods locally available.

4 egg yolks
¼ cup sugar
¼ cup dry white wine or Champagne

1 tablespoon fruit liqueur (see note below)
1 pint fresh berries or other fruit

1. Place the egg yolks and the sugar in the top of a double boiler or in a 1-quart saucepan and whisk together until a thick ribbon of mixture pours off the whisk.

2. Place the pan with the sugar-egg mixture over another pan containing hot, but not boiling water. The mixture shouldn't be so hot that it will cook the yolks.

3. Add the wine and liqueur to the sugar-yolk mixture and whisk constantly over the hot water for 3–4 minutes until a nice thick custard is formed.

4. When the custard has thickened, **immediately** remove from the heat or you will have fancy scrambled eggs!

5. Have your fresh berries or other fruit divided into 4 or 5 serving dishes or glasses. Pour the sabayon over the fruit and serve.

Note: Use the following brandies or liqueurs with the appropriate fruit:
  · Amaretto with raspberries or strawberries
  · Orange-flavored liqueur with oranges or any berry
  · Rum (if using) with almost all fruits

Yield: 8 servings

> ### TINA'S TIDBITS
>
> - *Israel has recently started to produce liqueurs that are kosher for Passover. Some companies in the United States are also producing some fruit-flavored brandies that can be used during Passover as well.*
> - *It is important to cook the yolks slowly so that they will incorporate air as you whisk. As the structure of the yolk firms up around the air, a light, foamy sauce will be created.*
> - *The trick with this sauce is not to undercook the yolks or they won't retain the air. However, at the first sign of solidification, get it off the heat. It is better to have a sauce that is runny than one that is firm and with lumps!*
> - *Sabayon does not hold for long periods of time. However, if you must make it before the meal, keep its consistency stabilized by placing the pan over warm water so that the sauce doesn't liquefy and settle to the bottom.*

IRENE'S PASSOVER STRAWBERRY FLUFF CAKE

This recipe is not difficult—no spending hours baking—but this cake is a hit with my guests every year that my good friend Irene makes it. Try other fruits that can break down easily, like raspberries or frozen mixed berries, which are softer.

⅔ of a can Passover almond macaroons
2 egg whites
2 pints or 2 cups sliced strawberries

1 tablespoon fresh lemon juice
1 cup sugar
1 teaspoon vanilla extract

1. Press the macaroons evenly into the bottom of a 9-inch springform pan.

2. Place the remaining ingredients in the bowl of an electric mixer.

3. Beat on high for 15–20 minutes or until the mixture has significantly increased (tripled) in volume and is light and foamy.

4. Carefully pour the strawberry mixture into the prepared pan. Decorate with some additional sliced strawberries and freeze uncovered for at least 2 hours or until firm. If not serving immediately, cover with plastic wrap and place in the freezer.

Yield: 15 or more servings

TINA'S TIDBITS

- *Any crust can be used as the base for this dessert. However, if you have to bake your crust first, make sure it and the pan are completely cool before adding the filling.*
- *Normally egg whites are beaten only with sugar to achieve a high volume. In this recipe it would be impossible to incorporate the strawberries if they were added at the end, so the long beating time is necessary to achieve a uniform consistency.*
- *If you want to serve more people with the same amount of filling, use the entire can of macaroons and press into the bottom of a 13 × 9-inch pan.*

PASSOVER PECAN BISCOTTI

One Passover season there was a nationwide shortage of kosher for Passover pareve margarine. This hampered baking because most desserts for the holiday do not contain dairy products so that they can be served at the end of the seder. I developed the following recipe using oil instead of margarine and the cookies came out great!

1 cup pecans
1¼ cups Passover cake meal
4 tablespoons potato starch
¼ teaspoon salt
½ teaspoon cinnamon

3 eggs
1 cup sugar
¾ cup vegetable oil
1½ teaspoons vanilla extract
2 tablespoons orange juice

1. Place the pecans in a processor work bowl and pulse the processor on and off until the nuts are finely ground.

2. Place the nuts in a small bowl and add the cake meal, potato starch, salt, and cinnamon. Stir well to combine.

3. Beat the eggs, sugar, and oil together until an emulsion is formed and no streaks of oil are visible. Add the vanilla and orange juice and mix to incorporate.

4. Add the dry ingredients to the egg mixture and stir to thoroughly combine.

5. Divide the dough into three strips on parchment paper and bake in a 350°F oven until golden brown.

6. Remove from the oven and cut each log crosswise into ½-inch slices. Place slices on their sides and bake for 5 minutes.

7. Remove from the oven and turn the cookies over. Bake for an additional 5 minutes to brown.

8. Cool and store in an airtight container.

Yield: 3–4 dozen

TINA'S TIDBITS

- *It is very important to thoroughly combine the eggs and oil together to make an emulsion before adding the dry ingredients. The end result is a cookie that is crisp and light without any greasy consistency.*
- *Twice baking the cookies not only browns them beautifully, but dries them out sufficiently so that they will stay fresh for a week or more.*
- *Adding potato starch creates a dough that is less rough than one made with just matzah cake meal, and it slices well.*

SHAVUOT

On the third new moon after the Israelites had gone forth
from the land of Egypt, on that very day, they entered the wilderness of Sinai.

EXODUS 19:1

Shavuot is the holiday that celebrates the giving of the Torah on Mount Sinai. It is called the Feast of Weeks because it occurs seven weeks after the end of Passover. It is also called Yom HaBikurim, "Day of the First Fruits." In biblical times Shavuot marked the end of the grain harvest (end of counting the Omer) and

the beginning of the harvest of the first fruits of the year. Two loaves of leavened bread were brought to the Temple to signify the conclusion of the counting of the Omer, and Jews brought the first fruits of the new crops as an offering to the Temple as well. Actually, the first fruits of a crop could be brought anytime between Shavuot and Sukkot. Once the Temple was destroyed in 70 c.e., there was no place to bring the harvest offerings. Since the giving of the Torah at Mount Sinai was in the month of Sivan, the holiday became more associated with the giving of the Torah than as one of the three harvest festivals.

Many symbolic customs and food traditions surround Shavuot. Greenery and flowers are placed in synagogues and homes to commemorate the lush,

green fields surrounding Mount Sinai. Spices and roses are also used for decorative purposes, possibly because one interpretation of the Bible was that the Israelites fainted when they heard the voice of God and they had to be revived with the smell of spices. In Eastern Europe, beginning in medieval times, a young boy was brought to the *cheder* (schoolroom) to begin his studies. To make the start of his education sweeter, a drop of honey was placed on each letter of the *alef-bet*. As he learned the letter, he was encouraged to lick off the honey.

Eating dairy foods instead of meat to celebrate the holiday is the most prevalent Shavuot food association. Although there is no definitive explanation for its origin, theories abound. These

LEFT: *Deluxe Noodle Kugel, page 338*

include that the laws of kashrut were given at Sinai, and the Jews knew their utensils were not kosher, so they ate uncooked dairy foods; the cattle were grazing on fresh grass, so their milk was rich and plentiful; God was bringing the people to the land of "milk and honey." Whatever the interpretation, dairy recipes are prepared for the holiday. Enjoy!

BLINTZES

It is not clear why blintzes are associated with Shavuot. Some say it is because they contain cheese and others because two blintzes on a plate side by side look like a Torah scroll. Whatever the theory, blintzes are great to eat anytime.

DOUGH:
2 large eggs
⅔ cup milk
⅓ cup water
Pinch of salt
1 cup flour
Butter for frying
Sour cream

FILLING:
7.5ounce package farmer cheese
8 ounces cream cheese
3 tablespoons sugar
2 eggs
½ teaspoon cinnamon
1½ teaspoons vanilla

1. To make the dough, beat the eggs until slightly mixed. Add the milk, water, and salt and beat until smooth.

2. Using a wire whisk, gradually beat the flour into the mixture until each addition is totally incorporated and the mixture is smooth.

3. When the batter is the consistency of heavy cream, stop adding the remaining flour. Tap the bowl on the table to remove air bubbles, and set the mixture aside for ½ hour while you make the filling.

4. To make the filling, beat the cheeses with a mixer or processor until smooth. Add the remaining ingredients and mix thoroughly to combine. Set aside.

5. To make the blintz crepes, lightly butter a 6- or 8-inch frying pan. When the butter is sizzling, pour in 2 or more tablespoons of batter (the amount depends on the size of the pan), and swirl it around in the pan to make a uniform pancake. Alternatively, you could add ¼ cup batter, let it set for 5 seconds, and then quickly pour out the excess.

6. When the pancake top is glistening and dry, flip it out onto a plate. Proceed with the remaining batter.

7. Place the pancakes brown side up and put 1 tablespoon of filling on each center. Fold up the bottom, fold in the sides, and roll up the blintz until the filling is sealed. Place seam side down on a plate until ready for frying.

8. Heat some butter in a pan, and when sizzling, add a few blintzes, seam side down. Fry on both sides until golden brown all over. Serve with sour cream.

Yield: Approximately 12 blintzes

TINA'S TIDBITS

- *If you allow the batter to rest for 1/2 hour, the flour will hydrate, which will make the batter smoother and thicker.*
- *Always put the filling on the side that was initially browned when making the crepe. That way the uncooked side is on the outside of the blintz when it is baked or fried and no side of the dough will be cooked twice, which would make it tough and rubbery.*

DELUXE NOODLE KUGEL

My friends call this "killer kugel." Joan Nathan ran this recipe in her New York Times *column one year, and, as a result, I received many e-mails thanking me for sharing this recipe. I joke that this is a poor excuse for a cheesecake. Rich, creamy, and utterly delicious, a kugel in a 13 × 9-inch baking pan should serve twenty-five people. However, one reader said she made two kugels for fifteen people and almost all of it was gone!*

½ pound medium or extra-wide noodles (see note under Tina's Tidbits)
1 pound cream cheese
½ pound unsalted butter
1 cup sugar
1 pint sour cream
1 teaspoon vanilla

8 eggs
1 small can mandarin oranges, drained
1 small can crushed pineapple, drained
4 ounces walnuts
⅓ cup sugar
1 teaspoon cinnamon
2 tablespoons butter

1. Cook the noodles according to package directions. Drain and place in a 4-quart bowl.

2. Combine the cream cheese and butter in a processor work bowl and blend until smooth. Scrape down the sides of the work bowl. Add the sugar and process until well combined. Add the sour cream, vanilla, and eggs and process until well mixed. Pour into the 4-quart bowl with the noodles.

3. Stir the fruits in by hand, and pour the mixture into a buttered 13 × 9-inch baking dish. The mixture will almost overflow. Cover with plastic wrap and refrigerate overnight.

4. When ready to bake, uncover and place in a preheated 350°F oven and bake for 50 minutes.

5. Combine the walnuts with the sugar and cinnamon and sprinkle on top of the kugel. Dot with the 2 tablespoons of butter and bake for 15 minutes more. Serve warm or at room temperature. This could be made totally in advance, but it won't be as light.

Yield: 15 or more servings

TINA'S TIDBITS

- *Large noodles will be more visible in this kugel but will provide a more cheesecake-like consistency in some areas. Medium noodles will be distributed more uniformly. Either way this is delicious.*
- *The easiest way to dot butter is to freeze a stick of butter and then grate it over the top of your casserole.*
- *Refrigerating the mixture overnight allows the butter and cream cheese to solidify around the eggs and sour cream. This creates a mixture that will trap the air and puff up better when baked.*
- *If you don't want to use nuts, try crushing cocoa crisp cereal, sprinkling it on top of the kugel, and then dotting it with butter. The original recipe, given to me over forty years ago, used this topping, but I can't teach it or I would lose my credibility!*

Rigatoni con Quattro Fromaggi (Rigatoni Pasta with Four Cheeses)

My students call this "adult macaroni and cheese"; I call it a perfect example of Italian cuisine at its richest, with a little tweaking to substitute the smoky pancetta ham with the substance and earthy character of porcini mushrooms. This is a very rich cheese entrée that needs only some crusty bread and a salad to round out the meal.

½ cup butter, divided use
8 ounces crimini or domestic mushrooms, cubed
1 ounce dried porcini mushrooms
½ cup mushroom broth prepared from bouillon cube or bought ready-made, boiling
1½ cups chopped onions
½ cup flour
1 quart milk

½ pound rigatoni
¾ cup cubed fontina cheese (about 3 ounces by weight)
¾ cup cubed Gruyère
¾ cup cubed Emmenthaler or Jarlsberg cheese
¾ cup cubed Bel Paese cheese
¼ cup freshly grated Parmesan cheese

1. Melt 1 tablespoon of the butter in a large sauté pan and sauté the mushrooms until lightly golden and soft, about 7 minutes.

2. Crush the dried porcinis in your hand and add to the fresh mushrooms. Add the boiling liquid and simmer for 5 minutes. Set aside.

3. Melt the remaining butter in a 3-quart saucepan and sauté the onions until soft and translucent.

4. Put the sautéed onions in a processor work bowl and pulse until the onions have been pureed. Return the onions to the saucepan.

5. Add the flour to the onion mixture and stir constantly with a wire whisk until smooth.

6. Heat the milk until scalded (little bubbles form around the edges). Put the milk in the processor work bowl and pulse on and off 2 or 3 times to "clean" the bowl. Add the milk to the onion-flour mixture and whisk until smooth and thick.

7. Cook the rigatoni according to package directions, and preheat the oven to 350°F.

8. Place half of the rigatoni in the bottom of a 2-quart casserole. Cover with half the mushroom mixture and then half of all the cheeses **except** the Parmesan. Spoon half of the sauce over all. Repeat the process using the remaining ingredients and topping the last layer of sauce with the Parmesan cheese.

9. Bake at 350°F for 30–35 minutes or until golden and bubbly.

Yield: 8–10 servings

TINA'S TIDBITS

- *Necessity is the mother of all inventions, and just as Jewish cooks had to make adjustments to local recipes centuries ago, so too did I have to find a good substitute for pancetta, Italian cured and spiced bacon. Dried, earthy porcini mushrooms add a smoky spice taste as a substitute.*
- *Rigatoni increases in size when boiled so that little shelves of pasta are distributed throughout the casserole.*
- *The rich onion-cream mixture created for the base of this sauce is called a soubise.*

MEDITERRANEAN CHEESE TORTA

All the flavors of the Mediterranean in one layered dish! I created this recipe after seeing a prominent department store advertise a cheese mold that was extremely expensive. This recipe made six molds for the price of one! As part of your dairy meal, serve this as an appetizer or accompanied by a warm pita or bagels.

10 sun-dried tomato halves
3.5 ounces jarred roasted red peppers, drained
20 pitted Calamata olives
8 ounces cream cheese
4 ounces unsalted butter
6 ounces Gorgonzola or other blue-veined cheese
8 ounces mascarpone
8 ounces cream cheese

1 cup firmly packed fresh basil leaves
2 large cloves garlic
3 tablespoons extra virgin olive oil
½ cup grated Parmesan cheese
2 tablespoons pine nuts
8 ounces cream cheese
4 ounces unsalted butter

1. Lightly grease one 4-cup mold or 5–6 six-ounce ramekins. Line the mold(s) with plastic wrap or cheesecloth and set aside.

2. Combine the first five ingredients in the processor work bowl and process until a smooth paste is formed. Pour the mixture into the 4-cup mold or divide evenly among the ramekins. Rinse the work bowl.

3. Combine the Gorgonzola with the mascarpone and cream cheese in the processor and process until smooth, stopping to scrape down the sides of the bowl if necessary. Pour the mixture evenly over the sun-dried tomato mixture in the mold(s). Rinse out the bowl.

4. Combine the basil with the garlic and oil in the processor work bowl and process until a fairly smooth paste is formed. Add the remaining ingredients and process until well combined and smooth, stopping to scrape down the sides of the bowl if necessary. Pour this mixture over the other layers and smooth evenly. Cover with plastic wrap until firm.

5. When ready to serve or package for gifts, unmold and carefully remove plastic wrap.

Yield: 8–10 servings per 1 mold

TINA'S TIDBITS

- *Cheese and cheese mixtures may be frozen as long as they do not have high moisture content. Freeze these tortas first in their molds, and then remove them with the plastic wrap and freeze in airtight freezer bags.*
- *Put a straw into an almost sealed freezer bag and suck out all the air. Remove straw and seal quickly. This stops the formation of ice crystals.*

ICONS OF JEWISH COOKING

CHICKEN SOUP

Chicken soup has been an icon of the Jewish table since early medieval times. Its presence defined the Shabbat table, and a Jewish wedding feast symbolically started with the soup. At a wedding, chicken soup was served to draw the parallel between the fecundity of chickens and the wish that the new couple be fruitful

and multiply. The golden droplets of chicken fat that pooled on the top of the soup also demonstrated the wealth of the host of the wedding. In those days, the rendered chicken fat in the soup was never discarded; on the contrary, it was a prized addition to the bowl.

In keeping with the imperative of Shabbat to perform *hidur mitzvah*, "glorifying the Sabbath," even the poorest of Jews would save their funds for a chicken to be the highlight of the Friday night meal. Our ancestors were resourceful and utilized as much of the chicken as possible. Imagine a poor family living in the Pale of Settlement in Eastern Europe—one chicken could provide three courses! The liver was cooked with onions and mixed with some of the *schmaltz* (chicken fat) to start the meal with some chopped liver. Then the chicken was boiled in water with some meager vegetables and became the wonderful soup course. Finally, the meat was eaten, and the bones were probably reserved to provide a base for a bean soup later

in the week! My father-in-law had an interesting custom of eating the soup after the entrée. He did it because that was how it was always done in his house. There is a Lithuanian tradition, according to Rabbi Gil Marks, that Jews saved the soup for last in case Elijah the prophet knocked on their door in the middle of dinner to take them to Jerusalem. This way they would have eaten enough to sate them on their long journey.

As far as the curative powers of chicken soup, recent studies conducted at the University of Nebraska Medical School (see www.unmc.edu/chickensoup/article.htm) identified some properties in chicken soup with vegetables that suggests it has an anti-inflammatory effect on our bodies that helps lessen the symptoms of the common cold. Moses Maimonides, the great scholar and physician of the twelfth century, prescribed chicken soup to the weak and the infirm in one of his medical writings, and this was thought to be based on earlier Greek texts.

Left: *Basic Chicken Soup, page 346*

BASIC CHICKEN SOUP

This is the way my mother taught me to make chicken soup. She always used fresh dill. My friend Leslie's mom always used thyme. Neither one was wrong. Each had her own tradition. In this section I will not tell you the "right" way to make a dish. Consider these recipes as building blocks, so you can tweak the recipe to your own personal memory.

One 4- to 5-pound fowl or yearling (soup chicken)—a roaster will do
5 quarts water or water to cover
1 parsnip, peeled and cut into thirds
1 large onion, peeled but left whole
1 turnip, peeled and cut into quarters
2 stalks celery with leaves, cut into thirds

3 or more carrots, peeled and sliced into 1-inch lengths
Fresh dill, 3 or more sprigs to taste
Fresh parsley, 2 sprigs or more if parsnip isn't being used
Salt and pepper to taste
Kreplach or matzah balls (optional; see recipes)

1. Cut the chicken into pieces. Place the pieces in a large soup pot and cover with water.

2. Bring the water to a boil and simmer for 30 minutes, skimming the top of the liquid to remove all of the brown foam.

3. Add the remaining ingredients and cook over low heat until the chicken is quite tender and the vegetables are soft, about 2–3 hours.

4. Remove the chicken with a slotted spoon. Discard the dill and parsley. Remove the vegetables to nibble on, and save the carrot for later use in the soup. Strain the soup so that it is nice and clear.

5. Place the soup in a clean pot, and add the carrots. Cooked kreplach or matzah balls may be added at this point. Heat until nice and hot. Serve.

Yield: 3 quarts soup

TINA'S TIDBITS

- *Always cut up your chicken before making soup. This will expose more of the interior of the meat to the water and will produce a much richer-flavored soup.*
- *Even if you don't keep kosher, use kosher chickens or organic chickens to make the soup. I once made this recipe in a friend's home using a well-known nonkosher chicken. The chicken shrank in half because it had been plumped with water, and the soup tasted like the chicken "ran" through it!*
- *An alternative to clear soup is to remove the vegetables and herbs from the broth and recombine the vegetables with the broth in a blender until the mixture is opaque and creamy.*
- *Another traditional way to serve chicken soup is to add the cooked vegetables and shredded chicken meat to the bowl for a hearty meal.*

CHICKEN SOUP WITH GHONDI (CHICKPEA MEATBALLS)

When I first tried to make these easy chicken meatballs, I thought that they gave new meaning to the word "sinkers." However, after consulting with Najmieh Batmanglij, one of the most renowned experts on Persian cooking, I learned a few tricks to make these toothsome morsels firm but not rocklike. Sautéing the onion adds extra flavor and more moisture to the ghondi, *and using dark chicken meat from the thigh makes the balls softer. If you can't get a butcher to grind the meat for you or you don't want to grind it at home in a grinder or processor, I suggest that you try ground turkey or ground veal.*

1 recipe for Basic Chicken Soup (see page 346)
1 teaspoon ground turmeric
Juice of ½ lemon (optional)
3 tablespoons extra virgin olive oil
1 medium onion (about 8 ounces), finely diced
8 ounces boneless chicken thighs, ground, or ground turkey

½ teaspoon ground cardamom
½ teaspoon cumin (optional)
⅛ teaspoon turmeric
¼ teaspoon kosher salt
10 grindings black pepper or to taste
½–¾ cup toasted chickpea flour

1. Prepare the basic chicken soup, but add the turmeric to the soup and the optional lemon juice after the soup is cooked and strained of all vegetables and chicken parts.

2. To prepare the *ghondi*, heat an 8-inch frying pan for 20 seconds. Add the 3 tablespoons olive oil and heat for an additional 10 seconds. Add the diced onions and sauté until they are soft and just lightly golden.

3. In a 2-quart bowl, add the ground chicken or turkey, the spices, and ½ cup of the chickpea flour. Add the onions and all of the oil from the pan to the bowl. Mix well with a fork at first and then with your fingers until all the ingredients are well combined. If the mixture is too moist, add some of the remaining chickpea flour. If the mixture is too dry, you can add a little bit of water.

4. Shape the mixture into balls about 1 inch in diameter. Place the balls in hot soup and simmer, covered, for 20 minutes or until they are done on the inside.

5. Serve with the soup or as a separate course with fresh herbs.

Yield: 8–10 servings

TINA'S TIDBITS

- *If you overwork ground meat by squeezing it a lot, you will toughen the meat, and ultimately your finished product will be tough and hard. Use a fork and then your fingertips to achieve a soft paste.*
- *Pamela Grau Twena's book,* The Sephardic Table, *suggests the nontraditional addition of cumin to the mixture, which tastes wonderful. She also recommends making enough to serve cold on Shabbat morning with pita and green vegetables.*
- *It is important to use toasted chickpea flour, which imparts a different taste and texture to the finished meatball than nontoasted chickpea flour.*

Sopa de Pollo con Albondigas (Chicken Soup with Meatballs)

I had the pleasure of meeting Anya Von Bremzen when she was in Dallas a few years ago. An accomplished travel and food writer, she, along with Penelope Casas, has enlightened the world to Spanish cuisine. The following is a variation of her recipe, adapted from The New Spanish Table, *that makes it easy to create a hearty soup in very little time.*

3 slices whole-wheat bread
½ cup water or chicken stock
1 large egg
½ teaspoon kosher salt
10 grindings of fresh white pepper or ⅛ teaspoon ground white pepper
10–15 grindings of fresh whole nutmeg or ⅛ teaspoon ground nutmeg
10 ounces ground turkey

⅓ cup all-purpose flour (approximately)
2 tablespoons extra virgin olive oil
Three 10.5-ounce cans of chicken broth concentrate or 64 ounces store-bought broth
7 tablespoons rice flour combined with ⅓ cup water or chicken stock
Chopped fresh chives or Italian flat leaf parsley for garnish (optional)

1. Remove and discard the crusts from the bread slices. Tear the bread into large pieces, and place in a small bowl containing ½ cup water or stock. Set aside for 5 minutes.

2. Whisk the egg in a medium bowl. Add all the spices and whisk to combine.

3. Gently squeeze the bread to remove the water, and place the bread in the bowl with the egg mixture. Stir to combine.

4. Add the ground turkey and gently mix with your fingertips until well combined. The mixture will be very loose.

5. Place the flour on a plate and drop teaspoon mounds of meat mixture onto the flour.

6. For each ball, lightly toss the meat in the flour, and then put the meat in your hand. Shake your hand with fingers slightly closed as if you were getting ready to roll dice. This method will lightly toss the meat in your hand and create a fairly uniform ball. Place the ball on the rim of the plate and proceed with the remaining meat.

7. Heat a large nonstick sauté pan over high heat for 15 seconds. Add oil and heat for 10 seconds.

8. Reduce the heat to moderate and add the meatballs. Shake the pan and gently turn the meat so that it is lightly golden on all sides.

9. Remove the meatballs from the pan and place on paper towels to absorb excess oil.

10. Meanwhile, reconstitute the canned broth and bring to a boil. Slowly whisk in the rice flour mixture and return to a boil. Cook until thickened, about 2 minutes. Add the meatballs and reheat. Serve with a garnish of chopped fresh chives or Italian flat leaf parsley.

Yield: 8 or more servings

TINA'S TIDBITS

- *Crusts of bread rarely soften the same as the interior bread and don't blend in as well. That is the main reason for slicing off the crusts.*
- *Good-quality canned or frozen chicken broth may be substituted for homemade, especially if other ingredients are added to enhance the flavor and texture of the broth. Make sure the broth is reconstituted if it is sold in concentrated form or it will have an overwhelming flavor and make your finished dish too salty.*
- *Ground turkey is moister than chicken and is readily available. If not, use ground chicken or grind your own in a processor work bowl. However, do not overprocess or meatballs will be tough when cooked.*

GREEK AVGOLEMONO SOUP

An extension of the agristada sauce, this soup is refreshing, with its lemon and dill. The use of oil points to the Jewish cook, because she had to devise a way to keep kosher and enjoy the foods of the land at the same time.

3 tablespoons extra virgin olive oil (preferably Greek oil)
1 large onion, cut into ¼-inch dice
8 cups chicken broth
½ cup long-grain rice
Salt and freshly ground black pepper, to taste

2–3 tablespoons fresh lemon juice
2 eggs
1 tablespoon chopped fresh dill
Sprig of dill for garnish (optional)
Zest of 1 lemon, cut into long, fine strips for garnish (optional)

1. Heat the oil in a 3-quart saucepan. Sauté the onions over moderate heat until soft and very lightly golden.

2. Add the chicken broth and bring to a boil. Add the rice.

3. Simmer the soup, covered, for 20 minutes or until the rice is tender. Season with salt and pepper to taste.

4. After the soup and rice are cooked, whisk the lemon juice with the eggs in a 1-quart bowl.

Whisking constantly, add ½ cup of the hot soup to the egg mixture to temper it.

5. With the soup on the lowest heat, add the lemon mixture slowly into the pot, whisking constantly until the mixture is thoroughly incorporated.

6. Add the chopped dill, and garnish with the thin strips of lemon zest and an additional sprig of dill.

Yield: 8–10 servings

TINA'S TIDBITS

- *Do not mix the egg yolk and lemon juice together if you are not prepared to finish the soup right away. The acid in the juice will curdle the egg yolk if they are combined for a long time.*
- *Adding some hot soup to the eggs before adding the eggs to the soup will temper the eggs and allow them to thicken the soup rather than seize and curdle and make the soup lumpy.*

Italian Stracciatella Soup

Stracciatella *means "little rags" in Italian, and it is descriptive of the egg-cheese mixture once it is cooked by the heat of the soup. Traditionally, the base of this soup is either chicken or beef broth. However, in order for the laws of kashrut to be observed, the broth needs to be pareve.*

2 eggs
2 tablespoons freshly grated parmesan cheese
2 tablespoons finely chopped fresh parsley
  (preferably Italian flat leaf)

Pinch of freshly ground nutmeg
Pinch of salt (optional)
1 quart high-quality imitation chicken broth or
  vegetable stock

1. In a small bowl, beat the eggs until they are just blended, and mix in the cheese, parsley, nutmeg, and salt.

2. Bring the stock to a bubbling boil in a heavy 2-quart saucepan.

3. Pour in the egg mixture, stirring gently and constantly with a whisk. Simmer for 2–3 minutes. The egg and cheese mixture will form tiny flakes in the stock.

4. Taste for seasoning. Ladle the soup into a tureen or individual soup bowls and serve at once.

Yield: 4 servings

TINA'S TIDBITS

- *There are many high-quality vegetarian "chicken" broths on the market today.*
- *Similar to egg drop soup, the cheese creates a more ragged appearance when it is melted in the egg mixture, and that's how it received its name.*

CHINESE HOT AND SOUR SOUP

Not exactly what you had in mind for Shabbat dinner? Well, the thousands of Jews who have lived in China over the last thirteen hundred years probably weren't eating kreplach soup. Actually they might have ... and just called it "wonton soup"! Using chicken soup as the base, hot and sour soup is not only iconic for Chinese cuisine, but it is representative of China's contribution to the chicken soup category.

4 large dried shitake mushrooms
6 tree ear mushrooms
6 dried tiger lily buds, stem (hard end) removed
1 tablespoon oil
1/4 pound finely julienned veal scaloppine
1 tablespoon light soy sauce
1/2 cup finely shredded bamboo shoots
5 cups chicken broth
Salt to taste

2–3 tablespoons Chinese black vinegar or red wine vinegar
1 teaspoon dark soy sauce
2 tablespoons cornstarch
3 tablespoons water
1 block firm white bean curd, cut into thin strips
1 tablespoon sesame seed oil
1 teaspoon freshly ground pepper
1 egg, slightly beaten
2 tablespoons chopped scallions

1. Place the black Chinese mushrooms, tree ears, and tiger lily buds in a glass bowl and cover with water. Microwave for 2 minutes, allow the dried vegetables to sit for 15 minutes or longer until soft, and drain.

2. Cut off and discard the stems of the mushrooms. Cut both the mushrooms and the tree ears into thin slices. With your fingers, shred the tiger lily buds, and if they are long, cut them in half.

3. Heat a wok or 3-quart saucepan for 20 seconds. Add the oil and heat for another 10 seconds. Add the julienned veal and stir-fry for 10 seconds. Add the light soy sauce and stir-fry for another 20 seconds or until the meat is about done.

4. Add the mushrooms, tree ears, tiger lily buds, and bamboo shoots. Stir-fry quickly for 30 seconds, and add the broth and salt to taste. Stir in the vinegar and dark soy sauce.

5. Combine the cornstarch and water, and stir into the simmering broth. When the mixture is slightly thickened, add the bean curd and bring to a boil.

6. Turn off the heat. Add the sesame seed oil and the pepper, and stir to blend.

7. Pour the soup into a hot tureen or keep it in the pot with the heat still turned off.

8. Add the lightly beaten egg in a steady stream as you slowly stir in a circular motion. Sprinkle with the scallions and serve at once.

Yield: 6 servings

TINA'S TIDBITS

- *The distinctive musty flavor of this soup comes from the tiger lily buds. These dried buds are from the tiger lily flower and are considered vegetarian and kosher.*
- *For an authentic taste, veal is the perfect substitute for pork in any Chinese dish. Similar in color and texture to pork, it does not alter the flavor or the look of the dish one iota.*
- *Cornstarch must be exposed to boiling liquid for it to thicken properly. If your soup doesn't look thick enough, combine another tablespoon of cornstarch with 2 tablespoons of cold water and stir it into the hot soup. The beauty of cornstarch is that it doesn't immediately swell and clump together when added to a hot liquid, so adjustments to the soup are easy to make.*

INDIAN MULLIGATAWNY SOUP

This soup hails from the Tamil region of southern India (the first Indian region inhabited by Jews). The name means "fire water," but this soup is not that spicy. It is loaded with flavor and packed with protein from the chicken as well as the chickpeas. It is very easy to make and fun to eat, especially if you serve it over rice, with peanuts, coconut, and raisins sprinkled on top.

One 3-pound chicken, cut up
6 cups chicken stock or water
1 onion stuck with 6 cloves
1 stalk of celery
1 carrot, coarsely chopped
1 bay leaf
2 sprigs of parsley
Salt to taste
15 whole peppercorns
1 cup packaged coconut
One 15-ounce can chickpeas, drained
6 tablespoons flour
1 tablespoon turmeric

$\frac{1}{2}$ teaspoon powdered ginger
1 tablespoon ground cumin
1 tablespoon ground coriander
$\frac{1}{8}$–$\frac{1}{4}$ teaspoon cayenne pepper
4 tablespoons margarine
2 cloves garlic, minced
1 cup soy creamer or water
Salt and pepper to taste
Basmati rice (optional)
Coconut (optional)
Raisins (optional)
Peanuts (optional)

1. Cook the chicken in a 4-quart pot with the next 8 ingredients for 1 hour or until the chicken is tender. Strain the broth, and remove the skin and bones from the meat.

2. Put 2 cups of the strained broth into a blender and add the cup of packaged coconut. Blend until the coconut is pulverized. You have now created fresh coconut milk. Strain this coconut milk over a bowl through cheesecloth or a double-mesh strainer to remove all the solid particles of coconut. Throw away any coconut solids.

3. If the blender is gritty, rinse out the container. Add the coconut milk and chickpeas to the blender and blend until smooth.

4. Combine all of the dried spices with the flour in a small bowl. Set aside. Melt the margarine in a 3-quart saucepan. Whisk in the flour mixture and the garlic, and stir for 1 minute.

5. Whisk in the coconut milk mixture and the remaining broth until smooth and thickened.

6. Add the creamer (or water) and the chicken pieces, and season to taste with the salt and pepper. Serve.

Yield: 8 servings

TINA'S TIDBITS

- *To make this soup into a meal, place a scoop of cooked basmati rice (very fragrant rice) in the bottom of the soup bowl. Pour the soup over the rice, and pass dishes of the optional condiments for guests to sprinkle on top of their soup.*
- *Coconut milk is not milk at all but the white liquid derived from grinding coconut with water and then squeezing the pulp to extract as much flavor as possible.*

Tom Kah Gai
(Thai Chicken in Coconut Curry Soup with Rice Stick Noodles)

At present there are three hundred Jews living in Thailand, all in Bangkok. Although the first documented Jew in Thailand was in the early seventeenth century, the present Jewish community established its earliest roots in 1890 when the Rosenberg family migrated to Thailand and established modern hotels in the country. There are three synagogues in Bangkok—one Sephardic, one Ashkenazic, and a Chabad house that is frequented by thousands of Jewish tourists every year. This chicken soup-based Thai soup is my homage to the tolerant, accepting Thai people, who have always welcomed our people.

4–6 ounces *Chantaboon* noodles or any flat, wide, rice stick noodle
2 tablespoons peanut oil
4 cloves garlic, finely minced
1 scallion, finely minced
Two 3-inch pieces of dried lemongrass or 1 fresh stalk of lemongrass, cut into 4 pieces
$\frac{1}{4}$ teaspoon freshly ground black pepper
1 teaspoon Thai red curry paste
$\frac{1}{2}$ serrano pepper, seeded and chopped
4 Kaffir lime leaves

1 piece dried galangal root or $\frac{1}{2}$-inch slice of fresh ginger root
4 cups water
$\frac{1}{2}$ pound boneless chicken breast, sliced into $\frac{1}{4}$ × 3-inch pieces
2 tablespoons cornstarch
One 14-ounce can coconut milk
One 15-ounce can straw mushrooms, drained
2 tablespoons light soy sauce or *nam pla* fish sauce
Juice from $\frac{1}{2}$ lime
$\frac{1}{4}$ cup chopped fresh cilantro

1. Bring 3 quarts of water to a boil. Add the noodles and stir constantly for 1 minute to prevent sticking together. Drain in a colander and rinse with cold water. Set aside.

2. Heat a 4-quart saucepan or soup pot over high heat for 20 seconds. Add the oil and heat for another 20 seconds. Reduce the heat to medium high, and add the garlic, scallion, lemongrass, black pepper, curry paste, serrano pepper, Kaffir leaves, and galangal root. Stir-fry for 2 minutes, until the seasonings are fragrant. Add the water and bring to a boil.

3. Place the chicken in a small bowl and lightly toss with the cornstarch to coat well. Add the chicken to the pot of soup. Reduce the heat to medium and simmer the chicken in the soup for 4 minutes or until the meat is thoroughly cooked.

TINA'S TIDBITS

- *Most, if not all, of the ingredients are available in local supermarkets throughout the country.*
- *Read the (very) fine print on the Thai red curry paste jar. Although most jarred paste is pareve, some follow the original recipe and contain 5 percent shrimp paste.*
- *The Chantaboon noodles are very wide, flat noodles of irregular shape from the Chantaboon region. They have a tendency to curl up into cylinders. If you prefer, any width rice stick noodle may be used.*

4. Add the remaining ingredients **except** the cilantro and continue cooking for another 2 minutes.

5. Add the reserved noodles and simmer for 5 or more minutes until the noodles are thoroughly swollen and the soup is slightly reduced.

6. Serve in soup bowls garnished with some chopped cilantro.

Yield: 8 servings

KNISHES, *BOREKAS,* AND FILLED PASTRIES

*L*ittle "pies" of dough filled with meat, cheese, or vegetables are ubiquitous in every region of the Jewish Diaspora. I think that this genre of food is illustrative of the history of the Jews. With the laws of kashrut and Shabbat dictating what ingredients could be used and what time was appropriate to cook the food, little

packets of food encased in dough could be made in advance and served at will. To those dictates add the extra burden of poverty and long hard toil in the fields and one can see why a food that provides sustenance, is portable, and relies more heavily on vegetables than meat would be popular among the Jewish community. Add symbolism and superstition to the equation and you have the ultimate Jewish finger food.

The Radenites, ninth-century Jewish traders along the Silk Road, are thought to be the original importers of Asian pocket foods. With their rise in popularity in the West, many of these filled pastries took on folkloric meaning. Hamantaschen were symbolic of the hated enemy of the Persian Jews, and the actual consumption of the baked good was a metaphor for "devouring our enemies." Kreplach, originally worn around the neck as an amulet at the time of the New Year, might not ward off evil decrees, but the superstitious medieval German Jews weren't taking any chances and hoped that their well-being would be "sealed" for good in the coming year. Some pockets of dough were shaped in half moons to represent political regimes that were at times hated, and thus consumed like hamantaschen. One interpretation of triangular shaped pastries is that

the points represent the three Patriarchs, Abraham, Isaac, and Jacob. Many celebrations included filled pockets of dough to symbolize that God surrounds us and protects our goodness from evil.

In North America, we have been exposed to the many names and permutations of these dishes. Due to the largest migration of Jews to the United States at the beginning of the twentieth century, the cooking of Eastern European and Russian Jews has left the most indelible mark on our culinary memories. Dense crusty dough filled with potato, kasha, or liver is known by all Americans as a knish. Today knishes are four-inch square pillows of dough bursting with popular potato-onion filling. Long ago they were bite-sized morsels served as part of a Russian *zakuski* (appetizer plate) or served at special events like a bris (*b'rit milah*), bar mitzvah, or wedding. *Piroshkies* can be sweet or savory, fried or baked. The Polish immigrants called them pierogis, and these pastries were often boiled instead of fried or baked.

If Shakespeare's Juliet could fret about "What's in a name?" the same holds true for these treasures from the kitchen. *Boyos, borekas, borekitas, sambousak, buricche, pasteles,* pierogis, *pastelikos,* empanadas, kreplach, phyllos, *cigares, bulemas, briks,* samosas, or wonton—all have made their way into the Jewish kitchen, and all can be created with the use of modern equipment or with purchased prepared dough. They are similar and yet literally worlds apart.

Fillings can be meat, fish, vegetable, or cheese. They can be baked, fried, or sometimes boiled. The dough can use oil, butter, or animal fat (chicken, goose, or beef). They can be leavened by yeast, baking powder, or air, in the case of strudel or *pâte à choux* (cream puff paste). They can be shaped in rounds, squares, half-moons, crescents, tight cylinders, triangles, or conical with the top opened to the delight of the gastronome. Flavors can be mild or spicy, sweet or tart, flavored with herbs or spices. Each little pocket tells a story of persistence and success.

Eastern European Potato Knishes

Not quite as heavy with crust as the commercial variety, here is one of many examples of the creative use of potatoes by the Jewish cook.

DOUGH:
2 cups all-purpose flour
1 teaspoon baking powder
$\frac{1}{2}$ teaspoon salt
2 tablespoons water
2 tablespoons vegetable oil
2 eggs, lightly beaten

FILLING:
2 large onions, diced
2 tablespoons rendered chicken fat or oil
2 pounds russet potatoes (approximately four 5-inch potatoes)
$\frac{1}{4}$ cup chopped parsley
1 large egg
Salt and freshly ground black pepper to taste
1 egg yolk mixed with 1 teaspoon water for glaze

1. Combine the flour, baking powder, and salt in a medium bowl, and form a well in the center of the flour mixture. Combine the water, oil, and eggs, and pour into the well. Mix the ingredients together to form a smooth dough. Cover the dough and let it rest while you make the filling.

2. Slowly cook the onions in the chicken fat or oil in a covered skillet over a low heat for 10 minutes. Remove the cover and fry over medium heat until golden brown.

3. Meanwhile, peel the potatoes and cut them in quarters. Put them in a pot with cold salted water to cover the potatoes and bring to a boil. Cook the potatoes until tender, about 20 minutes. Drain and cool for 5 minutes.

4. Mash the potatoes and add the parsley, egg, salt and pepper, and the sautéed onions and oil and mix thoroughly. Adjust the seasonings if necessary.

5. Preheat the oven to 350°F. Divide the dough in half, and roll each half to $\frac{1}{8}$-inch thickness in a rectangular shape. Spread some of the filling in a line about $\frac{1}{2}$ inch in from the bottom edge. Fold over the dough and roll until all of the filling is covered. Wet the edge of the dough with a little water and seal the edges of the dough. Cut the filled dough away from the remaining dough. Repeat with the remaining dough and filling, and then repeat with the other half of the dough.

6. Cut the roll into 2-inch pieces and place them on a greased or parchment-lined cookie sheet.

7. Brush with the beaten egg yolk mixed with water, and bake for 15 minutes or until golden brown.

Yield: 2 dozen

TINA'S TIDBITS

- *Flour, eggs, onions, potatoes—the most exotic item in this recipe is parsley! You may, however, choose to add any additional ingredients; just make sure they are cooked, like mushrooms, or need no cooking, like chopped fresh dill.*
- *It is easier to roll out two large rectangles and create two or three rolls of filled dough from each piece of dough than to roll out six small rectangles and fill them individually.*
- *These may be made in advance and refrigerated or frozen after baking until ready to use.*

GRANDMA GUSSIE'S POTATO KNISHES

In my family, knishes weren't the large, square, hard cushions of dough with potato on the inside. They were a soft patty of potato dough with fried onions encased in the center. No family function at my grandmother's house was without this treat, and you had to act fast or you didn't get to grab more than one. When she was recovering in the hospital from a heart attack, everyone centered their conversation on Grandma's knishes. Subliminally everyone knew that the precious recipe had not been written down. No one was able to comprehend "a bissel" (little) of this and "a shiterein" (handful) of that until one day I came across a recipe that reminded me of Grandma's knishes, and with a little tweaking, I now pass the recipe on to the next generation!

4½ cups dry mashed potato (no liquid or fat added)
3 eggs, lightly beaten with a fork
½ cup or more flour or matzah meal
¼ teaspoon freshly ground black pepper

3 teaspoons salt, divided use
¼ cup olive oil or chicken fat
3 large onions, finely diced
Additional olive or vegetable oil for frying knishes

1. Mix the potatoes, eggs, flour or matzah meal, pepper, and 2 teaspoons of salt together to form a smooth, but slightly sticky dough. Set aside for 20 minutes while you fry the onions.

2. Heat a 10-inch skillet over high heat for 20 seconds. Add the oil or chicken fat and heat for another 10 seconds, turning down the heat if the oil begins to smoke. Add the onions and sauté until the onions are dark golden brown but not burnt. Remove from the heat and stir in the remaining teaspoon of salt.

3. Heavily flour a board and your hands with flour or matzah meal. Take about 1 tablespoon of dough and, using your fingertips, flatten it in your palm or on the board until it is about a 2- to 3-inch circle. If dough is too sticky, roll in additional flour or matzah meal.

TINA'S TIDBITS

- *Cooked mashed potatoes tend to hydrate when they sit out for a long time. To prevent excess moisture, use within an hour of mashing or leave the potatoes whole until ready to proceed with a recipe.*
- *These knishes are perfect for Passover if you eliminate the flour. However, the dough will be smoother if flour is used.*
- *Matzah meal acts like a sponge, absorbing excess moisture in dough. To allow for this, the mixture must rest for 15-20 minutes before using.*
- *Sometimes tossing the dough very lightly on a floured board will make the dough less sticky and the process of shaping will be easier.*

4. Place a scant teaspoon of the onion mixture in the center of the circle, and fold the dough edges over the filling to meet in the center to create a smaller, filled circle of dough.

5. Place on a floured plate until ready to fry or fry immediately. **Note:** These should not stand too long or they will get soggy.

6. Heat a clean frying pan for 20 seconds. Add the additional oil to a depth of $1/4$ inch and heat for 15 more seconds.

7. Place the knish seam side (the side where the dough came together) down in the hot oil and fry over moderate heat for 4 minutes or until golden brown. Flip the knish over and fry until the other side is golden, about 2 minutes. Remove with a slotted spatula to paper towels to drain. Let cool for a minute or so.

8. Serve as soon as they are not too hot to handle. Enjoy!

Yield: 2–3 dozen

AUSTRIAN POTATO-MUSHROOM STRUDEL

Making strudel is much easier now that we have quality phyllo dough available in the supermarket. The lowly shtetl knish goes upscale with mushrooms, parsley, and Yukon Gold potatoes!

2 pounds Yukon Gold potatoes (approximately 4 potatoes)
½ ounce dried porcini mushrooms
4 ounces crimini or baby bella mushrooms
2 tablespoons vegetable oil
2 medium onions, diced
1½ teaspoons truffle-scented flour or all-purpose flour

2 tablespoons parsley
1 large egg, lightly beaten
1½ teaspoons salt
Freshly ground black pepper to taste
½ pound phyllo dough
1 stick unsalted butter, melted

1. Cook the whole, unpeeled potatoes in boiling salted water to cover for 25 minutes or until a knife easily pierces the potato. Drain and cool until easy to handle.

2. Place the porcini mushrooms in a 16-ounce bowl and cover with water. Microwave on high for 3 minutes. Allow the mushrooms to soak for 10 minutes or until soft. Gently squeeze some of the excess moisture out of the mushrooms and reserve the liquid for later. Chop the mushrooms into fine pieces. Set aside.

3. Chop the crimini or baby bella mushrooms into ¼-inch dice. Set aside.

4. Heat a 3-quart saucepan over high heat for 20 seconds. Add the oil and heat for 10 seconds. Add the diced onions and stir to coat with oil. Cover and cook over low heat for 10 minutes. Remove the cover and sauté over medium heat until golden brown.

5. Add the crimini or baby bella mushrooms to the onions and cook for 2 minutes. Add the chopped porcini mushrooms and ¼ cup of the soaking liquid. Be careful to remove the liquid from the top of the bowl to prevent inclusion of sediment from the bottom of the bowl. Cook for 2 minutes and add the flour. Stir to combine and cook for 1 minute more. Remove from the heat.

6. Peel the potatoes and mash until smooth. Add the onion-mushroom mixture, parsley, egg, salt, and pepper, and mix until thoroughly combined. Check for seasonings.

7. Place one sheet of phyllo dough, short side facing you, on a clean, large towel, and brush with some melted butter. Place a second sheet of dough to the right of the first but overlapping the first sheet by 2 inches. Brush the second sheet with butter.

8. Place a third sheet of dough directly below the first sheet but overlapping it by 2 inches. Brush with melted butter. Place the fourth sheet to the right of the third sheet, overlapping the bottom of the second sheet and the right side of the third. Brush with melted butter.

9. Place a 1-inch-thick line of the potato mixture 1 inch above the bottom of the dough and 2 inches in from each side. Brush the edges with some

butter. Fold the bottom up over the filling, and fold the sides in over the filling to conceal.

10. Tightly roll the dough up from the bottom, and place the log of strudel on a parchment-lined, rimmed cookie sheet. Brush the top with some melted butter.

11. Lightly score the dough in 1-inch intervals, and liberally sprinkle water all over the dough so that some of the water pools in the bottom of the pan.

12. Place in a 375°F oven and bake for 20 minutes or until the strudel is golden brown.

13. When ready to serve, cut the log into 1-inch pieces and serve.

Yield: 30 pieces

TINA'S TIDBITS

- *Oil or margarine can be used in place of butter to make this recipe pareve.*
- *Phyllo dough can be cut into 2-inch-wide strips, brushed with melted butter, and then folded like a flag into filled triangles.*
- *These knishes are delicious served with some sour cream to which some chopped chives have been added.*

TUNISIAN BRIKS

These wonderful pastries might be reminiscent of knishes, but they are literally worlds apart. Briks are the iconic street food of Tunisia. Street vendors sell these savory fried turnovers of dough filled with meat, fish, or vegetable stuffing all over Tunisia. Their popularity is similar to the sale of hot dogs in our country or falafel in Israel. Normally, briks are served with harissa, but here I have used some of the spicy relish to enhance the flavor of the sweet potato filling. In the sixteenth century, sweet potatoes were brought by the Portuguese from the New World to Africa, where they have been continuously cultivated to this day.

The following is a sweet potato adaptation of a brik recipe from Pamela Grau Twena's book The Sephardic Table.

1 tablespoon extra virgin olive oil
½ cup finely chopped onion
1 large clove garlic, finely minced
1 tablespoon finely chopped flat leaf parsley
1 medium sweet potato, about 8 ounces after cooking and peeling, preferably with pale flesh if available, or Yukon Gold potatoes

2 teaspoons harissa, or more to taste
1 egg, separated
Salt to taste
12–15 regular-sized (8-inch square) *lumpia* shells or thin spring roll skins
1 or more cups of vegetable oil for frying *briks*

1. Heat an 8-inch skillet over high heat for 20 seconds. Add olive oil and heat for 10 seconds more. Reduce the heat if the oil is smoking, and add the onion.

2. Sauté the onion until golden. Add the garlic and sauté another minute until the mixture is fragrant; do not let the garlic get too dark.

3. Remove the skillet with the onion mixture from the heat, and add the parsley and potato. Mash the potato well to mix all of the ingredients together. Add the harissa, egg yolk, and salt to taste, and stir to combine.

4. Combine the remaining egg white with 1 teaspoon of water.

5. Lay one *lumpia* shell or spring roll skin on a board or countertop. Place 1 heaping tablespoon of the potato mixture in the center. Using your finger, rub some egg white on the bottom and top edges of the shell or skin.

(See next page.)

TINA'S TIDBITS

- *Burnt garlic will impart a bitter taste to food. Always add the garlic after the onions are golden to add flavor and prevent burning.*
- *Egg white cooks immediately when exposed to high heat. It is a perfect sealant for that reason and will not splatter in the hot oil the way pure water would.*
- *Crumpling paper towels provides a larger surface area to absorb oil from fried foods and makes the food less greasy.*
- *Although briks are meant to be eaten right after cooking, these are good warm or at room temperature. Reheat in a 425°F oven until crisp if you want to serve them hot.*

6. Fold the bottom edge over the filling, and lightly press down along the long edge. Do the same with the top edge, bringing it down to the long edge, creating a rectangle.

7. Rub some egg white on the left and right edges of the formed rectangle. Fold the right edge over the filled section and gently press down to seal the edge. Repeat with the left edge, creating a packet that looks almost square. Place seam side down on a plate while you form the other packets.

8. Pour the oil into a flat-bottomed wok or a small saucepan so that the oil is 1 inch deep.

9. Heat the oil to 350°F on a frying thermometer until hot but not smoking.

10. Place the packets, 2 or 3 at a time, into the hot oil, seam side down. Fry until lightly golden and the tops begin to puff up a little. Turn the *briks* over and fry just until lightly browned. Immediately remove from the oil with a wire spatula or slotted spoon.

11. Drain on crumpled paper towels and serve. Additional harissa may be used for a dip, if desired.

Yield: 12–15 servings

INDIAN SAMOSAS

Is it possible that potatoes are the number-one culinary choice for stuffing, or does the choice of filling have more to do with the cost of food and being frugal? Whatever the answer, potatoes show up in India as well for wonderful little packets of spicy potato and pea filling. There is no need to make your own dough when wonton skins are readily available. Serve with some raw mango chutney.

2 tablespoons vegetable oil
1 teaspoon crushed red pepper
1 teaspoon chopped fresh ginger
1 teaspoon chopped fresh garlic
1 medium onion, cut into $^1\!/_4$-inch dice
$^1\!/_2$ teaspoon salt

3 medium Yukon Gold, California whites, or russet potatoes, peeled and cut into $^1\!/_4$-inch cubes
2 cups water
One 10-ounce package frozen peas, thawed
2 teaspoons curry powder
$^1\!/_2$ pound wonton skins
Oil for frying filled dough

1. Heat the 2 tablespoons oil in a large frying pan, and add the red pepper, ginger, garlic, and onion.

2. Sauté for 5 minutes or until the onion is golden. Do not burn the garlic.

3. Add the salt, potatoes, and water, and stir to combine. Cover and cook for 20 minutes over medium heat, until the potatoes are tender.

4. Add the peas and the curry powder, and cook until the peas are hot and any excess water is evaporated.

5. Brush the edges of the wonton skin with a little water. Place a teaspoon of the filling in the center and fold over into a triangle, sealing the edges well. Continue with the rest of the dough and filling.

6. Heat the oil to 375°F in a frying pan or wok to a depth of 2 inches. Do not let the oil smoke.

7. Fry a few samosas at a time in the hot oil until golden. Drain on paper towels and serve.

Yield: 1–2 dozen

TINA'S TIDBITS

- *Stir potato mixture occasionally, using a rubber spatula so that the potatoes don't break up. Yukon Golds or California long whites break up less than russet potatoes, which are the traditional choice.*
- *Do not use too much filling or the wontons will open in the hot oil and lose their contents.*
- *Use only enough water to dampen the edges so that they stick together. Too much water will cause steam when the samosas go into the oil and the wonton skins will open.*
- *Do not try to fry too many samosas at a time. If the samosas are not crowded when they are frying, the temperature of the oil won't drop and the dough won't absorb excess oil. The finished product will be light, crisp, and not greasy.*

Hungarian Mushroom Turnovers

Using dough similar to rugelach dough, these mushroom turnovers are rich and savory. You won't miss the cinnamon and sugar!

DOUGH:
4 ounces unsalted butter
4 ounces cream cheese
Pinch of salt
1 cup all-purpose flour

FILLING:
4 tablespoons butter
1 onion, finely chopped
½ pound fresh mushrooms
Salt and freshly ground pepper to taste
¼ teaspoon nutmeg
1 tablespoon cream sherry
1 egg yolk mixed with 1 teaspoon water for glaze
Sesame seeds

1. Cream the 4 ounces of butter, cream cheese, and salt in a mixer at high speed until well combined, light, and fluffy.

2. Add the flour. Mix on medium speed only until the flour is incorporated and the mixture just begins to hold together. Divide the dough into 4 equal pieces, and form each piece into a ball, flatten to 1 inch, and refrigerate for 20–30 minutes.

3. While the dough is chilling, sauté the onion in the 4 tablespoons of butter until lightly golden.

4. Wash and pat dry the mushrooms and place them in a processor. Pulse the processor on and off until the mushrooms are in uniform, fine pieces.

5. Add the mushrooms to the onions and sauté until they give up their juices and begin to appear dry.

6. Add the seasonings and the sherry.

7. Roll a ball of dough ⅛-inch thick on a lightly floured surface and cut into approximately six 2-inch circles.

8. Place a teaspoon of filling in the center of each circle. Dip your finger in water and brush the edges of the circle with it. Fold the circle in half. Pinch the edges together and use the tines of a fork to crimp the edges. Place on an ungreased cookie sheet and proceed with the rest of the dough in the same manner.

9. Brush the tops of the turnovers with the egg yolk glaze and sprinkle with some sesame seeds. Bake at 400°F for 15 minutes or until light and golden. Serve hot. Freeze leftovers only after turnovers have completely cooled.

Yield: 2 dozen turnovers

TINA'S TIDBITS

- *Beating the cream cheese and butter together helps to thoroughly combine the two ingredients and incorporates air into the dough to help make it light and flaky.*
- *Although the ancient city of Byzantium (now Istanbul) adopted the crescent shape as its symbol to honor the goddess Diana long before the Ottoman Empire was established, the crescent remained a symbol of that empire and the present country of Turkey. Legend has it that in 1793 when the Austrians defeated the Ottoman advance into their country, they celebrated by making pastries in the shape of a crescent so that they could symbolically devour their enemy. Although the symbolism is long forgotten, many countries that bordered or were a part of the empire have crescent-shaped pastries in their repertoire.*

Boston Chremslach (Stuffed Matzah Balls)

These little balls or pancakes can be filled with fruits and cinnamon and sugar or with meats. They are perfect for dinners the rest of Passover.

DOUGH:
1 recipe for matzah balls, yours or a prepared mix
1/4 teaspoon ground ginger

FILLING:
2 cups cooked meat, finely chopped (meat shreds from your sliced brisket are perfect!)

1/2 medium onion, finely grated
1 tablespoon chicken fat
Salt, pepper, and cinnamon to taste
3 quarts water with 2 good-quality chicken bouillon cubes
2 tablespoons oil or chicken fat for frying (optional)
1 onion, sliced (optional)

1. Make the dough for matzah balls, adding the ginger to the recipe, and set aside until ready to form the balls.

2. Combine the meat, grated onion, chicken fat, salt, pepper, and cinnamon for the filling.

3. Shape 2 tablespoons of the matzah ball mixture into a flat, thick disk.

4. Place a teaspoon of meat mixture into the center of the disk and pull up the sides of the dough over filling to shape the dough into a ball. Make sure no filling is exposed or it will open in the water. Repeat with the remaining dough and filling.

5. Combine the 3 quarts of water and two bouillon cubes in a large pot and bring to a boil.

6. Add the filled balls, cover the pot, reduce the heat, and simmer for 20 minutes.

7. To serve, fry the sliced onion in 2 tablespoons of oil or chicken fat and then lightly fry the cooked, stuffed matzah balls in the pan with the onions until golden. If necessary, more oil and more onion may be added to fry all of the stuffed matzah balls.

Yield: 12 servings

TINA'S TIDBITS

- Chremslach *are generally pancake-shaped and fried or baked. My version lets you use leftover matzah ball mixture and all the shreds from your sliced brisket!*
- *Leftover prepared matzah balls can be fried in a pan with the onions, too, and served with leftover meat and gravy days after the seder.*
- *Never lift the lid on the pot when the* chremslach *are boiling or they will shrink and be tough and raw on the inside. Boil for 20 minutes and* **don't peek!**

Eastern European Kreplach

The kreplach represent our fate being "sealed" for the coming year. They are often served in chicken soup on Rosh HaShanah or before sundown the evening Yom Kippur begins. Wonton dough makes it very easy to make kreplach, but they will be floppy and thin. Homemade dough or purchased ravioli dough will give the thickness reminiscent of your grandmother's.

½ pound homemade dough (see below), fresh ravioli
    dough, or wonton skins
2 cups cooked meat, finely chopped, or hamburger
    lightly sautéed
1 medium onion, finely chopped

1 teaspoon chicken fat
Salt and pepper to taste
1 egg, slightly beaten
Oil for frying (optional)

1. Cut the dough into 2-inch squares.

2. Combine the meat, onion, chicken fat, and seasonings in a small bowl. Beat the egg in a glass dish and add to the meat mixture. Add a little water to the dish used for the beaten egg.

3. Place a teaspoon of filling on each square.

4. Brush the top edges of the dough with the egg-water wash.

5. Fold the dough in half on the diagonal to make a triangle. Pinch the edges together to seal.

6. Cook in boiling salted water for 10 minutes or until done. Serve in the chicken soup or fry in a little oil.

Kreplach Dough

2 large eggs
1 tablespoon olive oil
2 tablespoons ice water
2 cups bread flour

1. Place eggs in the food processor work bowl. Add the olive oil and the water and mix by turning the processor on and off twice.

2. Add 1 cup of the flour and turn the processor on for 5 seconds. Scrape the sides of the bowl.

3. Add the other cup of flour and process for 10 seconds longer. Dough will be crumbly. Pinch a little bit of dough; if it holds together it is ready to be rolled.

4. Remove the dough and divide it in half. Place it on a lightly floured surface, cover and let it rest for 10 minutes or longer if you are rolling the dough by hand.

Yield: 18 or more pieces

TINA'S TIDBITS

- *Pasta or pastry dough must be allowed to rest for at least 15 minutes after it is formed so that the gluten in the dough will relax and roll out easily without shrinking back.*
- *When slicing pot roast, shards of meat invariably fall off the slices. Although tempting to eat right then, these bits of meat make great filling for kreplach, knishes, or chremslach. Freeze the meat bits, and defrost them when you're ready to make kreplach.*
- *If you're purchasing pasta dough to make any filled pasta form, never buy sheets of lasagna noodles. They are too thick when folded over and will be quite chewy. On the other hand, maybe that's the way your bubbe made them!*
- *Salt should never be used in pasta dough, as it will toughen the dough and make it very difficult to roll out. Always add the salt to the water when cooking the filled dough.*

Spanish Spinach Empanadas

Empanadas are sealed pockets of dough filled with a myriad of fillings. Here we see the classic Jewish Sephardic filling using spinach, pine nuts, and raisins.

2 tablespoons raisins
1/4 cup water
1 1/2 tablespoons extra virgin olive oil
One 10-ounce package frozen chopped spinach, thawed and squeezed very dry
Salt and pepper to taste

3 anchovies, mashed, or 1 teaspoon anchovy paste
2 cloves garlic, finely minced
3 tablespoons pine nuts
1 package frozen puff pastry sheets (preferably one containing butter, but not necessary), thawed
1 egg mixed with 1 teaspoon water for glaze

1. To make the filling, cover the raisins with the water in a small bowl and microwave for 1 minute. Set aside and soak until needed.

2. Heat the oil in a skillet and sauté the spinach until it gives up its juices. Add the salt, pepper, anchovies or anchovy paste, and garlic and cook for a minute.

3. Drain the raisins and finely chop them with the pine nuts in a food processor or by hand. Stir into the spinach mixture.

4. Defrost the dough according to package directions. Roll the puff pastry out on a lightly floured surface to a thickness of 1/8 inch. Cut the dough into 2- to 3-inch circles. Lightly brush the edges of the circle with a little bit of the egg-water mixture.

5. Place a teaspoon of the filling on each dough circle and fold it in half. Seal the edges by crimping with the tines of a fork, and brush the top with the egg glaze.

6. Line a cookie sheet with parchment paper. Preheat oven to 350°F. Place the empanadas on the cookie sheet and then bake for 15 minutes or until golden. Serve hot or at room temperature.

Yield: 18 pieces

TINA'S TIDBITS

- *Ten ounces of frozen chopped spinach is equivalent to one pound of large leaf spinach before cleaning off the sand and removing the stems.*
- *To avoid having the spinach turn green-gray from long cooking, squeeze small amounts of the defrosted spinach in your hand until no liquid can be seen. This will let you sauté the ingredients fast without having to spend time sautéing, so the excess water in the vegetables evaporates.*
- *Egg is needed to seal puff pastry because the egg will cook and seal the dough when exposed to the heat in the oven, whereas water might just evaporate and then the puff pastry dough would open up, exposing the filling.*

French Stuffed Brie en Croûte

I used to make my own brioche dough to wrap Brie, and then I discovered that prepared frozen pastry sheets are much easier to use and available in supermarket freezers. There are no potatoes here as in so many other stuffed pastries, but I suppose sautéed slices of potato and onion with chives could taste great on the inside. Create your own filling, or use one of the recipes below.

One 14-ounce wheel of Brie cheese
One 10 × 10-inch sheet of prepared frozen puff pastry (half of 17.3-ounce package)

1 egg
1 tablespoon water

1. Thaw the sheet of dough for 30 minutes, and preheat the oven to 400°F. Prepare your choice of filling (see recipes below).

2. Roll out one sheet of dough into a 14 × 14-inch square. Combine the egg and water, and brush over the sheet of dough.

3. Evenly cut the Brie in half horizontally. Place one half of the cheese, cut side up, on the egg-brushed dough. Place filling over the cheese and top with the other half of the cheese, cut side down.

4. Fold up the sides of the dough over the cheese, brushing the dough with extra egg wash to "glue" the dough edges together and trimming any excess dough. Press the edges to seal. Flip the covered Brie over and place seam side down on a parchment-lined cookie sheet.

5. Brush the top and sides of the dough with the egg wash, and use any remaining dough to decorate the top. Brush decorations with egg wash as well.

6. Either freeze at this point for later gift giving, or bake in the preheated oven for 20 minutes or until golden brown. Allow the cheese to sit at least $\frac{1}{2}$ hour before serving. Serve alone or with toasted French bread or crackers. Serves 12–15.

Apple-Cranberry Filling

$\frac{1}{3}$ cup sweetened dried cranberries
2 tablespoons orange juice
1 small Gala apple, peeled
1 teaspoon unsalted butter

1 tablespoon applejack or Grand Marnier
$\frac{1}{4}$ teaspoon cinnamon
$\frac{1}{4}$ cup chopped toasted pecans

1. Place the dried cranberries in the orange juice and microwave on high for 1 minute. Let the mixture rest while you prepare the rest of the filling.

2. Thinly slice the peeled apple, and sauté in a nonstick pan in the butter until slightly golden and soft. Add the soaking cranberries and the juice to the pan, and gently sauté until the juice is absorbed.

3. Add the applejack or Grand Marnier and the cinnamon. Reduce the mixture over high heat until the liquor is incorporated into the fruit. Add the chopped pecans, stir, and set aside while preparing the dough.

Mushroom-Chive Filling

½ tablespoon unsalted butter
1 clove garlic, finely minced
8 medium mushrooms, thinly sliced

Salt and freshly ground pepper to taste
1–2 tablespoons cream sherry
Six 8-inch stalks of fresh chives, finely chopped

1. Melt the butter in an 8-inch nonstick frying pan. Add the garlic and sauté over medium heat for 30 seconds or until the garlic is soft. **Do not brown** the garlic or it will be bitter.

2. Add the mushrooms and salt and pepper to taste, and sauté over medium heat until soft and lightly browned.

3. Add the cream sherry and increase the heat to incorporate the sherry and reduce the sauce to less than ½ tablespoon.

4. Turn off the heat and add the chopped fresh chives. Stir and set aside while you prepare the dough.

Yield: 25 servings

TINA'S TIDBITS

- *If you have leftover dough, you can patch it together, but you must keep the dough with its layers going in the same direction rather than just squeezing it into a ball. Once the dough is layered, it may be folded over and rolled out. This technique keeps the layers intact so the dough will puff up instead of spreading out in all directions.*
- *Fillings may be made in advance and refrigerated until ready to use.*
- *Each filling should be good for 2 to 3 small Brie. Use one and freeze the rest for a later date.*
- *Cut a decorative piece of dough for the top that will describe the filling inside.*

Greek Spanakopita

The best filling in my estimation. I used to make a thousand of these at a time for a large kosher caterer in Philadelphia. Worth the effort, I promise.

1 medium onion, finely diced
2 tablespoons unsalted butter
One 10-ounce package frozen chopped spinach, defrosted
½ pound feta cheese, crumbled
7.5 ounces farmer cheese (pot cheese)

3 eggs lightly beaten
Salt and freshly ground pepper to taste
Nutmeg, to taste
¼ cup dry bread crumbs, unseasoned
½ pound phyllo dough
¾ cup melted unsalted butter

1. Preheat the oven to 425°F.

2. Sauté the onion in the 2 tablespoons butter until golden. Squeeze out all of the excess moisture from the spinach. Add the spinach to the onions, and cook over low heat until most of the moisture has evaporated, stirring occasionally. Add the feta, farmer cheese, eggs, and seasonings and combine. Add the bread crumbs and cook, stirring constantly, for 3 minutes.

3. Cut through the roll of phyllo dough 2 inches from the end. Return the rest of the dough to its plastic sleeve and cover with plastic wrap and a damp towel. Unroll the cut phyllo and lay out 3 or 4 strips at a time. Cover the unused strips with plastic wrap and a damp towel to prevent them from drying out before using.

4. Brush the unrolled strips of dough with melted butter. Put 1 teaspoon of filling at the far right end of the strip. Fold the dough over the filling to form a right triangle. Continue folding the dough over and over to make a triangle (as if you were folding a flag). Make sure that one of the edges is always lined up with the top or bottom of the strip of dough.

5. Arrange the triangles on a baking sheet, seam side down, and brush with melted butter. Bake 15–20 minutes or until golden.

Yield: 5–6 dozen

TINA'S TIDBITS

- *May be frozen before or after baking.*
- *If freezing unbaked, do not brush with butter before freezing. Place foil between layers to prevent them from sticking together. Take them from the freezer and immediately proceed to step 5.*

SPINACH AND CHEESE FILLED RAVIOLI

Here, again, is the wonderful combination of spinach and cheese whose roots go back to Spain. The pasta dough is an easy, processor dough, and the filling could be poached in salted water without the dough. This is a modern dish called gnudi (pronounced "nudey"), I guess because it is devoid of its pasta.

FILLING:
One 10-ounce package frozen spinach
2 large eggs
¼ cup finally minced fresh parsley or 1 tablespoon dried
1 pound ricotta cheese, whole milk or part skim
¾ cup freshly grated parmesan cheese
2 teaspoons sugar
¼ teaspoon grated nutmeg

Salt and freshly ground black pepper to taste
Cornmeal for dusting

PASTA:
2 large eggs
1 tablespoon olive oil
2 tablespoons ice water
2 cups bread flour

1. To make the filling, thoroughly thaw the spinach and squeeze out all of the liquid. Add the remaining ingredients and mix thoroughly. Set aside while you make the pasta.

2. Place the eggs in the food processor work bowl. Add the olive oil and the water, and mix by turning the processor on and off twice.

3. Add 1 cup of the flour and turn the processor on for 5 seconds. Scrape the sides of the bowl.

4. Add the other cup of flour and process for 10 seconds longer. The dough will be crumbly. Pinch a little bit of dough; if it holds together, it is ready to be rolled. If it doesn't hold together then add water a teaspoon at a time to the dough while the processor is running.

5. Remove the dough and divide it in half. Place both halves on a lightly floured surface, cover them with an inverted bowl, and allow them to rest for 10 minutes or longer if you are rolling the dough by hand.

6. Prepare the pasta according to machine directions.

7. Fill the sheets of dough at intervals with a teaspoon of the filling.

8. Brush the area of dough around each filling mound with a little bit of water.

9. Cover the sheet with the filling with another sheet of dough, and press down with the sides of your pinkies around each mound of filling. Cut with a knife or fluted pastry cutter, or use a ravioli form and follow the manufacturer's directions.

10. As the ravioli are made, place them on a towel lightly sprinkled with cornmeal.

11. Bring a large pot of salted water to a boil and drop the ravioli in the pot. When the ravioli come to the surface, partially cover the pot and cook for 5 minutes or until done.

12. Serve with butter and parmesan cheese or casserole style with tomato sauce.

Yield: 4–6 servings

TINA'S TIDBITS

- *Bread flour has a higher gluten content than regular flour, so it mimics the semolina flour used in Italy.*
- *Italians always add a touch of sugar to counteract any bitterness that might be in the vegetable.*
- *Nutmeg should always be added in small quantity when working with cheese and/or spinach. It enhances the flavor of the filling. Don't use too much, however, or your ravioli will taste like egg nog!*

Bulgarian Potato-Cheese Borekas

As one moves closer to the Ottoman Empire and the Middle East, the dough and choice of cheese change. The finished result is flavorful but slightly different from the Ashkenazic preparation.

DOUGH:
½ cup extra virgin olive oil
1 cup water
½ teaspoon salt
1 tablespoon sugar
2¼ cups all-purpose flour

FILLING:
1 cup mashed potato (½ pound potato cooked in salt water and mashed)
½ cup grated *Kashkavel*, Jarlsberg, or Gouda cheese
¾ cup crumbled feta cheese
⅛ teaspoon nutmeg (or 2 good pinches)
4 grindings of black pepper (or to taste)
1 egg mixed with 1 tablespoon water for glaze
Sesame seeds for topping

1. Place olive oil, water, salt, and sugar in a 2-quart saucepan and bring to a boil. Remove from heat.

2. Immediately add the flour and stir with a wooden spoon or rubber spatula until the flour is thoroughly combined with the liquid. Turn the dough out onto a board or countertop, and gently knead about 8–10 times until the mixture is a smooth ball of dough (be careful, the dough is hot!). Turn the empty saucepan over to cover the dough on the counter for 15 minutes or until the dough can be handled.

3. While the dough is cooling, combine all of the filling ingredients together in a bowl.

4. Preheat the oven to 400°F.

5. Roll the dough out on a board or counter (no need to flour) to ⅛-inch thickness. Cut into 2½-inch circles. Pat each circle with your fingertips to make the dough thinner and the circle slightly wider.

6. Place 1 teaspoon of filling in the center of each circle. Fold the dough over to make a semicircle. Touch your pinkies together to make an arch, and press the sides of your pinkies down around the edge of the dough to seal in the filling.

7. Place on a parchment-lined cookie sheet. Continue with the rest of the dough and filling (you might have some extra filling, which can be refrigerated or frozen for later use). Gently curve each *borekas* to make a crescent, and press the tines of a fork around the edges to seal. Brush with the egg mixture, and sprinkle with sesame seeds.

8. Bake for 18–20 minutes or until golden. Serve warm or at room temperature. May be frozen and reheated for 10 minutes at 350°F.

Yield: 2–3 dozen

TINA'S TIDBITS

- *The American palate is not familiar with the lower-salt, lower-sugar dough of Europe. Those ingredients may be adjusted to accommodate your preferences.*
- *Using the tines of a fork to crimp the edges of the dough not only provides a decorative accent, but actually seals the dough as well.*
- *No amount of egg wash or crimping will compensate for overfilling the pastry. The steam created by the filling when baked will push open the dough if too much filling is used in one crescent pastry.*

BOLEMAS WITH PUMPKIN-CHEESE STUFFING

Bolemas *are small, snail-shaped filled pastries that are part of the Turkish culinary repertoire. Here the dough of choice is yeast dough. You may use your favorite yeast dough recipe; however, to save time, I use frozen bread or challah dough and it works beautifully.*

1½ pounds frozen bread dough, rolls, or the
  equivalent of your favorite bread recipe
1 small pie pumpkin or 1 cup canned pumpkin puree
1 large egg
½ cup shredded Monterey Jack or Jarlsberg cheese
⅓ cup feta cheese, crumbled
1 tablespoon grated Asiago or Parmesan cheese

1 tablespoon sugar
½ teaspoon salt
¼ teaspoon cinnamon
1 tablespoon fine semolina flour or cream of wheat
  cereal
1 egg mixed with 1 teaspoon water for glaze

1. Thaw the bread dough or rolls, and divide into 24 equal pieces. If you're making your own bread dough, weigh the dough to find the right amount (1½ pounds will probably be half your recipe), and divide it into 24 pieces. Set it aside while you make the filling.

2. If you're using fresh pumpkin, bake the whole pumpkin on a rimmed cookie sheet in a 350°F oven for 45–60 minutes. When it's cool enough to handle, split it open, remove the seeds and stringy membrane, and scoop out the soft flesh. You will have more than you need for this recipe, but the rest can be refrigerated or frozen for later use.

3. Combine the filling ingredients and set aside.

4. Roll out each piece of dough on a lightly floured board to approximately 4 × 7 inches. Place 1 tablespoon of filling in the center of the long edge, and use your fingers to create a line of filling about ½ inch wide parallel to the long edge. Roll the dough up tightly like a jelly roll and then coil the roll, pinching the end of the dough under to secure it while baking. Place it on a parchment-lined cookie sheet, and repeat with the remaining dough and filling. Set aside to rise for 15 minutes.

5. Brush the tops of the coils with the egg wash and bake in a preheated 350°F oven for 20 minutes or until the rolls are nicely browned. Serve warm or at room temperature.

Yield: 24 *bolemas*

TINA'S TIDBITS

- *The filling is not sweet, like pumpkin pie. You may add a little more spice or sugar if you think it is warranted, but use caution because the feta and Jarlsberg are very strong in flavor.*
- *Semolina or cream of wheat absorbs the excess moisture in fillings and swells up. The quality of the dough is intact, and the filling is moist.*

THAI VEGETARIAN SPRING ROLLS

No frying or grease, just the fresh, clean tastes of green herbs and sweet vegetables to delight your guests.

1 teaspoon sugar
2 tablespoons soy sauce
Juice from 1½ limes (approximately 3 tablespoons)
2.25 ounces thin rice stick noodles (rice vermicelli)
1 large carrot, peeled
½ cup roasted peanuts or cashews
½ teaspoon crushed red pepper flakes
1 English seedless cucumber, about 1 pound, peeled
Bunch of fresh Thai basil or fresh mint
Bunch of fresh cilantro
¼ pound extra firm tofu (optional)
8 rice paper disks, about 8 inches in diameter

DIPPING SAUCE:
¼ cup chunky peanut butter
¼ cup hoisin sauce
¼ cup water
1 tablespoon Thai chili sauce with garlic or Thai sweet chili sauce
1 tablespoon vegetable oil
Additional water as needed

1. Combine the sugar, soy sauce, and lime juice in a small bowl and set aside.

2. Bring 2 quarts of salted water to a boil and add the rice noodles. Cook for 4 minutes or until noodles are very tender. Drain and rinse with cold water to stop the cooking. Drain and combine the cooked noodles with 2 tablespoons of the soy-lime mixture. Set aside.

3. Cut the carrot into 3-inch lengths. Using the finest grating disk on your processor, lay the carrot down in the feed tube and process. The finished result will be the finest julienne of carrot. Another way to do this is to draw a 5-hole zester in long strokes down the sides of the carrot.

4. Pulse the nuts in a processor work bowl until nuts are chopped small but still have a coarse texture. Combine the carrot with the nuts. Add the crushed pepper flakes and 1½ tablespoons of the soy-lime mixture and set aside.

5. Cut the cucumber into 3-inch lengths. Using a large grating disk in the processor, lay the cucumber lengthwise in the feed tube and process to get a medium to thin julienne. You can also do this by slicing the sections of cucumber lengthwise into a fine julienne. Toss the cucumber with the remaining soy-lime mixture and set aside.

6. Tear off about 48 small leaves of cilantro or tear larger leaves in half so you have about 48 pieces. (This may be done in advance to make assembly faster.) Prepare the Thai basil in the same way,

7. To assemble the spring rolls, fill a large pie plate or casserole with very warm tap water. Place a damp towel on your counter.

8. Place one rice paper disk in the warm water for about 20 seconds or until it is pliable. Remove to the damp towel. Sprinkle 6 basil or mint leaves and 6 cilantro leaves all over the wrapper.

9. Place 1 tablespoon of cucumber horizontally 2 inches from the bottom of the wrapper. Place 1 stick of tofu over that, if using.

10. Spread 1 tablespoon of the carrot mixture over the cucumber. Place approximately 2 tablespoons of noodles over the carrots.

11. Fold the bottom up over the filling. Fold in the left and right sides of the wrapper to enclose all of the filling. Starting from the bottom, tightly roll up the wrapper, and place the finished roll on a lightly greased platter or on a bed of lettuce leaves. Continue with the remaining wrappers.

12. Cover the rolls with plastic wrap and keep refrigerated until ready to serve. They will hold for a number of hours, but they get watery as they sit. They may be made 4–5 hours in advance.

13. To make the sauce, combine all of the ingredients by hand or in a small processor work bowl. Thin with additional water if needed.

Yield: 15 rolls

TINA'S TIDBITS

- If all ingredients are prepared in advance, assembly is very easy. You could have your guests put their own together if the party is informal.
- Leftover dipping sauce can be tossed with pasta, cooked vegetables, and cooked chicken or fish for an easy meal.
- If there are any seeds in the cucumber, use the tip of a teaspoon and scrape them out before proceeding with the julienne.
- Rice paper gets its distinguishable design because it is made on bamboo woven mats and the design of the mat shows when it is dry.

CHINESE DEEP-FRIED WONTON

Who knows which came first, the Russian and Middle Eastern Jewish traders bringing their kreplach and borekas to China or the Chinese teaching the Jews how to make wontons? It doesn't really matter—they are all delicious to eat.

2 tablespoons oil
$\frac{1}{2}$ pound ground veal
2 tablespoons light soy sauce
1 tablespoon cream sherry
$\frac{1}{2}$ teaspoon salt
6 canned whole water chestnuts, finely chopped

1 scallion, finely chopped
1 teaspoon cornstarch dissolved in 1 tablespoon water
$\frac{1}{2}$ pound prepared wonton skins
3 cups oil for frying
1 jar plum sauce

1. To prepare the filling, set a 12-inch wok over high heat for 30 seconds. Pour in the 2 tablespoons of oil, swirl it about in the pan, and heat for another 30 seconds. Turn the heat down if the oil begins to smoke.

2. Add the veal and stir-fry for 1 minute or until it loses its pink color.

3. Add the soy sauce, sherry, salt, water chestnuts, and scallions, and stir-fry for 1 minute.

4. Give the cornstarch mixture a stir to recombine, and pour it into the pan. Stir constantly until the mixture thickens. Transfer the contents to a bowl and cool to room temperature before assembling the wonton.

5. Lay a wonton square so that the point is on top and looks like a diamond. Place $1\frac{1}{2}$ teaspoons filling on each wonton center.

6. Wet your finger with a little water, and brush the upper left and lower right edge with your wet finger.

TINA'S TIDBITS

- *Veal is a perfect substitute for pork. Its color, consistency, and flavor mimic those attributes of pork, allowing cooks to maintain the original flavor as well as the laws of kashrut.*
- *Because the filling is already cooked, all you need to do is focus on the color of the dough as it is frying. When golden, they are done!*
- *Crumpling up the paper towel creates more surface area for the oil to be absorbed.*
- *Because frying in deep oil often leaves those brown sticky lines all over the pan, it is advisable to keep one inexpensive steel wok on hand for frying in this manner. Woks are meant to be cleaned but left with that dark patina, so cleanup is much easier, with no hard scrubbing.*

7. Pretend that the diamond is like the points of a clock. Folding the dough in half, bring the point of dough at 6 o'clock up to just left of 12 o'clock. You now have a slightly off-center triangle. Wet the bottom left point of the dough with a little water.

8. Hold the bottom points in your left and right hands and pull down on the points so that the point in your right hand overlaps the wet point in your left hand. Pinch the dough together. Set aside while you fold the remaining wonton. This may be done an hour or so in advance. If the wontons have to sit longer, they should be covered with plastic wrap and refrigerated. Remove from the refrigerator at least $\frac{1}{2}$ hour before cooking.

9. To cook, place 3 cups of oil in a deep fryer or a clean 12-inch wok and heat the oil until it registers 375°F on a frying thermometer.

10. Deep-fry the wontons 6 at a time until they are golden. Transfer to crumpled paper towels to drain while you fry the rest. Serve with plum sauce.

Note: Fried wontons can be kept warm for an hour or so in a 250°F oven or reheated for 5 minutes in a 450°F oven.

Yield: 2–3 dozen

GEFILTE FISH

Gefilte fish is so much a part of the Jewish culinary psyche that we take it for granted that everyone loves it and eats it. But you know that statement is false if you have ever invited a non-Jewish friend for a Passover seder (for that matter, it's not always popular with every Jew around the table either). Gefilte fish is often approached by the uninitiated in the same way as haggis or headcheese—hesitantly. This simple ball of ground fish says volumes about the medieval Jewish world, Jewish laws, and rabbinic interpretations of those laws.

Gefilte fish was created in late medieval Germany. The Mishnah reinforced the rule of no work on Shabbat by including the prohibition of removing any inedible parts of a mixture from our food. This would include the bones of a fish. To enable fish consumption on Shabbat, the raw fish meat was removed, the bones were discarded, and the fish meat was mixed with eggs and seasonings and stuffed back into the whole fish carcass to be cooked. *Gefullte* means "stuffed" in German!

Over time, the recipe for stuffed whole fish became one for balls of ground fish mixture poached in a large pot of fish heads and skin accompanied by some onion, celery, and carrot and then cooked for about 1$\frac{1}{2}$ hours until the smell in the house was definitely going to ward off Elijah when he came to the seder door! This process existed for the sole purpose of creating the jelly for the chilled fish. If you don't want the jelly, then gefilte fish is as easy to make as meatballs without the spaghetti!

Aside from the strong smell in the house, the worst aspect of making gefilte fish the "old" way is that coagulated blood from the bones (the brown scum on the broth's surface) and some of the fish scales would stick to the fish, and that wasn't pleasant.

The following recipes take you from the classic preparation to a modern interpretation without losing the gestalt of the dish but lessening the time and odor in the kitchen significantly.

GEFILTE FISH AND HORSERADISH MOLD

*This could be the **only** time you will see flavored gelatin in one of my recipes! That said, an argument can be made for this easy, beautiful presentation. Making this recipe means you don't have to have those twenty glass plates with a leaf of lettuce, piece of carrot, and ball of gefilte fish precariously balancing on top of each other in your refrigerator taking up room. It also takes less time to serve, since it can be prepared on one platter that can be passed.*

One 3-ounce box of lemon gelatin
1 cup boiling water
1 cup fish broth from jar
One 6-ounce jar red horseradish, drained of excess
    liquid

1 or 2 jars gefilte fish
1 carrot for garnish (optional)
Scallion or chives for garnish (optional)

1. Remove gefilte fish from the jar, pat dry, and put in a large, shallow, slightly rimmed serving dish.

2. Place gelatin in a medium-sized bowl. Add boiling water and stir until dissolved. Add fish broth and horseradish, and stir until well blended.

3. Pour the liquid mixture around the gefilte fish pieces.

4. Slice the carrot into $1/8$-inch circles, and cut with a teeny flower-shaped cutter or with a knife to resemble a flower. Cook in boiling salted water until tender. Drain.

5. Cut thin curved slices from the green part of the scallion. Set aside.

6. Lightly dip the bottoms of the carrot flowers in some of the gelatin mixture and strategically place the carrot shapes on the gefilte fish pieces. Do the same with the curved slices of scallion to resemble the leaves. Chill and serve when firm.

Yield: 12 servings

TINA'S TIDBITS

- *Some prepared horseradish has such a high level of acid that it impedes the gelatin from setting completely. That's OK—just make sure that you arrange the gefilte fish and jelly in a rimmed platter and everything will still look and taste good.*
- *If you heat up the jelly in the jar until it is liquid, it will set the mixture better because the jelly is formed by the collagen in the fish bones and this will firm when chilled.*

Gefilte Fish

Making gefilte fish is just like making chicken soup and meatballs, especially if you follow my recipe below. So don't be afraid to try it!

Here's the classic preparation for you to "doctor" to fit your memories.

4 pounds whole fish (combination of carp, whitefish, pike, snapper, or sea trout)
2 carrots, cut into 1-inch lengths on a diagonal
2 stalks celery, cut into 2-inch lengths
1 pound yellow onions
1 bouquet garni (1 bay leaf, thyme, marjoram, and summer savory or parsley) wrapped in cheesecloth
2–3 quarts water

2 medium yellow onions
1 carrot
1/4 cup very loosely packed fresh parsley
2 eggs
1/3 cup water
1/2 cup matzah meal
Salt and pepper to taste
Garlic, ginger, sugar, dill, or whatever your bubbe used to use (regional options)

1. Fillet the fish or have the store do it for you.

2. Rinse out the head of the fish and make sure that any bloody masses are removed. Soak all of the bones and the head in cold salted water to cover for 15 minutes or longer. Drain the bones and discard the water.

3. Place the bones and the head on the bottom of a large Dutch oven, and cover with the carrots, celery, and thinly sliced onion. Add the bouquet garni and the 2–3 quarts of water to cover, and simmer for 1–1 1/2 hours. Strain the liquid, reserve the carrots, and set aside. Discard the bones and everything else.

4. To make the fish, grind the fish fillet twice in a grinder fitted with a fine blade or process in a food processor until a fairly smooth texture. Remove the fish to a large bowl.

5. Grind or process the onions, carrot, and parsley and add to the fish.

TINA'S TIDBITS

- *If you don't like the jelly with the fish, then you can skip the whole head and skin process! The collagen in the bone jells the liquid when it is chilled. The fish balls can be poached instead in salted water to which a little carrot, onion, and celery have been added.*
- *To grind fish in a processor, always use 1 pound of fish at a time, and always pulse (turn on and off rapidly) the machine so that you don't overgrind the fish and make it tough.*
- *Protein foods get tough when exposed to high temperatures, so keep the fish stock at a simmer when cooking the fish balls.*
- *When working with matzah meal, give the meal time to hydrate—absorb some of the moisture in the food—before you add additional matzah meal to your recipe.*
- *If you are using jarred gefilte fish, remove the liquid from the jar and reheat it with a fresh onion and cut-up carrot. When the liquid has cooled down, strain it into the jars with the gefilte fish. Add the carrot slices to the soup. This will make the broth, and subsequently the fish, taste more like homemade.*

6. Add the eggs, water, matzah meal, and salt and pepper, and mix well with a fork until light and fluffy. **Note:** To check for seasoning, cook 1 teaspoon of the fish mixture in salted water for 10 minutes. Taste and then adjust seasonings if necessary. Never taste freshwater fish raw.

7. Shape about $\frac{1}{3}$ cup of the fish mixture in your hands to form ovals, and gently place in a frying pan to which 1 inch of prepared fish stock has been added. Poach, covered, for 20–30 minutes (depending on size) over low heat or until the center of a fish ball appears white. Drain on a cloth towel and cool in previously made fish broth. Serve with horseradish.

Yield: 8–10 pieces

Algerian Fish Terrine for Passover

When I first came upon a variation of this recipe, I thought that it could definitely be an alternative to gefilte fish. And the fact that the hard-boiled eggs were in the loaf triggered elation that this might be the way to combine two Passover seder courses into one. But don't save it for Passover. Serve it at your next party.

1 carrot, peeled and coarsely chopped
1 stalk celery, cut into thirds
1 small onion, quartered
10 black peppercorns
2 cups water
2 cups dry white wine
2 pounds fish fillets (halibut, snapper, or tilapia)
2 large (3-inch) onions
2 roasted and peeled red bell peppers, jarred or fresh
$\frac{1}{2}$ teaspoon cinnamon
$\frac{1}{2}$ teaspoon nutmeg
Salt and freshly ground black pepper to taste
6 large eggs
$\frac{1}{2}$ cup matzah meal
Olive oil, for greasing the pan
3 peeled hard-boiled eggs
$\frac{1}{2}$ cup chopped Calamata olives

SAUCE:
$\frac{1}{2}$ cup mayonnaise
2 tablespoons ketchup
1 teaspoon prepared horseradish
1 or more teaspoons sweet vermouth or white wine for thinning sauce

1. Combine the first 6 ingredients in a large frying pan or a 3-quart saucepan. Bring to a boil. Reduce the heat and simmer for 20 minutes.

2. Strain the liquid and return the clear broth to the used pan. Bring the liquid to a simmer.

3. Rinse off the fillets and place them in the simmering broth. Cover the pan and cook the fish for 3–5 minutes or until the fish is cooked through.

4. Peel the onions and cut into quarters. Place them in a processor work bowl fitted with the metal blade. Pulse the machine on and off 20 times to create a coarse puree.

5. Rinse the red bell peppers and pat dry. Cut into eighths and add to the work bowl along with the cinnamon, nutmeg, salt, and pepper. Pulse on and off until the peppers are pureed. You may need to scrape down the sides of the bowl.

6. Drain the fish and add to the work bowl. Process until a smooth mass is formed.

7. Add the 6 raw eggs and the matzah meal, and turn the machine on long enough to incorporate all of the ingredients.

8. Lightly grease a loaf pan with some olive oil. Pour half of the fish mixture into the pan.

9. Using one of the hard-boiled eggs as your mold, make three indentations down the center of the fish mixture. Sprinkle $\frac{1}{2}$ of the chopped olives evenly into these indentations. Place the three hard-boiled eggs on top of the olives, and sprinkle the eggs with the remaining chopped olives.

10. Pour the remaining fish mixture into the loaf pan. Lightly press down on the mixture to thoroughly cover the eggs, and smooth out the top.

11. Place a paper towel in the bottom of a 13 × 9-inch pan. Set the loaf pan in the center, and pour hot water around the loaf pan to a depth of at least 1 inch.

12. Bake in a preheated 325°F oven for approximately 30 minutes or until the loaf is firm. Remove from the water bath. Cool to room temperature, and then cover and refrigerate until ready to serve.

13. To make the sauce, whisk the mayonnaise in a bowl until smooth. Add the ketchup and horseradish, and stir well. If necessary, add a small amount of sweet vermouth or wine to achieve the desired consistency.

14. To serve, remove the loaf from the pan, and slice into $1/4$- to $1/2$-inch slices. Drizzle a tablespoon or more of the sauce on a plate, and place the slice on top of the sauce.

Yield: 30 thin slices

TINA'S TIDBITS

- *Placing a paper towel in the bottom of your water bath will prevent the loaf pan or ramekins from sliding when you are removing the finished item from the hot oven.*
- *Small, individual servings can be made in 5- to 6-ounce ramekins using a few pieces of sliced egg in each ramekin instead of a whole egg.*
- *More matzah meal may be added to the mixture if you want a firmer loaf. However, make sure you allow some time for the matzah meal to hydrate before you bake the loaf.*

Quenelles

Quenelles are to gefilte fish what mousse is to a candy bar. These are light, delicate morsels of fish and cream that deserve to be tried at least once in your life. They are not necessarily appropriate for a seder unless yours is a small, dairy affair, but basically the same concept of ground fish poached in liquid. Enjoy!

1 pound fresh halibut, sea bass, or cod fillet
1 teaspoon salt
Freshly ground pepper to taste
$\frac{1}{8}$ teaspoon ground nutmeg
$1\frac{1}{2}$ cups heavy cream
1 egg
3 tablespoons unsalted butter
1 small shallot, finely minced
3 tablespoons flour

Salt and freshly ground pepper to taste
Big pinch of nutmeg
1 sprig of fresh thyme or lemon thyme
1 cup court bouillon (see recipe on following page) or fish stock
1 cup half and half cream
$\frac{1}{3}$ cup freshly grated Gruyère or Emmenthaler cheese
$\frac{1}{4}$ cup freshly grated Parmesan cheese
Additional Parmesan cheese for topping

1. Cut the fish fillets into cubes and place in a processor work bowl with the salt, pepper, and nutmeg. Process the fish for 30 seconds or until the metal blade has finely chopped the fish. Scrape down the sides of the work bowl, and pulse on and off a few more times until the mixture is fine.

2. With the processor running, slowly pour the heavy cream into the work bowl until all of the cream is incorporated. Stop and add the egg. Pulse 3 or 4 times to incorporate the egg completely. Transfer the mixture to a metal bowl, and place in the freezer for approximately 30 minutes until very cold but not frozen.

3. While the fish mixture is chilling, prepare the béchamel for the sauce. In a 2-quart saucepan, melt the butter and sauté the shallot for 3 minutes or until soft. Add the flour, salt, pepper, and nutmeg, and whisk for a minute to lightly toast the flour.

4. Whisk constantly as you add the court bouillon and the cream to prevent lumps. Continue stirring until the mixture is smooth and thick, about 4 minutes.

5. Strain the sauce into a 1-quart saucepan and add the cheeses. Stir over low heat until the cheeses are melted and the mixture is smooth. Turn off the heat, but keep warm until ready to use.

6. Bring a 5-quart saucepan filled with salted water to a boil. Keep the water at a low simmer while you make the quenelles.

7. To shape the quenelles, have two oval-shaped soup spoons and a glass of cold water available. Dip one spoon in the cold water, and scoop up some of the fish mixture. Dip the other spoon into the water, and shape the fish into an oval. Gently slide the quenelle into the water, and rapidly shape another fish oval. Cook 3–5 quenelles at a time in a covered pot for 2–3 minutes. Drain on paper towels, and place in a single layer in a buttered gratin dish or low-sided glass casserole. Continue with the remaining fish mixture until all the quenelles are prepared.

8. When all the quenelles have been poached, pour the reserved sauce over them and sprinkle with additional Parmesan cheese. Bake uncovered in a 425°F oven for 10 minutes. Transfer the pan to the broiler, and broil until the dish begins to lightly brown and appears to bubble on the sides, about 2 minutes. Serve immediately.

Note: The dish can be assembled up to 8 hours in advance and refrigerated. Remove from the refrigerator $1/2$ hour before serving and then proceed with the baking in step 8.

Court Bouillon

1 carrot
1 onion
$1/2$ stalk of celery
1 bay leaf
$1/2$ teaspoon fennel seed

8 peppercorns
1 teaspoon salt (optional)
2 cups white wine
2 cups water

1. Chop the carrot, onion, and celery into coarse pieces.

2. Mix the vegetables with the remaining ingredients in a saucepan and cook at a simmer for 15–20 minutes. Strain the liquid and put it in a large frying pan or a fish poacher. Bring the poaching liquid to a boil. Proceed to poach the fish or poultry as directed in the specific recipe.

Yield: 4 servings

TINA'S TIDBITS

- *Court bouillon can be used for poaching chicken or fish. After using, strain the liquid, mark whether it was for chicken or fish, and freeze the stock for future use.*
- *Salmon imparts a strong flavor to the stock. Do not reuse the stock unless it is for salmon.*

EGGPLANT

*T*he migration of the cultivation and consumption of eggplant over the last four thousand years began in the Southeast Asian region of India and Burma. The plant was introduced to the Chinese about fifteen hundred years ago. Both societies relished (not to pun) eggplant, which is a fruit, not a vegetable.

By the fourth century C.E., the consumption of eggplant in all forms followed the path of the Silk Road from China to the Near East, and eggplant dishes became popular throughout the Middle East and especially in Egypt and Turkey. In 711 C.E., the Moors conquered Spain and introduced eggplant to that region. Many believed that the fruit of the eggplant was an aphrodisiac, and it was called *berenganas*, "apple of love," in Spain.

When the Jews residing in Spanish territories, including Sicily, were expelled during the Inquisition, they brought their culinary expertise and fondness for eggplant to the mainland Italian states. Eating eggplant became associated with the Jews, and it was over a hundred years after their arrival before Italians would begin to eat the fruit. Italians and northern Europeans were very hesitant to eat this exotic food, grown and eaten by Jews, because it was a member of the nightshade family and they thought consuming the fruit would make you go mad. Even before the influx of Spanish-Jewish immigrants to Italy, Europeans were referring to eggplant as *mala insana*, "crazy spirit," and eggplants were called "crazy apples" throughout Europe until the mid-seventeenth century. What this means is that most traditional Italian eggplant dishes originated in Jewish kitchens!

By the sixteenth century, eggplant was widely popular in Mediterranean and southern European countries.

Eggplants come in many shapes and colors, although dark purple is the color we generally associate with the fruit. When brown and white varieties were grown in Europe, the eggplant gained more popularity. As a matter of fact, the English first saw the small, white, egg-shaped variety and coined the name "eggplant."

Eggplant made the journey across the Atlantic in the mid-seventeenth century when Spaniards (or more likely Jews fleeing continued persecution) brought the plant to Brazil, and it was Thomas Jefferson who introduced the new colonies to this plant in 1806. In the United States, eggplant was used mostly as an ornament and did not gain popularity until the 1950s.

All of the following selections are listed geographically from their origin of cultivation through the routes of the Diaspora. They make excellent appetizers served with sliced pita triangles, naan bread, or crackers. Placed in a lettuce cup and garnished with a radish rose, as my mother often did, these eggplant salads make a perfect light first course to a meal.

When buying eggplant, look for smooth, shiny skins with no brown spots, bruises, or indentations. Wrinkled, dull skin is a sign of age and will guarantee a bitter, spongy fruit. Smaller eggplants have fewer seeds and thinner skins—two parts of the plant that can make the cooked eggplant taste bitter. Eggplants are very perishable, so when you purchase them make sure they are very fresh. When you press your finger lightly against the skin, it should leave a subtle imprint. If the eggplant doesn't "give" at all under light pressure, it is underripe and will be bitter. If it gives too much, it is old and overripe and will not have a pleasant taste. Because of its perishability, eggplant should be cooked within 4 days of purchase and should not be stored in the cold part of your refrigerator.

Many recipes call for salting the eggplant for a half hour to remove excess water and bitterness. As it turns out, today's varieties do not require this step if they are fresh. Very large, hence old, eggplants might benefit from peeling, as much of the bitterness comes from just under the thick skin layer.

If you want to remove some of the moisture so that the eggplant doesn't sponge up oil during frying, you might try microwaving the eggplant slices on high for 4 minutes and then blotting away the excess water with paper towels before you proceed with your favorite recipe.

Because its cooked consistency resembles meat, eggplant is often used in vegetarian dishes. For the kosher cook, substituting eggplant for meat opens the door to many new recipes that normally would not be considered kosher because of the use of dairy products and meat products in the same dish.

Although the prime time to buy eggplant is August and September, eggplant is available all year round, and now might be a great time to start exploring its many uses in your favorite recipes.

COOKING WHOLE EGGPLANT

My grandmother, as well as many older cooks, used to roast their eggplants right on the top of a gas stove. I presume that either their culinary skills were great enough to know when to turn the eggplant so that no part of the skin would ever split and ooze out the eggplant's juices or they just didn't care if the stove top got messy and cleaned it up right away. In either case, the modern cook can replicate the results of stove-top broiling in an outdoor grill or in the oven. Either way, the method is easy as long as you don't get distracted and forget that the eggplant is roasting to a charred crisp inside and out!

To Grill Outside

Turn your grill on 15 minutes before using. Place the washed (don't forget to remove paper label if it is stuck to the eggplant) whole eggplant on the grill over medium-high heat, and close the lid (this also helps enhance the eggplant's smoky taste). Turn the eggplant after 10 minutes to the opposite side. Cover the grill and continue grilling for another 10 minutes. Check the eggplant and turn it on a third side if it doesn't look blackened. The goal is to have the eggplant nicely charred (can even be crisp in places) and completely deflated. If you think it needs a little more time, then lower the flame a little and let the eggplant cook another 5–10 minutes.

Remove the eggplant to a large bowl or colander, and slit the skin open on one side from near the stem all the way to the bottom. This will allow the bitter juices to run out and make your dish taste better. When cool enough to handle, peel off and discard the skin and stem, place the pulp and the seeds in a clean bowl, and proceed with your favorite recipe.

To Roast in an Oven

Preheat an oven to 425°F. Place the eggplant on a foil-lined cookie sheet that has sides (to catch any juices that might drip out). Prick the eggplant on one side with a fork to allow the steam to escape and prevent the eggplant from exploding all over your oven! Roast for about 30 minutes, turning the eggplant every 10 minutes so that all sides get exposed to the heat. The skin will appear wrinkly but might not be charred, since you are not using the broiler elements on top. When the eggplant feels soft and deflated, it is cooked. Remove it from the oven. Slit the eggplant open on one side, from stem to base, and let it drain, either in the pan or in a bowl until cool. When it is cool enough to handle, peel off and discard the skin and stem, place the pulp and the seeds in a clean bowl, and proceed with your favorite recipe.

Eggplant Bharta

The following recipe is adapted from a recipe by my friend June Penkar. June is a Bene Israel from India who now lives in Dallas. The Bene Israel trace their lineage back to the kohanim *who escaped Judea in the second century* B.C.E. *and were shipwrecked on the Konkan coast of India. They were discovered in the eighteenth century living in total isolation from Judaism but were identified as Jews by their observance of Shabbat, laws of kashrut, and the recitation of the* Sh'ma.

Eggplant has a prominent role in Indian cuisine. It is believed that the plant originated in India and spread throughout the Middle East and the Mediterranean through the spice trade routes and the Moors bringing eggplant to Spain. When Spain expelled the Jews, they brought eggplant to other parts of the Mediterranean.

2 large or 3 medium eggplants (about 2½ pounds)	1 teaspoon kosher salt
2 red bell peppers	1 large clove garlic, finely chopped
4 Roma tomatoes	1 jalapeño pepper, seeds removed and finely chopped
4 tablespoons vegetable oil, divided use	⅛–¼ teaspoon cayenne pepper, or more if desired
½ teaspoon salt	¼ teaspoon turmeric
Freshly ground black pepper	½ teaspoon garam masala
1 medium onion, finely diced (about 1½ cups)	Fresh chopped cilantro for garnish

1. Roast the eggplants on a low-rimmed cookie sheet in a 350°F oven for 30 minutes or until the eggplant is soft and deflated. Cool and scoop out the pulp, including the seeds. Set aside until needed.

2. Wash and cut the peppers in half lengthwise, and remove the stem, all seeds, and all membranes. Wash the tomatoes and cut them in half lengthwise.

3. Toss the red bell peppers and the tomatoes with 1 tablespoon of the vegetable oil, the ½ teaspoon salt, and a few grindings of black pepper. Roast, cut side down, on a rimmed cookie sheet (to catch any juices released) in a 400°F oven for 20 minutes.

4. When cool enough to handle, peel the peppers and tomatoes, and set aside with any accumulated juices.

5. Heat a 10-inch frying pan over high heat for 20 seconds. Add the remaining 3 tablespoons of oil and heat for 10 seconds. Add the finely diced onion and sauté for 5 minutes until lightly golden. If necessary, reduce the heat to medium high.

TINA'S TIDBITS

- *The liquid that collects within the roasted whole eggplant should be discarded before mashing the pulp, as it tends to be very bitter.*
- *Although this mixture is often served hot as part of a meal, the flavors are enhanced when allowed to meld for a few hours or overnight. Reheat or serve cold as a dip or side salad.*
- *Much of the heat from a jalapeño comes from the seeds and the membrane. Removal of these parts will reduce their "kick."*

6. While the onions are cooking, add the eggplant pulp to a food processor work bowl and pulse the machine on and off 5 times. Cut the roasted pepper into 4–6 pieces and add to the eggplant. Pulse the processor on and off 5 times. Add the roasted tomatoes and pulse on and off 5 times. The pieces should be small but not totally blended into the eggplant.

7. Add the eggplant mixture to the onions and sauté for 5 minutes. Add the 1 teaspoon kosher salt, garlic, jalapeño, cayenne, turmeric, and garam masala to the pan, and cook over low heat for 3 minutes or until nice and hot.

8. When ready to serve, garnish with chopped cilantro and accompany with soft pita bread, naan, or crackers.

Yield: 6–8 servings

INDIAN SPICE EGGPLANT

This recipe has been adapted for the modern cook. Traditionally, all whole spices are heated in a frying pan to bring out their flavors and then used whole or sometimes ground. This is an elaborate version of an Indian baigan bharta, *which might also contain sautéed onion and tomatoes.*

1 small eggplant ($^3/_4$–1 pound)
$^1/_2$ teaspoon freshly grated peeled ginger
1 serrano or $^1/_2$ long green Indian pepper, finely chopped
$^1/_2$ teaspoon ground coriander
$^1/_4$ teaspoon ground cumin
$^1/_4$ teaspoon ground turmeric
$^1/_8$ teaspoon ground cloves

$^1/_8$ teaspoon ground cinnamon
$^1/_8$ teaspoon ground cardamom
1 teaspoon sugar
2 teaspoons red wine vinegar
$^1/_2$ teaspoon kosher salt or to taste
2–3 tablespoons extra virgin olive oil
1 tablespoon finely chopped fresh mint or cilantro for garnish (optional)

1. Follow the directions for roasting an eggplant on the grill or in your oven. Place in a bowl, allowing the juices to drain until cool enough to handle.

2. Scoop out the flesh and the seeds from the eggplant and place in a 1-quart mixing bowl. It's OK if some of the charred skin or meat remains.

3. Using a knife and fork, cut through the eggplant as if you were cutting a steak. Cut in all directions. Next, use the fork to whip the eggplant into a relatively smooth mass.

4. Add all of the seasonings and stir with the fork to thoroughly combine.

5. Slowly add the oil as you whip the mixture with the fork.

6. Place in a serving bowl and refrigerate for at least $^1/_2$ hour for flavors to meld.

7. Garnish with the chopped mint or cilantro just before serving. Serve with naan, pita, or French bread.

Yield: 4 servings

TINA'S TIDBITS

- *Knock on an eggplant with your knuckles. A hollow sound means that the fruit is dry and shouldn't be selected.*
- *To prevent a bowl from spinning when both your hands are busy whisking in oil, place a damp cloth or paper towel on the counter under the bowl and the bowl will remain still.*
- *An easy way to mince a hot chili pepper without burning your skin is to hold it by the stem end and use a pair of sharp kitchen shears to cut the pepper into quarters lengthwise. Run the pepper (still holding onto the stem) under running water while you use the tip of the scissors to remove the seeds. Then just snip little pieces from the pepper using the scissors.*
- *This mixture may be combined in the processor, creating a very smooth dip, if preferred.*
- *Keep all your brown spices in the freezer and they will retain their flavor for a long time.*

BABA GHANOUSH

Baba ghanoush is probably the most popular Middle Eastern eggplant dish. Originally made with a sesame sauce that included garlic and lemon juice, it is now made with pure tahini, and garlic and lemon juice are added by the cook. Experiment with adding additional flavors such as cumin, smoked pimentón *paprika from Spain, or ginger and cilantro for your own ethnic twist.*

2 medium eggplants (about 2½ pounds total)
3 tablespoons tahini (sesame seed paste)
1 tablespoon water
Juice of 1 lemon
2 large cloves garlic, finely minced or pressed
   through a garlic press

2 tablespoons extra virgin olive oil
Salt and freshly ground black pepper
2 teaspoons chopped fresh mint or flat leaf parsley for
   garnish

1. Preheat the oven to 425°F. Wash and pat dry the eggplants, and prick them with the tines of a fork in many places to allow steam to escape when cooking. Place the eggplants on a rimmed cookie sheet and bake for 25–35 minutes, turning the eggplants every 10 minutes until the skin is black and crisp and the eggplants appear to be deflated.

2. Remove the eggplants to a colander, slit them open, and allow them to drain for 10 minutes or until cool enough to handle.

3. Remove and discard the skin and the seeds from the eggplant, and chop the meat of the eggplant in a bowl.

4. Combine the tahini with the water and lemon juice. Add this mixture and the garlic to the eggplant and mix well.

5. Whisk in enough olive oil to balance the lemon juice and tahini, and season with salt and pepper to taste.

6. Garnish the dish with the fresh mint or parsley. Serve with pita bread or crackers.

Yield: 6–8 servings

TINA'S TIDBITS:

- *To add a little more of the Middle East to your dish, serve the baba ghanoush with toasted pita triangles. Cut the pita rounds into wedges, and brush the tops with either plain olive oil or olive oil that has been flavored with 1 clove of minced garlic or with some zatar.*
- *Zatar is a commercially prepared mixed spice containing wild thyme, marjoram, sesame seeds, and ground sumac (no, not the poisonous one!).*

SYRIAN EGGPLANT WITH POMEGRANATE MOLASSES

I first discovered pomegranate molasses when I was slowly walking through a Middle Eastern market. I often use the syrup as a base for marinades or glazes for poultry and fish, and I created a salad dressing using the syrup with vanilla for my Rosh HaShanah menu (see Pomegranate Vanilla Vinaigrette, page 197). Finding out that the great Jewish cooks of Aleppo in Syria used the molasses with eggplant made me quite happy to explore that combination, and here is the result.

1 medium eggplant (1–1½ pounds)
2 tablespoons pomegranate molasses
2 large garlic cloves, finely minced or pressed
   through a garlic press

¼ teaspoon dried crushed red pepper flakes
3–4 tablespoons extra virgin olive oil
Kosher salt to taste
Pomegranate seeds for garnish (optional)

1. Roast the eggplant over a grill until all sides are charred and the eggplant is soft and deflated.

2. Remove to a colander, slit open on 1 side from stem to bottom, and let the juices run out for 10 minutes or until it is cool enough to handle.

3. Remove the skin and stem and discard them.

4. Place the eggplant pulp in a clean bowl, cut in all directions with a knife and fork, and continue to mix with the fork until no long strings of eggplant remain.

5. Add the pomegranate molasses, minced garlic, and red pepper flakes, and combine thoroughly.

6. Slowly add the oil as you whip the eggplant mixture with a fork until a smooth emulsion, or spread, is formed.

7. Season with salt to taste.

8. Spread the mixture on a 9-inch plate and make a slight well in the center. Drizzle with a little more olive oil, and sprinkle with some pomegranate seeds.

9. Serve with pita points or crackers.

Yield: 4 servings

TINA'S TIDBITS

- *Pomegranate molasses is very thick. After opening the bottle, store it in the refrigerator to keep it fresh, but bring it to room temperature before using so it will be easy to pour and combine with the other ingredients.*
- *If the mixture is too sweet for your taste, try adding 1 tablespoon of fresh lemon juice and possibly a little more oil to balance the flavors.*
- *This is a great sauce/condiment to serve over grilled fish or chicken—not traditional but delicious.*

Moroccan Eggplant Salad

Winding our way along the "eggplant route," we find ourselves in Morocco, where the Arab influence is prevalent and neighboring Spain tempers some of the heat from the North African cooking. I have added the wonderful flavor of Spanish pimentón *to this dish to transition the basic eggplant salad of the Middle East to the more northern Mediterranean palette. This salad is a perfect addition to your tapas table and easy to make.*

2 medium eggplants
2 large cloves of garlic, coarsely chopped
1 tablespoon lemon juice
Salt and pepper to taste
1 teaspoon cumin

1 teaspoon *pimentón de la Vera* (smoked Spanish paprika)
1 tablespoon sugar
¼ cup extra virgin olive oil

1. Grill the eggplants for 20–30 minutes, turning 2–3 times, until soft inside and charred outside. Drain the eggplants in a colander in the sink for 15 minutes.

2. Remove the peel, and place the eggplant pulp in a processor work bowl with all the other ingredients except the olive oil. Pulse the machine until the mixture is fairly smooth.

3. With the processor running, slowly drizzle the oil into the eggplant until it forms a smooth, creamy consistency. Refrigerate until serving. Serve as a dip or first course salad.

Yield: 4–6 servings

> ### TINA'S TIDBITS
>
> - *The flavor of garlic will always get more intense and sometimes even bitter when overprocessed in a processor. For that reason, always coarsely chop the garlic first; never add it whole to the work bowl, so that you use the processor for the minimum amount of time.*
> - *You can control the consistency of your mixture by pulsing the processor on and off until you achieve the desired texture. Just turning the machine on can easily overwork the food and make it too smooth, without any texture.*
> - *Adding oil slowly while a processor is on will create a type of emulsion like mayonnaise and will prevent the oil from weeping out while standing.*

NORTH AFRICAN EGGPLANT WITH HONEY

The spice trade route ended more or less in the ports of North Africa, and from there the spices were traded all over the Mediterranean and Europe. I love the mix of hot and sweet in dishes, and the concept of using honey with hot chili and garlic intrigued me when I saw this combination. Here I have created a dish that could be an appetizer for many or, using smaller eggplants, could be used for individual portions as a first course or over couscous as an entrée. However you choose to serve it, it is intriguing and delicious.

1 medium eggplant (about 4 inches wide and 9 inches long)
1 teaspoon kosher salt
3 tablespoons extra virgin olive oil, divided use
1 large clove of garlic, finely minced
1 heaping teaspoon freshly grated peeled ginger

½ teaspoon ground cumin
¼ teaspoon crushed chili flakes
3 tablespoons honey, wildflower or orange preferred
1 tablespoon fresh lemon juice
¼ cup water
1 French baguette, thinly sliced

1. Starting 1 inch from the stem end, slice the eggplant lengthwise into six ½-inch slices, keeping the slices intact.

2. Place the eggplant on a large plate, and fan the slices without tearing them away from the stem. Sprinkle the teaspoon of kosher salt over the slices. Place a heavy plate over the salted eggplant and weight the plate down with a heavy jar or can. Allow it to sit for 25 minutes.

3. Rinse the eggplant and pat it dry with a paper towel.

4. Brush about 2 tablespoons of the oil all over the exterior and interior surfaces of the eggplant. Fan out on a hot grill, and grill for 5 minutes. Carefully turn over the eggplant, and grill it for another 5 minutes. Remove it from the grill.

5. Meanwhile, heat a 10-inch frying pan for 20 seconds over high heat. Add 1 tablespoon of oil and heat for 10 seconds.

6. Reduce the heat to medium high. Add the garlic and sauté for 15 seconds. The garlic should not brown at all. Immediately remove pan from the heat.

7. Add the remaining ingredients and stir to thoroughly combine.

8. Carefully transfer the fanned eggplant into the frying pan, and spoon the sauce all over to cover the eggplant thoroughly. Cover the pan and return to a medium flame.

TINA'S TIDBITS

- *From a culinary point of view, eggplant is terrific because it provides substance to a dish while not adding a specific flavor to the finished product. In that respect it's like tofu; it absorbs the flavors of the other ingredients in the dish.*
- *Never use aluminum pans with eggplant, as it will cause discoloration.*
- *Garlic should never be allowed to get too dark or it will become bitter and ruin the flavor of a dish.*
- *Simmering means to keep a mixture at such a low boil that the bubbles form mainly around the perimeter of the pan.*

9. Gently simmer the eggplant for 10–15 minutes, basting the eggplant often until it is soft and most of the water has evaporated. The sauce will thicken when cool.

10. Remove the eggplant from the pan and transfer it to a serving plate. Cover with sauce. Serve cold with a small knife to cut into slices to be served on French bread.

Note: Small baby eggplants may be used for serving individual portions; however, adjust the grilling time accordingly so that they do not burn.

Yield: 4–6 servings

CAPONATA

When the Jews were expelled from Spain in 1492, there were forty thousand Jews on the island of Sicily, a Spanish territory at the time. The Jews left the island with the culinary traditions of their ancestors steeped in Moorish customs. The people of northern Italy were not accustomed to eggplant. They were fearful of this fruit, which they thought had the power to make you go mad, and they also viewed eggplant as "Jew food." As a result any old eggplant dish from Italy had its roots in a Jewish kitchen.

One of the most popular Italian eggplant dishes is caponata, an eggplant relish so ubiquitous that it can be found in cans on our own supermarket shelves. Caponata is actually a Jewish Sabbath dish. The vinegar and sugar preserve the mixture so that it can be made in advance of Shabbat and served at room temperature for the s'udah sh'lishit meal Saturday afternoon.

2 eggplants, 8 inches long
1¼ cups olive oil
2 large onions, cut into ½-inch dice
One 6-ounce can tomato paste
1 ounce drained capers

2 tablespoons sugar
¼ cup red wine vinegar
1 large clove garlic, minced
Salt and pepper to taste

1. Wash the eggplants, cut off the ends, and cut into ½-inch cubes.

2. Heat a 4-quart pot for 20 seconds. Add the oil and heat for another 10 seconds. Add the eggplant cubes and fry in the oil until the cubes are soft and particles on the bottom of the pan are golden. The eggplant will absorb the oil at first and then the oil will be released. Remove the eggplant cubes with a slotted spoon and place them in a bowl. Leave the remaining oil in the pot.

3. Add the onions to the pot and fry until slightly golden and soft.

4. Return the eggplant to the pot, and add the remaining ingredients. Cook for 20 minutes over low heat, until the flavors are well blended. Stir occasionally.

5. Serve warm, at room temperature, or cold. The caponata lasts for weeks in the refrigerator and always tastes better the longer it sits.

Yield: 10 or more servings

TINA'S TIDBITS

- *Eggplant soaks up a lot of oil but will release it once it starts to cook. The best way to prevent excess absorption is to make sure the oil is very hot but not smoking.*
- *Do not cut eggplant too small or it will disintegrate. However, if you cut eggplant too thick for this recipe or for recipes that call for whole slices, the eggplant won't cook evenly and you will get undercooked eggplant that is spongy and tasteless.*
- *After the caponata is made and refrigerated, excess oil can be blotted off the top by using a paper towel.*
- *As long as a thin film of oil is covering the top of the food, this dish will last weeks or longer in the refrigerator. Oil keeps out the air that would allow bacteria to grow.*

PATRAGEL

Every family function at my Romanian grandmother's home began with this dish, and my mother often started our dinner with a plate of lettuce topped with a scoop of patragel, *topped with a green pepper ring and a radish rose. This is my family's transliteration of her name for the dish. It is called* patlican *in Turkey; similar spellings exist throughout that part of the world. This is as simple as it gets!*

1 large eggplant
1 or more cloves of garlic, finely minced
Salt and freshly ground black pepper

1 or more tablespoons extra virgin olive oil
1 teaspoon sugar or to taste (optional)

1. Roast eggplant over a flame or in a 350°F oven until all sides of the eggplant are slightly charred and the eggplant is deflated, about 30 minutes.

2. Slit the sides of the eggplant and let it drain in a colander until cool.

3. Scoop out the eggplant pulp, and whip in the garlic, seasonings, and olive oil until smooth but not oily. Add sugar if desired. Serve with pita or crackers.

Yield: 4 servings

TINA'S TIDBITS

- *The "or more" of garlic in the recipe is there not to scare the faint of heart; Romanians eat **lots** of garlic on their food and often sweeten their dishes, even if it has an abundance of garlic in it.*
- *"Russian caviar" is basically this recipe with finely chopped onion and bell pepper in it; leave out the sugar, please!*

Eggplant Salad with Pine Nuts Kioupia

The island of Rhodes had a good-sized Jewish population before the Nazi occupation. Today there are very few Jewish families residing there, but one of the synagogues is still open for visitors, and it contains the nerot tamid, "eternal lights," from all of the destroyed synagogues on the island.

On a recent visit I drove four miles inland to a restaurant called Kioupia. Here we ate in a farmhouse courtyard, surrounded by whitewashed terraced walls whose ledges housed hundreds of votive candles twinkling in the night air, as we ate a twenty-five-course meal of assorted little mezes. Their eggplant dish was reminiscent of my Romanian grandmother's, but there was an added ingredient. I was informed that it was yogurt. Here is my version of that wonderful eggplant dip. Drizzle it with a little extra olive oil and serve it with some Greek olives and feta cheese and you could make it a meal.

2 large eggplants (about 2 pounds)
2 tablespoons extra virgin Greek olive oil
Juice of 1 small lemon
2 cloves of garlic, chopped

¼ cup Greek yogurt
Salt and freshly ground black pepper
2 tablespoons pine nuts

1. Wash the whole eggplants and pierce with a small, sharp knife in one or two places.

2. Place the eggplants on a rimmed cookie sheet and broil under the broiler in the oven or cook directly on an outdoor grill, turning every 10 minutes, until the eggplants are deflated and their skins are charred.

3. Remove the eggplants to a colander placed in the sink, and slit the skins open. Allow the eggplants to drain for at least 10 minutes or until they are cool enough to handle. If there is a large clump of seeds, remove some of it (you don't have to get all of them), and discard the stem and the skin. Place the pulp of the eggplant into a processor work bowl.

4. Add the olive oil, lemon juice, and garlic to the eggplant, and pulse on and off 7 times until the mixture is fairly smooth but still a little chunky. Pour the mixture into a bowl.

5. Whisk the Greek yogurt and salt and pepper into the mixture. Add more olive oil or lemon juice if the mixture appears too dry. Adjust the seasoning if necessary.

6. Toast the pine nuts on a cookie sheet in a 350°F oven for 5 minutes or until lightly golden. Do not burn.

7. Just before serving, fold the toasted nuts into the eggplant, reserving a few to garnish. Serve at room temperature or cold with crackers or wedges of pita.

Yield: 6–8 servings

TINA'S TIDBITS

- *Greek yogurt has the consistency of sour cream, and even the fat-free variety tastes richer than most sour creams on the market. Domestic yogurt is not as thick. It can be squeezed in some cheesecloth, but it won't have the same consistency. It is easier to just locate some good Greek or Bulgarian yogurt.*
- *Greek olive oil is pressed from Calamata olives and has a distinctive, slightly stronger flavor than Italian olive oil. Extra virgin olive oil of any variety should be used for a clean taste and a higher smoking point.*
- ***Never*** *use lemon juice from a bottle. It is not "real" in taste because of all the preservatives added to it.*
- *Lemons will give off more juice if they are stored at room temperature.*

Imam Bayaldi

One of the most famous Turkish dishes, the name says it all. Translated it means "the imam fainted." Small eggplants are slit, stuffed with sautéed onion, tomato, and spices, and slowly cooked in a lemon and olive oil sauce until the eggplants have absorbed most of the sauce and are luscious and soft. Some say this dish got its name because the dish is so wonderful; others suggest the great amount of oil used in the recipe caused the imam to assess the expense of this dish, which overwhelmed him, and he fainted. You be the judge.

10 small, round eggplants (2–3 ounces each)
2 quarts salted water for soaking eggplant, or enough to cover
⅓ cup extra virgin olive oil

FILLING:
2 tablespoons extra virgin olive oil
1 large onion, thinly sliced in semicircles (about 3 cups)
4 large cloves of garlic, finely minced (about 2 tablespoon)
One 14.5-ounce can diced tomatoes, drained
One 5.5-ounce can tomato juice (about ¾ cup)
Juice of ½ medium lemon
Kosher salt and freshly ground black pepper
1 tablespoon sugar, or to taste

1. Remove the leaves around the stem of the eggplant, keeping the stem attached.

2. Using a bar zester or vegetable peeler, cut away 4 strips of peel from around the eggplant to create a striped effect. Cut a slit down the middle from the stem to the bottom, being careful not to cut completely through to the other side. Place in the bowl of salted water.

3. When all of the eggplants are in the bowl of salted water, let them soak for 10 minutes. Drain and pat dry.

4. Heat a 10-inch frying pan for 20 seconds. Add the ⅓ cup olive oil and heat for another 10 seconds. Add all of the eggplants and cook over low heat for 5 minutes, turning occasionally to cook all sides.

TINA'S TIDBITS

- *Small baby eggplants are hard to find outside of Asian markets. However, small Italian eggplants can be used in the same manner. Portion size will be slightly larger but not significantly.*
- *When a recipe calls for sliced onions, it never means onion rings. Slice the onion in half from top to bottom, and then thinly slice with the grain (top to root end) or across to create half moons.*
- *A bar zester has a little notch on one side to deeply peel one strip of lemon for a "twist." This notch will also give you uniform lines on the eggplant.*
- *To avoid burning garlic and destroying the subtle flavor of the filling, add garlic to the pan when more moisture has accumulated from the onions. This will allow the flavors to meld without jeopardizing the garlic's flavor.*

5. Set the pan with the eggplant aside to cool while you make the filling.

6. To make the filling, heat a 10-inch skillet for 20 seconds over high heat, and add the remaining 2 tablespoons of olive oil. Heat the oil for 10 seconds, and add the sliced onions.

7. Sauté the onions over low heat for 7 minutes or until soft and very lightly golden. Add the garlic and sauté for 1 minute. Add the drained diced tomatoes and cook for 2 minutes. Set aside.

8. Fill each eggplant with some of the onion mixture and return to the oily pan in which they were fried, cut side up.

9. Combine the remaining ingredients and pour around the eggplant. Cover and simmer for 30 minutes or until the eggplants are soft to the touch but still hold their shape. Baste with the tomato-oil mixture. If there is too much sauce, simmer uncovered until the sauce is reduced.

10. Transfer the cooked eggplants and their liquid to a shallow-rimmed serving dish and cool to room temperature. Serve.

Note: Eggplants may be refrigerated for a few days for later use, but bring to room temperature before serving.

Yield: 5–10 servings

CHEESECAKE

The cheesecakes Judith fed to Holofernes bore no resemblance to the modern-day icon of Jewish cuisine. Her cakes were salty, to induce a thirst for wine and an eventual drunken stupor; these cheesecakes just induce high cholesterol!

For centuries Jews produced all the dairy products they needed. The family cow provided the milk products needed to produce cheese, cream, and butter, and ultimately her supervised slaughter could take care of the meat needs. She could be considered a walking cheesecake factory.

We don't need to have a cow in our backyard to provide us with the provisions to make a great cheesecake, just good recipes.

ITALIAN CHEESECAKE

It is rare that we can re-create a food memory from our childhood. Time and experience color our thoughts and palate. However, I was able to re-create the delicious, light cheesecake from Debold's Bakery in Hempstead, New York. They might not have considered it Italian, but with the ricotta instead of cream cheese and sour cream, it definitely hails from close to the Mediterranean.

CRUST:
1 cup plus 2 tablespoons flour
3 tablespoons sugar
6 tablespoons unsalted butter
1 egg
½ teaspoon vanilla

FILLING:
1 pound ricotta cheese
½ pound cream cheese
3 tablespoons flour
½ teaspoon salt
1 teaspoon vanilla
Grated zest of ½ lemon
2 eggs
4 egg whites
¾ cup sugar
¾ cup crushed pineapple, drained

1. Preheat the oven to 300°F, and butter the bottom and sides of a 10-inch springform pan.

2. Place the flour and sugar in a processor and pulse on and off to combine. Cut the butter into 6 pieces and add to the work bowl. Pulse the machine until the mixture looks like coarse meal.

3. Combine the egg and vanilla in a small dish, and add it to the work bowl with the processor running. As soon as a ball of dough begins to form, stop the processor and remove the dough.

4. Roll the dough ¼ inch thick between two sheets of plastic wrap or wax paper, and using the bottom of the pan as a pattern, cut out a 10-inch circle. Place the dough in the pan, prick it all over with a fork, and bake for 15 minutes. Cool.

5. Drain the ricotta, and place the 2 cheeses in the processor work bowl and process until the mixture is smooth. Add the flour, salt, vanilla, lemon zest, and 2 eggs, and process until smooth. Pour into a bowl.

6. In another bowl, beat the egg whites with the sugar until stiff, but shiny. Fold into the cheese mixture.

7. Spread the drained, crushed pineapple over the crust, and gently pour the cheese mixture over the pineapple. Bake for 45 minutes or until the cake is fairly set. Cool and serve.

Yield: 8–10 servings

TINA'S TIDBITS

- *The crust for this cake is a* murbeteig, *or German short crust. A firm cookie dough is needed so that the pineapple doesn't dissolve it during baking.*
- *Use whole-milk ricotta for a rich taste and lower water content.*
- *If cream cheese is at room temperature, it will blend well with other ingredients and no lumps will be apparent.*
- *Creating a meringue before adding to the cheese mixture not only incorporates air into the mixture but also ensures that the sugar will be completely dissolved.*

Rich Sour Cream Cheesecake

It doesn't get much richer than this! Firm but light because there is less cheese and more eggs and sour cream, this is a dessert to make any person living within the Pale feel rich!

CRUST:
10 double crackers of graham crackers (1 paper packet), broken in pieces
$\frac{1}{4}$ cup sugar
4 tablespoons unsalted butter

TOPPING:
16 ounces cream cheese
1 cup sugar
5 large eggs, separated
1 teaspoon vanilla extract
2 teaspoons lemon juice
1 pint sour cream

1. Place the broken pieces of graham crackers in a processor work bowl with the $\frac{1}{4}$ cup sugar. Pulse the machine on and off until the crackers are completely pulverized.

2. Add the butter and pulse on and off again until the butter is incorporated. Butter the sides of a 10-inch springform pan, and press the crumb mixture into the bottom of the pan, reserving $\frac{1}{2}$ cup of crumbs for later.

3. Bake in a preheated 400°F oven for 8 minutes or until lightly golden. Set aside.

4. Reduce the oven temperature to 300°F.

5. In a clean processor work bowl, combine the cheese and the sugar until smooth. You might have to stop and scrape down the sides of the bowl once. Add the egg yolks and process for 5 seconds or until combined.

6. Add the vanilla, lemon juice, and sour cream and pulse for 20 seconds or until the mixture is very smooth. Pour the mixture into a 2-quart bowl.

7. Using a handheld mixer, beat the egg whites until firm peaks form. Stir $\frac{1}{2}$ cup of these whites into the cream cheese to "lighten" the mixture a little. Add the remaining egg whites and fold gently but swiftly to produce a lighter but not streaked mix.

8. Pour the batter into the prepared pan with the crust. Smooth out the top and bake for 1 hour. Turn off the oven, but keep the cake in the oven for another $\frac{1}{2}$ hour. Open the oven door and let the cake cool in the oven for an hour or so.

9. Run a sharp knife along the edge of the pan and remove the springform sides. Gently press the reserved crumbs around the side of the cake. Refrigerate until serving. Serve plain or with a fruit topping of your choice.

Yield: 10–12 servings

TINA'S TIDBITS

- *Low heat and little air in the batter will do the most for preventing cracks in a cheesecake.*
- *The cake might seem a little soft at first, but it will firm up when cold.*
- *Eggs act like flour in this cake; they bind the ingredients together.*

New York Style Cheesecake

As much as I love my childhood Italian cheesecake, nothing sends me into rapture more than an ultrasmooth, ultrarich New York style cheesecake. I want it so smooth that you would be tempted to spread it on a bagel if it wasn't so rich and sweet. Here is my version, which I taught so long ago that I found it in my files printed in dot matrix!

CRUST:
1 cup flour
¼ cup sugar
1 teaspoon finely grated lemon zest
1 stick cold unsalted butter
¼ teaspoon vanilla extract
1 egg yolk

FILLING:
24 ounces good-quality, full-fat cream cheese
¾ cup sugar
Finely grated zest of ½ orange
Finely grated zest of 1 small lemon
1 teaspoon vanilla
3 eggs plus 2 egg yolks
¼ cup heavy cream

1. Place the flour, sugar, and teaspoon of lemon zest in a processor work bowl and pulse on and off 3 times to combine.

2. Cut the butter into 8 pieces and distribute in the work bowl. Pulse the machine for 5 seconds or until the mixture looks like coarse meal.

3. Combine the egg yolk and the vanilla and add to the work bowl while the processor is running. Mix only until the dough begins to clump together and starts to form a ball. Refrigerate for 15 minutes or longer, if necessary.

4. Preheat the oven to 400°F.

5. Pat the chilled dough over the bottom and 2 inches up the sides of a 9-inch springform pan. Bake for 10 minutes in the preheated 400°F oven. Cool while you make the filling.

6. Reduce the oven temperature to 275°F.

7. Using an electric mixer, beat the cream cheese until it is very smooth with no lumps. Scrape down the sides of the bowl if necessary. Add the sugar slowly and mix well to incorporate.

8. Add the remaining ingredients to the work bowl and mix thoroughly.

9. Pour the cheese mixture into the springform pan with the partially baked crust. Lightly tap the pan on the counter to bring any trapped air to the surface.

10. Bake the cake for 1 hour. Cool thoroughly before refrigerating or covering with a topping. Keep chilled in the refrigerator until ready to serve.

Yield: 12–15 servings

TINA'S TIDBITS

- *Processors generate a lot of heat, so it is best to have your butter cold when making dough.*
- *Never let the dough form a ball. At that stage, the gluten has been activated, and the dough could be tough and hard to roll.*
- *When egg or egg yolk is the only liquid except flavoring, make sure that the two ingredients are combined first so that they will be uniformly distributed without overworking the dough.*
- *Cream cheese must be smooth before other ingredients are added or the mixture will retain any lumps.*

CANNOLI CHEESECAKE

I developed this cheesecake after making mini cannoli for a Rosh HaShanah open house. With so much filling left over, I decided to transform the leftovers into a cheesecake. This is slightly grainy because it is based on ricotta and not cream cheese, but if you like cannoli you will be very happy with this alternative. Obviously, if you do not have any store-bought shells at your disposal, you can use one of the previous crust recipes for your base.

CRUST:
4 ounces of prepared cannoli shells (about 12 mini shells)
4 tablespoons unsalted butter
½ cup sugar
¼ teaspoon cinnamon

FILLING:
3 large eggs
1 cup sugar
1 teaspoon vanilla
5 cups leftover prepared cannoli filling (see recipe below)

1. Preheat the oven to 350°F.

2. Combine the cannoli shells with the butter, sugar, and cinnamon in a small processor work bowl and process until fine crumbs.

3. Press the crumbs into the bottom of one 9-inch springform pan or five 4½-inch mini springform pans. Place the prepared pans on a rimmed cookie sheet.

4. Bake the crust for 10 minutes at 350°F. Remove from the oven while preparing the filling.

5. Combine the eggs, sugar, and vanilla with a wire whisk. Add the cannoli filling and blend well.

6. Pour the filling into the prepared pan and place in the oven. Immediately reduce the temperature to 300°F and bake for 50 minutes or until the mixture is set but not dry.

7. Cool and then refrigerate until serving.

CANNOLI FILLING

1½ pounds whole-milk ricotta
8 ounces cream cheese, softened
1 tablespoon vanilla extract
1½ cups confectioners' sugar

½ teaspoon cinnamon
¾ cup mini chocolate chips
¼ cup finely chopped candied citron (optional)

1. Place the ricotta and the softened cream cheese in a large mixing bowl and beat with an electric mixer until smooth.

2. Add the vanilla, confectioners' sugar, and cinnamon and beat until the sugar is dissolved and the filling is smooth. Add the chocolate chips and the citron if using and stir by hand to combine.

Yield: 10–12 servings

TINA'S TIDBITS

- *To make the cake more dense, drain the ricotta cheese in a sieve or cheesecloth to extract some of the excess moisture.*
- *Confectioners' sugar is 3% cornstarch, which helps absorb excess moisture in the ricotta as well.*
- *To achieve a smoother cake consistency, do not add chocolate chips and citron to the batter; sprinkle the mini chips and citron over the top of the cake right after it is removed from the oven.*

PRALINE CHEESECAKE

Many years ago I freelanced for the largest kosher catering company in Philadelphia. I was asked to make sixteen of my praline cheesecakes for a bar mitzvah. Commercial mixers are identical to stand mixers in a home kitchen, just bigger. They also "attack" in the same way if you are not careful. When I added four dozen eggs to the cream cheese in the bowl and turned the mixer on, two eggs shot out into the room in opposite directions and they splattered on the floor fifteen feet away! The mixer does an excellent job of combining ingredients, but you need to turn the machine on slowly or you could repeat my performance. Here's the recipe I used that day, but only for one cake!

CRUST:
1 cup graham cracker crumbs
$\frac{1}{4}$ cup finely ground pecans
3 tablespoons sugar
$\frac{1}{2}$ stick unsalted butter

FILLING:
24 ounces cream cheese (3 packs)
$1\frac{1}{4}$ cups dark brown sugar
1 tablespoon cornstarch
3 large eggs
2 teaspoons vanilla
$\frac{1}{4}$ teaspoon cinnamon
Pure maple syrup
2 tablespoons large pecan halves, lightly toasted in the oven (at 350°F) for 4 minutes

1. Preheat the oven to 325°F.

2. Combine the crust ingredients in a bowl and work the mixture into a dough with your fingertips. Pat this dough into the bottom of a 9- or 10-inch springform pan. Bake for 6–8 minutes and remove from the oven.

3. In a processor work bowl, combine the cream cheese and sugar and pulse until the sugar is mixed in well and the cream cheese is smooth. Scrape down the sides of the bowl.

4. Add the cornstarch, eggs, vanilla, and cinnamon, and when the mixture is smooth, pour into the prepared crust.

5. Gently tap the cake pan on the counter to remove any excess air. Place the pan in the middle of the oven and bake for 40–50 minutes. Remove from the oven and let the cake cool completely.

6. Run a knife around the sides of the cake before removing the springform. Brush 1–2 tablespoons of pure maple syrup over the top of the cake, and place the toasted pecan halves in a decorative pattern on top. Chill before serving.

Yield: 8–10 servings

TINA'S TIDBITS

- *The shape of the springform pan sometimes leaves a depression in the cheesecake running parallel to the sides of the pan. This actually looks attractive and provides a rim for any topping you might add.*
- *If the top cracks, use the pecans to creatively cover those cracks with an interesting design. No one will know.*
- *Toasting nuts brings out their flavor, so it is an especially good idea to toast the pecans so that their rich flavor will complement the strong maple flavor of the syrup.*

CHAROSET

The Passover seder begins with the description of the items on the seder plate, and the anticipation mounts to the time in the "order" of this ceremony when participants will be eating their Hillel sandwich of matzah and bitter herbs. The first bite is plain and hot, but then they get a chance to eat those little shards of matzah with something special: the mixture called *charoset*, symbolizing the mortar that was used by the Jewish slaves in Egypt to hold the pyramid stones together.

What are the requirements for making *charoset*? Nothing, except a desire to have it look dark and muddy like cement. Any special ingredients? None, but creative cooks have always managed to find something indigenous to the area where they live to create this symbol. Whether a lumpy mixture of fresh and dried fruit, a smooth paste, a liquid, or a firm ball, charoset is an expression of the diversity of Jewish cultural backgrounds tied together by the single root planted firmly in the story of continuity and survival.

The following is a small sampling of *charoset* recipes from throughout the Diaspora, representing the bounty of the lands of their origin.

ASHKENAZIC CHAROSET

My job when I was a child was to chop the charoset *in the wooden bowl with a mezzaluna that looked more like a handheld guillotine than a moon-shaped chopper. Making the mixture gray to represent the mortar that was used to hold the bricks of the pyramids together was no problem, since it took a long time to chop the apples and they oxidized during the process.*

Before food processors the task was arduous, but the mixture held together while still being a little lumpy. Today, using the processor, the charoset *can be as smooth as paste, if you want it to be that way.*

Here is the classic Ashkenazic charoset *made in the United States over the last century.*

2 McIntosh apples, peeled and cored
1 cup walnut pieces
1½ teaspoons cinnamon or to taste

Sweet Concord grape or Malaga Passover wine
Matzah meal, if necessary

1. Combine the apples and walnuts in a wooden bowl, and chop to a fine consistency with a curved chopper or mezzaluna.

2. Add the cinnamon and wine to bind, and set aside, covered, in a glass bowl in the refrigerator until ready to use.

3. If the apples give up a great deal of juice, add a few tablespoons of matzah meal to bind the mixture together. Don't add too much matzah meal, as it swells and the mixture could become too thick.

Yield: 1½ cups

TINA'S TIDBITS

- *Since walnuts and soft McIntosh apples were most abundant in the states with the most Jewish immigrants, these ingredients were most often called for in printed recipes.*
- *The sweet wine most associated with Jewish ritual was a result of the availability of tart grapes that could only be made palatable by adding copious amounts of sugar to them while making the wine.*
- *Matzah meal can absorb excess liquid in the* charoset. *Use a little at a time because it will take about 15 minutes for the liquid to absorb, and if you add too much, you will have a dry mass that tastes like matzah instead of apples.*

TRADITIONAL CHAROSET TEXAS STYLE

For over twenty years our family has been spending the first night of Passover at the Friedlanders' home. Lynn is a native Texan with Ashkenazic roots. How does this lineage manifest itself in her charoset? The basic Ashkenazic formula is augmented with native Texas pecans and sugar. Migration changes recipes to conform to what is readily available . . .

8–10 sweet apples (Fuji, Gala, Honeycrisp, or Jonagold)
8–10 ounces pecans, toasted

1 tablespoon cinnamon, or to taste
$\frac{1}{3}$ cup sugar, or to taste
1 cup sweet Concord grape Passover wine

1. Peel, core, and cut the apples into 8 pieces.

2. Place $\frac{1}{2}$ of the apples in a processor work bowl and pulse until the pieces are about $\frac{1}{4}$ inch. Remove to a large glass bowl, and repeat with the remaining apples.

3. Toast the pecans at 350°F for 5 minutes. Cool slightly and add them to the work bowl. Pulse the machine on and off until the pecans are finely chopped. Add the pecans to the apples.

4. Add the cinnamon and sugar to the apple mixture and stir to combine.

5. Add the wine and mix well.

6. Cover and refrigerate at least overnight, but preferably 1–2 days.

7. If the mixture is watery, drain off the excess liquid and adjust the cinnamon, sugar, and wine as desired.

Yield: About $1\frac{1}{2}$ quarts

TINA'S TIDBIT

- *The choice of nut used in making charoset has more to do with availability than anything else. Walnuts were readily available in eastern Europe and parts of the Middle East; Texas has an abundance of pecans. Necessity opens the door to creativity. In this case there is no bitterness in pecans as there is in walnuts and the resulting mixture has a much sweeter, more well-rounded flavor.*

Jaroset
(Panamanian Halek)

This recipe comes from Rita Sasso, a Panamanian whose roots go back to Spain via Amsterdam and Curaçao, which had a significant Jewish population in the seventeenth and eighteenth centuries. Rita and I became pen pals when I published a recipe in my Reform Judaism *column that was given to me by a friend in Mexico. She recognized the recipe as her own. We have shared recipes ever since, and here is one she gave me with her permission to publish.*

4 ounces dried figs
4 ounces raisins
4 ounces prunes
4 ounces pitted dates
1½ cups peanut butter or almond butter

2–3 cups brown sugar, according to taste
½ cup sweet Passover wine, as needed
Cinnamon, enough to cover the balls of *charoset*
(approximately 1½ ounces)

1. Place the dried fruits in a processor work bowl and process until a relatively smooth paste is formed.

2. Add the peanut butter and brown sugar to the processor work bowl and pulse on and off a few times to begin to combine the ingredients. The machine will only begin the process, as the mixture will be thick.

3. Remove the mixture to a bowl, and continue to combine the ingredients, kneading with your hands.

4. Little by little add the wine to the mixture until you obtain a firm ball of fruit. This mixture will be quite sticky. If necessary, refrigerate for ½ hour until the mixture firms up a little.

5. Wet your hands periodically with cold water and form small balls of *charoset* about the size of a small walnut.

6. Place the balls on a parchment-lined cookie sheet and put them in the freezer until frozen.

7. Once the balls are hard, you can remove them to a freezer bag until needed.

8. Just before serving, defrost and roll each ball in cinnamon. Serve.

Yield: 4 dozen balls

TINA'S TIDBITS

- *Do not double this recipe unless you have a very large food processor or the mixture will be too difficult to combine thoroughly.*
- *Because of the strong Sephardic influence in Central America, peanuts are often found in foods for Passover. Observant Ashkenazic Jews will not eat peanuts during Passover so almond butter makes a good substitute in this recipe.*

Garosa
(Charoset from Curaçao)

Here's a recipe from modern-day Curaçao, whose Jewish roots go back over four hundred years.

2 ounces pitted dates, preferably Medjool
2 ounces pitted prunes
2 ounces dark raisins
2 ounces dried figs
2 cups unsalted peanuts
½ cup cashew nuts
Grated zest from 1 medium lemon

½ cup dark brown sugar
2 tablespoons honey
2 teaspoons cinnamon plus additional for coating
1–2 tablespoons sweet Passover wine
1 tablespoon orange juice
1 teaspoon lemon juice

1. Combine the dates, prunes, raisins, figs, peanuts, and cashews in a processor work bowl and pulse on and off until the contents are fairly small.

2. Add the zest and the remaining ingredients, and continue to process until the mixture is moist and relatively smooth and firm.

3. Roll the mixture into 1-inch balls, and roll each ball in cinnamon to coat well. Place in 1 layer on a flat plate until ready to serve.

Yield: 15–20 balls

TINA'S TIDBITS

- *One of the noticeable differences between Eastern European charoset and Middle Eastern or Sephardic charoset is that in the latter, the basis for the mixture is dried fruit, using what grew abundantly all around the Jews.*
- *Probably because the dried fruit is so sticky, most charoset from the Mediterranean are shaped into balls.*

ITALIAN CHAROSET

This recipe really tells a story. The Ottoman influence is seen with the dates, walnuts, and spices. The apples represent the immigrants from the north of Italy. The citrus fruits signal the presence of Jews in the citrus industry in Italy, and the cocoa and vanilla have to come from the Jewish traders who lived in South and Central America and traded with their brethren in Italy. The fact that this recipe, adapted from Edda Servi Machlin, incorporates the use of the processor shows that our traditions continue to adapt to the times and equipment readily available to us.

½ pound pitted dates
½ pound walnuts
3 large apples, peeled and cored
1 large whole seedless orange, washed and cut into
   chunks
3 large ripe bananas
⅓ cup sweet wine

½ teaspoon cinnamon
⅛ teaspoon cloves
1 tablespoon lemon juice
Matzah meal as needed
¼ cup unsweetened cocoa
¼ cup vanilla-flavored sugar

1. Place the dates, walnuts, apples, and orange chunks in a processor and process until very fine. Spoon into a medium bowl.

2. Peel and mash the bananas, and add to the other mixture in the bowl.

3. Add the wine, spices, and lemon juice and mix well. If the mixture is too moist or soft, then add a few tablespoons of matzah meal to the fruit mixture. Wait 10 minutes before proceeding so that the matzah meal can hydrate and absorb any excess moisture.

4. Mix together the cocoa and sugar.

5. Make little balls out of the paste, and roll them in the cocoa-sugar mixture.

Yield: 3–4 dozen balls

TINA'S TIDBIT

- *Because cocoa will hydrate easily, make the paste balls in advance, and roll them in the cocoa just before serving.*

Rhodesian Charoset

On the island of Rhodes, the charoset exemplifies its place in the Eastern Mediterranean by the use of only oranges and dates as the base, augmented with the spices from the nearby spice trade route and almonds. The addition of Concord grape wine (a wine commercially made only in the northeastern United States) shows the migration of the tradition across the Atlantic.

1 medium orange
Zest of ½ medium orange
18 pitted large dates, preferably Medjool
½ cup honey

½ teaspoon ground cinnamon
¼ teaspoon ground cloves
¼ cup sweet Concord grape Passover wine
⅓ cup toasted, finely chopped almonds

1. Zest half of the orange and put the peel in a processor work bowl.

2. Cut off the top and the bottom of the orange to reveal the fruit inside. Starting from the top, place your knife just under the peel and cut it away, following the curve of the orange. The first slice is the hardest, and then you can easily see how deep to cut to remove the peel without cutting into the fruit.

3. Cut the orange into 3 or 4 slices crosswise and place in the processor work bowl with the zest.

4. Pit the dates if necessary and add to the orange pieces. Process the mixture until a fairly smooth paste is formed.

5. Scrape the mixture into a 2-quart saucepan. Add the honey to the pot and cook over medium-low heat until the mixture thickens and the bubbles are so thick they can hardly come up through the paste. This will take about 10 minutes. Stir often to prevent scorching.

6. Remove from the heat and add the spices and wine. Stir over low heat until all the ingredients are well combined and the mixture begins to thicken again.

7. Remove from the heat, stir in the toasted finely chopped almonds, and place in a bowl. Cover and refrigerate for at least a few hours or longer to allow the flavors to meld.

Yield: 1½ cups

TINA'S TIDBIT

• *This recipe uses heat to reduce the liquid content of the* charoset *rather than adding matzah meal, which has only been in existence commercially for the last 150-plus years.*

ISRAELI CHAROSET

This recipe is an adaptation of the California-influenced Israeli charoset of the well-known kosher cooking instructor and cookbook author Judy Zeidler. This recipe truly tells a story since the ingredients are an amalgam of both Ashkenazic and Sephardic culinary traditions. Flavorful, intriguing, and a big hit at the seder.

⅔ cup pistachio nuts
2 apples (Gala or Empire), peeled, cored, and cut into chunks
15 pitted dates
2 bananas, peeled and cut into 1-inch pieces
1–2 tablespoons fresh lemon juice (depending on sweetness of fruits used)

Zest of ½ lemon
¼ cup fresh orange juice
Zest of ½ orange
1 teaspoon cinnamon
¼ cup sweet Concord grape Passover wine
4 tablespoons matzah meal

1. Place the pistachio nuts in a processor work bowl and pulse on and off until the nuts are ground fine but not forming butter.

2. Add the apples and dates, and pulse until the fruits are fairly well chopped.

3. Add the bananas, lemon juice and zest, orange juice and zest, and cinnamon, and pulse until the mixture is a coarse but combined mass.

4. Remove the mixture to a glass bowl, and stir in the wine and matzah meal. Chill, covered, until serving time.

Yield: 10–15 servings

TINA'S TIDBIT

- *Here the banana is used again, with its great ability to impart both sweetness and a dark brown color when the mixture oxidizes.*

EGYPTIAN CHAROSET

The Capsouto brothers left Cairo for Lyon when the lives of Jews became difficult in Egypt after the creation of the State of Israel. Their little synagogue in Lyon was gifted a Torah by the synagogue in Istanbul so that they could conduct services. They later settled in New York. In 1987, after a dramatic massacre that occurred at the Neve-Shalom Synagogue in Istanbul, Turkey—the brothers' parents were from Turkey—the Capsouto brothers began their tradition of holding a Passover seder at their New York City restaurant for charity. At first their efforts helped raise funds to rebuild the Istanbul synagogue, and now they donate the proceeds to a cause that the American Joint Distribution Committee feels is in need.

The following recipe, adapted from the Capsouto Frères menu, is the charoset served at these charitable seders.

8-ounce package of Medjool dates, pitted
2 Fuji or Gala apples

Water
1 cinnamon stick (optional)

1. Place the dates in a 2-quart saucepan with water and cook, covered, on medium high while you prepare the apples. The water should be reduced to below the level of the dates, and the dates should begin to soften.

2. Peel, core, and dice the apples into $\frac{1}{2}$-inch chunks. Add the apples and cinnamon stick (if using), and cook over low heat until the apples are soft. Do not let the water completely evaporate. It is rare that this happens, but if it does, add $\frac{1}{4}$ cup water to the pan.

3. Remove the cinnamon stick, if using. Pass the dates and apples through a food mill using the medium disk or use a processor, pulsing the machine on and off to get a rough puree of the ingredients. If the mixture is too watery, return it to the pan and cook on low heat until the desired thickness is achieved.

Yield: 2 cups

TINA'S TIDBITS

- *A food mill will puree mixtures while separating the skin from the pulp of the food. It is a hand-cranked, nonelectric utensil and a valuable tool to have in your kitchen.*
- *Apples may be left with their skin on prior to cooking, because the food mill will separate the skin from the fruit pulp. However, the pectin in the skin will create a thicker charoset when cooled, so don't let the water evaporate while cooking or your final, chilled mixture will be too thick.*
- *Cinnamon stick is my addition for the modern palate, but it bridges the gap from traditional Ashkenazic charoset to this Middle Eastern variety.*
- *This is actually a much easier and less labor intensive method of making halek (see page 433).*

NONTRADITIONAL TOMATO CHAROSET

OK, so sometimes creativity gets the best of us, but when I thought about creating this recipe, I knew I wanted it to be a paste that was dark like mortar and incorporated some of the foods of Israel. Everyone loved it, and I didn't tell them what they were eating until after the seder. Let's keep it our little secret, shall we?

1½ pounds small grape tomatoes
6 tablespoons granulated sugar, divided use
8 ounces whole almonds
¼ cup honey

Zest of ¼ medium orange
1½ teaspoons cinnamon
½ teaspoon ground ginger
¼ teaspoon ground cloves

1. Preheat the oven to 350°F (325°F for convection oven).

2. Line a large rimmed cookie sheet with parchment paper. Cut the tomatoes in half lengthwise and place cut side up on the cookie sheet.

3. Sprinkle 2 tablespoons of the sugar over the tomatoes and place in the oven for 15 minutes.

4. Remove the tomatoes from the oven and sprinkle them with another 2 tablespoons of sugar. Return to the oven and roast for 30 minutes or until the tomatoes are beginning to brown and the sugar is caramelizing. Do not let the sugar burn.

5. Remove from the oven and allow the tomatoes to cool.

6. Meanwhile, toast the almonds in the oven for 7–8 minutes, until fragrant. Do not let the almonds get too dark. Cool the almonds and finely grind them in a nut mill or food processor, using short pulses so that the nuts are ground fine without forming a butter. Place the nuts in a 1-quart bowl and set aside.

7. Place the tomato mixture in the processor work bowl and process until coarsely chopped. Add the honey, orange zest, spices, and remaining 2 tablespoons of sugar. Process to a smooth paste.

8. Add 1½ cups of the ground almonds to the tomato mixture and pulse on and off until the mixture is well blended. Transfer to a storage container and place in the refrigerator for 3 days.

9. When ready to serve, either serve in a dish with a spoon or shape into ¾-inch balls and roll in the remaining ground almonds. Serve cold.

Yield: 20 balls

TINA'S TIDBITS

- *Roasting the tomatoes serves two purposes: the flavor is enhanced by the caramelized sugar and juices, and it helps the tomato dry out so that the mixture won't be too thin and wet.*
- *One tablespoon of sugar and some cinnamon may be added to the remaining nuts for the coating.*

APPLES AND HONEY

*A*pples and honey. The words are bound together like peanut butter and jelly and are rife with memories. Ask Jewish preschoolers what these words bring to mind and they will shout out gleefully, "Rosh HaShanah!" Dipping sliced apple in honey in the Ashkenazic world and eating a sweet apple conserve with bread

in the Sephardic world are universal traditions to express our hope for a sweet and fruitful year. These apple traditions are not based on law or dictates but customs. Jewish customs often originate as a way of reinforcing Jewish identity and history and serve to bind Jews throughout the Diaspora to their heritage and homeland. The question is, why apples and honey?

Although most associate the apple with Adam and Eve's mishap in the Garden of Eden, the Bible never states what fruit was picked from the Tree of Knowledge—apples are most often used as metaphor for affection and association with God.

In the traditional interpretation of Song of Songs, the Jewish people are compared to an apple: "As the apple is rare and unique among the trees of the forest, so is my beloved [Israel] among the maidens [nations] of the world" (2:3). In medieval

times apples were considered so special that prayers were etched into the skin of the apple before it was eaten. Could this have led to the custom of using the apple as a symbol of our "wishes" for a fruitful year? Even the *Zohar*, a thirteenth-century Jewish mystical text of kabbalistic writings, states that beauty "diffuses itself in the world as an apple."

The use of honey seems obvious; it is sweet and therefore symbolically represents our hopes for a sweet year. Consuming honey during the High Holy Days was an old custom followed by Jews throughout the world. This custom was referenced in writings in the seventh century by Babylonian Talmudic scholars, although its practice is presumed to predate the writings. Eating apples and honey connects us to our ancient past and brings sweetness and hope for each new year and each new generation.

HALEK
(DATE HONEY)

This recipe is worth trying when you have a little time, because the resulting liquid has many culinary uses all year long. This is the honey referred to in the Torah when Israel is called the "Land of Milk and Honey."

2 cups pitted dates
5 cups water

1. Combine the dates and water in a 2-quart saucepan and bring to a rolling boil.

2. Remove from the heat and cover. Let the dates steep in the water for 4 hours or overnight. They will get very soft, and their skins will begin to peel off.

3. Cut out a 10-inch square of triple-layered cheesecloth, and place it in a small colander over a clean 1-quart saucepan.

4. Carefully pour the date-soaking liquid through the cheesecloth into the pan.

5. Working with $\frac{1}{2}$ cup of dates at a time, place the dates in the cheesecloth, and bring up the corners so that the dates are encased in the cloth.

6. Twist the cheesecloth over the pot, as tight as you can until the dates give up some more juice. Keep squeezing until it appears that the dates have been wrung dry.

7. Discard the used pulp and repeat with another $\frac{1}{2}$ cup of dates. Continue this process until all the dates have been used.

8. Return the pot to the stove and cook over moderate heat until the liquid is reduced to a syrupy consistency.

9. Pour this liquid into a 1-pint jar and refrigerate until ready to use.

Yield: $1\frac{1}{2}$–2 cups

TINA'S TIDBITS

- *This amount of dates makes about a pint of* halek. *Some people make 5-6 quarts at a time, but I assume friends come to help, because it could take all day to make that large a quantity.*
- *Because there is so much natural sugar in the dates, the boiling creates syrup as the water evaporates.*
- *The syrup will get thicker as it chills and will last for many months in the refrigerator.*

HONEYED CHERRY-PECAN BRIE

The ultimate Jewish mother feeding the masses is Ina Pinkney, the owner of Ina's in Chicago. Warm, loving, and nurturing, she can serve up the best stories with the best food while you dine in her casual eatery. Ina gave me the idea for this Brie. I've adapted it using Texas pecans and dried cherries, but sweetened dried cranberries or dried apricots, finely diced, would be delicious, too.

One 15-ounce wheel of Brie
²⁄₃ cup pecan halves, coarsely chopped
¹⁄₃ cup dried cherries, coarsely chopped if large
¹⁄₄ cup honey

1 tablespoon unsalted butter, melted
¹⁄₄ teaspoon cinnamon
¹⁄₄ teaspoon ground cardamom

1. Place the Brie on a large sheet of foil or a decorative disposable cake pan (if you're giving this as a gift).

2. Combine the remaining ingredients in a small bowl, and pour the mixture on top of the Brie.

3. When ready to bake, preheat the oven to 350°F. Bake the Brie, uncovered, for 15–20 minutes, until the cheese puffs slightly on the sides. Let rest for 15 minutes.

4. To serve, cut out a small wedge of cheese with a sharp knife; the cheese will ooze out. Serve with crackers or thinly sliced French bread.

Yield: 12–15 servings

TINA'S TIDBITS

- *Always place Brie on a pan with a slight rim (such as a pizza pan) when baking. Brie is considered a double crème cheese with a relatively high butterfat content. When it bakes, some oil often oozes out, so a pan with a rim is a good idea.*
- *This is enough topping for two 5-inch Brie wheels. One of these smaller wheels would serve 8-10 people if you had other hors d'oeuvres to serve.*
- *Refrigerate the Brie until the topping is firm and then cover it if you are transporting it to a friend.*

"WALDORFED" SPINACH SALAD

Much of fall's bounty finds its way into this salad bowl. This is a great salad to take to a friend's house for Rosh HaShanah, with the apples and honey already in it. Or bring this salad out to the sukkah for entertaining your own ushpizin (guests).

2 large Jonagold apples, peeled, cored, and sliced ¼ inch thick
Juice of 1 large lemon
Zest of ½ lemon
4 small scallions, thinly sliced
2 stalks of celery, finely diced
½ cup dark raisins

⅓ cup mayonnaise
¼ cup almond butter or peanut butter
2 tablespoons maple syrup or honey
5 cups baby spinach leaves
¼ cup toasted slivered almonds or peanuts
  (depending on which butter you are using)

1. Combine the apples with the lemon juice, zest, scallions, celery, and raisins in a large bowl.

2. In a small bowl, whisk together the mayonnaise, almond or peanut butter, and maple syrup or honey.

3. Toss this mixture with the apple mixture and chill until serving.

4. When ready to serve, toss the apple mixture with the spinach, and garnish with the toasted nuts.

Yield: 6–8 servings

TINA'S TIDBITS
• *When buying a lemon, lightly scratch the rind with your fingernail. The aroma that is given off will tell you if the zest will be sweet like a lemon lollipop or tart and if the flavor of the juice will be full-bodied and tart or tasteless and astringent.*
• *To remove the strings from a stalk of celery, just bend the large, white end back and pull down; a number of strings should pull away.*

Southwestern Honey Chicken Breast

I served this adaptation of a deep-fried chicken recipe, to two hundred women at a Dallas Akiba Academy luncheon to demonstrate that keeping kosher did not keep us out of the forefront in culinary trends.

1–2 pounds boneless chicken breast
1/2 cup honey
1/3 cup apple juice or cider
2 tablespoons applejack or brandy

1/2 cup whole-wheat flour
Salt and pepper to taste
4 tablespoons olive oil and/or butter

1. Remove the fillet from the chicken breast and lightly pound the breast for uniform thickness. Marinate the chicken in the honey, juice, and brandy for a few hours or overnight.

2. Combine the flour with the salt and pepper on a large plate.

3. Remove the meat from the marinade but **do not dry**. Dip in the seasoned flour and sauté in the hot olive oil until golden on both sides (about 3 minutes per side). Serve with black bean sauce and avocado-tomatillo relish (see recipes below).

Black Bean Sauce

1 can black beans, rinsed and drained
1 cup chicken broth
1 teaspoon minced garlic
3 serrano chilies, seeded and deveined
1 1/2 tablespoons chopped tomatillo
1 tablespoon chopped cilantro
1 tablespoon chopped onion
Lime juice to taste
Salt to taste

1. Combine all of the ingredients, except the lime juice and salt, in a medium saucepan and cook for 5 minutes.

2. Blend the mixture in a blender until smooth.

3. Season with the lime juice and salt. Serve warm with the chicken breasts.

Avocado-Tomatillo Relish

1 avocado, diced into 1/2-inch cubes
2 tablespoons diced tomatillo
1 tablespoon diced red bell pepper
1 tablespoon diced green bell pepper
1/2 teaspoon minced jalapeño pepper
1 tablespoon chopped scallions
3 tablespoons olive oil
Lime juice to taste
Salt to taste

1. Combine all of the ingredients in a bowl.

2. Season with lime juice and salt to taste. Chill until ready to serve.

Yield: 6–8 servings

TINA'S TIDBITS

- *Boneless chicken breast does not need tenderizing; marinating is purely for enhanced flavor.*
- *This flour coating is delicate, because there is no egg to adhere to. However, if your pan is sufficiently hot and there is enough oil in the pan, the delicate whole-wheat flour coating will adhere.*

German Apfelpfannkuchen (Apple Pancake)

German bakers used apples in many of their recipes. Jewish cooks were no exception. Apples were plentiful in Europe and Eastern Europe, but to the poor they were a delicacy that made a simple dish a special occasion food. Here, an oven-baked pancake is topped with a luscious apple topping. The really good news is that the topping can be made in advance and just reheated, and the pancake takes almost no time to prepare and cook.

1 Jonathan or Winesap apple, peeled and cored
1 tablespoon unsalted butter
¼ cup apricot preserves
½ teaspoon vanilla
Pinch of cinnamon
2 tablespoons sugar
2 eggs

½ cup milk
½ cup flour
Pinch of nutmeg
Zest of ¼ orange
1 stick unsalted butter
Confectioners' sugar for dusting

1. Prepare the topping by thinly slicing the peeled and cored apple.

2. Melt the 1 tablespoon butter in a frying pan and add the apples, apricot preserves, vanilla, cinnamon, and sugar. Sauté over low heat until the apples begin to give off some of their juices. Turn the heat up to medium and continue sautéing until the mixture becomes a little more syrupy. Cover and keep warm while you prepare the pancake **or** cover and refrigerate for up to 5 days until needed.

3. To make the pancake, preheat the oven to 475°F.

4. Combine the eggs, milk, flour, nutmeg, and orange zest in a blender and blend until smooth and well combined.

5. Place the butter in a 10-inch ovenproof frying pan, cast-iron skillet, or heavy metal pie pan that holds 2 quarts.

6. Heat the butter in the pan **in the oven** until the butter is melted.

7. Immediately add the batter to the hot pan. Return the pan to the oven and bake for 12 minutes or until golden. Remove from the oven and transfer to a hot pad or place the pancake on a plate.

8. Reheat the apple mixture in the sauté pan or in the microwave (if the mixture was made in advance and refrigerated), adding a little water, apple juice, or applejack if the mixture is too thick.

9. Place the apples on top of the pancake. Dust with confectioners' sugar and serve.

Yield: 4–6 servings

TINA'S TIDBITS

- *It is important to use a large, heavy frying pan or a rimmed pan for this recipe so that the batter will immediately sear when it comes in contact with the hot pan, and it will puff up enormously as a result.*
- *The choice of apple is really up to you in terms of taste, but make sure your choice is a firm, crisp apple, so that it will retain its shape after sautéing.*
- *The blender works better than a processor for this recipe because the liquid batter is drawn into the blade and will be rendered smooth. Liquid in a processor tends to hydroplane over the blades, and small particles escape, resulting in a lumpy or coarse-textured product.*

APPLE BROWN BETTY

The major connection to Jewish cooking in this recipe is the desire to create something wholesome and wonderful for our families. Actually this is my dessert of choice for Sukkot and for Erev Yom Kippur. This recipe is easily made pareve by substituting pareve margarine for the butter.

2 pounds or 4 cups chopped pared apples, about 3/4-inch chunks
1/4 cup orange juice
1 cup brown sugar
1/2 cup all-purpose flour

1/4 cup whole-wheat flour
1/2 teaspoon cinnamon
1/4 teaspoon ground nutmeg
1 stick unsalted butter

1. Butter a 9-inch pie plate or a 2-quart casserole. Place the apples in it and sprinkle with the orange juice.

2. Combine the remaining ingredients thoroughly with your fingertips or in a processor and crumble the sugar mixture on top of the apples.

3. Bake at 375°F for 45 minutes or until the apples are tender and the topping is crisp. Serve warm.

Yield: 6–8 servings

TINA'S TIDBITS

- *The whole-wheat flour not only adds more nutrients to this dessert, but also makes the topping extra crunchy.*
- *Overhandling flour with butter makes the flour tough and hard when baked; this is exactly what you want to do with this recipe! So let your kids help. They can't harm the finished product.*
- *The orange juice prevents the apples from turning brown, flavors the dish, and combines with some of the flour in the topping to create a subtly thickened sauce.*

APPLESAUCE

You will never want to buy applesauce again after tasting this. No sugar is needed for taste or consistency. And if you own a food mill, no peeling is required! Start to finish, this takes 15 minutes to prepare.

4–6 medium apples
¼–½ cup water

2-inch cinnamon stick or ½ teaspoon ground cinnamon
¼ cup sugar (optional)

1. Wash the apples, core, and cut them into eighths. Do not peel.

2. Combine the apples, water, and cinnamon in a saucepan. Cover the pot and simmer for 10 minutes or until the apples are very tender.

3. Remove the skins. Mash the apples until smooth and add sugar if desired.

Yield: 2–3 cups

TINA'S TIDBITS

- *It is not necessary to peel the apples before you cook them. If the apples are unpeeled, the natural pectin in the skins will thicken the sauce, and the skin will give the sauce a rosy color.*
- *To remove the apple skins, pass the apples through a food mill or just remove the skins by hand with a spoon.*
- *The flavor cells of an apple are just below the skin. Cooking the apple with the skin only enhances its flavor.*

Lekach
(Honey Cake)

Nothing says Rosh HaShanah or Shabbat Kiddushim more than the iconic honey cake. Moist and delicious, this cake definitely tastes even better when made a day in advance. The coffee and spices meld with the honey and brandy to give full flavor. Made with oil, the traditional way, this cake is pareve.

1 cup wildflower honey
½ cup strong coffee or 1 teaspoon instant espresso and ½ cup water
1 tablespoon brandy
2 eggs
1 tablespoon oil
¼ cup brown sugar
1¾ cups flour

Pinch of salt
½ teaspoon baking soda
1 teaspoon baking powder
½ teaspoon allspice
¾ teaspoon cinnamon
¼ teaspoon ground ginger
⅓ cup raisins (optional)
Whole blanched almonds for topping (optional)

1. Preheat the oven to 325°F.

2. Grease 2 loaf pans, 48 mini muffin pans, or 1 tube pan with cooking spray, or use paper liners in the muffin tins.

3. Bring the honey to a gentle boil and cool slightly. Add the coffee and brandy and set aside.

4. In a large bowl, beat the eggs until light and lemon-colored. Add the oil and gradually beat in the sugar.

5. In a separate bowl, combine the dry ingredients. Add the dry ingredients alternately with the honey mixture to the egg-sugar mixture. Mix well after each addition to thoroughly incorporate the ingredients.

6. If you are using raisins, dust them with a little additional flour so that they will not sink to the bottom of the cake. Fold the raisins into the cake batter, and pour the mixture into the prepared pans. If using, place one almond in the center of each muffin or in a line on the top of the cake.

7. Bake the muffins for 15–18 minutes or until a tester comes out clean. Loaf pans take up to 45 minutes and tube pans will take a little longer. Test with a toothpick. If you insert the toothpick in the cake and it comes out without any batter adhering to it then the cake is done. Muffins may be served with ginger-orange cream cheese spread.

Ginger-Orange Cream Cheese Spread

8 ounces cream cheese
1 tablespoon frozen orange juice concentrate
2 tablespoons milk
1 tablespoon brown sugar
1 tablespoon crystallized ginger, chopped

1. Combine all of the ingredients in a processor work bowl and process until smooth.

2. Serve alongside sweet quickbreads, such as honey cake or pumpkin bread, or pipe individual rosettes on top of the mini muffins of the above sweet breads.

Yield: 20 servings or 48 mini muffins

TINA'S TIDBITS

- *This cake is aromatic and tasty warm from the oven, but because of the brandy and spices, it tastes even better if it's allowed to sit a day or so wrapped in foil.*
- *Because the batter is high in sugar and relatively thin, the cake may have a tendency to sink in the middle if the pan is too deep. I recommend a tube pan because the open center can heat the cake more evenly.*
- *Mini muffins are great for a big party. Everyone wants a spiritual taste of the honey cake but only a small bite when many foods are offered.*

Quick Honey Cake

When I was creating my honey cake bread pudding recipe, it was July and no prepared honey cakes were available. I didn't have the time or desire to make a honey cake from scratch just to cut it up for an experiment, so I devised this simple way to make the base for my recipe. Turns out, this cake was good on its own—just as sticky on top and balanced with the coffee flavor and honey.

³/₄ cup warm coffee or 1 teaspoon instant espresso and ³/₄ cup water
¼ cup honey

One 14.5-ounce box gingerbread mix
Eggs, as needed in the mix
Oil or margarine, as needed in the mix

1. Microwave the coffee with the honey for 30 seconds. Stir to combine.

2. Prepare the cake following the package directions **except** substitute the warm coffee and honey for all of the liquid in the recipe. Use the appropriate amount of oil and eggs called for on the package.

3. Bake the cake according to the package directions. Cool completely and serve, or use in the Apples and Honey Cake Bread Pudding recipe (see page 444).

Yield: 8 servings

TINA'S TIDBITS

- *It is not always easy to find, but I keep a jar of Medaglia D'Oro instant espresso in my freezer for all the times a recipe calls for strong coffee or espresso. It dissolves immediately and is not bitter.*
- *Although most honey on the market is clover honey, I love wildflower honey. The floral undertones are terrific and are really pronounced in mild-flavored dishes.*

Apples and Honey Cake Bread Pudding with Butterscotch Sauce

I created this recipe when I had too much leftover honey cake. Moist and rich, this "bread" pudding is not overly sweet. Serve with some vanilla ice cream or whipped cream if you like, but I promise you the spiked butterscotch sauce is delicious over the warm dessert (see the recipe on the following page).

1 loaf honey cake (approximately 9 × 5 inches), store-bought or homemade
3 Jonagold, Fuji, or Gala apples
2 ounces (½ stick) unsalted butter
¼ cup sugar
½ teaspoon cinnamon

4 eggs
⅓ cup brown sugar
1 teaspoon vanilla
1 cup half-and-half cream
3 cups milk (whole or 2% preferred)

1. Butter a 13 × 9-inch glass pan. Preheat the oven to 350°F.

2. Cut the honey cake into ¾-inch cubes. Place in a 4-quart bowl and set aside.

3. Peel, core, and slice the apples into eighths. Cut each eighth crosswise into 3 or 4 chunks.

4. Heat a 10-inch skillet for 15 seconds. Add the butter and melt. Sauté the apples in the butter over medium-high heat until the apples give up some of their juice.

5. Add the sugar and cinnamon to the apples, and continue sautéing until the sugar is dissolved and the apples begin to brown and get softer. Remove from the heat and set aside until needed.

6. In a 2-quart bowl, whisk the eggs until lightly beaten. Whisk in the brown sugar and vanilla until thoroughly incorporated. Pour in the cream and milk and whisk to combine.

7. Place half of the honey cake cubes in the prepared pan. Cover with the reserved apples and then with the remaining honey cake cubes.

8. Pour the egg-milk mixture through a sieve directly over the entire surface of the honey cake. Lightly press down on the cake to make sure it is covered with the custard.

TINA'S TIDBITS

- *Because honey will absorb moisture in a baked product, it is important that there be enough liquid in the bread pudding to allow the cake to swell and soften.*
- *Bread puddings in general are best made with dry or dense bread so that they absorb more of the egg-milk mixture, creating a light, airy product. If your grandmother's recipe for honey cake is dry and hard, you can salvage your efforts with this recipe.*
- *Evaporated milk is often used in sauces because it provides the smooth consistency of cream and doesn't curdle easily.*

9. Place the pan in a larger pan, and pour hot water into the larger pan to a depth of 1 inch.

10. Bake in the preheated oven for 45 minutes or until a sharp, thin knife inserted into the center of the pudding comes out wet, but clear. Serve warm with optional sauce on the side.

Yield: 12–15 servings

HOMEMADE BUTTERSCOTCH SAUCE

1 cup light or dark brown sugar (see note below)
²⁄₃ cup light corn syrup
2 ounces (½ stick) unsalted butter

²⁄₃ cup evaporated milk
1 teaspoon vanilla extract
1–2 tablespoons Scotch or dark rum (optional)

1. In a medium saucepan, combine the sugar, syrup, and butter. Stir only until the butter is melted and the mixture comes to a full boil. Adjust the heat to medium high and boil without stirring for 1 minute. Remove from the heat.

2. Combine the milk with the vanilla and add to the pan. Stir only to combine. Add liquor, if using, and pour into a glass jar. Use immediately or refrigerate until ready to serve. May be warmed in the microwave or served cold.

Note: Light brown sugar is standard for butterscotch flavor, but dark brown sugar may be used for a stronger molasses flavor, if desired.

PICKLES AND PRESERVING

Originally cultivated in India and later in Mesopotamia and the Tigris Valley, the cucumber goes back to biblical times (Numbers 11:5 and Isaiah 1:8). And so does the art of pickling. During the age of exploration, Christopher Columbus brought cucumber plants to the New World on his voyages, and the pickles that

were aboard ship prevented the seamen from getting scurvy. For the Jews who lived in Eastern Europe before the great immigration to America, pickling served two purposes: it preserved, for future consumption, the meager amounts of produce and fish that were available, and it enabled women of the shtetl to earn a few extra kopeks so that their husbands could spend more time studying Talmud.

Is it any surprise that pushcarts with pickles found their way to the New World?

In the early 1900s, Jewish immigrants began New York City's first commercial pickle district. Many vendors started out with a rented pushcart to haul homemade pickles. In 1920, there were more than eighty pickle vendors in the vicinity of Hester Street. One of the most successful was Izzy Guss. That year he bought his own pickle store, which he named Guss' Pickles. Over time, with the decline in the economy and tougher immigration and pushcart laws, most of the pickle men went bust. Today, only one pickle store on Essex Street remains, and its owner, Alan Kaufman, learned the business from his mentor, Izzy Guss. He continues to pickle by hand,

the old-fashioned way, using the original Eastern European recipe. He can tell you why it's preferable to use salt (the shtetl way) instead of vinegar—vinegar will brown the pickle faster and sour it more quickly. And if you ask him the difference between a Polish pickle and a kosher dill pickle, he'll tell you that the Polish has more dill and the dill more garlic. Go figure.

For the home cook, there's more to pickling than pickles. All kinds of foods can be preserved through this process. Our Sephardic ancestors, for example, would roast produce and then preserve it in vinegar and olive oil. As far back as Roman times, mushrooms, zucchini and other squash of all shapes and sizes, turnips, eggplant, citrus fruits, and many other fruits and vegetables were seasoned and then immersed in a vinegar/salt bath. They were then allowed to marinate and cure. Not only did this save the food for future consumption, but it allowed the household to enjoy delicious foods on Shabbat without any last-minute preparation that was forbidden by Jewish law.

PICKLED CUCUMBERS

If you follow the recipe in one popular American cookbook, making pickles can take countless hours. Instead, I followed the advice of Alan Kaufman (the owner of The Pickle Guy, the only privately owned pickle store on the Lower East Side) and tried the following recipe—the pickles take about twenty minutes to make and need only two days of waiting time. And the addition of the ginger, cardamom, and cinnamon renders a subtle touch of the Middle East to these pickles.

12–16 small cucumbers, about 5 inches long
4 large cloves of garlic, cut in half, green stem removed
$\frac{1}{8}$ teaspoon coriander seed
2 bay leaves, crushed
$\frac{1}{2}$ teaspoon black peppercorns
$\frac{1}{4}$ teaspoon mustard seed

8 whole allspice berries
1-inch piece of crystallized ginger
$\frac{1}{2}$ stick cinnamon
6 cardamom pods
4 cups of water
$\frac{1}{2}$ cup distilled organic white vinegar
3 tablespoons coarse kosher salt

1. Slice the cucumbers crosswise into $\frac{1}{4}$-inch pieces and discard the ends.

2. Place the cucumbers in two 1-quart wide-mouthed jars. (I use leftover gefilte fish jars!)

3. Combine all of the spices and lightly crush with a mortar and pestle or the back of a spoon. (For a more Eastern European pickle, you can eliminate the allspice, ginger, cinnamon, and cardamom and replace with dried hot pepper, more garlic, and dill or dill seed.) Divide the spice mixture evenly between the two jars.

4. Bring the water to a boil in a stainless steel, glass, or enamel saucepan.

5. Add the vinegar and salt, and stir with a rubber spatula until the salt dissolves.

6. Pour the hot liquid evenly into the jars.

7. Let cool on the counter for about an hour, and then cover with the jar lids.

8. Shake the jars, turning over 2 times to distribute the spices in the water.

9. Place the jars in a closet or another cool dark place for 2 days to pickle and flavor the cucumbers properly. Then refrigerate until ready to eat.

10. Serve and enjoy! (The pickles may be stored in the refrigerator for up to 6 weeks or longer.)

Yield: 12–16 servings

TINA'S TIDBITS

- *Pickling in vinegar hastens the process of souring, but your vegetables will discolor faster.*
- *If fresh garlic turns blue/green in the pickling jar, the garlic is very fresh or there is not enough salt in the brine.*
- *Placing the pickles in the refrigerator immediately without waiting the two days will yield pickles that are bright green and crispier.*

ITALIAN MARINATED ROASTED RED BELL PEPPERS

The following recipe is based on the technique described in Classic Italian Jewish Cooking *by Edda Servi Machlin. My use of balsamic vinegar imparts a sweet taste to the peppers. Jewish cooks have been preparing peppers this way for centuries.*

3 very large sweet red peppers
½ cup balsamic vinegar
1 teaspoon salt

2 very large cloves of garlic, cut into quarters
Salt and freshly ground black pepper to taste
About ¾ cup extra virgin olive oil, enough to cover

1. Preheat the oven to 450°F.

2. Place the whole peppers on a baking sheet and roast them for 15 minutes or until the peel is blackened in spots.

3. Meanwhile, fill a large bowl with water and 8 ice cubes.

4. When the peppers are done, immediately plunge them into the bowl of ice water.

5. When the peppers are cool enough to handle, peel them under water. Remove the stem and seeds and any interior membrane.

6. Cut the peppers lengthwise into ½-inch strips. You may wish to cut the strips in half crosswise if the peppers are very long.

7. Bring the vinegar and salt to a boil in a stainless steel or enameled pan. Add the sliced peppers and cook for 3 minutes, stirring with a soft spoon or spatula.

8. Remove the peppers from the heat and allow the mixture to cool to room temperature.

9. Drain the peppers. Stir in garlic and salt and pepper to taste.

10. Place the mixture in a 1-quart wide-mouthed glass jar. Pour olive oil over the peppers to cover. Bang the jar on the counter to force any air bubbles to the surface; this will help prevent mold from forming inside the jar.

11. Close the lid tightly on the jar and refrigerate. The peppers may be eaten right away, but their flavor will be greatly enhanced after a day. They will last about 1–2 weeks in the refrigerator before spoiling, or you may freeze for later use. (If freezing, transfer to a freezer safe container or make sure there is enough room in the jar for the liquid to expand.)

Yield: 6 servings

TINA'S TIDBITS

- *Roasting peppers in a hot oven causes the peppers to blister, but the "meat" of the vegetable does not burn. You'll preserve the flesh of your peppers far better this way than roasting them on a grill.*
- *By far, the easiest way to peel peppers is immediately after water submersion.*
- *Any time you are boiling vinegar and salt, it must be in a nonreactive pan. Stainless steel, glass, or enamel is okay. Copper, brass, and aluminum will react with the liquid and ruin your recipe.*
- *Balsamic vinegar will impart a dark mahogany hue to the peppers. If you want them more natural looking, use apple cider vinegar or white wine vinegar instead.*

Harissa

Harissa is to Tunisia what ballpark mustard and ketchup are to America ... don't set the table without it! There are more variations in the recipe than there are cooks in Tunisia, but you can be assured that all harissas will contain a lot of heat and that caraway seed will find its way into the mix. Although harissa is readily available in many markets, I wanted to include a recipe for you to enjoy.

2-ounce package dried poblano or other hot chilies
$3/4$–1 cup water
2 large cloves of garlic, peeled and crushed
$1\frac{1}{2}$ teaspoons coriander seed, lightly crushed

1 teaspoon caraway seed, lightly crushed
1 teaspoon salt
3 tablespoons extra virgin olive oil plus 1 tablespoon for topping paste in jar

1. Carefully remove the stem and seeds from the chilies, and place the chilies in a glass bowl. Cover with the water and microwave on high for 2 minutes. Set the bowl aside and let the chilies soak and get soft, about 20 minutes.

2. Drain the chilies, reserving $\frac{1}{4}$ cup of the water.

3. Add the garlic, crushed coriander, and caraway seeds to a small processor work bowl, and process until a coarse mixture is formed.

4. Add the drained chili peppers and salt, and process to break up the peppers. You will need to stop the machine and scrape down the sides of the bowl a few times.

5. Add 2 tablespoons of the reserved chili water, and process until a coarse paste is formed. Scrape down the sides of the bowl again.

6. With the processor running, slowly add 3 tablespoons of the olive oil to the paste, and process until all the oil is incorporated and the mixture forms a spreadable, coarse paste.

7. Place the mixture in a clean 8-ounce jar, and pour the remaining tablespoon of olive oil over the top of the mixture to prevent it from drying out and spoiling. Refrigerate until needed.

Yield: $\frac{3}{4}$ cup

TINA'S TIDBITS

- *Some small processors can't quite grind the whole spices and chili peppers into a smooth paste. That is OK. However, if you don't want to sit with a mortar and pestle and pound your way to smoothness, you might want to try an immersion blender or a regular blender to get a smoother consistency. If you double the recipe, you will find it easier to puree in a big blender.*
- *When storing a prepared paste in the refrigerator, cover the top of the paste with 1/4 inch of oil before putting on the lid. The oil creates a barrier between the paste and the air, and mold is less likely to form.*

Amba
(Iraqi Pickled Mango)

Mangoes are the most popular fruit in the world and the third most popular fruit, after apples and bananas, in the United States. Although they are grown in many tropical and subtropical climates, the Middle East counts on the height of the growing season in India and Pakistan to get the best fruit. When they are plentiful, they can be eaten out of hand or used in preparing many dishes. When they are not reliably available, the mango aficionado has to rely on the fruits that were pickled to enjoy their taste. Here is one such favorite.

1 teaspoon turmeric
2 teaspoons curry powder
¼ teaspoon fenugreek seeds (optional)
10 grindings of black pepper (approximately ½ teaspoon)
2 tablespoons kosher salt

1 teaspoon citric acid
Zest of ¼ lemon
1 teaspoon ginger
1⅓ cups water (preferably filtered)
2 ripe unblemished mangoes

1. Combine the spices together with the water in a 2-quart bowl. Set aside while you cut the mangoes.

2. Mangoes are oval with two somewhat flat sides. A large flat seed is in the center. Slice the mango lengthwise along the flat side, running your knife along the seed. Repeat the same procedure on the other side. You now have two sides with pulp attached to the skin.

3. Cut lengthwise and crosswise lines ½ inch wide through the flesh to the skin, making a grid through the fruit. Turn the fruit "inside out" so the flesh sticks up. Carefully cut the cubes off into a small bowl.

4. Using a rubber spatula, stir to recombine the pickling solution. Carefully fold in the mangoes and coat with the spices.

5. Transfer the mixture to a clean 1-quart jar or two 1-pint jars, evenly distributing all of the ingredients. Screw the tops on tightly, and place in a cool dark place for 3 days. Gently turn the jars upside down periodically to disperse the spices.

6. *Amba* will last in the refrigerator for a month or more.

Yield: 1 quart

TINA'S TIDBIT

- *If you love mangoes, then you should invest in a mango slicer. It looks like an apple corer that slices apples into eighths, but it has two curved blades that core out the pit. You wind up with two perfect halves and enough fruit still attached to the pit to munch on before discarding.*

ENGLISH TOMATO CHUTNEY

I love chutney. The juxtaposition of the sweet and tart, the mild and hot, intrigues my palate. When I was in England, I was treated to a taste of this variety of chutney and couldn't wait to get home and re-create it.

2 medium-large tomatoes, seeded and chopped into ½-inch dice (approximately 3 cups)
1½ medium onions, cut into ½-inch dice (approximately 2 cups)
1¼ cups dark raisins
1¼ cups brown sugar
1 cup apple cider vinegar
¼ teaspoon salt

1½ teaspoons mustard seeds, slightly crushed
Dash of cayenne pepper
1 yellow or red bell pepper, cut into ½-inch dice
1½ teaspoons chopped candied ginger root
1 small clove of garlic, minced
¼ teaspoon turmeric
¼ teaspoon celery seed

1. Combine all of the ingredients in a heavy 3-quart saucepan.

2. Bring the mixture to a boil over high heat. Reduce the temperature until the mixture starts to simmer.

3. Simmer uncovered over low heat for approximately 2 hours or until most of the liquid has evaporated and the mixture has thickened. Stir periodically to prevent the mixture from sticking.

4. Pour into jars that have been sterilized (washed in a dishwasher and filled while still hot). Seal and store in the refrigerator.

5. Serve with meats or cheese or on a buttered baguette.

Yield: 1 quart

TINA'S TIDBITS

- *If you want slightly less "bite" to your chutney, try using unflavored rice wine vinegar or champagne vinegar instead of the apple cider variety.*
- *Two 1/4-inch slices of peeled fresh ginger may be used instead of candied ginger if that's not readily available. You can mince them or leave them whole for discarding later.*

Thai Basil–Jalapeño Pesto

You might question the inclusion of an herb paste with pickling, but the Italians knew that the addition of acid and oil would preserve the fresh taste of the herbs long after the frost had arrived. I created the following pesto recipe out of necessity: I had a bumper crop of Thai basil in my garden and wanted it to last. The pesto contains no butter or cheese, is sharp and tangy, and has a subtle Asian flavor. Toss with pasta or a favorite vegetable. It's also a great spread on a turkey sandwich.

³⁄₄ cup macadamia nuts or almonds, lightly toasted
3 jalapeños, seeds and membrane removed
2 large cloves of garlic, cut into quarters
2 cups firmly packed Thai basil leaves (Italian basil may be substituted)

3 tablespoons unseasoned rice wine vinegar
¹⁄₃ cup extra virgin olive oil
Salt and freshly ground pepper to taste

1. Add the nuts to the processor work bowl and pulse the processor on and off until the nuts are fairly fine.

2. Add the jalapeño and garlic and pulse 5 times. Scrape down the sides of the bowl with a spatula.

3. Add the basil and pulse about 10 times or until a coarse paste is formed.

4. Add the rice wine vinegar and pulse on and off a few times to combine.

5. Turn the processor on and slowly drizzle the olive oil into the pesto until the mixture looks creamy and fairly smooth.

6. Scrape into a bowl and season to taste with salt and pepper.

7. Refrigerate or freeze.

Yield: 1¹⁄₄ cups

TINA'S TIDBITS

- The "heat" in a jalapeño derives mostly from the seeds and the **white** interior membrane. The more seeds and membrane you leave, the hotter your dish will be.
- Pesto means "to pound." Traditionally, the basil leaves and nuts were pounded into a paste. Using a processor is much easier.
- Macadamia nuts are the hardest nuts in the world. Use almonds if you are making this pesto by hand.
- Be careful not to overprocess green herbs—you'll bring out the chlorophyll in the leaf and your mixture will taste more like grass than basil.

SPICY BLUEBERRY VINEGAR AND BLUEBERRY CHUTNEY

When I was Chef Field years ago, it was my job to experiment with foods and demonstrate their uses to the customers at Marshall Field's department store. I loved jarred blueberry chutney and its accompanying vinegar, but after a few years the product was no longer being sold. The following two recipes are good on their own, in salads and sandwiches, with cheese and with meats. The chicken recipe uses both these products to tenderize and flavor the meat. My creation of these recipes is no different than what our ancestors did when they arrived in a new country: take what's locally available, add personal preference and experience to the mix, and make sure it conforms to kashrut.

SPICY BLUEBERRY VINEGAR

2 cups fresh blueberries, rinsed and dried with paper towel
2 whole sticks cinnamon
1¼ cups unseasoned rice vinegar

1. Place the blueberries and the cinnamon in a clean pint jar.

2. Heat the vinegar in a microwave for 2–3 minutes until hot but not boiling.

3. Pour the vinegar into the jar with the blueberries, leaving ½ inch headroom.

4. Cover and store in a cool dark place for 10–14 days before using.

Yield: 1 ½ cups vinegar

BLUEBERRY CHUTNEY

2 cups fresh or frozen blueberries
1¼ cups sugar
½ cup white vinegar
½ teaspoon cloves
1 teaspoon cinnamon

1. Combine all of the ingredients in a stainless steel 2-quart pot, and cook over medium heat for 10–15 minutes or until slightly thickened.

2. Cool and place in clean jars. Keep refrigerated.

Yield: 2 cups

BAKED CHICKEN WITH BLUEBERRY CHUTNEY

½ cup spiced blueberry vinegar (see recipe above)
1 chicken, cut into 8 pieces
¾ cup or more blueberry chutney (see recipe above) or preserves

1. Marinate the chicken in the blueberry vinegar for at least 30 minutes.

2. Preheat the oven to 350°F.

3. Drain the chicken and place it in a foil-lined roasting pan.

4. Coat the chicken pieces on all sides with the blueberry chutney. Place the chicken pieces, skin side up, in the roasting pan.

5. Roast for 45 minutes or until the chicken is golden and the juices run clear when the meat is pierced with the sharp end of a knife. Serve.

Yield: 4–6 servings

TINA'S TIDBITS

- *Although chicken doesn't need tenderizing, marinating the meat in a vinegar solution will yield a more moist and tender finished product, much the same as brining.*
- *Blueberry chutney is sweet and tart at the same time. It is a perfect accompaniment to cheese. Try it poured over a wedge of Gorgonzola Dolce or even over a brick of cream cheese.*

INDEX

Numerals in italics signify pages of photographs

B

C

S

Florida
Real Estate
License
Exam Prep

All-in-One Review and Testing to Pass Florida's Real Estate Exam

Fourth Edition

Stephen Mettling
David Cusic
Ryan Mettling
Jane Somers

Performance Programs Company
6810 190th Street East
Bradenton, FL 34211
www.performanceprogramscompany.com

Material in this book is not intended to represent legal advice and should not be so construed. Readers should consult legal counsel for advice regarding points of law.

© 2023 by Performance Programs Company
6810 190th Street East, Bradenton, FL 34211
info@performanceprogramscompany.com
www.performanceprogramscompany.com

ISBN: 978-1955919265

Contents

Introduction

Welcome licensee candidates and future real estate professionals!

We know you have worked hard just to get here – you've completed or nearly completed your prelicense curricula, and now all you have to do is pass the state license exam. But easier said than done – and that's where we come in. We know the exam can be tough, and very nerve-wracking to prepare for. That's why we created the Florida Real Estate License Exam Prep (FL-RELEP) the way we did. Since we have been managing real estate schools and developing curriculum for forty years, we know how all this works – or fails to work. Let us assure you – you made the right decision buying this publication to prepare for your Florida exam. Here's why.

First, FL-RELEP is comprehensive. It contains both extensive content review as well as testing practice. And the text review, unlike most competing books, is Florida-specific – not just simplistic national content, but terse, relevant and accurate state and national laws and regulations presented as a set of 'key point reviews' ideal for pre-test memorization. FL-RELEP precisely follows the official 50+ page Florida syllabus topic by topic in the correct ordered sequence. Consequently, the material serves as a more user-friendly review for students who have taken pre-license courses throughout Florida containing this required content and organization. FL-RELEP's key point reviews are a succinct compression of tested principles and practices drawn from our own Florida textbook, Principles of Real Estate Practice in Florida – one of the most widely used principles textbooks in Florida. Finally, our review content and question selection is tailored to follow the state testing outline promulgated by the state of Florida. As such, the breadth and depth of the law reviews and test questions reflect the topic emphasis of Florida's license exam.

A word about the tests. The FL-RELEP's test questions are designed to cover the content covered by the law reviews – which reinforces your learning of the total body of information tested by the state of Florida. The questions are direct, to the point, and designed to test your understanding. When you have completed a given test, you can check your answers against the answer key in the appendix. You may also note that each question's answer is accompanied by a brief explanation to further reinforce your understanding.

Your particular study and testing practice strategy using FL-RELEP is up to you. But to fully exploit its comprehensive content coverage, you should try to review and memorize the key point reviews as much as possible. Then you should make every effort to take each exam, review your mistakes, and re-read the key point reviews that cover your weaker areas.

In the end, as you know, it's all up to you. Unlike other publications, we are not going to tell you that using this book will guarantee that you pass the Florida state exam. It still takes hard work and study to pass. But we have done our best here to get you ready. Following that, the most we can do is wish you the best of success in taking and passing your state exam. So good luck!!

About the authors

For over forty five years, Stephen Mettling and David Cusic, PhD, have operated Performance Programs Company, one of the nation's most successful training organizations specializing in real estate program development. Mr. Mettling and Dr. Cusic have jointly written over 100 books, courses, and custom programs in all facets of real estate for some of the country's largest real estate schools, associations and organizations.

Mr. Mettling has also served as vice president and author for the country's largest real estate training and publishing organization. Under various capacities, he has managed the acquisition, development, and sale of national real estate textbooks and publications, as well as directed the country's largest affiliated group of real estate schools.

Dr. Cusic, an author and educator with international real estate training experience, has been engaged in vocation-oriented education since 1966. Specializing in real estate training since 1983, he has developed numerous real estate training programs for corporate and institutional clients around the country.

Ryan Mettling, partner and currently general manager and marketing director of Performance Programs, is an accomplished online curriculum designer, author and course developer. Ryan is a co-author of the Real Estate License Exam Prep (RELEP) Series and Real Estate Math Express. Mr. Mettling is a member of the Real Estate Educators Association (REEA), and graduated Valedictorian from the University of Central Florida's College of Business Administration.

Jane Somers has been a writer and educator for more than 30 years. She has directed the academic programs for a multi-campus college and has in recent years become an accomplished developer of online and classroom real estate curricula for a national real estate licensing organization, specializing in state licensing laws. Ms. Somers is also active in condominium association management and has served as president of a condominium owners association for ten years.

PART ONE: LAW & PRACTICE REVIEW

SECTION 1: The Real Estate Business

Real Estate Professions

Real estate activities
- Create, improve, manage, maintain, demolish, own, regulate, and transfer real properties

Property type specializations
- Residential; residential income; office; retail; industrial; farm and ranch; special purpose; land

Why hire a Real Estate Professional
- Knowledge of property transfer, of market conditions & how to market real estate

Real estate brokerage
- Procure a buyer or tenant for an owner or landlord, or vice versa

Forms of specialization
- By property type; geographical area; type of transaction; type of client; by form of business organization; or by form of client relationship
- In addition to residential brokerage – property management, appraising, financing & counseling

Skills and knowledge
- Market conditions; law; financing; marketing; ethics; selling; communications; computer basics; and other skills

Professional organizations
- Promote interests of practitioners and enhance their professional standing

Development and Construction

Development and Construction
- process steps: acquire land; subdivide; financing; land/offsite development; construction; leasing; sale

Land acquisition
- developer conducts location analysis
- identify highest and best use; feasibility analysis and site selection
- master plan and proforma budget

Subdividing and development
- convert land to parcels; generate plat map
- construction plan; dedications

7

- construction

Residential construction
- spec homes
  - built without prior purchase, commitment from buyer
- custom homes
  - sale contract precedes construction
  - buyer preferences incorporated into improvement specs

- tract homes
  - builder offers choice of floor plans; buyer selects plan and a given lot

Regulation and Licensing

Regulation of business practices
- All facets of the industry are regulated by federal, state, and local laws; agents must understand relevant laws and adapt business practices accordingly

Real estate license laws
- The primary body of laws and regulations governing the licensure and conduct of real estate brokers and agents
- License laws are administered and enforced under the jurisdiction of the Florida Real Estate Commission

SECTION 2: Real Estate License Law and Qualifications for Licensure

Historical Perspective of FL License Law

Pre-1923
- Caveat emptor – let buyer beware

1923
- Real Estate License Law, Chapter 475 passed to protect public by regulating real estate brokers, sales, associates, and schools

1925
- Real Estate Commission created to administer and enforce license law, keep records, investigate, and grant, deny, suspend, revoke licenses

Present day
- Division of Real Estate (DRE) for Commission support services; DRE under Department of Business and Professional Regulation (DBPR)
- Regulation needed when
  - harm to public is potential and recognizable
  - danger greater than anticompetitive impact from regulation
  - other regulations do not sufficiently protect public
  - no less restrictive regulations exist

Definitions of Key Terms (475.01)

- **Broker** – person who performs real estate services for another person for compensation, including appraising, auctioning, selling, exchanging, buying, renting, or offering or negotiating to do any of these
- **Broker associate** – person who qualifies for a broker's license but operates as sales associate employed by another broker
- **Caveat emptor** – seller cannot be held responsible for the quality of product unless there is a warranty; let the buyer beware
- **Commission** – Florida Real Estate Commission (FREC)
- **Compensation** – something of value given, received, promised, expected as equivalent for services, debt, loss, etc.
- **Customer** – member of the public buying or selling real property and is or is not represented by a real estate licensee in brokerage relationship
- **Department** – Department of Business and Professional Regulation (DBPR)
- **Fiduciary** – broker in trust and confidence relationship with seller or buyer where duties include loyalty, confidentiality, obedience, full disclosure, accounting, and use of skill, care, and diligence
- **Florida resident** – resided in Florida continuously for 4 months or more in temporary or permanent location
- **Involuntary inactive status** – when license not renewed at end of license period as required by Department
- **Mutual recognition agreement** – contract between two states to recognize each other's real estate license education; in Florida, applicants must pass Florida real estate law exam
- **Nolo contendere** or **no contest** – defendant's pleading not admitting guilt but subjects him/her to punishment as though guilty plea entered
- **Owner-developer** – unlicensed entity that sells, exchanges, or leases its own property

- **Prima facie evidence** – evidence sufficient to establish fact, to raise presumption of fact, or prove case unless rebutted
- **Principal** – party with whom a real estate licensee entered into a single agent relationship
- **Real estate services** – real estate activity performed for another person for compensation, including appraising, auctioning, selling, exchanging, buying, renting, or offering or negotiating to do any of these
- **Real property** or **real estate** – interest or estate in land, business enterprises, or business opportunities, not to include cemetery lots, rights of burial in a cemetery, renting of mobile home lot or recreational vehicle lot in mobile home or travel park
- **Reciprocity** – agreement between two states that allows licensee in one jurisdiction to practice real estate in the other jurisdiction
- **Registration** – submitting information to the DBPR for their records
- **Sales associate** – performs real estate services for compensation under direction, control, or management of another person
- **Single agent** – broker who represents, as a fiduciary, either buyer or seller but not both in same transaction
- **Transaction broker** – represents buyer, seller, or both in real estate transaction but not in fiduciary capacity
- **Voluntarily inactive status** – license status when licensee asks to be placed on inactive status and pays applicable fee

Key Florida Real Estate Statutes and Rules

Florida Statute Chapter 475
- Regulates real estate brokers, sales associates, and schools by establishing licensees and appraisers' legal rights and responsibilities; interpreted and enforced by FREC; divided into four parts
  - **Part I** – covers real estate brokerage
  - **Part II** – establishes requirements for licensed and certified real estate appraisers in line with federal statutes
  - **Part III** – establishes broker's lien rights for earned commission on commercial property; known as the Commercial Real Estate Sales Commission Lien Act
  - **Part IV** – establishes broker's lien rights for earned commission related to brokerage agreement to lease commercial real estate; known as the Commercial Real Estate Leasing Commission Lien Act

Florida Statute Chapter 455
- Establishes the general provisions for Business and Professional Regulation, including provisions for
  - military personnel on active duty, spouses of military personnel on active duty, and immigrants practicing real estate
  - organization, compensation, etc. for the Commission
  - practicing without license
  - license examinations and professional testing services
  - regulation of licensees by the DBPR
  - discipline of licensees who fail to comply with Chapter 455

Florida Statute Chapter 120
- Establishes regulatory agencies' procedures for deciding and implementing agency action, including licensing and disciplining real estate licensees; called Administrative Procedure Act

Florida Statute Chapter 20
- Established Florida government's executive branch's organizational structure

Florida Administrative Code Chapter 61J2
- FREC's administrative rules pursuant to Chapter 120 that include detailed principles for real estate practice; expansion of Chapter 475 provisions

The DBPR's *Florida Candidate Information Booklet for the Real Estate Sales Associate Examination* lists 33 additional Florida Administrative Codes and 8 U.S. Federal Regulations that are important to know for the examination.

General Licensing Provisions (475.17; 455.213)

General licensing provisions
- 18 years of age
- High school diploma or equivalent
- Honest, trustworthy, of good character
- Good reputation for fair dealing
- Competent and qualified to make real estate transactions and conduct negotiations
- U.S. Social Security number
- Submission of application and fee
- No acts or attempts to act as broker or sales associate in violation of Chapter 475 for 1 year prior to application, unless legally exempt from licensure
- Completion of educational and examination requirements (see below)

Application requirements
- Disclose criminal and/or traffic offenses whether guilty, nolo contendere, adjudication withheld, or still under investigation
- Disclose if denied or license disciplined or pending discipline in any jurisdiction
- Disclose if guilty of grounds for suspension or revocation under Chapter 475
- License denied for failure to disclose offenses
- License revoked if offenses discovered after license issued
- Confirm criminal matter that has been expunged from criminal record
- Disclose aliases
- Submit scanned fingerprints
- Submit application fee
- 30 days to notify applicant of errors and omissions; failure to provide missing information not reason for license denial if no notice of insufficiency sent to applicant
- Application approved if not processed within 90 days
- Applicants with criminal history to be reviewed by FREC and possibly brought before FREC, after which application denial or approval will be determined
- Commission denials must list reason and give 21 days for applicant to request hearing.
- Application good for 2 years from receipt

Nonresident requirements
- U.S. citizenship not required
- Florida residency not required
- Disclose Florida non-residency on application
- Social Security number required
- 60 days to notify Commission when FL licensee becomes resident of another state; must keep mailing address current; cited and fined $300 if no notice to Commission
- Complete all Florida education requirements
- Exam taken in English unless 15 or more applicants request another language
- Comply with all FL Chapter 475 requirements and FREC rules
- Florida mutual recognition agreements with seven other states
- Florida reciprocity for U.S. military members and spouses who hold valid license in another state or foreign jurisdiction
- Mutual recognition applicants

- o   submit application
- o   submit certification of license history from state where licensed
- o   and pass FL licensing laws exam with score of 75% or higher
- No FL resident eligible for FL application for mutual recognition
- Under mutual recognition, no FL license issued for FL resident licensed in another state
- Mutual recognition licensees complete all FL required post and continuing education
- Requirements of other mutual recognition states vary

Sales Associate Licensing Requirements (475.161; 475.182)

Pre-license requirements
- Meet general licensing provisions (see above)
- 63 classroom hours of FREC-approved course or 4-year degree in real estate
- Florida attorneys are exempt from course requirement but must pass license exam
- Submit application, fingerprints, and fee
- Pass the state license exam with a grade of 75% or higher within 2 years of course completion
- Applicants who fail the exam are allowed to review the exam
- Activate license

Post-license education requirements
- 45-hour FREC-approved course prior to initial license expiration or 4-year degree in real estate to include a minimum of 15 hours of instruction
- Pass end-of-course exam with 75% score
- Failure to complete requirements by expiration date results in license becoming null and void
- Qualified hardship cases extend completion deadline to 6 months after expiration date

Continuing education requirements for active and inactive sales associates
- 14 classroom hours every 2 years
- 3 of the 14 hours to be core law; completed as classroom or online course
- 3 of the 14 hours to be Ethics and Business Practices
- 8 of the 14 hours to be specialty education (one-time attendance at Commission legal agenda session can count for 3 of these hours)
- A grade of 80% or higher on the Commission-prescribed continuing education course or courses examination

Broker Licensing Requirements (475.17)

Pre-license requirements
- Meet general licensing provisions (see above)
- Hold active sales associate license with completed post-license education
- 24 months real estate experience during previous 5 years as sales associate or broker in another state
- Current certification of license history from applicable state for non-FL experience
- 72 classroom hours pre-licensing course or 4-year degree in real estate
- Submission of application, fingerprints, and fee
- Pass the state broker exam with a grade of 75% or higher
- Activate license

Post-license education requirements
- 60-hour course prior to initial license expiration or 4-year degree in real estate
- Pass end-of-course exam with 75% score
- Failure to complete requirements by expiration date results in license becoming null and void

Continuing education requirements for active and inactive brokers
- 14 classroom hours every 2 years
- 3 of the 14 to be core law; completed as classroom or online course
- 3 of the 14 hours to be Ethics and Business Practices
- 8 of the 14 hours to be specialty education (one-time attendance at Commission legal agenda session can count for 3 of these hours)
- A grade of 80% or higher on the Commission-prescribed continuing education course or courses examination

Registration and Licensure (475.181)

Registration
- Provide licensed broker or sales associate's information to DBPR
  - name
  - name and address of each employer
  - license status
  - status as officer, director, or partner in real estate business
- Sales and broker associates allowed only one registered employer

Licensure
- Granted when license exam passed
- Allows legal practice of real estate
- Includes name, license status, effective and expiration dates, governor and DBPR secretary names, and type of license
- Licensees may print own license online rather than wait 7 to 10 days for DBPR to print and mail license

Real Estate Services: Activities Requiring a License (475.01)

Services requiring licensure when performed for compensation
- Selling or attempting to sell real property
- Buying or attempting to buy real property
- Leasing or attempting to lease real property
- Exchanging or attempting to exchange real property
- Negotiating or closing sale, exchange, purchase, or rental of real property or business enterprise
- Advertising or attempting to advertise real property
- Listing or selling timeshare periods
- Appraising or attempting to appraise real property
- Auctioning or attempting to auction real property
- Offering or attempting to perform real estate activities
- Procuring of sellers, purchasers, lessors, or lessees of real property or business enterprise
- Advertising or representing self as engaged in real estate services

Services not requiring licensure
- Onsite renting of apartments when employed by owner
- Owner selling timeshare period
- Renting or advertising licensed public lodging
- Tenant receiving $50 or less referral fee for referral of tenant
- Owner offering to sell real property

13

Individuals Exempted from Licensure (475.011)

Exemptions from licensure requirements

- An attorney at law
- A certified public accountant
- The personal representative, receiver, trustee, or general or special magistrate appointed by will or court order
- A trustee under deed of trust or trust agreement for charitable or natural right purposes
- Any individual or entity that sells, exchanges, or leases its own real property, except if employed or compensated for that purpose
- Any salaried employee of public utility, rural electric cooperative, railroad, or state or local government agency not otherwise compensated for buying, leasing, etc. for use of employer
- Any salaried employee leasing apartments from an onsite rental office
- Any salaried manager of condominium or cooperative apartment complex renting individual units within the complex for 1 year or less
- Any compensated person or entity who performs real estate services related to radio, television, or cable enterprises regulated by the FCC, except if sale or purchase of land, buildings, fixtures, and improvements involved
- Any full-time graduate student in appraising degree program at FL college who is under direct supervision of licensed broker
- Any full or part owner of timeshare period who offers period for sale
- An exchange company for timeshare period
- Any registered, licensed, or certified appraiser or appraiser trainee performing appraisals
- Any compensated person or entity who rents or advertises public lodging establishment
- Any dealer registered under Securities and Exchange Act of 1934 or federally insured depository institution or its parent, subsidiary, or affiliate who sells, exchanges, purchases, or rents a business enterprise to accredited investor
- Any property management company or owner of apartment complex who pays referral fee of $50 or less to tenant.
- Any person selling cemetery lots
- Any person who rents mobile home or recreational vehicle park lots

SECTION 3: Real Estate License Law and Commission Rules

Florida Real Estate Commission (475.02)

Purpose
- To protect the public by regulation of real estate and appraisal licensees through education and compliance

Composition
- 7 total members, 1 of whom must be 60 years or older
- 4 licensed brokers with active license for previous 5 years
- 1 licensed broker or licensed sales associate with active license for previous 2 years
- 2 members of the public who have never been brokers or sales associates
- All appointed by Governor for 4-year terms

Duties and powers
- Enact bylaws and rules for its own government
- Regulate professional practices
- Create and enforce license laws, rules, and regulations
- Educate real estate professionals in ethical, legal, and business principles
- Administer FL Real Estate Commission Education and Research Foundation
- Adopt seal used to authenticate its proceedings
- Establish fees for application, examination, reexamination, licensing and renewal, certification, reinstatement, and record making and keeping.
- License broker associates and sales associates, but not as general partner, member, manager, officer, or director of brokerage firm
- Deny application or renewal of license, registration, or permit
- Determine violations and impose penalties
- Notify Division of Florida Condominiums, Timeshares, and Mobile Homes of disciplinary action against licensee

Jurisdiction limitations
- Powers limited to administrative, not criminal
- No power to impose imprisonment as penalty

Department of Business and Professional Regulation (20.165; 455.01; 455.203)

Purpose
- To license and regulate real estate professionals in FL

Definitions
- **Board** – any board or commission authorized to exercise regulatory functions
- **Consumer member** – a non-real estate professional serving on a board
- **Department** – Department of Business and Professional Regulation
- **License** – any permit, registration, certificate, or license issued by the Department
- **Licensee** – any person issued a permit, registration, certificate, or license issued by the Department
- **Profession** – any activity, occupation, or vocation regulated by the Department

Composition
- Under executive branch of Governor and governed by Chapter 120, F.S.
- Headed by Secretary
  - appointed by Governor
  - confirmed by Senate
  - with no set term limits
- **Division of Professions** responsible for testing and licensing professionals
- **Division of Regulation** responsible for enforcement of licensed professions
- **Division of Real Estate** regulates real estate and appraisal licensees
  - responsible for examination, licensing, and regulation of real estate professionals and schools
  - administrative duties for Florida Real Estate Commission
- **Division of Service Operations** responsible for inquiries, processing applications and fees, and sending license and renewal notices
- **Division of Florida Condominiums, Timeshares, and Mobile Homes** provides education, complaint resolution, mediation, arbitration, and developer disclosure
- **Business Regulation** headed by Deputy Secretary of Business Regulation, responsible for licensing and regulating condominiums, timeshares, mobile homes, hotels, restaurants
- **Agency Clerk's Office** responsible for maintenance of filed documents

Duties and powers
- Approve license applications
- Renew broker, broker associate, or sales associate license when application and fee received with proof of completion of continuing education requirements
- Adopt rules establishing procedure for license renewals every 4 years
- Appoint executive director for each board
- Disclose licensees information to Department of Revenue
- Mail renewal and possible reversion notice 60 days prior to end of license period
- Inspect and audit any licensed broker or brokerage office for Chapter 475 violations
- Provide injunctive relief for violations

Real Estate Regulation: Licenses

Licensing examinations (475.175)
- Testing service contracted by Division of Professions (currently Pearson Vue)
- Exams measure applicant's ability to practice real estate
- Record of exam-related documents and scores stored for 2 years
- Grades and questions confidential
- Theft or copying of exam is a third degree felony

Fees (475.125)
- Initial application fee
- Exam and fingerprinting fee
- 2-year license fee
- Unlicensed activity fee with renewal
- Real Estate Recovery Fund fee
- Fees waived for military veterans and their spouses within 60 months of honorable discharge
- Fees waived for military personnel and their spouses or surviving spouses
- Fees waived for applicants with low incomes

License renewal (475.182)
- Initial effective date same as exam passing date, both sales associate and broker
- Initial license period 18-24 months
- License expiration every 24 months on either March 31 or September 30

- Renewal notice sent 90 days prior to expiration date
- Post-license education to be completed prior to first renewal
- Continuing education to be completed prior to subsequent renewals
- Renewal application and fee submitted attesting to completion of education
- Late fee for renewals after expiration date
- License reverts to involuntary inactive status if not renewed by expiration date (see below)
- 24-month grace period to renew license after expiration
- No practicing real estate with expired or inactive license
- Active duty military exempt from renewal fee requirements
- Out-of-state military spouse exempt from renewal fee requirements
- Active duty military exempt from renewal fee requirements for 2 years after discharge
- Surviving spouse of military member who died while on active duty and within 2 years preceding the spouse's license renewal date exempt from renewal fee requirements
- Exemption only if not engaging in real estate activities for profit
- Active duty military spouse may obtain 6-month temporary FL license if licensed in another state

License status
- **Active (475.182)**
  - required for real estate practice
  - achieved when sales associate is employed by broker
  - sustained when renewal requirements met
- **Voluntary inactive (475.183)**
  - licensee request to DBPR
  - renew by application to DBPR with 12 hours continuing education per year
- **Involuntary inactive (475.182; 31)**
  - non-renewed license automatically changed to involuntary inactive
  - reactivate before 12 months by request to DBPR with 14 hours continuing education
  - reactivate after 12 months and before 24 months with 28 hours continuing education
  - $100 fee for late renewal of inactive license plus renewal fee for each inactive period
  - inactive more than 2 years automatic expiration, null and void
  - notice sent 90 days prior to expiration
  - employer broker license suspended or revoked, sales associate automatically becomes involuntary inactive
  - reactivate with new employer broker
- **Void (475.183)**
  - when involuntary inactive for 2 years
  - when revoked after disciplinary action; permanent penalty
  - reinstate revoked license within 6 months if void due to illness or economic hardship
  - reinstate with continuing education, fees, and eligibility for renewal
  - reinstate as sales associate after 5 years if revoked due to no post- or continuing education completed
  - reinstate as sales associate after 5 years if revoked due to false information on application
- **Ineffective (475.31)**
  - voluntary or involuntary inactive
  - suspended
- **Cease to be in force (475.23)**
  - broker changes business address and does not notify Commission within 10 days
  - real estate school changes business address and does not notify Commission within 10 days
  - sales associate changes employer and does not notify Commission within 10 days

License types
- **Multiple Licenses (475.215)**
  - for brokers only when necessary to conduct separate brokerage businesses
  - must not be used in prejudicial or harmful manner
  - may be denied by Commission
- **Group Licenses (61J2-6.006)**
  - for owner/developer of properties through multiple, connected entities
  - for sales associate or broker associate to sell for all entities owned by owner/developer

Current mailing address (61J2-10.038)

- Current residential address of licensee for mail
- Must notify DBPR in writing of mailing, email, and place of practice addresses within 10 days of change
- Called address of record
- Failure to notify results in violation of 455 F.S., possible citation and $500 fine

SECTION 4: Authorized Relationships, Duties and Disclosure

Concepts of Agency

Levels of Agency: Universal / General / Special

Universal:	• represent in all matters • can contract for principal
General:	• represent in business matters • agent can contract for principal
Special:	• represent in single business transaction • normally agent cannot contract for principal • characterizes the brokerage relationship

---

Causes for agency relationship termination

- fulfillment
- expiration
- mutual agreement
- incapacity
- abandonment or destruction of property
- renunciation
- breach
- bankruptcy
- revocation of license

Fiduciary relationships

Agent's Fiduciary Duties to Client

Skill, care and diligence:	• proactive; competent; act within bounds of expertise
Loyalty:	• place client interest above customer and self
Obedience:	• provided actions, instructions are legal
Confidentiality:	• extends beyond listing term indefinitely
Full disclosure:	• property condition; customers; material facts
Accounting:	• proper handling of monies and documents

Obligations Owed Customers

- honesty and fair dealing
- reasonable care and skill
- proper disclosure

Types of agency: single / dual / subagency / no agency

Single agency:
- seller or buyer agency
- tenant or landlord representation

Subagency:
- outside brokers and agents who help listing agent
- listing broker's own agents

Dual agency:
- representing both sides
- potentially illegal or conflict of interest
- must disclose & obtain written consent
- voluntary by consent
- involuntary by actions of parties (implied agency)
- duties: all but full disclosure and loyalty

No agency:
- "facilitator" or "transaction broker"
- representing neither party in the transaction
- duties to both parties: accounting; skill, care and diligence; honesty and fair dealing; disclosures affecting property value

---

General disclosure rules

Objectives of disclosure:
- declare
- explain
- offer choice
- obtain documented consent

Seller agent disclosures to client:
- in writing
- on or before listing is executed

Seller agent disclosures to customer:
- in writing
- prior to substantive contact
- oral disclosure permitted but must have written follow-up

Buyer agent disclosures to seller:
- in writing
- upon first contact with listing agent or seller
- substantive contact is assumed

Dual agent disclosures:
- "informed, written consent"
- may not disclose price or financing positions or motivations unless authorized

Facilitator disclosures:
- on becoming transaction broker or on substantive contact, whichever is first

Florida Law of Agency (475.255)

Definitions
- **Principal** – person delegating authority to another person
- **Agent** – person authorized to act for another person
- **Universal agent** – authorized to perform all acts legally allowed
- **General agent** – authorized to perform acts associated with one job
- **Special agent** – authorized to perform specific transaction or act
- **Dual agent** – fiduciary broker to both buyer and seller in same transaction; illegal in Florida

Agency relationship
- Delegation of authority for one person to act on behalf of another
- No relationship with payment but no consideration of related facts
- Fiduciary relationship between agent and principal
- Accidental relationship created by words, not payment

Types of agency relationship laws
- Common – generally accepted and used; from judgments of courts
- Statutory – written legislative statutes
- Administrative – rules and regulations by administrative agencies

Relationships regulated by
- Real estate license law
- FREC

Authorized Brokerage Relationships (475.2701; 272; 278)

Definitions
- **Buyer** – transferee or lessee in real estate transaction
- **Seller** – transferor or lessor in real estate transaction
- **Transaction broker** – limited representation to either or both parties with no fiduciary and not single agent
- **Single agent** – fiduciary representation to either buyer or seller, but not both
- **Subagent** – authorized to help and represent agent

Brokerage Relationship Disclosure Act
- Purpose – eliminate customer confusion in real estate transactions regarding broker relationships and duties
  - revokes dual agency
  - establishes brokerage representation disclosure requirements
  - allows single agent to represent buyer or seller, but not both in same transaction
  - allows transaction brokers to provide limited nonfiduciary representation to buyer, seller, or both in same transaction
- Coverage – all brokerage relationship activities
- Disclosure requirements only to residential sales

Disclosure requirements
- Written disclosure of duties of single agent and no brokerage relationship
- Disclosure records to be maintained for 5 years after written contract to purchase
- No written disclosure requirement for transaction broker relationship

Designated sales associates
- Two associates act as single agents for buyer and seller in same transaction when
  - other than residential sale
  - each party has $1 million in assets
  - customers request
- Broker advises sales associates, not customers
- Disclose single agent duties
- Customers to sign disclosures regarding assets and request for sales associate
  - to include sales associate disclosure confidentiality clause
  - disclosures required or allowed by law acceptable
  - disclosure to broker acceptable for purpose of advice
  - disclosure to broker confidential and not used to detriment of other party

Brokerage relationships
- Transaction broker or single agent allowed in FL
- Agent may change from one relationship to the other with customer written consent and disclosure of new relationship duties to seller and buyer
- Presumed transaction broker unless single or no relationship established in writing

Residential sale definition
- Improved, 4 or fewer residential units
- Unimproved, 4 or fewer units for residential use
- 10 or fewer acres agricultural property
- No disclosure requirements for
  - licensee knows buyer or seller has single agent or transaction broker
  - nonresidential transactions
  - real property rental with no option to buy
  - bono fide open house
  - answering general questions
  - providing general information about broker and services
  - interest in business except with 4 or fewer residential units

Transaction broker
- With buyer, seller, or both and duties to
  - deal honestly and fairly
  - account for all funds
  - use skill, care, and diligence
  - disclose known material facts
  - present all offers on time
  - limited confidentiality unless waived
  - additional duties as agreed

Single agent
- With buyer or seller and duties to
  - deal honestly and fairly
  - be loyal
  - be confidential
  - obey
  - account for all funds
  - use skill, care, and diligence
  - present all offers on time
  - disclose known material facts
  - disclose and describe duties in writing before agreement or showing

No brokerage relationship
- With seller or buyer to facilitate sale or purchase of property
- Duties to
  - deal honestly and fairly

- o disclose known material facts
- o account for all funds
- o disclose and describe duties in writing before showing of property

Brokerage relationship restrictions
- Transaction broker relationship allowed with both buyer and seller
- No brokerage relationship allowed with both buyer and seller
- Brokerage firm providing single agent relationship with one party and transaction broker or no brokerage relationship with other party in same transaction is NOT allowed, even if handled by different sales associates in same firm

Transition to transaction broker
- With written consent to change relationship
- Duties of transaction broker will then apply

Terminating a broker relationship
- Fulfillment of agreement
- Mutual agreement
- Expiration of agreement terms
- Broker or customer gives notice
- Death of broker or customer
- Property lost / destroyed
- Bankruptcy

Misrepresentation and Fraud (455.227)

Definitions
- **Puffing** – licensee boasting about property's benefits
- **Misrepresentation** – misstatement or concealment of fact

Misrepresentation

Intentional misrepresentation:	• purposeful **misstatement** of material fact
Intentional omission:	• **purposeful concealment** of material fact
Negligent misrepresentation:	• **unintended misstatement** that agent should have known
Negligent omission:	• **unintended concealment** that agent should have known

Fraud
- Misstatement or failure to disclose material fact
- Knowledge that statement was false or fact should have been disclosed
- Party relied on misstatement
- Party was damaged by misstatement

Florida law prohibits
- Selling property covered by mortgage that covers other property
- Promises of future sale of property
- Offering property or price by chance
- Offering property or discount by solving puzzles
- Making deceptive representations regarding real estate practice
- Obtaining license by bribe or fraud

- Failing to perform legal obligations
- Employing tricks or schemes
- Practicing beyond scope of law
- Contracting for services by unqualified or unlicensed person

Professional Ethics

- Apply Golden Rule
- Does not have to conflict with profit
- Influenced by personal code of behavior
- Influenced negatively by employer's or other agents' bad behavior
- Not regulated by statute
- Support improved professional standards
- Act can be legal but unethical
- Code of Ethics and Standards of Practice
  - developed by the National Association of Realtors (NAR)
  - promotes fair dealings with public, clients, and other brokers

Sales Associate – Broker Relationship (475.161; 42)

- Every sales associate must be employed by registered broker
- May be employed by broker as independent contractor
- Cannot be registered or licensed as
  - general partner
  - member, manager
  - officer
  - director of brokerage firm
- May only collect transaction-related money in name of employer
- May only earn transaction-related money by permission of employer

SECTION 5: Real Estate Brokerage Activities: Guides for Sales Associates

Brokerage Offices (475.22)

Broker office requirements
- Must have at least one enclosed room in stationary building
- Must have sign at entrance of each branch
  - broker name, trade name, and licensed real estate broker
- For office outside FL, broker cooperate with FL Commission rules & investigations
- Office to be registered with DBPR
- Additional offices to be registered as branch offices
- Records and files to be kept in office
- Home offices to have entrance sign and comply with local zoning

Advertising (61J2-10.025; 501.2075)

Advertising
- Must include brokerage name; no blind advertising
- No fraudulent, deceptive, false, or misleading ads
- Broker's name as registered with Commission
- Brokerage name next to contact information in online ads
- Advertising real estate services = acting as broker
- No advertising in sales associate's name
- Must be clear advertiser is real estate broker
- Broker is responsible for content
- Must disclose if licensee owns interest in property
- Team advertising to be done in brokerage firm name in a manner which reasonable persons would know they are dealing with a team or group
- No blind or false advertising
- Internet advertising to include point of contact and brokerage firm name
- Licensees selling own property need not include they are licensees in advertising
- Restrictions on unsolicited email advertising; must have opt out option
- Must comply with do not call and no-sales-solicitation calls lists
- Willful violations = civil penalty up to $10,000

Escrow / Trust Accounts – General Rules (61J2-14)

Broker held
- Sales associate gives deposit to broker by end of following business day
- Broker deposit into escrow account within 3 business days of receipt
- Broker to be signatory on all escrow accounts
- Escrow accounts to be held at Florida banks, credit unions, and savings associations
- $1,000 broker personal funds per sales escrow account allowed
- $5,000 broker personal funds per property management account
- 30 days to correct account errors
- Broker has no right to or lien on escrow deposits
- No disbursement of funds until transaction closed

- Broker to make, date, and sign monthly account statement-reconciliation
- Provide records to DBPR as required
- Maintain escrow records for 5 years
- Broker can deposit into interest-bearing account upon consent of all parties; must be in insured account in FL; interest disposition to comply with Florida law
- Recommended to separate earnest money from rental deposits
- Conflicts over funds disposition to be reported to FREC within 15 business days
- Conflict settlement procedure (any of four) to be implemented within 30 days
- Disposition of conflicted funds determined by FREC

Attorney / Title Company held
- Licensee to name attorney or title company on sales contract
- Broker to request verification of receipt of deposit by attorney/title company within 10 business days of deposit due date
- Broker to provide seller's broker copy of deposit verification within 10 business days of request
- Licensee to provide copy of written verification to seller's broker or seller

---

Commingling & Conversion

Not allowed !!

Commingling:	• mixing broker's personal or business funds with trust funds
	• includes failure to deposit funds in a timely manner
Conversion:	• using trust funds for personal or business purposes

---

Broker-Agent Relationship

Broker-Agent Relationship Essentials

Legal relationship	• Sales associate or person acting as a broker associate:
	  - is agent & fiduciary of broker
	  - acts in broker's name
	  - is subagent of client
	• sales associates or broker associates may not:
	  - have two employers
	  - be paid by other parties
	  - bind clients contractually

Sales associate's employment status	• employee or independent contractor • defined by agreement

Obligations and responsibilities

- agent to broker:
  - obtain & sell listings
  - follow policies and employment provisions
  - promote ethics and broker's reputation
- broker to agent:
  - provide data, office support, compensation, training
  - uphold ethics, policies, and employment agreement

Agent compensation

- commissions per schedule after splits with cooperating brokers

Broker's Commission (542; 475.703; 713; 61J2.10; 475.23)

Antitrust laws

- Florida Chapter 542 known as "Florida Antitrust Act of 1980"
- To complement federal antitrust laws against restraints of commerce to foster effective competition
- Every contract, combination, or conspiracy in restraint of trade is illegal, including monopolization
- Two or more brokers are not allowed to agree to
  - set commission rates or
  - boycott competitor for discounting rates or
  - set percentage amount of commission splits offered in market or
  - fix time frame for listings or
  - have group of brokers treat 1 competitor differently
- No discriminatory trade practices based on sex, race, color, religion, ancestry, or national origin
- Violators guilty of felony with criminal or civil penalties
- Suits for damages result in recovery of 3 times the amount of damage
- Action must be within 4 years of cause

Lien law on real property

- Commercial brokers have liens against owner's net proceeds from sale of commercial property for earned commission
  - lien is against personal property, not against real estate
- Closing agent to seek adjudication for nonpaid commissions
- Residential brokers have no lien rights for unpaid commissions and prohibited from commission liens unless authorized in listing contract
- Brokers do have lien rights on commercial property for nonpayment of commission in both sales and leases
- Construction lien law allows liens on real property for unpaid professional services, labor, or materials for property improvements and construction

Sales associate commission

- May only collect commission or other monies in name of employer (broker) and with consent of employer
- May not do anything to earn a commission except on behalf of registered employer
- May not sue principal over unpaid commission
- Commission agreements to be included in broker's policy manual
- Procuring cause is attributed to the person who starts the chain of events that leads to the sale of the property

Math-commission
- Commission computed based on listing agreement provisions
- Broker commission split with any cooperating brokers
- Then split with sales associate based on sales associate percentage
- Example
  - commission = 6% of selling price
  - 3% to cooperating broker
  - 2% to sales associate
  - 1% to broker

Kickbacks
- Broker not to receive kickback or rebate for use of any particular business or servicer without advising all parties in transaction
- Kickback must be legal under FL regulations
- Not allowed for transactions involving title and casualty insurance
- Unlicensed individuals not to be paid for real estate services
- Shared brokerage compensation not kickback if fully disclosed to all parties

Change of employer
- Notify Commission of change within 10 days on prescribed form
- License ceases to be in force until change reported
- Confidentiality still in force after termination
- No duplication or removal of records

Business Entities and Registration

Requirements to register
- One active broker as officer, director, member, manager, or partner of entity
- Submit application and fee
- No sales associate as officer, director, member, manager, or partner of entity
- No broker-associate as officer, director, member, manager, or partner unless upgraded to active broker

May register as brokerage
- Sole proprietorship
- General and limited partnerships, not ostensible partnerships
- Corporation
- Limited liability company - LLC
- Limited liability partnership

May not register as brokerage
- Corporation sole
- Joint venture
- Business trust
- Cooperative association
- Unincorporated association

Trade Names (475.22) & LLC/PA Registration

- Must be included on office entrance sign
- Must be in Commission records and on broker's license
- Not to be used by sales associate

- Sales associates & broker associates can register with the state as limited liability companies (LLC) or professional associates (PA)
  - cannot use trade name or fictitious name
  - must register under their real name
  - only have the real name show on the license

Unlicensed Assistants

- Cannot perform real estate services without license
- Illegal to pay unlicensed assistant for performing real estate services
- May provide support services such as
  - submit listings to MLS
  - assemble documents
  - deposit trust monies
  - compute commission checks
  - place signs on properties
  - prepare advertising for broker approval
  - answer certain questions

SECTION 6: Violations of License Law, Penalties and Procedures

Legal Terms to Know

- **Administrative complaint** – contains allegations of facts and related charges against a broker; known as formal complaint
- **Breach of trust** – failure to carry out fiduciary duties
- **Citation** – issued to subject of complaint; includes statement of complaint, law violated, imposed penalty, with option to dispute; becomes final order if lack of dispute
- **Complaint** – a claim of dissatisfaction against a real estate professional
- **Commingle** – mix broker's personal funds with funds belonging to someone else in escrow account
- **Concealment** – not disclosing information or material facts
- **Conversion** – broker's personal use or misuse of money belonging to others
- **Culpable negligence** – criminal offense of gross acts of negligence that expose others to harm or threat of harm
- **Fraud** – deceit, trickery, breach of confidence for profit or to gain unfair advantage
- **Legally sufficient** – containing ultimate facts that violation occurred
- **Mediation** – informal process conducted by unbiased third party to reach an agreeable settlement of a complaint
- **Misrepresentation** – a false statement that induces a party to enter into a contract
- **Moral turpitude** – conduct contrary to community standards of justice, honesty, or good morals
- **Notice of noncompliance** – issued by DBPR as first response to a minor violation by a licensee, such as failure to maintain the office entrance sign as required and others listed in 61J2-24.003. It gives violators 14-days to correct the violation.
- **Probable cause** – reasonable grounds for prosecution
- **Recommended order** – issued by administrative law judge to include findings and recommended penalty
- **Stipulation** – DRE attorneys and licensee agree to case facts and penalty
- **Subpoena** – direct written order to appear at a certain time and place to testify
- **Summary suspension order** – issued when serious violation justifies immediately suspending licensee prior to hearing
- **Voluntary relinquishment for permanent revocation** – method of settlement offered in response to or anticipation of charges filed against licensee

Complaint Process (455.225; 120.68)

Process
- **File complaint**
  - must be in writing, signed by complainant, and legally sufficient
- **Investigation**
  - DBPR investigates complaints, even when withdrawn or by anonymous or confidential informant
  - may provide notice of noncompliance for first minor violation
  - may include summary suspension
- **Probable cause**
  - FREC closed probable cause hearing with decision within 30 days after final investigative report
  - no probable cause, case dismissed
  - probable cause, formal complaint filed and mailed to licensee
- **Formal or informal hearing**

- o licensee does or does not dispute allegations, requests or waives hearing
- o disputes go to formal hearing
- o non-disputes go to informal hearing
- o administrative law judge hears case and issues recommended order
- **Final order**
  - o FREC issues final order of innocence or guilt with appropriate penalty
- **Judicial review**
  - o accused licensee may seek appeal via judicial review within 30 days after final order
  - o enforcement of final order may be stayed with conditions via writ of supersedeas
  - o licensee may continue to perform during appeal if stay is obtained
  - o judicial review may result in corrective action of FREC or confirmation of findings

Violations and Penalties (475.17, 181, 25; 455.227)

Grounds for license denial
- Failure to meet basic licensure requirements: age, education, good character, honest, fair, competent
- Acting as broker or sales associate in the year prior to applying for license
- Failure to complete or correct application
- Failure to pay applicable fees
- Failure to successfully complete exam
- Cheating on exam
- Violations of F.S. 475 or F.S. 455

Grounds for suspension
- Can suspend license for up to 10 years for first offense
- Misleading, deceptive, or fraudulent real estate practices
- Crime related to practice of real estate
- Failure to comply with certain educational requirements
- Filing false complaint against another licensee
- Fraud or bribery in obtaining or renewing license
- Dishonesty or trickery in business transaction
- Violation of practice duties
- False, deceptive advertising
- Failure to deliver personal property at agreed-upon time
- Any other FL rules & regulations violations

Grounds for revocation
- Second suspension for same or different violation
- License issued via FREC mistake
- License obtained by fraud, misrepresentation, or concealment
- At FREC's discretion for any offense that is grounds for denial or suspension
- Sales associates employed by revoked broker placed in involuntary inactive status

Types of Penalties (475.42; 61J2-24; 120.695; 455.22)

Administrative
- Notice of noncompliance
- License denial
- License suspension
- License revocation
- Probation with conditions
- Reprimand

- Citations
- Up to $5,000 fine

Civil
- For practicing real estate without license; enforced by courts; loss of commission

Criminal
- Misdemeanor of second degree – violation of F.S. 475; up to $500 fine, up to 60 days jail
- Felony of third degree
  - false information when applying for license
  - theft or copying licensure exam
- FREC has no authority to order jail time or restitution

Other
- Violations of multiple statutes – fine and/or jail up to max of either statute violated
- Unlicensed real estate practice
  - hearing by DBPR; fines up to $5,000
  - cease and desist order
  - injunction by circuit court
  - civil court for unpaid fines
  - criminal prosecution for felony of third degree; up to $5000 fine, up to 5 years jail

Real Estate Recovery Fund (475.482)

Real Estate Recovery Fund
- To reimburse person or entity for adjudged monetary damages by violations of licensed broker
  - broker not seller, buyer, landlord, or tenant nor principal in business entity in transaction
  - broker solely licensee in transaction
- To reimburse broker required to pay damages for disbursing escrow funds in compliance with disbursement order; no reimbursement if broker fails to defend actions to Commission
- Funded by additional fees to licensees, by Commission fines, and by interest earned on investment of funds; fees charged to licensees when fund balance falls below $500,000

Conditions for recovery
- Final judgment of civil court
- Notice to Commission
- Claim within 2 years of damaging act or discovery of damaging act; no claim after 4 years
- Writ of execution issued
- Recovered amounts applied to damages
- No appeal of final judgment

Exemptions
- Spouse of judgment debtor
- Licensed broker acting as single or transactional agent in subject transaction
- Broker owned or controlled property in subject transaction
- Broker was unlicensed

Payments
- No more than $50,000
- Commission subrogated to right, title, and interest of claimant
- Amounts reclaimed go to Fund
- Limited to $50,000 per transaction regardless of number of claimants
- Limited to aggregate $150,000 per broker
- Broker license suspended upon date of payment from fund until licensee reimburses fund with interest

Disciplinary Guidelines (61J2-24)

- Set by FREC for imposing penalties for Chapter 455 and 475 violations
- Gives notice to licensees of range of penalties for each violation
- Order includes: reprimand, fine, probation, suspension, and revocation or denial
- Combinations of penalties allowed by law
- Penalty may also include probation with conditions
- Aggravating or mitigating circumstances allow deviation from guidelines

SECTION 7: Federal and State Laws Pertaining to Real Estate

Federal Fair Housing

Federal Fair Housing Law

Civil Rights Act of 1866:	• no discrimination in selling or leasing housing based on race
Executive Order 11063:	• no race discrimination involving FHA- or VA-backed loans
Fair Housing Act of 1968 (Title VIII):	• no discrimination based on race, color, religion, national origin

	• Exemptions:
	  - privately owned home where no broker is used and no discriminatory advertising is used
	  - rental of 1-4 unit building where owner is also an occupant; no discriminatory advertising
	  - facilities owned by private clubs; leased non-commercially to members
	  - facilities owned by religious organizations with non-discriminatory membership requirements

Jones v. Mayer:	• no race discrimination, without exception
Housing and Community Development Act of 1974:	• no discrimination based on sex
Fair Housing Amendments Act of 1988:	• no discrimination based on sex or against the handicapped or familial status
Equal Opportunity Poster:	• must be displayed by brokers

Prohibited Acts

Forms of illegal discrimination

discriminatory misrepresentation:	• misrepresenting facts in order to discriminate
advertising:	• ads that restrict availability
appraising:	• may not consider protected classes as a factor adversely affecting value
unequal services:	• not rendering same service to all parties
steering:	• channeling buyers to or away from neighborhoods

blockbusting:	• inducing sale or rent based on incoming minorities that will lower values
restricting MLS access:	• MLS restriction to protected classes
redlining:	• not making loans in certain areas for discriminatory reasons

Anti-Trust Laws

no collusion:	• two or more businesses conspiring to disadvantage a competitor
no price fixing:	• two or more brokers agreeing to fix prices
no market allocation:	• colluding to restrict competition in a market segment in exchange for a competitor's reciprocal agreement

Discriminatory Advertising (HUD)

Race, Color, Origin, Religion:	• cannot make limitations or preferences
Sex:	• no explicit preference
Familial Status:	• no preference or exclusion based on family makeup
Handicap:	• no exclusions based on physical capabilities

Violations & Enforcement

- File HUD complaint with Office of Fair Housing and Equal Opportunity
    - within one year
    - HUD investigates
    - attempt to resolve out of court

- May sue in court
    - within two years
    - can get restraining order, damages

- Violators are subject to criminal prosecution

Florida Fair Housing Law (760)

Definitions
- **Accessible** – public or common areas to be approached, entered, and used by physically handicapped
- **Common areas** – indoor or outdoor spaces or elements used by residents or guests
- **Conciliation** – attempted resolution of fair housing complaint through informal negotiations

- **Familial status** – individual or family with custody of children under 18 years old
- **Handicap** – person with physical or mental impairment that limits a major life activity

No discrimination
- Based on race, color, religion, sex, national origin, age, handicap, or marital status
  - in employment
  - in certain private club memberships
- Based on race, color, religion, sex, national origin, handicap, or familial status
  - in sale, rental, financing, appraisal, or insuring housing
  - in provision of real estate brokerage service
  - in advertising dwelling
- Based on race, color, creed, sex, national origin, or physical disability
  - in accommodations or service
- No steering or blockbusting
- No refusing to design or modify multi-family housing for mental or physical disabilities
- No refusing to make or modify rules, practices, or services to accommodate mental or physical disabilities
- No retaliating, harassing, coercing, intimidating, or interfering when exercising rights

Exemptions
- Single-family homes for rent or sale by owner of 3 or fewer houses
- Dwelling rooms or units for 4 or fewer families with owner residing in 1 unit
- Religious organizations
- Private clubs preferring membership for lodgings
- Dwellings with first occupancy prior to March 1991
- Familial status for housing for elderly
- Individuals who pose direct threat to health or safety of others
- Individuals convicted of illegal manufacture or distribution of controlled substance

Enforcement
- Complainant to file written complaint with FREC within 1 year of allegation
- FREC to investigate and give notice of intent to resolve within 100 days
- Conciliation attempt to resolve issue
- Complainant may file civil action if unresolved within 180 days of filing
- Burden of proof on complainant
- Fines up to $10,000 for first guilty finding; up to $25,000 for second; up to $50,000 for third

Florida Environmental Laws (380; 386)

FL Department of Environmental Protection (DEP)
- To create strong community partnerships
- To safeguard FL's natural resources
- To enhance FL ecosystems

Radon Gas
- Information about what radon gas is required on lease/sale agreement
- Radon gas testing not required

Florida Clean Indoor Air Act
- To protect public against health hazards of secondhand tobacco smoke
- Prohibits smoking in enclosed indoor workplace
- Prohibits smoking near schools by persons under 18 years of age
- No smoking signs to be posted
- Administered and enforced by Department of Health

Florida Fair Lending Act (494.0078-494.00797)

Florida Fair Lending Act
- To protect against equity-based rather than income-based lending
- To protect against unreasonable and unnecessary loan terms
- Prohibits
  - prepayment penalties
  - default interest rate
  - balloon payments for terms less than 10 years
  - negative amortization
  - prepaid penalties
  - extending credit regardless of borrower's payment ability
  - due-on-demand clause for high-cost loans
  - refinancing within first 18 months of loan
  - recommendation of default
- Certain disclosures to borrower required

Florida Deceptive and Unfair Trade Practices Act (501.201-501.213)

Deceptive and Unfair Trade Practices Act
- To protect public and businesses from unfair competition and trade practices
- To make state consumer protection consistent with federal consumer protection
- Prohibits
  - unfair methods of competition
  - unconscionable acts or practices
  - unfair or deceptive acts or practices in conduct of any trade or commerce
- Enforced by state attorney
- Civil penalties for violations

National Uniform Landlord Tenant Act (URLTA)

URLTA Essential Provisions

Leases:
- clear lease terms
- fair market rent
- cannot waive rights

Deposits:
- limits on amounts
- tenant's right to interest
- rules and deadlines for returning

Landlord Obligations:
- bargain in good faith
- provide maintenance and repairs
- comply with building codes
- provide safety and access
- procedure for delivery of notices

Tenant Obligations:
- maintain condition
- abide by rules and regulations

- no damage or abuse
- abide by approved uses
- no disturbance of other tenants

Lease Termination

Causes

- default
- notice
- property destruction
- death

- term expiration
- voluntary agreement
- condemnation
- abandonment under certain conditions

Florida Residential Landlord and Tenant Act (83)

Exclusions
- Medical, geriatric, educational, counseling, religious residency or detention; public or private
- Occupancy under contract of sale of dwelling unit
- Transient occupancy
- Cooperative apartment occupancy tenant
- Condominium owner occupancy

Security deposits
- Money held by landlord as security for performance of rental agreement
- To be held
  - in non-interest-bearing escrow account, or
  - in interest-bearing account and pay tenant at least 75% of annualized average interest or 5% simple interest per year, or
  - by posting surety bond with clerk of circuit court in same county as swelling
- Notify tenant within 30 days or in lease where money is being held
- Return to tenant within 15 days of vacating premises
- Notify tenant within 30 days of intent to claim all or part of deposit
- No notice, no claim allowed
- Disputes settled in court with prevailing party receiving court costs and attorney fees

Advance rentals
- Payments to be applied to future rent periods, not current rent period
- To be held
  - in non-interest-bearing escrow account, or
  - in interest-bearing account and pay tenant at least 75% of annualized average interest or 5% simple interest per year, or
  - by posting surety bond with clerk of circuit court in same county as swelling
- Notify tenant within 30 days or in lease where money is being held
- Landlord to transfer advance rents to landlord's own account when payments are due

Commingling
- No commingling of deposit or advanced monies with landlord's funds
- No hypothecating, pledging, or using monies until actually due to landlord

Lease approvals for active military personnel
- Protection for active military by requiring faster lease approvals
- Application approval or denial within 7 days with reason given for denial
- Application not processed within 7 days results in automatic lease

SECTION 8: Property Rights: Estates and Tenancies; Condos, Coops, CDDs, HOAs, and Time-Sharing

Nature of Property

Real vs. Personal Property; Fixtures

Real Property:
- land
- fixtures
- attachments

Personal Property:
- chattels
- trade fixtures
- emblements

Differentiation criteria:
- intention; adaptation; functionality; relationship of parties; contract provisions

Conversion:
- real to personal property-- severance personal to real property-- affixing

Emblements:
- plants or crops considered personal property

Trade fixtures:
- personal property items temporarily attached to real estate in order to conduct business

General Property Rights

Land / Real Estate / Real Property

Land:	surface, all *natural things* attached to it, subsurface, and air above the surface
Real estate:	land + **manmade** permanent attachments
Real property:	real estate + bundle of rights

Bundle of Rights

"PUTEE":	*P* ossess
	U se
	T ransfer
	E xclude
	E ncumber

Riparian / Littoral

Riparian Rights (Rivers and Streams)

- navigable: own land to water's edge
- *not navigable*: own underlying land to midpoint of stream

Littoral Rights (Lakes and Seas)

- own to high water mark

Memory Tip: R : River Riparian   L: Lake Littoral

Estates and Tenancies

Interests

Possession	Non-possession
• Estate	• Encumbrance • Public interest

Estates

Freehold (Own)	Leasehold (Lease)

• Fee simple
  - Absolute
  - Defeasible
• Life Estates
  - Conventional
  - Legal
	• Estate for years
	• Periodic
	• Estate at Will
	• Estate at Sufferance

Freeholds

Fee simple	• *not limited* by one's lifetime • absolute: *highest* form of ownership interest • defeasible: *reverts* to previous owner per conditions
Life estate	• passes *to another* upon death of a named party • remainder: *named party* to receive estate • reversion: *previous owner* to receive estate
Conventional life estate	• *limited* to lifetime of life tenant or named party • pur autre vie: limited to lifetime of another, passes to remainderman or previous owner

Legal life estate	<ul><li>created by operation of state law as opposed to a property owner's agreement</li><li>designed to protect family survivors</li><li>homestead: rights to one's **principal residence**</li><li>laws protect homestead from creditors☐</li><li>family must occupy the homestead</li><li>cannot be conveyed by one spouse</li><li>endures over life of head of household</li><li>interests extinguished if property destroyed</li></ul>

Leaseholds

Estate for years	• specific, **stated duration**, per lease
Periodic	• lease term **renews automatically** upon acceptance of rent
Estate at Will	• for **indefinite period** subject to rent payment; cancelable with notice
Estate at Sufferance	• tenancy **against landlord's will** and without an agreement

Forms of Ownership

Tenancy in severalty	• **sole** ownership
Tenancy in common	<ul><li>co-tenants individually own undivided interests</li><li>**any ownership share possible**</li><li>no survivorship</li><li>can convey to outside parties</li></ul>
Joint tenancy	<ul><li>equal undivided interest jointly owned</li><li>**survivorship**</li><li>requires **four unities** to create: time, title, interest, possession</li></ul>
Tenancy by the entireties	<ul><li>**husband and wife** own equal undivided interest</li><li>Now applies to same-sex couples in some states</li></ul>

Joint Tenancy & Four Unities

Unity of ownership	• owners hold single title jointly
Equal ownership	• owners always hold equal shares
Transfer	• may transfer to new owner as a tenancy in common interest with remaining joint tenants

| **Survivorship** | • on death, interests and rights pass to other joint tenants |
| **Creation** | • requires "four unities," *PITT*: |

1. *P*ossession: acquire same possessory rights
2. *I*nterest: acquire equal, undivided interests
3. *T*ime: acquire interests at same time
4. *T*itle: acquire interests with same deed

Homestead (222; 196)

Protection of Homestead
- From forced sale to satisfy judgment liens
- No protection from foreclosure
- From death of spouse when only spouse's name is on title

Tax exemption
- For real and personal property belonging to FL resident
- For leasehold interests in property in FL
- Requires legal title and permanent residency on homestead
- $25,000 exemption deducted from value of homestead for tax purposes
- Additional $25,000 deducted for levies valued greater than $50,000 other than school district levies
- Up to additional $25,000 exemption on assessed valuation greater than $100,000 for all levies other than school district levies
- Additional exemption up to $50,000 for 65 years or older and low income living in certain counties with refund of prior years' overpaid taxes
- Exemption for deployed servicemembers for specific military operations
- Additional exemption for disabled veterans
- Exemption for first responders with total and permanent disability from line-of-duty injury in Florida or another state during authorized operation if the responder is a permanent resident of Florida on January 1 of year exemption is claimed
- Properties used for religious, literary, scientific, government, or charitable purposes fully exempt
- Homestead considered abandoned if rented

Condominiums and Cooperatives

Condominiums

- ownership of a **unit of airspace** plus an **undivided interest** in the **common elements** as tenant in common with other owners
- may be sold, encumbered or foreclosed **without affecting other unit owners**
- creation: by developer's declaration

Florida New Unit Condominium Disclosures

- Prospectus
- Bylaws
- Declaration
- Rules and regulations
- FAQ
- Expected budget projection of association
- Articles of incorporation

Florida Resale Condominium Disclosures

- Current declaration
- Articles of incorporation
- Bylaws
- Rules of association
- FAQ
- Recent association financial report
- Governance form
- Assessments and condo estoppel letter
- Condo rider

Termination of Condominium Association

- Termination of covenants of declaration for specific reasons, such as maintenance of storm water management systems or conservation areas, protection of residents from health and safety hazards, etc.
- Optional termination with 80% approval of voting interests
- Termination not to proceed if rejected by 5% negative vote of voting interests

Note: A sales contract where these disclosures have not been made is voidable at the option of the buyer before closing.

Cooperatives
- ownership of *shares in owning corporation*, plus *proprietary lease* in a unit
- corporation has sole, undivided ownership

Homeowners' Associations (HOA's)
- F.S. Chapter 720 is known as the Homeowners' Association Act
- HOA is a FL corporation responsible for the operation of a community and the membership consists of the land parcel owners
- unpaid HOA fees/dues may result in a property lien

Community Development Districts (CDDs)
- CDDs are a local unit of special-purpose government created to serve the long-term specific needs of its community
- CDDs have the authority to plan, finance, construct, operative and maintain community-wide infrastructure
- Common responsibilities include water supply, sewer/wastewater management & street lights

Time Shares
- a lease (right-to-use) or ownership (interval ownership) interest in a property for the purpose of periodic use by the owners or tenants on a scheduled basis
- Right-to-use timeshare leases typically are for 20-40 years in Florida
- a Florida timeshare sales contract can be cancelled without any penalty within the first ten days

Community Property

Separate

- acquired *before marriage*
- acquired by *gift or inheritance*
- acquired with *separate-property funds*
- *income* derived from *separate property*

Community

- all other property earned or acquired during the marriage

SECTION 9: Title, Deeds and Ownership Restrictions

Title to Real Property

Bundle of Rights

"PUTEE":
- *P* ossess
- *U* se
- *T* ransfer
- *E* xclude
- *E* ncumber

Legal Title v. Equitable title

Legal title

- Full legal ownership of property and the bundle of rights as they apply to it. Contrasts with equitable title.

Equitable title

- An interest that gives a lienholder or buyer the right to acquire legal title to a property if certain contractual conditions occur

Acquiring & Recording Legal Title

Voluntary & Involuntary Alienation

Voluntary transfer	Involuntary transfer
• deed • will • public grant	• descent (without will, with heirs) • escheat (without will nor heirs) • foreclosure (loan default) • eminent domain (public good) • adverse possession (hostile, open use)

Note: Adverse possession in Florida must be continuous for seven years.

Notice

Notice:
- how ownership is evidenced to the public

Actual notice:
- *knowledge acquired directly* through demonstrable evidence, e.g., presenting or inspecting a deed, visiting a party in possession

45

Constructive notice:	• *knowledge one could have obtained*, as presumed by law; imparted by recording in public records "for all to see"

Evidence of Title

Forms of evidence to prove marketable title and ownership:

- title insurance
- attorney's opinion of abstract
- title certificates
- Torrens registration

Deeds

Deed Validity

Requirements:

1. grantor
2. grantee
3. in writing
4. legal description
5. granting clause
6. consideration
7. grantor's signature
8. acknowledgement
9. delivery and acceptance

Note: Two witnesses must sign the deed for validity in Florida.

Deed Clauses

Premises:	granting
Habendum:	type of estate
Reddendum:	restrictions
Tenendum:	other property included

Covenant/Warrant Clauses

Seisen:	assures right to convey
Quiet Enjoyment:	assures no 3rd party title disputes
Further Assurance:	assures assistance if title problems discovered later
Warranty of Title:	assures grantee will receive good title
Encumbrances:	assures no additional encumbrances
Against Grantor's Acts:	assures nothing done to impair title during fiduciary period

Deed Types

Bargain and sale:	"I own but won't defend"
General warranty:	"I own and will defend"
Special warranty:	"I own and warrant myself only"
Quitclaim:	"I may or may not own, and won't defend. I may have to get a judge to clear title. "

Special purpose deeds:	Used for different purposes, interests conveyed, or by different parties

Title Transfer by Descent

Testate / Intestate

Order of Title Transfer

Dies testate with heirs:
- first to creditors
- then to homestead
- then **to heirs by will**

Dies intestate with heirs:
- first to creditors
- then to homestead
- then *to heirs by laws of descent*

Dies intestate, no heirs:
- first to creditors
- then **to state by escheat**

Ownership Limitations and Restrictions: Encumbrances & Liens

Easements

Appurtenant
- *attaches* to the estate
- *dominant* tenement's *right to use* or restrict adjacent *servient* tenement
- *by necessity*, to *landlocked* owners
- party wall easement in a shared structure: to not damage or destroy

in Gross
- *does not attach* to the estate
- **Personal**-- not transferrable, ends upon death of easement holder
- **Commercial**-- transferrable, granted to a business

by Prescription
- obtainable through *continuous, open, adverse use* over a period

License
- *personal* right to use a property
- *does not attach*
- *non-transferrable*
- *revocable*

Note: In Florida, the period of time for an easement by prescription is 20 years.

Leases

Types of Leases

Gross lease	• landlord pays expenses; tenant pays higher rent than net
Net lease	• tenant pays some or all expenses; rent is less than gross
Percentage lease	• landlord receives rent minimum plus percentage of retailer's sales
Residential lease	• gross lease hybrid; short term; uniform terms reflect landlord-tenant standards
Ground lease	• landlord owns and leases ground but does not own improvements
Proprietary lease	• for cooperative unit owners; indefinite term; assigned to new unit owner on sale
Leasing of rights	• leasehold transfer of rights for limited use; examples: air, mineral, water rights

General and Specific Liens

Lien Types

Lien Types	Examples
voluntary / involuntary:	• mortgage lien / tax lien
general / specific:	• against any & all assets / against car or house
superior / junior:	• paid before juniors / paid after superiors by date of recording

Lien Priority

Superior Liens by rank

- Real estate tax liens
- Special assessment liens
- Federal estate tax liens
- State inheritance tax liens

Junior Liens by date of recording

- Federal income tax liens
- Judgment liens
- Mortgage liens
- Vendor's liens
- Mechanics liens (priority by date work performed)

Public / Government Restrictions

Public Land Use Controls
Zoning
- "police power" granted by state-level enabling acts; zoning ordinance: creates zones, usage restrictions, regulations, requirements
- enables urban land managers to create separate land uses that do not conflict with one another nor create incompatible adjacencies

Eminent Domain
- allows a government entity to purchase a fee or easement interest in privately owned real property for the **public good** and for **public use** in exchange for "just compensation"

Subdivision Regulations
- location, grading, alignment, surfacing, street width, highways
- sewers and water mains
- lot and block dimensions
- building and setback lines
- public use dedications
- utility easements
- ground percolation

Building Codes
- comprehensive onsite and offsite construction and materials standards; must be met to receive certificate of occupancy

Environmental Restrictions
- Flood control; solid waste disposal; air quality; water quality; marine protection; noise control; toxic substances controls; lead paint; CERCLA; Superfund

Deed Restrictions

Deed restriction
- single-property use restriction as stipulated in a deed; may not be discriminatory

- examples: minimum area of a residence; setbacks; limits on other structures; conducting commercial activities

Declaration restriction
- use restriction in multiple-property declarations; enforced by court injunction

Deed condition
- usage restriction that can trigger repossession by a previous owner if violated

SECTION 10: Legal Descriptions

Purpose and Types of Legal Descriptions

Purpose
- to accurately locate and identify the boundaries of a parcel of real property to a degree acceptable by courts of law in the state where the property is located
- general criterion is that it alone provides sufficient data for a surveyor to locate the parcel

Metes and Bounds Method
- describes perimeter by landmarks, monuments, distances, angles
- usable within rectangular survey system
- starting at point of beginning (POB), follow perimeter, **return to POB**

Lot and Block System
- Used to describe properties in residential, commercial, industrial subdivisions
- Tracts of land divided into lots, then grouped into blocks

Rectangular Survey System

Meridians:	north-south lines six miles apart
Parallels:	east-west lines six miles apart
Range:	north-south strip between meridians
Tier:	east-west strip of area between parallels; also called township strip
Township:	the six-mile by six-mile square at the intersection of a range and a tier
Section of a township:	a 1 mile x 1 mile square; 1 section = 640 acres; 36 sections per township
Fractions of a section:	going from the smallest to largest unit, indicate size and location within successively larger quarters or halves of the section: E 1/2 of the NE 1/4 of the NE 1/4 of Section 8
Check:	correction lines used in the Rectangular Survey System to correct distortions in vertical lines caused by the curvature of the earth and lines slowly coming closer to each other. Occurs every 24 miles north and south of the baseline.
Government lot:	a tract of land normally described by a lot; typically an irregular portion of a section formed by a meandering body of water or other impassable object

SECTION 11: Real Estate Contracts

Definition, Preparation of Contracts (725)

Contract defined
- An agreement between two or more parties who have a "meeting of the minds," and have pledged to perform (or refrain from performing) some act.
- A *valid* contract is *legally enforceable* by meeting certain requirements of contract law.
- If a contract does not meet requirements, it is not valid and the parties to it cannot resort to a court of law to enforce its provisions

Florida contract law
- Contract = enforceable promise
- Must be drafted by attorney
- Licensees can assist buyer or seller with filling in blanks for
  - listing agreement
  - buyer brokerage agreement
  - sale and purchase contract
  - option contract
- Licensees may not draft
  - deeds
  - mortgages
  - promissory notes
  - leases but can fill in blanks for leases less than 1 year
- Use of standardized contracts preferred, including "As Is" sale and purchase contract
  - Typically available through local Realtor Boards
- FL's statute of frauds covers
  - purchase and sale contracts
  - option contracts
  - deeds and mortgage instruments
  - leases for more than 1 year
  - listing agreements for more than 1 year

Essentials of a Contract

Contract Classifications

Oral vs. written:	• oral, or parol, contract may not be enforceable
Express vs. implied:	• express: all terms expressly agreed to • implied: unintentional agreement deemed to exist due to terms implied by actions
Bilateral vs. Unilateral:	• bilateral: both parties promise to perform • unilateral: one party performs only if other party performs
Executed vs. Executory:	• executed: fully performed • executory: performance yet to be completed

Contract Status

Valid:	•	meets all requirements
Valid but unenforceable:	•	certain oral contracts; if performed, cannot change outcome
Void:	•	not valid; unenforceable
Voidable:	•	may be rescinded due to subsequent discoveries: if performed, cannot change outcome

---

Contract validity

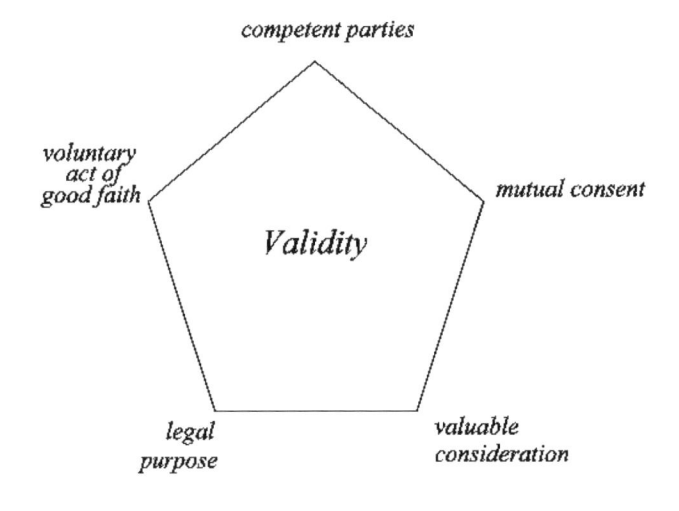

Competent parties
- legal age
- mental competency
- legitimate authority

Mutual consent
- clear and unequivocal **offer and acceptance** with an underlying **meeting of the minds**

Valuable consideration
- two-way exchange of valuable consideration for performance by the other party; not "love and affection"

Legal purpose
- promise, intent and content must be lawful; if illegal, contract is void – cannot contract to break the law

Voluntary, good faith
- no duress, coercion, fraud or misrepresentation

Contract Negotiation: Offer / Counteroffer / Acceptance

Offer:	•	intention to enter into contract
	•	must contain all intended terms
	•	must be in writing
	•	expires in "reasonable time" or date and time specified

Acceptance:	• unequivocal and manifest agreement to offer • no changes to offer whatsoever • signed, preferably dated
Completed contract:	• communication of acceptance to offeror • if by mail, offer is communicated upon mailing
Counteroffer:	• new or amended terms of a received offer • original offer is void
Revoking an offer:	• may be done at any time prior to offeree's communication of acceptance

Termination

Causes:

- Performance
- Infeasibility
- Mutual agreement
- Cooling-period rescission
- Revocation
- Abandonment
- Lapse of time
- Invalidity of contract

Breach & Remedies

Rescission:	• cancel contract; return deposits
Forfeiture:	• defaulting party gives up something according to contract terms
Liquidated damages:	• damages due a damaged party as stated in contract
Suit for damages:	• civil suit for money damages not covered by contract
Specific performance:	• suit to force party to fulfill contract promises

Enforcement Limitations

Statute of limitations.
- Restricts the time period for which injured party has the right to rescind or disaffirm contract.
- A party to a voidable contract must act within the statutory period.

Statute of frauds.
- Requires that certain contracts be in writing to be enforceable.
- Real property fee conveyance contracts fall in this category
- Exception - lease of one year's duration or less may be oral..
- Exclusive listing agreements must be in writing.

Contracts: Listings

Characteristics

Parties:
- listing broker-- fiduciary of buyer client or seller client
- subagent-- fiduciary of listing broker's client
- customer-- non-fiduciary principal in transaction

Fiduciary duties:
- to client: loyalty; obedience; disclosure; care; diligence; accounting
- to customer: honesty, care and disclosure

Authority:
- limited agency agreement
- broker may not contract for client unless specifically authorized
- clients liable only for broker's acts within scope of authority

Contract law:
- unilateral contract
- oral listing is valid and enforceable
- exclusive listing in some states must be written to be enforceable
- personal service contract-- not assignable

Types of Listings

Exclusive right-to-sell:
- given to one broker
- usually must be written
- must expire
- broker gets commission if property transfers during period

Exclusive agency:
- exclusive excepting owner
- oral or written
- must expire
- broker gets commission unless owner sells

Open listing:
- non-exclusive
- oral or written
- no stated expiration
- procuring cause gets commission
- no commission if client procures customer

Net listing:
- all sale proceeds above a seller's minimum price go to the broker
- discouraged, if not illegal in Florida

Buyer agency agreements:
- create a fiduciary relationship with the buyer
- if exclusive, buyer agrees to only work with the buyer representative in procuring a property
- must have an expiration date along with other requirements of a valid listing

Listing Compensation & Termination

Compensation:
- negotiated between agent and principal
- where disputed among agents, agent with procuring cause is owed commission
- based on results: find ready willing and able customer

Causes for termination:
- performance
- infeasibility
- mutual agreement
- revocation
- abandonment
- breach
- expiration
- invalidity
- incapacitation or death
- involuntary transfer
- destruction of property

Agent's performance:
- may perform only authorized tasks
- must verify owner and property data
- may delegate duties to sales associates and other brokers

Revoking a listing:
- clients always have power to revoke during period
- may incur liability for commission or damages

Contracts: Option Contracts

Essentials
- optionor gives option to optionee
- unilateral contract: seller must perform, buyer need not
- if option is exercised, option becomes bilateral sale contract

Contract requirements
- non-refundable consideration for the option right
- price and terms of the sale
- option period expiration date
- legal description
- must be in writing
- must meet contract validity requirements

Common clause provisions
- how to exercise option
- terms of option money forfeiture
- how option money will be applied to purchase price

Contracts: Sale and Purchase Contracts

Characteristics

- binding, bilateral contract for purchase and sale
- the enforceable "blueprint" for closing
- contract is executory, or to be fulfilled
- expires upon closing
- must be in writing
- for validity, must
  - contain valuable consideration
  - identify property
  - be signed by all

Creation / Deposit / Contingencies

Creation:
- created by unqualified acceptance of an offer
- gives buyer equitable title, and power to force specific performance

Deposit, or earnest money escrow:
- secures contract validity and buyer's equitable interest
- varies in amount
- deposit controlled by disinterested party who must act according to escrow instructions

Contingencies:
- conditions that must be met for the contract to be enforceable
- must be clear
- have expiration date
- require diligence to satisfy

Primary Clauses

- parties
- consideration
- legal description
- price and terms
- loan approval provisions
- earnest money
- escrow
- closing and possession dates
- conveyed interest
- type of deed
- title evidence
- property condition warranty/disclosures
- closing costs
- damage and destruction
- default
- broker's agency disclosure and who pays commission
- seller's representations: property condition, marketable title

Secondary Clauses

- inspections
- owner's association disclosure
- survey
- environmental hazards, compliance with laws
- rental property tenant's rights
- FHA or VA financing condition
- flood plain and flood insurance
- condominium assessments

- due-on-sale and seller financing disclosure
- foreign seller withholding
- tax-deferred exchange
- boilerplate: merger of agreements, notices, time of the essence, fax transmission, survival, dispute resolution, addenda

Sale Contracts: Mandatory Disclosures (475; 404)

Material defects
- Seller must truthfully disclose property condition and defects that affect property value
- Broker must disclose if known or should have known

Radon gas
- Radioactive gas
- Lease or sale agreement must contain explanation/disclosure of what radon gas is
- No testing required

Lead-based paint
- Presence must be disclosed by sellers and landlords
- Disclosure on sale contracts
- EPA pamphlet given to buyers or tenants prior to signing lease or sale contract
- Buyers allowed 10 days to test for lead-based paint
- Licensee to make seller comply

Energy Efficiency Brochure
- Must be given to buyer prior to sale contract
- Gives buyer option to receive rating on building

Homeowners association
- Sellers to disclose mandatory homeowners association
- Provide buyer with
  - disclosure summary of association
  - existence of restrictive covenants
  - imposed assessments

Property tax
- Ad valorem tax disclosure summary prior to or at sale contract signing
- Disclosure attached to sale contract or as wording within the contract
- Discloses future tax may be different than current tax

Building code
- Disclose previous, unresolved building code violations
- Include nature of violation, proceedings, copy of pleadings, documents received by seller
- Disclose buyer's responsibility for compliance with code and court orders

SECTION 12: Residential Mortgages

Mortgage Concepts

Lien vs. Title Theory State
- **lien theory state** -- lender of mortgaged property holds equitable title rather than legal title; borrower holds legal title. FL is a lien theory state.

- **title theory state** – lender holds legal title to the mortgaged property until the mortgagor satisfies the terms and obligations of the loan.

Hypothecation
- Use of real property as collateral for a mortgage loan

Lien priority
- Order in which liens against a property are satisfied
- The highest priority lien is paid by foreclosure proceeds before any other lien

Superior Liens by rank	Junior Liens by date of recording
• Real estate tax liens	• Federal income tax liens
• Special assessment liens	• Judgment liens
• Federal estate tax liens	• Mortgage liens
• State inheritance tax liens	• Vendor's liens
	• Mechanics liens (priority by date work performed)

Transaction Instruments, Components & Mechanics

Mortgage Instruments & Mechanics

Elements:
- promissory note: promise to repay loan
- mortgage: pledge of property as collateral for loan

Mechanics:
- borrower gives lender promissory note and mortgage
- lender gives borrower funds and records a lien

Trust Deed Transaction

Elements:
- promissory note: trustor's promise to repay loan
- deed of trust: title to property as collateral for loan

Mechanics:
- trust deed conveys title from the borrower/trustor to a third-party trustee
- trustee holds title on behalf of the lender/beneficiary until the debt is repaid

Promissory note
- legal instrument executed by borrower stating debt amount, loan term, method and timing of repayment, interest rate, promise to pay; may repeat other provisions from mortgage

58

document or deed of trust; negotiable instrument assignable to a third party

Financial components

- original principal: capital amount borrowed on which interest payments are calculated
- loan balance: remaining unpaid principal at any point in the life of the loan
- interest: charge for the use of money; rate fixed or variable
- Annual Percentage Rate (APR) includes interest and all other finance charges; lender must disclose on residential properties
- point: one percent of the loan amount
- loan origination fee: charged by lender at origination to obtain required return
- term: period of time for repayment of interest and principal
- payment: the periodic payment of interest and/or principal
- down payment: borrower's cash payment applied to the purchase price
- loan-to-value ratio: the loan's share of the total value of the property
- equity: at closing, the borrower's cash invested in the property; thereafter, the difference between the market value and the loan balance

Mortgage Clauses

Payment of Principal and Interest: Prepayment and Late Charges

- Borrower must make timely payments according to the terms of the note
- Late payments or early payoffs may trigger penalties

Funds for Taxes and Insurance

- Borrower must make monthly payments to cover taxes and hazard insurance
- Borrower may also have to pay flood insurance and mortgage insurance premiums
- **Escrow account**: reserve account for periodic payments of taxes and insurance.
- Real Estate Settlement Procedures Act (RESPA) limits funds the lender can require for this purpose.

PITI

- Borrower's monthly payment for principal and interest is called the **P&I** payment (principal and interest)
- The amount which includes the escrow payment is called **PITI** (principal, interest, taxes, insurance).

Charges and Liens

- Borrower is liable for paying any charges, liens, or other expenses that may have priority over the mortgage or trust instrument.

Hazard or Property Insurance

- Borrower must keep property insured as the lender requires.

Occupancy, Preservation, Maintenance and Protection of the Property

- Borrower must take and maintain occupancy as the borrower's principal residence according to requirements
- Borrower must not abuse or neglect the including use for illegal purposes, creating hazardous waste on the property, or destroying the improvements

Protection of Lender's Rights in the Property
- Lender may take actions to protect its rights in the property if the borrower jeopardizes the property's value. The costs of these actions would be charged to the borrower

Mortgage Insurance
- Lender may require *private mortgage insurance, or PMI* which protects the lender against loss from borrower default
- Applies to loans that are not backed by the Federal Housing Administration (FHA) or Veterans Administration (VA) and that have a down payment of less than 20% of the property value

Inspection
- Lender may inspect the property with reasonable cause to fear damage to the collateral

Condemnation
- If the property is condemned or taken by eminent domain, lender reserves a claim on any resulting proceeds

Transfer of the Property or a Beneficial Interest in Borrower
- If borrower sells the property without the lender's approval, the lender may demand immediate repayment of the loan balance. This **alienation** clause, aka a **due-on-sale** clause, allows lender to prevent unapproved loan assumptions
- The requirement to repay the loan before the scheduled due date is called **acceleration**.

Borrower's Right to Reinstate
- If lender holds borrower in default, borrower has the right to reinstatement by performing certain actions, usually paying overdue payments plus expenses the lender
- Clause is called a **redemption** clause
- Gives the borrower time to satisfy obligations and prevent a forced sale

Release
- Agreement to release the lien obligation when borrower has paid off the loan
- Release clause, aka **defeasance** clause, may require lender to execute a **satisfaction of mortgage,** aka **release of mortgage**
- If deed of trust, lender directs trustee to execute a **release deed** or **deed of reconveyance** to the borrower as trustor.
- Release deed or satisfaction should be recorded as necessary

Escalation Clause
- Allows lender to increase the loan's interest rate

Contracts: Contract for Deed

Essentials	• purchase price is paid over time in installments • seller retains title, buyer takes possession • at end of period, buyer pays balance, gets legal title
Interests and rights	• seller may encumber or assign interest • seller remains liable for underlying mortgage • buyer may use, possess, or profit

- buyer must make periodic payments, maintain the property, and purchase at the end of the term

Default and recourse
- buyer may sue for cancellation and damages or specific performance
- seller may sue for specific performance or damages, or may need to foreclose

Land Development & Construction Loans

Land development loans overview

- land development loans - finance infrastructure construction to a tract of land
- construction loans - used to finance improvements
- blanket loan - hypothecates other properties as collateral for additional financing
- takeout commitment – pledge to grant longer-term loan on given portions of completed construction
- buydowns – developer assistance to buyers to effectively lower interest rate for the borrower

Default and Foreclosure

Foreclosure

Mortgage lien foreclosure:
- liquidation of collateral property by *judicial, non-judicial,* or *strict* foreclosure

Judicial foreclosure:
- lawsuit and court-ordered public sale; *deficiency judgments*, *redemption rights*

Non-judicial foreclosure:
- *"power of sale"* granted to lender; no suit; *no deficiency* judgment; *no redemption* period after sale

Strict foreclosure:
- court orders *legal transfer of title directly to lender* without public sale

Deed in lieu of foreclosure:
- defaulted *borrower deeds property to lender* to avoid foreclosure

SECTION 13: Types of Mortgages and Sources of Financing

Note: see also finance computations in Part Two: Real Estate Math Review, Finance Section

Types of Mortgages

Conventional mortgages

- Originated by banks and private financial institutions
- No government-related insurance or guarantees as with FHA or VA
- Typically require 20% down payments; smaller down payments may require PMI
- Assumptions require approval

Government loan programs

- **FHA** – federally insured loan programs (see following)
- **VA** – federally guaranteed loan programs (see following)

Amortized fixed-rate v adjustable loans

- **Amortized:** payments include increasing increments of principal which retire loan balance over loan term
- **Fixed rate:** interest rate does not change – can have for amortized or interest-only loans
- **Adjustable loans:** interest rate fluctuates up or down with an index; payments may also vary

Adjustable Loan Characteristics

- **Mechanics**: rate adjusts up or down with index; payments may or may not change;
- **Negative amortization**: loan balance increases if payments are less than what is owed given the balance and rate, i.e., unpaid monthly amounts are added to the principal balance
- **Rate and payment caps**: maximum amounts the interest rate or payments can increase in a given adjustment period or over the life of the loan; protects borrower from unaffordable increases
- **Index and margin**: interest rate tied to any number of financial indices. Margin equals a fixed point spread between the index and the interest rate
- **Teaser rates:** to attract borrowers, adjustable loans may have low initial rates which increase over subsequent adjustment periods to a more permanent market level.

Custom Mortgages

- **Partially amortized with a balloon:** payments will not retire principal balance over life of the loan, thus requiring a lump-sum payment, or "balloon" payment at end of term
- **Interest-only loans:** loans where payments are interest only, and the principal balance is retired in full at maturity using a balloon payment
- **Biweekly mortgage:** loan payments are every-two weeks, a device that reduces total interest paid, but also shortens risk period for the lender
- **Package mortgage:** mortgage loans which also finance articles of personal property as part of the purchase transaction
- **Home equity loans:** funds borrowed using the homeowners equity for collateral; funds can be used for any purpose

- **Purchase money mortgage:** a seller-financed loan to the buyer of portions of the purchase price using the property as collateral. Usually accompanied by a senior underlying first mortgage
- **Reverse annuity mortgage:** a financial arrangement where the homeowner pledges equity to a lender in exchange for periodic payments of the pledged equity. In essence it is the periodic receipt of equity liquidation in exchange for an increase of debt owed on the property.

FHA Loans

Insured loans granted by approved lenders to qualified borrowers.

Loan term:	• 15, 30 years
Qualifying ratios:	• income: 31% • debt: 43%
Minimum downpayment:	• 3.5%
Mortgage insurance:	• required at 78% LTV or above • premium = one-time 1.75-2.25% of loan amount, plus annual premium
Points:	• None
Maximum loan amount:	• varies by Metropolitan Statistical Area

---

VA Loans

Guaranteed loans:	• granted by approved lenders to qualified veterans
Qualifying ratios:	• depends on lender
Minimum downpayment:	• None
Points:	• 1.25 - 3.3, depending on downpayment, type of loan, type of veteran

---

Loan Qualification

Equal Credit Opportunity Act
- lender must evaluate applicant according to applicant's own income and credit information

Income qualification
- income ratio and debt ratio qualify borrower's income; income ratio applied to gross income determines housing expense maximum; debt ratio takes revolving debt into account
- income ratios: 25-28% conventional; 31% FHA-insured
- debt ratios: 36% conventional; 43% FHA and 41% VA

Cash qualification
- lender verifies applicant's sources of cash for down payment; extra cash enhances income qualification evaluation

Net worth
- extent to which applicant's assets exceed liabilities as a further source of reserves

Credit evaluation
- lender obtains credit reports to evaluate applicant's payment behavior

Loan commitment
- written pledge by lender to grant loan under specific terms; firm, lock-in, conditional, take-out

The Mortgage Market

Supply and demand for money
- relationship between supply and demand for money affects interest rates, consumer prices, availability of mortgage money; regulated by Federal Reserve

Federal Reserve control of money supply among banks
- Sells T-bills to reduce money supply and increase interest rates; buys T-bills to increase supply and decrease rates
- Sets the reserve requirement for member banks
  - increase reserves to tighten money and raise interest rates
  - decrease reserves to loosen money and lower interest rates
- sets the discount rate for member banks
  - increase rate to tighten money
  - decrease rate to increase money supply

Federal Home Loan Bank System (FHLBS)
- Counterpart to the Fed for savings and loan associations

Federal Deposit Insurance Corporation (FDIC)
- Insures deposits up to $250,000 per depositor, per insured bank, for each account ownership category

The primary mortgage market
- Originates mortgage loans directly to borrowers;
- Includes savings and loans, commercial banks, mutual savings banks, life insurance companies, mortgage bankers, credit unions

The secondary mortgage market
- Buys existing loans to provide liquidity to primary lenders; Fannie Mae, Ginnie Mae, Freddie Mac, investment firms, life insurance companies, pension funds

Role of FNMA, GNMA, and FHLMC
- FNMA buys conventional, FHA- and VA-backed loans and pooled mortgages; guarantees payment on mortgage-backed securities
- GNMA guarantees payment on certain types of loans
- FHLMC buys and pools mortgages; sells mortgage-backed securities

Mortgage loan originator v. lender/banker v. broker
- Mortgage loan originator: solicits, negotiates mortgage loans; requires MLO license
- Mortgage broker: an intermediary who brings mortgage borrowers and mortgage lenders together, but does not use its own funds to originate mortgages
- Mortgage banker: person or entity who funds or services loans for others and/or who sells mortgages to the secondary market

Truth-in-Lending and Regulation Z

- Reg Z implements Truth-in-Lending Simplification and Reform Act and Consumer Credit Protection Act
- Provisions: lender must disclose finance charges and APR prior to closing; borrower has limited right of rescission; lender must follow disclosure requirements in advertising

Equal Credit Opportunity Act

- ECOA prohibits discrimination in lending

Real Estate Settlements and Procedures Act

- RESPA standardizes settlement practices
- provisions: lender must provide CFPB booklet explaining loans, settlement costs and procedures
- lender must provide CFPB Loan Estimate of settlement costs within three days of application
- lender must provide CFPB Closing Disclosure three days before loan consummation; buyer to have three days to review form prior to closing; if changes are made, closing must wait another three days

National Flood Insurance Act

- borrowers of "federally-related loans" must obtain flood insurance if property is in designated flood-hazard area
- requires disclosure that flood insurance is obtained under a separate policy issued by F.E.M.A.

SECTION 14: Closing of Transactions

Note: see also closing computations (costs and prorations) in Part Two: Real Estate Math Review

Closing Essentials

Settlement process
- Identify selling terms & costs
- Determine non-prorated debits and credits
- Complete prorated debits and credits
- Complete closing statement
- Disburse funds

RESPA

Applicability	• for residential property • first or second mortgage • federally-related mortgage, or • assumption modifying loan terms
Information booklet	• lender must provide CFPB booklet, "Your Home Loan Toolkit"
Loan Estimate	• lender must provide CFPB's H-24 Loan Estimate of settlement costs within three days of application
Closing Disclosure	• lender must use CFPB's H-25 Closing Disclosure
Referral fees and kickbacks	• RESPA prohibits payment of referral fees and kickbacks • business relationships between firms involved in the transaction must be disclosed

Debits & Credits

Amount buyer must produce: excess of *buyer's debits* over credits

Amount seller must receive: excess of *seller's credits* over debits

Buyer's credits
- earnest money
- loan amount
- seller's share of prorations buyer will pay

Buyer's debits
- purchase price
- expenses (per agreement or custom)
- buyer's share of prorations prepaid by seller

Seller's credits

- purchase price
- buyer's share of prorated items prepaid by seller

Seller's debits

- expenses (per agreement or custom)
- seller's share of prorated items the buyer will pay
- loan balance and other liens to be paid off

Non-prorated expenses

Buyer usually pays	Seller usually pays
Mortgage recording fees Documentary stamp tax Intangible tax on mortgage Mortgage-related fees: appraisal, credit, survey, loan origination Impound reserves: insurance, taxes Attorney fees	Stamp tax on deed Title insurance Brokerage fee Inspection fees Title-related expenses Attorney fees

Prorated items

	arrears	advance
real estate taxes	x	
insurance premiums		x
mortgage interest	x	
rents received by seller		x
utilities	x	

30-Day 12-Month Proration

Formula: Monthly Amount = (Annual amount ÷ 12)
Daily Amount = (Monthly amount ÷ 30)
Proration = (Monthly amount x no. of months) + (Daily amount x no. of days)

Example: An annual tax bill is $1,800. Closing is on April 10. What is the seller's share of the taxes?

1. ($1,800 ÷ 12) = $150 monthly amount
2. ($150 ÷ 30) = $5.00 daily amount
3. ($150 x 3 months) = $450 Jan - Mar; ($5 x 10) = $50 Apr 1 - Apr 10; ($450 + 50) = $500 seller's share

---

365-Day Method

Formula: Daily amount = Annual amount ÷ 365 days; or
Daily amount = Monthly amount ÷ no. of days in month
Proration = (Daily amount x no. of days)

Example: An annual tax bill is $1,800. Closing is on April 10. What is the seller's share of the taxes?

1. ($1,800 ÷ 365) = $4.93 daily amount
2. Jan 1 thru April 10 = (31 + 28 + 31 + 10) days, or 100 days
3. ($4.93 x 100 days) = $493 seller's share

Truth-in-Lending/RESPA Integrated Disclosures Rule

Forms and Procedures
- effective since October 3, 2015
- mandatory: Your Home Loan Toolkit booklet at loan application
- Loan Estimate form: 3 business days after loan application
- Closing disclosure: 3 business days before consummation

Good faith (Loan Estimate Statement)
- Loan Estimate costs based on best information available
- Closing Disclosure costs equal estimate costs within certain tolerances

Types of charges
- no limitation on increase over estimate
- 10% tolerance charges
- 0 tolerance charges

Applicable transactions
- most closed-end consumer mortgages, including: construction loans, loans secured by vacant land, loans to trusts
- not covered: home equity loans, reverse mortgages, loans on mobile homes, loans by small lenders (no more than 5 loans per year)

The H-25 form (the Closing Disclosure Statement)
- 5 pages, variable by loan type
- Includes closing cost details, cash to close calculations, and summaries of transactions

Physical Characteristics of Real Estate

Physical characteristics
- Immobility; indestructibility; heterogeneity.

Immobility
- Land cannot be moved from one site to another; its location is forever fixed

Indestructibility
- Land is permanent and cannot be destroyed since by definition it extends below ground and into the sky
- Since land is permanent, it does not depreciate
- Only improvements depreciate and are insurable

Non-homogeneity
- Land is non-homogeneous; no two parcels of land are exactly the same since they have a different location

Physical aspects of real estate

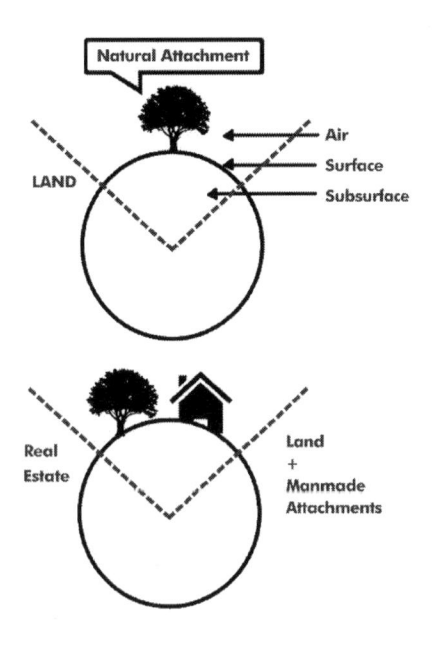

Economic Characteristics of Real Estate

Supply
- the quantity of a product or service available for sale, lease, or trade at any given time

Demand
- is the quantity of a product or service that is desired for purchase, lease, or trade at any given time

Supply / Demand / Price

Real Estate Supply:	• property available for sale or lease; measured in dwelling units, square feet, acres
Real Estate Demand:	• buyers and tenants wishing to acquire property and leaseholds; measured in households, square feet, acres
Interaction:	• if supply increases relative to demand, price decreases; • if demand increases relative to supply, price increases

Market Indicators and the Supply-Demand Cycle

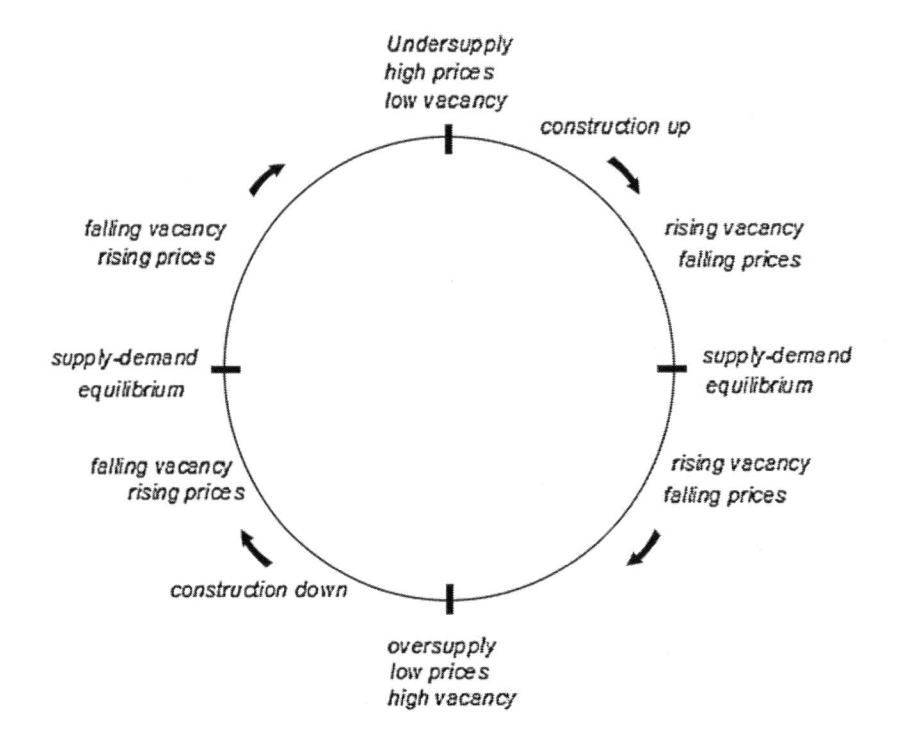

cycle repeats

Factors Influencing Supply and Demand
- cost, availability of financing
- availability of developable land
- construction costs
- capacity of infrastructure
- governmental regulation and police powers
- changes in the economic base
- in- and out-migrations of major employers
- labor availability
- land availability

Government Influences on the Real Estate Market

- local zoning power
- local control and permitting of new development
- local taxing power
- federal influence on interest rates
- environmental legislation and regulations

Market Indicators

- **Vacancy rates**
  - increases indicate buyer / tenant market & falling prices / rents
  - decreases indicate seller / landlord market & rising prices / rents

- **Building permits** – increases indicate declining vacancy; increasing prices & construction

- **Prices**
  - increases indicate rising demand or declining supply or both
  - decreases indicate falling demand or rising supply or both

SECTION 16: Real Estate Appraisal

Note: see also valuation computations in Part Two: Real Estate Math Review, Appraisal & Value Section

---

Regulation of Appraisal Practice

FIRREA

- Financial Institutions Reform, Recovery and Enforcement Act (**FIRREA**) enacted in 1989 to regulate appraisal practices
- Requires that competent individuals whose professional conduct is properly supervised perform all appraisals used in federally-related transactions
- As of January 1, 1993, federally-related appraisals must be performed only by state-certified appraisers
- **USPAP** - Uniform Standards of Professional Appraisal Practice – competency standards established by the **Appraiser Qualifications Board** of the Appraisal Foundation

Florida appraisal license types

- Registered Trainee Appraiser
- Certified Residential Appraiser
- Certified General Appraiser

Florida Value Adjustment Board

- at county level
- handles challenges to Truth in Millage (TRIM) value assessments
- property owners represented by attorney, agent, appraiser

Florida Property Owner Bill of Rights

- county appraisers required to publish list of constitutionally protected property rights on their websites

---

Concepts and Principles of Value

Supply and demand

- When demand exceeds supply, scarcity exists, values rise.
- When supply exceeds demand, surplus exists, values decline.
- When supply and demand are, the market is in balance, values stabilize.

Utility

- A property's use in the marketplace contributes to the demand for it.

Transferability

- How readily or easily title or rights to real estate can be transferred affects the property's value.

Anticipation

- The benefits a buyer expects to derive from a property over a holding period influence what the buyer is willing to pay for it.

Substitution
- A buyer will pay no more for a property than the buyer would have to pay for an equally desirable and available substitute property

Contribution
- The contribution to value of an improvement is equal to the change in market value that the addition of the improvement causes

Change
- Market conditions affect the benefits that can arise from the property

Highest and best use
- A property achieves its maximum value when it is put to whichever use generates the greatest income and return. The highest and best use must be legally permissible, physically possible, financially feasible, and maximally productive

Conformity
- A property's maximal value is attained when its form and use are consonant with surrounding properties and uses

Progression and regression
- The value of a property is influenced by the values of neighboring properties

Assemblage
- Conjoining adjacent properties can create a combined value in excess of the values of the unassembled properties. This excess value is called **plottage value**

Subdivision
- The division of a single property into smaller properties can result in a higher total value

Types of Value

Market value
- Market value is an estimate of the price at which a property will sell at a particular time. This type of value is the one generally sought in appraisals and used in brokers' estimates of value

Insured value
- Insured value is the face amount a casualty or hazard insurance policy will pay in case a property is rendered unusable

Reproduction value
- Reproduction value is the value based on the cost of constructing a precise duplicate of the subject property's improvements, assuming current construction costs.

Replacement value
- Replacement value is the value based on the cost of constructing a functional equivalent of the subject property's improvements, assuming current construction costs

Salvage value

- Salvage value refers to the nominal value of a property that has reached the end of its economic life. Salvage value is also an estimate of the price at which a structure will sell if it is dismantled and moved.

Assessed value

- Assessed value is the value of a property as estimated by a taxing authority as the basis for ad valorem taxation

Depreciated value

- Depreciated value is a value established by subtracting accumulated depreciation from the purchase price of a property

Book value

- Book value is the value of the property as carried on the accounts of the owner. The value is generally equal to the acquisition price plus capital improvements minus accumulated depreciation.

Investment value

- The value of an income property as indicated by the capitalized value of the cash flow the property generates

Market Value Requirements

The price willing buyer and seller would agree on given:

- a cash transaction
- reasonable market exposure
- parties have market and property use information
- there is no pressure to complete the transaction
- transaction is arm's length: parties are not related
- marketable title
- no hidden influences

The Appraisal Process

Appraisal Process

1. Identify the purpose
2. Assimilate the relevant data
3. Assess the highest and best use
4. Estimate the value of the land
5. Apply the three approaches to value
6. Reconcile the values from the approaches
7. Compile the report

Value Approaches: Sales Comparison Approach

Sales Comparison Approach

1. Identify comparable sales
2. Compare comps to the subject and make adjustments to the comparables
3. Weight values indicated by adjusted comparables for the final value estimate of the subject

Adjusting Comparables

Rules for selecting comparables:
- must be physically similar
- in subject's vicinity
- recently sold in arm's length sale

Rules for adjusting comparables:
- never adjust the subject!
- deduct from comparable if better than subject
- add to comp if worse than subject
- Remember: ("Subtract if Superior !")

Weighting adjustments:
- best indicator has fewest and smallest adjustments and smallest net adjustment from the sale price

Value Approaches: Cost Approach

Cost Approach

1. Estimate land value
2. Estimate replacement cost of improvements
3. Estimate total depreciation
4. Subtract: (improvements - depreciation)
5. Add: (land value + depreciated improvements)

Forms of Value Loss

Depreciation:
- **loss of value** from deterioration, functional obsolescence, or economic obsolescence

Deterioration:
- **wear and tear** from use and aging

Functional Obsolescence:
- **outmoded** physical or design **features**: curable or incurable

Economic Obsolescence:
- loss of value due to adverse **changes in surroundings**: incurable

Curability:
- curable: cost to cure is less than resulting contribution to value

- incurable: cost to cure exceeds contribution to value

Value Approaches: Income Approach

Income Approach

- Based on the principle of anticipation: the expected future income stream of a property underlies what an investor will pay for the property
- Also based on the principle of substitution: that an investor will pay no more for a subject property with a certain income stream than the investor would have to pay for another property with a similar income stream.

Steps in the Income Approach

1. Estimate potential gross income (units x rent)
2. Estimate effective gross income (potential - vacancy)
3. Estimate net operating income (NOI) (effective income - expenses)
4. Select and apply capitalization rate (NOI ÷ cap rate)

Gross Rent Multipliers

Gross rent multiplier

- Simplified income-based methods to estimate value
- Method consists of applying a multiplier to the estimated gross rent of the subject
- Multiplier is derived from market data on sale prices and gross rent
- Does not necessarily produce accurate value estimates

Formula:

- GRM = price divided by monthly rent
- Value = GRM times monthly rent

Preparing a Comparative Market Analysis

Steps

1. Identify comparables sold, for sale properties, and expired listings
2. Compile comparison data for each comparable: price, sale date, location, age, lot size, site aspects, living area, bedrooms, etc.
3. Complete adjustments for differences; rules:
   a. Never adjust the subject
   b. Add value to the comparable if a feature is inferior to the subject
   c. Subtract value from the comp if a feature is superior to the subject
4. Derive total adjustments for each comparable
5. Reconcile all value-adjusted comps to the subject to identify a value estimate

SECTION 17: Real Estate Investments and Business Opportunity Brokerage

Note: see also investment computations in Part Two: Real Estate Math Review, Investment Section

Investment Terminology

Appreciation
- An increase in the value of a property owing to economic forces beyond the control of the investor

Asset
- A tangible or intangible item of value

Basis
- A measurement of how much is invested in the property for tax purposes; **adjusted basis** is the original cost of the asset plus capital improvements minus depreciation

Capital gain (or loss)
- The difference between the net sales proceeds of an asset and its adjusted basis

Cash flow
- The remaining positive or negative amount of income an investment produces after subtracting all operating expenses and debt service from gross income

Equity
- That portion of a property's value owned by the legal owner, expressed as the difference between the property's market value and all loan balances outstanding on the property

Leverage
- The relationship between the yield rate of an investment and the interest rate of funds borrowed to finance the investment. If the yield rate is greater than the loan rate, positive leverage results. If the yield rate is less than the loan rate, negative leverage results

Liquidity
- The degree to which an investment is readily marketable, or convertible to another form of asset. If immediately salable, an investment is liquid; the longer it takes to sell, the more illiquid the investment. Real property is relatively illiquid in comparison with other types of investment

Tax shelter
- An investment that produces depreciation or other non-cash losses that a taxpayer can deduct from other income to reduce tax liability

Investment Characteristics

Ownership benefits:
- income
- appreciation
- tax shelter: depreciation and interest deductions
- inflation hedge: moves with inflation increases
- equity build-up: equity increases as loan is paid down

Ownership risks:
- relatively illiquid: not readily marketable
- management intensive: doesn't "manage" itself; requires professional oversight and maintenance
- negative leverage and price movements

Investment Entities

Direct:
- investor buys directly and manages personally

General partnership:
- all members own and manage

Limited partnership:
- general partner manages; limited partners own but do not manage

Real Estate Investment Trust:
- investors buy trust certificates; trust invests in real estate assets
- investors share returns per ownership percent

Risk Assessment

Market risk
- Changes in the demand may cause investment to lose value and become illiquid

Business risk
- Changes in the operation of a business impacting the investment may reduce the income and appreciation capacity of the investment

Purchasing power risk
- Changes in the value of money as an exchange medium, such as through inflation, may decrease the practical value of your invested resource

Financial risk
- Changes in financial markets & interest rates may reduce the value of the investment by making it less desirable and more expensive to maintain

Business Brokerage

Licensed activity
- Business brokers must be licensed in real estate
- Involves lease or fee conveyancing or dispositions

Business enterprise v business opportunity brokers
- Business enterprise brokers – engage in corporate transactions to sell or buy businesses that sell goods or services

- Business opportunity brokers – sell or buy small businesses

Comparisons between business and real property brokerage
- Different to real estate brokerage –
  - involves non-real-estate assets
  - business valued differently than real estate
  - may include corporate stock
  - may involve assuming short- and long-term liabilities
  - business market unlimited in geographic scope

- Experience & knowledge needed beyond real estate
  - corporate finance
  - business accounting
  - business valuation
  - business laws

SECTION 18: Taxes Affecting Real Estate

Note: see also taxation computations in Part Two: Real Estate Math Review, Taxation Section

Real Property Taxation

Contesting assessed value
- Obtain adjustments to assessed value with county property appraiser; 25-day deadline
- File appeal with Value Adjustment Board
- May pursue relief with the courts

Property exemptions
- Immune property: government property
- Exempt property: religious organization and nonprofit facilities
- Partial exemption: homestead exemption

Homestead exemptions
- For Florida residents' principal residence
- Must make an initial filing by March 1st
- Amount: $25,000 exemption of assessed value for total assessed values to $50,000; $50,000 exemption if assessed value is greater than $75,000; if value is between $50,000 and $75,000, exemption is $25,000 plus value amount in excess of $50,000
- Additional exemptions: $500 for blind homeowners, widows, and completely disabled residents and $5,000 for qualified disabled veterans

Greenbelt exemption
- Exemption from increasing assessed values for agricultural properties caused by growth and increasing feasibility for development

Special Assessments
- One-time tax levies for specific improvements to groups of properties; levies are applied only to those properties benefitting from the improvement

Tax lien enforcement
1. unpaid taxes →
2. tax sale ordered →
3. equitable right of redemption →
4. tax sale to pay taxes, interest, and charges →
5. statutory right of redemption →
6. tax deed to successful bidder or holder of tax certificates

Federal Income Taxes

Principal residence taxation
- Taxpayers can deduct mortgage interest, ad valorem taxes, and fees relating to mortgage loan acquisitions including points
- May also deduct portions of living area used for in-home business, with qualifications

80

Investment property income taxation

- Tax is payable on net income after mortgage interest, depreciation, and operating expenses
- Owners may not deduct reserves from income, nor loan principal
- Taxable income is payable at ordinary income tax rates
- Annual depreciation allowed is equal to the improvement value divided by the number of years in the depreciation term (established by IRS); cannot depreciate the land portion of total value

Capital gain taxation of income property

- Taxes are charged on the capital gain realized from the sale of income properties
- Capital gain is equal to the amount realized at closing (price – selling costs) minus the adjusted basis of the property (beginning basis + improvements – total depreciation)

SECTION 19: Planning and Zoning

Definitions

Building code: A standard of construction of an improved property established by local government officials

Certificate of occupancy: A document confirming that a newly constructed or renovated property has fully complied with all building codes and is ready for occupancy

Concurrency: A planning policy that requires developers to correct foreseen negative impacts of a development during the construction period of the project itself rather than afterwards

Condemnation: 1. A decree that a parcel of private property is to be taken for public use under the power of eminent domain. 2. A government order that a is no longer fit for use and must be demolished.

Deed restriction: A provision in a deed that limits or places rules on how the deeded property may be used or improved

Eminent domain: A power of a government entity to force the sale of private property for subsequent public use

Florida's Growth Management Act of 2011: Florida enacted this legislation to reduce urban sprawl.

Land use control: Regulation of how individual owners use property in a municipality or planning district. Control patterns are in accordance with a master plan

Master plan: An amalgamated land use plan for a municipality, county, or region which incorporates community opinion, the results of intensive research, and the various land use guidelines and regulations of the state. Acts as a blueprint for subsequent zoning ordinances and rulings

Non-conforming use : A legal or illegal land use that is not consistent with the current zoning ordinance

Police power: A government's legal authority to create, regulate, tax, and condemn real property in the interest of the public's health, safety, and welfare

Restriction: A limitation on the use of a property imposed by deed, zoning, state statute, or public regulation

Special exception: A land use in conflict with current zoning that is authorized because of its perceived benefit to the public welfare

Variance: A land use that conflicts with current zoning but is authorized for certain reasons, including undue hardship to comply and minimal negative impact to leave it alone

Zoning ordinance: A municipal land use regulation

Land Use Planning

Goals of land use control
- preserve property values; promote highest and best use; safeguard public health, safety and welfare; control growth; incorporate community consensus
- process: develop plan; create administration; authorize controls

The master plan
- long term growth and usage strategies; often required by state law
- local plans fuse municipal goals and needs with state and regional laws (the Florida's Growth Policy and Community Planning Act)

Planning objectives
- control growth rates: how much growth will occur and at what rate
- control growth patterns: type of growth desired, where it should be located
- accommodate demand for services and infrastructure
- save tax money
- establish adequate services
- protect against environmental issues

Plan development
- research trends and conditions; blend local and state objectives into master plan

Planning management
- commission makes rules, approves permits, codes, and development plans

Public Land Use Control

Zoning
- "police power" granted by state-level enabling acts; zoning ordinance: creates zones, usage restrictions, regulations, requirements
- Enables urban land managers to create separate land uses that do not conflict with one another nor create incompatible adjacencies

Types of zone
- residential, commercial, industrial, agricultural, public, PUD
- residential zoning regulates density or number of dwellings in an area
- commercial zoning regulates intensity, or how much commercial activity is permitted in relation to size of the site

Zoning administration
- Zoning Board of Adjustment oversees rule administration and appeals

Zoning Appeals

Nonconforming use:	- legal if use existed prior to zone creation, illegal otherwise
Variance:	- use exception granted based on hardship
Special exception:	- based on public interest
Amendment:	- change of zones; rezoning

Planned Unit Development (PUD)
- PUD zoning designed to regulate use of whole tracts of land with a singular design
- Design purposes are to achieve optimum space efficiency and open space

Subdivision regulation
- plat of subdivision and relevant requirements must be met and approved; must meet FHA requirements for insured financing

Building codes
- comprehensive onsite and offsite construction and materials standards; must be met to receive certificate of occupancy

Public acquisition and ownership
- eminent domain: public power to acquire property for public use

---

Private Land Use Control

Deed restriction
- single-property use restriction as stipulated in a deed; may not be discriminatory

Declaration restriction
- use restriction in multiple-property declarations; enforced by court injunction

Deed condition
- usage restriction that can trigger repossession by a previous owner if violated

---

Environmental Controls

Areas of concern
- air, soil, water quality; ambient health hazards; natural hazards

Major legislation
- limits damage to environment; standards for air, land, water, materials use

Responsibilities & liabilities
- disclosure and information for practitioners; remediation for owners

---

Environmental Laws

Legislation	Date	Regulated
Solid Waste Disposal Act (later part of RCRA)	1965 (1976, 1999, 2002)	landfills
Air Quality Act, Clean Air Act	1967 (1970)	air quality standards
National Environmental Policy Act (NEPA)	1969 (1970)	created EPA
Flood Control Act	amended 1969	building in flood zones; flood insurance
Resource Recovery Act	1970	solid waste disposal
Water Quality Improvement Act	1970	dumping in navigable waters; wetlands
Water Pollution Control Act amendment	1972	dumping in navigable waters; wetlands

Clean Water Act	1972 (1977)	dumping in navigable waters; wetlands
Lead-based paint ban (US Consumer Product Safety Commission rule)	1978	lead-based paint in residences
PCB ban (EPA rule)	1979	polychlorinated biphenyls
RCRA amendment	1984	underground storage tanks
Comprehensive Environmental Response, Compensation and Liability Act (CERCLA)	1980	hazardous waste disposal
Superfund Amendment and Reauthorization Act	1986	hazardous waste cleanup costs
Asbestos ban (EPA rule)	1989	asbestos in building materials
Residential Lead-based Paint Hazard Reduction Act (EPA and HUD rule)	1992 (1996)	lead-based paint disclosure and treatment
Flood Insurance Reform Act	1994	flood insurance in flood zones
Brownfields legislation	2002	industrial site cleanup
Florida's SB 552	2016	Statewide water management program

Testable Dates to Remember

Legal circumstance	Timeframe / Deadline
Eligibility period for taking state exam after passing prelicense course	2 years
DBPR to approve or deny license application	90 days of receipt
Upon application, broker applicants must have maintained an active license	2 of past 5 years
To be licensed as a Florida resident, must have continuously resided in FL (or presently with intent to reside) for	4 months
License expiration periods	every 2 years
14 hours of CE or initial post-license course must be completed by	March 31 or September 30
Florida Real Estate Commissioners serve terms of	4 years
Deadline after which license becomes null and void via voluntary non-renewal, non-completion of post-license course, or failure to activate an inactive license	2 years
Must notify FREC of mailing address change within	10 days
Florida resident licensee becoming a nonresident must notify FREC within	60 days
Brokers must retain records for	5 years
Deadline for sales associates to convey trust funds to broker	End of following business day
Broker must deposit trust funds received	Immediately or end of 3rd business day following receipt
If there is an escrow account disbursement dispute, broker must notify FREC within	15 days
Deadline to notify FREC of employer change	10 days following change
Complaints against licensees must be filed within	5 years of violation
Fair housing complaints must be made to the FL Commission on Human Relations or HUD within	1 year (2 years if suing)
FREC can suspend a license for up to	10 years
Landlord must return tenant deposit in	15 days if full; 30 days claiming a portion

Upon default, a lease termination by the landlord or tenant requires	7-day written notice
The rescission period for condominium and cooperative units is	15 days if new; 3 days if resale
The rescission period for timeshares is	10 days
Recission period for a purchased property with a homeowner's association	3 days after receipt of HOA disclosure summary
Period of continuous occupation to claim adverse possession	7 years
Easement by prescription period	7 years
Lender must provide Loan Estimate (H-24) within _____ of receiving the loan application and allow the buyer to see the Closing Disclosure (H-25) _____ before loan consummation	3 days 3 days
Buyer's right to receive copy of appraisal	3 or more business days before closing
Loan applicants must receive the CFPB booklet "Your Home Loan Toolkit" within _____ of receiving a loan application.	3 days
Homeowners can protest the assessed value of their house after the TRIM notice is mailed within	25 days
Property taxes due dates	November 1st ; delinquent on April 1st
Right of redemption period in foreclosure	Up until foreclosure sale completed
Right of redemption period in tax certificate sale	Two years from date of sale
"As-in" inspection period following sale contract execution	15 days
Copies of legal documents to principals	Upon execution

PART TWO: REAL ESTATE MATH REVIEW

Basic Math

Fractions

Adding and subtracting same denominator:

      Formula: $a/c + b/c = (a + b) \div c$

      Example: $1/2 + 1/2 = (1 + 1)/2 = 2/2 = 1$

Adding and subtracting different denominators:

      Formula: $a/c + b/d = (ad + bc)/cd$

      Example: $1/2 + 1/3 = (3 + 2)/6 = 5/6$

Multiplying:

      Formula: $(a/c) \times (b/d) = ab/cd$

      Example: $(2/5) \times (4/6) = 8/30 = 4/15$

Decimals and Percents

Converting decimals to percentages

      Formula: *Decimal number x 100 = Percentage number*

      Example: $.022 \times 100 = 2.2\%$

Converting percentages to decimals

      Formula: *Percent number $\div$ 100 = Decimal number*

      Example: $2.2 \div 100 = .022$

Multiplying percents

      Formula: *1. Percent number $\div$ 100 = Decimal number*

                       2. Beginning number x Decimal number = Product

      Example: 75% of 256 (75% x 256) = ?

                      1. $75 \div 100 = .75$

                      2. $256 \times .75 = 192$

Dividing by percents

Formula: *1. Percent number ÷ 100 = Decimal number*

                 2. Beginning number ÷ Decimal = Dividend

Example: 240 ÷ 75% = ?

                1. 75% ÷ 100 = .75

                2. 240 ÷ .75 = 320

Decimals, Fractions, and Percentages

Converting fractions to percents

Formula: (1)   a / b or a ÷ b = a divided by b = decimal number

               (2)   decimal number x 100 = percent number

Example: (1)   2 / 5 = 2 divided by 5 = 0.4

               (2)   .4 x 100 = 40%

Converting a percent to fraction and reducing it

Formula: (1)   X% = X ÷ 100 or X / 100

               (2) $\dfrac{X \div a}{100 \div a}$ where a is the largest number that divides evenly into both numerator and denominator

Example: (1)   40% = 40 ÷ 100, or 40 / 100

               (2) $\dfrac{40 \div 20}{100 \div 20} = \dfrac{2}{5}$

Converting fractions to decimals and percentages

Formula: *Decimal x 100 = Percent number*

Example: .75 x 100 = 75%

Equations

Additions and Subtractions

Formula: *if*   *a = b + c*

               then   *b = a - c (subtracting c from both sides)*

               and   *c = a - b (subtracting b from both sides)*

Example: 10   = 6 + 4

$$6 \quad = 10 - 4$$

$$4 \quad = 10 - 6$$

Multiplications and Divisions

Formula: *if* $a = b \, x \, c$

                then $b \, = \, a \, / \, c$ *(dividing both sides by c)*

                and $c \, = \, a \, / \, b$ *(dividing both sides by b)*

Example: $10 = 2 \, x \, 5$

                $2 \, = \, 10 \div 5$

                $5 \, = \, 10 \div 2$

Linear and Perimeter Measurement

Linear measure of rectangles

Formula: *Side A = Area ÷ Side B*

Example: A rectangular house has one side 40' side long and area of 1,200 SF. What is the length of the other side?

                Side A = (1,200' ÷ 40') = 30'

Perimeter measurement

Formula: *Perimeter = Sum of all sides of an object*

Example: A five-sided lot has the following dimensions:

                Side A = 50' Side B = 60'
                Side C = 70' Side D = 100'
                Side E = 30'

                What is the perimeter of the lot?

                P = 50' + 60' + 70' + 100' + 30' = 310'

Area Measurement

Square and rectangle

Formula: *Area = Width x Depth (Horizontal) or Width x Height (Vertical)*

                Width = Depth (Height) ÷ Area

                Depth (Height) = Width ÷ Area

Example: A house is 40' deep and 30' wide. What is its area?

Area = 40' x 30' = 1,200 SF

Triangle

Formula: *Area = (Height x Base) ÷ 2*

Note: Base is also sometimes referred to as "width"

Example: An A-frame house has a front facade measuring 30' across and 20' in height. What is the area of the facade?

Area = (30' x 20') ÷ 2 = 300 Square feet (SF)

Square foot-to-acre conversion

Formula: *Acres = Area SF ÷ 43,560 SF*

Example: How many acres is 196,020 SF?

196,020 SF ÷ 43,560 SF = 4.5 acres

Acre-to-square foot conversion

Formula: *SF = Number of acres x 43,560 SF*

Example: How many square feet is .75 acres?

.75 acres x 43,560 SF = 32,670 SF

Linear and Area Conversion Chart

Linear measures

(cm = centimeter; m = meter; km = kilometer)

1 inch	=	1/12 foot	=	1/36 yard		
1 foot	=	12 inches	=	1/3 yard		
1 yard	=	36 inches	=	3 feet		
1 rod	=	16.5 feet	=	1/320 mile		
1 mile	=	5280 feet	=	1760 yards	=	320 rods
1 centimeter	=	1/100 m				
1 meter	=	100 cm	=	1/1000 km		
1 kilometer	=	1,000 m				

Area measures

1 square inch	=	1/144 sq. foot				
1 square foot	=	1/9 sq. yard	=	144 sq. inches		
1 square yard	=	9 sq. feet	=	1,296 sq. inches		
1 acre	=	1/640 sq. mi	=	43,560 SF	=	208.71 ft x 208.71 ft
1 square mile	=	640 acres	=	1 section	=	1/36 township
1 section	=	1 mi x 1 mi	=	640 acres	=	1/36 township
1 township	=	6 mi x 6 mi	=	36 sq. mi	=	36 sections

Metric conversions

(cm = centimeter; m = meter; km = kilometer)

1 inch	=	2.54 cm				
1 foot	=	30.48 cm	=	.3048 m		
1 yard	=	91.44 cm	=	.9144 m		
1 mile	=	1609.3 m	=	1.60 km		
1 centimeter	=	.3937 inch				
1 meter	=	39.37 inches	=	3.28 feet	=	1.094 yards
1 kilometer	=	3,281.5 feet	=	.621 mile		

Fractions of sections, acres, and linear dimensions

Fraction		# Acres
1 section	=	640 acres
1/2 section	=	320 acres
1/4 section	=	160 acres
1/8 section	=	80 acres
1/16 section	=	40 acres
1/32 section	=	20 acres
1/64 section	=	10 acres

Calculating Area from the Legal Description

Formula:

(1) *First multiply all the denominators of the fractions in the legal description together.*

(2) *Then divide 640 by the resulting product.*

Examples: How many acres are in the Northern 1/2 of the Southwestern 1/4 of Section 6?

640 / (2 x 4) = 640 / 8 = 80 acres

How many acres are in the Western 1/2 of the Northwestern 1/4 of the Northeastern 1/4 of Section 8?

640 / (2 x 4 x 4) = 640 / 32 = 20 acres

Volume Measurement

Formula: *Volume = Width x Height x Depth*   *(assume objects with 90 degree angles)*

Base = (Height x Depth) ÷ Volume

Height = (Base x Depth) ÷ Volume

Depth = (Base x Height) ÷ Volume

Example: What is the volume of a 40' x 30' x 20' house?

40' x 30' x 20' = 24,000 cubic feet

Ownership

Condominium Assessment Calculation

Formula: *Monthly assessment = (Total annual building budget x Condo unit % of value) ÷ 12*

Example: Assume a condominium complex with a $300,000 budget and a unit that comprises 1.48% of the total value of the complex. Monthly assessment?

($300,000 x .0148) ÷ 12 = $370 monthly assessment.

Leases

Percentage Lease Rent Calculation

Formula: *Monthly percentage rent = Sales x percent of sales charged*

Example: A store generates $50,000 per month. The lease calls for 1.5% percentage rent. Monthly rent amount?

($50,000 x .015) = $750 / month

Contracts for the Sale of Real Estate

Percentage of Listing Price Calculation

Formula: *Percentage of listing price = Offer ÷ Listing price*

Example: A property listed for $150,000 receives an offer for $120,000. The offer's percentage of listing price is:

$120,000 ÷ $150,000 = 80%

Earnest Money Deposit Calculation

Formula: *Deposit = Offering price x required or market-accepted percentage*

Example: A seller requires a 2% deposit on a property listed for $320,000. The required deposit (assuming a full price offer) is:

$320,000 x 2% = $6,400

Appraisal & Value

Adjusting Comparables

Rules:
1. Never adjust the subject!

2. If the comparable is superior to the subject, subtract value from the comparable.

3. If the comparable is inferior to the subject, add value to the comparable.

Example: The subject has a $10,000 pool and no porch. A comparable that sold for $250,000 has a porch ($5,000), an extra bathroom ($6,000), and no pool.

Adjustments to comp: $250,000 (+10,000 - 5,000 - 6,000) = $249,000 indicated value of subject

Gross Rent Multiplier

Formulas: *Sales price = Monthly rental income x GRM*

Monthly rental income = Sales price / Gross Rent Multiplier

Note: Gross rent multiplier is often abbreviated as GRM.

Examples: 1. What is the value of a fourplex with monthly rent of $2,800 and a GRM of 112?

$2,800 rent x 112 GRM = $313,600

2. What is the GRM of a fourplex with monthly rent of $2,800 and a value of $313,600?

313,600 price ÷ $2,800 rent = 112 GRM

Gross Income Multiplier

Formulas   *Gross Income Multiplier = Sales price ÷ Annual income*

Sales price = Annual income x Gross Income Multiplier

Annual income = Sales price ÷ Gross Income Multiplier

Note: Gross income multiplier is often abbreviated as GIM.

Examples: 1. What is the value of a commercial property with an annual income of $33,600 and a GIM of 9.3?

$33,600 income x 9.3 GIM = $312,480

2. What is the GIM of a commercial property with annual income of $33,600 and a value of $312,480?

$313,600 price ÷ $33,600 = 9.3 GIM

Cost Approach Formula

Formula: *Value = Land value + (Improvements + Capital additions - Depreciation)*

Example: Land value = $50,000; home replacement cost = $150,000; new garage added @ $30,000; total depreciation = $10,000

94

Value = $50,000 + (150,000 + 30,000 - 10,000) = $220,000

Depreciation

Formulas: *Annual depreciation = Beginning depreciable basis ÷ Depreciation term*

Depreciable basis = (Initial property value + Any capital improvements - Land value)

Note: The depreciation term is in number of years.

Example: Property value = $500,000; land value = $110,000; depreciation term = 39 years

Step 1: ($500,000 - $110,000) = $390,000 depreciable basis

Step 2: ($390,000 ÷ 39 years) = $10,000 annual depreciation

Income Capitalization Formula

Formulas: *Value = Annual Net Operating Income ÷ Capitalization rate*

Capitalization rate = Annual Net Operating Income ÷ Value

Annual Net Operating Income = Value x Capitalization rate

Examples:
1. A property generates $490,000 net income and sells at a 7% cap rate. What is its value?

   $490,000 ÷ 7% = $7,000,000 value

2. A property has a net income of $490,000 and sells for $7,000,000. What is its cap rate?

   $490,000 ÷ 7,000,000 = .07, or 7%

3. A property's value is $7,000,000 and the cap rate is 7%. What is the property's net operating income?

   $7,000,000 x .07 = $490,000

Net Operating Income (NOI, Net Income)

Formula: *NOI = Potential rent - Vacancy loss + Other income - Operating expenses*

Note: NOI does not include debt payments!

Example: A building has 10 office suites generating annual potential rent of $10,000 each. Vacancy = 10% and annual expenses are $35,000. Vending machines yield $5,000. What is the NOI?

95

$100,000 rent - 10,000 vacancy + 5,000 other income - 35,000 expenses = $60,000 NOI

Finance

Points

Definition: 1 point = 1% of the loan amount or .01 x loan amount

Formulas: *Points = Fee paid ÷ Loan amount*

    Fee paid = Loan amount x Points

    Loan amount = Fee paid ÷ Points

Examples:
1. A borrower pays $500 for a $10,000 loan. How many points are paid?

    $500 ÷ 10,000 = .05 = 5 points

2. A borrower pays 5 points on a $10,000 loan. What is the fee paid?

    $10,000 x .05 = $500

3. A borrower pays $500 as 5 points on a loan. What is the loan amount?

    $500 ÷ .05 = $10,000

Rules of Thumb: 1 point charged raises lender's yield by .125%

    8 points charged raises lender's yield by 1%

Example: A lender wants to yield 7% on a 6.5% loan. How many points must he or she charge?

    (7% - 6.5%) = .5%

    .5% ÷ .125% = 4 points

Interest Rate, Principal and Payment

Caveat!

    Interest rates in mortgage financing apply to the <u>annual</u> interest payment and <u>exclude</u> principal payment. Remember to convert annual payments to monthly or vice versa as the question requires, and to exclude principal payments from your calculations!

Formulas: *Payment = Principal x Rate*

    Principal = Payment ÷ Rate

    Rate = Payment ÷ Principal

Examples:
1. A borrower has a $100,000 loan @ 6% interest. What are the annual and monthly payments?

Annual payment = $100,000 x .06 = $6,000
Monthly payment = $6,000 ÷ 12 = $500

2. A borrower has a $500 monthly payment on a 6% loan. What is the loan principal?

Principal = ($500 x 12) ÷ 6% = ($6,000 ÷ .06) = $100,000

3. A borrower has a $500 monthly payment on a $100,000 loan. What is the loan rate?

Rate = ($500 x 12) ÷ $100,000 = ($6,000 ÷ 100,000) = .06 = 6%

Total Interest, Interest Rate, and Loan Term

Formulas: *Interest-only loan:*   *Total interest = Loan amount x Rate x Term in years*

               Amortized loan: *Total interest = (Monthly PI payment x 12 x term) - Loan amount*

Examples: 1. A borrower obtains a 10-year interest only loan of $50,000 @ 6%. How much interest will he or she pay?

               ($50,000 x .06 x 10) = $30,000

            2. A borrower obtains a 10-year amortized loan of $50,000 @ 6% with monthly payments of $555.10. How much interest will he or she pay?

               ($555.10 x 12 x 10) - $50,000 = $16,612

Amortization Calculation

Formulas: *Month 1:*   *Principal paid = Monthly payment - (Loan amount x Rate ÷ 12)*

               Month 2:   *New loan amount = (Previous month principal - Principal paid)*

                              Principal paid = Monthly payment - (New loan amount x Rate ÷ 12)

Example: A borrower obtains a 30-year $100,000 amortized loan @ 7% with a $665.31 monthly payment. What is the principal paid in the second month?

               Month 1:   Principal paid = $665.31 - ($100,000 x 7% ÷ 12) = $665.31 - (583.33 interest paid) = $81.98

               Month 2:   New loan amount = $100,000 previous month beginning loan amount - $81.98 principal paid = $99,918.02

                            Principal paid = $665.31 - ($99,918.02 x 7% ÷ 12) = $665.31 - (582.86 interest paid) = $82.45

Loan Constants

Formulas: *Monthly payment = (Loan amount x Loan constant) / 1000*

Loan amount = (Monthly payment ÷ Loan constant) x 1000

Loan constant = (Monthly payment ÷ Loan amount) x 1000

Examples:
1. A borrower obtains a loan for $100,000 with a 6.3207 constant. What is the monthly payment?

    Monthly payment = ($100,000 ÷ 1,000) x 6.3207 = $632.07

2. A borrower has a monthly payment of $632.07 on a loan with a monthly constant of 6.3207. What is the loan amount?

    Loan amount = ($632.07 ÷ 6.3207) x 1000 = $100,000

3. A borrower obtains a loan for $100,000 with a monthly payment of $632.07. What is the loan constant?

    Loan constant = ($632.07 ÷ $100,000) x 1,000 = 6.3207

Loan - to - Value Ratio (LTV)

Formulas: *LTV ratio = Loan ÷ Price (Value)*

Loan = LTV ratio x Price (Value)

Price (Value) = Loan ÷ LTV ratio

Examples:
1. A borrower can get a $265,600 loan on a $332,000 home. What is her LTV ratio?

    LTV Ratio = $265,600 ÷ 332,000 = 80%

2. A borrower can get an 80% loan on a $332,000 home. What is the loan amount?

    Loan = $332,000 x .80 = $265,600

3. A borrower obtained an 80% loan for $265,600. What was the price of the home?

    Price (value) = $265,600 ÷ .80 = $332,000

Financial Qualification

Income ratio qualification

Formula: *Monthly Principal & Interest (PI) payment = Income ratio x Monthly gross income*

Example: A lender uses a 28% income ratio for the PI payment. A borrower grosses $30,000 per year. What monthly PI payment can the borrower afford?

Monthly PI payment = ($30,000 ÷ 12) x .28 = $700

How much can the borrower borrow if the loan constant is 6.3207? (See also- loan constants)

Loan amount = ($700 ÷ 6.3207) x 1,000 = $110,747.22

Debt ratio qualification

Formulas: *Debt ratio = (Housing expense + Other debt payments) ÷ Monthly gross income*

Housing expense = (Monthly gross income x Debt ratio) - Other debt payments

Example: A lender uses a 36% debt ratio. A borrower earns $30,000 / year and has monthly non-housing debt payments of $500. What housing payment can she afford?

Housing expense = ($30,000 ÷ 12 x .36) - 500 = ($900 - 500) = $400

Investment

Appreciation Calculations

Simple appreciation

Formulas: *Total appreciation = Current value - Original price*

Total appreciation rate = Total appreciation ÷ Original price

Average annual appreciation rate = Total appreciation rate ÷ number of years

One year appreciation rate = (Annual appreciation amount) ÷ (Value at beginning of year)

Examples: 1.   A home purchased for $200,000 five years ago is now worth $300,000. What are the total appreciation amount, total appreciation rate, and average appreciation rate?

Total appreciation = ($300,000 - 200,000), or $100,000

Total appreciation rate = ($100,000 ÷ 200,000), or 50%

Average annual appreciation rate = 50% ÷ 5 years = 10%

2. A home costing $250,000 is worth $268,000 one year later. What is the one-year appreciation rate?

One-year appreciation rate = ($18,000 ÷ 250,000) = 7.2%

Compounded appreciation

Formula: *Appreciated value = Beginning value x (1+ annual rate) x (1+ annual rate) ......*
for the number of years in question

Example: A $100,000 property is expected to appreciate 5% each year for the next 3 years. What will be its appreciated value at the end of this period?

Appreciated value = $100,000 x 1.05 x 1.05 x 1.05 = $115,762.50

Rate of Return, Investment Value, Income

Formulas: Where Income = net operating income (NOI); Rate = rate of return, cap rate, or percent yield; and Value = value, price or investment amount:

Rate = Income ÷ Value

Value = Income ÷ Rate

Income = Value x Rate

Examples: 1. An office building has $200,000 net income and sold for $3,200,000. What was the rate of return?

Rate = ($200,000 NOI ÷ 3,200,000 price) = 6.25%

2. An office building has $200,000 net income and a cap rate of 6.25%. What is its value?

Value = ($200,000 ÷ 6.25%) = $3,200,000

3. An office building sells for $3,200,000 at a cap rate of 6.25%. What is its NOI?

Income = $3,200,000 x 6.25% = $200,000

Basis, Adjusted Basis, and Capital Gain

Formulas: *Capital gain = Amount realized - Adjusted basis, where*

Amount realized = Sale price - Selling costs

Adjusted basis = Beginning basis + Capital improvements - Total depreciation

Total depreciation = (Beginning depreciable basis ÷ Depreciation term in years) x Years depreciated

Depreciable basis = Initial property value + Capital improvements - Land value

Example: Tip: work example backwards from last formula to first formula.

An apartment building was purchased for $500,000, with the land value estimated to be $100,000. The owner added a $100,000 parking lot. The property was depreciated on a 40-year schedule (for present purposes!). Three years later the property sold for $700,000, and selling costs were $50,000. What was the capital gain?

1. depreciable basis = $500,000 purchase price + 100,000 parking lot - 100,000 land = $500,000

2. total depreciation = ($500,000 ÷ 40 years) x 3 years = $37,500

3. adjusted basis = $500,000 purchase price + 100,000 parking lot - 37,500 total depreciation = $562,500

4. amount realized = $700,000 sale price - 50,000 selling costs = $650,000

5. capital gain = $650,000 amount realized - 562,500 adjusted basis = $87,500

Depreciation

Formulas: *Annual depreciation = (Beginning depreciable basis) ÷ (Depreciation term in number of years)*

Depreciable basis = (Initial property value + Capital improvements - Land value)

Example: Property value = $500,000; land value = $110,000; depreciation term = 39 years

1. ($500,000 - 110,000) = $390,000 depreciable basis

2. ($390,000 ÷ 39 years) = $10,000 annual depreciation

Equity

Formula: *Equity = Current market value - Current loan balance(s)*

Example: A home that was purchased for $150,000 with a $100,000 loan is now worth $300,000. The current loan balance is $80,000. What is the homeowner's equity?

Equity = $300,000 value - $80,000 debt = $220,000

Net Income

Formula: *NOI = Potential rent - Vacancy loss + Other income - Operating expenses*

Note: NOI does not include debt payments!

Example: A building has 10 office suites generating annual potential rent of $10,000 each. Vacancy = 10% and annual expenses are $35,000. Vending machines yield $5,000. What is the NOI?

$100,000 rent - 10,000 vacancy + 5,000 other income - 35,000 expenses = $60,000 NOI

Cash Flow

Formula: *Cash flow = (Net Operating Income - Debt service) where debt service is PI payment*

Example: A building generates $100,000 NOI after expenses and has a debt payment of $40,000. What is its cash flow?

Cash flow = $100,000 - 40,000 = $60,000

Investment Property Income Tax Liability

Formula: *Tax liability = (NOI + Reserves - Interest expense - Depreciation) x Tax bracket*

Example: An office building has NOI of $200,000, an annual reserve expense of $20,000, interest expense of $130,000 and annual depreciation of $50,000. Assuming a 28% tax bracket, what is its income tax liability?

Tax liability = ($200,000 + 20,000 - 130,000 - 50,000) x 28% = $11,200

Return on Investment

Formula: *ROI = NOI ÷ Price*

Example: An investment property generates a cash flow of $100,000 and appraises for $1,500,000. What is the owner's return on investment?

ROI = $100,000 ÷ 1,500,000 = 6.67%

Return on Equity

Formula: *ROE = Cash flow ÷ Equity*

Example: An investment property generates a cash flow of $100,000. The owner has $500,000 equity in the property. What is the owner's return on equity?

ROE= $100,000 ÷ 500,000 = 20%

Real Estate Taxation

Converting Mill Rates

Definition: 1 mill = $.001; a mill rate of 1 mill per $1,000 = .1%; a 1% tax rate = 10 mills

Formula: *Tax = (Taxable value ÷ 1000)   x Mill rate*

Example: A tax rate on a house with a $200,000 taxable value is 7 mills per thousand dollars of assessed valuation. What is the tax?

Tax = ($200,000 ÷ 1,000) x 7 mills = $1,400

Tax Base

Formula: *Tax base = Assessed valuations – Exemptions*

Example: A town has a total assessed valuation of $20,000,000 and exemptions of $4,000,000. What is the tax base?

$20,000,000 - 4,000,000 = $16,000,000

Tax Rate, Base, and Requirement

Formulas: *Tax rate = Tax requirement ÷ Tax base*

Tax base = Tax requirement ÷ Tax rate

Tax requirement = Tax base x Rate

Example: A town has a tax base of $160,000,000 and a budget of $8,000,000. What is the tax rate?

Tax rate = ($8,000,000 ÷ 160,000,000) = .05, or 5%, or 50 mills

Special Assessments

Formula: *Special assessment = Total special assessment cost x Homeowner's share*

Example: A homeowner owns 100' of an 800' seawall that must be repaired. The total assessment will be $80,000. What is the homeowner's assessment?

1.   Homeowner's share = 100' ÷ 800' = .125, or 12.5%

2.   Special assessment = $80,000 x 12.5% = $10,000

Commissions

Commission Splits

Formulas:

Total commission = Sale price x Commission rate

Co-brokerage split = Total commission x Co-brokerage percent

Agent split = Co-brokerage split x Agent percent

Broker split = Co-brokerage split - Agent split

Example:

A $300,000 property sells at a 7% commission with a 50-50 co-brokerage split and a 60% agent split with her broker. What are total, co-brokerage, agent's, and broker's commissions?

Total commission = $300,000 x .07 = $21,000

Co-brokerage splits = $300,000 x .07 x .50 = $10,500

Agent split = $10,500 x .60 = $6,300

Agent's broker's split = $10.500 - 6,300 = $4,200

Seller's Net

Formula:

Seller's net = Sale Price - (sale price x commission) - Other closing costs - Loan balance

Example:

A home sells for $260,000 and has a loan balance of $200,000 at closing. The commission is 7% and other closing costs are $2,000. What is the seller's net?

Seller's net = ($260,000 - (260,000 x .07) - 2,000 - 200,000) = $39,800

Price to Net an Amount

Formula:

Sale Price = (Desired net + Closing costs + Loan payoff)) (1 - Commission rate)

Example:

A homeseller wants to net $50,000. The commission is 7%, the loan payoff is $150,000, and closing costs are $4,000. What must the price be?

Sale price = ($50,000 + 4,000 + 150,000) ÷ .93 = $219,355

Closing Costs, Prorations

30-Day 12-Month Method

Formulas:

Monthly amount = Annual amount / 12

Daily amount = Monthly amount / 30

> *Proration = (Monthly amount multiplied by the # months) + (Daily amount multiplied by the # days)*

Example: An annual tax bill is $1,800. Closing is on April 10. What is the seller's share of the taxes?

  1. Monthly amount = ($1,800 ÷ 12) = $150; no. of months = 3

  2. Daily amount = ($150 ÷ 30) = $5.00; no. of days = 10

  3. Proration = ($150 x 3) + ($5 x 10) = ($450 + 50) = $500 seller's share

365-Day Method

Formula: *Daily amount = (Annual amount ÷ 365) or (Monthly amount ÷ Length of month)*

Proration = Daily amount multiplied by the # days

Example: An annual tax bill is $1,800. Closing is on April 10. What is the seller's share of the taxes?

  1. Daily amount = ($1,800 ÷ 365) = $4.93

  2. Jan 1 thru April 10 = (31 + 28 + 31 + 10) days, or 100 days

  3. Proration = $4.93 x 100 days = $493 seller's share

Income Received in Advance (Rent)

Logic: *Credit buyer and debit seller for buyer's share*

Example: Seller receives $1,000 rent. The month is ¾ over.

  1. Buyer's share is ($1,000 x 25%) = $250

  2. Credit buyer / debit seller $250.

Expenses paid in Arrears (Tax)

Logic: *Credit buyer and debit seller for seller's share*

Example: Buyer will pay $1,000 taxes. The year is ¾ over.

  1. Buyer's share is ($1,000 x 25%) = $250

  2. Credit buyer / debit seller $750.

Insurance Coverage

Recovery with Co-Insurance Clauses

Formula: Recovery = (Damage claim) x (Percent replacement cost covered ÷ Minimum coverage requirement)

Example: An owner insures a home for $100,000. Replacement cost is $150,000. A co-insurance clause requires coverage of 80% of replacement cost to avoid penalty. Fire destroys the house. What can the owner recover from the insurer?

Claim recovery = $150,000 x (67% cost covered ÷ 80% required) = $125,625

PART THREE: PRACTICE TESTS

Section 1 Test: The Real Estate Business

1.1   Real estate brokerage is primarily concerned with which of the following activities?

    a. Locating buyers for a seller's residence and a seller's residence for a buyer's purchase.
    b. Procuring a buyer or a tenant for an owner or landlord, and vice versa.
    c. Managing sales agents in a brokerage office.
    d. Managing real estate portfolios of every property type.

1.2   The principal forms of property-type specializations are which of the following?

    a. Agricultural, commercial, and residential properties
    b. Residential, retail, industrial, office, farm and land and special purpose properties
    c. Residential, industrial, and retail properties
    d. Owned and leased properties

1.3   Real estate license laws are commonly created and administered at what level of government?

    a. Municipal jurisdictions
    b. County government
    c. State government
    d. Federal government

1.4   Isabella is looking to buy a new home. She went to a subdivision developer who offered a choice of floor plans and lots to choose from. What type of home is Isabella considering in this example?

    a. A spec home
    b. A special assessment home
    c. A tract home
    d. A corporate home

1.5   Isabella decided to purchase an empty lot and is working with a builder on what features she wants the new house to have. She has signed a sales contract before the construction has started. What type of home has Isabella decided to go with in this example?

    a. A spec home
    b. A custom home
    c. A cooperative home
    d. A proforma home

Section 2 Test: Florida License Law & Qualifications for Licensure

2.1 Harold filed his application for sales associate licensure 31 days ago. To date he has not heard if his application has been approved or not. What is the status of Harold's application?

    a. It is still pending approval until 60 days have passed.
    b. It is still pending approval until 90 days have passed.
    c. It is automatically approved because 30 days have passed.
    d. It is automatically denied because 30 days have passed.

2.2 A licensed broker in Georgia moved to Florida 6 months ago and now wants to apply for a Florida broker's license under the mutual recognition agreement between Florida and Georgia. What must the broker do to obtain the Florida license under this agreement?

    a. The broker must complete Florida's post-license educational requirements and pass the licensure exam.
    b. The broker must pass the license law exam and pay the application fee.
    c. The broker must submit an application and a certification license history from Georgia.
    d. The broker is not eligible for a Florida license under the mutual recognition agreement.

2.3 Which of the following is the most accurate definition of real estate broker?

    a. A person who buys and sells real estate for others, regardless of compensation
    b. A person who buys, sells, and manages real estate for a broker employer for compensation
    c. A person who buys or sells real estate on behalf of others for compensation
    d. A person who buys, sells, or manages real estate on behalf of others

2.4 Which Florida statute establishes real estate licensees' legal rights and responsibilities?

    a. Chapter 455
    b. Chapter 475
    c. Chapter 120
    d. Chapter 61J2

2.5 What is the best definition for "real estate"?

    a. Selling, buying, leasing, appraising, auctioning, exchanging for compensation
    b. Interest in land, business enterprises, or business opportunities with some exceptions
    c. Houses, apartments, mobile homes, condominiums, or commercial space for rent or sale
    d. The business of creating a brokerage for offering specific services

2.6 Which of the following is a requirement of the general licensing provisions?

    a. 21 years of age
    b. 2 year college degree
    c. U.S. citizen
    d. Social Security number

2.7 Florida sales associate educational requirements include

    a. 75 hours of FREC-approved courses
    b. 55 hours of post-licensing coursework prior to initial license expiration
    c. 14 hours of continuing education every 2 years
    d. 2-year college degree in real estate

2.8   Florida broker pre-license requirements include

    a. passing the broker exam with a score of 60%.
    b. 3 years of real estate experience during the previous 5 years.
    c. holding a Florida sales associate license for previous 12 months.
    d. 72 hours of pre-licensing coursework.

2.9   Which of the following real estate services can legally be offered by someone not licensed as a real
       estate broker, broker associate, or sales associate?

    a. An individual negotiating a sale of real property
    b. A property management firm paying a $200 referral fee to an unlicensed apartment tenant
    c. An apartment complex owner's employee working from an offsite office
    d. An individual renting properly licensed public lodging

2.10   Which of the following must be licensed as a real estate broker, broker associate, or sales associate?

    a. Anyone acting as an attorney
    b. Anyone procuring purchasers of business opportunities
    c. Anyone selling cemetery lots
    d. Anyone renting mobile home park lots

2.11   Lisa is a full-time graduate student in an appraising degree program at the University of South
       Florida. All of Lisa's appraisal activities are being supervised by Ken who is a licensed real estate
       broker. What type of license must Lisa have to perform the appraisal activities she is involved in?

    a. Sales associate license
    b. Appraiser license
    c. Broker associate license
    d. No license

2.12   If Charlie submits an application for licensure, completes the educational requirements, but does not
       pass the licensing exam, when will Charlie's application expire?

    a. 30 days after failing the exam
    b. 2 years after it was received
    c. 1 year after failing the exam
    d. Never

2.13   To meet the continuing education requirements for either a sales associate or a broker, what can a
       licensee substitute for 3 classroom hours of coursework?

    a. Attendance at a legal agenda session of the Commission
    b. An approved course on real estate issues relevant to the modern practice of real estate by a
       licensee
    c. An approved course on technology used in the real estate industry
    d. Any of the above

2.14   A broker's post-license education requirement includes

    a. passing end-of-course exam.
    b. 72 classroom hours of coursework.
    c. 60 hours of coursework within 30 days of initial license expiration.
    d. 14 classroom hours every 2 years.

2.15 Ted is a licensed real estate broker in Florida, but he is moving to North Dakota to live. What should Ted do about his Florida broker license?

a. Apply to use his Florida license in North Dakota through a mutual recognition agreement
b. Notify the Commission of his change of residency and comply with nonresident requirements
c. Exchange his Florida license for a North Dakota license within 60 days of arriving in that state
d. Use his Florida license in North Dakota since the licensing requirements there are the same as in Florida

2.16 If an applicant omitted information on the license application, within what time frame must the applicant be notified to correct the error?

a. 10 days
b. 30 days
c. 60 days
d. 90 days

2.17 If an applicant makes an error on the license application, the license may be denied if the error is not corrected. What is the exception to this rule?

a. The error was accidental.
b. The applicant was not notified of the error within the designated time period.
c. The application was from a licensed sales associate applying for a broker's license.
d. The error was not in regard to civil or criminal offenses.

2.18 Which Florida statute or code covers the Commission's administrative rules that include detailed principles for real estate practice?

a. Chapter 61J2
b. Chapter 20
c. Chapter 475
d. Chapter 455

2.19 Which statute established general provisions for the Department of Business and Professional Regulation?

a. Chapter 475
b. Chapter 455
c. Chapter 20
d. Chapter 120

3.1 The Florida Real Estate Commission consists of

    a. seven members, all appointed by the Governor.
    b. seven members, only 4 of whom are appointed by the Governor.
    c. nine members, all appointed by the Governor.
    d. four members, all licensed brokers and appointed by the Governor.

3.2 Which of the following is true regarding the Florida Real Estate Commission?

    a. Members may not teach real estate courses.
    b. Disciplinary powers of the Commission may be delegated to any member.
    c. Any attorney employed by the Commission may prosecute a matter.
    d. The Commission is responsible for fostering the education of brokers in the principles that should govern their conduct.

3.3 If a broker's license has become void during a period of economic hardship, when can his license be reinstated?

    a. It can be reinstated after 2 years.
    b. It can be reinstated within 6 months.
    c. It can be reinstated as sales associate license after 5 years.
    d. It cannot be reinstated.

3.4 Tania has just received her sales associate license. When must she complete her post-license education requirements?

    a. Within the first year after licensure
    b. Prior to the first renewal of her license
    c. Within 1 year after the renewal of her license
    d. Prior to receiving the 90-day renewal notice

3.5 Broker John changed his business address and did not notify the Commission during the required time period. What is the status of John's license?

    a. It is void.
    b. It is in voluntary inactive status.
    c. It has ceased to be in force.
    d. It has been suspended.

3.6 Which of the following is a duty or power of the Department of Business and Professional Regulation?

    a. Suspend the license of a broker who is not in compliance with a support order
    b. Establish license and examination fees
    c. Adopt a seal for authenticating its proceedings
    d. Educate real estate professionals in ethical, legal, and business principles

4.1   An agency relationship is formed when a customer

    a. asks for information about a particular property.
    b. asks questions about a broker's services and qualifications.
    c. pays a broker for help.
    d. gives a broker authority to act on his/her behalf.

4.2   Which type of agency is illegal in Florida?

    a. Universal
    b. Dual
    c. Special
    d. General

4.3   What is the purpose of the Brokerage Relationship Disclosure Act?

    a. To provide customers with a greater understanding of real estate transactions and broker relationships
    b. To discipline real estate brokers for not complying with the requirements for disclosures in real estate transactions
    c. To outline the duties of designated sales associates in real estate transactions
    d. To give real estate customers options for action against brokers who misrepresent their relationship and duties to customers

4.4   The disclosure requirements for authorized brokerage relationships apply only to

    a. commercial property.
    b. agricultural property.
    c. residential property.
    d. nonresidential property.

4.5   The best definition of designated sales associates is

    a. individuals who have obtained their sales associate licensure.
    b. the sales associates who work for a particular real estate firm.
    c. sales associates who are acting as single agents under certain conditions in the same transaction.
    d. sales associates who are assigned to one particular customer.

4.6   A customer must sign a disclosure showing his or her assets are $1 million or more when in a brokerage relationship with a

    a. transaction broker.
    b. subagent.
    c. single agent.
    d. designated sales associate.

4.7   Which type of property would not be classified as residential?

    a. Single family house
    b. 5 acres of agricultural property
    c. 10 residential units in one building
    d. Residential triplex

4.8   Which of the following is a duty of a transaction broker but not a duty of a single agent?

   a. Limited confidentiality
   b. Disclosure of known material facts
   c. Disclosure of duties in writing
   d. Obedience

4.9   Florida's real estate disclosure requirements apply in which of the following situations?

   a. The transaction involves a nonresidential property.
   b. The 3-residential-unit property is being rented with an option to buy.
   c. The signing of a simple month-to-month lease by a residential tenant.
   d. The broker is engaged in a conversation with an industrial tenant where no confidential
      information is exchanged.

4.10   A broker who represents as a fiduciary both the buyer and seller in a real estate transaction is a

   a. transaction broker.
   b. single agent.
   c. dual agent.
   d. subagent.

4.11   In Florida, it is presumed that all licensees are operating as transaction brokers unless

   a. the customer asks for a single agent relationship.
   b. the broker designates a sales associate to act as a single agent.
   c. another type of relationship is established in writing.
   d. the customer wants no brokerage relationship.

4.12   In a brokerage relationship that involves designated sales associates, what is the role of the broker?

   a. To advise and assist the sales associates
   b. To advise the customers about all facets of the transaction
   c. To coordinate the relationship between the customer and the sales associate
   d. To coordinate the sharing of all confidential information between the seller and the buyer

4.13   The Brokerage Relationship Disclosure Act

   a. re-establishes dual agency.
   b. establishes brokerage representation disclosure requirements.
   c. allows a single agent to represent both the buyer and the seller in the same transaction.
   d. requires transaction brokers to provide fiduciary representation to the buyer, the seller, or both in
      the same transaction.

4.14   The disclosure requirements covered in the Brokerage Relationship Disclosure Act only apply to

   a. commercial properties being sold.
   b. properties rented with an option to buy.
   c. agricultural properties with 10 or more acres.
   d. residential sales.

4.15   The main difference between a single agent and a transaction agent is

   a. the duty to disclose known material facts.
   b. the fiduciary representation to one customer.
   c. when offers must be presented to the seller.
   d. accounting for funds.

4.16 Chuck is selling a duplex he owns. He has asked Broker Terrance to simply show the property for him. What type of broker relationship do these two men have?

   a. Transaction broker relationship
   b. Single agent relationship
   c. Subagent relationship
   d. No brokerage relationship

4.17 In the practice of real estate, what is the common term used if a licensee brags that a property located near a large park is "in the best part of town"?

   a. Misrepresentation
   b. Fraud
   c. Puffing
   d. Exaggeration

4.18 Florida law prohibits a real estate agent from making deceptive representations related to the practice of real estate. Which of the following would be considered a deceptive representation of the practice?

   a. A broker encourages a client to contact to contact a lawyer about the status of their property's title.
   b. A broker informs a potential buyer that the area's zoning will soon change.
   c. A sales associate claiming her license allows her to open her own real estate firm.
   d. A sales associate helping their client fill in the blanks of prepared sales contract.

4.19 What might be the best way to conduct an ethical real estate practice?

   a. Copy the behavior of any other agent
   b. Apply the Golden Rule
   c. Research statutes for ethics regulation
   d. Simply follow what is legal

4.20 When may a sales associate be registered as a general partner in a brokerage firm?

   a. When designated as such by the employer broker
   b. When registered under the directing broker of the firm
   c. When employed as full time employee and not independent contractor
   d. May not under Florida statutes regarding registration of general partners

4.21 Under what conditions may a sales associate collect a commission for a real estate transaction?

   a. If the sales association obtains permission from his or her employer to collect the commission in the sales associate's name
   b. If the sales associate collects the commission in his or her own name
   c. If the sales associate has permission from his or her employer to collect the commission and collects it in the employer's name
   d. If the sales associate performed all acts for the transaction

4.22 Sales associate Ken wants to sell Susan's property and earn a commission for doing so. How may Ken legally sell the property and earn the commission?

   a. Ken would follow the same steps any broker would follow to sell the property.
   b. Ken would need to act under his registered employer and collect the commission in his employer's name.
   c. Ken would surprise his employer by selling the property on his own and then collect the commission in his own name.
   d. There is no way for Ken to legally sell the property and earn the commission.

4.23 The agency relationship is defined by

    a. the Realtor Code of Ethics.
    b. the laws of agency, or in some states, by statute.
    c. the law of real estate contracts.
    d. the agreement between a principal and an agent.

4.24 Which of the following is true of the connection between compensation and the agency relationship?

    a. An agreement to give and receive compensation creates an agency relationship.
    b. If an agency relationship exists, the principal must provide valuable consideration to the agent.
    c. The relationship is independent of any compensation arrangement.
    d. If an agency relationship exists, the agent is entitled to compensation.

4.25 One of the parties to an agency relationship defaults, and the agreement terminates. Which of the following is true?

    a. All obligations are extinguished.
    b. Both parties must continue to perform all other obligations of the agreement.
    c. The defaulting party may have a financial consequence.
    d. The damaged party has no claim against the defaulting party.

4.26 Among the fiduciary duties imposed on a real estate agent is the requirement to

    a. refuse offers the agent knows will be unacceptable to the principal.
    b. present all offers to the principal regardless of their amount.
    c. advise the principal against accepting an offer that is below full price.
    d. advise a prospect that the principal will not accept the prospect's offer in order to elicit a better offer.

4.27 One of the agent's fiduciary duties that continues even after a listing agreement expires is

    a. obedience.
    b. diligence.
    c. confidentiality.
    d. disclosure.

4.28 The standard of care and competence that a principal can expect from an agent is generally that which is

    a. specified in the agency agreement.
    b. necessary to earn the promised compensation.
    c. necessary to procure a customer.
    d. comparable to that of other practitioners in the area.

4.29 Agent Michael is showing his new listing to a buyer who informs him that he has just inherited five million dollars. Michael is now bound by fiduciary duty to

    a. keep the information in confidence.
    b. disclose the information to the buyer's agent.
    c. disclose the information to the seller.
    d. verify the buyer's statements before disclosing them to the client.

4.30 Agent Gerry has executed an exclusive buyer broker agreement with the Andersons. The agent subsequently places an offer with Melinda, the exclusive selling agent for the Lincolns, to buy their lakefront property. The offer contains provisions for the Lincolns to pay the brokerage commission, which the Lincolns agree to. Given this set of circumstances, Gerry owes the full set of fiduciary duties to

a. the Andersons.
b. the Lincolns.
c. Gerry's broker.
d. Melinda's broker.

4.31 A subagent is the agent of

a. the seller.
b. the buyer.
c. a broker who has an agency relationship with a client.
d. the client's and the customer's agents.

4.32 Which of the following is a dual agency situation?

a. Two agents share the exclusive right to represent the same client on all transactions.
b. One agent represents both sides in a transaction.
c. A selling agent from one brokerage works with a listing agent from another brokerage to complete a transaction.
d. One agent represents two sellers at the same time.

4.33 The duties of a transaction broker or facilitator include

a. preserving the confidentiality of information received from either party.
b. helping the two parties achieve their respective objectives.
c. disclosing material facts that affect the value of the property to both parties.
d. choosing to obey the instructions of one party and informing the other party of the decision.

4.34 In which of the following contact situations would a seller's agent be expected to disclose his agency relationships?

a. The agent is showing the client's property to a prospective buyer.
b. The agent tells an acquaintance at a party about the client's property.
c. The agent answers questions about the client's property for a telephone caller responding to a newspaper ad.
d. The agent is showing a potential buyer houses in a certain price range in the multiple listing book.

4.35 The essential foundation of the agency relationship consists of

a. mutual respect, compensation, and confidentiality.
b. diligence, results, and compensation.
c. service, marketing, and respect.
d. good faith, trust and confidence.

4.36 Audrey wants to take a vacation. To do so, she authorizes an agent to conduct the operations of one of her business enterprises. The kind of agency she has established is

a. limited.
b. general.
c. universal.
d. special.

4.37 A property seller empowers an agent to market and sell a property on his behalf. The kind of agency represented is

a. general.
b. special.
c. universal.
d. no agency.

4.38 Implied agency arises when

a. an agent accepts an oral listing.
b. a principal accepts an oral listing.
c. a party creates an agency relationship outside of an express agreement.
d. a principal agrees to all terms of a written listing agreement, whether express or implied.

4.39 An agency relationship may be involuntarily terminated for which of the following reasons?

a. Condemnation of the property.
b. Mutual consent.
c. Full performance.
d. Renewal of the agent's license.

4.40 A principal discloses that she would sell a property for $500,000. During the listing period, the house is listed and marketed for $530,000. No offers come in, and the listing expires. Three weeks later, the agent confides to a customer that the seller would have sold for less than the listed price. Which of the following is true?

a. The agent has violated the duty of confidentiality.
b. The agent has fulfilled all fiduciary duties, since the listing has expired.
c. The agent is violating the duties owed this customer.
d. The agent has created a dual agency situation with the customer.

4.41 A principal instructs an agent to market a property only to families on the west side of the university campus. The agent refuses to comply. In this case,

a. the agent has violated fiduciary duty.
b. the agent has not violated fiduciary duty.
c. the agent is liable for breaching the listing terms.
d. the agent should obey the instruction to salvage the listing.

4.42 An owner's agent is showing a buyer a residential property for sale. The buyer notices water stains on the foundation walls and floor, and informs the agent. The appropriate course of action for the agent is to

a. immediately contract to paint the ceiling.
b. immediately contract to repair the roof.
c. suggest the buyer make a lower-price offer.
d. inform the seller.

4.43 The meaning and salient characteristics of the agency relationship should be disclosed to the client

a. prior to completing a listing agreement.
b. prior to or upon completion of an offer.
c. upon the initial contact with the person.
d. prior to showing properties.

4.44   When must a listing agent disclose his or her agency relationship to prospective tenants or buyers?

     a. Immediately prior to the initial contact.
     b. Upon initial contact.
     c. Whenever substantive communication is made beyond casual conversation.
     d. Immediately following any offer executed by the customer.

4.45   A buyer agent or tenant representative should disclose his or her agency relationship to the owner's agent

     a. immediately prior to the initial contact.
     b. upon initial contact.
     c. immediately prior to substantive contact.
     d. immediately following any offer executed by the landlord.

4.46   An agent is operating as a disclosed dual agent on a transaction. In this case, the agent

     a. may not represent one party's interests to the detriment of the other.
     b. must operate without a listing agreement.
     c. must be obedient and loyal to both parties.
     d. must require that the principals refrain from disclosing any material facts to him.

4.47   An agent informs a buyer that a provision in a contract is very commonplace. After explaining the clause, the agent assures the buyer that the clause does not mean anything significant. If something goes wrong with the transaction, the agent could be liable for

     a. violating duties owed a customer.
     b. misinterpreting the clause.
     c. intentional misrepresentation.
     d. practicing law without a license.

Section 5 Test: Real Estate Brokerage Activities and Procedures

5.1   Which of the following is required of a brokerage office?

    a. Locked file cabinets
    b. At least three total rooms
    c. Entrance sign
    d. Separate conference room

5.2   Which of the following statements is FALSE?

    a. All advertising must include the brokerage phone number and image of the broker.
    b. Advertising must not be deceptive.
    c. The broker's name must appear on advertising as it is registered with the FREC.
    d. In online ads, the brokerage name must appear in close proximity to the contact information.

5.3   Regarding escrow accounts, which of the following is true?

    a. Sales associates must deposit funds into the account the same day they are received.
    b. A broker may designate a sales associate to be signatory on all accounts.
    c. The brokers has a lien on all escrow deposits.
    d. The broker has 30 days to correct any account errors.

5.4   If escrow funds are held by a title company,

    a. the title company must provide a deposit receipt within 5 days of deposit being received.
    b. the title company must provide written verification of receipt of a deposit directly to the seller if the seller is represented by a broker.
    c. the licensee must name the title company on the sales contract.
    d. the licensee must provide verification of deposit receipt within 10 days of deposit due date.

5.5   Examples of antitrust violations would include which of the following?

    a.   Blockbusting and adverse possession
    b.   Redlining and police powers
    c.   Point of beginning and market rebalancing
    d.   Collusion, price fixing, and market allocation

5.6   The Florida Antitrust Act of 1980 was enacted

    a. to complement the federal antitrust laws.
    b. to replace federal antitrust regulations in Florida.
    c. because federal antitrust laws are outdated.
    d. because there are no federal antitrust laws.

5.7   A broker has not violated Florida antitrust laws if he/she

    a. meets with another brokerage to compare listed properties.
    b. meets with another brokerage to set the percentage amount of commission splits offered in the market.
    c. gets other brokers to boycott a competitor for discounting rates.
    d. agrees with another brokers to set commission rates.

5.8   A sales associate may collect a commission directly from the seller only when

   a. he/she has performed real estate services for the seller.
   b. his/her employer consents.
   c. he/she has sued the seller.
   d. he/she collects the commission in his/her own name.

5.9   If Sales Associate Bob is working with a listing agreement that provides for a 7% commission, how much would Bob actually receive if the selling price of the property is $200,000 and the buyer's broker is to receive half of the overall commission and Bob is to receive half of his broker employer's cut?

   a. $14,000
   b. $7,000
   c. $3,500
   d. $1,750

5.10   What is a kickback?

   a. The action taken when a new employer kicks the sales associate back to a previous employer
   b. The action taken when a broker applicant fails the license examination and must retake it
   c. Monies paid to the FREC when renewing a license
   d. Monies paid to a broker for using a particular service provider during a real estate transaction

5.11   If a broker receives a kickback, what must he or she do?

   a. Disclose it to all involved parties
   b. Deposit the funds into an escrow account
   c. Notify his or her employer
   d. Never use the particular service provider again

5.12   Which of the following statements is true regarding a sales associate's changing employers?

   a. The former employer must notify the FREC within 30 days of the associate's termination.
   b. Unless the former employer's license has been suspended, the associate's license remains in force during the change of employer.
   c. The associate must notify the FREC on a prescribed form within 5 days of termination.
   d. The associate may not remove any records from the former employer's office.

5.13   Which of the following statements is false when a business entity wishes to register as a brokerage?

   a. The entity must have at least one active broker or sales associate as an officer, director, member, manager, or partner.
   b. The entity must submit an application for brokerage and pay a fee.
   c. A broker-associate may be an officer, director, member, manager, or partner of the entity only if he/she has been upgraded to an active broker.
   d. A sales associate may not be an officer, director, member, manager, or partner of the entity.

5.14   Which of the following business entities may not register as a brokerage?

   a. Sole proprietorship
   b. Corporate sole
   c. General partnership
   d. LLC

5.15 A trade name must not

   a. be included on an office entrance sign.
   b. be included in the FREC's records.
   c. be on a broker's license.
   d. be used by a sales associate.

5.16 An unlicensed associate may not

   a. compute commission checks.
   b. sign a listing agreement.
   c. prepare advertising for broker approval.
   d. deposit trust monies.

5.17 A broker-associate may be a business entity officer, director, or partner if he/she

   a. works for a broker.
   b. has an active broker-associate license.
   c. upgrades to an active broker.
   d. manages the entity.

5.18 If a sales associate terminates his employment with one broker and becomes employed with another
      broker, what happens to the associate's license?

   a. It is suspended.
   b. It ceases to be in force.
   c. It is revoked.
   d. It remains inactive.

5.19 Broker Chad received an under-the-table payment from Tom's Home Inspection Services for
      recommending Tom to a home buyer.

   a. Chad must not tell the seller about the payment.
   b. Chad must not claim the payment on his income taxes.
   c. Chad must deposit the payment into an escrow account related to the same transaction.
   d. Chad must tell everyone involved in the same transaction about the payment.

5.20 Broker Sal sold Owner John's home and is not being paid his commission. What type of lien rights
      does Sal have for the unpaid commission?

   a. Sal has lien rights against John's net proceeds from the sale of the property.
   b. Sal has a lien on John's real property for the unpaid commission.
   c. Sal has no lien rights for the unpaid commission.
   d. Sal has lien rights limited to the value of the property, regardless of the sale price.

5.21 In what they believed was a smart business decision, Roy's Realty and Wescott brokerages have
      created a monopoly for real estate services in their small town of Bakersville. Was this indeed a
      smart business decision? Why or why not?

   a. Yes, because it will allow substantial business growth
   b. Maybe, maybe not, depending on how many other brokerages are in the area
   c. No, because the town is small and doesn't afford the growth potential they are looking for
   d. No, because they have violated antitrust laws

5.22 What is the statute of limitation for filing any action in a claim for an antitrust law violation?

   a. 30 days
   b. 90 days
   c. 3 years
   d. 4 years

5.23 Florida allows brokers to deposit personal funds into a sales escrow account. What is the allowed limit of personal funds?

a. $500
b. $1,000
c. $1,500
d. $5,000

5.24 Florida allows brokers to deposit personal funds into a property management escrow account. What is the allowed amount of personal funds in this type of account?

a. $500
b. $1,000
c. $1,500
d. $5,000

5.25 When may escrow account funds be disbursed?

a. As needed
b. When the transaction closes
c. When depositor determines
d. When seller agrees

5.26 What is the broker's monthly responsibility regarding all escrow accounts?

a. Disburse funds where needed
b. Deposit received funds into accounts and pay interest to FREC
c. Create a written statement of liabilities and balances
d. Provide DBPR with copies of all deposit slips for the accounts

5.27 Which of the following information is not required as part of the minimum information to be included in an escrow account statement-reconciliation?

a. Reconciliation date
b. Names of depositors
c. Outstanding checks
d. Name of bank

5.28 Under Florida Deceptive and Unfair Trade Practices, the penalty for willful unfair or fraudulent advertising is

a. civil penalty of not more than $10,000.
b. loss of real estate license.
c. reprimand by FREC.
d. $25,000 fine.

5.29 Additional brokerage offices are deemed as branch offices if

a. the same broker works from all of the offices.
b. the name of the broker is displayed on all the offices.
c. they are all in the same city.
d. they are all in the same county.

5.30   If a broker's registered office is located outside Florida, which of the following is correct?

    a. The broker must pay an annual $300 foreign office fee to FREC.
    b. The broker is not regulated by FREC if their office is outside Florida, even if they practice real estate in Florida.
    c. The broker must personally appear at any office of the FREC if requested in relation to an investigation.
    d. FREC will not issue licenses to brokers with offices outside Florida.

5.31   If a broker conducts business at a location other than the principal brokerage office, what is the broker required to do?

    a. Include the address of the second location on all advertising for the principal brokerage
    b. Register the second location as a branch office
    c. Actively work from both offices
    d. Staff both offices with sales associates and unlicensed assistants

5.32   A broker is required to immediately deposit any trust funds received. Under Florida real estate law, how is "immediately" defined?

    a. As soon as the funds are received
    b. By the end of the same day
    c. Within 3 business days
    d. Within 5 days

5.33   Where may trust funds not be deposited?

    a. Credit union
    b. Broker's business account
    c. Savings and loan
    d. Title company with trust powers

5.34   If an escrow account's record shows a negative balance, what must the broker do?

    a. Personally make up the difference to bring the account back into a positive balance
    b. Meet with bank personnel to determine the cause for the negative balance
    c. Transfer funds from another account to remove the negative balance
    d. Note the cause and corrective action taken

5.35   If there is a dispute involving the amount of the broker's commission, what may the broker do regarding the trust funds in the associated escrow account?

    a. Disburse the commission payment to him/herself
    b. Retain the commission amount in the account until the dispute is resolved
    c. Move the commission amount to another escrow account until the dispute is resolved
    d. Nothing; the funds do not belong to the broker.

5.36   A sales associate may form which of the following types of company using the name they are legally licensed under?

    a. A C corporation
    b. A limited liability corporation
    c. A S corporation
    d. A partnership

5.37   Violators of Florida antitrust laws can be sued for recovery of

    a. three times the amount of the damage.
    b. a maximum of $5,000.
    c. a minimum of $10,000.
    d. the exact amount of damage.

6.1   Which of the following is not required when filing a complaint against a licensee for a rule or regulation violation?

    a. Complaint must be in writing.
    b. Complaint must be signed by the complainant.
    c. Complaint must be legally sufficient.
    d. Complaint must include witnesses to the action.

6.2   Which of the following is not an option for the respondent to a filed complaint?

    a. Dispute the allegations and be provided an informal hearing
    b. Not dispute the allegations and waive the right to a hearing
    c. Dispute the allegations and request a formal hearing
    d. Not dispute the allegations and request an informal hearing

6.3   A licensee who has received a final order of guilty for a violation complaint may appeal the order

    a. to the probable cause panel.
    b. within 30 days after the final order.
    c. only if the licensee initially disputed the allegations.
    d. only if the licensee was provided an informal hearing.

6.4   What happens if a complainant withdraws a complaint against a licensee?

    a. The complainant is always disciplined for filing an erroneous complaint.
    b. The complaint may not be refiled at any time.
    c. The complaint may be investigated anyway.
    d. The licensee must file suit against the complainant.

6.5   If an applicant for licensure has not successfully passed the licensure examination,

    a. his/her license can be canceled.
    b. his/her license can be denied.
    c. he/she can be fined.
    d. he/she must submit a new application within 30 days.

6.6   To avoid denial of licensure, an applicant

    a. must be 21 years old.
    b. must not have been disbarred.
    c. must have performed real estate services for 1 year prior to application for licensure.
    d. must hold a college degree.

6.7   The FREC may suspend a license

    a. for a period no longer than 2 years.
    b. for a period no longer than 3 years.
    c. for a period no longer than 5 years.
    d. for a period no longer than 10 years.

6.8   Revocation of a license

    a. is limited to a period of 1 year.
    b. is limited to a period of 5 years.
    c. is limited to a period of 10 years.
    d. is permanent.

6.9   If Broker Bob knowingly files a false complaint against Broker Tom, what can happen to Bob?

a. He may be fined $5,000.
b. His license may be canceled.
c. He may be barred from practicing real estate for 15 years.
d. His license may be suspended.

6.10 If Broker Bob knowingly files a second and then third false complaint against Broker Tom, what can happen to Bob?

a. He may be fined $5,000.
b. His license may be canceled.
c. He may be barred from practicing real estate permanently.
d. His license may be suspended.

6.11 Which of the following is not an administrative penalty for law or rules violations?

a. Reprimand
b. License cancelation
c. Probation
d. Fine

6.12 What is the maximum imprisonment time allowed for a misdemeanor of the second degree?

a. 60 days
b. 6 months
c. 1 year
d. No prison time

6.13 Being compensated for practicing real estate without a license is a

a. misdemeanor of the second degree.
b. misdemeanor of the third degree.
c. felony of the first degree.
d. felony of the third degree.

6.14 A notice of noncompliance may be issued for a minor violation. Which of the following falls within the statutory guidelines of a "minor violation"?

a. Broker Hale failed to maintain a sign at his brokerage office.
b. Broker Terry misappropriated $15,000 worth of escrow funds.
c. Sales associate Randy intentionally did not disclose to a buyer that a property's basement floods.
d. Sandra does not have a real estate license but has sold over 5 houses for compensation.

6.15 Property Seller Sue believes she has a valid case against Broker Bob because Sue suffered monetary damages due to Bob's action as her real estate agent. Before Sue can seek recovery payment from the Florida Real Estate Recovery Fund, who must determine whether or not she suffered the damages?

a. The FREC
b. The DBPR
c. A civil court
d. A probable cause panel

6.16 To qualify for recovery funds, the complainant must file a claim within

a. 6 months of discovery of the damaging act.
b. 90 days of discovery of the damaging act.
c. 2 years of discovery of the damaging act.
d. 5 years of discovery of the damaging act.

6.17   A person may be qualified to make a claim for recovery from the Real Estate Recovery Fund if

    a. the person is thc debtor's spouse.
    b. the person is the licensed single agent in the transaction listed in the claim.
    c. the licensee is the owner of the property involved in the transaction.
    d. the person notified the FREC of the claim by certified mail.

6.18   Payments from the Real Estate Recovery Fund are limited for each broker to an aggregate

    a. $50,000
    b. $100,000
    c. $150,000
    d. $250,000

6.19   When the DRE attorneys and the licensee and his/her attorneys come to an agreement regarding the statement of facts and the imposed penalty associated with a complaint, this is known as

    a. mediation.
    b. probable cause.
    c. voluntary relinquishment for permanent revocation.
    d. stipulation.

6.20   Charlene, who is located in Michigan, is looking to purchase a home in Florida based solely on her broker's recommendations because she will not see the home prior to purchase. Her broker has told her that he found a beautiful home on a lake that is just what she is looking for. In actuality, the home is a fixer-upper at best, and the lake is infested with alligators and poisonous snakes. Which of the following statements is FALSE?

    a. Charlene may use the broker's email describing the house and photos of the house received after closing as legally sufficient grounds for filing a complaint against the broker.
    b. The broker has demonstrated moral turpitude.
    c. The broker is guilty of breach of trust.
    d. Charlene should file a citation against the broker.

6.21   If a licensee is suspended prior to any hearing for a complaint of a serious law violation, this action is known as a

    a. summary suspension order.
    b. subpoena.
    c. probable cause
    d. stipulation.

6.22   What is the purpose of the Disciplinary Guidelines set forth by the FREC?

    a. To limit the penalties the FREC may impose
    b. To provide complainants with anticipated results of complaints
    c. To give notice to licensees of the range of penalties allowed for each count during a hearing
    d. To outline penalties allowed for mitigating circumstances

Section 7 Test: Federal and State Laws Pertaining to Real Estate

7.1 The fair housing law that first protected people against discrimination in housing based on race was the

    a. Civil Rights Act of 1866.
    b. Civil Rights Act of 1968.
    c. Executive Order 11063 of 1962.
    d. Title VIII amendment to the Fair Housing Act.

7.2 The classes protected against discrimination by the Fair Housing Act of 1968 are

    a. race only.
    b. religion and gender only.
    c. race, color, religion, and national origin.
    d. age and gender only.

7.3 An agent is committing an act of discriminatory advertising by doing which of the following?

    a. Telling prospective buyers about the positive and negative aspects of a certain neighborhood.
    b. Telling a prospective seller that now would be a good time to put a property on the market.
    c. Advertising a property as available to individuals of a particular race.
    d. Telling a prospective buyer that the agent is too busy to show the buyer properties personally on a given day.

7.4 Which of the following is an example of blockbusting?

    a. An agent shows a minority home buyer properties located in a neighborhood where there are no other minority home owners.
    b. An agent persuades a minority home buyer to avoid looking in a neighborhood where there are no minority home owners.
    c. An agent persuades a family to put their house on the market because ethnic minority families are beginning to move into the neighborhood.
    d. An agent persuades a minority home buyer to buy a property located in an area where most of the home owners belong to minority groups.

7.5 The practice of redlining is specifically prohibited by

    a. The Home Mortgage Disclosure Act.
    b. The Real Estate Settlement Procedures Act.
    c. The Civil Rights Act of 1866.
    d. The Americans with Disabilities Act.

7.6 Title VIII of the Civil Rights Act of 1968 applies to the sale of

    a. all single-family residences.
    b. all privately owned single-family residences.
    c. privately owned single-family residences listed with a broker.
    d. privately owned single-family residences for sale by owner.

7.7 A broker signs a listing agreement to sell a home for $200,000. An immigrant couple are interested in the house and ask the agent the price. The agent states the price as $210,000. According to the fair housing laws, such an action is

    a. illegal, because the agent changed the terms of the sale to discourage this particular couple.
    b. illegal, because the agent violated the listing agreement.
    c. legal, because the quoted price increase did not exceed 10% of the listing price.
    d. legal, because the increased price does not necessarily exclude the couple.

7.8 Which of the following actions is allowed under federal fair housing laws?

    a. A broker, following the instructions of the seller, advertises the property as for sale to Christian families only.
    b. A home seller, acting without a broker, places a "for sale-- mature, single men only" sign in front of the house.
    c. The owner of four rental houses advertises one of the properties for rent to married couples, no children, no pets.
    d. The owner of a duplex who resides in one of the units refuses to rent the other unit to a non-Christian.

7.9 Cecily Longstreet believes a real estate agent has kept her from seeing a certain property for rent because she is a woman. What actions should she take if she wants legal satisfaction for her complaint?

    a. File charges of illegal discrimination with the police department that has jurisdiction over the local area.
    b. File a complaint with HUD and/or file suit against the offending parties in a state or federal court within the prescribed time period.
    c. Wait two years and then file a civil suit in federal court.
    d. Sue HUD for damages under the Civil rights Act of 1866.

7.10 George Scott hires Shannon Lang to sell his house, with the condition that he will not be the first one in the neighborhood to sell to members of a certain ethnic group. What should Shannon do about this condition?

    a. Inform Scott that the condition is illegal and that she cannot comply with it.
    b. Note the condition on the listing agreement and have Scott initial it.
    c. Pretend that she did not hear the condition and proceed to market the property to all groups.
    d. Tell Scott that she will try to discourage members of that group from looking at the property, but that she cannot control cooperating brokers.

7.11 Under federal fair housing laws, the owner of a ten-unit apartment building may legally

    a. advertise that the property is not available to anyone requiring wheelchair access.
    b. refuse to rent to aliens.
    c. require families without children to pay the same security deposit that families with children must pay.
    d. require tenants to move out when they become 62 years old.

7.12 Sam Gough wants to rent out his home, but wants to exclude families with children because of his belief that they cause damage. Under what conditions would federal fair housing laws allow Gough to rent on these terms?

    a. The owner has a consistent no-children policy in all his rental properties.
    b. The owner can prove that costs to repair damage caused by previous tenants with children exceeded the tenants' security deposit.
    c. It is a single-family house that is part of a federally-designated planned unit development.
    d. It is a single-family house, and the owner owns only one other rental home in addition to his own residence.

7.13 Which of the following laws or rulings extended discrimination to include gender, handicapped status, and family status?

a. Executive Order 11063.
b. the Civil Rights Act of 1968.
c. the Fair Housing Amendments Act of 1988.
d. Jones v Mayer.

7.14 The Wallaces, a minority family, would like to buy a home in a certain price range. Agent Ambrose shows the family all available properties in a neighborhood of families with similar backgrounds. Ambrose does not mention a number of homes in the family's price range in other neighborhoods. This agent could be liable for

a. blockbusting.
b. providing unequal services.
c. steering.
d. nothing; his services were legal and acceptable.

7.15 An agent does not like a particular minority buyer, and is very short with the person, refusing to engage in lengthy conversation or show him any properties. A second minority party visits the office the next day. The agent is very forthcoming, and shows the person five prospective properties. This agent could be liable for

a. providing unequal services.
b. steering.
c. misrepresentation.
d. nothing; both parties were minorities, and therefore no discrimination occurred.

7.16 Following the client's recommendation, an agent conceals the availability of a property from an employed but pregnant and unmarried minority woman. This agent could be liable for

a. discriminatory misrepresentation by omission.
b. steering.
c. violating fiduciary duty.
d. nothing: an agent may show or not show any property at his or her discretion.

7.17 Discrimination based on age is expressly prohibited in which of the following?

a. Advertising housing
b. Housing sale
c. Employment
d. Real estate brokerage service

7.18 An aggrieved person must file a fair housing complaint with the FREC

a. immediately when alleged discrimination occurs.
b. within 100 days of discrimination allegation.
c. within 6 months of discrimination allegation.
d. within 1 year of discrimination allegation.

7.19 Sinkholes are common in Florida where there are limestone deposits. Which Florida agency would be most helpful to contact if a sinkhole develops on your property?

a. FL Department of Environmental Protection
b. FL Real Estate Commission (FREC)
c. FL Department of the Interior
d. FL Housing Division

7.20 Which of the following is covered by the provisions of the Florida Residential Landlord and Tenant Act?

a. A private drug rehabilitation facility
b. A hotel
c. A leased condominium
d. A leased cooperative apartment

7.21 If a landlord intends to claim a security deposit to cover damages by the vacating tenant, what must the landlord do?

a. File suit in circuit court
b. Notify the tenant before he/she has vacated the premises
c. Notify the tenant within 30 days of his/her vacating the premises
d. Simply transfer the security deposit to the landlord's personal account

7.22 Under the Florida Constitution, homesteads are protected from

a. property taxes.
b. tax liens for unpaid taxes.
c. forced sale to satisfy liens.
d. foreclosure.

7.23 Which of the following is not a basis for the granting of additional homestead ?

a. Familial status
b. Disability
c. Age
d. Non-school-district levies

7.24 Which of the following is allowed by the Florida Fair Lending Act?

a. Penalties for paying loan in full before due date
b. Lender requiring borrowers to refinance every 18 months
c. Lender recommending the borrower default on the loan
d. Lending based on borrower income

7.25 Which of the following contracts would be covered by Florida's Statute of Frauds?

a. A 3-month lease
b. A six month listing agreement
c. A purchase contract on a property for $109,000
d. A 7-month lease

7.26 Which of the following must be disclosed regarding radon gas?

a. The date testing was completed
b. The level of gas found as a result of testing
c. An explanation of what radon gas is
d. Testing compliance requirements

7.27 What is the purpose of the property tax disclosure?

a. To notify the buyer that a homestead tax exemption is available
b. To notify the buyer that future taxes may be different than the current taxes
c. To notify the buyer how much income taxes will be due from the sale
d. To notify the buyer that the seller has unpaid property taxes

7.28 One feature common to both real estate brokerage and business brokerage is

    a. valuation methodologies.
    b. assumption of short- and long-term liabilities.
    c. unlimited geographic scope.
    d. real property transactions.

8.1   Which of the following would be defined as real estate as opposed to real property?

      a. Wells, driveways, and signs on a parcel of land.
      b. Mobile homes temporarily parked on a parcel of land.
      c. Timber that has been cut and is lying on a parcel of land.
      d. Business equipment an owner or tenant has placed on a parcel of land.

8.2   Which of the following would be considered a property improvement?

      a. An alteration to land to make it more useful.
      b. An increase in the value of a property.
      c. A chicken coop permanently attached to land.
      d. A set of farming tools located in the tool shed.

8.3   Which of the following best describes the physical boundaries of land?

      a. The surface of the earth and infinite space above the surface.
      b. The center of the earth and infinite space above the earth.
      c. The surface of the earth and all water and minerals on or below the surface to the center of the earth.
      d. The surface of the earth and the air rights above the surface to the point defined by local zoning.

8.4   The "bundle of rights" refers to a set of rights

      a. enjoyed by the owner of a property.
      b. that is synonymous with the Bill of Rights.
      c. guaranteed to citizens by the Statute of Rights.
      d. specified in a deed or land contract.

8.5   Which of the following best describes the legal concept of personal property?

      a. Any item which is acquired in a fee simple sale transaction.
      b. Any item of property that is not definable as real property.
      c. Any movable property owned by an individual, partnership, or corporation.
      d. Any item that is not a natural item affixed to the earth.

8.6   The right to encumber a property means that the owner can

      a. sell the property to an encumbered party.
      b. pledge the property as collateral for debt.
      c. lease the property.
      d. assign the bundle of rights to another.

8.7   A property owner leases 60 acres of agricultural land for a renewable period of 5 years. In the context of real estate rights, this lease represents a(n)

      a. transfer of a portion of the bundle of rights.
      b. encroachment on the bundle of rights.
      c. conveyance of the complete bundle of rights.
      d. encumbrance of the tenant's rights.

8.8   A homeowner is very upset over a drone that a neighbor flies over his house. He takes his case to
       court to end this possible violation of rights. Does he have a case, and on what basis?

       a. No. The neighbor is not physically on his property.
       b. No. The drone is in the air, so he cannot exercise any surface rights.
       c. Yes. The owner has the right to stop encroachments.
       d. Yes. The drones infringe on his air rights.

8.9   Littoral rights apply to which of the following?

       a. Boatable ponds entirely contained within the boundaries of an owner's property.
       b. Streams and rivers.
       c. Navigable lakes, seas, and oceans.
       d. Navigable streams and rivers.

8.10   A retired couple has just bought a retirement home with a pier on a large lake. In this case the
       retirees' water rights extend to

       a. the high water mark of the body of water at the shoreline.
       b. the low water mark of the body of water at the shoreline.
       c. the center of the lake.
       d. the end of the pier.

8.11   A waterfront homeowner has just died. What will become of the water rights the owner enjoyed
       while living in the home?

       a. They revert to the state when the property is sold.
       b. They are extinguished.
       c. They are a personal right belonging to an individual owner, not attaching to the real property.
       d. They transfer with the property when the property is sold.

8.12   Riparian rights concern which of the following bodies of water?

       a. Lakes.
       b. Seas and oceans.
       c. Streams and rivers.
       d. Navigable lakes.

8.13   Which of the following best describes a "fixture?"

       a. Any item of personal property positioned within the boundaries of a parcel of real estate.
       b. An item of personal property that has been converted to real property.
       c. An item of real property temporarily placed on land for the purpose of conducting a business.
       d. An item of personal property that has been left in one location for a period of six months.

8.14   An item may be considered personal property as opposed to real property provided that

       a. the owner intended to remove it after a period of time.
       b. it can be removed without altering the appearance of the structure.
       c. it is unnecessary to the physical integrity of the structure.
       d. the owner installed it at some time after acquiring the real property.

8.15   Two people own a house, each having an undivided equal interest. Which of the following best
       describes what each party owns?

       a. Fifty percent of the physical house and the land it rests on.
       b   One hundred percent of the home and the land.
       c. Fifty percent of the estate consisting of the indivisible whole of the real property.
       d. Each owns one hundred percent of the estate represented by the real property and fifty percent of
           the physical house and the land it rests on.

8.16 A real property interest that includes the right to possess is considered

   a. an estate in land.
   b. a leasehold estate.
   c. a fee simple estate.
   d. the bundle of rights.

8.17 The right to control land usage by zoning and eminent domain is an example of

   a. a public interest.
   b. a police interest.
   c. an encumbrance.
   d. an estate in law.

8.18 If the duration of an owner's rights in an estate is not determinable, the owner has

   a. a tenancy at sufferance.
   b. a leased fee simple estate.
   c. a freehold estate.
   d. a leasehold estate.

8.19 The distinguishing feature of a leasehold estate is

   a. ownership of an interest by a tenant.
   b. temporary ownership of the full bundle of rights in a property.
   c. unlimited ownership of one right in the bundle of rights in a property.
   d. that the estate is limited by a lease term.

8.20 Paul gives Dennis a life estate and designates Lucy as the remainderman. Dennis sells the property to Allen. When Dennis dies who owns the property as a fee simple estate?

   a. The state of Florida
   b. Dennis
   c. Paul
   d. Lucy

8.21 Ned grants his sister Alice an estate for as long as she lives. Her descendants, however, cannot inherit the estate. What kind of estate is it?

   a. An estate pur autre vie.
   b. An estate for years.
   c. An ordinary life estate.
   d. A legal life estate.

8.22 Homestead estates are examples of

   a. a conventional life estate.
   b. a legal life estate.
   c. an estate created by an owner's agreement.
   d. a fee simple absolute.

8.23 Louis owned a boat and a house before marrying Barbara. While she was single, Barbara owned a new car. The two got married and bought a second home. As a wedding present, Barbara's father bought Louis a motorcycle. Under the law of community property, what property can Louis sell without his wife's consent or signature?

   a. The boat and house.
   b. The boat, house, and motorcycle.
   c. The second home and the motorcycle.
   d. The boat and motorcycle.

8.24 Katelyn rents an apartment for one year. What rights has she acquired under the leasehold?

   a. The right to exclude everyone from the premises.
   b. The right to encumber the fee interest.
   c. The right to sell the premises.
   d. The right to possess and use the premises.

8.25 An estate from period-to-period will continue as long as

   a. the tenant makes, and landlord accepts, regular rent payments.
   b. the term specified in the lease.
   c. the period is less than a year.
   d. the landlord has not sold the property.

8.26 An estate at will
   a. cannot be terminated.
   b. is terminated only if so stated in the lessee's last will and testament.
   c. terminates on the death of lessor or lessee.
   d. terminates on the date specified in the lease agreement.

8.27 A tenant continues to occupy an apartment after lease expiration without the consent of the landlord. This type of estate is called

   a. an estate at sufferance.
   b. a holdover estate.
   c. a canceled leasehold.
   d. a hostile leasehold.

8.28 A tenant without a lease has been sending the landlord monthly rent checks, and the landlord continues to accept the payments. What kind of leasehold estate exists?

   a. Estate for years.
   b. Estate from period to period.
   c. Estate at will.
   d. Estate at sufferance.

8.29 A fee or life estate is held by an individual. This form of estate is referred to as a(an)

   a. tenancy in severalty.
   b. tenancy by the entireties.
   c. absolute fee simple.
   d. legal fee simple.

8.30 Six people have identical rights in a property and enjoy an indivisible interest. However any of the owners may sell or transfer his/her interest without consent of the others. This form of ownership is a

   a. joint tenancy.
   b. homestead ownership.
   c. tenancy in common.
   d. estate in severalty.

8.31 The "four unities" required to create a joint tenancy include which of the following conditions?

a. Parties must acquire respective interests at the same time.
b. Parties must be residents of the same state at the time of acquiring the interest.
c. Parties must be family members.
d. Parties must have joint financial responsibility.

8.32 Unlike tenants in common, joint tenants

a. own distinct portions of the physical property.
b. cannot will their interest to a party outside the tenancy.
c. may own unequal shares of the property.
d. cannot encumber their interest to outside parties.

8.33 Which of the following life estates is created by operation of law rather than by the owner?

a. Conventional life estate.
b. Ordinary life estate.
c. Legal life estate.
d. Community property life estate.

8.34 Which of the following is true of a homestead?

a. A homestead interest cannot be conveyed by one spouse.
b. A homestead interest cannot be passed to the children of the head of household.
c. A homestead interest is a form of conventional life estate.
d. A homestead is a primary or secondary residence occupied by a family.

8.35 A tenant in common can

a. sell or transfer his interest without the consent of the other tenants in common.
b. use his or her interest in the estate to encumber the entire estate.
c. sell, encumber or transfer his or her interest only to the other tenants in common.
d. sell, encumber or transfer his or her interest only with the consent of all the other tenants in common.

8.36 Which of the following would be considered community property?

a. Property acquired before the marriage
b. A motorcycle bought after the marriage with separate property marital funds
c. Income derived from community property during the marriage
d. A mother's heirloom wedding ring gifted to the wife after her wedding

8.37 When real property is held in a land trust, who controls the property?

a. The trustor
b. The trustee
c. The beneficiary
d. The mortgagee

8.38 In a separate property state, John marries Patricia. Prior to the marriage John owned an SUV. During the marriage, John bought a Buick, John and Patricia bought a second property with money earned from Patricia's job, and each individual received a motorcycle from Patricia's uncle as a gift. What property will be split during the divorce?

a. The SUV, the Buick, and the second property.
b. The SUV, the Buick, the second property, and the motorcycles.
c. The Buick and the second property.
d. The Buick, the second property, and the motorcycles.

136

8.39   Which of the following is true of a cooperative?

a. A cooperative may hold an owner liable for the unpaid operating expenses of other tenants.
b. The owners have a fee simple interest in the airspace of their respective apartments.
c. Owners may sublease their apartments even if they sell their stock in the cooperative.
d. The proprietary lease is guaranteed to have a fixed rate of rent over the life of the lease term.

8.40   Which of the following is true of a tenancy in common?

a. The co-owners must be related.
b. The owners enjoy an indivisible interest.
c. The tenants must acquire their interests at the same time.
d. The tenants must pay equal amounts for their interest in the estate.

8.41   Carissa and Robert acquire a condominium as tenants in common. In this circumstance, Carissa can

a. sell her interest to a third party without the consent of Robert.
b. use her interest in the estate to mortgage the entire estate.
c. sell her interest only to Robert.
d. sell encumber or transfer her interest only with the consent of Robert.

8.42   When a tenant in common dies, what happens to the tenant's interest in the estate?
a. It is divided equally among the surviving tenants in common.
b. The surviving tenants must buy the interest from the deceased tenant's heirs or sell their interests to the heirs.
c. It becomes a joint tenancy.
d. It passes by probate to the deceased tenant's heirs.

8.43   Which of the following is true of a joint tenancy?

a. The tenants can determine the size of the share owned by each tenant.
b. The size of the tenant's shares is determined by the amount of equity each has invested in the property.
c. The tenants have an equal and indivisible ownership interest.
d. There can be no more than two co-owners, and each has a fifty percent interest.

8.44   In contrast to a tenancy in common, in a joint tenancy

a. there is a single title to the property.
b. there are as many titles to the property as there are co-owners.
c. title is held by a trustee.
d. co-owners who are married hold separate titles.

8.45   If a joint tenant sells his or her interest to an outside party,

a. the new owner becomes a tenant in common with the other owners, who continue to hold a joint tenancy with each other and a tenancy in common with the new owner.
b. the joint tenancy continues with the new owner as the third joint tenant.
c. the joint tenancy terminates and all owners become tenants in common.
d. the joint tenancy terminates and the owners must create a new joint tenancy to include the new owner.

8.46   When a joint tenant dies, what happens to the tenant's interest in the estate?

a. It passes to the decedent's heirs, who become joint tenants.
b. It passes as a tenancy in common to the decedent's heirs.
c. The joint tenancy terminates and becomes a tenancy in common with the decedent's heirs and the surviving tenants as co-owners.
d. It passes to the surviving joint tenants.

8.47   Under what conditions can two individuals own a property as tenants by the entireties?

   a. If they so elect at the time of acquiring title.
   b. If they are blood relatives.
   c. If they are married.
   d. If they incorporate.

8.48   When an estate is held in a trust, which party holds legal title?

   a. The beneficiary.
   b. The trustor.
   c. The trustee.
   d. The grantor.

8.49   Tanya buys a 4-bedroom condominium. As the new owner, she has the right to

   a. sell or mortgage the unit without impediment from individual owners of neighboring units.
   b. sell the interest in the physical unit separately from the interest in the common elements.
   c. prevent non-owners from using the unit owner's portion of the common elements.
   d. exclusively possess and use those portions of the common areas structurally or functionally necessary for the operation of the unit.

8.50   A condominium owner's share of maintenance and operations expenses are based on

   a. the unit's pro rata share of floor space.
   b. the unit's pro rata share of the property value as defined in the declaration.
   c. the number of shares the owner purchased in the condominium association.
   d. the assessed value of the condominium unit.

8.51   By contrast to a condominium, the owner of a cooperative owns

   a. shares in a corporation or association and a proprietary lease in a physical unit.
   b. a fee simple interest in a physical unit plus a tenancy in common in common elements.
   c. a tenancy in common in a physical unit and the common areas.
   d. a ground lease in the physical unit's pro rata share of land and a proprietary lease in the unit.

8.52   In a cooperative, real property is owned only by

   a. the individual unit owners.
   b. the individual unit owners and the cooperative association.
   c. the cooperative developer.
   d. the corporate entity of the cooperative association.

8.53   In a time-share freehold, owners acquire

   a. undivided interests in the property as tenants in common.
   b. a renewable periodic tenancy from for a portion of a year.
   c. a pro rata share of a leased fee.
   d. a tenancy in severalty for a portion of a year.

8.54   Which of the following types of leasehold estate lacks a specific term?

   a. Estate for years.
   b. Estate from period-to-period.
   c. Estate at will.
   d. Estate by the entireties.

9.1   Which of the following describes an encumbrance?

    a. A third party's right encroach upon a property without the permission of the property owner.
    b. A third party's right to claim the sale proceeds of a property that has been mortgaged as collateral for a loan.
    c. A third party's interest in a real property that limits the interests of the freehold property owner.
    d. Another's right to acquire a freehold interest in a property against the property owner's wishes.

9.2   Which of the following is true of easements in general?

    a. They involve the property that contains the easement and a non-owning party.
    b. They apply to a whole property, not to any specific portion of the property.
    c. They only involve the legal owner of the property.
    d. They may require a specific use, but cannot prohibit one.

9.3   Mr. King wants to offer 100 acres of his property for sale. Since the property is landlocked, he will have to put in a driveway to the road that will run across his remaining property. What kind of easement will he have to grant?

    a. An easement in gross.
    b. A commercial easement.
    c. A personal easement.
    d. An easement appurtenant.

9.4   If property Alpha has a court-ordered easement across property Beta in order for Alpha to have access to a public road, the easement is a(n)

    a. easement by prescription.
    b. personal easement.
    c. easement by necessity.
    d. easement in gross.

9.5   An encroachment is

    a. an easement that has not been recorded on the title of the burdened property.
    b. an unauthorized physical intrusion of one property into another.
    c. a right granted by a property owner to the owner of an adjoining property to build a structure that protrudes across the property boundary.
    d. a structure that does not comply with a zoning ordinance.

9.6   A court might grant an easement by prescription if

    a. a town needs to dig a trench across an owner's property to install a sewer line to a neighboring property, and the owner refuses permission.
    b. a property owner sells the front half of a lot and wants to continue using the driveway to access the rear of the lot.
    c. a trespasser has been using an owner's property for a certain period with the owner's knowledge but without permission.
    d. a property owner wants to prevent the owner of an adjoining property from building a an improvement that blocks her view.

9.7 The purpose of a deed restriction is to enable an owner to specify

a. the form of ownership in which a property may be held.
b. how long a property must be owned before it can be legally transferred.
c. what groups of people are legally excluded from future ownership of a property.
d. how a property may be used and what improvements may be built on it.

9.8 Melinda purchases a house and finances it. The lender in turn places a lien on Melinda's title. The lien in this mortgage transaction is

a. evidence of debt incurred by a property owner.
b. a promissory note granted by a property owner as security for a debt.
c. the creditor's claim against the property as collateral security for the loan.
d. the document required to clear clouded title.

9.9 In a lien-theory state, what kind of interest does a mortgage lender have in the liened property?

a. A possessory interest.
b. A tenancy-by-mortgagee interest.
c. A legal interest in a pro rata share of the property.
d. An equitable interest.

9.10 How is a lien terminated?

a. Payment of the debt that is the subject of the lien and recording of the satisfaction.
b. Transfer of the property that has the lien.
c. Recording of another lien that is superior.
d. Death of the lienor or lienee.

9.11 A judge rules in favor of the creditor in a court proceeding and places a judgment lien against all the debtor's assets, including his real property. This is an example of a(n)

a. voluntary junior lien.
b. involuntary superior lien.
c. involuntary specific lien.
d. involuntary general lien.

9.12 A real estate tax lien, a federal income tax lien, a judgment lien, and a mortgage lien are recorded against a property. Which lien will be paid first when the property is sold?

a. Real estate tax lien.
b. Federal income tax lien.
c. Judgment lien.
d. Mortgage lien.

9.13 A lien holder can change the lien priority of a junior lien by agreeing to

a. change the date of recording.
b. lower the amount of the claim.
c. cancel the lien.
d. subordinate the lien.

9.14 Which of the following accurately describes the act of foreclosure?

a. A court-ordered acceleration of loan payments.
b. The final step in a bankruptcy filing.
c. A proceeding to enforce a lien by forcing the sale or transfer of a secured property.
d. A proceeding to take equitable title to a property that was liened as security for a mortgage loan.

9.15 A property is secured by a mortgage that does not contain a "power of sale" clause. To foreclose, the lien holder will have to

a. file a deficiency suit.
b. file a foreclosure suit.
c. file a suit to quiet title.
d. obtain a quit claim deed.

9.16 A homeowner defaults on his mortgage loan. In the subsequent foreclosure action, the lender takes title to the liened property directly instead of initiating a court-ordered public sale. This is an example of

a. strict foreclosure.
b. judicial foreclosure.
c. non-judicial foreclosure.
d. deed in lieu of foreclosure.

9.17 A property owner gives Deanna permission to cross his property as a shortcut to her kindergarten school bus. One day the property owner dies. What right was Deanna granted originally, and will it survive the owner's death?

a. A personal easement in gross, which continues after the owner's death.
b. An easement by prescription, which continues after the owner's death.
c. A license, which continues after the owner's death.
d. A license, which terminates upon the owner's death.

9.18 On two adjacent properties, there is an easement that allows property A to use the driveway that belongs to property B. After how many years will this become an easement by prescription?

a. 7 years
b. 10 years
c. 15 years
d. 20 years

9.19 A property owner who is selling her land wants to control how it is used in the future. She might accomplish her aim by means of

a. an injunction.
b. a deed restriction.
c. an easement.
d. a land trust.

9.20 What distinguishes a lien from other types of encumbrance?

a. It involves a monetary claim against the value of a property.
b. It lowers the value of a property.
c. It is created voluntarily by the property owner.
d. It attaches to the property rather than to the owner of the property.

9.21 Which of the following defines actual notice?

a. It is notice published in a newspaper.
b. It is knowledge one could have or should have obtained.
c. It is notice explicitly stated in a legal document.
d. It is knowledge received or imparted through direct experience.

9.22 Which of the following defines constructive notice?

    a. It is notice published in a newspaper.
    b. It is knowledge one could have or should have obtained.
    c. It is notice explicitly stated in a legal document.
    d. It is knowledge received or imparted through direct experience.

9.23 Ownership of real estate can be transferred voluntarily or involuntarily. The three ways title can be transferred voluntarily are by

    a. grant, deed, and will.
    b. escheat, deed, and covenant.
    c. title certificate, will, and deed.
    d. sale contract, deed, and warrant of seizin.

9.24 What is the function of recording a deed?

    a. It makes the deed valid.
    b. It causes title to pass.
    c. It gives constructive notice of ownership.
    d. It removes all prior recorded encumbrances.

9.25 The only clause that is actually required in a deed is the

    a. habendum clause.
    b. granting clause.
    c. reserving clause.
    d. tenendum clause.

9.26 The type of deed that offers the grantee the fullest protection against claims to the title is the

    a. general warranty deed.
    b. special warranty deed.
    c. quitclaim deed.
    d. bargain and defend deed.

9.27 What is one of the purposes of a lawsuit to "quiet title"?

    a. To force the grantor to defend the title against a third party claim.
    b. To terminate a co-ownership estate when one co-owner is unwilling.
    c. To keep the owner's name out of the title records.
    d. To have an encumbrance removed if the lienholder cannot prove its validity.

9.28 Which of the following best describes the documentary stamp tax?

    a. A transfer tax based on the price of the property being conveyed.
    b. A tax a title company must pay in order to examine title records in the recorder's office.
    c. A tax collected by attorneys and paid to the state when transfer documents are prepared.
    d. A tax on stamps used to certify the authenticity of a conveyance.

9.29 The court proceeding that generally settles a decedent's estate is called

    a. testate.
    b. probate.
    c. escheat.
    d. distribution.

9.30 If an owner of real property dies intestate and has no legal heirs, what will happen to the property?

a. It will escheat to the state or county.
b. It will transfer to the decedent's executor.
c. It will be divided equally among adjoining property owners.
d. It will become a public easement.

9.31 A municipality wants to build a sewage treatment facility which will require the acquisition of several parcels of privately owned land. What legal power enables the municipality to buy the necessary properties, even against the owners' wishes?

a. Estoppel.
b. Escheat.
c. Alienation.
d. Eminent domain.

9.32 An adverse possessor must be able to successfully demonstrate that he or she has been

a. openly possessing and claiming the property without the owner's consent.
b. occupying the property without an occupancy permit.
c. using the property intermittently and without permission over a period of years.
d. building a permanent structure on the property.

9.33 A buyer has signed a contract to purchase a property, but is uncertain of the condition of the title. Which of the following parties is legally responsible for knowing the condition of the title?

a. The County Recorder.
b. The seller's agent.
c. The buyer.
d. The mortgage lender.

9.34 A break in the chain of title to a property results in

a. a clouded title.
b. a title plant.
c. a lien of indeterminate ownership.
d. a duplicate title.

9.35 Wayne and Leota obtain an insurance policy that protects them from liabilities and losses resulting from title defects. The kind of policy they bought is a

a. a homeowner's insurance policy.
b. standard owner's title insurance policy.
c. lender's title insurance policy.
d. private mortgage insurance policy.

9.36 An owner transfers title to a property to a buyer in exchange for a motorcycle. This is an example of

a. voluntary alienation.
b. involuntary liquidation.
c. hypothecation.
d. 1031 exchange.

9.37 A person wishes to convey any and all interests in a property to another without assurance of the property's marketability. This party would most likely use which of the following types of deed?

a. A sheriff's deed.
b. A special warranty deed.
c. A partition deed.
d. A quitclaim deed.

9.38 Jennifer owns a one-half interest in a condominium as a tenant in common with her business partner. If Jennifer has several heirs and dies without a will, the property will

a. pass to the heirs by the laws of descent and distribution.
b. escheat to the state.
c. pass to the surviving spouse based on homestead law.
d. pass to the surviving heirs according to the provisions of the will.

9.39 A drifter secretly lives in an abandoned shack on a large ranch property. After twenty years, the person makes a claim of ownership to the shack and the land immediately surrounding it that he had cleared. This claim will likely be

a. upheld through adverse possession.
b. upheld because of the length of possession.
c. declined through the doctrine of prior appropriation.
d. declined because possession was secretive.

9.40 To be marketable, title must be

a. insured.
b. free of undisclosed defects and encumbrances.
c. abstracted by an attorney.
d. guaranteed by a title certificate.

9.42 A landlord generally has the right to enter the leased premises

a. at any time without notice.
b. for specified reasonable purposes.
c. provided the tenant gives prior permission.
d. only thirty days prior to lease expiration.

9.43 When a tenant rents an apartment, he or she is usually responsible for

a. compliance with the rules and regulations of the building.
b. payment for any alterations to the leased space.
c. recording the lease in title records.
d. occupying the premises throughout the lease term.

9.44 Under landlord-tenant laws, landlords must treat tenants fairly and honestly. In a residential leasehold, this requirement would include

a. insuring the tenant against loss of personal property.
b. providing required building support and services.
c. guaranteeing that a fair rent is being charged.
d. insuring the property for the value of the leasehold.

9.45 While a one-year lease is in effect, the tenant dies of a sudden illness. In this situation,

a. the lease automatically terminates.
b. the tenant's estate has the option of canceling the contract.
c. the landlord can record a lien against the leased fee interest.
d. the tenant's estate is still obligated under the lease.

9.46 Three students rent a house together, and all three sign a one-year lease. Six months later, two students move out. Which of the following is true of the remaining rent obligation?

a. The remaining tenant is responsible for the full rent obligation.
b. The remaining tenant is responsible for one third of the rent obligation.
c. The lease is cancelled due to abandonment. Therefore, the rent obligation is extinguished.
d. The departing tenants have no further rent obligation.

9.47 A tenant transfers a portion of the leasehold interest to another party. The instrument that accomplishes this transfer is a(n)

a. deed.
b. novation.
c. sublease.
d. reconveyance

9.48 Vijay enters into a lease for his new store. The provisions of the lease require Vijay to pay the operating expenses of the premises such as janitorial and repair expenses. This is an example of a

a. gross lease.
b. percentage lease.
c. land lease.
d. net lease.

9.49 A tenant obtains a full-service lease where the landlord agrees to pay all operating expenses in exchange for an additional $5.00 rent per square foot. Another term for this lease is a(n)

a. gross lease.
b. proprietary lease.
c. exchange lease.
d. full service net lease.

9.50 Which of the following circumstances is the most likely scenario for a ground lease?

a. A developer wants to acquire a necessary parcel that separates two parcels she already owns.
b. An owner-developer wants to retain ownership of the land portion of the improved real property.
c. A fast food company wants to place a restaurant in an existing building without buying either land or improvement.
d. A farmer wants to sell his property to a mining company.

9.51 A tenancy at will can usually be terminated by

a. either party giving proper notice.
b. either party without notice.
c. a sublease, with the lessor's approval.
d. an assignment by the lessor.

9.52 Under the Uniform Residential Landlord and Tenant Act, if a lease does not state a clear expiration date, the lease is regarded as

a. invalid.
b. a tenancy from period-to-period.
c. a tenancy at will.
d. a tenancy for years.

9.53   The Uniform Residential Landlord and Tenant Act generally does not apply to

   a. a hotel.
   b. a single-family residence.
   c. a unit in an apartment building that has fewer than ten units.
   d. a duplex in which the owner occupies one of the units.

9.54   In executing a condominium lease, a tenant has acquired

   a. a temporary transfer of legal title.
   b. a limited freehold interest in the air space of her unit.
   c. a temporary possessory interest.
   d. a title conveyance in exchange for rent.

9.55   When a tenant acquires a leasehold estate through a lease, what does the property owner acquire?

   a. A freehold estate for years.
   b. A reduced leasehold estate.
   c. A defeasible estate.
   d. A leased fee estate.

9.56   When an owner leases her property, she temporarily relinquishes the right to

   a. transfer the property.
   b. encumber the property.
   c. occupy the property.
   d. maintain the property.

9.57   Which of the following happens when a leased property is sold?

   a. The buyer acquires title subject to the lease, which remains in effect.
   b. The lease is cancelled.
   c. The lease expires within thirty days unless renewed.
   d. A new lease is automatically executed.

9.58   If a lease does not state a specific ending date, when does it terminate?

   a. Immediately, since it is an invalid lease.
   b. After one year.
   c. When either party gives proper notice.
   d. Whenever the property is sold.

9.59   In accordance with the statute of frauds,

   a. leases in excess of one year must be recorded to be enforceable.
   b. oral leases are not enforceable.
   c. a five-year lease must be in writing to be enforceable.
   d. an unwritten lease is fraudulent.

9.60   Which of the following is true of a sublease?

   a. The subtenant takes over sole responsibility for performance of the original lease contract.
   b. The original tenant retains primary responsibility for performance of the original lease contract.
   c. It does not convey any of the leasehold interest.
   d. It conveys the entire leasehold interest.

Section 10 Test: Legal Descriptions

10.1 A legal description of a property is one which

    a. accurately identifies the boundaries of the property as distinct from all other properties.
    b. accurately describes the location and dimensions the lot and improvements on the property.
    c. is accepted by a licensed surveyor as suitable for inclusion in a survey of the property.
    d. is written by an attorney licensed to practice real estate law in the state in which the property is located.

10.2 The essential elements of the metes and bounds system are

    a. parallels, base lines, and meridians.
    b. boundaries, distances, and a base line.
    c. reference points, angles, and distances.
    d. lot numbers, sections, and ranges.

10.3 In the Rectangular Survey System, a range is the area in between

    a. any row of sections in a township.
    b. two consecutive meridians.
    c. a principal meridian and a base line.
    d. a parallel and a meridian.

10.4 In the Rectangular Survey System, a tier is defined by

    a. six consecutive sections of a township.
    b. two consecutive meridians.
    c. two consecutive parallels.
    d. a parallel and a meridian.

10.5 In the Rectangular Survey System, what are the dimensions of a township?

    a. One mile square.
    b. Six miles by six miles, or 6 miles square.
    c. Thirty-six miles square.
    d. The north and south boundaries are one mile apart; the east and west boundaries are indeterminate.

10.6 What portion of a section is ten acres?

    a. 1/8.
    b. 1/16.
    c. 1/32.
    d. 1/64.

10.7 The lot and block system of legally describing property is used for

    a. farm properties.
    b. any property in an unincorporated area.
    c. properties where metes and bounds is not acceptable.
    d. properties in a subdivision.

10.8 A certain legal description contains the phrase, "...northwesterly along Erie Road to the POB...". What kind of description is this?

a. Plat survey.
b. Government grid.
c. Metes and bounds.
d. Rectangular survey.

10.9 How many sections are there in a township?

a. One.
b. Six.
c. Twelve.
d. Thirty-six.

10.10 In the Rectangular Survey System, a section contains how many acres?

a. 640.
b. 320.
c. 160.
d. 40.

11.1 The valuable consideration necessary to make a contract valid must be

   a. money.
   b. something tangible.
   c. something of value traded in exchange for something of value.
   d. something of equal value with whatever is received in exchange.

11.2 A real estate sales contract, to be enforceable, must

   a. contain a legal description of the property.
   b. be written on a form approved by the state bar association.
   c. be acknowledged by three witnesses.
   d. be recorded within three days to be enforceable.

11.3 How much time does a seller have to accept a buyer's offer?

   a. Forty-eight hours from the time of the offeror's signing of the offer.
   b. Twenty-four hours from the time of the offer's delivery to the seller.
   c. Within 24 hours following the stated expiration.
   d. A reasonable time, or until the expiration date on the offer.

11.4 A buyer submits an offer to a seller and then dies in a car accident. Before learning of the buyer's death, the seller accepts the offer. Which of the following is true?

   a. The seller can force the buyer's estate to go through with the purchase.
   b. The buyer's death terminated the offer.
   c. The seller must make a new offer with the same terms to the buyer's heirs.
   d. The buyer's heirs have the option of enforcing the contract.

11.5 Which of the following contracts can be assigned to another party?

   a. An exclusive listing agreement.
   b. A personal services agreement.
   c. A contract for the sale of undeveloped land.
   d. An employment contract between a broker and a sales associate.

11.6 An implied agency relationship may be deemed to exist if

   a. the parties do not disavow an express contract that has expired.
   b. the parties act is if there is a contract.
   c. an offering party does not receive written notice that the offer has been rejected.
   d. the parties promise to perform their part of the agreement if the other party performs.

11.7 Which of the following is an executory contract?

   a. An expired lease.
   b. A sale contract before closing.
   c. A recorded sale contract.
   d. An option to buy after it is exercised.

11.8 A bilateral contract is one in which

   a. both parties promise to do something in exchange for the other party's performance.
   b. both parties receive equal consideration.
   c. two parties agree to perform a service together.
   d. both parties promise to do something if the other party performs first.

11.9   A homeseller signs a listing agreement with a broker then subsequently revokes the listing. Which of the following is true?

a. The seller continues to have contractual obligations to the broker.
b. The contract remains in full force until the expiration date.
c. The broker may have a claim for marketing expenses expended during the listing term.
d. The seller cannot sign a listing agreement with another broker.

11.10 A breach of contract is

a. a termination of the contract by the mutual consent of the parties.
b. financial damage suffered by a party because another party has nullified a contract provision.
c. a lawsuit to force a party to discharge the contract.
d. the failure of a party to perform according to the terms of the contract.

11.11 What is rescission?

a. The act of withdrawing an offer before it has been accepted.
b. The act of declaring that a contract is no longer in effect for a given party.
c. The act of declaring a contract unenforceable.
d. The act of modifying the terms of an offer.

11.12 To be valid, a valid contract must

a. reflect a mutual understanding or agreement.
b. use precise wording in a document.
c. not be executable.
d. be created only by an attorney.

11.13 Two parties enter into a contract. The agreement fulfills all the requirements for a valid contract, with no disqualifying circumstances. Given this situation, it is still possible that the contract may be

a. void.
b. illegal.
c. unenforceable.
d. voidable.

11.14 The guardian for a mentally incompetent party enters into an oral contract with another party to buy a trade fixture on behalf of the incompetent party. This contract

a. does not meet validity requirements.
b. is possibly valid and enforceable.
c. must be in writing to be valid.
d. is valid but unenforceable.

11.15 A prospective homebuyer submits a signed offer with the condition that the seller pay for the inspection at closing. The seller disagrees, crosses out the provision, then signs and returns the document to the buyer. At this point, assuming all other contract validity items are in order, the original offer is now

a. an accepted offer, therefore a valid contract.
b. an executable option.
c. a counteroffer.
d. an invalid offer.

11.16 A construction contractor executes a contract with a buyer. In the agreement, the contractor promises to complete construction by November 20. This promise can be construed as

    a. an option.
    b. mutual consent.
    c. a meeting of the minds.
    d. valuable consideration.

11.17 A seller contracts to sell a property that she does not own. The sale contract for this transaction

    a. is executable.
    b. must be in writing.
    c. is void.
    d. is illegal yet potentially enforceable.

11.18 The statute of limitations requires that parties to a contract who have been damaged or who question the contract's provisions

    a. must act within a statutory period.
    b. must select a specific, limited course of action for recouping their losses.
    c. must arbitrate prior to taking court action.
    d. must wait a statutory period before they may take legal action.

11.19 The purpose of the statute of frauds is to

    a. invalidate certain oral contracts.
    b. require certain conveyance-related contracts to be in writing.
    c. nullify oral leases and listing agreements.
    d. eliminate fraud in real estate contracts.

11.20 A seller immediately accepts a buyer's offer but waits ten days before returning the accepted document to the buyer. Meanwhile, the offer has expired. Which of the following is true?

    a. The buyer is bound to the contract since it was accepted immediately.
    b. The buyer has no obligations to the seller whatsoever.
    c. The buyer may not rescind the expired offer.
    d. The seller may sue for specific performance.

11.21 When a broker enters into a listing agreement, the broker has agreed to accept which of the following?

    a. Fiduciary and contractual obligations with the client.
    b. Fiduciary relationships with client and customer.
    c. Contractual obligations with cooperating brokers.
    d. Fiduciary obligations with the customer.

11.22 The degree of authority granted by a residential brokerage listing agreement generally allows the agent to

    a. create contractual obligations for the client.
    b. negotiate the selling price between client and customer.
    c. hire inspectors, and other individuals to prepare the property for marketing.
    d. market, sell and show the property.

11.23 A sales associate, without an oral or written listing agreement, brings potential buyers to the seller. The seller says, "You can bring me buyers if you want, but I'm not paying you a commission." The sales associate then continues to direct buyers to the property. Which of the following is true about this situation?

   a. There is no agency relationship, and therefore the seller will owe no commission if one of the sales associate's buyers buys the property.
   b. An implied agency may have been created, with obligations to perform for both seller and agent.
   c. The seller and agent have an illegal, undisclosed agency relationship.
   d. The agent has an open exclusive agency listing with no commission agreement, and therefore owes no fiduciary duties to the seller.

11.24 An agent enters into a listing agreement with a homeseller, but then becomes too busy to professionally fulfill the terms of the agreement. To solve the dilemma, the agent assigns the agreement to another licensee in the office. Which of the following is true about this situation?

   a. The agent cannot assign the listing agreement.
   b. The new listing agent acquires the full set of fiduciary duties owed to the client.
   c. The new broker has to split any commission that results with the assigning broker.
   d. The original broker has to disclose the assignment to the seller.

11.25 From an agent's point of view, the most desirable form of listing agreement is a(n)

   a. exclusive agency.
   b. exclusive right to sell.
   c. open listing.
   d. net listing.

11.26 What is a multiple listing?

   a. A listing shared by a listing agent and a selling agent.
   b. A listing that a listing agent delegates to a subagent.
   c. A listing that is entered in a multiple listing service to enable cooperation with member brokers.
   d. A listing that authorizes a listing agent to market more than one property for a seller.

11.27 Which of the following conditions is necessary for a customer to qualify as "ready, willing, and able" in the context of a commissionable transaction?

   a. The customer's offer must be accepted.
   b. The customer must be legally competent to undertake the transaction.
   c. The customer must have a commitment from a lender.
   d. The customer must have no business relationship with the agent.

11.28 Although a listing broker may delegate listing tasks to an employed licensee, the broker may not delegate the authority to

   a. obtain and distribute compensation.
   b. provide cooperating brokers with information about the property.
   c. advertise the property.
   d. inspect the property for hazardous substances.

11.29 Agent Peter has an open listing with Frank. Paul is Peter's broker. Agent Perry's customer buys Frank's house. Patrick has a commission agreement with Frank. Who is most likely to be compensated in this scenario?

   a. Peter, since he has a written listing agreement.
   b. Paul, since he is Peter's broker
   c. Perry, since he found the customer.
   d. Patrick, since he has a commission agreement.

11.30 If an agent has an exclusive listing to sell a property, and the property is then taken by eminent domain, what is the status of the listing?

a. The seller's obligations under the listing are assigned to the agency that takes the property.
b. It becomes a voidable contract.
c. The commission clause of the agreement is canceled.
d. It may be terminated against the agent's will.

11.31 A broker obtains an exclusive listing to sell a house, but after two months, he abandons the listing because the seller is too demanding and hot-tempered. What can the seller do in this situation?

a. Have the licensee's license revoked for negligence.
b. Sue the broker for money damages.
c. Sign a listing agreement with another broker and force the first broker to pay the commission.
d. Force the broker to perform the contract without compensation.

11.32 An owner agrees to pay a broker for procuring a tenant unless it is the owner who finds the tenant. This is an example of a(n)

a. exclusive right-to sell agreement.
b. exclusive agency agreement.
c. open listing.
d. net listing.

11.33 A landlord promises to compensate a broker for procuring a tenant, provided the broker is the procuring cause. This is an example of a(n)

a. exclusive right-to rent agreement.
b. exclusive agency agreement.
c. open rental listing.
d. net lease listing.

11.34 A property owner agrees to pay a broker an open-ended commission as the difference between the sale price and a net amount, provided the owner receives a minimum amount of proceeds from the sale at closing. This is an example of a(n)

a. exclusive right-to sell agreement.
b. exclusive agency agreement.
c. open listing.
d. net listing.

11.35 In the context of agency law, the legal difference between an owner representation agreement and a buyer representation agreement is

a. the client.
b. the commission amount.
c. fiduciary duties.
d. regulatory approvals.

11.36 A multiple listing authorization gives a broker what authority?

a. To list the owner's property in a multiple listing service.
b. To sell several properties for the owner at once.
c. To represent both seller and buyer, if necessary, in selling the property.
d. To delegate the listing responsibilities to other agents.

11.37 A real estate sale contract is an executory contract until

   a. the completed sale transaction is recorded.
   b. the buyer and seller have agreed to all provisions and have signed the contract.
   c. all the obligations and promises are performed and the transaction is closed.
   d. the loan has been approved, the title insurance has been obtained, and the closing date is set.

11.38 In assisting a buyer or seller to complete an offer to purchase, what should an agent do to reduce the risk of committing an unauthorized practice of law?

   a. Use a standard contract promulgated by a state agency or a real estate board.
   b. Observe ethical standards promulgated by real estate trade organizations.
   c. Offer legal advice only on points of the contract that the agent is absolutely certain about.
   d. Write contract terms that are fair to both buyer and seller.

11.39 To be enforceable, a contract for the conveyance of real estate must

   a. be acknowledged by witnesses.
   b. be written.
   c. be recorded.
   d. have an expiration date.

11.40 A buyer makes an offer to purchase a house, and the seller accepts the offer. However, before the sales associate can inform the buyer of the seller's decision, the buyer delivers a written notice that she is opting out and cancelling the agreement. At this point, which of the following is true?

   a. The contract has been legitimately cancelled and is null and void.
   b. The seller must give the buyer an opportunity to make a new offer.
   c. The buyer must perform under the terms of the contract
   d. The seller must notify the buyer in writing that the buyer is in default.

11.41 Which of the following is an essential element of a valid contract for the sale of real estate?

   a. A valid blank form that the contract is written on.
   b. A habitable property.
   c. An offer and acceptance.
   d. A marketable title.

11.42 What kind of interest does the buyer acquire once a real estate sale contract is signed by the principal parties?

   a. Legal title.
   b. Lienholder interest.
   c. Reversionary interest.
   d. Equitable title.

11.43 A contingency in a sale contract is

   a. a promise by buyer or seller to perform a specific action.
   b. a condition that, if unmet, renders the contract unenforceable.
   c. one of several alternative actions that buyer or seller may take to satisfy contract requirements.
   d. an optional, unilateral action that either party may take at the request of the other party.

11.44 A clause in a sale contract stipulates that the seller must provide evidence that the property is free of active termite infestation. On the day of closing, the buyer learns that inspection service did not provide the required written documentation. The buyer then proceeds to declare that the sale is off. Which of the following is true of this situation?

a. The seller can sue for specific performance.
b. The buyer will be in default, and liable for damages, if he does not complete the transaction.
c. The buyer may be able to have the contract canceled.
d. The contract is automatically void.

11.45 A buyer signs an earnest money agreement and gives it to the broker who showed her the property she is buying. After leaving the broker's office, she reconsiders and decides she prefers a different property. How long does she have to take back her offer?

a. Until the seller communicates acceptance of the offer.
b. Until the earnest money deposit check is cashed.
c. She can take it back at any time, but must forfeit the earnest money.
d. She cannot take it back until after the expiration date of the offer.

11.46 On Wednesday, Fred offers to sell his property to Jack for $275,000, with the offer to remain open until 5 p.m. the next day. On Thursday morning, Sally offers Fred $280,000 for the property and Fred accepts. At 1 p.m. on Thursday afternoon, Jack accepts. Which of the following is true of this situation?

a. The acceptance by Sally creates a contract and terminates Fred's offer to Jack.
b. Fred has entered into contracts with both Jack and Sally to sell the same property.
c. Fred's acceptance of Sally's offer is invalidated by Jack's acceptance, because Fred's offer to Jack was made prior to Sally's offer to Fred.
d. No contract has been created because it is impossible to have two valid sale contracts for the same property.

11.47 Among the items that normally must be disclosed in a sale contract or its addenda is/are the

a. buyer's financial capability.
b. buyer's source of funds for the down payment.
c. seller's acceptable price range.
d. agency relationships and property condition.

11.48 To create an enforceable option-to-buy contract, there must be an exchange of

a. a promise to sell and a promise to buy.
b. valuable consideration and a right to buy.
c. valuable consideration and a promise to buy.
d. a down payment and a post-dated contract for sale.

11.49 Mary Carboy buys a house from Jim Schmidt and at the same time obtains an option to purchase the adjoining vacant lot for $10,000 within one year. A few months later, Carboy informs Schmidt that she is ready to exercise her option, but finds that Schmidt has received an offer of $12,000 from another party. Schmidt states that he will accept the offer unless Carboy is willing to match the $12,000 offer. Which of the following is true of this situation?

a. Schmidt must sell to Carboy for $10,000.
b. Carboy must pay $12,000 or lose the property.
c. Schmidt may sell to Carboy or the other party, but the price cannot exceed $10,000.
d. If the other party delivers payment before Carboy does, the option is canceled.

11.50 Which of the following is true regarding the assignability of an option?

   a. It is assignable only if the contract specifically allows assignment.
   b. It is never assignable.
   c. It is assignable only if the option is exercised.
   d. It is always assignable unless the contract prohibits assignment.

11.51 Which of the following is true of a contract for deed transaction?

   a. At the end of the contract period, the vendee receives equitable title, provided all required periodic payments have been made.
   b. The vendee has no right to possess or occupy the property during the contract period.
   c. At the end of the contract period, the vendor conveys legal title, provided the vendee has fulfilled all obligations.
   d. The vendor may cancel the contract at any time before the final payment has been received.

11.52 Several buyers are competing for the last available home in a desirable new subdivision. One buyer calls the owner-developer directly on the phone and offers $20,000 over and above the listed price. The developer accepts the offer. At this point,

   a. the parties have a valid, enforceable sale contract on the home.
   b. the parties have completed a verbal, executory contract.
   c. the parties may not cancel their contract.
   d. the developer could not entertain other offers on the property.

11.53 An owner completes a sales contract on her property with a buyer. Before closing, the seller runs into financial trouble and assigns the contract to her principal creditor. The buyer cries foul, fearing the property will be lost. Which of the following is true?

   a. The buyer can sue the assignee to disallow the illegal assignment.
   b. The buyer can take legal action against the assignor.
   c. The assignor has completed a legal action.
   d. The sale contract is nullified.

11.54. A due-on-sale clause in a sale contract puts parties on notice that

   a. the full price of the property is due the seller at closing.
   b. any loans surviving closing become immediately payable.
   c. all of the seller's debts must be retired before or upon closing.
   d. any conveyance may trigger an acceleration of any loans secured by the property.

11.55 A tenant has an option-to-purchase agreement with the landlord that expires on June 30. On July 1, the tenant frantically calls the landlord to exercise the option, offering the apology that she was busy with a death in the family. Which of the following is true?

   a. Since options contain grace periods, the landlord must sell.
   b. The tenant loses the right to buy, but can claim the money paid for the option from the landlord.
   c. The landlord does not have to sell, but must renew the option.
   d. The option is expired, and the tenant has no rightful claim to money paid for the option.

11.56 Two parties enter into a contract for deed agreement. In this form of agreement,

   a. title is conveyed to the buyer, but the seller retains possession for a stipulated time period.
   b. the buyer contracts to pay all cash at closing in exchange for the deed.
   c. the seller retains legal title while the buyer makes partial payments until the contract is fully executed.
   d. the buyer immediately acquires legal title and takes possession.

12.1 What is a lien-theory state?

    a. A state in which a mortgagee holds legal title to a secured property.
    b. A state in which a mortgagee has equitable title to a secured property.
    c. A state that allows a real estate owner's creditors to record liens against the owner's property.
    d. A state in which a lien is considered as a conveyance.

12.2 What is the function of a note in a mortgage or trust deed financing arrangement?

    a. It is the lender's security instrument in the collateral property.
    b. It is evidence of ownership of the mortgage or trust deed.
    c. It contains the borrower's promise to maintain the value of the property given as collateral for a loan.
    d. It is evidence of the borrower's debt to the lender.

12.3 When homebuyer Henry pledges his newly purchased home as collateral for a mortgage loan, the evidence of the pledge is the

    a. trust deed or mortgage.
    b. promissory note.
    c. loan commitment.
    d. loan receipt.

12.4 The borrower in a mortgage loan transaction is known as the

    a. mortgagee.
    b. mortgagor.
    c. lienor.
    d. trustee.

12.5 If a borrower obtains an interest-only loan of $200,000 at an annual interest rate of 6%, what is the monthly interest payment?

    a. $1,200.
    b. $600.
    c. $500.
    d. $1,000.

12.6 If a borrower's monthly interest payment on an interest-only loan at an annual interest rate of 6% is $500, how much was the loan amount?

    a. $72,000.
    b. $100,000.
    c. $120,000.
    d. $50,000.

12.7 A borrower of a $50,000 interest-only loan makes annual interest payments of $3750. What interest rate is the borrower paying?

    a. 7.5%.
    b. .75%.
    c. 3.75%.
    d. 8.5%.

12.8 Maria borrows $100,000 and pays two points for the loan. How much does she pay in points?

    a. $200.
    b. $2,000.
    c. $1,200.
    d. It depends on the interest rate.

12.9 Which of the following is true of an amortizing loan?

    a. The amount of annual interest paid is the same for every year of the loan term.
    b. Part of each periodic payment is applied to repayment of the loan balance in advance and part is applied to payment of interest in arrears.
    c. Except for any points that may be paid, the interest on the loan balance is usually paid in advance.
    d. The interest rate is reduced each year to maintain equal payments even though the outstanding loan balance is smaller.

12.10 For a loan that is not backed by the Federal Housing Administration or Veterans Administration, and for which the borrower is making a down payment of less than 20%, the lender is likely to require the borrower to obtain

    a. a subrogation agreement.
    b. private mortgage insurance.
    c. a letter of credit.
    d. a co-signer on the note.

12.11 What is a loan-to-value ratio?

    a. The percentage of a lender's portfolio that is composed of mortgage loans.
    b. The ratio of borrowed principal plus total interest to the appraised value of the collateral property.
    c. The ratio of a lender's return on a mortgage loan to the value of the collateral property.
    d. The fraction of the appraised value of the property offered as collateral which the lender is willing to lend.

12.12 The difference between what a borrower has to pay to purchase a property and the amount a lender will lend on the property is the

    a. mortgage insurance coverage amount.
    b. lender's profit margin.
    c. buyer's down payment.
    d. origination fee.

12.13 A lender lends money to a homeowner and takes legal title to the property as collateral during the payoff period. They are in a

    a. title-theory state.
    b. lien-theory state.
    c. state allowing land trusts.
    d. state where hypothecation is illegal.

12.14 A lender who charges a rate of interest in excess of legal limits is guilty of

    a. redlining.
    b. usury.
    c. profit-taking.
    d. nothing; there are no legal limits to interest rates.

12.15 A lender is charging 2 points on a $60,000 loan. The borrower must therefore pay the lender an advance amount of
   a. $120.
   b. $300.
   c. $1,200.
   d. $3,000.

12.16 The difference between a balloon loan and an amortized loan is
   a. an amortized loan is paid off over the loan period.
   b. a balloon loan always has a shorter loan term.
   c. an amortized loan requires interest-payments.
   d. a balloon loan must be retired in five years.

12.17 A distinctive feature of a promissory note is that

   a. it is not assignable.
   b. it must be accompanied by a mortgage.
   c. it is a negotiable instrument.
   d. it may not be prepaid.

12.18 When the terms of the mortgage loan are satisfied, the mortgagee

   a. may retain any overage in the escrow account.
   b. may inspect the property before returning legal title.
   c. may be entitled to charge the borrower a small fee to close the loan.
   d. may be required to execute a release of mortgage document.

Section 13 Test: Types of Mortgages and Sources of Financing

13.1 The Equal Credit Opportunity Act prohibits a lender from

    a. refusing a loan because the borrower does not match the lender's target market.
    b. including income from self-employment in the borrower's qualifying income.
    c. requiring both spouses to sign the loan application form.
    d. refusing a loan because a borrower has a defective credit report.

13.2 A loan applicant has an annual gross income of $72,000. How much will a lender allow the applicant to pay for monthly housing expense to qualify for a loan if the lender uses an income ratio of 28%?

    a. $2,160.
    b. $1,680.
    c. $1,068.
    d. $840.

13.3 AMC Bank discovers, in considering buyer Bob's application for a mortgage loan, that Bob has borrowed the down payment from an uncle and has to repay that loan. Bob should expect that AMC Bank will

    a. refuse the application.
    b. adjust the applicant's debt ratio calculation and lower the loan amount.
    c. increase the loan amount to enable the borrower to pay off the loan to the relative.
    d. require the borrower to make payments to an escrow account for repayment of the relative's loan.

13.4 The Federal Reserve's Regulation Z applies to which loans?

    a. All loans.
    b. All loans secured by real estate.
    c. All loans secured by a residence.
    d. All loans over $25,000.

13.5 If a particular loan falls under Regulation Z's right of rescission provision,

    a. the lender has the right to change the terms of the loan within a certain period.
    b. the lender has the right to accelerate repayment of the loan because of a change in the borrower's credit status.
    c. the borrower has the right to pay off the loan ahead of schedule with no penalty.
    d. the borrower has a limited right to cancel the transaction within a certain period.

13.6 Under the Equal Credit Opportunity Act, a lender, or a real estate agent who assists a seller in qualifying a potential buyer, may not

    a. tell a rejected loan applicant the reasons for the rejection.
    b. ask the buyer/borrower about his/her religion or national origin.
    c. ask the buyer/borrower to explain unconventional sources of income.
    d. use a credit report that has not been provided to the borrower.

13.7 A conventional mortgage loan is one that is

    a. backed by the Federal National Mortgage Association.
    b. insured under Section 203(b) of the Federal Housing Administration loan program.
    c. guaranteed by the Government National Mortgage Association.
    d. not FHA-insured or VA-guaranteed.

13.8 The assumability of an FHA-insured loan is

    a. unrestricted.
    b. limited by when the loan was originated.
    c. limited to owner-occupied properties.
    d. prohibited on all existing loans under current regulations.

13.9 A VA certificate of eligibility determines

    a. how long an individual served in the military.
    b. the maximum loan amount an approved lender can give to veterans.
    c. how much of a loan the VA will guarantee.
    d. whether a lender is approved to issue VA-guaranteed loans.

13.10 A borrower obtains a 30-year, fully amortizing mortgage loan of $50,000 at 8%. What is the principal balance at the end of the loan term?

    a. $2,000.
    b. $50,000.
    c. $220.
    d. Zero.

13.11 Which of the following describes a purchase money mortgage financing arrangement?

    a. A bank gives a buyer a senior mortgage loan that fully covers the cost of purchasing the property.
    b. The buyer gives the seller a mortgage and note as part of the purchase price of the property.
    c. A land trust holds title to the property while the buyer makes periodic installment payments to the seller.
    d. The seller uses the purchase money obtained from the buyer's mortgage loan to repay the seller's outstanding loan balance.

13.12 A homeowner borrows money from a lender and gives the lender a mortgage on the property as collateral for the loan. The homeowner retains title to the property. This is an example of

    a. intermediation.
    b. forfeiture.
    c. hypothecation.
    d. subordination.

13.13 Which of the following correctly describes the flow of money and documents in a mortgage loan transaction?

    a. The borrower gives the lender a note and a mortgage in exchange for loan funds.
    b. The lender gives the borrower a mortgage and receives a note in exchange for loan funds.
    c. The borrower receives a note in exchange for a mortgage from the lender.
    d. The lender gives the borrower a note, loan funds and a mortgage.

13.14 In a deed of trust transaction, which of the following occurs?

    a. The beneficiary conveys title to a trustee in exchange for loan funds.
    b. The trustee conveys title to a beneficiary in exchange for loan funds.
    c. The trustor conveys title to a trustee in exchange for loan funds from the beneficiary.
    d. The trustee conveys title to a trustor in exchange for loan funds from the beneficiary.

13.15 In addition to income, credit, and employment data, a mortgage lender requires additional documentation, usually including

    a. an appraisal report.
    b. a criminal record report.
    c. a subordination agreement.
    d. a default recourse waiver.

13.16 The three overriding considerations of a lender's mortgage loan decision are

    a. points, interest rate, and loan term.
    b. the location of the mortgaged property, the borrower's cash, and the amount of the borrower's equity.
    c. the ability to re-pay, the value of the collateral, and the profitability of the loan.
    d. the amount of the loan, the borrower's income, and the down payment.

13.17 The reason lenders consider the loan-to-value ratio important in underwriting is that

    a. they don't want to lend borrowers any more money than necessary.
    b. they want to ensure there is more than enough collateral to cover the loan amount.
    c. borrowers can only afford to borrow a portion of the entire purchase price.
    d. the higher the loan-to-value ratio, the more profitable the loan.

13.18 The Equal Credit Opportunity Act (ECOA) requires lenders to

    a. extend equal credit to all prospective borrowers.
    b. consider the income of a spouse in evaluating a family's creditworthiness.
    c. discount the income of a person involved in child-rearing or child-bearing.
    d. specialize lending activity by geographical area for improved customer service.

13.19 Lenders use an income ratio in qualifying to

    a. insure a borrower has the earning power to make the loan payments.
    b. compare a borrower's earnings to the borrower's short-term debt.
    c. identify the highest possible interest rate that the borrower can afford.
    d. quantify the borrower's assets to the fullest extent.

13.20 The debt ratio formula used to qualify borrowers is

    a. total debt divided by debt payments.
    b. gross income divided by assets.
    c. gross income divided by debts.
    d. debt payments divided by gross income.

13.21 At the closing of a mortgage loan

    a. the borrower pays off the note and receives clear title.
    b. the lender issues a firm loan commitment.
    c. the parties complete all loan origination documents and the loan is funded.
    d. the borrower's loan application is complete and the file closed.

13.22 Which laws or regulations require mortgage lenders to disclose financing costs and annual percentage rate to a borrower before funding a loan?

    a. The Equal Credit Opportunity Act.
    b. Truth-in-Lending laws and Regulation Z.
    c. The Real Estate Settlement and Procedures Act.
    d. Federal Fair Housing Laws.

13.23 Which laws or regulations prevent mortgage lenders from discriminating in extending credit to potential borrowers?

    a. The Equal Credit Opportunity Act.
    b. Truth-in-Lending laws.
    c. The Real Estate Settlement and Procedures Act.
    d. Federal Fair Housing Laws.

13.24 Which laws or regulations require mortgage lenders to provide an estimate of closing costs to a borrower and forbid them to pay kickbacks for referrals?

    a. The Equal Credit Opportunity Act.
    b. Truth-in-Lending laws.
    c. the Real Estate Settlement and Procedures Act.
    d. Federal Fair Housing Laws.

13.25 Which of the following are methods used by the Federal Reserve System to regulate the money supply?

    a. Selling securities, printing money, and controlling lending underwriting requirements.
    b. Buying securities, changing the discount rate, and controlling banking reserves.
    c. Printing money, changing interest rates, and selling T-bills.
    d. Controlling the prime rate, trading securities, and purchasing loans.

13.26 How does the secondary mortgage market aid borrowers seeking a mortgage loan?

    a. It cycles funds back to primary lenders so they can make more loans.
    b. It issues second mortgages and sells them in the home equity market.
    c. It lends funds to banks so they can make more loans.
    d. It pays off defaulted loans made by primary mortgage lenders.

13.27 The major organizations operating in the secondary mortgage market are

    a. Fannie Mae, Freddie Mac, and Ginnie Mae.
    b. Fannie Mae, GMAC, and MGIC.
    c. Freddie Mac, FHA, and VA.
    d. Fannie Mae, Freddie Mac, and the Federal Reserve.

13.28 What is the role of Fannie Mae in the secondary mortgage market?

    a. It guarantees FHA-backed and VA-backed loans.
    b. It insures FHA-backed and VA-backed loans.
    c. It purchases FHA-backed and VA-backed loans.
    d. It originates FHA-backed and VA-backed loans.

13.29 What is the role of the Federal Housing Authority in the mortgage lending market?

    a. It guarantees loans made by approved lenders.
    b. It insures loans made by approved lenders.
    c. It purchases loans made by approved lenders.
    d. It originates loans made by approved lenders.

13.30 What is the role of the Veteran's Administration in the mortgage lending market?

    a. It guarantees loans made by approved lenders.
    b. It insures loans made by approved lenders.
    c. It purchases loans made by approved lenders.
    d. It originates loans made by approved lenders.

13.31 In a graduated payment mortgage loan,

  a. loan funds are disbursed to the borrower on a graduated basis.
  b. the interest rate periodically increases in graduated phases.
  c. the loan payments gradually increase.
  d. the loan payments gradually increase and the loan term gradually decreases.

13.32 In a buydown,

  a. the lender lowers the interest rate on a loan in exchange for a prepayment of principal.
  b. the borrower pays additional interest at the onset in order to obtain a lower interest rate.
  c. the lender requires the borrower to buy down the price of the property by increasing the down payment.
  d. the borrower pays the lender additional funds to buy down the term of the loan.

Section 14 Test: Real Estate Computations and Closing Transactions

14.1 The conditions of an escrow agreement cannot be met and the related transaction cannot be completed. In such a case, the escrow agent

  a. levies a fine against the defaulting party.
  b. assigns his or her fiduciary responsibilities to the seller's broker.
  c. returns funds to the buyer.
  d. cancels the sale contract and destroys the transaction documents.

14.2 To avoid violating the Real Estate Settlement Procedures Act, parties who are providing services to the buyer or seller in a transaction must

  a. be paid before the closing date for any service they provide.
  b. inform the closing agent of the cost of their services at least one week before the closing date.
  c. receive payment only from the funds held in escrow, not directly from buyer or seller.
  d. disclose in writing any business relationships they have with other parties involved in the transaction.

14.3 A certain item is to be prorated between a buyer and seller. If no outside party is concerned, which of the following statements is true?

  a. The item must be prorated and recorded as a debit to one party and a credit to the other party for the same amount.
  b. The item must be prorated and recorded as a debit to one party; the remainder is recorded as a credit to the other party.
  c. The party who is owed money receives a credit for the entire item and a debit for the prorated amount.
  d. The party who owes money receives a debit for the portion owed and a credit for the portion that is not owed.

14.4 An item is said to be paid in arrears if it is normally paid

  a. on a monthly or yearly basis.
  b. at some time after the expense is incurred.
  c. only after it is billed.
  d. whenever it is incurred.

14.5 A seller received a rental payment of $900 in advance. At closing, the seller has earned only $320 of this rent. What should appear on the closing statement?

  a. A debit to the seller and credit to the buyer for $320.
  b. A debit to the seller for $580 and a credit to the buyer for $320.
  c. A debit to the seller for $320 and a credit to the buyer for $900.
  d. A debit to the seller and credit to the buyer for $580.

14.6 A buyer will receive a water bill for an estimated $100 at the end of the month. At closing, the seller has used an estimated $43 in water. What should appear on the closing statement?

  a. A debit to the seller and credit to the buyer for $57.
  b. A debit to the seller and credit to the buyer for $43.
  c. A debit to the buyer and credit to the seller for $57.
  d. A debit to the buyer and credit to the seller for $43.

14.7 A sale transaction closes on April 1, the ninety-first day of the tax year. The day of closing belongs to the seller. Real estate taxes for the year, not yet billed, are expected to be $2,190. According to the 365-day method, what is the seller's share of the tax bill?

a. $1,644.00.
b. $546.00.
c. $959.30
d. $1,364.66.

14.8 A sale transaction closes on July 4. The day of closing belongs to the seller. On January 1, the seller paid a hazard insurance premium of $375 for the calendar year. According to the 12-month/30-day method, what is the seller's share of the insurance premium?

a. $183.33.
b. $187.50.
c. $189.05.
d. $191.67.

14.9 Waldo is buying Marianne's house. The closing date (day belongs to seller) of the sale transaction is September 1 (day 244 of the year). Current Year real estate taxes are $1,100 (will be billed to buyer next year). Use the 365-day method for prorating. What is Marianne's share of the real estate taxes?

a. $364.66.
b. $367.67.
c. $732.33.
d. $735.34.

14.10 Christie is buying John's house. The closing date (day belongs to seller) of the sale transaction is September 1 (day 244 of the year). Existing hazard insurance of $350 has been paid by John through December 31. Use the 365-day method for prorating. What is Christie's share of the existing hazard insurance already paid in full?

a. $116.03.
b. $117.99.
c. $232.01.
d. $233.97.

14.11 Julie is buying Florence's house. The closing date (day belongs to seller) of the sale transaction is September 1 (day 244 of the year). The buyer's loan amount is $78,750 (90%; 30 years @ 8%). The monthly payment on this loan is $577.84, with $525 going to interest in the first month. At closing, Julie must pre-pay interest for the period of Sept. 2-Sept. 30. Use the 365-day method for prorating. What is Julie's prepaid interest amount?

a. $507.50.
b. $525.00.
c. $543.10.
d. $558.58.

14.12 Melissa is buying Raymond's house. Melissa's loan amount is $88,750. She has agreed to pay 2 points at closing. How much will Melissa pay for points?

a. $157.50.
b. $177.50.
c. $1,775.00.
d. $887.50.

14.13 Tina is buying Terrell's house for $187,500. The broker's commission, to be paid by the seller, is 6%. How much will Terrell pay the broker?

    a. $31,250.
    b. $2,625.00.
    c. $4,725.
    d. $11,250.

14.14 A sale contract stipulates that a buyer is to pay the seller's transfer tax expenses. This practice is not customary in the area. In this case,

    a. the buyer and seller must amend the contract before closing.
    b. the contract is voidable, since the seller must pay the expense.
    c. the buyer may pay or not pay the expense, at his or her option.
    d. the buyer must pay the expense.

14.15 What a buyer has to pay at closing is equal to

    a. the excess of the buyer's debits over the buyer's credits.
    b. the excess of the buyer's credits over the buyer's debits.
    c. the excess of the seller's debits over the seller's credits.
    d. the excess of the seller's credits over the seller's debits.

14.16 The standard E & O policy covers damages resulting from

    a. failure to disclose an environmental condition.
    b. antitrust violations.
    c. mishandling of earnest money deposits.
    d. negligence, error or omission in carrying out professional services.

15.1 If the price of an item is increasing, one can usually assume that

   a. demand for the item is decreasing in relation to supply of the item.
   b. demand for the item is increasing in relation to supply of the item.
   c. supply of the item is increasing.
   d. demand for the item and supply of the item are increasing.

15.2 When the market for an item has achieved market equilibrium, which of the following statements is true?

   a. New suppliers will enter the market and drive the price down.
   b. Demand will slowly taper off, driving the price down.
   c. Unmet demand for the item is directed toward demand for some other item.
   d. Supply and demand are equal, and price and value are equal.

15.3 As an economic product, real estate is distinguished by

   a. its homogeneity.
   b. its variety.
   c. the uniqueness of every parcel.
   d. its ability to appreciate in value.

15.4 The city of Stevensville has declared a moratorium on new construction. If demand is increasing, what will be the likely effect on real estate prices in the area?

   a. Prices level off.
   b. Prices continue to follow the trend that preceded the moratorium.
   c. Prices fall.
   d. Prices rise.

15.5 If Okapi, Inc., a company that markets its sports clothing worldwide, moves into Stevensville and hires 100 employees, it is reasonable to expect that the town will experience

   a. an immediate rise in the demand for industrial real estate, but no other changes in the real estate market.
   b. an increase in demand for all types of real estate.
   c. a housing boom, but no other changes in the real estate market.
   d. an immediate increase in the prices for industrial and office real estate, but no impact on the residential market.

15.6 What is "absorption?"

   a. The amount of new space that is added to available space over a period of time.
   b. The number of houses that are built over a period of time.
   c. The amount of space that is occupied at any given time.
   d. The number of available units that become occupied over a period of time.

15.7 When vacancies are declining in a real estate market, it is common for the market to experience

   a. rising prices.
   b. falling prices.
   c. falling construction activity.
   d. falling absorption.

15.8 The price for any product is a function of four fundamental determinants of value. These are

    a. durability, feasibility, mobility, and location.
    b. desire, utility, scarcity, and purchasing power.
    c. popularity, recognizability, promotion, and rebate.
    d. fungibility, costs, convenience, and uniqueness.

15.9 A town is rapidly growing, but all the buildable vacant lots in the most desirable area have already been occupied. In this case, it is likely that the price of existing homes in that area

    a. will stabilize, since the population must stabilize.
    b. will increase.
    c. will decline, since no further building can take place.
    d. will not show any predictable movement.

15.10 If there is a significant undersupply of homes in a market, construction will tend to increase. This is an example of

    a. supply outstripping demand.
    b. demand outstripping value.
    c. consumer optimism.
    d. the market tending toward equilibrium.

15.11 If commercial real estate rental prices are falling in a market, it is likely that
    a. demand has outstripped supply of space.
    b. the market is in equilibrium.
    c. the market is over-supplied.
    d. employment is increasing.

15.12 A construction boom in a market is an indication that prices

    a. have been increasing.
    b. have been declining.
    c. have been in equilibrium.
    d. have exceeded supply.

15.13 Why is real estate traditionally considered a relatively illiquid economic product?

    a. Its physical form is fixed.
    b. Real estate is defined as land, not water.
    c. It is often difficult to convert to cash.
    d. It cannot be moved.

15.14 What does "base employment" refer to in the context of real estate demand?

    a. The lowest category of employment in terms of wages and desirability
    b. The number of persons employed in base industries in an area
    c. The number of persons employed on military bases in an area
    d. The labor pool available for employment in all industries in an area

15.15 What is "vacancy" in real estate market economics?

    a. A property that has no owner-occupant
    b. The total number of properties of a certain type that are on the market at a given time
    c. The absence of certain types of users in a given market area
    d. The total existing space of a certain type that is unoccupied at a given time

15.16 A moratorium on new construction is an example of

    a. local government influencing the real estate market, regardless of demand.
    b. the natural result of demand exceeding supply in a local market.
    c. government promotion of the free market concept in the local real estate market.
    d. a government policy that aims to restrain a trend of rising prices in the local real estate market.

15.17 Of the following potential influences on a local real estate market, which one would be considered local, rather than regional, national, or global?

    a. Changes in money supply
    b. Federal Reserve interest rates
    c. In- and out-migrations of major employers
    d. Trade imbalances with foreign trading partners

15.18 There is a lot of new construction going on in the town of Florence. Which of the following would most likely be the immediate effect on the real estate market?

    a. Demand increases and prices rise.
    b. Vacancy rises and prices fall.
    c. Absorption and vacancy decrease.
    d. Supply decreases relative to demand.

15.19 What kind of real estate users are most concerned with neighborhood quality, access to services, property amenities, and quality of life in their demand for real estate?

    a. Retail
    b. Office
    c. Industrial
    d. Residential

15.20 One distinguishing feature of real estate as an economic product is

    a. its easy convertibility to cash.
    b. its quick response to changes in supply-demand balance.
    c. its susceptibility to swings in the local economy.
    d. the easy substitutability of one item for another.

16.1 Bill Parsons paid $150,000 for a house to operate as a rental property, figuring that he could rent it out at a rate of $900 a month. In paying a price based on the property's ability to generate a desired future income, Parsons was motivated by the economic principle known as

a. substitution.
b. anticipation.
c. supply and demand.
d. utility.

16.2 Which of the following situations illustrates the principle of contribution?

a. A homebuyer makes a down payment of 20% instead of the 10% the lender requires.
b. A homeowner adds a third bathroom to a house and thereby increases the appraised value by $10,000.
c. The appraised value of a house goes up by $20,000 over a two-year period because of the prices recently paid for other houses in the neighborhood.
d. Because of a decline in mortgage interest rates, a homeowner in a certain market is able to list her house at a higher price.

16.3 When a property owner combines two adjacent properties to create a single property with a higher value than the sum of the values of the two separate properties, the applicable principle of value is called

a. assemblage.
b. accretion.
c. progression.
d. subdivision.

16.4 What is the difference between market value and market price, if any?

a. There is no difference.
b. Market value is a broker's estimate; market price is a precise number derived by a licensed appraiser.
c. Market value is an average price derived from comparable sales; market price is a price based on the cost of creating the property.
d. Market value is an estimate; market price is the price at which a property sold.

16.5 The first step in the appraisal process, regardless of the appraisal method, is to

a. identify the highest and best use of the property to be appraised.
b. collect and analyze property data.
c. estimate the value of the land as if it were vacant.
d. define the appraisal problem and the purpose of the appraisal.

16.6 In the final step of an appraisal, the appraiser reconciles the value estimates derived by the various appraisal approaches by

a. disregarding the high and low extreme results.
b. averaging the results of all three approaches.
c. weighing the applicability of the approaches and considering the quality of data supporting each approach.
d. choosing the result that is closest to the average for properties in the immediate neighborhood.

16.7 Which of the following statements properly describes the central concept of the sales comparison approach?

a. Find the median price of recently sold comparable properties and add or subtract dollar amounts in the subject property to account for competitive differences.
b. Make dollar adjustments to the sale prices of comparable properties to account for competitive differences with the subject.
c. Find at least three comparable properties that are currently for sale and make dollar adjustments to the listing prices to account for competitive differences with the subject.
d. Apply an appreciation factor to the price at which the subject property most recently sold and make dollar adjustments to account for competitive differences with comparable properties currently for sale.

16.8 One of the strengths of the sales comparison approach is that it

a. takes into account the subject property's investment value.
b. reveals the profit margin of the builder or developer of the subject property.
c. discovers the underlying value of the subject property apart from the influence of competing properties.
d. takes into account the competitive value of specific amenities of the subject property.

16.9 In making dollar adjustments in the sales comparison approach, the appraiser

a. adds value to a comparable that is inferior to the subject property.
b. adds value to the subject property if it is inferior to a comparable.
c. subtracts value from a comparable that is inferior to the subject property.
d. subtracts value from the subject property if it is inferior to a comparable.

16.10 The best comparable property for use in the sales comparison approach is the one that

a. requires the most and largest adjustments.
b. requires the fewest and smallest adjustments.
c. sold most recently at the highest price.
d. is located closest to the subject property.

16.11 A house is being appraised using the sales comparison approach. The house has three bedrooms, two bathrooms, and a patio. The appraiser selects a comparable house that has three bedrooms, 3 bathrooms, and no patio. The comparable house just sold for $200,000. A bath is valued at $7,000, and a patio at $2,000. Assuming all else is equal, what is the adjusted value of the comparable?

a. $202,000.
b. $207,000.
c. $195,000.
d. $205,000.

16.12 Which of the following statements properly describes the central methodology of the cost approach to appraisal?

a. Apply a depreciation factor to the reported actual cost of acquiring and improving the subject property.
b. Estimate the cost of building the improvements on the subject property.
c. Estimate the land value and add to this the actual cost of the improvements adjusted for competitive differences with similar properties.
d. Add the estimated land value and cost of improvements and subtract the accrued depreciation of the improvements.

16.13 One of the strengths of the cost approach is that it

    a. takes into account the amount of money required to develop a similar property.
    b. is very accurate for a property with new improvements that represent the highest and best use.
    c. results in an actual price in dollars instead of an estimated value.
    d. reveals the owner's return on money invested in the cost of development.

16.14 The principle underlying depreciation from physical deterioration is that

    a. eventually, a property loses all of its value.
    b. a property loses a portion of its value each year because of economic obsolescence.
    c. a property loses the same increment of value each year over the economic life of the property.
    d. the value lost to depreciation is incurable.

16.15 A property is being appraised by the cost approach. The appraiser estimates that the land is worth $30,000 and the replacement cost of the improvements is $95,000. Total depreciation from all causes is $10,000. What is the indicated value of the property?

    a. $135,000.
    b. $130,000.
    c. $125,000.
    d. $115,000.

16.16 Which of the following statements properly describes how to apply the income capitalization approach to appraisal?

    a. Apply a rate of return to the price paid for an income property.
    b. Divide the income a property generates by a rate of return.
    c. Estimate the amount of income a property must generate to return the capital amount invested in it.
    d. Estimate the rate of return a property owner receives from income generated by the property.

16.17 A strength of the income capitalization approach is that it

    a. uses a rate of return that is required for all potential purchasers in a market.
    b. yields an accurate projection of investment income.
    c. uses a method that is also used by investors to determine how much they should pay for an investment property.
    d. can be used with any type of property in any market.

16.18 A property is being appraised using the income capitalization approach. Annually, it has an estimated gross income of $60,000, vacancy and credit losses of $3,000, and operating expenses of $20,000. Using a capitalization rate of ten percent, what is the indicated value (to the nearest $1,000)?

    a. $370,000.
    b. $400,000.
    c. $570,000.
    d. $600,000.

16.19 An apartment building that sold for $450,000 had monthly gross rent receipts of $3,000. What is its monthly gross rent multiplier?

    a. 12.5
    b. .01.
    c. .08.
    d. 150.

16.20 A rental house has monthly gross income of $1,200. A suitable gross income multiplier derived from market data is 14.1. What estimated sale price (to the nearest $1,000) is indicated?

a. $169,000.
b. $102,000.
c. $203,000.
d. $173,000.

16.21 A certified appraiser is one who has received certification by

a. a licensed real estate school.
b. the Appraisal Institute.
c. the state in which the appraiser operates.
d. the Appraisal Review Board.

16.22 The act that required federally-related appraisals to be conducted by a certified appraiser is known as

a. The Financial Institutions Reform, Recovery and Enforcement Act (FIRREA).
b. The Uniform Standards of Professional Appraisal Practice Act (USPAPA).
c. The Appraisal Foundation Authorization and Reform Act (AFAR).
d. The Federal Institution for Regulation and Enforcement of Appraisal Act (FIREAA).

16.23 As a component of real estate value, the principle of substitution states that

a. if two similar properties are for sale, a buyer will purchase the cheaper of the two.
b. if one of two adjacent homes is more valuable, the price of the other home will tend to rise.
c. if too many properties are built in a market, the prices will tend to go down.
d. people will readily move to another home if it is of equal value.

16.24 Highest and best use of a property is that use which

a. is physically and financially feasible, legal, and the most productive.
b. is legal, feasible, and deemed the most appropriate by zoning authorities.
c. entails the largest building that zoning ordinances will allow developers to erect.
d. conforms to other properties in the area.

16.25 Lynne just bought a house. She paid $187,500, for it, even though it had been listed at $195,000. An adjoining property owner, Ken, had tried to buy the property for $185,000, but had been refused. He now offers Lynne $190,000 for the house. Lynne is interested, so she hires an appraiser. The appraiser returns an estimate of value of $200,000. Which of these numbers can be called the market value?

a. $187,500.
b. $190,000.
c. $195,000.
d. $200,000.

16.26 A notable weakness of the sales comparison approach to value is that

a. there may be no recent sale price data in the market.
b. the approach is not based on the principle of substitution.
c. the approach is only accurate with unique, special purpose properties.
d. sale prices cannot be compared, since all real estate is different.

16.27 In the market data approach, an appraiser

a. chooses nearby comparables, adjusts the subject for differences, and estimates the value.
b. gathers relevant price data, applies the data to the subject, and estimates the value.
c. selects comparable properties, adjusts the comparables, and estimates the value.
d. identifies the price previously paid, applies an appreciation rate, and estimates the value.

174

16.28 In the sales comparison approach, an adjustment is warranted if

    a. the buyer obtains conventional financing for the property.
    b. the seller offers below-market seller financing.
    c. a comparable is located in another, albeit similar neighborhood.
    d. one property has a hip roof and the other has a gabled roof.

16.29 To complete the sales comparison approach, the appraiser

    a. averages the comparable values.
    b. weights the comparables.
    c. identifies the subject's value as that of the middle value of the comparables.
    d. identifies the subject's value as that of the nearest comparable.

16.30 One weakness of the cost approach for appraising market value is that

    a. builders may not pay market value for materials or labor.
    b. market value is not always the same as what the property cost.
    c. comparables used may not have similar quality of construction.
    d. new properties have inestimable costs and rates of depreciation.

16.31 The cost of constructing a functional equivalent of a subject property is known as

    a. reproduction cost.
    b. replacement cost.
    c. restitution cost.
    d. reconstruction cost.

16.32 An office building lacks fiber optic cabling to accommodate the latest communications equipment. This is an example of

    a. physical deterioration.
    b. economic obsolescence.
    c. incurable depreciation.
    d. functional obsolescence.

16.33 A home is located in a neighborhood where homeowners on the block have failed to maintain their properties. This is an example of

    a. curable external obsolescence.
    b. incurable economic obsolescence.
    c. functional obsolescence.
    d. physical deterioration.

16.34 In appraisal, loss of value in a property from any cause is referred to as

    a. deterioration.
    b. obsolescence.
    c. depreciation.
    d. deflation.

16.35 In the cost approach, after estimating the value of the land and the cost of the improvements, the appraiser

    a. estimates depreciation, subtracts depreciation from cost of improvements, and adds back the land value.
    b. subtracts deterioration from cost, estimates land depreciation, and totals the two values.
    c. estimates depreciation of land and improvements and subtracts the total from original cost.
    d. estimates obsolescence and subtracts from the cost of land and improvements.

Section 17 Test: Real Estate Investments

17.1 When an investor has to pay a lender more to finance the investment than the investment property generates in income, the investor suffers from

  a. negative amortization.
  b. negative leverage.
  c. a reverse mortgage.
  d. a debt investment.

17.2 Cost recovery is allowed as a federal tax deduction on

  a. principal residences that do not have a home office.
  b. income properties.
  c. land.
  d. commercial properties owned by the federal government.

17.3 A homeowner paid $200,000 for a house three years ago. The house sells today for $239,000. How much has the property appreciated?

  a. 8.4 %.
  b. 6.5 %.
  c. 19.5 %.
  d. 16.3 %.

17.4 The primary tax benefit in owning a non-income property such as a residence is

  a. depreciation of improvements.
  b. appreciation of land.
  c. a deduction for costs of operating the property.
  d. a deduction for mortgage interest.

17.5 A house sold for $250,000. The seller paid a brokerage commission of six percent, legal fees of $600, and had other closing costs of $1,500. What are net proceeds from the sale?

  a. $235,000.
  b. $234,000.
  c. $233,500.
  d. $232,900.

17.6 A homeowner bought a house five years ago for $150,000. Since then, the homeowner has spent $3,000 to pave the driveway and has added a central heating/airconditioning system at a cost of $4,000. What is the homeowner's adjusted basis if the house is sold today?

  a. $156,000.
  b. $157,000.
  c. $144,000.
  d. $145,000.

17.7 A homeowner sold her house and realized a net proceeds amount of $210,000. Her adjusted basis in the home was $176,000. She immediately bought another house for $200,000. What was her capital gain?
  a. $10,000.
  b. $24,000.
  c. $34,000.
  d. None.

17.8 After five years of owner-occupancy, Simon Wilson sells his principal residence for a gain of $150,000, and the next month buys another principal residence that costs more than the adjusted sale price of the old home. Which of the following is true of the treatment of the tax on gain?

a. There is no taxable gain.
b. It must be paid in the year of the sale.
c. The homeowner may choose to pay it or defer it.
d. Tax is due on the difference between the cost of the new home and adjusted basis of the old one.

17.9 Ralph Roberts buys a small office building as an investment and participates actively in the management and operation of the building. This is an example of

a. syndication.
b. equity investment.
c. direct investment.
d. illiquidity.

17.10 Elmo Gilmore owns a small retail property that he inherited from his father. There are no mortgages or interest expenses connected with the property. Elmo takes an annual cost recovery expense of $5,000. The property has a monthly gross income of $1,500 and monthly operating expenses of $500. Elmo's taxable income from this property will be taxed at a rate of 30%. What is the tax liability for the year?

a. $2,100.
b. $3,600.
c. $3,900.
d. $7,000.

17.11 All investors desire their investments to increase in value. However,

a. the degree of return is inversely related to the degree of risk.
b. the more the investor stands to gain, the greater the risk that the investor may lose.
c. investments requiring intense management have lesser returns.
d. the more liquid an investment is, the greater the chances are that the investment will not appreciate.

17.12 Two of the financial rewards that investments offer are

a. income and tax benefits.
b. negative leverage and appreciation.
c. appreciation and taxation.
d. positive leverage and prestige.

17.13 Because a real estate investment can take a long time to sell, real estate investments are considered to be

a. management intensive.
b. insensitive to marketing.
c. vulnerable to seller's markets.
d. relatively illiquid.

17.14 Compared to a stock portfolio, a real estate investment would be considered

a. a riskier investment.
b. a more management-intensive investment.
c. a shorter-term investment.
d. a more leveraged investment.

17.15 Six investors purchase a shopping center. One investor manages the tenants and another handles the marketing and leasing. Two investors manage accounting and finance, and the remaining two run the management office. This is a possible example of

a. a general partnership.
b. a limited partnership.
c. a real estate investment trust.
d. an investment conduit.

17.16 The formula for determining taxable income produced by an income property is

a. gross income minus expenses plus land and building depreciation.
b. gross income minus expenses minus land and building depreciation.
c. gross income minus building depreciation plus land depreciation.
d. gross income minus expenses minus building depreciation.

17.17 In deriving taxable income on an investment property, it is generally legal to

a. deduct principal and interest payments from income.
b. deduct principal payments from income.
c. deduct interest payments from income.
d. deduct principal and interest payments from income and capital gain.

17.18 Jake does not use any part of his principal residence as a home office. Which of the following is true of the tax treatment of this property?

a. The owner may deduct the property's interest and principal from ordinary income.
b. The owner may depreciate the property and deduct depreciation expenses from ordinary income.
c. The owner can deduct any capital gain when the property is sold.
d. The owner may be able to avoid capital gain tax when the property is sold.

17.19 An investment property seller pays $14,000 in closing costs. These costs

a. may be deducted from personal income.
b. may be deducted from the property's income.
c. may be deducted from the sale price for gains tax purposes.
d. may be deducted from the adjusted basis for gains tax purposes.

17.20 The formula for calculating capital gain tax is the taxpayer's tax bracket multiplied by

a. the sum of the beginning basis plus gain.
b. the difference between amount realized and adjusted basis.
c. the sum of net sale proceeds and capital gain.
d. the difference between net sale proceeds and capital gain.

Section 18 Test: Taxes Affecting Real Estate

18.1 Which of the following entities can legally levy annual real property taxes?

a. The Internal Revenue Service.
b. A utility company.
c. A tax district.
d. A court of law.

18.2 Certain classes of property owner and types of property are exempted or immune from real property taxation in many areas. The protected categories usually include

a. recreational properties.
b. properties owned by a government agency.
c. properties that comply with the Americans with Disabilities Act.
d. properties occupied by single-parent families.

18.3 What is the purpose of an equalization factor in ad valorem taxation?

a. It modifies a local tax rate to bring it into conformity with statutory tax rates.
b. It changes the assessed value of an individual property to make it reflect the assessed values of other properties in the same neighborhood.
c. It adjusts assessments in a locality to make them more consistent with an average level for the state or other higher level jurisdiction.
d. It adjusts the amount of the homestead exemption in a certain area to make it proportionally equivalent to the average homestead exemption in other areas.

18.4 A school district's tax rate is 10 mills. The school district's required revenue from real estate taxes is $20,000,000. What is the tax base of the area?

a. $20,000,000.
b. $200,000,000.
c. $2,000,000,000.
d. $200,000,000,000.

18.5 A homeowner receives a tax bill that includes an amount for the library district, taxed at $1.00 per $1,000, and the fire protection district, taxed at $2.00 per $1,000. How much does the taxpayer have to pay for these two items if the property's taxable value is $147,000?

a. $1,567.
b. $157.
c. $1,410.
d. $441.

18.6 A town is replacing a sidewalk that serves five homes. The length of the sidewalk is 200 feet. Mary's property has 38 feet of front footage. If the cost of the project to be paid by a special assessment is $30,000, what will Mary's assessment be?

a. $6,000.
b. $5,700.
c. $789.
d. $1,579.

18.7 What is a tax deed?

    a. A conveyance instrument for a property that is sold to enforce a tax lien.
    b. A document recorded in title records showing that property taxes have been paid.
    c. A notice to a homeowner that a tax lien has been entered against the property.
    d. A document that gives a municipal authority the power to collect an individual tax bill.

18.8 If a property owner has the right to redeem his or her property after a tax sale, the owner has

    a. a legal right of rescission.
    b. an equitable right to acquire title.
    c. a right of homestead exclusion.
    d. a statutory right of redemption.

18.9 The formula for deriving a municipal jurisdiction's ad valorem tax base is

    a. the jurisdiction's annual budget times the tax rate.
    b. the total of all assessed values of properties minus exemptions.
    c. the total amount of ad valorem taxes required by the budget.
    d. the municipality's budget multiplied times the millage rate.

18.10 A homeowner's total tax bill is derived by

    a. dividing the tax requirement by the tax base.
    b. multiplying each district's tax rate times the market value of the property.
    c. multiplying each district's tax rate times the taxable value of the property.
    d. averaging the tax rate for each tax district, and multiplying the average tax rate times the assessed value.

19.1   Which of the following is true regarding master planning and zoning?

   a. The aggregate of zoning ordinances is the master plan.
   b. A master plan eliminates the need for zoning ordinances.
   c. Master planning is a county-level function; zoning is limited to the city level.
   d. Zoning ordinances are a primary means of keeping land use in harmony with the master plan.

19.2   The basic intent of zoning ordinances is to

   a. establish the basis for public ownership of land for the common good.
   b. establish subdivision rules and regulations.
   c. specify usage for every parcel within the zoning authority's jurisdiction.
   d. restrict development in unincorporated areas.

19.3   Why do zoning authorities create different types of zones?

   a. To ensure that a variety of building structures are available in the community.
   b. To separate land uses so that they do not interfere with each other.
   c. To preserve high density land uses.
   d. To discourage industrial and commercial users from relocating.

19.4   The key consideration in granting a zoning exception known as a special exception is which of the following?

   a. Hardship.
   b. Change of zones.
   c. The public interest
   d. The use was legal prior to the new zone creation

19.5   The intensity of land usage generally refers to what?

   a. The number of residential building lots per acre.
   b. The number of people per square mile.
   c. The number of building permits issued per year within a zoning jurisdiction.
   d. The area of a commercial or industrial facility in relation to the size of the site.

19.6   How does Planned Unit Development zoning vary from ordinary zoning?

   a. It applies only to office parks.
   b. It incorporates a number of different zones within a single property boundary.
   c. It requires that multiple tracts of land be developed according to a single design.
   d. It requires developers to obtain a separate building permit for every structure.

19.7   Which of the following situations is most likely to represent an illegal nonconforming use?

   a. A homeowner in a residential zone converts her residence to a private school.
   b. A homeowner builds a toolshed in a neighborhood where there are no toolsheds.
   c. A storeowner remodels a storefront in accordance with regulations, and then the zoning is changed to residential.
   d. A new zoning ordinance outlaws two-story additions after a homeowner completes an addition.

19.8   What is the difference between a variance and a nonconforming use?

   a. A variance, once granted, is unconditional and permanent.
   b. A variance is granted by the zoning board if the owner has a justifiable reason.
   c. A nonconforming use is allowed if the owner requests it in advance of building.
   d. A nonconforming use violates current zoning, but a variance does not.

19.9   A document certifying that a structure complies with building codes and is ready for use is referred to as a(n)

   a. inspection report.
   b. satisfaction bond.
   c. certificate of occupancy.
   d. user permit.

19.10   Which of the following is true of an eminent domain proceeding?

   a. It cancels the property owner's mortgage loan balance.
   b. It leaves the property owner with equitable title in place of legal title.
   c. It conveys legal title to the acquiring entity.
   d. It clouds the chain of title by canceling the original grant.

19.11   Among other provisions, the Superfund Act (CERCLA) and Superfund Amendment and Reauthorization Act of 1986 provided that

   a. large development projects undergo an environmental impact survey immediately after completion of construction.
   b. industrial users of real estate comply with air quality standards.
   c. the EPA would give financial help to homeowners to remedy any hazardous situation resulting from radon, asbestos, or lead-based paint.
   d. parties responsible for improper disposal of hazardous waste could be charged for the cleanup costs.

19.12   Public land use planning strives to balance which of the following potentially conflicting interests?

   a. Individual property rights and the public's interest.
   b. Public policy makers and community business leaders.
   c. Tenant occupancy specifications and construction contractors.
   d. Individual property owners and municipal planning agencies.

19.13   Zoning, building codes, and environmental restrictions are forms of local land use control known as
   a. master planning.
   b. preemption.
   c. police power.
   d. concurrency.

19.14   If a municipality exerts its power of eminent domain against a certain property owner, what happens?

   a. The owner must pay higher property taxes or give up the property.
   b. The owner must cede an easement without receiving any compensation.
   c. The municipality annexes the property.
   d. The owner must sell the property in exchange for market-value compensation.

19.15   To be valid, a local zoning ordinance must

   a. reasonably promote community health, safety and welfare.
   b. comply with federal zoning laws.
   c. apply only to unique properties.
   d. published periodically in the local newspaper.

19.16 Why do communities require building permits?

    a. To promote development.
    b. To establish the basis for an inspection.
    c. To promote certificates of occupancy.
    d. To ensure that improvements comply with codes.

19.17 What is the purpose of residential zoning?

    a. To increase home values in a neighborhood.
    b. To regulate the density of dwellings in the residential zone.
    c. To prevent families from residing in commercial and industrial sites.
    d. To maximize intensity of usage.

19.18 A non-profit organization wants to erect an urgent care facility in a residential zone. Given other favorable circumstances, the local authorities may grant permission by allowing

    a. a special exception.
    b. an illegal nonconforming use.
    c. an easement.
    d. a license.

19.19 A property that conformed with zoning ordinances when it was developed but does not conform to new ordinances is said to be

    a. an illegal special exception.
    b. a variance.
    c. a legal nonconforming use.
    d. unmarketable.

19.20 The approval process for development of multiple properties in an area includes submission of

    a. a covenant of restriction.
    b. a plat of subdivision.
    c. a court order.
    d. a developer's pro forma.

20.1   A licensee sells 5/6 of an acre for $28,000, and receives a 6% commission. If she splits with her broker 50-50, what did she receive per square foot?

   a. $.023 / SF
   b. $.046 / SF
   c. $.037/ SF
   d. $.002 / SF

20.2   Lots in the South Hyde subdivision are selling for approximately $.50 / SF. The Grandersons want to build a 2,500 SF home on a 1.5 acre corner lot. The custom builder can build the home for $135 / SF. What will the completed property cost the Grandersons?

   a. $359,170
   b. $370,170
   c. $32,670
   d. $374,070

20.3   Ivan owned a 1/4 acre lot. He wanted to construct a 120' x 80' tennis court on the lot. What approximate percentage of the lot will be left over, if any, when he has completed the construction?

   a. 12%
   b. 88%
   c. 3%
   d. 15%

20.4   A developer wants to develop a 16-acre subdivision. He figures that the streets and common area will take up about 30% of this overall area. If the minimum lot size is to be 12,000 SF, how many lots can the developer have on this property?

   a. 42
   b. 487
   c. 40
   d. 57

20.5   A homeowner wants to insulate the new recreation room in her basement. She has been told that 3" of insulation would do the job. The walls are all 9' high and respectively measure 13', 13', 18', and 18' in length. How many rolls will she need if each roll measures 3" x 2' x 50'?

   a. 6
   b. 56
   c. 5
   d. 9

20.6   Maria plans to mulch the flower area around her house. The house measures 40' x 30', and she figures she'll mulch an area 8' in width to form a big rectangle all around the perimeter. What is the square footage of the resulting mulched area?

   a. 64 SF
   b. 2,576 SF
   c. 1,824 SF
   d. 1,376 SF

20.7. Calculate how many acres are in the Southeastern ¼ of the Western ½ of the Eastern ½ of Section 9.

    a. 20 acres
    b. 40 acres
    c. 60 acres
    d. 5 acres

20.8. Homeowner Savannah owns the Southeastern ¼ of the Southwestern ¼ of the Northwestern ¼ of Section 4. How many acres is that property?

    a. 4 acres
    b. 40 acres
    c. 10 acres
    d. 8 acres

20.9 Yard of Pizza has a percentage lease on its 1,800 SF space in Lincoln Shops. The terms are $1.40 / SF / month rent plus 1.75% of the store's gross income. If monthly sales averaged $41,500 last year, how much annual rent did Yard of Pizza pay last year?

    a. $38,955
    b. $43,420
    c. $30,240
    d. $21,525

20.10 A home appreciated 2 2/3% one year, then 5 1/5% the next year, then 7 1/4% the third year. What was the average appreciation over the 3-year period expressed as a decimal?

    a. 5.04%
    b. 15.24%
    c. 7.56%
    d. 4.8%

20.11 A homeowner paid $185,000 for a house three years ago. The house sells today for $239,000. How much has the property appreciated?

    a. 23 %
    b. 77 %
    c. 29 %
    d. 123 %

20.12 Seller Frank receives an offer of $290,000 on a property he listed at $308,000. How much is the offer as a percent of the listing price?

    a. 87%
    b. 91%
    c. 94%
    d. 106%

20.13 A property is being appraised using the income capitalization approach. Annually, it has potential gross income of $30,000, vacancy and credit losses of $1,500, and operating expenses of $10,000. Using a capitalization rate of 9%, what is the indicated value (to the nearest $1,000)?

    a. $206,000
    b. $167,000
    c. $222,000
    d. $180,000

20.14 If gross income on a property is $75,000, net income is $30,000 and the cap rate is 8%, the value of the property using the income capitalization method is

a. $625,000
b. $375,000
c. $3,750,000
d. $937,500

20.15 The roof of a property cost $16,000. The economic life of the roof is 20 years. Assuming the straight-line method of depreciation, what is the depreciated value of the roof after 3 years?

a. $16,000
b. $13,600
c. $18,400
d. $12,000

20.16 Lee had to report his home office depreciation for the tax year. He has a 2,500 SF home and a 500 SF office area. Lee paid $280,000 for his home, and he figures the land portion carries about 25% of that value. If Lee depreciates on a 39-year basis, how much can he write off for his home office depreciation per year?

a. $1,077
b. $1,436
c. $5,384
d. $2,108

20.17 A property is being appraised by the cost approach. The appraiser estimates that the land is worth $40,000 and the replacement cost of the improvements is $175,000. Total depreciation from all causes is $27,000. What is the indicated value of the property?

a. $148,000
b. $228,000
c. $162,000
d. $188,000

20.18 An apartment owner paid $500,000 for her complex 5 years ago. An appraiser at that time valued the land @ $100,000, but land has appreciated 25% over this period. The investor has used a 40-year straight-line depreciation method to depreciate the property. What is its current value using the cost approach?

a. $437,500
b. $462,500
c. $475,000
d. $546,875

20.19 An apartment building that recently sold for $400,000 had monthly gross rent receipts of $3,200. What is its monthly gross rent multiplier?

a. 80
b. .01
c. 110
d. 125

20.20 A rental home has monthly gross income of $1,100. A suitable gross income multiplier derived from market data is 14.7. What estimated sale price (to the nearest $1,000) is indicated?

a. $99,000
b. $162,000
c. $194,000
d. $173,000

20.21 Amy obtains a 75% LTV loan on her new $200,000 home with an annual interest rate of 6%. What is the first month's interest payment?

a. $900
b. $250
c. $1,000
d. $750

20.22 Emily has an interest-only home equity loan at an annual interest rate of 5.3%. If her monthly payment is $790, how much is the loan's principal balance (to the nearest $1,000)?

a. $222,000
b. $179,000
c. $95,000
d. $146,000

20.23 The loan officer at Sixth Fourth Bank tells Amanda she can afford a monthly payment of $1,000 on her new home loan. Assuming this is an interest-only loan, and the principal balance is $249,000, what interest rate is Amanda getting?

a. 4.82%
b. 5.03%
c. 6.25%
d. 3.69%

20.24 The Keegans obtain a fixed-rate amortized 30-year loan for $280,000 @ 6.25% interest. If the monthly payments are $1,724, how much interest do the Keegans pay in the second month of the loan?

a. $1,748.33
b. $1,456.95
c. $1,458.33
d. $1724.00

20.25 A lender offers the Greys two alternative loan packages for their $60,000 home equity application. One option is an interest-only loan for 5 years @ 6.5% interest with no points, and the second, a 6.25% interest-only loan for 5 years with 1 point to be paid at closing. Which loan will cost the Greys less total interest, and by how much?

a. The first option, by $150.
b. The second option, by 150.
c. The second option, by $750.
d. Both options charge the same amount of interest.

20.26 Jose recently obtained a 90% loan on his $410,000 home, and he had to pay $6,150 for points. How many points did he pay?

a. 1.4 points
b. 1.67 points
c. 2.48 points
d. 1.5 points

20.27 Mack is buying Roy's house for $500,000. Mack's loan amount is $325,000. He has agreed to pay 1.5 points at closing. How much will Mack pay for points?

a. $450
b. $4,500
c. $4,875
d. $7,500

20.28 A lender determines that a homebuyer can afford to borrow $130,000 on a mortgage loan. The lender requires an 80% loan-to-value ratio. How much can the borrower pay for a property and still qualify for this loan amount?

a. $138,000
b. $104,000
c. $162,500
d. $170,000

20.29 Home buyer Janet pays $1,600 / month for the interest-only loan on her new house. The loan's interest rate is 6.75%. If she obtained a 75% loan, what was the purchase price?

a. $313,333
b. $31,604
c. $379,259
d. $256,000

20.30 Loan applicant Taylor has an annual gross income of $76,000. How much will a lender allow Taylor to pay for monthly housing expense to qualify for a loan if the lender uses an income ratio of 30%?

a. $2,160
b. $1,900
c. $1,215
d. $4,433

20.31 An investor paid $80,000 for a lot and $600,000 to have an apartment building constructed on it. He has depreciated the property for the past 10 years on a 39-year straight-line schedule. If he sells the property this year and realizes $780,000, what is his capital gain?

a. $253,846
b. $274,000
c. $100,000
d. $179,000

20.32. A homeowner bought a house five years ago for $250,000. Since then, the homeowner has spent $2,000 to build a screened porch and has added a central air-conditioning system at a cost of $5,000. What is the homeowner's adjusted basis if the house is sold today?

a. $256,000
b. $257,000
c. $244,000
d. $245,000

20.33 A homeowner sold her house and had net proceeds of $265,000. Her adjusted basis in the home was $231,000. She immediately bought another house for $301,000. What was her capital gain?

a. $265,000
b. $36,000
c. $34,000
d. None

20.34 Debra bought a home for $120,000, paying $24,000 down and taking a mortgage loan of $96,000. The following year she had a new roof put on, at a cost of $5,000. What is Debra's adjusted basis in the house if she now sells the house for $150,000?
a. $29,000
b. $96,000
c. $101,000
d. $125,000

20.35 A certain investor wants an 11% return on investment from any real estate investment. A property priced at $360,000 has gross income of $60,000 and expenses of $22,000. Approximately how much too high or too low is the price of this property for the investor to obtain her desired return exactly?

a. $1,000 overpriced.
b. $8,000 underpriced.
c. $15,000 overpriced.
d. $16,000 underpriced.

20.36 An office building investor sees a listing of an office building which is priced at $2 million. He loves the property, but he knows he needs to make a return of at least 8% to satisfy his partners. If the building is 25,000 SF, rents for $10/SF per year, has 5% vacancy, and annual expenses of $70,000, should he buy it? What is his return?

a. No, since he will yield 2.00%.
b. Yes, since he will yield 8.375%.
c. Yes, since he will yield 8%.
d. Yes, since he will yield 9.125%.

20.37 Chad owns a small retail property that he inherited from his father. There are no mortgages or interest expenses connected with the property. Chad takes an annual cost recovery expense of $7,000. The property has a monthly gross income of $1,650 and monthly operating expenses of $600. Chad's taxable income from this property will be taxed at a rate of 30%. What is the tax liability for the year?

a. $1,680
b. $5,940
c. $2,100
d. $7,000

20.38 A property has a net income of $150,000, interest payments of $105,000, principal payments of $30,000, and annual cost recovery of $7,000. The property's tax rate is 28%. What is the property's annual tax on income?

a. $14,550
b. $40,040
c. $10,640
d. $2,240

20.39 An investor bought 4 oversized lots in order to subdivide. He paid $70,000 for the lots. After subdividing, the investor was able to sell each lot for $23,000. Excluding commissions and closing costs, what per cent profit did the investor realize?

a. 0%
b. 45%
c. 23.9%
d. 31.4%

20.40 A school district's tax rate is 10 mills. The school district's required revenue from taxes is $10,000,000. What is the tax base of the area?

a. $10,000,000
b. $100,000,000
c. $1,000,000,000
d. $100,000,000,000

20.41 A homeowner's residence has an assessed valuation of $140,000, and a market value of $170,000. The homestead exemption is $25,000. Tax rates for the property are 7 mills for schools; 3 mills for the city; 2 mills for the county; and 1 mill for the local community college. What is the homeowner's tax bill?

a. $1,495
b. $1,820
c. $1,150
d. $2,210

20.42 The village of Goodsprings has an annual budget requirement of $8,000,000 to be funded by property taxes. Assessed valuations are $400,000,000, and exemptions total $25,000,000. What must the tax rate be to finance the budget?

a. 2.00%
b. 2.13%
c. 1.32%
d. 21.33%

20.43 A property has sold for $127,000. The listing agreement calls for a commission of 7%. The listing broker and selling broker agree to share the commission equally. What will the listing agent receive if the agent is scheduled to get a 40% share from his broker?

a. $4,445
b. $3,556
c. $2,667
d. $1,778

20.44 Kevin, who works for selling broker Paul, sells a house listed by listing broker Adams. The house sells for $325,000. The co-brokerage split between Paul and Adams is 50-50. Kevin is on a 65% commission schedule with Paul. If the total commission rate is 6.5%, what is Kevin's commission?

a. $6,866
b. $5,282
c. $10,563
d. $13,731

20.45. A sale transaction closes on April 1, the ninety-first day of the tax year. The day of closing belongs to the seller. Real estate taxes for the year, not yet billed, are expected to be $3,150. According to the 365-day method, what should appear on the closing statement?

a. A debit to the buyer and credit to the seller for $2,364.62
b. A debit to the buyer and credit to the seller for $785.34
c. A credit to the buyer and debit to the seller for $785.34
d. A credit to the buyer and debit to the seller for $2,364.62

20.46 Alexis is buying Jack's house. The closing date (day belongs to seller) of the sale transaction is September 1 (day 244 of the year). Her loan has a monthly payment of $577.84, with $525 going to interest in the first month. At closing, Alexis must pre-pay interest for the period of Sept. 2-Sept. 30. Use the 365-day method for prorating. What is her prepaid interest amount?

a. $507.50
b. $525.00
c. $543.10
d. $558.58

20.47 A sale transaction on rental property closes on December 16. The landlord received the December rent of $1,380 on December 1. Assuming the closing day is the buyer's, and that the 365-day method is used for prorating, which of the following entries would appear on the settlement statement?

a. Debit seller $667.74.
b. Credit seller $1,380.00.
c. Debit buyer $712.26.
d. Credit buyer $712.26.

20.48 A home sells for $322,600 in Primm County. Here, transfer taxes are set at $1.00 per $500 of the sale price. Title insurance runs $450, and the attorney costs $550. The agent's commission is 7%, and the mortgage balance is $210,000. Annual real estate taxes are estimated to be $4,000, half of which will have to be charged to the seller. If the seller pays all of these expenses, what will she net at closing?

a. $86,873
b. $88,371
c. $81,372
d. $86,372

20.49 A farmer wants to net at least $5,000/acre on the sale of his 300-acre property. If he allows for 10% commissions and closing costs, and to allow for negotiating room, he wants to get 95% of the listing price as the selling price, what should his listing price be per acre?

a. $5,750
b. $5,882
c. $4,250
d. $5,848

20.50. The Wildes have purchased a $740,000 home. The land is worth 25%, and they insure the improvements @ 75% of their replacement value. If the Wildes suffer damage estimated at $500,000, and they have an 80% co-insurance clause, what will their recovery be from the policy?

a. Zero
b. $531,915
c. $500,000
d. $468,750

20.51 The Uptons carry a $140,000 property insurance policy which covers 75% of the replacement cost of their insurable property, valued at $190,000. They have an 80% co-insurance requirement in the policy. If the family incurs a $150,000 loss, what if any amount will the Uptons recover?

a. $159,999
b. $140,625
c. $140,000
d. $187,500

PART FOUR: FLORIDA LICENSE EXAM SIMULATION TEST

S 1.   A farmer temporarily installs produce coolers in a leased farm stand in order to prevent spoilage. The coolers would be considered which of the following?

    a.   Trade fixtures that are real property.
    b.   Trade fixtures that are personal property.
    c.   Temporary real property.
    d.   Emblements.

S 2.   Property can be converted from real to personal property and from personal property to real property by means of which processes, respectively?

    a.   Assemblage and plottage.
    b.   Application and dissolution.
    c.   Severance and affixing.
    d.   Planting and harvesting.

S 3.   The highest form of ownership interest one can acquire in real estate is the

    a.   legal life estate.
    b.   conventional life estate.
    c.   defeasible fee simple estate.
    d.   absolute fee simple estate.

S 4.   The distinguishing feature of a defeasible fee simple estate is that

    a.   it can be passed on to heirs.
    b.   it has no restrictions on use.
    c.   the estate may revert to a grantor or heirs if the prescribed use changes.
    d.   it is of unlimited duration.

S 5.   Maria acquires a property from her uncle Alfonso. When Maria dies, the estate will pass to Alfonso's other niece, Serena. The type of estate that Maria has in the property is a

    a.   conventional life estate.
    b.   legal life estate.
    c.   fee simple defeasible estate.
    d.   tenancy by the entireties.

S 6.   One difference between a cooperative estate and a condominium estate is that

    a.   a condominium owner owns a unit of air space whereas the co-op owner owns a proprietary lease.
    b.   a condominium sale adversely affects other unit owners.
    c.   the coop owner owns stock and a freehold real estate interest whereas the condominium owner simply owns a proprietary lease.
    d.   the condominium owner owns the common elements and the airspace whereas the coop owner only owns the apartment.

S 7. Who are the essential parties involved in an estate in trust?

    a.   Owner, trustor and lawyer.
    b.   Owner, trustor and trustee.
    c.   Trustee, title company, and beneficiary.
    d.   Trustor, trustee and beneficiary.

S 8. A condominium owner enjoys a

    a.   share in an association that owns one's apartment.
    b.   tenancy in common interest in airspace and common areas of the property.
    c.   fee simple ownership of the airspace in a unit and an undivided share of the entire property's common areas.
    d.   fee simple ownership of a pro rata share of the entire property.

S 9. With various types of junior liens, the order of payment priority is generally established according to

    a.   the date of recordation.
    b.   what form of tax is in question.
    c.   the order of disbursement.
    d.   whether the lien was subordinated.

S 10. What is a lien-theory state in contrast to a title-theory state?

    a.   A state in which liens are given priority over other encumbrances.
    b.   A state in which a mortgagor retains title to the property when a mortgage lien is created.
    c.   A state in which the holder of a mortgage lien receives title to the mortgaged property until the debt is satisfied.
    d.   A state in which liens must be recorded to be enforceable.

S 11. A property owner has an easement appurtenant on her property. One day the property is sold to another party who is opposed to the easement. Following the closing, this particular form of easement

    a.   terminates.
    b.   transfers with the property.
    c.   transfers with the owner to a new property.
    d.   becomes a license on the property.

S 12. What fundamental legal purpose is fulfilled by title records?

    a.   Keeping the county apprised of tax payments.
    b.   Preventing identity theft.
    c.   Giving constructive notice of one's rights and interests in the property.
    d.   Assembling all relevant documents in a single place.

S 13. What is "chain of title?"

    a.   The list of all parties who have ever owned real estate.
    b.   The bundle of rights linked to the recorded title to a parcel.
    c.   A chronology of successive owners of record of a parcel of real estate.
    d.   Involuntary conveyance of title by statutory rules of descent.

S 14. Which of the following provides the strongest evidence of marketable title?

    a.   A general warranty deed.
    b.   A title certificate.
    c.   Title insurance.
    d.   An attorney's opinion.

S 15. A store owner enters into a lease that charges rent per square foot, a common area fee, and a portion of the store owner's gross income from the property. This kind of lease is a

a. triple charge, or triple net lease.
b. proprietor's lease.
c. percentage lease.
d. retailer's gross lease.

S 16. An owner leases a property to a business in exchange for rent. The tenant is required to pay all operating expenses as well. This is an example of a

a. proprietary lease.
b. percentage lease.
c. gross lease.
d. net lease.

S 17. A lease automatically terminates under which of the following circumstances?

a. The tenant fails to pay rent.
b. The leased property is foreclosed.
c. The tenant goes out of business.
d. The landlord cancels the lease.

S 18. A county or municipal authority usually grants a certificate of occupancy for new construction only after

a. all contractors' work has been inspected.
b. all work has been completed for at least sixty days.
c. the construction conforms to building codes.
d. the tax assessor has valued the improvement.

S 19. A property owner is precluded by deed restriction from developing a thirty foot boat dock. The limitation prompts the owner to sell to another party. The new owner

a. is free to build the dock since the next door neighbor built a similar dock two weeks later.
b. takes title subject to the same restriction.
c. can build the dock with special permission from the zoning board.
d. may build, since the restriction is extinguished by the sale.

S 20. Emily sells Rycole a property containing a deed condition. The condition stipulates that the forested portion of the property must never be razed for development. Three months later, Rycole proceeds to harvest the trees and turn the area into an executive golf course. What recourse, if any, does Emily have under the deed condition?

a. She has the right to re-possess the property because the grantee has violated the condition.
b. The condition has ceased to apply because she allowed the violation to continue for a certain period of time.
c. She can claim the proceeds from the harvested trees.
d. She can force Rycole to sell the property to a new owner who agrees to comply with the condition.

S 21. What is the essential purpose of legal descriptions of real property?

a. To create a consistent, unchanging standard for uniquely locating a property.
b. To enable courts and attorneys to calculate property size accurately.
c. To comply with common law for real property.
d. To eliminate cumbersome metes and bounds descriptions.

194

S 22. Which of the following characterizes metes and bounds descriptions?

   a.   They use meridians and base lines.
   b.   They identify an enclosed area, beginning and ending at the same point.
   c.   They use lot and block numbers.
   d.   They incorporate elevation into the descriptions.

S 23. A buyer agrees to all terms of a seller's offer except the length of time for a contingency to procure financing. The buyer extends the financing period in the offer by one week, signs the form, and mails it back to the seller. At this point, the seller's offer

   a.   is void.
   b.   becomes an executory contract.
   c.   becomes a counteroffer.
   d.   has been accepted, since the modification was a contingency.

S 24. Real estate contracts that are not personal service contracts

   a.   may be assigned.
   b.   are not assignable.
   c.   must be in writing.
   d.   are exempt from the statute of frauds.

S 25. Which of the following contracts must be in writing to be enforceable?

   a.   A parol contract.
   b.   A six-month lease.
   c.   A two-year lease.
   d.   An executory contract.

S 26. Agent Bob, who works for Broker Bill, obtains an owner listing to lease a building. Bill's other agent, Sue, locates a tenant for Bob's listing. Broker Bill in this instance is

   a.   an implied agent.
   b.   a dual agent.
   c.   a single agent.
   d.   a subagent.

S 27. A transaction broker should disclose his or her agency relationship to prospective buyers and sellers

   a.   upon first substantive communication.
   b.   upon completion of the listing agreement.
   c.   immediately following completion of any offer.
   d.   Immediately prior to closing.

S 28. A transaction facilitator in a residential transaction represents

   a.   the seller.
   b.   the buyer.
   c.   both seller and buyer.
   d.   neither seller nor buyer.

S 29. A principal instructs an agent to inform minority buyers that the property for lease was just leased an hour ago and is no longer available. The agent refuses to comply. In this case,

   a.   the agent should exercise caution until the listing expires, then decline to renew it.
   b.   the principal has proposed an illegal act, which should not be obeyed.
   c.   the agent is liable for breaching the listing terms.
   d.   the agent may sue the principal for discrimination and misrepresentation.

S 30. The amount of a real estate broker's commission is established by

    a. agreement among competing brokers.
    b. negotiation with clients.
    c. the local Board of Realtors®.
    d. state real estate license law.

S 31. A client revokes an exclusive right-to-sell listing two months prior to expiration. The reason stated: the client is too busy to meet with the agent. In this case,

    a. the client is criminally liable for negligence.
    b. the client may be liable for a commission and marketing expenses.
    c. the agent can sue the client for specific performance, even if no customer had been located.
    d. the agent must accept the revocation without the possibility of damage recovery.

S 32. A protection period clause in an exclusive listing provides that

    a. the owner is protected from all liabilities arising from the agent's actions performed within the agent's scope of duties.
    b. the agent has a claim to a commission if the owner sells or leases to a party within a certain time following the listing's expiration.
    c. agents are entitled to extend a listing agreement's term if a transaction is imminent.
    d. an owner is not liable for a commission if a prospective customer delays in completing an acceptable offer.

S 33. Real estate advertising must conform to regulatory standards and requirements. One requirement is

    a. a broker may only place blind ads in social media outlets.
    b. a broker must have all advertising approved by the local real estate board.
    c. the advertising must not be deceptive.
    d. sales agents may only advertise in their own name.

S 34. The three principal brokerage firms in a market agree to pay sales agents 15% more than any other competitor currently in practice. This is an example of

    a. collusion.
    b. price fixing.
    c. allocation of markets.
    d. steering.

S 35. Two leading agencies jointly agree to raise commissions charged to residential sellers to 7.5% of the sales price. Which of the following is true?

    a. This is a perfectly legitimate business practice.
    b. The brokers have illegally fixed prices.
    c. The brokers have allocated markets.
    d. The brokers have engaged in legal collusion.

S 36. A sale contract contains an open-ended financing contingency: if the buyer cannot obtain financing within a reasonable time, the deal is off. Six months later, the buyer still cannot secure financing. Which of the following is true?

    a. The seller may cancel the contract, since it can be ruled invalid.
    b. The buyer can continue indefinitely to seek financing, and the seller's property must remain off the market, since "reasonable" is not defined.
    c. The escrow agent is entitled to the buyer's deposit.
    d. The seller can force a lender to commit to a loan under fair financing laws.

S 37. In the event of a buyer's default, a provision for liquidated damages in a sale contract enables a seller to

    a. sue the buyer for specific performance.
    b. force the buyer to quitclaim equitable title.
    c. sue the buyer for the broker's marketing expenses.
    d. claim the deposit as compensated damages for the buyer's failure to perform.

S 38. Which of the following is true of an option-to-buy agreement?

    a. The potential buyer, the optionee, is obligated to buy the property once the option agreement is completed.
    b. The optionor must perform if the optionee takes the option, but the optionee is under no obligation to do so.
    c. The contract can be executed at no cost to the optionee.
    d. It is a bilateral agreement.

S 39. If a manufacturer that is the major employer in a small city moves its operations to another city, it is reasonable to expect

    a. a fall in housing demand, but no other changes in the real estate market.
    b. a decline in demand for all types of real estate in the real estate market.
    c. an immediate fall in the demand for industrial real estate, but no other changes in the real estate market.
    d. an immediate decline in the prices for industrial and office real estate, but no impact on the residential market.

S 40. If a commercial real estate market is undersupplied, it is likely that

    a. rental prices in that market will fall.
    b. rental prices in that market will rise.
    c. rental prices will remain stable until equilibrium is reached.
    d. construction will increase to the point of equilibrium.

S 41. The amount of available property that becomes occupied over a period of time is called

    a. vacancy.
    b. absorption.
    c. equilibrium.
    d. occupation.

S 42 The roof of a property cost $20,000. The economic life of the roof is 20 years. Assuming the straight-line method of depreciation, what is the depreciated value of the roof after 3 years?

    a. $20,000.
    b. $17,000.
    c. $14,000.
    d. $3,000.

S 43. The income capitalization approach to appraising value is most applicable for which of the following property types?

    a. Single family homes.
    b. Apartment buildings.
    c. Undeveloped land.
    d. Churches.

S 44. In the income capitalization approach, an appraiser

   a. estimates gross income and multiplies times the gross income multiplier.
   b. estimates effective income, subtracts tax, and applies a capitalization rate.
   c. estimates net income and applies a capitalization rate to it.
   d. estimates potential income and applies a capitalization rate to it.

S 45. Net operating income is equal to

   a. potential income minus expenses minus debt service.
   b. effective gross income minus potential income.
   c. potential gross income minus vacancy and credit loss minus expenses.
   d. effective gross income minus vacancy and credit loss.

S 46. If net income on a property is $40,000 and the cap rate is 10%, the value of the property using the income capitalization method is

   a. $100,000.
   b. $400,000.
   c. $1,000,000.
   d. $4,000,000.

S 47. The key feature of an adjustable mortgage loan is that

   a. the interest rate may vary.
   b. the monthly payment increases over the life of the loan.
   c. the principal balance does not amortize.
   d. the loan term can be shortened or lengthened.

S 48. Why is a wraparound mortgage loan potentially interesting to a home seller as an investment?

   a. It is a senior loan that can be easily subordinated for additional debt.
   b. A wraparound lender can profit when the interest rate of the wraparound exceeds that of the underlying mortgage.
   c. The underlying loan is retired early.
   d. The second mortgage borrower may make payments directly to the first mortgage lender.

S 49. A builder is required to secure a loan with mortgages on three properties. This is an example of

   a. a participation mortgage loan.
   b. a blanket mortgage loan.
   c. a permanent mortgage loan.
   d. a bridge loan.

S 50. Which of the following is true of a loan with negative amortization?

   a. The interest rate on the loan increases as the principal balance decreases.
   b. Payments are not sufficient to retire the loan.
   c. The loan balance is diminishing, or going negative.
   d. Additional interest is being added to the monthly payment.

S 51. The loan-to-value ratio is used as an underwriting mechanism because

   a. the LTV determines the profitability of the loan.
   b. the loan amount needs to be less than the property's value.
   c. borrowers tend to inflate the true value of the property.
   d. a full-price loan overfinances the borrower.

S 52. In the past, borrowers were often surprised by unexpected or undisclosed borrowing fees and expenses at closing. This phenomenon has been largely corrected through disclosure requirements mandated by which of the following laws?

a. Equal Credit Opportunity Act
b. Truth-in-Lending laws
c. National Disclosure Procedures Act
d. Federal Fair Housing Laws

S 53. Which of the following is an important function of the secondary mortgage market?

a. Participants borrow funds from banks so the banks can make more loans.
b. Participants issue tax certificates and sell them to primary lenders.
c. Participants purchase pools of defaulted loans from lenders to keep them solvent.
d. Participants sell mortgage-backed securities in order to buy pools of loans.

S 54. Cash flow is a measure of how much pre-tax or after-tax cash an investment property generates. To derive cash flow it is therefore necessary to exclude

a. cost recovery expense.
b. interest expense.
c. loan principal payments.
d. net operating income.

S 55. The method for deriving an investor's return on investment, or ROI, is by

a. dividing net operating income by cash flow.
b. multiplying the required yield times after-tax cash flow.
c. dividing net income by the price paid for the property.
d. multiplying cash flow times the price paid for the property.

S 56. Which of the following items would affect a homeowner's adjusted basis?

a. Installing a higher capacity air conditioning and purifying system.
b. Replacing a washing machine.
c. Stripping and staining hardwood floors.
d. Replacing a broken picture window.

S 57. Which of the following is true with respect to real property taxation by the federal government?

a. It imposes ad valorem property taxes and capital gain tax.
b. It may not impose property taxes or tax liens.
c. There are no federal ad valorem taxes on real property.
d. It imposes ad valorem tax, but not capital gain tax.

S 58. Ad valorem taxes are based on

a. the replacement value of property.
b. the assessed value of property.
c. the millage value of property.
d. the broker's estimate of value.

S 59. A retirement facility prohibits ownership of any unit by persons under 55 years of age. The association claims it has made the prohibition properly. Which of the following is true?

a. They are violating the Civil Rights Act of 1866.
b. They are violating the Fair Housing Amendments Act of 1988.
c. They are guilty of age discrimination.
d. The prohibition may be legal if performed correctly.

S 60. An agent receives a full-price offer from a minority party. The agent presents the offer to the seller and discloses the buyer's minority status. The seller at that point instructs the agent to inform the buyer that the property has just gone under contract. The agent duly complies, telling the offeror that the home has just been temporarily removed from the market and is unavailable – but may be available soon if the contract falls through. Which party or parties, if any, have violated fair housing laws?

    a. The agent only.
    b. The owner only.
    c. The agent and the owner.
    d. Neither agent nor owner.

S 61. Which of the following are examples of closing items not prorated between buyer and seller?

    a. Taxes.
    b. Inspection fees.
    c. Utilities.
    d. Condominium assessments.

S 62. Which of the following activities is not allowed under the Real Estate Settlements and Procedures Act?

    a. A broker having any business relationship with an insurance company that is involved in the broker's transaction.
    b. A broker pre-qualifying a buyer for a mortgage loan.
    c. A lender requiring a deposit from a borrower for a tax and insurance escrow account.
    d. A lender paying a fee to a broker for referring a borrower to the lender.

S 63. Which of the following communication records must (as opposed to should) be kept?

    a. Notes on every conversation.
    b. Copies of required communications to principals.
    c. Notes from company training sessions.
    d. Business cards of licensees one meets at open houses.

S 64. To minimize the risk of violating fair housing laws, a licensee should

    a. refuse to use terms that refer to or describe any of the classes of persons protected by the laws.
    b. avoid working in neighborhoods that are predominantly occupied by a single ethnic group.
    c. make discriminatory or derogatory remarks in conversation only, never in writing.
    d. give better service to members of a protected class than is standard for other clients or customers.

S 65. What are "tenant improvements?"

    a. Modifications to a rental suite to conform to a tenant's usage specifications
    b. Marketing programs that yield a higher quality of tenant
    c. Increased revenue resulting from a rise in rental rates
    d. Increased occupancy resulting from a population increase in the market area

S 66. For the proper handling of client and owner monies, a property manager is generally required to

    a. deposit all funds every month in the management firm's central operating account.
    b. employ a notary to witness and record every deposit or payment received.
    c. maintain a special trust account in a qualified financial depository.
    d. disburse all funds to their legal owners on a weekly basis.

S 67. Jennifer advised her clients they needed to paint their living room before showing the property. The walls of these rooms were all 8' high. The wall lengths were 14', 18', 16', and 18'. If a gallon of paint covers 200 SF, how many whole gallons would the homesellers have to buy?

    a.   1
    b.   2
    c.   3
    d.   6

S 68. An investor just purchased a rectangular 2-acre retail lot for $250 a frontage foot. If she paid $100,000 total, what was the depth of the lot?

    a.   400'
    b.   250
    c.   871'
    d.   218'

S 69. Andra can afford to spend $5,000 in closing costs to refinance her home. The lender quotes closing costs of $800 plus 2 points. The house appraised out at $240,000, and she can get an 80% loan. Can Annika afford to refinance?

    a.   No, she is short by $64.
    b.   No, she is short by $1,600.
    c.   Yes, with $360 left over.
    d.   Yes, she in fact breaks even.

S 70. A lender offers an investor a maximum 70% LTV loan on the appraised value of a property. If the investor pays $230,000 for the property, and this is 15% more than the appraised value, how much will the investor have to pay as a down payment?

    a. $93,150
    b. $79,350
    c. $90,000
    d. $69,000

S 71. A house is being appraised using the sales comparison approach. The house has three bedrooms, two bathrooms, and a patio. The appraiser selects a comparable house that has three bedrooms, 2.5 bathrooms, and no patio. The comparable house just sold for $100,000. A half-bath is valued at $5,000, and a patio at $1,000. Assuming all else is equal, what is the adjusted value of the comparable?

    a. $100,000
    b. $104,000
    c. $96,000
    d. $106,000

S 72. A family purchased a $90,000 lot to build a custom home. At the date of closing, the lot was assessed at $84,550 and the tax rate was $1.91 / $100 assessed valuation. When they completed the home, the assessment increased by $235,000 to include the new construction. If the monthly tax escrow is based on the assessed value, what will the monthly tax escrow be?

    a. $517
    b. $6096
    c. $508
    d. $367

S 73. The James family purchased a home for $180,000 five years ago and obtained an 80% LTV loan. Now the property has appreciated 25%. In addition, the loan has been paid down $11,000. What is the James's current equity in the home?

    a. $47,000
    b. $81,000
    c. $45,000
    d. $92,000

S 74. George and Mary have owned a rental house for 10 years. They bought it for $240,000 and estimated the land value @ 25%. If the property is depreciated on a 39-year schedule, and appreciation totals 50% over the period, what is their gain if they sell the property today?

    a. $159,230
    b. $166,150
    c. $181,538
    d. $120,000

S 75. Adelpha's home is valued at $250,000. She has insurance coverage of $160,000 with an 80% co-insurance clause. If Adelpha has a damage claim amounting to $100,000, how much will she receive from her policy?

    a. $32,000
    b. $60,000
    c. $80,000
    d. $100,000

S 76. When applying for a Florida real estate license, the applicant must disclose if his or her license has been disciplined in any other jurisdiction, or

    a. he or she can be fined $500.
    b. his or her license can be converted to inactive status.
    c. his or her Florida license can be denied.
    d. he or she can be permanently barred from licensure in Florida.

S 77. Fred lives outside Florida and practices real estate in a mutual recognition state. To practice real estate in Florida, which of the following is required of Fred?

    a. Fred must become a Florida resident.
    b. Fred must pay FREC a one-time $1,000 activation fee.
    c. Nothing, Fred is already eligible to practice real estate in FL.
    d. Fred must pass FL licensing laws exam with score of 75% or higher.

S 78. To meet the educational requirements for a broker's license, what can be substituted for the 72 classroom hour pre-licensing course?

    a. 24 months of real estate experience during previous 5 years
    b. Certification of 3 years of real estate experience from state other than Florida
    c. 4-year college degree in real estate
    d. Active sales associate license with completed 14 hours of continuing education

S 79. In which of the following situations would a sales associate's license be placed in involuntary inactive status?

    a. When no transactions have been completed by the licensee over the last 12 months
    b. When the sales associate has been guilty of misconduct in practicing real estate
    c. When the sales associate's license has not been renewed at the end of the license period
    d. When the sales associate acted as a licensee within 1 year prior to actually becoming licensed

202

S 80. James is unhappy as a sales associate with Johnson Realty. James decides to quit and go to work immediately for a competitor, Benson Realty. What must James do to qualify as a sales associate for Benson?

a. He must request his license be placed on voluntary inactive status.
b. He must notify the Commission of the change within 10 days.
c. He doesn't have to do anything since he has already qualified for his sales associate license.
d. He must complete 14 hours of continuing education.

S 81. Cassandra is a sales associate who wants to work for two real estate firms. Should she apply for multiple licenses?

a. Yes – she's required to hold a separate license for each broker employer
b. Yes – since the license indicates the name of her supervising broker, she'll need multiple licenses for multiple supervising brokers
c. No – she only needs one license to practice real estate for the two firms
d. No – she is allowed to work for only one employer, and multiple licenses are only for brokers

S 82. Which type of agent has limited representation to either or both parties?

a. Single agent
b. Transaction broker
c. Subagent
d. Transitional broker

S 83. Which of the following is a duty of a broker facilitating a sale when no brokerage relationship exists?

a. Disclosure of known material facts
b. Confidentiality
c. To withhold or refuse to present all offers less than 90% of the listing price
d. Loyalty

S 84. Broker Phillip is representing Seller Tara as a single agent. Phillip would like to transition to a relationship that allows him to represent both Tara and Buyer Stan in the sale of Tara's duplex. Phillip is legally allowed to make the transition if he is not a fiduciary to either and if

a. he believes it will benefit both Tara and Stan.
b. Stan enters into an agency relationship with Phillip.
c. both Tara and Stan agree to the transition in writing.
d. Florida changes its laws to allow dual agents.

S 85. Which of the following would not be considered fraud?

a. A licensee knew about a sink hole that had previously occurred on a property but didn't tell the buyer.
b. A licensee knew the seller was HIV-positive but didn't tell the buyer.
c. A licensee did not tell a buyer about mold on the property, and the buyer's child became extremely ill from exposure to the mold.
d. A licensee knew the city was planning to build a super highway in close proximity to the property but didn't tell the buyer.

S 86. The requirements for a broker placing deposits into an interest-bearing escrow account do not include

a. consent of all involved parties.
b. account to be insured.
c. deposit owner (e.g., buyer) to be signatory on account.
d. account to be in Florida.

S 87. Who has lien rights against real property?

    a. Commercial brokers
    b. Residential brokers
    c. Construction service providers
    d. Closing agents

S 88. When is sharing a brokerage compensation with a party to the real estate transaction a legal kickback?

    a. When an agreement is made prior to the closing of the transaction
    b. When the other party is unlicensed
    c. When full disclosure is made to all interested parties
    d. When the amount of compensation shared is less than 50 percent of the amount received

S 89. To conduct an open house, an assistant needs

    a. a broker's approval.
    b. help from another assistant.
    c. a real estate license.
    d. an employer who is a licensed broker.

S 90. What is the penalty for violations of statutes regarding rental information lists?

    a. $1,500 fine
    b. Up to 5 years prison time
    c. License suspension
    d. Community service

S 91. What is the limit for broker personal funds or brokerage funds allowed in any escrow account?

    a. $1,000
    b. $5,000
    c. $10,000
    d. $25,000

S 92. A sales associate who is advertising real estate services must

    a. use his/her own name.
    b. include his/her trade name.
    c. not disclose he/she is a sales associate.
    d. advertise under his/her broker employer's name.

S 93. If escrow funds are to be placed in an interest-bearing account, which of the following requires written consent of all parties to the transaction?

    a. Bank to be used
    b. Rate of interest to be earned
    c. Designation of party to receive the interest
    d. Whether to commingle the escrow funds with brokerage funds

S 94. Who initially hears the case when a complaint goes to a formal hearing?

    a. The probable cause panel
    b. The FREC
    c. The judicial review committee
    d. The administrative law judge

S 95. Which of the following offenses is not grounds for license suspension?

    a. Cheating on the licensure end-of-course examination
    b. Deceptive advertising
    c. Filing a false complaint against another licensee
    d. Failure to share all offers with clients

S 96. In what situation may the Commission deviate from penalty or discipline guidelines?

    a. Licensee's first offense
    b. Lack of harm to consumer or public
    c. Mitigating circumstances
    d. Chapter 455 violation

S 97. What happens to a broker's license if payments are made from the Real Estate Recovery Fund for a claim made against the broker?

    a. The license is suspended.
    b. The license is revoked.
    c. The license is placed on voluntary inactive status.
    d. Nothing happens to the license.

S 98. Buyer Hannah is accusing Broker Gary of discriminating against her when she was purchasing seller Yvonne's house. Who faces the burden of proof in this Florida Fair Housing case?

    a. Hannah
    b. Gary
    c. Yvonne
    d. FREC

S 99. The Florida Clean Indoor Air Act protects the quality of indoor air by

    a. regulating mold cleanup inside buildings.
    b. requiring radon detectors in multi-family residential buildings.
    c. prohibiting smoking in workplaces.
    d. requiring smoke detectors inside public facilities.

S 100. It is permissible for real estate licensees to draft

    a. option contracts.
    b. deeds.
    c. promissory notes.
    d. no legal documents.

PART FIVE: ANSWER KEY & EXPLANATIONS

SECTION 1 TEST: The Real Estate Business

1.1 (b) Procuring a buyer or a tenant for an owner or landlord, and vice versa.
Brokerage is the business of completing real estate conveyance transactions as opposed to managing personnel or portfolios. Such transactions can be residential or commercial.

1.2 (b) Residential, retail, industrial, office, farm and land and special purpose properties
Improved real property is categorized as residential, commercial and special purpose properties. Within the commercial property category, you have office, industrial, and retail properties. Additionally, it is common to put land and agricultural property in their own category.

1.3 (c) State government
License laws are enacted by state legislatures, and regulations that enforce the statutes are promulgated by real estate commissions and agencies at the state level. Federal laws and local building codes also impact real estate practice, but these are not generally considered to be "license laws."

1.4 (c) A tract home
With tract homes, the builder offers a choice of floor plans and the buyer selects a plan and a given lot. Spec homes are build without prior purchase or commitment from buyer.

1.5 (b) A custom home
With custom homes, the blue prints are often unique and the buyer has a sales contract before construction starts. The buyer is often very involved in the design of the new home.

SECTION 2 TEST: Florida License Law & Qualifications for Licensure

2.1 (b) It is still pending approval until 90 days have passed.
"Any application for a license which is not approved or denied within the 90-day or shorter time period, within 15 days after conclusion of a public hearing held on the application, or within 45 days after a recommended order is submitted to the agency and the parties, whichever action and timeframe is latest and applicable, is considered approved..." 120.60(1)

2.2 (d) The broker is not eligible for a Florida license under the mutual recognition agreement.
Licensing under the mutual recognition agreement is for nonresidents only. 475.180
"For purposes of s. 475.180(1), Florida Statutes, a 'resident' of Florida is defined as:
(1) a person who has resided (regardless of whether the place or base of residence is a recreational vehicle, hotel, rental unit, or any other temporary or permanent situs) in Florida, continuously for a period of 4 calendar months or more, within the preceding one year..." 61J2-26.002
The broker in question is a 6-month resident of Florida.

2.3 (c) A person who buys or sells real estate on behalf of others for compensation
"Broker means a person who, for another, and for a compensation or valuable consideration directly or indirectly paid or promised, expressly or impliedly, or with an intent to collect or receive a compensation or valuable consideration therefor, appraises, auctions, sells, exchanges, buys, rents, or offers, attempts or agrees to appraise, auction, or negotiate the sale, exchange, purchase, or rental of business enterprises or business opportunities or any real property or any interest in or concerning the same..." 475.01(1)(a)

2.4 (b) Chapter 475
"Purpose.—The Legislature deems it necessary in the interest of the public welfare to regulate real estate brokers, sales associates, and schools in this state." 475.001

2.5 (b) Interest in land, business enterprises, or business opportunities with some exceptions
"'Real property' or 'real estate' means any interest or estate in land and any interest in business enterprises or business opportunities, including any assignment, leasehold, subleasehold, or mineral right; however, the term does not include any cemetery lot or right of burial in any cemetery; nor does the term include the renting of a mobile home lot or recreational vehicle lot in a mobile home park or travel park." 475.01(1)(i)

2.6 (d) Social Security number
"Any person desiring to be licensed shall apply to the department in writing. The application for licensure shall be submitted on a form prescribed by the department and must include the applicant's social security number." 455.213(1)

2.7 (c) 14 hours of continuing education every 2 years
"The renewal application for an active license as broker, broker associate, or sales associate shall include proof satisfactory to the commission that the licensee has, since the issuance or renewal of her or his current license, satisfactorily completed at least 14 classroom hours of 50 minutes each of a continuing education course during each biennium of a license period, as prescribed by the commission." 475.182(1)(a)

2.8 (d) 72 hours of pre-licensing coursework.
"The course or courses required for one to become initially licensed shall not exceed a total of 63 classroom hours of 50 minutes each, inclusive of examination, for a sales associate and 72 classroom hours of 50 minutes each, inclusive of examination, for a broker." 475.17(2)(a)1.

2.9 (d) An individual renting properly licensed public lodging
"Any person, partnership, corporation, or other legal entity which, for another and for compensation or other valuable consideration, rents or advertises for rent, for transient occupancy, any public lodging establishment licensed under chapter 509." 475.011(11) Exemptions

2.10 (b) Anyone procuring purchasers of business opportunities
"... or who takes any part in the procuring of sellers, purchasers, lessors, or lessees of business enterprises or business opportunities or the real property of another..." 475.01(1)(a)

2.11 (d) No license
"Any full-time graduate student who is enrolled in a commission-approved degree program in appraising at a college or university in this state, if the student is acting under the direct supervision of a licensed broker or a licensed or certified appraiser and is engaged only in appraisal activities related to the approved degree program." 475.011(7) Exemptions

2.12 (b) 2 years after it was received
"The application shall expire 2 years after the date received if the applicant does not pass the appropriate examination." 475.181(2)

2.13 (d) Any of the above
"Approval or denial of a specialty course must be based on the extent to which the course content focuses on real estate issues relevant to the modern practice of real estate by a real estate licensee, including technology used in the real estate industry. The commission may accept as a substitute for such continuing education course, on a classroom-hour-for-classroom-hour basis, any satisfactorily completed education course that the commission finds is adequate to educate licensees within the intent of this section, including an approved distance learning course. ... The commission may accept as a substitute for 3 classroom hours, one time per renewal cycle, attendance at one legal agenda session of the commission." 475.182(1)(a) and (b)

2.14 (a) passing end-of-course exam.
"The commission may prescribe a postlicensure education requirement in order for a person to maintain a valid broker's license, which shall not exceed 60 classroom hours of 50 minutes each, inclusive of examination, prior to the first renewal following initial licensure." 475.17(4)(a)

2.15 (b) Notify the Commission of his change of residency and comply with nonresident requirements

"Any resident licensee who becomes a nonresident shall, within 60 days, notify the commission of the change in residency and comply with nonresident requirements. Failure to notify and comply is a violation of the license law, subject to the penalties in s. 475.25." 475.180(2)(a)

2.16 (b) 30 days

"Upon receipt of a license application, an agency shall examine the application and, within 30 days after such receipt, notify the applicant of any apparent errors or omissions and request any additional information the agency is permitted by law to require." 120.60(1)

2.17 (b) The applicant was not notified of the error within the designated time period.

"An agency may not deny a license for failure to correct an error or omission or to supply additional information unless the agency timely notified the applicant within this 30-day period." 120.60(1)

2.18 (a) Chapter 61J2

Chapter 61J2 is the Florida Real Estate Commission's administrative rules pursuant to Chapter 120 that include detailed principles for real estate practice. It is an expansion of the Chapter 475 provisions. 61J2

2.19 (b) Chapter 455

Florida Statute Chapter 455 establishes the general provisions for Business and Professional Regulation, including provisions for military personnel on active duty, spouses of military personnel on active duty, and immigrants practicing real estate.

SECTION 3 TEST: Real Estate License Law and Commission Rules

3.1 (a) seven members, all appointed by the Governor.

"There is created within the department the Florida Real Estate Commission. The commission shall consist of seven members who shall be appointed by the Governor, subject to confirmation by the Senate." 475.02(1)

3.2 (d) The Commission is responsible for fostering the education of brokers in the principles that should govern their conduct.

"The commission shall foster the education of brokers, broker associates, sales associates, and instructors concerning the ethical, legal, and business principles which should govern their conduct." 475.04(1)

3.3 (b) It can be reinstated within 6 months.

"The commission may reinstate the license of an individual whose license has become void if the commission determines that the individual failed to comply because of illness or economic hardship, as defined by rule. The individual must apply to the commission for reinstatement within 6 months after the date that the license becomes void." 475.183(4)

3.4 (b) Prior to the first renewal of her license

"The commission may prescribe a postlicensure education requirement in order for a person to maintain a valid sales associate's license, which shall not exceed 45 classroom hours of 50 minutes each, inclusive of examination, prior to the first renewal following initial licensure." 475.17 (3)(a)

3.5 (c) It has ceased to be in force.

"A license shall cease to be in force whenever a broker changes her or his business address... The licensee shall notify the commission of the change no later than 10 days after the change..." 475.23

3.6 (a) Suspend the license of a broker who is not in compliance with a support order

"The department shall, when directed by the court or the Department of Revenue pursuant to s. 409.2598, suspend or deny the license of any licensee found not to be in compliance with a support order, subpoena, order to show cause, or written agreement entered into by the licensee with the Department of Revenue." 455.203(9)

SECTION 4 TEST: Authorized Relationships, Duties and Disclosure

4.1 (d) gives a broker authority to act on his/her behalf.
"Determination of agency or transactional brokerage relationship.—Without consideration of the related facts and circumstances, the mere payment or promise to pay compensation to a licensee does not determine whether an agency or transactional brokerage relationship exists between the licensee and a seller, landlord, buyer, or tenant. " 475.255

4.2 (b) Dual
"Disclosed dual agency as an authorized form of representation by a real estate licensee in this state is expressly revoked..." 475.272(1)

4.3 (a) To provide customers with a greater understanding of real estate transactions and broker relationships
"In order to eliminate confusion and provide for a better understanding on the part of customers in real estate transactions, the Legislature finds that the intent of the Brokerage Relationship Disclosure Act is to provide that:
(1)   Disclosed dual agency as an authorized form of representation by a real estate licensee in this state is expressly revoked;
(2)   Disclosure requirements for real estate licensees relating to authorized forms of brokerage representation are established;
(3)   Single agents may represent either a buyer or a seller, but not both, in a real estate transaction; and
(4)   Transaction brokers provide a limited form of nonfiduciary representation to a buyer, a seller, or both in a real estate transaction." 475.272

4.4 (c) residential property.
"The disclosure requirements of s. 475.278 apply only to residential sales as defined in s. 475.278(5)(a). " 475.274

4.5 (c) sales associates who are acting as single agents under certain conditions in the same transaction.
"For purposes of this part, in any real estate transaction other than a residential sale as defined in s. 475.278(5)(a), and where the buyer and seller have assets of $1 million or more, the broker at the request of the customers may designate sales associates to act as single agents for different customers in the same transaction." 475.2755(1)

4.6 (d) Designated sales associate
"... the buyer and seller as customers shall both sign disclosures stating that their assets meet the threshold described in this subsection and requesting that the broker use the designated sales associate form of representation." 475.2755(1)

4.7 (c) 10 residential units in one building
"As used in this subsection, the term 'residential sale' means the sale of improved residential property of four units or fewer, the sale of unimproved residential property intended for use of four units or fewer, or the sale of agricultural property of 10 acres or fewer." 475.278(5)(a)

4.8 (a) Limited confidentiality
"TRANSACTION BROKER RELATIONSHIP... The duties of the real estate licensee in this limited form of representation include the following: ... Limited confidentiality, unless waived in writing by a party." 475.278(2)(f)

4.9 (b)   The 3-residential-unit property is being rented with an option to buy.
"The real estate licensee disclosure requirements of this section do not apply to: nonresidential transactions; the rental or leasing of real property, unless an option to purchase all or a portion of the property improved with four or fewer residential units is given;..." 475.278(5)(b)2

4.10 (c) dual agent.
"As used in this section, the term 'dual agent' means a broker who represents as a fiduciary both the

prospective buyer and the prospective seller in a real estate transaction." 475.278(1)(a)

4.11 (c) another type of relationship is established in writing.
"Presumption of transaction brokerage.—It shall be presumed that all licensees are operating as transaction brokers unless a single agent or no brokerage relationship is established, in writing, with a customer." 475.278(1)(b)

4.12 (a) To advise and assist the sales associates
"However, Florida law allows a designated sales associate to disclose information allowed to be disclosed or required to be disclosed by law and also allows a designated sales associate to disclose to his or her broker, or persons specified by the broker, confidential information of a customer for the purpose of seeking advice or assistance for the benefit of the customer in regard to a transaction." 475.2755(1)

4.13 (b) establishes brokerage representation disclosure requirements.
"… the Legislature finds that the intent of the Brokerage Relationship Disclosure Act is to provide that:… Disclosure requirements for real estate licensees relating to authorized forms of brokerage representation are established;…" 475.272

4.14 (d) residential sales.
"Scope of coverage.—The authorized brokerage relationships described in ss. 475.2755 and 475.278 apply in all brokerage activities as defined in s. 475.01(1)(a). The disclosure requirements of s. 475.278 apply only to residential sales as defined in s. 475.278(5)(a)." 475.274

4.15 (b) the fiduciary representation to one customer.
"TRANSACTION BROKER RELATIONSHIP.—A transaction broker provides a limited form of representation to a buyer, a seller, or both in a real estate transaction but does not represent either in a fiduciary capacity or as a single agent." 475.278(2)

4.16 (d) No brokerage relationship
Unless Chuck and Terrance enter into an agency agreement, there is no brokerage relationship. Terrance can help facilitate the sale of the property and even be paid commission for the sale, but without a relationship agreed upon either verbally or in writing, it does not exist. However, the broker must still disclose his duties to the seller in writing prior to showing the property. 475.278(4)

4.17 (c) Puffing
Puffing is extravagant claims about the good points of real property and is based on opinion rather than fact, As long as the statement is not an outright lie (or a Fair Housing violation, etc.), puffing is not illegal.

4.18 (c) A sales associate claiming her license allows her to open her own real estate firm.
Only licensees with broker licenses can open their own real estate brokerage. The other answers have actions that licensees can/should do.

4.19 (b) Apply the Golden Rule.
Do unto others as you would have them do unto you is the ethical code that directs you to treat others as you would want to be treated. It is also known as the ethic of reciprocity. The behavior of any other agent cannot be relied upon to be ethical, and ethics are not regulated by statutes. Therefore, an act can be legal but not ethical.

4.20 (d) May not under Florida statutes regarding registration of general partners
"This section shall not operate to permit a broker associate or sales associate to register or be licensed as a general partner, member, manager, officer, or director of a brokerage firm…" 475.161

4.21 (c) If the sales associate has permission from his or her employer to collect the commission and collects it in the employer's name
"A sales associate may not collect any money in connection with any real estate brokerage transaction, whether as a commission, deposit, payment, rental, or otherwise, except in the name of the employer and with the express consent of the employer…" 475.42(1)(d)

4.22 (b) Ken would need to act under his registered employer and collect the commission in his employer's name.

"…no real estate sales associate, whether the holder of a valid and current license or not, shall commence or maintain any action for a commission or compensation in connection with a real estate brokerage transaction against any person except a person registered as her or his employer at the time the sales associate performed the act or rendered the service for which the commission or compensation is due." 475.42(1)(d)

4.23 (b) the laws of agency, or in some states, by statute.

In every state, a body of law, generally called the law of agency, defines and regulates the legal roles of this relationship. While the relationship is subject to contract law, agency law dictates how the relationship will achieve its purposes, regardless of what the listing contract states.

4.24 (c) The relationship is independent of any compensation arrangement.

It is important to understand that the agency relationship does not require compensation or any form of consideration. Nor does compensation define an agency relationship: a party other than the principal may compensate the agent.

4.25 (c) The defaulting party may have a financial consequence.

Involuntary termination of the relationship may create legal and financial liability for a party who defaults or cancels. For example, a client may renounce an agreement but then be held liable for the agent's expenses or commission.

4.26 (b) present all offers to the principal regardless of their amount.

A conventional listing agreement does not authorize an agent to obligate the client to contracts, and it does not allow the agent to conceal offers to buy, sell, or lease coming from a customer or another agent. Further, since a client relies on a broker's representations, a broker must exercise care not to offer advice outside of his or her field of expertise.

4.27 (c) confidentiality.

The confidentiality standard is one of the duties that extends beyond the termination of the listing: at no time in the future may the agent disclose confidential information.

4.28 (d) comparable to that of other practitioners in the area.

The agent is hired to do a job, and is therefore expected to do it with diligence and reasonable competence. Competence is generally defined as a "standard of practice" equal to the level of real estate marketing skills and knowledge of other practitioners in the area.

4.29 (c) disclose the information to the seller.

An agent has the duty to inform the client of all material facts, reports, and rumors that might affect the client's interests in the property transaction. This includes: the agent's opinion of the property's condition; information about the buyer's motivations and financial qualifications; discussions between agent and buyer regarding the possibility of the agent's representing the buyer in another transaction.

4.30 (a) the Andersons.

Since Gerry executed an agency agreement with the Andersons, they become the client and the Lincolns the customer, regardless of who pays the commission.

4.31 (c) a broker who has an agency relationship with a client.

In a subagency, a broker or licensed sales associate works as the agent of a broker who is the agent of a client. Subagents might include a cooperating licensed broker, that broker's licensed sales associates, and the listing broker's licensed sales associates, all of whom agree to work for the listing broker on behalf of the client.

4.32 (b) One agent represents both sides in a transaction.

Dual agency means representing both principal parties to a transaction. The agent represents both buyer and seller or tenant and owner.

4.33 (c) disclosing material facts that affect the value of the property to both parties.

In the role of facilitator, the broker's only fiduciary duties and standards of conduct are those of accounting;

skill, care, and diligence; honesty and fair dealing; and disclosure to both parties of all material facts in residential sale transactions affecting the property's value. Some states do not allow for this form of relationship in a real estate transaction.

4.34 (a) The agent is showing the client's property to a prospective buyer.
Agency disclosure must occur upon "substantive contact" between the listing agent and a customer. Examples of substantive contact include: showing the prospect a property; eliciting confidential information from a prospect regarding needs, motivation, or financial qualification; and executing a contractual offer to sell or lease.

4.35 (d) trust, confidence, and good faith.
The essence of the agency relationship is trust, confidence, and mutual good faith. The principal trusts the agent to exercise the utmost skill and care in fulfilling the authorized activity, and to promote the principal's best interests. The agent undertakes to strive in good faith to achieve the desired objective, and to fulfill the fiduciary duties.

4.36 (b) general.
In a general agency, the principal delegates to the agent ongoing tasks and duties within a particular business or enterprise. Such delegation may include the authority to enter into contracts.

4.37 (b) special.
Under a special agency agreement, the principal delegates authority to conduct a specific activity, after which the agency relationship terminates. In most cases, the special agent may not bind the principal to a contract. Real estate brokerage is commonly based on a special agency.

4.38 (c) a party creates an agency relationship outside of an express agreement.
An agency relationship can arise by implication, intentionally or unintentionally. Implication means that the parties act as if there were an agreement. For example, if an agent promises a buyer to do everything possible to find a property at the lowest possible price, and the buyer accepts the proposition, there may be an implied agency relationship even though there is no specific agreement.

4.39 (a) Condemnation of the property
An agency relationship may terminate contrary to the wishes of the parties by reason of: death or incapacity of either party; abandonment by the agent; condemnation or destruction of the property; renunciation; breach; bankruptcy; or revocation of the agent's license.

4.40 (a) The agent has violated the duty of confidentiality.
An agent may not disclose any information that would harm the client's interests or bargaining position, or anything else the client wishes to keep secret. The confidentiality standard is one of the duties that extends beyond the termination of the listing: at no time in the future may the agent disclose confidential information.

4.41 (b) the agent has not violated fiduciary duty.
Since it is illegal to refuse to show buyers the property based on where the buyers live, the agent has not violated fiduciary duty. The duty of obedience only applies to legal activities.

4.42 (d) inform the seller.
An agent has the duty to inform the client of all material facts, reports, and rumors that might affect the client's interests in the property transaction.

4.43 (a) prior to completing a listing agreement.
An agent who intends to represent a seller or owner must disclose the import of the proposed agency relationship in writing before the listing agreement is executed.

4.44 (c) Whenever substantive communication is made beyond casual conversation.
A listing agent must disclose in writing to a buyer or tenant that the agent represents the owner in the transaction. This disclosure must occur before or at the first "substantive contact" with the customer prospect. In some states, buyer representatives must disclose the agency relationship to sellers or their agents upon initial contact.

4.45 (b) upon initial contact.
A buyer agent must disclose the agency relationship to the seller or seller's agent on first contact. Substantive contact is assumed to occur immediately in this circumstance.

4.46 (a) may not represent one party's interests to the detriment of the other.
A dual agent's first duty is to disclose the agency relationship to both principal parties or to withdraw from one side of the duality. After disclosing, the agent must obtain the written consent of both parties. If both parties accept the dual agency, the agent owes all the fiduciary duties to both parties except full disclosure, undivided loyalty, and exclusive representation of one principal's interests.

4.47 (d) practicing law without a license.
An agent should not act or speak outside the agent's area of expertise. A customer may rely on anything an agent says, and the agent will be held accountable. For example, an agent represents that a property will appreciate. The buyer interprets this as expert investment advice and buys the property. If the property does not appreciate, the buyer may hold the agent liable.

SECTION 5 TEST: Real Estate Brokerage Activities and Procedures

5.1 (c) Entrance sign
"Each active broker shall maintain a sign on or about the entrance of her or his principal office and each branch office" 475.22

5.2 (a) All advertising must include the brokerage phone number and image of the broker.
While the brokerage name is required, the phone number and picture of the broker are not.

5.3 (d) The broker has 30 days to correct any account errors.
"A broker shall be provided a reasonable amount of time to correct escrow errors if there is no shortage of funds and such errors pose no significant threat to economically harm the public. For purposes of this subsection, reasonable amount of time shall be defined as 30 days from the date the last reconciliation statement was performed or should have been performed." 61J2-14.010

5.4 (c) the licensee must name the title company on the sales contract.
"When a deposit is placed or to be placed with a title company or an attorney, the licensee who prepared or presented the sales contract ('Licensee'), shall indicate on that contract the name, address, and telephone number of such title company or attorney. Within ten (10) business days after each deposit is due under the sales contract, the Licensee's broker shall make written request to the title company or attorney to provide written verification of receipt of the deposit, unless the deposit is held by a title company or by an attorney nominated in writing by a seller or seller's agent. Within ten (10) business days of the date the Licensee's broker made the written request for verification of the deposit, the Licensee's broker shall provide Seller's broker with either a copy of the written verification, or, if no verification is received by Licensee's broker, written notice that Licensee's broker did not receive verification of the deposit. If Seller is not represented by a broker, then Licensee's broker shall notify the Seller directly in the same manner indicated herein." 61J2-14

5.5 (d) collusion, price fixing, and market allocation.
Antitrust laws primarily focus on promoting fair trade and fair trade practices. Among the most common antitrust violations are collusion, price fixing and market allocation. In every case a market competitor is guilty of attempting to acquire an unfair competitive advantage over another competitor.

5.6 (a) to complement the federal antitrust laws.
"The Legislature declares it to be the purpose of this act to complement the body of federal law prohibiting restraints of trade or commerce in order to foster effective competition." 542.16

5.7 (a) meets with another brokerage to compare listed properties.
Comparing listed properties does not constitute any form of trade restraints, conspiracy, monopolization, etc.

5.8 (b) his/her employer consents.
Sales associates may only collect commissions in the name of the employer and with the consent of the employer and may only perform real estate services on behalf of employer. Sales associates may not sue the principal to obtain the commission.

5.9 (c) $3,500
7% of $200,000=$14,000. Half to the buyer's broker=$7,000. The other half goes to Bob's broker who gives Bob half to = $3,500.

5.10 (d) Monies paid to a broker for using a particular service provider during a real estate transaction
The definition of kickback is payment of something of value to a recipient as compensation or reward for providing favorable treatment to another party. In real estate, most kickbacks involve mortgage providers, inspectors, or home improvement providers.

5.11 (a) Disclose it to all involved parties
"Any real estate licensee who receives, or makes any arrangement or agreement to receive, directly or indirectly, any kickback or rebate... shall have fully advised the principal if any and all affected parties in the transaction(s), which the licensee is handling, of all facts pertaining to the arrangement of kickbacks or rebates. " 61J2-10.028

5.12 (d) The associate may not remove any records from the former employer's office.
"A license shall cease to be in force whenever a broker changes her or his business address, a real estate school operating under a permit issued pursuant to s. 475.451 changes its business address, or a sales associate working for a broker or an instructor working for a real estate school changes employer. The licensee shall notify the commission of the change no later than 10 days after the change, on a form provided by the commission." 475.23

5.13 (a) The entity must have at least one active broker or sales associate as an officer, director, member, manager, or partner.
The entity must have at least one active broker, but a sales associate may not be an officer, director, member, manager, or partner.

5.14 (b) Corporate sole
Only sole proprietorships, general and limited partnerships, corporations, LLCs, and limited liability partnerships can register.

5.15 (d) be used by a sales associate.
Sales associates are required to use their legal names.

5.16 (b) sign a listing agreement.
Unlicensed individuals may not perform any real estate services.

5.17 (c) upgrades to an active broker.
Broker-associates are not allowed to be an officer, director, member, manager, or partner of a business entity unless they upgrade to active licensed brokers.

5.18 (b) It ceases to be in force.
"A license shall cease to be in force whenever a broker changes her or his business address, a real estate school operating under a permit issued pursuant to s. 475.451 changes its business address, or a sales associate working for a broker or an instructor working for a real estate school changes employer." 475.23

5.19 (d) Chad must tell everyone involved in the same transaction about the payment.
"Any real estate licensee who receives, or makes any arrangement or agreement to receive, directly or indirectly, any kickback or rebate, for the placement of, or favor in, any business transaction which forms a part of, or is incident to, any transaction(s) negotiated or handled by said licensee, is a violation of Section 475.25(1)(b) or (d), Florida Statutes, or both of said subsections of the Florida Statutes, unless prior to the time of the placement of, or favor in, said business transaction, the licensee shall have fully advised the principal if any and all affected parties in the transaction(s), which the licensee is handling, of all facts pertaining to the arrangement of kickbacks or rebates." 61J2-10.028

5.20 (c) Sal has no lien rights for the unpaid commission.
Residential brokers have no lien rights for unpaid commission.

5.21 (d) No because they have violated antitrust laws
"It is unlawful for any person to monopolize, attempt to monopolize, or combine or conspire with any other person or persons to monopolize any part of trade or commerce in this state." 542.19

5.22 (d) 4 years
"Any action brought under s. 542.21 or s. 542.22 must be commenced within 4 years after the cause of action accrues." 542.26

5.23 (b) $1,000
"A broker may place and maintain up to $1,000 of personal or brokerage funds per each sales escrow account." 61J2-14

5.24 (d) $5,000
"A broker may place and maintain up to $5,000 of personal or brokerage funds per each property management escrow account." 61J2-14

5.25 (b) When the transaction closes
"A broker shall not deliver the deposit to the other party to the transaction until such transaction is closed…" 61J2-14

5.26 (c) Create a written statement of liabilities and balances
"Once monthly, a broker shall cause to be made a written statement comparing the broker's total liability with the reconciled bank balance(s) of all trust accounts." 61J2-14

5.27 (b) Names of depositors
"The minimum information to be included in the monthly statement-reconciliation shall be the date the reconciliation was undertaken, the date used to reconcile the balances, the name of the bank(s), the name(s) of the account(s), the account number(s), the account balance(s) and date(s), deposits in transit, outstanding checks identified by date and check number, an itemized list of the broker's trust liability, and any other items necessary to reconcile the bank account balance(s) with the balance per the broker's checkbook(s) and other trust account books and records disclosing the date of receipt and the source of the funds." 61J2-14

5.28 (a) civil penalty of not more than $10,000.
"Except as provided in s. 501.2077, any person, firm, corporation, association, or entity, or any agent or employee of the foregoing, who is willfully using, or has willfully used, a method, act, or practice declared unlawful under s. 501.204, or who is willfully violating any of the rules of the department adopted under this part, is liable for a civil penalty of not more than $10,000 for each such violation." 501.2075

5.29 (b) the name of the broker is displayed on all the offices.
"Any office shall be deemed to be a branch office if the name or advertising of a broker having a principal office located elsewhere is displayed in such a manner as to reasonably lead the public to believe that such office is owned or operated by such broker." 475.24

5.30 (c) The broker must personally appear at any office of the FREC if requested in relation to an investigation.
"If the department sends, by certified mail to the broker at the broker's last known business address as registered with the department, a notice or request to produce any documents or to appear for an interview with an authorized representative of the department and the broker fails to substantially comply with that request or notice, then such failure by the broker is a violation of the license law, subject to the penalties of s. 475.25." 475.22

5.31 (b) Register the second location as a branch office
"Whenever any licensee desires to conduct business at some other location, either in the same or a different municipality or county than that in which she or he is licensed, such other place of business shall be registered as a branch office, and an annual registration fee prescribed by the commission, in an amount not

exceeding $50, shall be paid for each such office." 475.24

5.32 (c) Within 3 business days
"'Immediately' means the placement of a deposit in an escrow account no later than the end of the third business day following receipt of the item to be deposited." 61J2-14.008

5.33 (b) Broker's business account
"'Trust' or 'escrow' account means an account in a bank or trust company, title company having trust powers, credit union, or a savings and loan association within the State of Florida." 61J2-14.008

5.34 (d) Note the cause and corrective action taken
"… whenever an account has a negative balance, the reconciliation shall disclose the cause(s) of the returned check or negative balance and the corrective action taken." 61J2-14.012

5.35 (b) Retain the commission amount in the account until the dispute is resolved
"In case of a dispute as to the amount of the commission, or the time of payment, the broker may retain only the amount of the claim in said account and in trust, until the dispute is settled by agreement, arbitration, mediation or court proceedings, as provided in Section 475.25(1)(d)1., Florida Statutes." 61J2-14.011

5.36 (b) A limited liability corporation
" A sales associate may only create a limited liability corporation (LLC) or a professional association (PA). These business entities may only be formed in the name they are licensed under. They may not use a tradename."

5.37 (a) three times the amount of the damage.
"Any person who shall be injured in her or his business or property by reason of any violation of s. 542.18 or s. 542.19 may sue therefor in the circuit courts of this state and shall recover threefold the damages by her or him sustained, and the cost of suit, including a reasonable attorney's fee." 542.22

SECTION 6 TEST: Violations of License Law, Penalties & Procedures

6.1 (d) Complaint must include witnesses to the action.
Witnesses are not required when filing a complaint.

6.2 (a) Dispute the allegations and be provided an informal hearing
"A formal hearing before an administrative law judge from the Division of Administrative Hearings shall be held pursuant to chapter 120 if there are any disputed issues of material fact." 455.225

6.3 (b) within 30 days after the final order.
"All proceedings shall be instituted by filing a notice of appeal or petition for review in accordance with the Florida Rules of Appellate Procedure within 30 days after the rendition of the order being appealed." 120.68

6.4 (c) The complaint may be investigated anyway.
"The department may investigate, and the department or the appropriate board may take appropriate final action on, a complaint even though the original complainant withdraws it or otherwise indicates a desire not to cause the complaint to be investigated or prosecuted to completion." 455.225

6.5 (b) his/her license can be denied.
Passing the examination is a requirement of initial licensure.

6.6 (b) must not have been disbarred.
"If the applicant has been denied registration or a license or has been disbarred … the applicant shall be deemed not to be qualified…"475.17

6.7 (d) for a period no longer than 10 years.
"The commission may deny an application for licensure, registration, or permit, or renewal thereof; may

place a licensee, registrant, or permittee on probation; may suspend a license, registration, or permit for a period not exceeding 10 years;" 475.25

6.8 (d) is permanent.
"In the event the board, or the department when there is no board, determines that revocation of a license is the appropriate penalty, the revocation shall be permanent." 455.227

6.9 (d) His license may be suspended.
Filing false complaints against other licensees is grounds for license suspension.

6.10 (c) He may be barred from practicing real estate permanently.
Committing the same violation more than once can result in license revocation, which is permanent.

6.11 (b) License cancelation
"For purposes of this rule, the order of penalties, ranging from lowest to highest, is: reprimand, fine, probation, suspension, and revocation or denial." 61J2-24

6.12 (a) 60 days
For violations of F.S. 475, a misdemeanor in the second degree, the maximum penalty is a fine up to $500 and/or up to 60 days imprisonment.

6.13 (d) felony of the third degree.
"A person may not operate as a broker or sales associate without being the holder of a valid and current active license therefor. Any person who violates this paragraph commits a felony of the third degree..." 475.42

6.14 (a) Broker Hale failed to maintain a sign at his brokerage office.
"A violation is a minor violation if it does not demonstrate a serious inability to practice the profession, result in economic or physical harm to a person, or adversely affect the public health, safety, or welfare or create a significant threat of such harm." 455.225
Failing to hang a sign is a minor violation unlike the other answer choices which are more serious.

6.15 (c) A civil court
"The Florida Real Estate Recovery Fund shall be disbursed as provided in s. 475.484, on order of the commission, as reimbursement to any person, partnership, or corporation adjudged by a court of competent civil jurisdiction in this state to have suffered monetary damages by reason of any act committed, as a part of any real estate brokerage transaction involving real property in this state, by any broker or sales associate..." 475.482

6.16 (c) 2 years of discovery of the damaging act.
"A claim for recovery is made within 2 years from the time of the act giving rise to the claim or within 2 years from the time the act is discovered or should have been discovered with the exercise of due diligence." 475.483

6.17 (d) the person notified the FREC of the claim by certified mail.
"Any person is eligible to seek recovery from the Real Estate Recovery Fund if:...At the time the action was commenced, such person gave notice thereof to the commission by certified mail..." 475.483

6.18 (c) $150,000
"Payments for claims based upon judgments against any one broker or sales associate may not exceed, in the aggregate, $150,000." 475.484

6.19 (d) stipulation.
A stipulation is an agreement between the DRE attorneys and the licensee regarding facts and penalty related a complaint.

6.20 (d) Charlene should file a citation against the broker.
A citation is not filed or issued by the complainant.

6.21 (a) summary suspension order.
Summary suspension orders are issued when a licensee has committed a law violation that is so serious that action cannot wait until the results of a hearing and final order.

6.22 (c) To give notice to licensees of the range of penalties allowed for each count during a hearing
"The purpose of the disciplinary guidelines is to give notice to licensees of the range of penalties which normally will be imposed for each count during a formal or an informal hearing." 61J2-24

SECTION 7 TEST: Federal and State Laws in Real Estate

7.1 (a) Civil Rights Act of 1866.
The original fair housing statute, the Civil Rights Act of 1866, prohibits discrimination in housing based on race. The prohibition relates to selling, renting, inheriting, and conveying real estate.

7.2 (c) race, color, religion, and national origin.
Title VIII of the Civil Rights Act of 1968, known today as the Fair Housing Act, prohibits discrimination in housing based on race, color, religion, or national origin.

7.3 (c) Advertising a property as available to individuals of a particular race. The prohibition against discriminatory advertising states that an agent may not advertise residential properties in such a way as to restrict their availability to any prospective buyer or tenant.

7.4 (c) An agent persuades a family to put their house on the market because ethnic minority families are beginning to move into the neighborhood.
Blockbusting, a prohibited activity, is the practice of inducing owners in an area to sell or rent to avoid an impending change in the ethnic or social makeup of the neighborhood that will cause values to go down.

7.5 (a) The Home Mortgage Disclosure Act.
The Home Mortgage Disclosure Act requires lenders involved with federally guaranteed or insured loans to exercise impartiality and non-discrimination in the geographical distribution of their loan portfolio. In other words, the act is designed to prohibit redlining, the practice of restricting loans by geographical are(a)

7.6 (c) privately owned single-family residences listed with a broker.
Among the circumstances where the Fair Housing Act might allow for an exemption is: a privately owned single-family home where no broker is used, with certain additional conditions. In other words, as soon as a broker is used in the sale, the law applies.

7.7 (a) illegal, because the agent changed the terms of the sale to discourage this particular couple.
The Fair Housing Act prohibition against discriminatory misrepresentation states that an agent may not conceal available properties, represent that they are not for sale or rent, or change the sale terms for the purpose of discriminating.

7.8 (d) The owner of a duplex who resides in one of the units refuses to rent the other unit to a non-Christian.
The Fair Housing Act would exempt the owner in this situation because it involves rental of an apartment in a 1-4 unit building where the owner is also an occupant and there is no discriminatory advertising.

7.9 (b) File a complaint with HUD and/or file suit against the offending parties in a state or federal court within the prescribed time period.
The Fair Housing Amendments Act of 1988 prohibits discrimination based on sex. If May feels she has been discriminated against in this way, she may file a complaint with the Office of Fair Housing and Equal Opportunity (OFHEO) in HUD within one year or file suit in a federal or state court within two years of the alleged violation.

7.10 (a) Inform Scott that the condition is illegal and that she cannot comply with it.
Scott is not allowed to discriminate based on race, color, religion, national origin, sex, family status, or handicap. If an agent goes along with a client's discriminatory act, the agent is equally liable for violation

218

of fair housing laws. It is thus imperative to avoid complicity with client discrimination. Further, an agent should withdraw from any relationship where client discrimination occurs.

7.11 (c) require families without children to pay the same security deposit that families with children must pay.
Fair housing laws prohibit discriminatory advertising, discrimination on the basis of national origin, discrimination based on age in dwellings of more than four units, and discrimination against families with children. The fact that the owner is requiring the same deposit from tenants with and without children does not discriminate against families with children but actually favors them.

7.12 (d) It is a single-family house, and the owner owns only one other rental home in addition to his own residence.
Federal fair housing laws do not prohibit age and family status discrimination in residential dwellings of four units or less and in single family houses if sold or rented by owners who have no more than three houses.

7.13 (c) the Fair Housing Amendments Act of 1988.
The Fair Housing Amendments Act of 1988 prohibited discrimination based on sex and discrimination against handicapped persons and families with children. Executive Order 11063 concerned racial discrimination in housing where federal funding was involved; the Civil Rights Act of 1968 concerned discrimination based on race, color, religion, and national origin; Jones v Mayer concerned racial discrimination.

7.14 (c) steering.
Steering is the illegal practice of limiting customers' choices by encouraging or discouraging them about the suitability of an area and directing them only to areas the agent deems suitable for them.

7.15 (a) providing unequal services.
The agent may be illegally providing unequal services by altering the nature or quality of brokerage services to a party based on race, color, sex, national origin, or religion.

7.16 (a) discriminatory misrepresentation by omission.
Discriminatory misrepresentation is the concealing of available properties, representing that they are not for sale or rent, or changing the sale terms for the purpose of discriminating.

7.17 (c) Employment
"To discharge or to fail or refuse to hire any individual, or otherwise to discriminate against any individual with respect to compensation, terms, conditions, or privileges of employment, because of such individual's race, color, religion, sex, national origin, age, handicap, or marital status." 760.10

7.18 (d) within 1 year of discrimination allegation.
"A complaint under subsection (1) must be filed within 1 year after the alleged discriminatory housing practice occurred." 760.34

7.19 (a) FL Department of Environmental Protection
The FL Department of Environmental Protection would be most helpful in regard to sinkholes. According to the FL DEP website, "for sinkhole questions, please call 850-245-2118."

7.20 (c) A leased condominium
Only condominiums occupied by the owner are excluded.

7.21 (c) Notify the tenant within 30 days of his/her vacating the premises
"…the landlord shall have 30 days to give the tenant written notice by certified mail to the tenant's last known mailing address of his or her intention to impose a claim on the deposit and the reason for imposing the claim. 83.49

7.22 (c) forced sale to satisfy liens.
"Whenever any natural person residing in this state desires to avail himself or herself of the benefit of the provisions of the constitution and laws exempting property as a homestead from forced sale under any process of law, he or she may make a statement..." 222.01

7.23 (a) Familial status
Exemptions are given to qualified individuals, so familial status is not a basis for additional exemptions.

7.24 (d) Lending based on borrower income
Income-based lending is allowed and preferred over equity-based income.

7.25 (c) A purchase contract on a property for $109,000
FL's statute of frauds covers, purchase and sale contracts, option contracts, deeds and mortgage instruments, leases for more than 1 year, and listing agreements for more than 1 year.

7.26 (c) An explanation of what radon gas is
No testing is required, but information about radon gas is required to be disclosed on the lease or sale agreement.

7.27 (b) To notify the buyer that future taxes may be different than the current taxes
The purpose of the disclosure is so the buyer will not expect future taxes to be the same as the current taxes and, thus, will not be surprised if they are different.

7.28 (d) real property transactions.
Both business and real estate brokerages handle the sale, purchase, or lease of real property.

SECTION 8 TEST: Property Rights, Estates and Tenancies

8.1 (a) Wells, driveways, and signs on a parcel of land.
The legal concept of real estate encompasses land and all man-made structures that are "permanently" attached to the land. The phrase "permanently attached" refers primarily to one's intention in attaching the item. Obviously, very few if any man-made structures can be permanently attached to the land in the literal sense. But if a person constructs a house with the intention of creating a permanent dwelling, the house is considered real estate. By contrast, if a camper affixes a tent to the land with the intention of moving it to another camp in a week, the tent would not be considered real estate.

8.2 (c) A chicken coop permanently attached to land.
Improvements to real estate include such things as fences, streets, buildings, wells, sewers, sidewalks and piers. Modifications to land or a developer's preparations of a parcel of land can include such activities as grading or clearing, neither of which are considered to be "improvements" in this sense of the word.

8.3 (b) The center of the earth and infinite space above the earth.
The legal concept of land encompasses the surface area of the earth; everything beneath the surface of the earth extending downward to its center; all natural things permanently attached to the earth; and the air above the surface of the earth extending outward to infinity. Land, therefore, includes minerals beneath the earth's surface, water on or below the earth's surface, and the air above the surface.

8.4 (a) enjoyed by the owner of a property.
This group of rights includes the right to Possess, Use, Transfer, Encumber, and Exclude others from using the property. (Remember: "PUTEE") Transfer rights include the right to sell, rent, donate, assign, or bequeath. The owner may also encumber the item by mortgaging it as collateral for debt.

8.5 (b) Any item of property that is not definable as real property.
Personal property is any owned item which is not real estate, and the rights associated with owning the personal property item. Items of personal property are also called chattels or personalty.

8.6 (b) pledge the property as collateral for debt..
The right to encumber the property essentially means the right to mortgage the property as collateral for debt. There may be restrictions to this right, such as a spouse's right to limit the degree to which a homestead may be mortgaged.

8.7 (a) transfer of a portion of the bundle of rights.
An ordinary lease is a common example of the transfer of a portion of one's bundle of rights. The owner relinquishes the right to possess portions of the surface, perhaps a building, in return for rent. The tenant enjoys the rights to possess and use the building over the term of the lease, after which these rights revert to the landlord. During the lease term, the tenant has no rights to the property's subsurface or airspace other than what the building occupies. Further, the tenant does not enjoy any of the other rights in the bundle of rights: he or she cannot encumber the property or transfer it. To a limited degree, the tenant may exclude persons other than the legal owner from the property.

8.8 (d) Yes. The drones infringe on his air rights.
Air rights apply to the space above the surface boundaries of the parcel, as delineated by imaginary vertical lines extended to infinity. Since the advent of aviation, property owners' air rights have been curtailed to allow aircraft to fly over one's property provided the overflights do not interfere with the owner's use and enjoyment of the property. The issue of violation of air rights for the benefit of air transportation is an ongoing battle between aircraft owners, airlines, airports, and nearby property owners.

8.9 (c) Navigable lakes, seas, and oceans.
Littoral rights concern properties abutting bodies of water that are not moving, such as lakes and seas. Owners of properties abutting a navigable, non-moving body of water enjoy the littoral right of use, but do not own the water nor the land beneath the water. The legal premise underlying the definition of littoral rights is that a lake or sea is a navigable body of water, therefore, public property owned by the state. By contrast, a body of water entirely contained within the boundaries of an owner's property is not navigable. In such a case, the owner would own the water as well as unrestricted rights of usage.

8.10 (a) the high water mark of the body of water at the shoreline.
Ownership extends to the high-water mark of the body of water. The low water mark would imply that the owner owned the water itself at times of high water levels!

8.11 (d) They transfer with the property when the property is sold.
Littoral rights attach to the property. When the property is sold, the littoral rights transfer with the property to the new owner.

8.12 (c) Streams and rivers.
Riparian rights concern properties abutting moving water such as streams and rivers. If a property abuts a stream or river, the owner's riparian rights are determined by whether the water is navigable or not navigable. If the property abuts a non-navigable stream, the owner enjoys unrestricted use of the water and owns the land beneath the stream to the stream's midpoint. If the waterway in question is navigable, the waterway is considered to be a public easement. In such a case, the owner's property extends t the water's edge as opposed to the midpoint of the waterway.

8.13 (b) An item of personal property that has been converted to real property.
A personal property item that has been converted to real property by attachment to real estate is called a fixture. Typical examples are chandeliers, toilets, water pumps, septic tanks, and window shutters. The owner of real property inherently owns all fixtures belonging to the real property. When the owner sells the real property, the buyer acquires rights to all fixtures.

8.14 (a) the owner originally intended to remove it after a period of time.
One's original intention can override the test of movability in determining whether an item is a fixture or not. If someone attached an item to real property, yet intended to remove it after a period of time, the article may be deemed personal property. If a person intended an article to be a fixture, even though the item is easily removable, the article may be deemed a fixture. For example, an apartment renter installs an alarm system, fully intending to remove the system upon lease expiration. Here, the alarm system would be considered personal property.

8.15 (c) Fifty percent of the estate consisting of the indivisible whole of the real property.
An undivided interest is an owner's fractional interest in an entire (undivided) estate, but not in a physical portion of the real property itself. An owner who has an undivided equal interest with another cannot exercise exclusive rights over a portion of the real estate, which is an indivisible whole.

8.16 (a) an estate in land.
Interests are principally distinguished by whether they include possession. If the interest-holder enjoys the right of possession, the party is considered to have an estate in land, or, familiarly an estate. Freehold and leasehold estates in land are further distinguished by whether the duration of the owner's rights can be determined.

8.17 (a) a public interest.
Public entities may own or lease real estate, in which case they enjoy an estate in land. However, government entities also have non-possessory interests in real estate which act to control land use for the public good within the entity's jurisdiction. The prime example of public interest is police power, or the right of the local or county government to zone. Another example of public interest is the right to acquire ownership through the power of eminent domain.

8.18 (c) a freehold estate.
In a freehold estate, the duration of the owner's rights cannot be determined: the rights may endure for a lifetime, for less than a lifetime, or for generations beyond the owner's lifetime. By contrast, leasehold estates have expirations.

8.19 (d) that the estate is limited by a lease term.
A leasehold estate is distinguished by its specific duration, as represented by the lease term. Further, leasehold tenants only enjoy limited property rights: use; temporary possession, and limited exclusion.

8.20 (d) Lucy
Once Dennis dies, the estate goes to Lucy. The state of Florida would not be involved after Dennis's death as it would be clear the property is to go to Lucy.

8.21 (c) An ordinary life estate.
A life estate is limited in duration to the life of the owner or other named person. Upon the death of the owner (ordinary life estate) or other named individual (pur autre vie life estate), the estate passes to the original owner (a reversionary interest) or another named party (a remainder interest). Thus with the life estate, the owner enjoys full ownership rights during the estate period, and holders of the future interest own either a reversionary or a remainder interest.

8.22 (b) a legal life estate.
Homestead, dower, and curtesy are legal life estates. A legal life estate is created by state law as opposed to being created by a property owner's agreement. The focus of a legal life estate is defining and protecting the property rights of surviving family members upon the death of the husband or wife.

8.23 (b) The boat, house, and motorcycle.
Separate property consists of: property owned by either spouse at the time of the marriage; property acquired by either spouse through inheritance or gift during the marriage; property acquired with separate-property funds; and income from separate property. Community property consists of all other property earned or acquired by either party during the marriage. A spouse owns separate property free and clear of claims by the other spouse. He or she can transfer it without the other spouse's signature. Upon the death of the separate property owner, the property passes to heirs by will or laws of descent. Community property cannot be transferred or encumbered without the signatures of both spouses. Upon the death of either spouse, half of the deceased's community property passes to the surviving spouse, and the other half passes to the decedent's heirs.

8.24 (d) The right to possess and use the premises.
Leasehold tenants are entitled to possess and use the leased premises during the lease term in the manner prescribed in the lease. They also have restricted rights to exclusion.

8.25 (a) the tenant makes, and landlord accepts, regular rent payments.
In an estate from period-to-period, also called a periodic tenancy, the tenancy period automatically renews as long as the tenant pays rent in a timely manner and the landlord accepts it. At the end of a tenancy period, if the landlord accepts another regular payment of rent, the leasehold is considered to be renewed for another period. A conveyance of leased property does not cancel a leasehold interest.

8.26 (c) terminates on the death of lessor or lessee.
The estate at will, also called a tenancy at will, has no definite expiration date and hence no "renewal" cycle. The landlord and tenant agree that the tenancy will have no specified termination date, provided rent is paid on time and other lease conditions are met. For example, a son leases a house to his father and mother "forever," or until they want to move. The estate at will is terminated by proper notice, or by the death of either party.

8.27 (a) an estate at sufferance.
In an estate at sufferance, a tenant occupies the premises without consent of the landlord or other legal agreement with the landlord. Usually such an estate involves a tenant who fails to vacate at the expiration of the lease, continuing occupancy without any right to do so. For example, a tenant violates the provisions of a lease and is evicted. The tenant protests and refuses to leave despite the eviction order.

8.28 (b) Estate from period to period.
In an estate from period-to-period, also called a periodic tenancy, the tenancy period automatically renews for an indefinite period of time, subject to timely payment of rent. At the end of a tenancy period, if the landlord accepts another regular payment of rent, the leasehold is considered to be renewed for another period.

8.29 (a) tenancy in severalty.
If a single party owns the fee or life estate, the ownership is a tenancy in severalty. Synonyms are sole ownership, ownership in severalty, and estate in severalty.

8.30 (c) tenancy in common.
The tenancy in common, also known as the estate in common, is the most common form of co-ownership when the owners are not married (though tenants in common can be married). The defining characteristics are: two or more owners; identical rights; interests individually owned; electable ownership shares; no survivorship; and no unity of time. With "identical rights", co-tenants share an indivisible interest in the estate, i.e., all have equal rights to possess and use the property subject to the rights of the other co-tenants.

8.31 (a) Parties must acquire respective interests at the same time.
To create a joint tenancy, all owners must acquire the property at the same time, use the same deed, acquire equal interests, and share in equal rights of possession. These are referred to as the four unities.

8.32 (b) cannot will their interest to a party outside the tenancy. The survivorship feature of joint tenancy presents an advantage to tenancy in common, in that interests pass without probate proceedings. On the other hand, joint tenants relinquish any ability to will their interest to parties outside of the tenancy.

8.33 (c) Legal life estate.
A legal life estate is created by state law as opposed to being created by a property owner's agreement. The focus of a legal life estate is defining and protecting the property rights of surviving family members upon the death of the husband or wife.

8.34 (a) A homestead interest cannot be conveyed by one spouse.
A homestead is one's principal residence. Homestead laws protect family members against losing their homes to general creditors attempting to collect on debts. Homestead laws generally provide that: the homestead interest cannot be conveyed by one spouse; both spouses must sign the deed conveying homestead property.

8.35 (a) sell or transfer his interest without the consent of the other tenants in common.
All tenants in common have distinct and separable ownership of their respective interests. Co-tenants may sell, encumber, or transfer their interests without obstruction or consent from the other owners. A co-tenant may not, however, encumber the entire property.

8.36 (c) Income derived from community property
If an income-producing property has been defined as community property, the revenue accruing from the investment is likewise community property.

8.37 (c) The beneficiary
A land trust allows the trustor to convey the fee estate to the trustee and to name himself or herself the

beneficiary. The land trust applies only to real property, not to personal property. The agreement, or deed in trust, grants the beneficiary the rights to possess and use the property, and to exercise control over the actions of the trustee.

8.38 (c) The Buick and the second property

Separate property belongs to one spouse. Separate property is that property which is acquired prior to the marriage, by gift or inheritance during the marriage, property acquired by separate-property funds, or income from separate property.

8.39 (a) A cooperative may hold an owner liable for the unpaid operating expenses of other tenants.
Since the corporation owns an undivided interest in the cooperative property, debts and financial obligations apply to the property as a whole, not to individual units as in a condominium.

8.40 (b) The owners enjoy an indivisible interest.
The tenancy in common, also known as the estate in common, is the most common form of co-ownership when the owners are not married (though tenants in common can be married). The defining characteristics are: two or more owners; identical rights; interests individually owned; electable ownership shares; no survivorship; and no unity of time. With "identical rights," co-tenants share an indivisible interest in the estate, i.e., all have equal rights to possess and use the property subject to the rights of the other co-tenants.

8.41 (a) sell her interest to a third party without the consent of Robert
All tenants in common have distinct and separable ownership of their respective interests. Co-tenants may sell, encumber, or transfer their interests without obstruction or consent from the other owners. A co-tenant may not, however, encumber the entire property.

8.42 (d) It passes by probate to the deceased tenant's heirs.
A deceased co-tenant's estate passes by probate to the decedent's heirs and devisees rather than to the other tenants in common. Any number of heirs can share in the ownership of the willed tenancy.

8.43 (c) The tenants have an equal and indivisible ownership interest.
In a joint tenancy, two or more persons collectively own a property as if they were a single person. Rights and interests are indivisible and equal: each has a shared interest in the whole property which cannot be divided up. Joint tenants may only convey their interests to outside parties as tenant-in-common interests. One can not convey a joint tenant interest.

8.44 (a) there is a single title to the property.
Whereas tenants in common hold separate title to their individual interests, joint tenants together hold a single title to the property. This is referred to as unity of ownership.

8.45 (a) the new owner becomes a tenant in common with the other owners, who continue to hold a joint tenancy with each other and a tenancy in common with the new owner.
A joint tenant may transfer his or her interest in the property to an outside party, but only as a tenancy in common interest. Whoever acquires the interest co-owns the property as a tenant in common with the other joint tenants. The remaining joint tenants continue to own an undivided interest in the property, less the new co-tenant's share.

8.46 (d) It passes to the surviving joint tenants.
In most states, joint tenants enjoy rights of survivorship: if a joint tenant dies, all interests and rights pass to the surviving joint tenants free from any claims of creditors or heirs. When only one joint tenant survives, the survivor's interest becomes an estate in severalty, and the joint tenancy is terminated.

8.47 (c) If they are married.
Tenancy by the entireties is a form of ownership reserved exclusively for husband and wife. It features survivorship, equal interests, and limited exposure to foreclosure.

8.48 (c) The trustee.
In an estate in trust, a fee owner-- the grantor or trustor-- transfers legal title to a fiduciary-- the trustee-- who holds and manages the estate for the benefit of another party, the beneficiary. The trust may be created by a deed, will, or trust agreement.

8.49 (a) sell or mortgage the unit without impediment from individual owners of neighboring units.
Condominium units can be individually sold, mortgaged, or otherwise encumbered without interference from other unit owners. An owner may not sell interests in the apartment separately from the interest in the common elements. Unit owners exclusively possess their apartment space, but must share common areas with other owners.

8.50 (b) the unit's pro rata share of the property value as defined in the declaration.
The unit's pro rata share of the property's ownership as defined in the declaration determines the amount of a unit owner's assessment. For example, if a unit represents a 2% share of the property value, that unit owner's assessment will be 2% of the property's common area expenses.

8.51 (a) shares in a corporation or association and a proprietary lease in a physical unit.
In a cooperative, or co-op, one owns shares in a non-profit corporation or cooperative association, which in turn acquires and owns an apartment building as its principal asset. Along with this stock, the shareholder acquires a proprietary lease to occupy one of the apartment units.

8.52 (d) the corporate entity of the cooperative association.
The corporate entity of the cooperative association is the only party in the cooperative with a real property interest. The association's interest is an undivided interest in the entire property. There is no ownership interest in individual units, as with a condominium.

8.53 (a) undivided interests in the property as tenants in common.
In a freehold time-share, or interval ownership estate, tenants in common own undivided interests in the property. Expense prorations and rules governing interval usage are established by separate agreement when the estate is acquired.

8.54 (c) Estate at will.
Three of the four principal types of leasehold estate are: the estate for years, which has a specific lease term; the estate from period-to-period, where the lease term of a specific period automatically renews; and the estate at will, which has no specified lease term. The fourth principal type, the estate at sufferance, is a tenancy without consent that therefore also has no specific term.

SECTION 9 TEST: Title, Deeds and Ownership Restrictions

9.1 (c) A third party's interest in a real property that limits the interests of the freehold property owner.
An encumbrance is an interest in and right to real property that limits the legal owner's freehold interest. In effect, an encumbrance is another's right to use or take possession of a legal owner's property, or to prevent the legal owner from enjoying the full bundle of rights in the estate.

9.2 (a) They involve the property that contains the easement and a non-owning party. An easement is an interest in real property that gives the holder the right to use portions of the legal owner's real property in a defined way. One cannot own an easement over one's own property. Easement rights may apply to a property's surface, subsurface, or airspace, but the affected area must be defined. An easement may be affirmative, allowing a use, such as a right-of-way, or negative, prohibiting a use, such as an airspace easement that prohibits one property owner from obstructing another's ocean view.

9.3 (d) An easement appurtenant.
An easement appurtenant gives a property owner a right of usage to portions of an adjoining property owned by another party. The property enjoying the usage right is called the dominant tenement, or dominant estate. The property containing the physical easement itself is the servient tenement, since it must serve the easement use.

9.4 (c) easement by necessity.
An easement by necessity is an easement appurtenant granted by a court of law to a property owner because of a circumstance of necessity, most commonly the need for access to a property. Since property cannot be legally landlocked, or without legal access to a public thoroughfare, a court will grant an owner

of a landlocked property an easement by necessity over an adjoining property that has access to a thoroughfare.

9.5 (b) an unauthorized physical intrusion of one property into another.
An encroachment is the unauthorized, physical intrusion of one owner's real property into that of another. Examples of encroachments are: a tree limb extending into the neighbor's property, violating his or her airspace; a driveway extending beyond the lot line onto the neighbor's land; and a fence built beyond the property line.

9.6 (c) a trespasser has been using an owner's property for a certain period with the owner's knowledge but without permission.
If someone uses another's property as an easement without permission for a statutory period of time and under certain conditions, a court order may give the user the easement right by prescription, regardless of the owner's desires. For a prescriptive easement order to be granted, the following circumstances must be true: the use has been occurring without permission or license; the owner knows or is presumed to have known of the use; and the use has been generally uninterrupted over the statutory prescriptive period.

9.7 (d) how a property may be used and what improvements may be built on it.
A deed restriction is a limitation imposed on a buyer's use of a property by stipulation in the deed of conveyance or recorded subdivision plat. A deed restriction may apply to a single property or to an entire subdivision. A developer may place restrictions on all properties within a recorded subdivision plat. Subsequent re-sales of properties within the subdivision are thereby subject to the plat's covenants and conditions.

9.8 (c) the creditor's claim against the property as collateral security for the loan.
A lien is a creditor's claim against personal or real property as security for a debt of the property owner. If the owner defaults, the lien gives the creditor the right to force the sale of the property to satisfy the debt. For example, a homeowner borrows $5,000 to pay for a new roof. The lender funds the loan in exchange for the borrower's promissory note to repay the loan. At the same time, the lender places a lien on the property for $5,000 as security for the debt. If the borrower defaults, the lien allows the lender to force the sale of the house to satisfy the debt.

9.9 (d) An equitable interest.
A lienor generally has an equitable interest in the property, but not legal ownership. The exception is a mortgage lien on a property in a title-theory state. In these states, the mortgage transaction conveys legal title to the lender, who holds it until the mortgage obligations are satisfied. During the mortgage loan period, the borrower has equitable title to the property.

9.10 (a) Payment of the debt that is the subject of the lien and recording of the satisfaction.
A lien terminates on payment of the debt and recording of documents. Payment of the debt and recording of the appropriate satisfaction documents ordinarily terminate a lien. If a default occurs, a suit for judgment or foreclosure enforces the lien. These actions force the sale of the property.

9.11 (d) involuntary general lien.
A general lien is one placed against any and all real and personal property owned by a particular debtor. An example is an inheritance tax lien placed against all property owned by the heir. A specific lien attaches to a single item of real or personal property and does not affect other property owned by the debtor. In addition, judgment liens are junior, involuntary liens.

9.12 (a) Real estate tax lien.
The category of superior, or senior, liens ranks above the category of inferior, or junior, liens, meaning that superior liens receive first payment from the proceeds of a foreclosure. The superior category includes liens for real estate tax, special assessments, and inheritance tax. Other liens, including income tax liens, mortgage liens and judgment liens, are inferior.

9.13 (d) subordinate the lien.
A lienor can change the priority of a junior lien by voluntarily agreeing to subordinate, or lower, the lien's position in the hierarchy. This change is often necessary when working with a mortgage lender who will not originate a mortgage loan unless it is senior to all other junior liens on the property. The lender may require the borrower to obtain agreements from other lien holders to subordinate their liens to the new

mortgage.

9.14 (c) A proceeding to enforce a lien by forcing the sale or transfer of a secured property.
All liens can be enforced by the sale or other transfer of title of the secured property, whether by court action, operation of law, or through powers granted in the original loan agreement. The enforcement proceedings are referred to as foreclosure. Note that lienors already possess equitable title, so they do not need to undertake a legal proceeding to establish this.

9.15 (b) file a foreclosure suit.
Judicial foreclosure occurs in states that use a two-party mortgage document (borrower and lender) that does not contain a "power of sale" provision. Lacking this provision, a lender must file a foreclosure suit and undertake a court proceeding to enforce the lien.

9.16 (a) strict foreclosure. Strict foreclosure is a court proceeding that gives the lender title directly, by court order, instead of giving cash proceeds from a public sale. On default, the lender gives the borrower official notice. After a prescribed period, the lender files suit in court, whereupon the court establishes a period within which the defaulting party must repay the amounts owed. If the defaulter does not repay the funds, the court orders transfer of full, legal title to the lender.

9.17 (d) A license, which terminates upon the owner's death.
A license is a personal right that a property owner grants to another to use the property for a specific purpose (to reach the kindergarten school bus). Unlike a personal easement in gross, which terminates only on the death of the grantee (Betty Luanne, in this instance), a license is revocable at any moment, is not transferable and does not attach to the land. It ceases on the death of either party, or on the sale of the property.

9.18 (d) 20 years
An easement by prescription is created after 20 years of open possession and use of another person's property.

9.19 (b) a deed restriction.
A private party who wants to control the quality and standards of a property can establish a deed restriction. Deed restrictions take precedence over zoning ordinances if they are more restrictive.

9.20 (a) It involves a monetary claim against the value of a property.
A lien is a creditor's claim against personal or real property as security for a debt of the property owner. If the owner defaults, the lien gives the creditor the right to force the sale of the property to satisfy the debt. Liens do not necessarily alter the property value. Liens can be involuntary as well as voluntary. Finally, liens attach to the property, but so do other encumbrances.

9.21 (d) It is knowledge received or imparted through direct experience.
The term "notice" is synonymous with "knowledge." A person who has received actual notice has actual knowledge of something. Receiving actual notice means learning of something through direct experience or communication. Thus, a document in itself cannot be actual notice. It is the seeing of the document that makes it actual notice.

9.22 (b) It is knowledge one could have or should have obtained. Constructive notice, or legal notice, is knowledge of a fact that a person could have or should have obtained. The foremost method of imparting constructive notice is by recordation of ownership documents in public records, specifically, title records. Since public records are open to everyone, the law generally presumes that when evidence of ownership is recorded, the public at large has received constructive notice of ownership.

9.23 (a) grant, deed, and will.
Voluntary transfer, or voluntary alienation, is an unforced transfer of title by sale or gift from an owner to another party. If the transferor is a government entity and the recipient is a private party, the conveyance is a public grant. If the transferor is a private party, the conveyance is a private grant. A living owner makes a private grant by means of a deed of conveyance, or deed. A private grant that occurs when the owner dies is a transfer by will.

9.24 (c) It gives constructive notice of ownership.
Recording is not necessary to make a deed valid. However, it is in the grantee's best interests to do so. Recording the deed gives the public constructive notice of the grantee's ownership.

9.25 (b) granting clause.
The granting, or premises, clause is the only required clause. It contains the conveyance intentions; names the parties; describes the property; and indicates a nominal consideration.

9.26 (a) general warranty deed.
The general warranty deed, or warranty deed for short, contains the fullest possible assurances of good title and protection for the grantee. The deed is technically a bargain and sale deed in which the grantor promises to defend against any and all claims to the title. The overall general warranty covenant is: "I own and will defend."

9.27 (d) To have an encumbrance removed if the lienholder cannot prove its validity.
Where there is a possibility that prior errors in deeds or other recorded documents might cloud (encumber) the title, the relevant parties execute a quitclaim deed to convey "any and all" interest to the grantee. If a party responsible for encumbering title refuses to quitclaim the interest, the owner may file a quiet title suit. This requires the lienor to prove the validity of an interest. If the defendant is unable to do so, the court removes the cloud by decree.

9.28 (a) A transfer tax based on the price of the property being conveyed.
State law usually requires payment of a documentary stamp tax on a conveyance of real property. The tax is based on the actual price of the property conveyed, thus enabling taxing authorities to ascertain current market value for ad valorem tax purposes. Payment of the tax is evidenced on the deed.

9.29 (b) probate.
A court proceeding called probate generally settles a decedent's estate, whether the person has died testate (having left a valid will) or intestate (having failed to do so).

9.30 (a) It will escheat to the state or county by escheat.
If an intestate decedent has no heirs, the estate escheats, or reverts, to the state or county after all claims and debts have been validated and settled.

9.31 (d) Eminent domain.
Various government and public entities can transfer private property to the public sphere by the power of eminent domain. The transfer is involuntary, even though the owner receives compensation. For example, a city government wants to widen a highway to accommodate growth. The government uses eminent domain to condemn and purchase all properties abutting the thoroughfare in order to complete the construction project.

9.32 (a) openly possessing and claiming the property without the owner's consent.
To claim legal title, the adverse possessor must be able to show a claim of right or color of title as reason for the possession; have notorious possession, which is possession without concealment; maintain a consistent claim of hostile possession, which is a claim to ownership and possession regardless of the owner's claims or consent; occupy the property continuously for a statutory period of time; in some states, pay taxes.

9.33 (c) The buyer.
Title records protect the buyer by revealing whether a property has marketable title, one free of undesirable encumbrances. The buyer is legally responsible for knowing the condition of title, since it is a matter of public record.

9.34 (a) a clouded title.
Chain of title refers to the succession of property owners of record dating back to the original grant of title from the state to a private party. If there is a missing link in the chronology of owners, or if there was a defective conveyance, the chain is said to be broken, resulting in a clouded title to the property.

9.35 (b) standard owner's title insurance policy.
An owner's policy may have standard coverage or extended coverage. Standard coverage protects against

title defects such as incompetent grantors, invalid deeds, fraudulent transaction documents, and defects in the chain of title. Extended coverage protects against liabilities that may not be of public record, including fraud, unrecorded ownership claims, unintentional recording errors, and unrecorded liens.

9.36 (a) voluntary alienation.
Voluntary alienation is an unforced transfer of title by sale or gift from an owner to another party.

9.37 (d) A quitclaim deed.
A quitclaim deed transfers real and potential interests in a property, whether an interest is known to exist or not. The grantor makes no claim to any interest in the property being conveyed and offers no warrants to protect the grantee. Where there is a possibility that prior errors in deeds or other recorded documents might cloud (encumber) the title, the relevant parties execute a quitclaim deed to convey "any and all" interest to the grantee.

9.38 (a) pass to the heirs by the laws of descent and distribution.
In this circumstance, the estate, including real property, will pass to lawful heirs according to the state's laws of descent and succession or distribution. These laws apportion the estate without regard to the wishes of the heirs or the intentions of the decedent. Escheat, by which the state takes the property, applies only if there are no legal heirs.

9.39 (d) declined because possession was secretive.
One of the preconditions for a claim of ownership based on adverse possession is notorious possession, or possession without concealment. Even if the length of possession in this case meets the statutory requirement, the drifter's secretiveness would invalidate the claim.

9.40 (b) free of undisclosed defects and encumbrances.
Marketable title is, by definition, one that is free and clear of undesirable and unknown encumbrances, claims, clouds, or other defects. Attorney's abstracts and title certificates do not guarantee that a title is marketable.

9.42 (b) for specified reasonable purposes.
A tenant has the sole right to occupy and use the premises without interference from outside parties, including the landlord. The landlord may enter the premises for specified purposes such as inspections, but the interference must be reasonable and limited. In addition, the landlord can do nothing outside of the lease's express provisions that would impair the tenant's enjoyment of income deriving from use of the premises.

9.43 (a) compliance with the rules and regulations of the building.
The lease defines the tenant's obligations, which principally are to pay the rent on time; maintain the property's condition; and comply with the rules and regulations of the building.

9.44 (b) providing required building support and services.
The lease defines the landlord's obligations, which principally are to provide the necessary building support and services, and maintain the condition of the property. It is the tenant's responsibility to obtain insurance and to determine the fairness of the rent.

9.45 (d) the tenant's estate is still obligated under the lease.
A valid lease creates obligations that survive the death of the landlord or tenant, with certain exceptions. A tenant's estate remains liable for payment of rent if the tenant dies; the landlord's estate remains bound to provide occupancy despite the landlord's death.

9.46 (a) The remaining tenant is responsible for the full rent obligation.
Multiple tenants who sign a single lease are jointly and severally responsible for fulfilling lease obligations. Thus, if one renter abandons an apartment, the other renters remain liable for rent.

9.47 (c) sublease.
Subletting (subleasing) is the transfer by a tenant, the sublessor, of a portion of the leasehold interest to another party, the sublessee, through the execution of a sublease. The sublease spells out all of the rights and obligations of the sublessor and sublessee, including the payment of rent to the sublessor. The sublessor remains primarily liable for the original lease with the landlord. The subtenant is liable only to

the sublessor.

9.48 (d) net lease.

A net lease requires a tenant to pay for utilities, internal repairs, and a proportionate share of taxes, insurance, and operating expenses in addition to rent. In effect, the landlord "passes through" actual property expenses to the tenant rather than charging a higher rent level. Net leases vary as to exactly what expenses the tenant is responsible for. The purest form of net lease requires tenants to cover all expenses, including major repairs and property taxes.

9.49 (a) gross lease.

2.49 A gross lease, or full service lease, requires the landlord to pay the property's operating expenses, including utilities, repairs, and maintenance, while the tenant pays only rent. Rent levels under a gross lease are higher than under a net lease, since the landlord recoups expense outlays in the form of added rent.

9.50 (b) An owner-developer wants to retain ownership of the land portion of the improved real property.

Ground leases are primarily used when an owner wishes to lease raw land to an agricultural or mining interest; when unimproved property is to be developed and the owner wants to retain ownership of the land; when the developer or future users of the property do not want to own the land; or when the owner of an improved property wishes to sell an interest in the improvements while retaining ownership of the underlying land.

9.51 (a) either party giving proper notice.

In the absence of an explicit term with beginning and ending date, a court will generally construe the lease to be a tenancy at will, cancelable upon proper notice.

9.52 (b) a tenancy from period-to-period.

URLTA sets standards for improving oral, vague, or unbalanced lease agreements. In the case of an unclear lease expiration date, the lease is generally deemed to be a periodic tenancy.

9.53 (a) a hotel.

State laws based on URLTA generally do not apply to transient occupancies, such as hotel and motel rentals, proprietary leases in cooperatives, or to occupancy in a residence that is under a contract for deed.

9.54 (c) a temporary possessory interest.

A lease is both an instrument of conveyance and a contract between principal parties to uphold certain covenants and obligations. As a conveyance, a lease conveys an interest, called the leasehold estate, but does not convey legal title to the property. For this reason, a leasehold is also called a less-than-freehold estate.

9.55 (d) A leased fee estate.

In conveying the leasehold estate, the landlord acquires a leased fee estate, which entails the rights to: receive rent; re-possess the property following the lease term; and monitor the tenant's obligations to maintain the premises.

9.56 (c) occupy the property.

The legal essence of a valid lease is that it conveys an exclusive right to use and occupy a property for a limited period of time in exchange for rent and the return of the property after the lease term is over.

9.57 (a) The buyer acquires title subject to the lease, which remains in effect.

The landlord may sell, assign, or mortgage the leased fee interest. However, transferring and encumbering the leased property do not extinguish the obligations and covenants of a lease. Buyers and creditors, therefore, must take their respective interests subject to the terms of the lease.

9.58 (c) When either party gives proper notice.

In the absence of an explicit term with beginning and ending date, a court will generally construe the lease to be a tenancy at will, cancelable upon proper notice.

9.59 (c) a five-year lease must be in writing to be enforceable.
Generally, a lease for a period exceeding one year cannot be oral but must be in writing to be enforceable because of the statute of frauds.

9.60 (b) The original tenant retains primary responsibility for performance of the original lease contract.
In a sublease-- a transfer of a portion of the leasehold-- the sublessor (original tenant) remains primarily liable for the original lease with the landlord. The subtenant is liable only to the sublessor.

SECTION 10 TEST: Legal Descriptions

10.1 (a) accurately identifies the boundaries of the property as distinct from all other properties.
A legal description of real property is one which accurately locates and identifies the boundaries of the subject parcel to a degree acceptable by courts of law in the state where the property is located. The general criterion for a legal description is that it alone provides sufficient data for a surveyor to locate the parcel. A legal description identifies the property as unique and distinct from all other properties.

10.2 (c) reference points, angles, and distances.
A metes and bounds description identifies the boundaries of a parcel of real estate using reference points, distances, and angles. The description always identifies an enclosed area by starting at an origination point, called point of beginning, or POB, and returning to the POB at the end of the description.

10.3 (b) two consecutive meridians.
The "vertical" area between consecutive meridians is called a range. A range is identified by its relationship to the principal meridian. All ranges are six miles wide.

10.4 (c) two consecutive parallels.
The "horizontal" area between two parallels is called a tier, or a township strip. A tier is identified by its relationship to the base parallel. All tiers are six miles wide.

10.5 (b) Six miles by six miles, or 6 miles square.
A township is the area enclosed by the intersection of two consecutive meridians and two consecutive parallels. Since the parallels and meridians are six miles apart, a township is a square with six miles on each side. Its area is therefore 36 square miles. Remember to differentiate square miles from miles square: 4 square miles is a measure of area (2 miles x 2 miles); 4 miles square is a representation of the sides of a square (4 miles by 4 miles).

10.6 (d) 1/64.
The size in acres of a subsection of a township is a fraction of 640 acres, since there are 640 acres in a section. Thus ten acres is 10/640, or 1/64th of a section.

10.7 (d) properties in a subdivision.
The recorded plat method, also called the lot and block system, is used to describe properties in residential, commercial, and industrial subdivisions. Under this system, tracts of land are subdivided into lots. The entire group of lots comprises the subdivision. In a large subdivision, lots may be grouped together into blocks for ease of reference.

10.8 (c) Metes and bounds.
A metes and bounds description identifies the point of beginning and describes the distance and direction from that point to the first monument, and thence to subsequent monuments and back to the beginning to define the property's enclosed perimeter.

10.9 (d) Thirty-six.
The rectangular survey system divides a township into thirty-six sections.

10.10 (a) 640.
Each side of a section is one mile in length. Thus the area of a section is one square mile, or 640 acres.

SECTION 11 TEST: Real Estate Contracts

11.1 (c) something of value traded in exchange for something of value.
A contract must contain a two-way exchange of valuable consideration as compensation for performance by the other party. The contract is not valid or enforceable if just one party provides consideration. Valuable consideration may be something of tangible value, such as money, or something the party promises to do. It may also be something intangible that a party must give up.

11.2 (a) contain a legal description of the property.
In addition to satisfying the requirements of a valid contract in general, a contract that conveys an interest in real estate must be in writing, contain a legal description of the property, and be signed by one or more of the parties.

11.3 (d) A reasonable time, or until the expiration date on the offer.
If an offer contains an expiration date and the phrase "time is of the essence," the offer expires at exactly the time specified. In the absence of a stated time period, the offeree has a "reasonable" time to accept an offer.

11.4 (b) The buyer's death terminated the offer.
Any of the following actions or circumstances can terminate an offer: acceptance; rejection; revocation; lapse of time; counteroffer; or death or insanity of either party.

11.5 (c) A contract for the sale of undeveloped land.
A real estate contract that is not a personal contract for services can be assigned to another party unless the terms of the agreement specifically prohibit assignment. Listing agreements, for example, are not assignable, since they are personal service agreements between agent and principal. Sales contracts, however, are assignable, because they involve the purchase of real property rather than a personal service.

11.6 (b) the parties act is if there is a contract.
An implied contract is an unstated or unintentional agreement that may be deemed to exist when the actions of any of the parties suggest the existence of an agreement.

11.7 (b) A sale contract before closing.
An executory contract is one in which performance is yet to be completed. A sales contract prior to closing is executory: while the parties have agreed to buy and sell, the buyer has yet to pay the seller and the seller has yet to deed the property to the buyer.

11.8 (a) both parties promise to do something in exchange for the other party's performance.
A bilateral contract is one in which both parties promise to perform their respective parts of an agreement in exchange for performance by the other party. An example of a bilateral contract is an exclusive listing: the broker promises to exercise due diligence in the efforts to sell a property, and the seller promises to compensate the broker when and if the property sells.

11.9 (c) The broker may have a claim for marketing expenses expended during the listing term.
The damaged party may elect the following legal remedies: rescission; forfeiture; suit for damages; or suit for specific performance. However, the broker must show that the seller has breached the contract.

11.10 (d) the failure of a party to perform according to the terms of the contract.
A breach of contract is a failure to perform according to the terms of the agreement.

11.11 (b) The act of declaring that a contract is no longer in effect for a given party.
Parties to a contract may rescind a contract by mutual consent, or a damaged party may rescind the contract unilaterally. This act of rescission cancels the contract and returns the parties to their pre-contract condition, including the refunding of any monies already transferred.

11.12 (a) reflect a mutual understanding or agreement.
Mutual consent, also known as offer and acceptance and meeting of the minds, requires that a contract involve a clear and definite offer and an intentional, unqualified acceptance of the offer.

232

11.13 (c) unenforceable.
A valid contract that is in writing is enforceable within a statutory time period. A valid contract that is made orally is also generally enforceable within a statutory period, with the exception that some contracts are enforceable only if they are in writing. These laws apply in particular to the transfer of interests in real estate. A void or voidable contract was not a truly valid contract.

11.14 (b) is possibly valid and enforceable.
Incompetent parties, or parties of "unsound mind," may not enter into enforceable contracts. However, during the period of one's incompetency, a court may appoint a guardian who may act on the incompetent party's behalf with court approval.

11.15 (c) a counteroffer.
By changing any of the terms of an offer, the offeree creates a counteroffer, and the original offer is void. At this point, the offeree becomes the offeror, and the new offeree gains the right of acceptance. If accepted, the counteroffer becomes a valid contract provided all other requirements are met.

11.16 (d) valuable consideration.
Valuable consideration can be something of tangible value, such as money, or something a party promises to do or not do. For example, a home builder may promise to build a house for a party as consideration for receiving money from the home buyer.

11.17 (c) is void.
The content, promise, or intent of a contract must be lawful. A contract that proposes an illegal act is void.

11.18 (a) must act within a statutory period.
The statute of limitations restricts the time period for which an injured party in a contract has the right to rescind or disaffirm the contract. A party to a voidable contract must act within the statutory period.

11.19 (b) require certain conveyance-related contracts to be in writing.
The statute of frauds requires that certain contracts must be in writing to be enforceable. Real estate contracts that convey an interest in real property fall in this category, with the exception that a lease of one year's duration or less may be oral.

11.20 (b) The buyer has no obligations to the seller whatsoever.
The mutual consent required for a valid contract is reached through the process of offer and acceptance. If the offeree accepts all terms without amendment, the offer becomes a contract. The exact point at which the offer becomes a contract is when the offeree gives the offeror notice of the acceptance. If an offer contains an expiration date and the phrase "time is of the essence," the offer expires at exactly the time specified.

11.21 (a) Fiduciary and contractual obligations with the client.
A listing agreement establishes an agency relationship between agent and client that commits the agent to the full complement of fiduciary duties to the client in fulfilling the agreement.

11.22 (d) market, sell and show the property.
Special agency limits the scope of the broker's authority to specific activities, generally those which generate customers and catalyze the transaction. A special agency agreement usually does not authorize a broker to obligate the client to a contract as a principal party. Normally, principals do not delegate the authority to negotiate price to an agent in a residential transaction.

11.23 (b) An implied agency may have been created, with obligations to perform for both seller and agent.
Clients and agents may also create an implied agency listing based on substantive actions rather than on an express agreement. For example, if a seller allows a broker to undertake certain activities toward effecting a transaction without a specific authorization, but with full knowledge and consent, an implied agency may have been created.

11.24 (a) The agent cannot assign the listing agreement.
Since a listing agreement is a personal service contract, it is not assignable. In particular, a broker cannot

assign a listing to another broker.

11.25 (b) exclusive right to sell.
The exclusive right to sell listing, or "exclusive," gives the agent the most control over the property and the greatest likelihood of being compensated for his or her marketing efforts.

11.26 (c) A listing that is entered in a multiple listing service to enable cooperation with member brokers.
Though not a distinct type of listing agreement, multiple listing is a significant feature of brokerage practice. Multiple listing is an authorization to enter a listing in a multiple listing service.

11.27 (b) The customer must be legally competent to undertake the transaction.
Effecting a completed transaction means finding a customer who is not only ready, willing, and able, but one who makes an acceptable offer. A ready, willing, and able customer is one who is: amenable to the terms of the transaction (ready and willing), and is financially capable of paying the price and legally capable of completing the transaction (able).

11.28 (a) obtain and distribute compensation.
In the normal course of business, a listing broker delegates marketing responsibilities to sales associates and broker associates. A sales associate or broker associate may not, however, seek compensation directly from a client. Only the broker can obtain and disburse the compensation.

11.29 (c) Perry, since he found the customer.
The two principal determinants of procuring cause are being first to find the customer, and being the one who induces the customer to complete the transaction.

11.30 (d) It may be terminated against the agent's will.
A listing may terminate on grounds of: performance; infeasibility; mutual agreement; revocation; abandonment; breach; lapse of time; invalidity of the contract; incapacitation of either party; destruction of the property; or, in this case; involuntary title transfer.

11.31 (b) Sue the broker for money damages.
If the broker cancels the listing or otherwise defaults, the client may sue the broker for money damages.

11.32 (b) exclusive agency agreement.
An exclusive agency listing authorizes a single broker to sell the property and earn a commission, but leaves the owner the right to sell the property without the broker's assistance, in which case no commission is owed.

11.33 (c) open listing.
An open listing is a non-exclusive authorization to sell or lease a property. The owner may offer such agreements to any number of brokers in the marketplace. With an open listing, the broker who is the first to perform under the terms of the listing is the sole party entitled to a commission.

11.34 (d) net listing.
A net listing is one in which an owner sets a minimum acceptable amount to be received from the transaction and allows the broker to have any amount received in excess as a commission, assuming the broker has earned a commission according to the other terms of the agreement.

11.35 (a) the client.
Generally, buyer and tenant representation agreements are subject to the same laws and regulations as those applying to owner listings. The only difference is the client and his or her transaction expectations.

11.36 (a) To list the owner's property in a multiple listing service.
A multiple listing is not a distinct listing contract but rather a provision in an exclusive listing authorizing the broker to place the listing into a multiple listing service. A multiple listing service is an organization of member brokers who agree to cooperate in the sale of properties listed by other brokers in exchange for a share of the broker's resulting commission.

11.37 (c) all the obligations and promises are performed and the transaction is closed.
An executory contract is one for which the signatories have yet to perform their respective obligations and promises. Upon closing, the sale contract is fully performed and no longer exists as a binding agreement.

11.38 (a) Use a standard contract promulgated by a state agency or a real estate board.
It is advisable, and legally required in most states, for a broker to use a standard contract form promulgated by state agencies or real estate boards, as such forms contain generally accepted language. This relieves the broker of the dangers of creating new contract language, which can be construed as a practice of law for which the broker is not licensed.

11.39 (b) be written.
A contract for the sale of real estate is enforceable only if it is in writing. A buyer or seller cannot sue to force the other to comply with an oral contract for sale, even if the contract is valid.

11.40 (a) The contract has been legitimately cancelled and is null and void.
To be valid, a contract must meet the criteria of: competent parties, voluntary act of good faith, mutual consent, legal purpose, and valuable consideration. The buyer broke the mutual consent requirement by opting out before being told of the seller's acceptance. Thus, there is no valid contract.

11.41 (c) An offer and acceptance.
A contract of sale is created by full and unequivocal acceptance of an offer. Offer and acceptance satisfy the mutual consent requirement for a valid contract. The offeree must accept the offer without making any changes whatsoever.

11.42 (d) Equitable title.
A sale contract gives the buyer an interest in the property that is called equitable title, or ownership in equity. If the seller defaults and the buyer can show good faith performance, the buyer can sue for specific performance, that is, to compel the seller to transfer legal title upon payment of the contract price.

11.43 (b) a condition that, if unmet, renders the contract unenforceable.
A contingency is a condition that must be met before the contract is enforceable. If one party cannot meet a contingency condition by a specified deadline, the other party may cancel the contract.

11.44 (c) The buyer may be able to have the contract canceled.
The termite inspection clause is a contingency clause. If one party cannot meet a contingency condition by a specified deadline, the other party may cancel the contract. Did the clause state that the inspector had to be properly licensed? If so, the buyer has a good case for cancellation.

11.45 (a) Until the seller communicates acceptance of the offer.
An offeror may revoke an offer for any reason prior to communication of acceptance by the offeree.

11.46 (b) Fred has entered into contracts with both Jack and Sally to sell the same property.
Jack's acceptance of Fred's offer creates a valid contract, just as Fred's acceptance of Sally's offer creates a valid contract. Fred should have revoked his offer to Jack before accepting Sally's offer.

11.47 (d) agency relationships and property condition.
It is common for the seller to disclose the property condition requiring the buyer to acknowledge receipt of the disclosure. The broker discloses the applicable agency relationships in the transaction and names the party who must pay the brokerage commission.

11.48 (b) valuable consideration and a right to buy.
An option-to-buy is an enforceable contract in which a potential seller, the optionor, grants a potential buyer, the optionee, the right to purchase a property before a stated time for a stated price and terms. In exchange for the right of option, the optionee pays the optionor valuable consideration.

11.49 (a) Schmidt must sell to Carboy for $10,000.
Mary's option-to-buy contract is enforceable, assuming she paid a consideration for it.

11.50 (d) It is always assignable unless the contract prohibits assignment.
A real estate contract that is not a personal service contract can be assigned to another party unless the

terms of the agreement specifically prohibit assignment. An option-to-buy is therefore assignable in the absence of such a prohibiting clause.

11.51 (c) At the end of the contract period, the vendor conveys legal title, provided the vendee has fulfilled all obligations.

A contract for deed is a bilateral agreement between a seller, the vendor, and a buyer, the vendee, in which the vendor defers receipt of some or all of the purchase price of a property over a specified period of time. At the end of the period, the buyer completes payment to the vendor of the full purchase price and the vendor deeds legal title to the vendee.

11.52 (b) the parties have completed a verbal, executory contract.

As a sale contract created by an offer and acceptance, the parties have an executory contract: the parties have yet to perform their respective obligations and promises. However, as a contract for the sale of real estate, this verbal contract is not enforceable. An enforceable real estate sale contract must be in writing.

11.53 (c) The assignor has completed a legal action.

Either party to a sale transaction can assign the sale contract to another party, subject to the provisions and conditions contained in the agreement.

11.54 (d) any conveyance may trigger an acceleration of any loans secured by the property.

The mortgage agreement may or may not state that the seller's loan will be accelerated by the lender and called due on sale. The due-on-sale clause in the sale contract merely stipulates that the buyer and seller recognize the possibility that loans that survive the closing may be called due.

11.55 (d) The option is expired, and the tenant has no rightful claim to money paid for the option.

The option automatically expires at the end of the option period. The landlord has no obligation, either to sell the property or to return the consideration, after the expiration date.

11.56 (c) the seller retains legal title while the buyer makes partial payments until the contract is fully executed.

In a contract for deed, the seller, or vendor, defers receipt of some or all of the purchase price of a property over a specified period of time. During the period, the vendor retains legal title and the vendee acquires equitable title. At the end of the period, the buyer pays the vendor the full purchase price and the vendor deeds legal title to the vendee.

SECTION 12 TEST: Residential Mortgages

12.1 (b) A state in which a mortgagee has equitable title to a secured property.

States differ in their interpretation of who owns mortgaged property. Those that regard the mortgage as a lien held by the mortgagee (lender) against the property owned by the mortgagor (borrower) are called lien-theory states. Those that regard the mortgage document as a conveyance of ownership from the mortgagor to the mortgagee are called title-theory states.

12.2 (d) It is evidence of the borrower's debt to the lender.

A valid mortgage or trust deed financing arrangement requires a note as evidence of the debt.

12.3 (a) trust deed or mortgage.

The mortgage or trust deed is evidence of the collateral pledge of the purchased property as security for the loan.

12.4 (b) mortgagor.

The mortgagor is the borrower and the mortgagee is the lender. As a memory aid, notice that "lender" and "mortgagee" both have two "e"s. "Mortgagor" and "borrower" both have two "o"s.

12.5 (d) $1,000.

Multiply the rate times the loan amount and divide by 12 to calculate monthly interest. Thus, ($200,000 x 6%) ÷ 12 = $1,000.

12.6 (b) $100,000.
The equation for the loan amount is (annual interest divided by the interest rate) = loan amount. Thus, ($500 x 12) ÷ .06 = $100,000.

12.7 (a) 7.5%.
The equation for the interest rate is (annual payment / loan amount) = interest rate. Thus ($3750 / $50,000) = 7.5%.

12.8 (b) $2,000.
A discount point is one percent of the loan amount. Thus, one point on a $100,000 loan equals ($100,000 x 2%) or ($100,000 x .02), or $2,000.

12.9 (b) Part of each periodic payment is applied to repayment of the loan balance in advance and part is applied to payment of interest in arrears.
In an amortizing loan, part of the principal is repaid periodically along with interest, so that the principal balance decreases over the life of the loan. The annual interest is never the same, since the principal balance to which the interest rate applies changes every year. Interest on a loan is always paid in arrears, not in advance.

12.10 (b) private mortgage insurance.
Mortgage insurance protects the lender against loss of a portion of the loan (typically 20-25%) in case of borrower default. Private mortgage insurance generally applies to loans that are not backed by the Federal Housing Administration (FHA) or Veterans Administration (VA) and that have a down payment of less than 20% of the property value. The FHA has its own insurance requirement for loans with a down payment of less than 20%.

12.11 (d) The fraction of the appraised value of the property offered as collateral which the lender is willing to lend.
The relationship of the loan amount to the property value, expressed as a percentage, is called the loan-to-value ratio, or LTV. If the lender's loan to value ratio is 80%, the lender will lend only $80,000 on a home appraised at $100,000. The difference between what the lender will lend and what the borrower must pay for the property is the amount the borrower must provide in cash as a down payment.

12.12 (c) buyer's down payment.
Price less loan is the down payment. This is also the buyer's initial equity.

12.13 (a) title-theory state.
States that regard the mortgage document as a conveyance of ownership from the mortgagor to the mortgagee are called title-theory states. However Florida is a lien-theory state.

12.14 (b) usury.
Many states have laws against usury, which is the charging of excessive interest rates on loans. Such states have a maximum rate that is either a flat rate or a variable rate tied to an index such as the prime lending rate.

12.15 (c) $1,200.
A point is one percentage point of a loan amount. Thus, 2 points on a $60,000 loan equal (.02 x $60,000), or $1,200.

12.16 (a) an amortized loan is paid off over the loan period.
Amortized loans retire the principal balance over the loan period. If a loan does not do this, one must make a balloon payment at the end of the loan term to complete the loan payoff.

12.17 (c) it is a negotiable instrument.
A promissory note is a negotiable instrument, which means the payee may assign it to a third party. The assignee would then have the right to receive the borrower's periodic payments.

12.18 (d) may be required to execute a release of mortgage document.
Lenders may be required to release the mortgage or trust document to the borrower when the borrower has paid off the loan and all other sums secured by the document. The release clause, also known as a

defeasance clause, may specify that the mortgagee will execute a satisfaction of mortgage (also known as release of mortgage and mortgage discharge) to the mortgagor.

SECTION 13 TEST: Types of Mortgages and Sources of Financing

13.1 (a) refusing a loan because the borrower does not match the lender's target market.
The Equal Credit Opportunity Act (ECOA) requires a lender to evaluate a loan applicant on the basis of that applicant's own income and credit rating, unless the applicant requests the inclusion of another's income and credit rating in the application. In addition, ECOA has prohibited a number of practices in mortgage loan underwriting, including refusing a loan on a property based on an applicant's demographic characteristics.

13.2 (b) $1680.
Monthly income qualification is derived by multiplying monthly income by the income ratio. Thus (72,000 / 12) x .28 = $1680. Remember to first derive the monthly income.

13.3 (b) adjust the applicant's debt ratio calculation and lower the loan amount.
Since a lender lends only part of the purchase price of a property according to the lender's loan-to-value ratio, a lender will verify that a borrower has the cash resources to make the required down payment. If someone is lending an applicant a portion of the down payment with a provision for repayment, a lender will consider this another debt obligation and adjust the debt ratio accordingly. This can lower the amount a lender is willing to lend.

13.4 (c) All loans secured by a residence.
Regulation Z applies to all loans secured by a residence. It does not apply to commercial loans or to agricultural loans over $25,000. Its provisions cover the disclosure of costs, the right to rescind the credit transaction, advertising credit offers, and penalties for non-compliance with the act.

13.5 (d) the borrower has a limited right to cancel the transaction within a certain period.
A borrower has a limited right to cancel the credit transaction, usually within three days of completion of the transaction. The right of rescission does not apply to "residential mortgage transactions," that is, to mortgage loans used to finance the purchase or construction of the borrower's primary residence. It does, however, apply to refinancing of mortgage loans, and to home equity loans. State law may require a rescission period and notice on first mortgage loan transactions as well.

13.6 (b) ask the buyer/borrower about his/her religion or national origin.
ECOA prohibits discrimination in extending credit based on race, color, religion, national origin, sex, marital status, age, or dependency upon public assistance. A creditor may not make any statements to discourage an applicant on the basis of such discrimination or ask any questions of an applicant concerning these discriminatory items. A real estate licensee who assists a seller in qualifying a potential buyer may fall within the reach of this prohibition.

13.7 (d) not FHA-insured or VA-guaranteed.
A conventional mortgage loan is a permanent long-term loan that is not FHA-insured or VA-guaranteed. FNMA does not "back" loans; FHA only insures FHA loans; and the VA, not GNMA guarantees loans.

13.8 (b) limited by when the loan was originated.
Rules for assumability vary according to when the FHA-insured loan was originated and whether the original loan was for an investment property or an owner-occupied principal residence. Loans originated before December 1, 1986, are generally assumable without restriction. Loans originated after December 1, 1986, require that the assumer show creditworthiness. Some mortgages executed from 1986 through 1989 contain language that is not enforced as a result of later Congressional action. Mortgages from that period are now freely assumable, despite any restrictions stated in the mortgage.

13.9 (c) how much of a loan the VA will guarantee.
A veteran must apply for a Certificate of Eligibility to find out how much the VA will guarantee in a particular situation.

13.10 (d) Zero.
If a loan is fully amortizing, its loan balance is zero at the end of the loan term.

13.11 (b) The buyer gives the seller a mortgage and note as part of the purchase price of the property.
With a purchase money mortgage, the borrower gives a mortgage and note to the seller to finance some or all of the purchase price of the property. The seller in this case is said to "take back" a note, or to "carry paper," on the property.

13.12 (c) hypothecation.
The process of securing a loan by pledging a property without giving up ownership of the property is called hypothecation.

13.13 (a) The borrower gives the lender a note and a mortgage in exchange for loan funds.
When a borrower gives a note promising to repay the borrowed money and executes a mortgage on the real estate for which the money is being borrowed as security, the financing method is called mortgage financing.

13.14 (c) The trustor conveys title to a trustee in exchange for loan funds from the beneficiary.
A deed of trust conveys title to the property in question from the borrower (trustor) to a trustee as security for the loan. The trustee is a third party fiduciary to the trust. While the loan is in place, the trustee holds the title on behalf of the lender, who is the beneficiary of the trust.

13.15 (a) an appraisal report.
Loan underwriting is the process of assessing the lender's risk in giving a loan. Mortgage underwriting includes: evaluating the borrower's ability to repay the loan; appraising the value of the property offered as security; and determining the terms of the loan.

13.16 (c) the ability to re-pay, the value of the collateral, and the profitability of the loan.
A lender assesses risks by examining, or qualifying, both borrower and property. In qualifying a borrower, an underwriter weighs the ability of the borrower to repay the loan. In qualifying a property, an underwriter assesses the ability of the property value to cover potential losses. In this evaluation, a lender requires that the appraised value of the property be more than adequate to cover the contemplated loan and costs. Finally, the loan must make money for the lending organization as a basic business precept.

13.17 (b) they want to ensure there is more than enough collateral to cover the loan amount.
Without an ample difference between the property value and the loan amount, a drop in property values could cause the loan balance to exceed the collateral itself. This greatly increases the risk of a loan loss should the borrower default since the balance could not be completely recovered in a foreclosure sale.

13.18 (b) consider the income of a spouse in evaluating a family's creditworthiness.
The Equal Credit Opportunity Act (ECOA) requires a lender to evaluate a loan applicant on the basis of that applicant's own income and credit rating, unless the applicant requests the inclusion of another's income and credit rating in the application. In such a case, a lender may not discount or disregard income from part-time work, a spouse, child support, alimony, or separate maintenance.

13.19 (a) insure the buyer has the earning power to make the loan payments.
Both the income and debt ratios in borrower qualification quantify how much a borrower can safely afford to pay on a mortgage loan. The income ratio focuses on the borrower's earning power.

13.20 (d) debt payments divided by gross income.
The debt ratio formula is (debt obligations) ÷ (income).

13.21 (c) the parties complete all loan origination documents and the loan is funded.
Closing of a mortgage loan normally occurs with the closing of the real estate transaction. At the real estate closing, the lender typically has deposited the funded amount with an escrow agent, along with instructions for disbursing the funds. The borrower deposits necessary funds with the escrow agent, executes final documents, and receives signed copies of all relevant documents.

13.22 (b) Truth-in-Lending laws and Regulation Z.
Regulation Z, which implements the Truth-in-Lending Act, applies to all loans secured by a residence. It does not apply to commercial loans or to agricultural loans over $25,000. It prescribes requirements to lenders regarding the disclosure of costs, the right to rescind the credit transaction, advertising credit offers, and penalties for non-compliance with the Truth-in-Lending Act.

13.23 (a) The Equal Credit Opportunity Act.
ECOA prohibits discrimination in extending credit based on race, color, religion, national origin, sex, marital status, age, or dependency upon public assistance.

13.24 (c) the Real Estate Settlement and Procedures Act.
RESPA is a federal law which aims to standardize settlement practices and ensure that buyers understand settlement costs. RESPA applies to purchases of residential real estate (one- to four-family homes) to be financed by "federally related" first mortgage loans. In addition to imposing settlement procedures, RESPA provisions prohibit lenders from paying kickbacks and unearned fees to parties who may have helped the lender obtain the borrower's business.

13.25 (b) Buying securities, changing the discount rate, and controlling banking reserves.
The Federal Reserve System regulates the money supply by means of three methods: selling or re-purchasing government securities, primarily Treasury bills, changing the reserve requirement for member banks; changing the interest rate, or discount rate, the system charges member institutions for borrowing funds from the Federal Reserve System.

13.26 (a) It cycles funds back to primary lenders so they can make more loans.
Secondary mortgage market organizations buy pools of mortgages from primary lenders and sell securities backed by these pooled mortgages to investors. By purchasing loans from primary lenders, the secondary market returns funds to the primary lenders, thereby enabling the primary lender to originate more mortgage loans.

13.27 (a) Fannie Mae, Freddie Mac, and Ginnie Mae.
As major players in the secondary market, the Federal National Mortgage Association (FNMA, "Fannie Mae"), Government National Mortgage Association (GNMA, "Ginnie Mae), and Federal Home Loan Mortgage Corporation (FHLMC, "Freddie Mac") tend to set the standards for the primary market. FHA, VA, and the Federal Reserve are not organizations in the secondary mortgage market.

13.28 (c) It purchases FHA-backed and VA-backed loans.
Fannie Mae buys conventional, FHA-backed and VA-backed loans; gives banks mortgage-backed securities in exchange for blocks of mortgages; and sells bonds and mortgage-backed securities. It does not guarantee, insure, or originate loans.

13.29 (b) It insures loans made by approved lenders.
The Federal Housing Administration (FHA) does not lend money, but insures permanent long-term loans made by others. The lender must be approved by the FHA, and the borrower must meet certain FHA qualifications.

13.30 (a) It guarantees loans made by approved lenders.
The Veterans Administration (VA) offers loan guarantees to qualified veterans. The VA partially guarantees permanent long-term loans originated by VA-approved lenders on properties that meet VA standards. The VA's guarantee enables lenders to issue loans with higher loan-to-value ratios than would otherwise be possible.

13.31 (c) the loan payments gradually increase.
Graduated payment mortgages allow for smaller initial monthly payments which gradually increase. The interest rate remains fixed as does the loan term.

13.32 (b) the borrower pays additional interest at the onset in order to obtain a lower interest rate.
A buydown loan entails a prepayment of interest on a loan. The prepayment effectively lowers the interest rate and the periodic payments for the borrower. Buydowns typically occur in a circumstance where a builder wants to market a new development to a buyer who cannot quite qualify for the necessary loan at market rates.

SECTION 14 TEST: Real Estate-Related Computations and Closings

14.1 (c) returns funds to the buyer.
If for any reason the transaction cannot be completed, the escrow instructions usually provide a mechanism for reconveying title to the seller and funds to the buyer. In such a case, both parties return to their original status as if no sale had occurred.

14.2 (d) disclose in writing any business relationships they have with other parties involved in the transaction.
Business relationships and affiliations among real estate firms, mortgage brokers, title insurance firms and other such companies that are involved in a transaction are permitted, provided the relationships are disclosed in writing to the consumer, the consumer is free to go elsewhere for the relevant service, and the companies do not exchange fees for referrals.

14.3 (a) The item must be prorated and recorded as a debit to one party and a credit to the other party for the same amount.
An income or expense item that affects both parties is apportioned, or prorated, to each party to reflect the proper amount that each owes or should receive. A prorated item is treated as a debit to one party and a credit to the other party for the same amount.

14.4 (b) at some time after the expense is incurred.
Items paid in arrears are paid after the expense has been incurred.

14.5 (d) A debit to the seller and credit to the buyer for $580.
For income the seller received in advance, the buyer receives a credit and the seller receives a debit. In effect, the seller has received some of the buyer's income, and the seller must pay this share to the buyer. Therefore the seller is debited and the buyer is credited the $580 the buyer is entitled to earn as the new owner.

14.6 (b) A debit to the seller and credit to the buyer for $43.
For an item the buyer will pay in arrears, the buyer receives a credit and the seller receives a debit. In effect, the seller has incurred some of the expenses that the buyer will be paying for after closing. Thus the seller must pay the buyer the used portion of the expense, or $43.

14.7 (b) $546.00.
The daily tax expense, first, is ($2,190 ÷ 365) or $6.00. Since the buyer will pay the taxes after closing, the seller will owe the buyer his or her portion of the tax bill, which is the 91 days from the beginning of the year through closing. Therefore, credit the buyer and debit the seller ($6.00 x 91), or $546.00.

14.8 (d) $191.67.
This method assumes all months are 30 days and the year is 360 days. The daily proration is therefore $375 ÷ 360, or $1.04. The closing occurs on the 184th day of the year. Thus, ($1.04 x 184) = $191.67. Note that if the day of closing is the buyer's, there would be 183 day's worth of prorated expense.

14.9 (d) $735.34.
Assuming a 365 day year, the daily tax expense is ($1,100 ÷ 365), or $3.013. As taxes are paid in arrears, the buyer will be paying the annual bill. Thus, he will be owed a credit for the seller's share of the bill, which is $3.013 x 244 days, or $735.34.

14.10 (a) $116.03.
The buyer's share is the unused portion, or (365 days – 244 days), or 121 days. The daily expense is ($350 ÷ 365), or $.9589. ($.9589 x 121) = $116.03. The seller receives this amount as a credit and the buyer a debit.

14.11 (a) $507.50.
If the buyer pays $525 interest for 30 days, the daily expense is ($525 ÷ 30), or $17.50. If there are 29 days of pre-paid expense, the buyer's charge is ($17.50 x 29), or $507.50.

14.12 (c) $1,775.
$88,750 x .02 = $1,775. Remember, one point = 1% of the loan amount.

14.13 (d) $11,250.
$187,500 x 6% = $187,500 x .06 = $11,250.

14.14 (d) the buyer must pay the expense.
Explicit agreements in the sale contract supercede traditional expense-payment responsibilities which can vary from state to state.

14.15 (a) the excess of the buyer's debits over the buyer's credits.
To determine how much money the buyer owes at closing, the buyer's debits are totaled and compared with the total of the buyer's credits. The excess of debits over credits is the amount the buyer must bring to the closing.

14.16 (d) negligence, error or omission in carrying out professional services.
A standard E&O policy provides coverage for "damages resulting from any negligent act, error or omission arising out of Professional Services." It does not cover dishonest or illegal acts, including environmental violations and mishandling of funds.

SECTION 15 TEST: Real Estate Markets and Analysis

15.1 (b) demand for the item is increasing in relation to supply of the item.
In a market economy, the primary interactions between supply, demand and price are: if supply increases relative to demand, price decreases; if supply decreases relative to demand, price increases; if demand increases relative to supply, price increases; and if demand decreases relative to supply, price decreases.

15.2 (d) Supply and demand are equal, and price and value are equal.
A market tends toward a state of equilibrium in which supply equals demand, and price, cost, and value are identical. According to this principle, market demand moves to meet supply, and supply moves to meet demand. If there is an extreme shortage of an item for which there is normally a strong demand, suppliers will rush to increase production to close the gap. If inventories of an item are very high, suppliers will stop production until the oversupply has been depleted.

15.3 (c) the uniqueness of every parcel.
In comparison with other economic products and services, real estate has certain unique traits. Traits of real estate include: inherent product value; uniqueness of every property; demand must come to the supply; illiquidity; slow to respond to changes; and a decentralized local market.

15.4 (d) Prices rise.
If demand is increasing and a moratorium slows supply, demand will begin to outpace supply, forcing prices to rise as the product becomes scarcer in relation to demand.

15.5 (b) an increase in demand for all types of real estate.
New businesses will arise to support the new company. They will hire new employees, some from out of town. The new employees will need housing. Hence the demand for residential real estate, as well as for commercial and industrial, will intensify, and it will also stimulate new construction.

15.6 (d) The number of available units that become occupied over a period of time.
Absorption is the amount of available property that becomes occupied over a period of time.

15.7 (a) rising prices.
Within the business cycle of real estate, declining vacancy indicates a combination of increasing demand which "fills up" supply which in turn decreases. As space becomes scarcer, rents for available space increase.

15.8 (b) desire, utility, scarcity, and purchasing power.
The value of something is based on the answers to four questions: how much do I desire it; how useful is it; how scarce is it; and am I able to pay for it.

15.9 (b) will increase.
If there is no longer a supply to meet the increasing demand of a growing population, prices for existing supply will rise.

15.10 (d) the market tending toward equilibrium.
A market tends toward a state of equilibrium in which supply equals demand, and price, cost, and value are identical. Thus if supply is scarce, construction will increase to stabilize the imbalance.

15.11 (c) the market is over-supplied.
Falling prices indicate an oversupply of commercial properties in relation to demand. In this case, construction of new supply will also slow down.

15.12 (a) have been increasing.
A rise in prices is a market signal that there is an undersupply of product in relation to demand. As the market moves toward equilibrium, builders construct more buildings to meet the unmet demand.

15.13 (c) It is often difficult to convert to cash.
Since real estate is often a large, long-term investment that has no exact duplicate, the process of a buyer's evaluating and choosing the right property is long and complex; hence, finding a buyer at a desired price can take a long time.

15.14 (b) The number of persons employed in base industries in an area
Base employment is the number of persons employed in the base industries that represent the economic foundation of an area. It is the driving component of total employment, which includes secondary and support industries, and which creates demand for all types of real estate.

15.15 (d) The total existing space of a certain type that is unoccupied at a given time
Vacancy is the amount of total real estate inventory of a certain type that is unoccupied at a given time. It is often stated as a percentage of total inventory, the vacancy rate for that property type.

15.16 (a) local government influencing the real estate market, regardless of demand.
Local governments sometimes declare a moratorium on new construction because of present or projected inadequacies of the infrastructure—water, sewer, power, roads, etc.—or because of the desire to conform to a master plan. The result may be to drive up prices, as supply cannot freely increase to meet demand.

15.17 (c) In- and out-migrations of major employers
Changes in employment numbers in a local market area, especially in major industries, have a direct impact on real estate demand in the area. Money supply, interest rates, and trade imbalances also have an impact, but they are regional or national factors rather than strictly local.

15.18 (b) Vacancy rises and prices fall.
New construction generally occurs to meet an excess of demand. By adding supply, it tends to increase vacancy and lower prices until supply-demand equilibrium is achieved.

15.19 (d) Residential
While all types of users may have these needs, they are most prominent for residential users because of concerns for family comfort and safety. Retail users are more concerned with competitive features of the trade area; office users care more about occupancy costs and suitability for the business; industrial users care more about such features as functionality, accessibility, and the labor pool.

15.20 (c) its susceptibility to swings in the local economy.
Because a real property cannot be transferred to a large, central real estate marketplace, its marketability is closely tied to local conditions. Investors and users must come to the product, unlike other types of economic product that can be moved to a place in search of greater demand

SECTION 16 TEST: Real Estate Appraisal

16.1 (b) anticipation.
Anticipation is the value principle that a buyer will pay a price based on the benefits the buyer expects to derive from a property over a holding period. For example, if an investor anticipates an annual rental income from a leased property to be one million dollars, this expected sum has a direct bearing on what the investor will pay for the property.

16.2 (b) A homeowner adds a third bathroom to a house and thereby increases the appraised value by $10,000.
The principle of contribution focuses on the degree to which a particular improvement affects market value of the overall property. In essence, the contribution of the improvement is equal to the change in market value that the addition of the improvement causes. For example, adding a bathroom to a house may contribute an additional $15,000 to the appraised value. Thus the contribution of the bathroom is $15,000.

16.3 (a) assemblage.
Assemblage, or the conjoining of adjacent properties, sometimes creates a combined value that is greater than the values of the unassembled properties. The excess value created by assemblage is called plottage value.

16.4 (d) Market value is an estimate; market price is the price at which a property sold.
Market value is an estimate of the price at which a property will sell at a particular time. The market price, as opposed to market value, is what a property actually sells for. Market price should theoretically be the same as market value if all the conditions essential for market value are present. Market price, however, may not reflect the analysis of comparables and of investment value that an estimate of market value includes.

16.5 (d) define the appraisal problem and the purpose of the appraisal.
The first step in the process is to define the appraisal problem and the purpose of the appraisal. This involves identifying the subject property by legal description; specifying the interest to be appraised; specifying the purpose of the appraisal; specifying the date for which the appraisal is valid; and identifying the type of value to be estimated.

16.6 (c) weighing the applicability of the approaches and considering the quality of data supporting each approach.
The final step in the appraisal process is to reconcile the value estimates produced by the three approaches to value into a final value estimate. To do this, an appraiser must weigh the appropriateness of a particular approach to the type of property being appraised and take into account the quality and quantity of data obtained in each method.

16.7 (b) Make dollar adjustments to the sale prices of comparable properties to account for competitive differences with the subject. The sales comparison approach consists of comparing sale prices of recently sold properties that are comparable with the subject, and making dollar adjustments to the price of each comparable to account for competitive differences with the subject. After identifying the adjusted value of each comparable, the appraiser weights the reliability of each comparable and the factors underlying how the adjustments were made. The weighting yields a final value range based on the most reliable factors in the analysis.

16.8 (d) takes into account the competitive value of specific amenities of the subject property.
The sales comparison approach is widely used because it takes into account the subject property's specific amenities in relation to competing properties. In addition, because of the currency of its data, the approach incorporates present market realities.

16.9 (a) adds value to a comparable that is inferior to the subject property.
If the comparable is inferior to the subject in some characteristic, an amount is added to the price of the comparable. If the comparable is better than the subject in some characteristic, an amount is deducted from the sale price of the comparable. This neutralizes the comparable's competitive advantage or disadvantage in an adjustment category. For example, a comparable has a swimming pool and the subject does not. To equalize the difference, the appraiser deducts an amount, say $6,000, from the sale price of the comparable.

16.10 (b) requires the fewest and smallest adjustments.
As a rule, the fewer the total number of adjustments, the smaller the adjustment amounts, and the less the total adjustment amount, the more reliable the comparable.

16.11 (c) $195,000.
Since the comparable has an extra bath, it is adjusted downward to equalize with the subject. Conversely, since it has no patio, the appraiser adds value to the comparable. Thus, $200,000 minus $7,000 plus $2,000 equals $195,000.

16.12 (d) Add the estimated land value and cost of improvements and subtract the accrued depreciation of the improvements.
The cost approach consists of estimating the value of the land "as if vacant;" estimating the cost of improvements; estimating and deducting accrued depreciation; and adding the estimated land value to the estimated depreciated cost of the improvements.

16.13 (b) is very accurate for a property with new improvements that represent the highest and best use.
The strengths of the cost approach are that it: provides an upper limit for the subject's value based on the undepreciated cost of reproducing the improvements. It is also very accurate for valuing a property with new improvements which are the highest and best use of the property.

16.14 (c) a property loses the same increment of value each year over the economic life of the property.
All property improvements have an economic life, which becomes incrementally shorter year after year as physical deterioration takes its toll. The property as a whole does not lose value, since land itself does not depreciate. Similarly, an improvement can regain value if it is repaired or updated. Finally, not all properties lose value from economic obsolescence.

16.15 (d) $115,000.
To appraise value using the cost approach, add the land value to the value of the depreciated improvement. Thus you have $30,000 + ($95,000 - 10,000), or $115,000.

16.16 (b) Divide the income a property generates by a rate of return.
An appraiser obtains an indication of value from the income capitalization method by dividing the estimated net operating income for the subject by the rate of return, or capitalization rate. The formula is: NOI / Cap rate = Value.

16.17 (c) uses a method that is also used by investors to determine how much they should pay for an investment property.
The strength of the income approach is that it is used by investors themselves to determine how much they should pay for a property. Thus, in the right circumstances, it provides a good basis for estimating market value. The approach, however, does not project what an income property's future income will be. Moreover, it is not an applicable method for estimating value if the subject is a non-income producing property.

16.18 (a) $370,000.
First, identify net income by subtracting out vacancy and expenses. Then divide by the capitalization rate. Thus, ($60,000 –3,000 – 20,000) ÷ 10% = $370,000.

16.19 (d) 150.
The monthly gross rent multiplier for a property is equal to the price divided by the monthly rent. Thus, ($450,000 ÷ $3,000) = 150.

16.20 (c) $203,000.
Multiply the monthly gross income times 12 to derive annual income. Multiply annual income times the gross income multiplier to derive the estimate of price. Thus, $1,200 times 12 equals $14,400. This times 14.1 equals $203,040, or $203,000 rounded.

16.21 (c) the state in which the appraiser operates.
A state-certified appraiser is one who has passed the necessary examinations and competency standards as established by each state in conformance with the federal standards.

16.22 (a) The Financial Institutions Reform, Recovery and Enforcement Act (FIRREA).
Title XI of FIRREA requires that competent individuals whose professional conduct is properly supervised perform all appraisals used in federally-related transactions. As of January 1, 1993, such federally-related appraisals must be performed only by state-certified appraisers.

16.23 (a) if two similar properties are for sale, a buyer will purchase the cheaper of the two.
According to the principle of substitution, a buyer will pay no more for a property than the buyer would have to pay for an equally desirable and available substitute property. For example, if three houses for sale are essentially similar in size, quality and location, a potential buyer is unlikely to choose the one that is priced significantly higher than the other two.

16.24 (a) is physically and financially feasible, legal, and the most productive.
This valuation principle holds that there is, theoretically, a single use for a property that produces the greatest income and return. A property achieves its maximum value when it is put to this use. The use must however be legal.

16.25 (d) $200,000. Market value is an opinion of the price that a willing seller and willing buyer would probably agree on for a property at a given time if: the transaction is for cash; the property is exposed on the open market for a reasonable period; buyer and seller have full information about market conditions ; there is no abnormal pressure on either party; it is an "arm's length" transaction; title is marketable; and the price does not include hidden influences such as special financing deals. The amount Lynne actually paid is the market price. The previous listing price and Ken's offer might be interesting data for the appraiser, but the appraisal must also consider other market data, such as comparable sales.

16.26 (a) there may be no recent sale price data in the market.
The sales comparison approach is limited in that every property is unique. As a result, it is difficult to find good comparables, especially for special-purpose properties. In addition, the market must be active; otherwise, sale prices lack currency and reliability.

16.27 (c) selects comparable properties, adjusts the comparables, and estimates the value.
The steps are to first identify comparable sales; then compare comparables to the subject and make adjustments to comparables; then, finally, weigh values indicated by adjusted comparables for the final value estimate of the subject.

16.28 (b) the seller offers below-market seller financing.
The principal factors for comparison and adjustment are time of sale, location, physical characteristics, and transaction characteristics. An adjustment may be made for such differences as mortgage loan terms, mortgage assumability, and owner financing.

16.29 (b) weights the comparables.
The last step in the approach is to perform a weighted analysis of the indicated values of each comparable. The appraiser, in other words, must identify which comparable values are more indicative of the subject and which are less indicative. However, all comparables are taken into account, not simply the nearest comparable.

16.30 (b) market value is not always the same as what the property cost.
The limitations of the cost approach are that: the cost to create improvements is not necessarily the same as market value; and depreciation is difficult to measure, especially for older buildings.

16.31 (b) replacement cost.
Reproduction cost is the cost of constructing, at current prices, a precise duplicate of the subject improvements. Replacement cost is the cost of constructing, at current prices and using current materials and methods, a functional equivalent of the subject improvements.

16.32 (d) functional obsolescence.
Functional obsolescence occurs when a property has outmoded physical or design features which are no

longer desirable or acceptable to current users.

16.33 (b) incurable economic obsolescence.
Economic (or external) obsolescence is the loss of value due to adverse changes in the surroundings of the subject property that make the subject less desirable. Since such changes are usually beyond the control of the property owner, economic obsolescence is considered an incurable value loss.

16.34 (c) depreciation.
Depreciation is the loss of value in an improvement over time. The loss of an improvement's value can come from any cause, such as deterioration, obsolescence, or changes in the neighborhood.

16.35 (a) estimates depreciation, subtracts depreciation from cost of improvements, and adds back the land value.
The steps in the costs approach are: (1) estimate land value; (2) estimate reproduction or replacement cost of improvements; (3) estimate accrued depreciation; (4) subtract accrued depreciation from reproduction or replacement cost; and (5) add land value to depreciated reproduction or replacement cost.

SECTION 17 TEST: Real Estate Investments

17.1 (b) negative leverage.
Leveraging is borrowing funds in order to make an investment that is larger than your own resource permits you to do directly. In negative leverage situations, your cost of borrowing funds to make the investment becomes greater than the income the investment returns to you.

17.2 (b) income properties.
Cost recovery, or depreciation, allows the owner of income property to deduct a portion of the property's value from gross income each year over the life of the asset. Principal residences cannot be depreciated (unless portions are treated as a home office.) Further, land cannot be depreciated.

17.3 (c) 19.5 %.
Appreciation amount is the current value of the property minus the original cost. The total appreciation rate is derived by dividing the appreciation amount by the original cost. Subtract the estimated current market value from the price originally paid (239,000 - 200,000 = 39,000) and then divide the result by the original price (39,000 / 200,000 = . 195 or 19.5%).

17.4 (d) a deduction for mortgage interest.
Deducting mortgage interest is a significant tax advantage of owning one's residence. Depreciation and cost-deductions do not apply to a non-income producing residence. Appreciation is a benefit, but not a tax benefit.

17.5 (d) $232,900.
The figure for net proceeds from sale is expressed by the formula: sale price - costs of sale = net proceeds. Thus $250,000 - (6% x 250,000) – 600 – 1,500 = $232,900.

17.6 (b) $157,000.
The beginning basis is the cost of acquiring a property. Basis is increased by capital improvements and decreased by depreciation. The basic formula for adjusted basis is Beginning basis ($150,000) + capital improvements ($3,000 + $4,000) - depreciation ($0) = adjusted basis ($157,000).

17.7 (c) $34,000.
The gain on sale (capital gain) of a primary residence is represented by the basic formula: amount realized (net sales proceeds, $210,000) - adjusted basis ($176,000) = gain on sale ($34,000). Note the purchase price of the second house is irrelevant.

17.8 (a) There is no taxable gain.
There is no taxable gain because the gain falls under the exclusion limit of $250,000. As of August 5, 1997, tax law provides an exclusion of $250,000 for an individual taxpayer and $500,000 for married taxpayers filing jointly on the gain from sale of a principal residence. The seller must have owned the property for at

least two years during the five years preceding the date of sale; used the property as principal residence for a total of two years during that five-year period; and have waited two years since the last use of the exclusion for any sale.

17.9 (c) direct investment.

Individuals, corporations, or other investor entities may invest as active investors in a property by buying it directly and taking responsibility for managing and operating the property. This investment mode is called direct investment.

17.10 (a) $2,100.

Annual gross operating income ($1,500 x 12 = $18,000) - annual operating expenses ($500 x 12 = $6,000) = annual net operating income ($12,000); annual net operating income ($12,000) - cost recovery expense ($5,000) = taxable income ($7,000); taxable income ($7,000) x tax rate (30%) = tax liability ($2,100).

17.11 (b) the more the investor stands to gain, the greater the risk that the investor may lose.

The general rule in investments is that the safer the investment, the more slowly it gains in value. The more you want it to gain, and the more quickly, the more you must risk losing it. Reward in investing corresponds directly to the degree of risk.

17.12 (a) income and tax benefits.

The basic financial rewards of an investment include income, appreciation in asset value, positive borrowing leverage, and tax benefits.

17.13 (d) relatively illiquid.

Real estate is by nature more difficult to convert to cash than many other types of investment. Compare the selling of a home with the ease of drawing money out of a bank account or selling a stock.

17.14 (b) a more management-intensive investment.

Real estate tends to require a high degree of investor involvement in management of the investment. Even raw land requires some degree of maintenance to preserve its value. Improved properties often require extensive management, including repairs, maintenance, onsite leasing, tenant relations, security, and fiscal management.

17.15 (a) a general partnership.

A general partnership is a syndicate in which all members participate equally in managing the investment and in the profits or losses it generates.

17.16 (d) gross income minus expenses minus building depreciation.

Taxable income from investment real estate is the gross income received minus any expenses, deductions or exclusions that current tax law allows. Depreciation of land is not allowed.

17.17 (c) deduct interest payments from income.

Taxable income is net operating income minus all allowable deductions. The interest portion of debt service is allowed and is deducted from Net Operating Income as interest expense. Principal repayment is not an allowable deduction on investment properties. Capital gain derivation does not involve interest or principal payments.

17.18 (d) The owner may be able to avoid capital gain tax when the property is sold.

Provided the owner meets certain ownership and use tests, there is no capital gain tax on sale of the property unless the gain exceeds $250,000 for a single taxpayer or $500,000 for married taxpayers who file jointly. Since the property is not used for business, deductions for expenses against income are not allowed.

17.19 (c) may be deducted from the sale price for gains tax purposes.

Selling costs include such expenses as brokerage commissions, relevant advertising, legal fees, seller-paid points and other closing costs. These costs are deducted from the selling price to get the amount realized, which is reduced by the adjusted basis to calculate gain on sale for gains tax purposes.

17.20 (b) the difference between amount realized and adjusted basis.

The formula for gain tax is Taxable Gain on Sale x the owner's marginal tax bracket. The formula for gain

on sale is: Amount Realized - Adjusted Basis = Gain on Sale. The formula for Amount Realized is: Selling Price - Selling costs = Amount Realized. Therefore, the gain tax = (Amount Realized - Adjusted Basis) x tax rate.

SECTION 18 TEST: Taxes Affecting Real Estate

18.1 (c) A tax district.
Real estate property taxes are imposed by "taxing entities" or "taxing districts" at county and local levels of government. States may legally levy taxes on real property, but most delegate this power to counties, cities, townships and local taxing districts. The federal government does, however, tax income derived from real property and gains realized on the sale of real property.

18.2 (b) properties owned by a government agency.
Certain types of property are exempt from property taxes. Certain classes of property owner may also be exempted or have a reduced liability. Exemptions include government-owned properties, real properties owned by churches, and properties owned by other non-profit organizations.

18.3 (c) It adjusts assessments in a locality to make them more consistent with an average level for the state or other higher level jurisdiction.
Equalization factors level out the unevenness of valuations for groups of properties. For instance, if assessed values of properties in one county are consistently ten percent below the average for other counties, an equalization board may multiply each assessed value in that county by a factor of 110% to raise them to the average level for the state.

18.4 (c) $2,000,000,000.
The mill rate = (tax requirement / the tax base). A mill is one one-thousandth of a dollar ($.001). To solve for the tax base, reconfigure this formula to be: Base = Tax Requirement / Mill Rate. Thus the Base = $20,000,000 / .010, or $2,000,000,000.

18.5 (d) $441.
The library tax is ($1.00 x 147) and the fire district tax is ($2.00 x 147). Thus the tax is $441.

18.6 (b) $5,700.
Special assessments are based on the cost of the improvement and apportioned on a pro rata basis among benefiting properties according to the value that each parcel will receive from the improvement. Here, Mary's share is 38 / 200, or 19%. 19% x $30,000 = $5,700.

18.7 (a) A conveyance instrument for a property that is sold to enforce a tax lien.
A tax deed is a legal instrument for conveying title when a property is sold for non-payment of taxes. The application for a tax deed causes the taxing agency to institute a tax sale or tax foreclosure.

18.8 (d) a statutory right of redemption.
If the taxpayer can redeem the property after the tax sale, this right is known as a statutory right of redemption. In this case, the taxpayer must pay the amount paid by the winning bidder at the tax sale, plus any charges, additional taxes, or interest that may have accumulated.

18.9 (b) the total of all assessed values of properties minus exemptions.
The tax base of an area is the total of the appraised or assessed values of all real property within the area's boundaries, excluding partially or totally exempt properties such as those owned by the government or non-profit organizations.

18.10 (c) multiplying each district's tax rate times the taxable value of the property.
Each property owner's tax bill is determined by multiplying the tax rate for each taxing district times the taxable value of the property. Taxable value is the assessed value after all exemptions and adjustments have been taken into account.

SECTION 19 TEST: Planning, Zoning and Environmental Hazards

19.1 (d) Zoning ordinances are a primary means of keeping land use in harmony with the master plan.
The master plan fuses state and regional land use laws with local land use objectives that correspond to the municipality's social and economic conditions. The completed plan becomes the overall guideline for creating and enforcing zones, building codes, and development requirements.

19.2 (c) specify usage for every parcel within the zoning authority's jurisdiction.
The intent of zoning ordinances is to specify land usage for every parcel within the jurisdiction. In some areas, state laws permit zoning ordinances to apply to areas immediately beyond the legal boundaries of the city or county.

19.3 (b) To separate land uses so that they do not interfere with each other.
One of the primary applications of zoning power is the separation of residential properties from commercial and industrial uses. Proper design of land use in this manner preserves the aesthetics and value of neighborhoods and promotes the success of commercial enterprises through intelligently located zones. Six common types of zone are: residential; commercial; industrial; agricultural; public; and planned unit development (PUD).

19.4 (c) The public interest
The principal forms of exceptions to a conforming use is legal nonconforming use (grandfathered in); variance based on hardship; and special exception based on the public interest.

19.5 (d) The area of a commercial or industrial facility in relation to the size of the site.
Commercial zoning regulates intensity of usage by limiting the area of store or office per site area. Intensity regulation is further achieved by minimum parking requirements, setbacks, and building height restrictions.

19.6 (c) It requires that multiple tracts of land be developed according to a single design.
Planned unit development zoning restricts use to development of whole tracts that are designed to use space efficiently and maximize open space. A PUD zone may be for residential, commercial, or industrial uses, or combinations thereof.

19.7 (a) A homeowner in a residential zone converts her residence to a private school.
A legal nonconforming use can be illustrated as follows. A motel is situated in a residential area that no longer allows commercial activity. The zoning board rules that the motel may continue to operate until it is sold, destroyed or used for any other commercial purpose. An illegal nonconforming use is one that conflicts with ordinances that were in place before the use commenced. For instance, if the motel in the previous example is sold, and the new owner continues to operate the property as a motel, the motel is now an illegal, nonconforming use.

19.8 (b) A variance is granted by the zoning board if the owner has a justifiable reason.
A nonconforming use is one that clearly differs from current zoning and is subject to change upon conveyance. A zoning variance allows a use that differs from the applicable ordinance for a variety of justifiable reasons.

19.9 (c) certificate of occupancy.
Building inspectors inspect a new development or improvement for code compliance. If the work complies, the municipality or county issues a certificate of occupancy which officially clears the property for occupation and use.

19.10 (c) It conveys legal title to the acquiring entity.
Eminent domain allows a government entity to purchase a fee, leasehold, or easement interest in privately owned real property for the public good, regardless of the owner's desire to sell or otherwise transfer any interest. In exchange for the interest, the government pays the owner a "just" compensation. To acquire a property, the public entity initiates a condemnation suit. Transfer of title extinguishes all existing leases, liens, and other encumbrances on the property.

19.11 (d) parties responsible for improper disposal of hazardous waste could be charged for the cleanup costs.
Under CERCLA and the Superfund Amendment of 1986, current landowners as well as previous owners of a property may be held liable for environmental violations, even if "innocent" of a violation. Sellers often carry the greatest exposure, and real estate licensees may be held liable for improper disclosure.

19.12 (a) Individual property rights and the public's interest.
The optimum management of real property usage must take into account both the interests of the individual and the interests of the surrounding community. While maintaining the value of an individual estate is important, the owner of an estate must realize that unregulated use and development can jeopardize the value not only of the owner's estate but of neighboring properties.

19.13 (c) police power.
At the local level, county and city governments control land use through the authority known as police power. The most common expressions of police power are county and municipal zoning.

19.14 (d) The owner must sell the property in exchange for market-value compensation.
Eminent domain allows a government entity to purchase a fee, leasehold, or easement interest in privately owned real property for the public good, regardless of the owner's desire to sell or otherwise transfer any interest. In exchange for the interest, the government pays the owner a "just" compensation.

19.15 (a) reasonably promote community health, safety and welfare.
Local planners do not have unlimited authority to do whatever they want. Their zoning ordinances must be clear in import, apply to all parties equally, and promote health, safety, and welfare of the community in a reasonable manner.

19.16 (d) To ensure that improvements comply with codes.
Local governments enforce zoning ordinances by issuing building permits to those who want to improve, repair, or refurbish a property. To receive a permit, the project must comply with all relevant ordinances and codes.

19.17 (b) To regulate the density of dwellings in the residential zone.
Residential zoning regulates density, by limiting the number and size of dwelling units and lots in an area.

19.18 (a) a special exception.
A special exception grant authorizes a use that is not consistent with the zoning ordinance in a literal sense, yet is clearly beneficial or essential to the public welfare and does not materially impair other uses in the zone.

19.19 (c) a legal nonconforming use.
An illegal nonconforming use is one that conflicts with ordinances that were in place before the use commenced. For instance, if a motel that was allowed as a legal nonconforming use is sold, and the new owner continues to operate the property as a motel, the motel is now an illegal, nonconforming use.

19.20 (b) a plat of subdivision.
In addition to complying with zoning ordinances, a developer of multiple properties in a subdivision must meet requirements for subdivisions, including submission of a plat of subdivision.

TEST 20: Real Estate Mathematics

20.1 (a) $.023 / SF
5/6ths of an acre = (5 x 43,560 SF) / 6, or 36,300 SF. Her commission was (.06 x $28,000) x .50, or $840. $840 / 36,300 SF = $.023 / SF.

20.2 (b) $370,170
The land costs $.50 x 43,560 SF/ac. x 1.5 ac, or $32,670. The home will cost $135 / SF x 2,500, or $337,500. The total property will cost $370,170.

20.3 (a) 12%
The lot measures 43,560 / 4, or 10,890 SF. The tennis court will take up 9,600 SF, leaving 1,290 SF. This amount is 11.8% of the total lot area.

20.4 (c) 40
The total area available for lots is 11.2 acres (16 acres x 70% for houses), or 487,872 SF (11.2 x 43,560). Dividing this area by 12,000 SF / lot = 40.66. Thus he can have a 40-lot subdivision.

20.5 (a) 6
First, the requirement = 2(13'x 9') +2 (18'x 9') =558 SF. Each roll is 2'x 50', or 100 SF. Thus she will need 6 rolls.

20.6 (d) 1,376 SF
First figure the area to be mulched. If the home is 40 x 30, the flower area adds 8' to each side of the house. Thus the outside perimeter of the flowered area is (40+8+8) by (30+8+8), or 46' by 56'. The area of the flowered area is (46' x 56') minus the house area of 1,200 SF. This is 1,376 SF.

20.7 (b) 40 acres
First, remember that a section contains 640 acres. The area in question is a forth of a half of a half of the total section. So divide 640 by (4 x 2 x 2). 4 x 2 x 2 is 16 and 640/16= 40 acres.

20.8 (c) 10 acres
This key to this question is to recall that a section has 640 acres. Theresa's property only is a ¼ of a ¼ of a ¼ of the entire section. Multiply 4 x 4 x 4 which equals 64. Savannah owns 1/64 of the section. Divide 640 by 64 and you get the answer of 10 acres.

20.9 (a) $38,955
Their fixed rent is (1,800 SF x $1.40/SF) x 12 months, or $30,240. The percentage rent is ($41,500 x .0175) x 12, or $8,715. Total rent is ($30,240 + 8,715), or $38,955.

20.10 (a) 5.04%
First, convert to decimals: 2 2/3 % = 2.67%; 5 1/5% = 5.2%; 7 1/4% = 7.25%. Thus total appreciation = (2.67% + 5.2% + 7.25%), or 15.12%. Divide by 3 to derive the average: 15.12% / 3 = 5.04%

20.11 (c) 29 %.
Appreciation as a per cent can be estimated by (1) subtracting the estimated current market value from the price originally paid (239,000 - 185,000 = 54,000) and (2) dividing the result by the original price (54,000 / 185,000 = . 29 or 29%).

20.12 (c) 94%
To find the percent of listing price the offer is, divide the offer by the listing price. In this question the offer is $290,000 and the listing price is $308,000. $$\frac{\$290,000}{\$308,000} = 94\%$$

20.13 (a) $206,000.
Remember the formula V = I / R where V is value, I is annual income, and R is the cap rate. Variations of this are: R = I / V in solving for the cap rate, and I = V x R in solving for income. Here, first identify net income by subtracting out vacancy and expenses. Then divide by the capitalization rate. Thus, ($30,000 – 1,500 – 10,000) / 9% = $205,555, or $206,000 rounded.

20.14 (b) $375,000.
Value = Income / Cap rate. Thus, V= $30,000 / .08 = $375,000.

20.15 (b) $13,600.
First derive the annual depreciation which is the cost divided by the economic life. Then multiply annual depreciation times the number of years to identify total depreciation. Remember to subtract depreciation from the original cost if the question asks for the ending value. Thus, ($16,000 / 20 years x 3 years) = $2,400 total depreciation. The ending value is $16,000 –2,400, or $13,600.

20.16 (a) $1,077
First, Lee's depreciable basis, without the land, is $280,000 x 75%, or $210,000. The annual depreciation for the entire home is ($210,000 / 39 years), or $5,384.61. Second, his office is 20% of the house (500 sf / 2,500 sf). Therefore Lee can take annual depreciation of ($5,384.61 x 20%), or $1,076.92.

20.17 (d) $188,000.
Cost Approach formula: Land + (Cost of Improvements + Capital Additions – Depreciation) = Value. Thus you have $40,000 + ($175,000 - 27,000), or $188,000.

20.18 (c) $475,000
Use the same Cost Approach formula: Land + (Cost of Improvements + Capital Additions – Depreciation) = Value. The land is worth (100,000 x 125%), or $125,000. Remember, you cannot depreciate the land, only the cost of the improvements. Therefore, annual depreciation is ($400,000 / 40), or $10,000. Total depreciation is ($10,000 x 5 years), or $50,000. Thus the value is ($125,000 + 400,000 – 50,000), or $475,000.

20.19 (d) 125.
Use the formula: GRM = Price / Monthly Rent. Thus, $400,000 / $3,200 = 125.

20.20 (c) $194,000.
Use the formula: GIM = Price / Annual Income. To solve for price convert the formula to Price = GIM x Annual Income. Thus, ($1,100 x 12) equals $13,200 annual income. ($13,200 x 14.7 GIM) = $194,040, or $194,000 rounded.

16.21 (d) $750
The loan amount is $200,000 x .75, or $150,000. The first month interest equals ($150,000 x 6%) / 12 months, or $750.

20.22 (b) $179,000.
The equation for the loan amount is (annual interest divided by the interest rate) = loan amount. Thus, ($790 x 12) / .053 = $178,868 or $179,000 rounded.

20.23 (a) 4.82%.
The equation for the interest rate is (annual payment / loan amount) = interest rate. Thus ($1,000 x 12) / $249,000 = 4.82%.

20.24 (b) $1,456.95
In the first month they pay interest of ($280,000 x 6.25%) / 12, or $1,458. If their fixed payment is $1,724, they paid down the principal by $266 ($1,724 - 1,458). Now they must pay 6.25% interest on the new principal balance of $279,734. This equals (279,734 x .0625) / 12, or $1,456.95.

20.25 (b) The second option, by 150.
The first option's interest total is (6.5% x $60,000) x 5 years, or $19,500. The second option will charge (6.25% x $60,000) x 5 years, plus $600, or a total of $19,350. The 2nd option is $150 cheaper.

20.26 (b) 1.67 points
A discount point is one percent of the loan amount. Jose's loan is ($410,000 x 90%), or $369,000. If he paid $6,150, he paid 1.67% of the loan amount ($6,150 / 369,000), or 1.67 points.

20.27 (c) $4,875.
$325,000 x .015 = $4,875. Remember, one point = 1% of the loan amount.

20.28 (c) $162,500
Use the formula: Price x LTV Ratio = Loan. Then plug in the figures and calculate: Price x .80 = $130,000. Therefore, Price = $130,000 / .80 = $162,500.

20.29 (c) $379,259
First, the annual interest paid is $1,600 x 12, or $19,200. The interest rate is 6.75%. Using the formula (Loan = Interest / Rate), the loan amount is $19,200 / 6.75%, or $284,444. As this is 75% of the price, the price is ($284,444 / .75), or $379,259.

20.30 (b) $1,900.
Monthly income qualification is derived by multiplying monthly income by the income ratio. Thus (76,000 / 12) x .30 = $1,900. Remember to first derive the monthly income.

20.31 (a) $253,846
Total depreciation on this property = ($600,000 / 39 years) x 10 years, or $153,846. His adjusted basis is therefore ($680,000 original price – 153,846 depreciation taken), or $526,154. The gain is then ($780,000 – 526,154), or $253,846.

20.32 (b) $257,000.
Adjusted basis = beginning basis ($250,000) + capital improvements ($2,000 + $5,000) – depreciation (0) = adjusted basis ($257,000).

20.33 (c) $34,000.
Capital gain = amount realized (net sales proceeds, $265,000) - adjusted basis ($231,000) = ($34,000).

20.34 (d) $125,000.
The basic formula for adjusted basis is: Beginning Basis + Capital Improvements - Exclusions and Credits = Adjusted Basis. Debra's adjusted basis is therefore $120.000 + $5,000 = $125,000. The financing terms and subsequent selling price are not relevant.

20.35 (c) $15,000 overpriced.
Use the same formula V = I / R where V is the price and R is the rate of return. Then plug in the numbers to solve for V. The NOI of this property is ($60,000 - $22,000), or $38,000. The return is 11%. Therefore, the value to get this return must be $38,000 / .11, or $345,455. Since the price is $360,000, the price exceeds the amount needed for an 11% return by approximately $15,000 ($360,000 - $345,455 = $14,545).

20.36 (b)   Yes, since he will yield 8.375%
Use the same formula R = I / V where V is the $2 million price, and R is the cap rate or rate of return. To identify income: (25,000 SF x $10/SF) = $250,000 gross income, minus 5% vacancy (.05 x $250,000), or $12,500, minus expenses of $70,000 = $167,500 net income. ($250,000 – 12,500 – 70,000)   Now divide net income of $167,500 by $2,000,000 to derive the return of 8.375%.

20.37 (a) $1,680.
Annual gross operating income ($1,650 x 12 = $19,800) - annual operating expenses ($600 x 12 = $7,200) = annual net operating income ($12,600); annual net operating income ($12,600) - cost recovery expense ($7,000) = taxable income ($5,600); taxable income ($5,600) x tax rate (30%) = tax liability ($1,680).

20.38 (c) $10,640
The basic formula for tax liability is: Taxable Income x Tax Rate = Tax Liability. Taxable Income is Net Operating Income - Interest Expense - Cost Recovery Expense. Therefore, the annual tax is $150,000 (NOI) - $105,000 (Interest Expense) - $7,000 (Cost Recovery Expense) x 28% = $10,640. Note that the principal payment is not deductible in calculating taxable income.

20.39 (d) 31.4%
The formula for profit % is (profit / initial investment). The profit made was ($23,000 x 4) – 70,000 initial investment, or $22,000. Dividing this by the amount invested derives a profit percent of 31.4%.

20.40 (c) $1,000,000,000.
The mill rate = (tax requirement / the tax base). A mill is one one-thousandth of a dollar ($.001). To solve for the tax base, reconfigure this formula to be: Base = Tax Requirement / Mill Rate. Thus the Base = $10,000,000 / .010, or $1,000,000,000.

254

20.41 (a) $1,495
First, always use the assessed valuation, not the market value. Subtract out the homestead exemption to derive taxable value, or $140,000 – 25,000 = $115,000. As a shortcut to calculating the tax bill, simply add up all the mills, multiply them times .001 to convert mills to decimals, then multiply this number times the taxable value. Thus (7 + 3 + 2 + 1) x .001 x $115,000 = $1,495.

20.42 (b) 2.13%
The rate = budget / tax base. Thus, $8,000,000 / (400,000,000 – 25,000,000) = 2.13%

20.43 (d) $1,778.
First calculate the total commission, then the co-brokerage splits, then the agent-broker split. Thus: $127,000 x 7% = $8,890 total commission. ($8,890 x 50%) = $4,445 total listing broker share. ($4,445 x 40% = $1,778 agent's share.

20.44 (a) $6,866
Figure the total commission, then the co-brokerage splits, then the broker-agent splits. Thus, ($325,000 x 6.5%) = $21,125. ($21,125 x 50%) = $10,563. ($10,563 x .65) = $6,866.

20.45 (c) A credit to the buyer and debit to the seller for $785.34.
The daily tax expense, first, is ($3,150 / 365) or $8.63. Since the buyer will pay the taxes after closing, the seller must pay the buyer his or her portion of the tax bill at closing, which is the 91 days from the beginning of the year through closing. Therefore, credit the buyer and debit the seller ($8.63 x 91), or $785.34.

20.46 (a) $507.50.
If the buyer pays $525 interest for 30 days, the daily expense is ($525 / 30), or $17.50. If there are 29 days of pre-paid expense, the buyer's charge is ($17.50 x 29), or $507.50.

20.47 (d) Credit buyer $712.26.
For the monthly proration using the 365-day method, solve first for the daily rent amount: ($1,380 / 31), or $44.52. Since the landlord received the rent and owes the buyer portions of the rent, the buyer will be credited. The owed amount is for the 16th through the 31st, or 16 days, since the closing day belongs to the buyer. Therefore, credit the buyer and debit the seller ($44.52 x 16),or $712.26.

20.48 (d) $86,372
First calculate the transfer tax: ($322,600 / 500) = 645.2 units of $500. Round this up to 646, then multiply times $1.00 to get $646 transfer tax cost. Next figure the commission @ ($322,600 x .07), or $22,582. Next, the seller's real estate tax proration charge will be $2,000. Then, add up the expenses: ($646 transfer tax + 450 title + 550 attorney + 22,582 commission + 210,000 loan payoff + 2,000 tax proration) = $236,228. Subtracting this from the sale price = $86,372.

20.49 (d) $5,848.
Be careful here. Since the net price is $5,000, the taking price (TP) minus the commission must equal the net price. In other words, the net price is 90% of the taking price. Since TP x 90% = Net, TP = Net / 90%. So the taking price is $5,556 ($5,000 / .9). Apply the same logic to deriving the asking price: the taking price is 95% of the list price, therefore the list price = (taking price / 95%), or $5,848. Now work backwards to prove your answer: (5,848 x 95% margin x .90 net of commission) = $5,000

20.50 (d) $468,750
Use the formula: (Percent of insurable property value carried / 80% replacement cost) x claim = recovery, where the insurable property value variable excludes the land value and is valued at replacement cost. Here, the insurable portion of the property is ($740,000 - 25% land value), or $555,000. The Wildes are carrying insurance to cover 75% of the replacement cost of the entire property. Their recovery amount is therefore (75% / 80%) x $500,000, or $468,750.

20.51 (c) $140,000
Use the formula: (Percent of insurable property value carried / 80% replacement cost) x claim = recovery. Thus, (75% / 80% x $150,000) = $140,625. However, the face value of the policy is the maximum they can receive, which is $140,000

LICENSE EXAM SIMULATION TEST

S 1. (b) Trade fixtures that are personal property.
Trade fixtures are items of a tenant's personal property that the tenant has temporarily affixed to a landlord's real property in order to conduct business. Trade fixtures may be detached and removed before or upon surrender of the leased premises. Should the tenant fail to remove a trade fixture, it may become the property of the landlord through accession. Thereafter, the fixture is considered real property.

S 2. (c) Severance and affixing.
Severance is the conversion of real property to personal property by detaching it from the real estate; affixing, or attachment, is the act of converting personal property to real property by attaching it to the real estate, such as by assembling a pile of bricks into a barbecue pit, or constructing a boat dock from wood planks.

S 3. (d) absolute fee simple estate.
The fee simple freehold estate is the highest form of ownership interest one can acquire in real estate. It includes the complete bundle of rights, and the tenancy is unlimited, with certain exceptions. The fee simple absolute estate is a perpetual estate that is not conditioned by stipulated or restricted uses.

S 4. (c) the estate may revert to a grantor or heirs if the prescribed use changes.
The defeasible fee estate is perpetual, provided the usage conforms to stated conditions. Essential characteristics are: the property must be used for a certain purpose or under certain conditions; and, if the use changes or if prohibited conditions are present, the estate reverts to the previous grantor of the estate.

S 5. (a) conventional life estate.
A conventional life estate is a freehold estate that is limited in duration to the life of the owner or other named person. Upon the death of the owner or other named individual, the estate passes to the original owner or another named party. A legal life estate is created by law as opposed to a property owner's choice.

S 6. (a) a condominium owner owns a unit of air space whereas the co-op owner owns a proprietary lease.
The owner of a condominium has a fee-simple ownership interest in his/her unit and its air space. Whereas, a co-op owner has a leasehold, not fee-simple, interest with the property's corporation. Since the corporation owns an undivided interest in the cooperative property, debts and financial obligations apply to the property as a whole, not to individual units as in a condominium.

S 7. (d) Trustor, trustee and beneficiary.
In an estate in trust, a fee owner-- the grantor or trustor-- transfers legal title to a fiduciary-- the trustee-- who holds and manages the estate for the benefit of another party, the beneficiary.

S 8. (c) fee simple ownership of the airspace in a unit and an undivided share of the entire property's common areas.
A condominium is a hybrid form of ownership of multi-unit residential or commercial properties. It combines ownership of a fee simple interest in the airspace within a unit with ownership of an undivided share, as a tenant in common, of the entire property's common elements, such as lobbies, swimming pools, and hallways.

S 9. (a) the date of recordation.
Among junior liens, date of recording determines priority. The rule is: the earlier the recording date of the lien, the higher its priority. For example, if a judgment lien is recorded against a property on Friday, and a mortgage lien is recorded on the following Tuesday, the judgment lien has priority and must be satisfied in a foreclosure ahead of the mortgage lien.

S 10. (b) A state in which a mortgagor retains title to the property when a mortgage lien is created.
In lien-theory states, laws give a lender on a mortgaged property equitable title rather than legal title. The

mortgagor in a lien theory state retains legal title.

S 11. (b) transfers with the property.
The term appurtenant means "attaching to." An easement appurtenant attaches to the estate and transfers with it unless specifically stated otherwise in the transaction documents.

S 12. (c) Giving constructive notice of one's rights and interests in the property.
Recorded instruments may include deeds, mortgages, liens, easements, sale contracts, and marriage, probate and tax records. The primary purpose of recording and maintaining records of these instruments is to provide constructive notice of the conditions of a property's title-- who owns it, who maintains claims against it.

S 13. (c) A chronology of successive owners of record of a parcel of real estate.
Chain of title refers to the succession of owners of record dating back to the original grant of title from the state to a private party. It is thus more than a mere list; it is a chronological list as reflected in title records.

S 14. (c) Title insurance.
A title insurance policy indemnifies the policy holder against losses arising from defects in the title and is thus generally accepted as the best evidence of marketability after a Torrens certificate, which is not available in every jurisdiction. A signed deed is no evidence of marketability, only of an intent to convey title. An attorney's opinion and a title certificate, while forms of evidence of marketability, do not guarantee clear title or offer any protection against a defective title.

S 15. (c) percentage lease
A percentage lease allows the landlord to share in the income generated from the use of the property. A tenant pays percentage rent, or an amount of rent equal to a percentage of the tenant's periodic gross sales.

S 16. (d) net lease.
A net lease requires a tenant to pay for utilities, internal repairs, and a proportionate share of taxes, insurance, and operating expenses in addition to rent.

S 17. (b) The leased property is foreclosed.
A foreclosure extinguishes all prior interests in a property, including a leasehold.

S 18. (c) the construction conforms with applicable building codes.
Building inspectors inspect a new development or improvement for code compliance. If the work complies, the municipality or county issues a certificate of occupancy which officially clears the property for occupation and use.

S 19. (b) takes title subject to the same restriction.
Deed restrictions attach to the title of the property. Therefore, the restriction passes to the new buyer.

S 20. (a) She has the right to re-possess the property because the grantee has violated the condition.
A deed condition may restrict certain uses of a property, much like a deed restriction. However, violation of a deed condition gives the grantor the right to re-take possession of the property and file suit for legal title.

S 21. (a) To create a consistent, unchanging standard for identifying a property's unique location.
A legal description of real property is one which accurately locates and identifies the boundaries of the subject parcel to a degree acceptable by courts of law in the state where the property is located. The general criterion for a legal description is that it alone provides sufficient data for a surveyor to locate the parcel. A legal description identifies the property as unique and distinct from all other properties.

S 22. (b) They identify an enclosed area, beginning and ending at the same point.
The metes and bounds description always identifies an enclosed area by starting at an origination point, called point of beginning, or POB, and returning to the POB at the end of the description.

S 23. (a) is void.
By changing any of the terms of an offer, the offeree creates a counteroffer, and the original offer is void. At this point, the offeree becomes the offeror, and the new offeree gains the right of acceptance. If

accepted, the counteroffer becomes a valid contract provided all other requirements are met.

S 24. (a) may be assigned.
A real estate contract that is not a personal contract for services can be assigned to another party unless the terms of the agreement specifically prohibit assignment. Listing agreements, for example, are not assignable, since they are personal service agreements between agent and principal. Sales contracts, however, are assignable, because they involve the purchase of real property rather than a personal service.

S 25. (c) A two-year lease.
A contract may be in writing or it may be an oral, or parol, contract. Certain oral contracts are valid and enforceable, others are not enforceable, even if valid. For example, most states require listing agreements, sales contracts, and leases exceeding one year to be in writing to be enforceable.

S 26. (b) a dual agent.
Dual agency occurs whenever a single broker represents both principal parties to a transaction. Here, since Bob and Sue work for Bill, Bill is the dual agent.

S 27. (a) upon first substantive communication.
The agent must provide written notice to all parties or their agents as soon as substantive communication occurs, which can include initial face-to-face contact.

S 28. (d) neither seller nor buyer.
In recent years, the brokerage industry has striven to clear up the question of who works for whom, and who owes fiduciary duties to whom. One solution allows a broker to represent no one in a transaction. That is, the broker acts as a transaction broker, or facilitator, and has no allegiance to buyer or seller.

S 29. (b) the principal has proposed an illegal act, which should not be obeyed.
An agent must comply with the client's directions and instructions, provided they are legal. If the directive is illegal, the agent must also immediately withdraw.

S 30. (b) negotiated with clients.
The amount of a broker's commission is whatever amount the client and broker have agreed to.

S 31. (b) the client may be liable for a commission and marketing expenses.
With an exclusive right-to-sell listing, if the property sells during the term of the revoked listing, the client is liable for the commission. If the property does not sell, the client is liable for the broker's actual costs.

S 32. (b) the agent has a claim to a commission if the owner sells or leases to a party within a certain time following the listing's expiration.
Many listings include a protection clause stating that, for a certain period after expiration, the owner is liable for the commission if the property sells to a party that the broker procured, unless the seller has since listed the property with another broker.

S 33. (c) the advertising must not be deceptive.
Advertising may not be misleading or deceptive in promoting the brokerage or listed properties. Blind ads are also prohibited without exception. Sales agents, moreover, must identify their employer.

S 34. (a) collusion.
Collusion is the illegal practice of two or more businesses joining forces or making joint decisions which have the effect of putting another business at a competitive disadvantage.

S 35. (b) The brokers have illegally fixed prices.
Price fixing is the practice of two or more brokers agreeing to charge certain commission rates or fees for their services, regardless of market conditions or competitors.

S 36. (a) The seller may cancel the contract, since it can be ruled invalid.
A contingency that is too broad, vague, or excessive in duration may invalidate the entire contract on the grounds of insufficiency of mutual agreement. To avoid problems, the statement of a contingency should be explicit and clear, have an expiration date, and expressly require diligence in the effort to fulfill the requirement.

S 37. (d) claim the deposit as compensated damages for the buyer's failure to perform.
If a buyer fails to perform under the terms of a sale contract, the breach entitles the seller to legal recourse for damages. The usual remedy is forfeiture of the buyer's deposit as liquidated damages, provided the deposit is not grossly in excess of the seller's actual damages.

S 38. (b) The optionor must perform if the optionee takes the option, but the optionee is under no obligation to do so.
An option-to-buy places the optionee under no obligation to purchase the property. However, the seller must perform under the terms of the contract if the buyer exercises the option. An option is thus a unilateral agreement. Exercise of the option creates a bilateral sale contract where both parties are bound to perform.

S 39. (b) a decline in demand for all types of real estate in the real estate market.
Businesses that support the departing company will lay off or fire new employees, causing some to leave town in search of work. Some of these businesses may also have to cease operations. Hence the demand for residential real estate, as well as for commercial and industrial, will decline, and new construction will probably also halt until some other factor increases demand again.

S 40. (b). rental prices in that market will rise
An undersupply of commercial properties in relation to demand will most likely increase prices, as renters have fewer choices and less bargaining power.

S 41. (b) absorption.
Absorption is the amount of available property that becomes occupied over a period of time, usually measured in square feet.

S 42. (b) $17,000.
First derive the annual depreciation, which is the cost divided by the economic life. Then multiply annual depreciation times the number of years to identify total depreciation. Remember to subtract depreciation from the original cost if the question asks for the ending value. Thus, ($20,000 ÷ 20 years x 3 years) = $3,000 total depreciation. The ending value is $20,000 – 3,000, or $17,000.

S 43. (b) Apartment buildings.
The income capitalization approach, or income approach, is used for income properties and sometimes for other properties in a rental market where the appraiser can find rental data. The approach is based on the principle of anticipation: the expected future income stream of a property underlies what an investor will pay for the property.

S 44. (c) estimates net income and applies a capitalization rate to it.
The steps are: estimate potential gross income; estimate effective gross income (potential minus vacancy and credit losses); estimate net operating income (effective minus total operating expenses); select a capitalization rate; and apply the capitalization rate. Use the formula: income ÷ cap rate = value.

S 45. (c) potential gross income minus vacancy and credit loss minus expenses.
Net operating income, or NOI, is always income after vacancy, credit loss and expenses. It does not, however, include debt service.

S 46. (b) $400,000.
Value = Income ÷ Cap rate. Thus, V= $40,000 ÷ .10 = $400,000.

S 47. (a) the interest rate may vary.
Adjustable rate mortgages (ARMs) allow the lender to change the interest rate at specified intervals and by a specified amount. Federal regulations place limits on incremental interest rate increases and on the total amount by which the rate may be increased over the loan term.

S 48. (b) A wraparound lender can profit when the interest rate of the wraparound exceeds that of the underlying mortgage.
In a wraparound loan arrangement, the seller receives a junior mortgage from the buyer, and uses the buyer's payments to make the payments on the original first mortgage. This potentially enables the seller to

profit from any difference between a lower interest rate on the senior loan and a higher rate on the wraparound loan.

S 49. (b) a blanket mortgage loan.
A blanket mortgage is secured by more than one property, such as multiple parcels of real estate in a development.

S 50. (b) Payments are not sufficient to retire the loan.
Negative amortization causes the loan balance to increase over the term. This occurs if the borrower's periodic payment is insufficient to cover the interest owed for the period. The lender adds the amount of unpaid interest to the borrower's loan balance.

S 51. (b) the loan amount needs to be less than the property's value.
Lenders must have a margin of borrower equity to protect against falling real estate values which increase the risk of the loan. Without this margin, a lender can incur a loan loss in a foreclosure sale since the proceeds may be less than the loan amount.

S 52. (b) Truth-in-Lending laws
Truth-in-Lending Laws, implemented by the Federal Reserve's Regulation Z, regulate the disclosure of costs, the right to rescind the credit transaction, advertising credit offers, and penalties for non-compliance with the act.

S 53. (d) Participants sell mortgage-backed securities in order to buy pools of loans.
Secondary mortgage market organizations buy pools of mortgages from primary lenders and sell securities backed by these pooled mortgages to investors. By selling securities, the secondary market brings investor money into the mortgage market. By purchasing loans from primary lenders, the secondary market returns funds to the primary lenders, thereby enabling the primary lender to originate more mortgage loans.

S 54. (a) cost recovery expense.
Cash flow is the difference between the amount of actual cash flowing into the investment as revenue and out of the investment for expenses, debt service, and all other items. Cash flow concerns cash items only, and therefore excludes depreciation (cost recovery), which is not a cash expense.

S 55. (c) dividing net income by the price paid for the property.
The investment return measure known as return on investment (ROI) is calculated by dividing net income by the value of the investment. This yields a rate of return on investment.

S 56. (a) Installing a higher capacity air conditioning and purifying system.
Basis is increased by the cost of capital improvements made to the property. Examples of capital improvements are: putting on an addition, paving a driveway, replacing a roof, adding central air conditioning, and rewiring the home. Repairs, maintenance, and redecorating are not generally considered capital improvements.

S 57. (c) There are no federal ad valorem taxes on real property.
There are no federal taxes on real property. The Constitution of the United States specifically prohibits such taxes. The federal government does, however, tax income derived from real property and gains realized on the sale of real property.

S 58. (b) the assessed value of property.
General property taxes are levied on an ad valorem basis, meaning that they are based on the assessed value of the property. Assessed value is determined according to state law, usually by a county or township assessor or appraiser.

S 59. (d) The prohibition may be legal if performed correctly.
The condominium association may be exempt from fair housing prohibitions against age discrimination if it is established as a retirement community in which 80 % of the dwellings have one person who is 55 years of age or older and it has amenities for elderly residents.

S 60. (c) The agent and the owner.
The owner has illegally discriminated, and the agent, by going along with the owner, is equally guilty of violating fair housing laws.

S 61. (b) Inspection fees.
Prorated items are expenses that both parties must share. Non-prorated items are one-time individual charges such as sale commissions, recording fees, and title insurance.

S 62. (d) A lender paying a fee to a broker for referring a borrower to the lender.
RESPA prohibits the payment of fees as part of a real estate settlement when no services are actually rendered. This prohibition includes referral fees for such services as title searches, title insurance, mortgage loans, appraisals, credit reports, inspections, surveys, and legal services.

S 63. (b) Copies of required communications to principals.
Some communications with transaction parties are good and necessary for business. Others are required by law, and records of them must be maintained for a statutory period. Required records typically include listing agreements, offers, contracts, closing statements, agency agreements, disclosure documents, correspondence and other communication records, notes and any other relevant information.

S 64. (a) refuse to use terms that refer to or describe any of the classes of persons protected by the laws.
Before entering into a listing agreement, a licensee should explain that it is necessary to comply with fair housing laws and obtain the potential client's acknowledgment and agreement. The agent should make it clear that the agent will reject the use of terms indicating race, religion, creed, color, national origin, sex, handicap, age or familial status to describe prospective buyers. Such terms should be avoided in conversation as well as in advertising.

S 65. (a) Alterations to a rental space made to fit a particular tenant
Alterations made specifically for certain tenants are called build-outs or tenant improvements. The work may involve merely painting and re-carpeting a rental space, or erecting new walls and installing special electrical or other systems.

S 66. (c) maintain a special trust account in a qualified financial depository.
State laws and real estate commission rules specify how a property manager is to manage trust funds. In general, the agent is to maintain a separate bank account for these funds, with special accounting, in a qualified depository institution. The rules for how long an agent may hold trust funds before depositing them, and how the funds are to be disbursed, are spelled out. The fundamental requirements are that the owners of all funds must be identified, and there must be no commingling or conversion of client funds and agent funds.

S 67. (c) 3
The total area of the living room is (8' x 14' + 8' x 18' + 8' x 16' + 8' x 18') = 528 SF. They will therefore need 528 / 200 SF, or 3 whole gallons.

S 68. (d) 218'
Since the investor paid $100,000 total, and that equals $250 per frontage foot, there are 400 frontage feet (100,000 / 250). If the property is two acres, it totals 87,120 SF. Dividing this by 400 produces a lot depth of 217.8'.

S 69. (c) Yes with $360 left over.
The loan she can get amounts to ($240,000 x 80%), or $192,000. The points charge is ($192,000 x .02), or $3,840. Total closing costs are then $3,840 + 800, or $4640. Thus she has $360 to spare.

S 70. (c) $90,000
First, the sale price is 115% of the appraised value, so the appraised value is $230,000 / 115%, or $200,000. The lender will lend $140,000 (70% of appraised value), so the investor will have to come up with $90,000 ($230,000 – 140,000).

S 71. (c) $96,000.
Since the comparable has an extra half-bath, it is adjusted downward to equalize with the subject. Conversely, since it has no patio, the appraiser adds value to the comparable. Thus, $100,000 minus $5,000 plus $1,000 equals $96,000.

S 72. (c) $508
The total assessed value is ($84,550 + 235,000), or $319,550. The annual tax is based on ($319,550 / 100) = 3195.5 100's. Round up to 3196. To derive the annual tax, multiply 3,196 x 1.91, or $6,104.36. Divide this by 12 for the monthly escrow: ($6,104 / 12) = $508.

S 73. (d) $92,000
The formula for equity is (current value – indebtedness). The current value is ($180,000 + 25% x 180,000), or ($180,000 x 125%), or $225,000. The current debt is ($180,000 x 80%) - $11,000, or $133,000. Their equity is therefore $92,000.

S 74. (b) $166,150
Use the formula: Gain = (Net selling price – adjusted basis) where adjusted basis = (beginning cost – depreciation). The selling price is $240,000 x 5% annual appreciation x 10 years, or ($240,000 + 50% x 240,000), or $360,000. Since land cannot be depreciated, the depreciable basis is ($240,000 total cost – 60,000 land value), or $180,000 (land = 25% total value). Annual depreciation = ($180,000 / 39 years), or $4,615. Thus total depreciation is ($4,615 x 10 years), or $46,150. The adjusted basis is therefore ($240,000 – 46,150), or $193,850. The total gain is therefore ($360,000 – 193,850), or $166,150.

S 75. (c) $80,000
Applying the formula (percent of insurable property value carried / 80% replacement cost) x claim = recovery), divide the amount of coverage carried ($160,000) by 80% of the insurable property value ($250,000) to get the percent of the claim the company will pay (80%). Multiply this percentage by the claim amount to get $80,000, what the company will pay.

S 76. (c) his or her Florida license can be denied.
"When the board, or the department when there is no board, finds any person guilty of the grounds set forth in subsection (1) or of any grounds set forth in the applicable practice act, including conduct constituting a substantial violation of subsection (1) or a violation of the applicable practice act which occurred prior to obtaining a license, it may enter an order imposing one or more of the following penalties: (a) Refusal to certify, or to certify with restrictions, an application for a license." 455.27(2)

S.77 (d) Fred must pass FL licensing laws exam with score of 75% or higher.
Mutual recognition applicants must submit application, submit certification of license history from state where licensed, and pass FL licensing laws exam with score of 75% or higher.

S 78. (c) 4-year college degree in real estate
"The postlicensure education requirements of this section, and the education course requirements for one to become initially licensed, do not apply to any applicant or licensee who has received a 4-year degree, or higher, in real estate from an accredited institution of higher education." 475.17(6)

S 79. (c) When the sales associate's license has not been renewed at the end of the license period
"'Involuntarily inactive status' means the licensure status that results when a license is not renewed at the end of the license period prescribed by the department. " 455.01(1)(g)

S 80. (b) He must notify the Commission of the change within 10 days.
"A license shall cease to be in force whenever a broker changes her or his business address, a real estate school operating under a permit issued pursuant to s. 475.451 changes its business address, or a sales associate working for a broker or an instructor working for a real estate school changes employer." 475.23

S 81. (d) No – she is allowed to work for only one employer, and multiple licenses are only for brokers.
"A licensed broker may be issued upon request additional licenses as a broker, but not as a sales associate or as a broker associate…" 475.215(1)
"A sales associate or broker associate shall have no more than one registered employer at any one time." 475.215(2) "A sales associate or broker associate may only be employed by one broker or by one owner-

developer." 61J2.6.006(1)

S 82. (b) Transaction broker
"Transaction brokers provide a limited form of nonfiduciary representation to a buyer, a seller, or both in a real estate transaction. " 475.272(4)

S 83. (a) Disclosure of known material facts
"No brokerage relationship–duties.—A real estate licensee owes to a potential seller or buyer with whom the licensee has no brokerage relationship the following duties:
1. Dealing honestly and fairly;
2. Disclosing all known facts that materially affect the value of the residential real property which are not readily observable to the buyer; and
3. Accounting for all funds entrusted to the licensee." 475.278(4)(a)

S 84. (c) both Tara and Stan agree to the transition in writing.
"This part does not prevent a licensee from changing from one brokerage relationship to the other as long as the buyer or the seller, or both, gives consent as required by subparagraph (3)(c)2. before the change and the appropriate disclosure of duties as provided in this part is made to the buyer or seller." 475.278(1)(a)

S 85. (b) A licensee knew the seller was HIV-positive but didn't tell the buyer.
Even when no brokerage relationship exists, the broker is required by law to disclose all known facts that materially affect the value of the residential property which are not readily observable to the buyer. A seller being HIV-positive (or AIDS if that is the case) is not a material fact that affects the value of the property, but sink holes, mold, and super highways are material facts. Failure to disclose material facts is illegal. 475.278

S 86. (c) deposit owner (e.g., buyer) to be signatory on account.
Broker or designated broker licensee must be signatory on escrow account, not the buyer, seller, or other party.

S 87. (c) Construction service providers
"A materialman or laborer, either of whom is in privity with the owner, or a contractor who complies with the provisions of this part shall, subject to the limitations thereof, have a lien on the real property improved for any money that is owed to him or her for labor, services, materials, or other items required by, or furnished in accordance with, the direct contract and for unpaid finance charges due under the lienor's contract." 713.05

S 88. (c) When full disclosure is made to all interested parties
"The sharing of brokerage compensation by a licensee with a party to the real estate transaction with full disclosure to all interested parties is not considered a violation of Chapter 475, Part I, Florida Statutes." 61J2-10.028

S 89. (c) a real estate license.
A license is required for anyone who performs real estate services, such as conducting an open house.

S 90 (c) License suspension
"(d) $1,000, when the conviction is of a misdemeanor of the first degree. (e) $500, when the conviction is of a misdemeanor of the second degree or a noncriminal violation." 775.083
"In addition to the penalty prescribed in paragraph (a), the license of any broker or sales associate who participates in any rental information transaction which is in violation of the provisions of subsection (1) shall be subject to suspension or revocation by the commission in the manner prescribed by law." 475.453

S 91. (b) $5,000
"Personal or brokerage funds in any escrow account shall not exceed $5,000 per account." 61J2-14

S 92. (d) advertise under his/her broker employer's name.
Sales associates are not allowed to advertise under their own names.

S 93. (c) Designation of party to receive the interest
"The placement of escrow monies in an interest-bearing account, designation of the party who is to receive

the interest, and the time the earned interest must be disbursed, must be done with the written permission of all the parties to the transaction." 61J2-14.014

S 94. (d) The administrative law judge
"A formal hearing before an administrative law judge from the Division of Administrative Hearings shall be held pursuant to chapter 120 if there are any disputed issues of material fact." 455.225

S 95. (a) Cheating on the licensure end-of-course examination
Cheating on the pre-license examination is grounds for license denial, not suspension.

S 96. (c) Mitigating circumstances
"When either the Petitioner or Respondent is able to demonstrate aggravating or mitigating circumstances to the Commission in a Section 120.57(2), F.S., hearing or to a Division of Administrative Hearings hearing officer in a Section 120.57(1), F.S., hearing by clear and convincing evidence, the Commission or hearing officer shall be entitled to deviate from the above guidelines in imposing or recommending discipline, respectively, upon a licensee." 61J2-24

S 97. (a) The license is suspended.
"Upon the payment of any amount from the Real Estate Recovery Fund in settlement of a claim in satisfaction of a judgment against a broker or sales associate as described in s. 475.482(1), the license of such broker or sales associate shall be automatically suspended upon the date of payment from the fund." 475.484

S 98. (a) Hannah
The burden of proof is on complainant in Fair Housing cases, which in this case is buyer Hannah.

S 99. (c) prohibiting smoking in workplaces.
A person may not smoke in an enclosed indoor workplace..." 386.204

S 100. (d) no legal documents.
Only attorneys should draft legal contracts. Licensees should only use standardized forms and help their clients fill in blanks.

Appendix: Useful Websites

Florida Real Estate Candidate Handbook
This contains crucial information regarding the Florida Real Estate Exam. Make sure to download and read this participant booklet to fully understand the entire test taking process.

www.myfloridalicense.com/dbpr/servop/testing/documents/RE_sales_cib.pdf

Key Florida Contacts

Florida Department of Business and Professional Regulation
1940 North Monroe Street
Tallahassee, FL 32399
850-487-1395
www.myfloridalicense.com/dbpr/index.html

Florida Division of Real Estate
400 West Robinson Street, N801
Orlando, FL 32801
850-487-1395
www.myfloridalicense.com/dbpr/re/index.html

Pearson Vue Testing Service
5601 Green Valley Drive
Bloomington, MN 55437
952-681-3000
https://home.pearsonvue.com/Home.aspx

Florida Association of Realtors
7025 Augusta National Dr.
Orlando, FL 32822-5017
407-438-1400
www.floridarealtors.org/

If you liked Florida Real Estate License Exam Prep, check out the other titles of Performance Programs Company!

Cramming for the Florida real estate exam? You need Florida Real Estate License Exam Prep!

Where can you buy Florida Real Estate License Exam Prep?
Florida Real Estate License Exam Prep is available as a printed book or e-book through nearly all online retailers.

Looking for a Florida-specific real estate principles textbook? Get what all the students love -- Principles of Real Estate Practice in Florida!

Principles of Real Estate Practice in Florida is invaluable reference material for real estate professionals. Its 540 pages contain the essentials of real estate law, principles, and practices taught in real estate schools and colleges across Florida.

Where can you buy Principles of Real Estate Practice in Florida?
Principles Real Estate Practice in Florida is available as a printed book or e-book through nearly all online retailers.

Struggling with real estate math? The solution to that equation is Real Estate Math Express!

Real Estate Math Express is a concise, easy-to-study test preparation guide to help real estate students improve their real estate math scores to pass the state licensing test. The primary feature of Real Estate Math Express is that it contains all necessary formulas and practice questions in 70+ pages.

Where can you buy Real Estate Math Express?
Real Estate Math Express is available as a printed book or e-book through nearly all online retailers.

Publisher Contact
Ryan Mettling
Performance Programs Company
6810 190th Street East, Bradenton, FL 34211
ryan@performanceprogramscompany.com
www.performanceprogramscompany.com